# *CONTEMPORARY INVESTMENTS*

**James P. Hoban, Jr.**
*Ball State University*

**Gene W. Hoban**
*Alma College*

**Carlene Creviston**
*Ball State University*

**ALLYN AND BACON**
*Boston    London    Sydney    Toronto*

*Editorial-production service:* Graphic Design and Production Services
Text designer: Sylvia Dovner
*Cover administrator:* Linda Dickinson
*Production administrator:* Lorraine Perrotta
*Manufacturing buyer:* Bill Alberti
*Series editor:* Rich Wohl
*Senior editorial assistant:* Kelley Saunders-Butcher

Copyright © 1990 by Allyn and Bacon
A Division of Simon & Schuster, Inc.
160 Gould Street
Needham Heights, Massachusetts 02194

**Library of Congress Cataloging-in-Publication Data**

Hoban, James P.
    Contemporary investments / James P. Hoban, Jr., Gene W. Hoban,
    Carlene Creviston.
      p.    cm.
    Includes index.
    ISBN 0–205–11924–7
    1. Investments—Handbooks, manuals, etc.    I. Hoban, Gene W.
II. Creviston, Carlene, 1937–   .    III. Title.
HG4527.H65   1990
332.6′78—dc20                   89–34965
                                        CIP

Printed in the United States of America
1  2  3  4  5  6  7  8  9  10—94  93  92  91  90

# CONTENTS

**PART III** ——————————————————————————————————

*Choosing Investments     199*

# PREFACE

Investments is a popular course for undergraduate business students. Most of these students take the course in order to learn how to invest the money they expect to earn after graduation. They want to know how they can make their own money grow by wise investment in the financial markets. Other students enroll in investments courses because they are considering careers in the securities industry (as brokers, traders, analysts, or portfolio managers). Others know that an investments course will be valuable to their planned career in insurance, real estate, banking, or financial advising.

This book serves all these students. However, it differs from its competition in that it is written in a style which capitalizes on the students' strong interest in their own investments. Because the book assumes that the reader (rather than an employer) is the investor, it stresses, on a personal level, the applicability of the subject matter to the reader. However, our less formal writing style and our practical approach still allow us to cover the complex investment vehicles and sophisticated concepts so important in the current world of investment strategies. Practice problems and many examples will help the student understand the concepts presented. In addition to describing in detail financial instruments and markets, risk-return relationships and a portfolio approach to investment decisions are emphasized. Modern financial theory is not ignored. Instead, it is presented in a manner that emphasizes its applicability to both the individual investor and the portfolio manager.

## ORGANIZATION OF THE BOOK

The book is divided into six units. The first unit, "Basic Concepts and Definitions," starts with a chapter titled "The Investment Setting." It begins by discussing why readers might accumulate wealth and then outlines the attributes they might seek in their investments. The second chapter describes how the financial markets are organized. Chapter 3, "Participating in the Financial Markets," describes how the reader can buy and sell securities. Chapter 4 teaches the reader how to measure the expected returns and the risks of securities. Because we believe the use of compound interest and present value tables is becoming obsolete, we assume the reader has a financial calculator. Chapter 5 introduces the securities issued by corporations while Chapter 6 describes the securities issued by the federal, state, and local governments.

Unit two describes "The Investment Environment." Chapter 7 discusses where to find the information necessary for investment decisions. Included in it are sections on the use of computerized information services and how to interpret stock market averages. Chapter 8 covers in detail "Security Laws and Ethics." Chapter 9 explores the relationship between "The Stock Market and the Economy."

The third unit, "Choosing Investments," shows the reader how to pick common stocks, bonds, and convertible securities. Chapter 10 is "Common Stock." Chapter 11, "Analyzing the Individual Firm," includes analysis of financial statements. Chapter 12 explains technical analysis. Chapter 13 is "Bonds" and it includes appendices on the yield curve and duration. Chapter 14 is "Convertible Securities, Warrants, and Rights."

Unit four, "Other Investment Vehicles," has six chapters. Chapter 15 is "Investment Companies." Since options have been receiving so much investor interest in recent years, all of Chapter 16 is used to explain them. Chapter 17 is "Commodity and Financial Futures." Chapter 18 discusses the advantages and means of international investing. Unlike most other investment books, this book has an entire chapter (19) on investment in real estate and an entire chapter (20) on investment in precious metals and collectibles.

Unit five, "Portfolio Considerations," introduces the reader to the recent work on market efficiency and its implications (Chapter 21) and portfolio theory (Chapter 22).

Unit six, "An Individual's Portfolio of Wealth," highlights this book's emphasis on the individual investor. Chapter 23 looks at "Financial Planning." Chapter 24 is "Tax Planning."

# STRENGTH OF THE BOOK

This book's strength is its combining of the theoretical and descriptive aspects of investments into a comprehensive practical textbook. Examples of how thoroughly it presents descriptive material are: Chapter 6—Government Securities, Chapter 8—Security Laws and Ethics, Chapter 19—Real Estate, Chapter 20—Precious Metals and Collectibles, Chapter 23—Financial Planning, Chapter 24—Tax Planning, and Appendix 3A—The Money Market.

Examples of how this book presents theoretical issues in an understandable manner are: Chapter 21—Market Efficiency, Chapter 22—Portfolio Theory, Appendix 13A—The Term Structure of Interest Rates, and Appendix 13B—Duration and Immunization.

# CHAPTER PEDAGOGY

The format of this book should aid in the learning process. Each chapter begins with chapter objectives and ends with a detailed summary. Each chapter has questions for review and most chapters have cases or problems which the student can use to apply what he has learned.

# SOFTWARE AVAILABLE WITH THIS TEXT

*Invest!: Investment Analysis and Portfolio Management*, by Hadi Salavitabar, © 1990 by Allyn and Bacon, is available. This self-contained software package is designed to take the user through different stages of investment analysis and portfolio management. This software and its user's manual can be ordered with *Contemporary Investments* at a specially reduced price. This combined shrink-wrapped package (value-pak) is available in both 3.5″ and 5.25″ disk sizes for DOS-based machines. While extensive in the techniques used, this software is extremely user-friendly and requires no previous experience with microcomputers.

*Educational Version of Twin Advanced* is another software package that is available to accompany *Contemporary Investments*. This software package, while limited in the number of rows and columns, includes all of the features of the popular spreadsheet package developed by Mosaic® software. It too is available as a specially priced value-pak. It is designed to run on DOS machines and is fully compatible with Lotus 1-2-3- files.

# INSTRUCTOR'S MANUAL

An instructor's manual is available, listing additional sources of instructional materials, as well as containing the answers to the questions, problems, and cases in the book. It also contains true/false and multiple-choice test questions and problems for each chapter, as well as additional problems. A computerized test bank, *The Allyn and Bacon Test Manager System,* containing those true/false and multiple-choice questions is also available to adopters of the book. The *INVEST!* software package described above offers the instructor great flexibility in designing the course. The instructor's manual includes ideas on integrating *INVEST!* with this text. It also indicates which text problems are the most suitable for use with *INVEST!*

# ACKNOWLEDGMENTS

We would like to extend our thanks to all those previously and presently at Allyn and Bacon who were involved with this project. Specifically, we would like to acknowledge the help and support of Rich Wohl, executive editor at Allyn and Bacon. We would also like to acknowledge the early support and guidance of Richard Carle, senior editor, and Cary Tengler, finance editor. Finally, we would like to thank Kelley Saunders-Butcher, senior editorial assistant, who worked very efficiently with us on a day-to-day basis.

Producing this book involved the efforts of many people, including: Judy Fiske, Linda Dickinson, Lorraine Perrotta, and Tamara Johnson, all from Allyn and Bacon; Sylvia Dovnar and Betty O'Bryant from Technical Texts, Inc.; and Karen Mason of Graphic Design and Production Services. We thank them.

For their reviews of parts or all of this manuscript, we are indebted to:

| | |
|---|---|
| Donald R. Chambers | C. Thomas Howard, Ph.D. |
| University of Maryland | University of Denver |
| Robert A. Connolly | Jack H. Rubens |
| University of North Carolina at Greensboro | Cleveland State University |

James F. Feller
Middle Tennessee State University

Cheryl Warren
Angelo State University

Jerry Blum
University of Nevada at Reno

George Traughton
California State University at Chico

John Dunkelberg
Wake Forest University

# BASIC CONCEPTS AND DEFINITIONS

# The Investment Setting

## OUTLINE

## OBJECTIVES

When you have finished studying this chapter you should understand

1. What investment is.

2. The significance of five attributes—returns, risk, liquidity, tax aspects, and manageability—in evaluating an investment.

3. The factors that determine the rate of return which an investor demands on an investment.

4. The value of viewing each asset you own as part of your total portfolio of wealth.

5. The importance of stock and bond investments in the wealth of individuals and institutions.

## *Do We Save Enough?*

Historically, saving has been considered a virtue and a necessity for economic growth. However, since 1978 the percentage of their incomes that people in the United States save has fallen from 7.1 percent to less than 4 percent. This is the lowest percentage since the Depression and is much below the savings rates in other industrial countries. Many economists argue that this amount of personal savings is not enough to provide for the new investment that the economy needs. However, there is much confusion over the savings rate, its significance, and the causes of its decline.

Measuring the personal savings rate in an economy and assessing its importance is difficult for several reasons. First, business and government savings are more important than personal savings. Savings by business is five times larger than personal savings. The federal deficit can be viewed as "dissavings" and a small reduction in it would increase the total national savings rate significantly. Second, the Commerce Department figures quoted above are based on a narrow definition of savings that does not include pensions of government workers, contributions to social security, purchases of consumer durables, or expenditures for education. If these were included, the rate would be much higher. Third, the Commerce Department's figure is obtained by subtracting personal expenditures from personal income. These variables are difficult to measure; small errors greatly affect the much smaller personal savings figure.

Several reasons are given for the decline in the personal savings rate: (1) the post-World War II baby boomers are at a high spending period in their life cycle; (2) the growth of social security benefits and of pension plans reduces the need to save for retirement; (3) large increases in stock prices and housing values might substitute for savings in a family's long-term financial planning; and (4) taxes on interest, dividends, and capital gains tend to discourage savings.

## INTRODUCTION

The objective of this book is to provide the reader with knowledge about investment opportunities and with a framework for choosing among competing alternatives. In this first chapter, we define investment and examine the investment attributes of return, risk, liquidity, tax aspects, and manageability. Next, we look at today's investment environment and then stress the importance of taking a broad view toward investment. In the final section, we discuss the importance of securities and look at stock ownership.

---

# INVESTMENT DEFINED

As you go through life, you must continually decide whether to spend now or invest for the future. When you invest, you do so with the expectation that your accumulated wealth will provide increased future wealth. Therefore, **investment** is defined as foregoing current consumption of wealth in order to obtain greater future benefits. Because the future is uncertain, investment has two aspects: time and risk. The sacrifice is now and its amount is certain. The benefit is in the future and its amount is uncertain. People differ greatly in their willingness to forego current consumption in order to invest for the future. Some will invest a lot in exchange for a small increase in future benefits. Others will demand a greater increase in the future benefits before they invest.

There is real growth in the economy if resources are used wisely. For example, as time passes cattle multiply and crops grow. Likewise, if capital is properly combined with labor, additional wealth can be created. Available growth opportunities influence how much the users of capital will pay to investors. These supply and demand forces for investment funds determine a **real rate of interest** in the economy. The real rate of interest compensates investors for the time value of money, but it does not compensate for risk or inflation.

# INVESTMENT ATTRIBUTES

Five attributes are related to investments: return, risk, liquidity, tax aspects, and manageability.

## Return

Not only do investors seek a positive return, but the higher the return, everything else being equal, the better. This preference is based on the fact that each additional dollar of return gives the investor the opportunity to satisfy more economic needs and desires. Return on an investment may come in one or both of two forms.

**1.** The investment may provide regular periodic income. Interest paid on bonds and dividends paid on stocks are examples of this form of return. Some investors, such as retired persons, seek return in the form of regular periodic income because they need it to meet current expenditures.

**2.** The other form of return is **capital appreciation,** which occurs when the investment is sold for more than it cost. Real estate and certain types of stocks can provide capital appreciation. Some investors seek investments that provide return in the form of capital appreciation rather than periodic income because they do not need income now; they want their investments to pay off in the future.

## Risk

Risk is a negative attribute of an investment. **Risk** is the chance that the investment will not achieve the expected return. Risk also includes the possibility that part or all of the investment will not be returned to the investor. Some assets, such as short-term accounts in depository institutions, have very little risk because their returns are certain. Other assets, such as stocks, are more risky because they may fluctuate greatly in value.

Although people vary in their degree of risk tolerance, observation and analysis of investor behavior lead to the conclusion that most people dislike risk; that is, they have **risk aversion.** For example, given the choice between two investments with the same expected return and different amounts of risk, most individuals will choose the one with the lower risk. However, the exact degree of risk aversion varies from person to person. Therefore, if one investment offers both more expected return and more risk than another, the investor will have to decide whether the additional return is enough compensation for bearing the additional risk. Some people will bear more risk in the hope of higher returns while others prefer lower risk and lower returns.

Because most investors are risk averse, a risk-return tradeoff exists in the investment opportunities of the financial markets. Normally, low-risk investments provide low returns and high-risk investments have the potential for high returns. This tradeoff is reflected in Exhibit 1–1, which displays expected rate of return as a function of risk.

---

**EXHIBIT 1–1   Risk-Return Tradeoff**

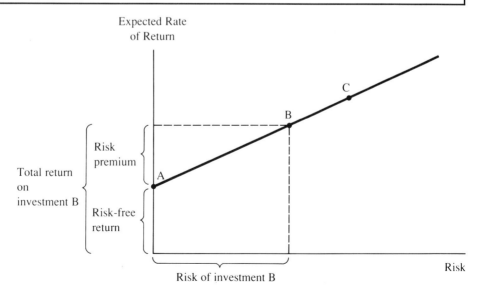

The horizontal axis in this figure reflects the amount of risk in an investment. The vertical axis reflects the expected rate of return. Line ABC intersects with the vertical axis at point A, which represents the risk-free rate of return. U.S. Treasury bills and short-term accounts in insured depository institutions are close to being risk free. A more risky investment, as represented by point B, offers an expected rate of return that consists of the risk-free return and a risk premium. The **risk premium** compensates the investor for bearing the additional risk. An even riskier investment, which is shown as point C, would have a higher risk premium and, therefore, a higher expected rate of return.

The line ABC on the graph reflects the risk-return tradeoff available on investments sold in the financial markets. The investor's attitude toward risk will greatly influence the investments which he or she chooses. Before making any investment, investors should attempt to assess the risk involved and decide if it is compatible with their risk preferences.

## Liquidity

**Liquidity** is a measure of how quickly an asset can be converted to currency with little or no loss in value. The last phrase is important; most assets can be sold quickly if the price is lowered substantially. However, an asset is not liquid if a price reduction is necessary in order to convert it to currency. An asset is highly liquid if it can be redeemed for cash in the near future or if there are good markets in which to sell it.

Degree of liquidity is measured on a continuum from perfectly liquid to extremely illiquid. Currency is by definition perfectly liquid; checking accounts are very liquid because depository institutions will convert a depositor's check to cash "on demand." Savings accounts are slightly less liquid. Although they can usually be converted to currency on request, depository institutions have the right to require a few days' notice before currency can be obtained. Stocks and bonds traded on the securities exchanges are quite liquid because the existence of good markets permits them to be converted into cash at full value quickly. Other investments, such as real estate, small businesses, and stocks not actively traded, are fairly illiquid. They either take a long time to sell or may sell below their value. Normally, less liquid investments pay a higher return than liquid ones, although the extra return on illiquid investments is not as great as the extra return on high-risk investments.

## Tax Aspects

In addition to return, risk, and liquidity, another attribute to be considered in an investment is its tax aspect. Three tax factors are important.

- Can you invest without paying income tax on the principal first?
- Can you control when investment income is recognized for tax purposes?
- How is the return taxed?

A few provisions of the tax law allow money to be invested without paying income tax on it first. Examples include employer contributions to retirement plans and sometimes your contributions to individual retirement accounts (IRAs). Tax-deferred earnings are normally taxed when the proceeds of the investment are paid out to the investor. Meanwhile the investor has a larger amount earning interest or dividends. Also, investors usually can control when they receive the proceeds so that taxes can be minimized.

This relates to the second issue: controlling when the investment income is recognized for tax purposes. Normally, investors want to delay recognizing taxable income so they can keep the money that would go to taxes and earn a return. Also, investors want to time the gains and losses so that taxes are minimized. One common practice for obtaining this objective is to delay recognizing gains until low earning years, often the retirement years.

The third issue is how the return is taxed. Some forms of returns are not taxed; for example, interest earned on most state and local bonds is exempt from federal income tax. The Tax Reform Act of 1986 divided income into three categories: active income (a person's salary), portfolio income (income from stocks and bonds), and passive income (income from a limited partnership which owns real estate). Your tax situation can determine what types of investments you should undertake.

## Manageability

The final investment attribute to be considered is the manageability of the investments. The question is, "How much work is required by me and do I enjoy this type of activity?" Some forms of investment require little effort. After you open an account with a depository institution or mutual fund, more money can be invested just by mailing it in. Each January you will receive a statement showing what to report for taxes. No other work is involved.

On the other hand, managing your own stock investments requires more work. Analysis of individual companies is necessary. Keeping track of the information required for taxes is more difficult. An example of an investment requiring even more work is owning rental properties. Unless a manager is hired, you may have to handle frequent tenant turnover, complaints from tenants, maintenance problems, and rent collections.

# TODAY'S ENVIRONMENT

The nominal long-term rate of return on investments depends on the real growth in the economy, the risk of the investments, and the rate of inflation.

Exhibit 1–2 presents the annual growth rates in the gross national product after adjusting for inflation. After performing poorly during the 1980–1982 period, the economy began a seven-year expansion in November 1982. The expansion was accompanied by low interest rates, low inflation, and record stock market highs.

## Interest Rates

Exhibit 1–3 reports historical interest rates on three-month U.S. Treasury bills, six-month commercial paper, and top quality (AAA) corporate bonds. The Treasury bill

---

**EXHIBIT 1–2  Percent Changes in Real Gross National Product in 1982 Dollars**

| Year | Percent Change in Real GNP (After Inflation) |
|------|----------------------------------------------|
| 1975 | −1.3 |
| 1976 | 4.9 |
| 1977 | 4.7 |
| 1978 | 5.3 |
| 1979 | 2.5 |
| 1980 | −0.2 |
| 1981 | 1.9 |
| 1982 | −2.5 |
| 1983 | 3.6 |
| 1984 | 6.8 |
| 1985 | 3.4 |
| 1986 | 2.8 |
| 1987 | 3.4 |

Source: *Economic Report of the President* (Washington, D.C.: U.S. Government Printing Office, 1989), Table B-5, p. 315.

---

**EXHIBIT 1–3  Historic Variations in Various Rates of interest**

| Year | 3-Month Treasury Bills (%) | 6-Month Commercial Paper (%) | AAA Grade Corporate Bonds (%) |
|------|----------------------------|------------------------------|-------------------------------|
| 1975 | 6.01 | 6.32 | 8.83 |
| 1976 | 5.12 | 5.34 | 8.43 |
| 1977 | 5.41 | 5.61 | 8.02 |
| 1978 | 7.46 | 7.99 | 8.73 |
| 1979 | 10.45 | 10.91 | 9.63 |
| 1980 | 12.02 | 12.29 | 11.94 |
| 1981 | 14.75 | 14.76 | 14.17 |
| 1982 | 11.14 | 11.89 | 13.79 |
| 1983 | 8.94 | 8.89 | 12.04 |
| 1984 | 9.95 | 10.16 | 12.71 |
| 1985 | 7.73 | 8.01 | 11.37 |
| 1986 | 6.16 | 6.39 | 9.02 |
| 1987 | 5.99 | 6.85 | 9.38 |
| 1988 | 6.90 | 7.68 | 9.71 |

Source: *Economic Report of the President* (Washington, D.C.: U.S. Government Printing Office, 1989), Table B-71, p. 390.

rate is the best proxy for a risk-free rate that exists in the U.S. economy. The six-month commercial paper rate is the short-term interest rate paid by very credit-worthy corporations, while the AAA corporate bond rate is the long-term rate paid by these corporations. Exhibit 1–3 shows drastic fluctuations in rates, especially the short-term rates.

In the long run, the level of interest rates depends on two factors. The first factor has already been discussed. It is the willingness of individuals to forego current consumption and invest. As this willingness to invest increases, the supply of funds available for investment increases and the cost of investment funds, the interest rate, goes down. The second factor is the demand for funds, or the investment opportunities that exist in the economy. The better the investment opportunities, the greater will be the demand for funds and, therefore, the higher the interest rates. A discussion of investment opportunities would involve a detailed analysis of tax policy, other governmental policies, available capital, and human and natural resources.

In the short run, the level of interest rates is influenced by current market conditions—the demand for and supply of money to lend. The demand for funds may change as households, businesses, and governmental bodies change their borrowing plans. The short-run supply of funds is greatly influenced by the nation's central bank, the Federal Reserve. By increasing or decreasing the supply of money, the Fed expects to improve economic conditions. However, its policies can cause sudden changes in interest rates.

## Inflation

Exhibit 1–4 reports recent inflation rates as measured by changes in the consumer price index. Like interest rates, inflation rates have fluctuated drastically in recent years. In 1980, inflation was above 13 percent, while by 1986 it was down to just below 2 percent.

It was pointed out above that investors demand payments of the real risk-free rate of return because of the time value of money, and they demand payment of a risk premium that depends on the investment's degree of risk. They also demand an **inflation premium** that adjusts the rate of return for the expected inflation. Therefore, as shown in Equation 1–1, the total required rate of return is the sum of the real risk-free rate of return, the inflation premium, and the risk premium.

$$\begin{array}{c} \text{required rate} \\ \text{of return} \end{array} = \begin{array}{c} \text{real risk-free} \\ \text{rate of return} \end{array} + \begin{array}{c} \text{inflation} \\ \text{premium} \end{array} + \begin{array}{c} \text{risk} \\ \text{premium} \end{array} \qquad (1\text{--}1)$$

For example, if the real risk-free rate were 3 percent, expected inflation was 6 percent, and the investor required a 7 percent risk premium for this investment, he or she would demand a 16 percent return. However, this example does not consider the effect of income tax on the investor's return. If the tax is considered, a larger inflation premium will be demanded, one that will provide 6 percent after tax.

Because investors tend to adjust their required rate of return to reflect anticipated inflation, it is the unanticipated inflation that harms their purchasing power. In fact,

---

**EXHIBIT 1–4**   *Annual Changes in Consumer Price Index*

| Year | Percent Change |
|------|----------------|
| 1975 | 9.1 |
| 1976 | 5.8 |
| 1977 | 6.5 |
| 1978 | 7.7 |
| 1979 | 11.3 |
| 1980 | 13.5 |
| 1981 | 10.4 |
| 1982 | 6.1 |
| 1983 | 3.2 |
| 1984 | 4.3 |
| 1985 | 3.6 |
| 1986 | 1.9 |
| 1987 | 3.6 |

Source: *Economic Report of the President* (Washington, D.C.: U.S. Government Printing Office, 1989), Table B-61, p. 377.

---

if inflation were less than expected, they would gain from the unduly high inflation premiums that they receive.

Often, for convenience of expression, the inflation premium is included in the risk-free rate. In other words, the nominal risk-free rate consists of the real risk-free rate plus the inflation premium.

# PORTFOLIO VIEW OF WEALTH

When you invest, you must choose specific assets in which to hold wealth. A **portfolio** is the combination of all your individual assets. If you view your wealth as a portfolio, you do not think of particular investments in isolation; rather you consider all your assets when making investment decisions. It is best to take a broad view of your wealth and include social security benefits, pension funds, and cash value of life insurance in your portfolio. A house, farm, small business, and real estate are assets whose attributes must be considered along with the attributes of stocks and bonds or savings accounts.

## Forms of Wealth

Wealth may be accumulated in many forms, which fall into two categories—financial assets and real assets. Exhibit 1–5 lists the most common financial and real assets. **Financial assets** are pieces of paper that represent claims on wealth held by others. **Real assets** are physical goods such as furniture, cars, houses, farms, small businesses,

---

**EXHIBIT 1–5   Classification of Assets**

---

*Financial Assets*
Currency
Accounts in depository institutions
U.S. savings bonds
Cash value of insurance, pensions, and annuities
U.S. Treasury bills, notes, and bonds
Municipal notes and bonds
Corporate notes and bonds
Stocks
Investment company shares
Other securities: warrants, options, futures, etc.

*Real Assets*
Houses
Cars, boats, recreational vehicles, etc.
Appliances, furniture, clothing, etc.
Real estate
Farms
Small businesses
Collectibles: art, antiques, stamps, coins, etc.
Precious stones and metals: jewelry, gold, silver, etc.

---

and precious metals and stones. Some real assets provide a current benefit. For example, a house provides a place to live and a car provides transportation. Other real assets, such as gold bullion, do not provide current benefits. However, gold in the form of jewelry can be worn. Real assets may increase or decrease in value as time passes. For example, in the 1970s most used houses steadily increased in value while the value of gold fluctuated.

Exhibit 1–6 shows financial assets as a percentage of the total assets held by consumers. After falling during most of the 1970s, this percentage has been increasing in the 1980s. As a reference point, notice that in recent years financial assets have never been less than one-half or greater than two-thirds of consumers' total assets.

## Diversification

An important consideration when you view your portfolio is the degree of diversification. **Diversification** is distributing your wealth among many assets in order to minimize the risk of loss. Wealth should be dispersed so that the loss of any one asset or the poor performance of one type of asset does not cause great loss.

Diversification takes place on two levels. The first relates to types of assets. You should avoid having most of your wealth in one type of asset, such as stocks, bonds, or real estate. A decline in the value of this type of asset could cause you substantial harm.

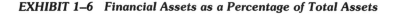

**EXHIBIT 1–6   *Financial Assets as a Percentage of Total Assets***

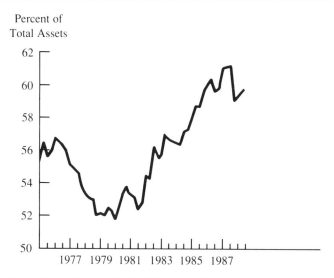

Source: Federal Reserve Bank of Cleveland, *Economic Trends,* (December 1988), p. 7.

On the second level, diversification is important among assets of the same type. For example, if you want to deposit more money in a savings account than the federal insurance agencies will cover, you should spread your deposits among several institutions. If you choose to invest money in securities, you should purchase stocks or bonds issued by several corporations. It is disheartening to read the articles that follow the failure of a large corporation—there are always stories of individuals who had a large share of their wealth invested in that one stock or bond issue and whose standard of living will be lowered because of the failure.

## Systematic Versus Unsystematic Risk

Stocks' return and risk characteristics have been studied more than those of any other assets. Therefore, more is known about how to diversify holdings of stocks. As shown in Equation 1–2, the total risk of a stock can be viewed as the sum of two components—systematic and unsystematic risk.

$$\frac{\text{total}}{\text{risk}} = \frac{\text{systematic}}{\text{risk}} + \frac{\text{unsystematic}}{\text{risk}} \qquad\qquad (1\text{--}2)$$

**Systematic risk** originates in the general economy and affects all stocks. Forces such as the level of economic activity, inflation, productivity, tax policy, and international relations cause systematic risk. The sensitivity of firms to these general ec-

## *Human Capital*

Human capital is the result of investment in people for the purpose of increasing future earnings potential. Education and occupational training in fields that will have a high demand in the future increase human capital. For most young people, human capital is their most valuable asset. Human capital differs from other forms of wealth in that it cannot legally be taken by others, it is not taxed, nor is it subject to bankruptcy court action. The amount of human capital that a person has will influence investment decisions. For example, a young person with high human capital may be more willing to start a business because he or she knows that in case of failure, the human capital will not be lost. Likewise, a young person with a secure,

high-paying job may be more willing to undertake risky investments than a person without the expected income from employment.

The chart below relates lifetime income to education. It is based on the mean income of year-round, full-time workers 25 years and over. It is based on the assumptions that persons with no college experience start working at age 18, that those who go to college start working at age 22, and that everyone retires at age 65. This analysis of the relationship between lifetime income and education could be refined in many ways; however, the basic fact that level of education strongly influences income would still be shown.

*Lifetime Income and Education*

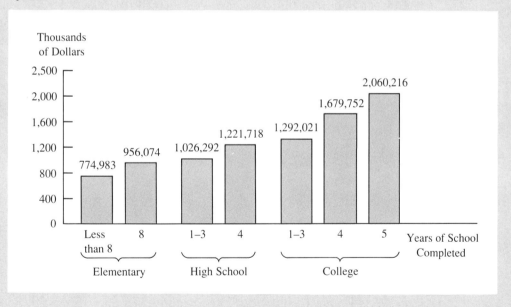

Source: Adapted from data in U.S. Bureau of the Census, "Money Income of Households, Families, and Persons in the United States: 1980," *Current Population Reports,* Series P-60, no. 156 (Washington, D.C.: U.S. Government Printing Office, 1987), Table 35, p. 134.

onomic conditions varies. In other words, firms vary in their degree of systematic risk. Some firms, such as automobile manufacturers, steel companies, and commercial airlines, are very sensitive. Other firms, such as utility companies and producers of low-cost consumer items, do not vary much in good or bad economic times.

**Beta** is a number that measures the sensitivity of a stock to systematic risk. A stock's beta can be found in several financial publications. The beta of the stock market as a whole is 1. Sensitive stocks have betas greater than 1. One would expect a stock with a beta of 2 to increase twice as much as the market in good times and to decrease twice as much as the market in bad times. Low beta stocks are those that are not sensitive to market movements. For example, one would expect a stock with a beta of .5 to increase only half as much as the market in good times and to fall only half as much in bad times.

In theory, the range of possible betas is unlimited. Negative betas are possible and would indicate that a stock moves in an opposite direction to the market. The firms whose stocks have negative betas are probably selling contracyclical products—things that people consume more in bad times such as replacement auto parts. (In bad times, consumers repair their old cars instead of buying new ones.)

In practice, few negative beta stocks exist because so few products are contracyclical. Investors who want low beta stocks can purchase stocks with betas between 0 and 1. On the other hand, stocks that are very sensitive to economic conditions have betas between 1.5 and 2.5. Stocks with betas greater than 2.5 are rare; few firms are so extremely sensitive to economic conditions. Exhibit 1–7 lists the betas of the stocks of some well-known companies.

---

**EXHIBIT 1–7   *Systematic Risk (Beta) of Some Well-Known Stocks***

| Stock | Beta |
| --- | --- |
| Lennar | 2.4 |
| Apple Computer | 1.9 |
| Mesa Petroleum | 1.9 |
| Amdahl Corporation | 1.6 |
| Mattel, Inc. | 1.6 |
| MCI Communications | 1.5 |
| Faberge, Inc. | 1.4 |
| Sheller-Globe | 1.2 |
| International Business Machines | 1.0 |
| General Electric | 1.0 |
| RCA Corporation | 1.0 |
| Denny's | .8 |
| Quaker Oats | .8 |
| McDonald's | .6 |
| Cincinnati Gas | .6 |
| Proctor & Gamble | .5 |
| Bell Canada | .5 |
| General Mills | .4 |

Investors can use betas to build stock portfolios that reflect the market sensitivity that they seek. Some investors may want the price stability that comes from portfolios containing low beta stocks. Others seek the higher potential returns that come with portfolios having higher beta (higher risk) stocks.

Of course, only part of a stock's risk is the systematic kind that originates in the general economy. **Unsystematic risk** is unique to the particular stock. A strike, fire, or product failure causes unsystematic risk. Because unsystematic risk is unique to a particular stock, it can be diversified away if you buy many stocks. This occurs because enough unexpected good things will happen to some of your stocks to offset the unexpected bad things that happen to others. How many stocks do you need to own in order to diversify away unsystematic risk? Empirical studies have shown that holding as few as eight stocks is adequate to diversify away almost all unsystematic risk. Therefore, if a substantial portion of your wealth is invested in stocks, be sure to own at least eight.

---

**EXHIBIT 1–8   Value of Stocks Listed on Exchanges (Billions of Dollars)**

| As of December 31 | New York Stock Exchange | American Stock Exchange | Exclusively on Other Exchanges | Total |
|---|---|---|---|---|
| 1940 | 41.9 | 8.6 | | 50.5 |
| 1945 | 73.8 | 14.4 | | 88.2 |
| 1950 | 93.8 | 13.9 | 3.3 | 111.0 |
| 1955 | 207.7 | 27.1 | 4.0 | 238.8 |
| 1960 | 307.0 | 24.2 | 4.1 | 335.3 |
| 1965 | 537.5 | 30.9 | 4.7 | 573.1 |
| 1970 | 636.4 | 39.5 | 4.8 | 680.7 |
| 1971 | 741.8 | 49.1 | 4.7 | 795.6 |
| 1972 | 871.5 | 55.6 | 5.6 | 932.7 |
| 1973 | 721.0 | 38.7 | 4.1 | 763.8 |
| 1974 | 511.1 | 23.3 | 2.9 | 537.3 |
| 1975 | 685.1 | 29.3 | 4.3 | 718.7 |
| 1976 | 858.3 | 36.0 | 4.2 | 898.5 |
| 1977 | 776.7 | 37.6 | 4.2 | 818.5 |
| 1978 | 822.7 | 39.2 | 2.9 | 864.8 |
| 1979 | 960.6 | 57.8 | 3.9 | 1,022.3 |
| 1980 | 1,242.8 | 103.5 | 2.9 | 1,349.2 |
| 1981 | 1,143.8 | 89.4 | 5.0 | 1,238.2 |
| 1982 | 1,305.4 | 77.6 | 6.8 | 1,389.7 |
| 1983 | 1,522.2 | 80.1 | 6.6 | 1,608.8 |
| 1984 | 1,529.5 | 52.0 | 5.8 | 1,587.3 |
| 1985 | 1,882.7 | 63.2 | 5.9 | 1,951.8 |
| 1986 | 2,128.5 | 70.3 | 6.5 | 2,205.3 |

Source: *Fifty-Third Annual Report,* U.S. Securities and Exchange Commission (Washington, D.C.: U.S. Government Printing Office, 1988), Table 22, p. 131.

**EXHIBIT 1–9  Holdings of New York Stock Exchange Listed Stock by Institutions (Billions of Dollars)**

| Type of U.S. Institution | Year End—1960 | 1965 | 1970 | 1975 | 1980 |
|---|---|---|---|---|---|
| Insurance companies | | | | | |
| Life | $ 3.2 | $ 6.3 | $ 11.7 | $ 21.6 | $ 38.1 |
| Nonlife | 6.0 | 10.1 | 12.2 | 11.6 | 26.9 |
| Investment companies | | | | | |
| Open-end | 12.4 | 29.1 | 39.0 | 35.0 | 38.1 |
| Closed-end | 4.2 | 5.6 | 4.1 | 5.5 | 5.1 |
| Noninsured pension funds | | | | | |
| Corporate and other private | 14.3 | 35.9 | 60.7 | 82.5 | 166.0 |
| State and local government | 0.3 | 1.4 | 9.6 | 24.4 | 53.0 |
| Nonprofit institutions | | | | | |
| Foundations | 8.0 | 16.4 | 17.0 | 20.8 | 32.4 |
| Educational endowments | 2.9 | 5.9 | 6.6 | 7.7 | 12.1 |
| Common trust funds | 1.4 | 3.2 | 4.1 | 5.2 | 9.5 |
| Mutual savings banks | 0.2 | 0.5 | 1.4 | 2.4 | 1.5 |
| Subtotal | $ 52.9 | $114.4 | $166.4 | $216.7 | $382.7 |
| Foreign Institutions | N/A | N/A | N/A | 25.1 | 57.5 |
| Total | $ 52.9 | $114.4 | $166.4 | $241.8 | $ 440.2 |
| Market value of all NYSE-listed stock | $307.0 | $537.5 | $636.4 | $685.1 | $1,242.8 |
| Estimated % held by institutional investors | 17.2% | 21.3% | 26.1% | 35.3% | 35.4% |

N/A  Not Available. Source: *Fact Book 1985* (New York: New York Stock Exchange, 1985), p. 55.

**EXHIBIT 1–10  Highlights of New York Stock Exchange Shareowner Surveys**

| | 1965 | 1970 | 1975 | 1980 | 1985 |
|---|---|---|---|---|---|
| Number of individual shareowners (thousands) | 20.120 | 30,850 | 25,270 | 30,200 | 47,040 |
| Number owning shares listed on NYSE (thousands) | 12,430 | 18,290 | 17,950 | 23,804 | 25,263 |
| Adult shareowner incidence in population | 1 in 6 | 1 in 4 | 1 in 6 | 1 in 5 | 1 in 4 |
| Median household income (prior year) | $9,500 | $13,500 | $19,000 | $27,750 | $36,800 |
| Number of adult shareowners with household income | | | | | |
| Under $10,000 (thousands) | 10,080 | 8,170 | 3,420 | 1,742 | 2,151 |
| $10,000 and over (thousands) | 8,410 | 20,130 | 19,970 | 25,715 | 40,999 |
| $15,000 and over (thousands) | 3,796 | 12,709 | 15,420 | 22,535 | 39,806 |
| $25,000 and over (thousands) | 1,073 | 4,114 | 6,642 | 15,605 | 32,690 |
| $50,000 and over (thousands) | N/A | N/A | 1,216 | 3,982 | 11,321 |
| Number of adult female shareowners (thousands) | 9,430 | 14,290 | 11,750 | 13,696 | 22,509 |
| Number of adult male shareowners (thousands) | 9,060 | 14,340 | 11,630 | 14,196 | 22,484 |
| Median age | 49 | 48 | 53 | 46 | 44 |

Note: Characteristics are for all individual shareowners, except where "adult" is designated. N/A  Not Available.
Source: *Fact Book 1988* (New York: New York Stock Exchange, 1988), p. 61.

**EXHIBIT 1–11**   *Characteristics of Individual Shareowners (Thousands of Shareowners)*

|  | 1965 | 1970 | 1975 | 1980 | 1985 |
|---|---|---|---|---|---|
| *Age* | | | | | |
| Under 21 | 1,280 | 2,221 | 1,818 | 2,308 | 2,260 |
| (21 and over) | 18,490 | 28,271 | 23,388 | 27,892 | 44,780 |
| 21–34 | 2,626 | 4,500 | 2,838 | 6,407 | 11,093 |
| 35–44 | 4,216 | 5,801 | 3,976 | 5,925 | 10,982 |
| 45–54 | 4,752 | 7,556 | 5,675 | 5,456 | 7,899 |
| 55–64 | 3,549 | 6,084 | 5,099 | 5,144 | 8,217 |
| 65 and over | 3,347 | 4,330 | 5,088 | 4,589 | 6,589 |
| *Education* | | | | | |
| 3 years high school or less | 3,106 | 3,566 | 1,621 | 1,746 | 2,513 |
| 4 years high school | 5,344 | 8,697 | 6,580 | 5,737 | 7,869 |
| 1–3 years college | 4,012 | 5,867 | 5,301 | 9,353 | 13,937 |
| 4 years college or more | 6,028 | 9,999 | 9,886 | 10,613 | 19,854 |
| *Occupation* | | | | | |
| Professional and technical | 3,136 | 6,320 | 4,273 | 6,096 | 9,725 |
| Clerical and sales | 2,903 | 4,415 | 3,399 | 3,928 | 6,288 |
| Managers and proprietors | 2,330 | 3,981 | 3,726 | 5,322 | 8,399 |
| Craftsmen and foremen | 924 | 1,377 | 1,154 | 1,548 | 2,821 |
| Operatives and laborers | 647 | 849 | 748 | 1,321 | 2,346 |
| Service workers | 414 | 622 | 452 | 236 | 1,372 |
| Farmers and farm laborers | 64 | 170 | 234 | 147 | 382 |
| Housewives, retired persons, and nonemployed adults | 8,072 | 10,320 | 9,402 | 8,108 | 11,819 |
| *Household Income* | | | | | |
| Under $5,000 | 2,977 | 2,389 | 780 | — | — |
| $5,000–$9,999 | 7,100 | 5,779 | 2,636 | 1,742 | 2,151 |
| $10,000–$14,999 | 4,862 | 8,346 | 4,552 | 3,180 | 1,193 |
| $15,000–$24,999 | 2,477 | 7,670 | 8,778 | 6,930 | 7,116 |
| $25,000 and over | 1,073 | 4,114 | 6,642 | 15,605 | 32,690 |
| *Portfolio* | | | | | |
| Under $10,000 | N/A | 8,810 | 11,647 | 17,912 | 24,292 |
| $10,000–$14,999 | N/A | 9,001 | 3,072 | 2,290 | 2,674 |
| $15,000–$24,999 | N/A | 8,272 | 2,760 | 1,847 | 3,214 |
| $25,000 and over | N/A | 4,437 | 5,909 | 4,489 | 8,019 |

Note: Except for age, selected characteristics are those of adult shareowners only.

Source: *Fact Book 1988* (New York: New York Stock Exchange, 1988), p. 62.

# STOCK OWNERSHIP

Stocks and bonds constitute an important segment of U.S. wealth. The market value of stocks and bonds listed on the stock exchanges at the end of 1986 was over $3.7 trillion. Of this total, the value of the stocks was $2.2 trillion and the value of the bonds was $1.5 trillion. However, most bonds are traded over-the-counter and not on the exchanges; therefore, the value of all the bonds outstanding is much greater than this amount. Exhibit 1–8 shows how the value of the stocks listed on the exchanges has fluctuated over the market cycles. Notice that the 1985 figure is more than double the 1978 value.

The New York Stock Exchange (NYSE) conducts periodic studies of the ownership of the stocks listed on that exchange. Exhibit 1–9 shows that among U.S. institutions, pension funds are by far the largest holder of NYSE stock. Other major institutional owners are insurance companies, investment companies, and nonprofit institutions. The exhibit also shows the dramatic increase over the past 25 years in the percentage of stock owned by institutions.

Most Americans benefit in some way from the institutional holdings listed in Exhibit 1–9. Anyone who owns a life insurance policy, participates in a pension or deferred profit-sharing plan, has an account in a mutual savings bank, or receives a scholarship from a college endowment fund may be considered an **indirect shareowner.** The NYSE estimates that at the end of 1980, there were 133 million indirect shareowners, more than three times the number of individuals who own stock directly.

Approximately one in four adults in the U.S. owns stock directly. Exhibits 1–10 and 1–11 summarize some of the characteristics of NYSE shareowners. These 47 million direct shareowners are in addition to the 133 million indirect shareowners. Although most direct owners are also indirect owners, they were eliminated in computing the indirect shareowner figure in order to avoid double counting.

# SUMMARY

Investment is foregoing current consumption of wealth in order to obtain greater future benefits. The assets to invest in should be chosen based on the attributes of return, risk, liquidity, tax aspects, and manageability. The rate of return which an investor demands depends on the real risk-free rate of return, anticipated inflation, and the risk of the investment.

There are two categories of assets: financial and real. An important concept is to view each asset as part of your total portfolio of wealth. In order to reduce risk, you should diversify a total portfolio and consider the relationship among the specific investments. The total risk of an investment is the sum of its systematic and unsystematic risk.

Most people in the United States are either direct or indirect owners of securities. Indirect ownership occurs when you own a life insurance policy, participate in a pension or deferred profit-sharing plan, have an account in a mutual savings bank, or receive a scholarship from a college endowment fund. Institutions, such as insurance companies, investment companies, and pension funds, now own over 35 percent of the stock listed on the NYSE.

## QUESTIONS

1. What is investment? How does it involve both risk and time?
2. Define the five attributes important in choosing investments.
3. What two forms of return might an investment provide? Give examples of investments that provide each form of return.
4. Discuss how different investments require varying amounts of work by the investor.
5. In the long run, what factors determine the level of interest rates? In the short run, what factors are important?
6. What factors determine the rate of return an investor demands on an investment?
7. Is anticipated or unanticipated inflation most harmful to an investor? Why?
8. What is the difference between real and financial assets? Give examples.
9. Why is diversification important? Explain how it is achieved.
10. What is the difference between systematic and unsystematic risk?
11. What does beta measure? What kinds of companies have high betas?
12. Who are indirect shareholders? How does the number of indirect shareholders compare to the number of direct shareholders?
13. What institutions are large owners of stocks?

## PROBLEMS

1. Given the following projections, what annual rate of return would you require on stock ABC (ignore taxes):

    — real risk-free rate of return = 3%
    — anticipated inflation = 5%
    — appropriate risk premium = 8%

2. Given the following projections, what annual rate of return would you require on stock XYZ (ignore taxes):

    — real risk-free rate of return = 2%
    — anticipated inflation = 7%
    — appropriate risk premium = 9%

## CASE PROBLEMS

1. Answer each of the questions below.

    a. What percentage of your income do you save? Are you satisfied with this percentage?
    b. Are you averse to risk? If yes, how averse?

    c. What is your preference for degree of liquidity? Why?

    d. What types of investments would you enjoy managing?

    e. How diversified is your wealth?

**2.** Describe how you think your life will be ten years from now. What do you think your answers to the above questions will be then?

# READINGS

Amihud, Yakov, and Mendelson, Haim. "Liquidity and Stock Returns," *Financial Analysts Journal* 42 (May–June 1986): 43–48.

    *This article examines the role of liquidity considerations in the pricing of stocks.*

Bruyn, Severyn T. *The Field of Social Investment.* Cambridge: Cambridge University Press, 1987.

    *Some churches, universities, unions, insurance companies, banks, mutual funds, and individuals are beginning to use social criteria in investment decisions. This book interprets the meaning of social investment and describes current practices.*

New York Stock Exchange. *Fact Book.* New York: New York Stock Exchange, Annual.

    *This publication provides the public, securities industry, government, and financial press with a reference manual on NYSE activities.*

U.S. Securities and Exchange Commission. *Annual Report.* Washington, D.C.: U.S. Government Printing Office, Annual.

    *This publication's text and tables record the activity and current regulation issues in the securities markets.*

Warschauer, Thomas, and Cherin, Antony. "Optimal Liquidity in Personal Financial Planning," *The Financial Review* 22 (November 1987): 355–368.

    *This article addresses the question of optimal personal liquidity in a personal financial-planning framework. A variety of motives for maintaining liquidity are examined in depth.*

# Financial Markets

## OUTLINE

## OBJECTIVES

When you have finished studying this chapter you should understand

1. What securities markets are and how they are organized.
2. How the original sale of a security takes place.
3. How a stock exchange operates.
4. The objectives of the national market system mandated by Congress.

# 2

## *Specialists and Liquidity*

"How the Stock Market Died and Rose Again a Day After the Crash" was the lead story in the November 20, 1987, *Wall Street Journal*. Its subtitle was "Credit Dried Up for Brokers and Especially Specialists Until Fed Came to Rescue." The article reported how on October 20, the day after the largest drop ever in stock prices, trading in stocks, options, and futures almost came to a halt. Many investors could not sell their securities; trading in major stocks, such as IBM and Merck, had stopped. Many securities firms were near failure as banks refused them loans. A "meltdown" of the markets was feared. If markets had closed, when and how would they have reopened? What would their closing have done to the economy and to international markets? What changes should be made in market structure to prevent a repeat of October 19 and 20, 1987? There is no agreement on the answers to these difficult questions, but this chapter provides some background for intelligent discussion of the future development of financial markets.

## INTRODUCTION

In this chapter, we introduce the reader to the securities markets. We explain how investment banking firms assist corporations wanting to sell securities to investors. Then, we explain how the investor can resell securities on the stock exchanges or in the over-the-counter market. In the last part of the chapter, we look at market efficiency and the government's attempt to improve it through the development of a national market system.

# SECURITIES MARKETS

A **securities market** is a mechanism for bringing together people who want to buy and sell financial assets. Securities markets are classified by the maturity of the financial assets bought and sold there. The **money market** is where large denomination debt instruments with original maturities of less than a year are bought and sold. The market in which the maturity period is longer than a year is the **capital market.** Stocks and bonds are bought and sold there.

Another way to segment securities markets is into primary and secondary markets. The original sale of a security takes place in the **primary market.** The money paid for the security goes to its issuer. Subsequent sales of the security take place in the **secondary market,** where the money paid for the security goes to its previous owner.

## *Investment Banking*

Important to the functioning of the primary market are investment banking firms. An **investment banking firm** is the middleman between firms wishing to raise money by selling securities and investors wanting to buy securities. An investment banking firm provides four services for the firm which plans to issue securities to the public: providing advice, underwriting, selling the securities, and providing an after-market.

***Providing Advice*** The investment banking firm advises the issuing firm about the financial markets. The investment banking firm's employees know what potential purchasers seek and what they are willing to pay. Similar to the practice of a corporation's using the same law firm for all its legal advice for many years, a corporation usually uses the same investment banking firm every time it has securities to sell. Therefore, any time the corporation seeks advice about its financing plans, the investment banking firm will review the plans and discuss the prices, advantages, and disadvantages of selling stocks or bonds now or in the future. In that way, the investment banking firm can help the corporation design an optimal long-range plan for raising money in the financial markets.

***Underwriting*** **Underwriting** is the process in which the investment banking firm bears the risk of the sale by purchasing the securities from the issuer and then reselling them to the public. The investment banking firm pays the issuer the agreed price. If the offering price to the public is too high and has to be reduced in order to sell the securities, the investment banking firm will have to lower its offering price, thereby reducing its expected profits or perhaps taking a loss.

The importance of the risk-bearing function provided by the investment banker is demonstrated by a 1979 debt offering by IBM. The $1 billion offering was evenly divided between 7-year notes and 25-year debentures. The group of investment bankers handling the issue started selling it on Thursday, October 4. On Saturday, October 6, the Federal Reserve Board announced a number of credit tightening measures, and on Monday morning bond prices fell drastically as interest rates went up. The investment bankers, not IBM, took a $20 million loss on the one-third of the debt issue that they had not sold to the public by Monday.

In some instances, the investment banking firm might consider underwriting a new or small firm's securities too risky; or, perhaps, the issuer and the investment banking firm cannot agree on the issue size or price. In these circumstances, instead of purchasing and reselling the securities, the investment banking firm could work as the issuing firm's agent in trying to sell the securities to the public. This is called a **best efforts arrangement.** The issuing firm pays the investment banking firm a commission for each share sold but the investment banking firm does not guarantee to sell a specific number of shares.

A third form of agreement between an issuing firm and an investment banking firm is a **standby offering.** It is usually used when the firm is selling additional shares to its existing stockholders through a rights offering. The issuer and the investment banking firm agree that the investment banking firm will underwrite and sell any portion of the offering not purchased by existing stockholders. This assures the issuer that all of the shares will be sold.

An exception to the normal long-term relationship between an investment banking firm and an issuing firm also exists. Because financing costs affect utility rates, utility regulators demand that **competitive bidding** by investment banking firms be used when utilities have securities to issue. Under a competitive bidding arrangement, the issuing firm solicits bids for the securities from investment banking firms. The investment banking firm offering the highest price purchases the securities for resale to the public.

A few large nonutility firms also sell securities to investment banking firms using competitive bidding. These firms do not need the advice investment banking firms offer their clients because they employ their own experts in financial markets, and they believe that competitive bidding provides them a better price for their securities.

***Selling the Securities***    The third service of the investment banking firm is selling the securities to the public. The firm's salespeople will be calling potential buyers and explaining the possibilities of the investment. The salespeople are paid a commission by the investment banking firm; therefore, customers can buy a new issue without paying an additional commission.

Usually, an investment banking firm is not financially strong enough or large enough to underwrite and sell the issue by itself. Therefore, it forms a syndicate with other investment banking firms. The **syndicate,** or a group of investment banking firms, shares the risk of underwriting the issue and provides additional salespeople. The inclusion of regional brokerage firms in the syndicate helps ensure that the securities are well placed. That is, they are sold to many investors in all parts of the country. This promotes broad interest in the firm and helps minimize potential control controversies. Large issues may require more salespeople than are available in the syndicate. In these cases, additional brokerage firms will be brought in as part of a selling group. Exhibit 2–1 is an advertisement showing the members of an investment banking syndicate.

The difference between the gross proceeds from the issue and the net amount paid to the issuer is called the **spread.** About 20 percent of the spread is a management

**EXHIBIT 2–1   Advertisement Showing Members of an Investment Banking Syndicate**

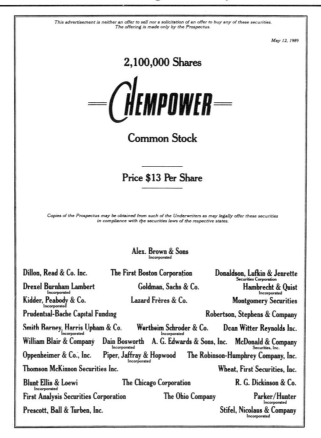

Source: Courtesy of Wertheim Schroder & Company, Inc.

fee paid to the investment banking firm that arranged the issue. About 50 percent of it is used to pay the selling commission. This is allocated based on the shares sold. The remainder pays the underwriters for their risk-bearing function.

Exhibit 2–2 shows the cost to a firm of selling new securities. The cost is stated as a percentage of the gross proceeds. The total cost of a new issue includes the underwriting fees and legal, administrative, and printing costs. Notice that small issues are much more expensive in terms of percentage of gross proceeds. Also, notice that common stock issues are more expensive than preferred stock or bond issues. This higher cost reflects two factors. First, most common stock issues are sold in smaller quantities to many investors while most bond and preferred stock issues are sold in larger quantities to few investors. Second, common stock is more difficult to price because the price depends greatly on expectations of future performance. Bonds and

---

**EXHIBIT 2–2** *Costs of Issuing Securities as Percent of Gross Proceeds*

| | *Selected Security Sizes*[a] | | | | | |
|---|---|---|---|---|---|---|
| | *2–5* | *5–10* | *10–20* | *20–50* | *50–100* | *Average All Deals*[b] |
| *Bonds* | | | | | | |
| Underwriting | 4.02 | 2.36 | 1.24 | 1.00 | .89 | 1.14 |
| Other | 2.21 | .78 | .65 | .43 | .28 | .45 |
| Total | 6.23 | 3.14 | 1.89 | 1.43 | 1.17 | 1.59 |
| *Common Stock* | | | | | | |
| Underwriting | 8.19 | 6.70 | 5.52 | 4.41 | 3.94 | 8.41 |
| Other | 3.71 | 2.03 | 1.11 | .62 | .31 | 4.02 |
| Total | 11.90 | 8.73 | 6.63 | 5.03 | 4.25 | 12.43 |
| *Preferred Stock* | | | | | | |
| Underwriting | — | 1.88 | 1.37 | 1.37 | 1.35 | 1.52 |
| Other | — | .66 | .42 | .29 | .20 | .39 |
| Total | — | 2.54 | 1.79 | 1.66 | 1.55 | 1.91 |

[a] In millions of dollars.

[b] Includes some smaller and some larger issues.

Source: U.S. Securities and Exchange Commission, ''Cost of Flotation of Registered Issues, 1971–1972'' (Washington, D.C.: U.S. Government Printing Office, December, 1974), pp. 9, 24, and 29.

---

preferred stock prices are based on interest and dividend rates and default risk. Therefore, underwriting common stock is more risky for the investment banking firm.

**Providing an After-Market**  The fourth service the investment banking firm provides is maintaining an after-market. The investment banking firm maintains a small inventory of the stock and stands ready to buy or sell it. This provides liquidity to the shareholders who purchased the stock. This market-making function will be examined in more detail when we look at the over-the-counter market for securities.

## Organized Exchanges

While the first sale of securities takes place in the primary market, most investors would not purchase securities unless there existed a secondary market where the securities could be resold. The secondary market provides liquidity for the securities. The secondary market is divided into the organized exchanges and the over-the-counter market.

A **stock exchange** is a not-for-profit corporation that provides a place where its members can come together for the purpose of buying and selling securities. Stock exchanges are grouped into two categories—national and regional. Large firms, such as IBM, Litton, and General Motors, may apply to have their stock listed for trading

---

**EXHIBIT 2–3   Requirements to be Listed on the New York Stock Exchange**

| Category | Minimum Amount |
| --- | --- |
| Pre-tax income last year | $ 2,500,000 |
| Pre-tax income each of the previous two years | $ 2,000,000 |
| Net tangible assets | $18,000,000 |
| Shares publicly held | 1,100,000 |
| Number of round-lot holders | 2,000 |
| Market value publicly held shares | $18,000,000 |

Source: Data compiled from *Fact Book 1988* (New York: New York Stock Exchange, 1988), pp. 22–23.

---

on one of the national exchanges. The two national exchanges, the New York Stock Exchange (NYSE) and the American Stock Exchange (AMEX), are both located in New York City. The exchange reviews a firm's listing application, considering in particular the degree of national interest in the company, its relative position and stability in its industry, and the future of its industry. Although each firm is considered on its own merits, some normal minimum requirements are published. Exhibit 2–3 displays these requirements for listing on the NYSE and Exhibit 2–4 displays the requirements for listing on the AMEX. Notice that the requirements of the NYSE are much stricter than those of the AMEX.

The listing requirements of the regional exchanges are less stringent than the AMEX. Regional exchanges provide markets for the securities of some regional firms. Membership on a regional exchange also provides an opportunity for nonmembers of the national exchanges to engage in the trading of securities. Therefore, many stocks are listed both on a national exchange and one or more regional exchanges in order to facilitate trading. The regional exchanges are much smaller than the national exchanges.

---

**EXHIBIT 2–4   Requirements to be Listed on the American Stock Exchange**

| Category | Minimum Amount |
| --- | --- |
| Pre-tax income last year | $ 750,000 |
| Stockholders' equity | $4,000,000 |
| Shares publicly held | 500,000 |
| Number of stockholders | 800 |
| Market value publicly held shares | $3,000,000 |
| Price per share | $3.00 |

Source: Data compiled from *AMEX Fact Book* (New York: American Stock Exchange, 1987), p. 11.

---

**EXHIBIT 2–5  Stock Trading Volume on the Exchanges, 1986**

| Exchange | Number of Shares (1,000) | Total Share Volume (%) | Market Value ($1,000) | Total Market Value (%) |
|---|---|---|---|---|
| New York | | | | |
| Stock Exchange | 39,258,480 | 81.22 | 1,450,150,125 | 85.05 |
| American | | | | |
| Stock Exchange | 2,998,859 | 6.20 | 43,432,469 | 2.55 |
| Midwest | | | | |
| Stock Exchange | | | | |
| (Chicago) | 2,783,626 | 5.76 | 102,362,283 | 6.00 |
| Pacific | | | | |
| Stock Exchange | | | | |
| (San Francisco, | | | | |
| Los Angeles) | 1,750,361 | 3.62 | 50,757,818 | 2.98 |
| Philadelphia | | | | |
| Stock Exchange | 742,819 | 1.54 | 26,866,492 | 1.57 |
| Boston | | | | |
| Stock Exchange | 647,135 | 1.34 | 24,604,904 | 1.44 |
| Cincinnati | | | | |
| Stock Exchange | 145,261 | .30 | 6,936,151 | .41 |
| Others | 11,153 | .02 | 13,711 | .00 |
| Total | 48,337,694 | 100.00 | 1,705,123,953 | 100.00 |

Source: Adapted from data in *Securities and Exchange Commission Annual Report*—1987 (Washington, D.C.: U.S. Government Printing Office, 1988), Tables 16A and 16B, pp. 123–24.

---

Exhibit 2–5 shows the number of and the dollar volume of the shares on the NYSE, AMEX, and regional exchanges.

As mentioned earlier, an exchange is a place where members come together to buy and sell securities. The members are classified according to their functions. Each class of members performs a specific function. The discussion here is based on the NYSE; however, other exchanges have similar organizations. Exhibit 2–6 is a picture of the trading floor of the NYSE.

The NYSE membership is fixed at 1,366. A person becomes a member by buying a membership from someone willing to sell it. Usually about 100 memberships are transferred each year. The highest price ever paid for a membership was $1.15 million (1987), the lowest price paid in recent years was $35,000 (1977). Each applicant for membership has to be approved by the exchange and each membership is in a specified class. There are commission brokers, specialists, floor brokers, odd lot dealers, registered competitive market makers, and bond dealers.

---

**EXHIBIT 2–6**  *New York Stock Exchange Trading Floor*

---

Source: Photo Courtesy of the New York Stock Exchange.

---

***Commission Brokers***  *Commission broker* memberships are held by officers of brokerage firms; some large brokerage firms have more than one member. Each membership allows the firm to have one person on the floor of the exchange to handle customer orders. The majority of members are commission brokers.

If you place an order with an office of a brokerage firm that is a member of the NYSE, the local office will immediately enter the order into its computer. The order will be printed out on a terminal beside the NYSE trading floor. Clerks working for your local firm hand the order to their commission broker as soon as he or she is available to handle it. The commission broker will then take the order onto the exchange floor where each stock is traded in a specific location. Your firm's broker will bargain with the brokers from other firms in order to buy or sell your stock at the best possible price. This bargaining means the organized exchanges are auction markets. **Auction markets** determine prices by the active competition of several parties willing to buy and sell.

The exact purchase price that the broker obtains will be immediately reported for everyone to see on the electronic ticker and entered into the brokerage firm's computer.

Normally the firm's local office can confirm that the order was transacted and tell you the exact price within a few minutes of the time you placed it.

***Specialists*** Specialists are members who make a continuous orderly market in stocks assigned them by the exchange. A specialist might make a market in one to three heavily traded stocks and five to ten less actively traded stocks. When your firm's commission broker took your order onto the floor of the exchange, he or she went to the specialist who makes a market in that stock. This location is known as a specialist's post. About one-fourth of the exchange members are specialists.

A continuous market requires that trading not stop because of a lack of buy or sell orders. The specialist maintains a continuous market by buying or selling for him or herself when a broker arrives at the specialist's post with an order and there is no other broker there with an offsetting order. For example, if your broker was executing a buy order for you and if there were no brokers with sell orders, your broker would purchase the stock from the specialist. This market-making function is somewhat comparable to the dealer's role in the OTC market.

In an orderly market prices move up or down gradually instead of changing drastically on succeeding sales. If there happen to be many sell but only a few buy orders, the specialist must sell; thus the stock's price moves up gradually.

Occasionally an event, announcement, or rumor will cause so many buy or sell orders that it is impossible for the specialist to maintain a continuous orderly market. In these cases, the exchange officers will halt trading in the security for hours or days. When the vital information is public and the number of orders can be estimated, the trading will be resumed. Usually, the price will then be very different from that before trading was halted. When a major tragedy occurs, such as the shooting of the president, all trading is stopped on the exchange.

The specialist's second function is to help the commission brokers execute orders. This service is very important in the case of limit orders and other special orders. A **limit order** is a buy or sell order with a price restriction on it. When you place a limit order to buy, you state the maximum price you are willing to pay. When you place a limit order to sell, you state the minimum price you are willing to accept. An order without any price restriction is called a **market order.**

When you place a limit order, the commission broker takes it to the specialist's post. If it is possible to get a price at least as good as you demand, the order will be transacted as a market order. If the broker cannot get the price you demand, your order is left with the specialist who will execute it if the market price rises (for a sell order) or falls (for a buy order) enough to meet your requirement. The specialist separately keeps track of all buy and sell limit orders by the required price. If two or more limit orders are for the same price, they are filed according to the time they were received. Although now computerized, the lists of limit orders to buy and sell are called the specialist's book.

---

**EXAMPLE** | You place a limit order to buy 100 shares of Ester Electronics at a price no higher than $32 a share. When the commission broker takes your order to the specialist's post, Ester is selling for $33. Therefore, he leaves your order with the specialist. Later in the day the price begins to drop. When the price gets to $32, the specialist executes your order. □

When you place a limit order, it is important to specify an expiration date. Although that date can be anytime, it is most common to have the limit order expire at the end of the day it was placed or to be in effect until you cancel it. Obviously, it is important not to forget or lose track of your limit order. If you have several limit orders pending and the market rises or falls sharply, several of your orders could be executed on the same day. If this happens, in the case of buy orders, you suddenly would need the money to pay for the stocks you bought.

There is another type of limit order, a stop loss order, that the specialist keeps track of for the commission broker. This order is used when you already own the stock and you want to limit the loss if the stock's price drops. A **stop loss order** instructs the specialist to sell your stock if the market price drops to the price you specify.

| EXAMPLE |

You purchase 500 shares of Ester Electronics at $33 a share. You considered how much you were willing to lose and decided you would want to sell if the price dropped to $30. Therefore, you placed a stop loss order for $30 a share. If the stock were to fall to that price, your order would become a sell order and your stock would be sold, limiting your loss. □

| EXAMPLE |

After two months the price of Ester's stock has risen to $37. You want to protect your paper gain. Therefore, you cancel your stop loss order for $30 a share and place a new one for $35 a share. If the price falls to $35 a share your stock will be sold, protecting some of the profit you have gained. □

There are two problems with a stop loss order. First, if the stock price is declining rapidly and there are many stop loss orders pending, the specialist can get permission from the officials of the exchange to suspend temporarily all stop loss orders in order to keep the market for the stock orderly. In this case, your order is suspended exactly when you need it.

The second problem occurs when an announcement or a rumor of important unfavorable news causes a sudden steep drop in price. Your order becomes a market order when the stock reaches the price you specified. However, it is possible that when this happens there will not be enough buy orders for your stock to be sold at that price. Therefore, the specialist will sell your stock at the best price possible, which could be much less than the price you specified in the stop loss order. This situation could be harmful to you if, after your stock is sold at the low price, more news reaches the market and the price recovers because the situation is not as bad as originally thought.

| EXAMPLE |

You place a stop loss order on your Ester Electronics stock at $35. Unexpectedly one morning, an Ester's customer announces that it is filing suit claiming its plant was seriously damaged because of a design defect in one of Ester's products. A few minutes after the wire services carry this report, there are sell orders for 955,000 shares and few buy orders. Within a half hour the price of Ester's stock falls to $32. Although your stop loss order becomes a market order when the price plummets through $35, there are not any buy orders for the specialist to match with it until the market price reaches $32. In the afternoon, Ester announces that its product was not at fault, that it can successfully defend itself in court, and that it has adequate insurance if it were to lose. This news causes the market price to recover to $35.75. Unfortunately, your stock was sold at $32. ☐

**Floor Brokers**   The third class of membership of the NYSE, floor brokers, like commission brokers, are permitted to execute orders on the floor of the exchange. However, floor brokers are not employed by brokerage firms that originate orders. When a commission broker cannot handle the large volume of orders coming in, floor brokers help execute the orders for a fee. Floor brokers are used by many firms on busy days and by some firms regularly. The firms regularly using them may have more orders than their own commission brokers can handle but not enough to justify another commission broker membership. Floor brokers help prevent bottleneck situations on the exchange and help smooth the transactions flow. This is especially important on heavy volume days.

**Odd Lot Dealers**   On the NYSE, stocks trade in round lots. A **round lot** of stock is usually 100 shares; although for a few less actively traded, higher-priced stocks, it is 10 shares. When 100 shares is specified as a round lot, an **odd lot** is any number of shares from 1 to 99. When 10 shares is specified as a round lot, an odd lot is from 1 to 9 shares. Odd lot dealers, the fourth class of NYSE members, combine odd lots to buy and sell on the floor of the exchange in round lots. In another location, the odd lot dealer's firm buys and sells in odd lots.

If you purchase or sell an odd lot, the order can be handled in any one of three ways. The first, traditional, way is for the brokerage firm you place the order with to forward it to the odd lot firm which would buy or sell the stock at the price of the next round lot sales on the NYSE and charge an odd lot differential fee of 12.5 or 25 cents a share. Second, starting more recently, some odd lot orders are sent electronically to the specialist who acts as an odd lot dealer from his or her inventory. Finally, some brokerage firms fill their customer's odd lot orders from the firm's inventory.

| EXAMPLE |

You place an order to buy 550 shares of Ester Electronics. The 500 share order would go to the firm's commission broker on the floor of the exchange. The remaining 50 share order would be handled by your brokerage firm using one of the methods for odd lots. ☐

**Registered Competitive Market Makers**   Formerly called registered traders, these are the fifth class of membership of the NYSE. They are on the floor of the exchange buying and selling for their own account and, like specialists, have some specific trading obligations. They do not execute orders for others but provide liquidity to the market with their buying and selling. They also are an important part of the process by which stock prices adjust to new information. Above the floor of the exchange, general and business news is electronically displayed as it is reported by the news services. A registered competitive market maker can see an unexpected news report that affects a stock and immediately go to the specialist's post to buy or sell the stock. This buying and selling partially causes the stock price to adjust quickly to the release of new information.

**Bond Dealers and Brokers**   This is the final class of membership to be discussed. Bonds are traded on an annex to the main trading floor of the NYSE. Bond dealers and brokers make markets and transact trades in the bonds listed on the exchange. Most of the bonds are issued by U.S. companies; some are issued by the U.S. government, foreign governments, foreign companies, and international banks.

## The Over-the-Counter Market

The **over-the-counter (OTC) market** consists of all trading of securities except that which takes place on the organized exchanges. Since municipal securities, most Treasury securities, and most stocks and bonds are traded in the OTC market, it is a much broader market than the organized exchanges. The OTC market does not have a specific trading location; it is made up of thousands of securities dealers and brokers located with and working for firms in financial centers across the country. Large dealer firms include Shearson Lehman Hutton, which makes markets in about 1,700 OTC stocks, and Merrill Lynch and Dean Witter Reynolds, which make markets in over 1,000 OTC each. Small regional firms may make markets in only a few stocks of local interest.

Dealers in the OTC market make markets for securities by continually quoting the prices at which they will buy or sell those securities. The price at which the dealer offers to buy is called the **bid price.** The price at which the dealer offers to sell is called the **ask price.** The difference between the bid and ask prices is the **spread.** The spread allows the dealer to make money. Prices in the OTC market are negotiated prices; that is, the dealers and the customers (through their brokers) can bargain about the price. The dealers may be willing to lower the price at which they will sell a stock or raise the price at which they will buy.

| EXAMPLE |

Immediately after an investment banking firm has sold a new stock issue to the public at $27 per share, the over-the-counter trading might start at $26.50 bid and $28 ask. If there had been high demand for the stock, the initial bid and ask prices would be higher. If there had been difficulty selling the stock at $27, the initial bid and ask prices probably would be lower.         □

If there is extensive trading in the stock, another dealer might consider it profitable to make a market in the stock and is free to do so. This dealer would be competing with the first dealer. If the second dealer were aggressive, he or she might narrow the spread and offer better bid and ask prices than the first dealer.

| EXAMPLE | If the first dealer were offering $26.50 bid and $28 ask, the competing dealer might offer $26.75 bid and $27.75 ask. □

Stocks actively traded in the OTC market have several competing dealers making a market in them. As the above example shows, this competition results in smaller spreads and better prices for sellers and buyers. If you place an order to buy or sell an OTC stock, your broker should determine who is dealing in the stock and what their bid and ask prices are. If there are competing dealers, your broker should send your order to the dealer offering the best price.

| EXAMPLE | You decide to purchase 100 shares of Ester Electronics, which is traded in the OTC market. You place your order with your broker who checks and finds there are two dealers who make markets in Ester's stock. One is offering $26.00 bid and $27.50 ask. The other is offering $26.25 bid and $27.75 ask. Your broker offers to buy the stock from the first dealer at $27.25 and the dealer agrees to sell at that price. You will pay $2,725 plus your broker's commission. □

| EXAMPLE | Six months later you decide to sell your 100 shares of Ester Electronics. You phone your sell order to your broker who checks and finds one dealer is quoting $27 bid and $28.50 ask and the second dealer is quoting $27.50 bid and $28.50 ask. Your broker offers to sell your stock to the second dealer at $27.50, and the dealer agrees. You will receive $2,750 minus your broker's commission. □

Trading and prices of OTC securities are reported daily to brokerage firms by the National Quotation Bureau, a private agency. Its "pink sheets" report on trading in 11,000 stocks while its "yellow sheets" report on bonds and other debt securities.

The **National Association of Security Dealers (NASD)** is the self-regulatory organization of the securities industry which oversees the OTC market. It was established under the authority of 1938 amendments to the Securities Exchange Act of 1934. Its objectives are to promote the investment banking and securities business, to standardize the principles and practices followed, and to promote high ethical standards and observance of federal and state securities laws. Almost all broker/dealers are members of NASD which is governed by a member-controlled board and a system of committees.

In 1971, the NASD brought computerized communications to the OTC market with a system called **NASD Automated Quotations (NASDAQ)** which electronically links brokers with over 500 OTC market makers. A broker can obtain in seconds up-to-the-minute quotes on over 5,500 OTC securities. These securities average 8 dealers;

## Market-Making Risks

During March and April of 1987, major Wall Street firms took huge losses in their market-making activities. These losses caused some observers to question the amount of risk the firms took as well as their internal controls.

For five years, the bond and stock markets had been moving up. Therefore, even poor market makers could make money on their inventories. Because market making was profitable, most firms expanded their activities in this area, some on a worldwide basis. Then, in March and April, interest rates suddenly went up and the value of bond inventories went down drastically. Most firms had losses in their market-making activities; some of the losses were very large.

When the losses occurred, the firms began to examine the risks they were taking in their market-making activities. (Better late than never!) They looked at how much should be invested in securities inventory, what level of management should supervise trading functions, how the risks taken in different areas complement each other, and whether hedging strategies protect the firm from unfavorable market moves.

some very popular issues have over 45 dealers. This system makes it easy for your broker to route your order to the dealer offering the best price.

Over 2,600 of the most actively traded OTC stocks are included on **NASDAQ's National Market System** list. The transactional information reported on these stocks is as complete as the information reported on the stocks listed on the exchanges. For other NASDAQ stocks, bid, ask, and last prices along with the high and low prices are available on the computer but volume data are available only at the end of the trading day.

NASDAQ continues rapidly to expand the number of securities and volume of trading its system can handle. Among its innovations is the Small Order Execution System which automatically executes small orders against the best prices available. This allows the market makers to handle greater volume more efficiently.

Before the 1980s, companies whose stock qualified for trading on a national exchange usually applied to have the stock listed there. Recently, over 1,800 companies listed on NASDAQ were eligible for national exchange listing but did not apply for it. Many of these companies believe the competing OTC dealers make as liquid a market as the specialist on the exchange would. NASDAQ officers argue that this is evidence of a significant change in market structure. They believe that competing dealers linked by modern communications with brokers will form the securities markets of the future instead of organized exchanges.

## The Third Market

Historically, NYSE member firms charged fixed commissions with no discounts for large orders. For example, the commission on a 1,000 share order was ten times the commission on a 100 share order. Brokerage firm costs, however, do not increase significantly on the large orders. The high profits on large orders from institutional investors enticed brokerage firms which were not members of the exchange to develop an alternative, the third market.

The **third market** refers to OTC trading of securities that are listed on the exchanges. Because exchange rules generally prohibit member firms from trading listed securities anywhere but on the exchange, third market trading is carried out by broker-dealer firms that are not exchange members. From the third market's development in 1963 until fixed commission rates were abolished in 1975, the exchanges lost a significant amount of trading volume to the third market. For example, in 1971, more than 17 percent of the trading of NYSE listed stocks occurred on the regional exchanges or in the third market. Since fixed commission rates were ended in 1975, the size of the third market has declined greatly.

## The Fourth Market

The **fourth market** refers to institutional investors buying and selling securities without using brokerage firms. Like the third market, it developed during the period of fixed commission rates. A fourth market trade occurs when a portfolio manager contacts other portfolio managers to inquire if they want to buy (or sell) the securities that he or she plans to sell (or buy). If another portfolio manager wants to buy (or sell) the securities, both the buying and selling institutions save the commission charges.

The fourth market remained a small telephone-based market until electronic technology came to it in 1987. In that year, Instinet, a provider of computer services, initiated its electronic trading service for institutions. Large institutions, such as pension and mutual funds, subscribe to the service. When they want to buy or sell, they enter their transaction. The computer matches buy and sell orders. Although matches only can be found for a small percentage of orders, institutions can try Instinet first and then place the order elsewhere if no match is found.

# MARKET EFFICIENCY

Securities markets are a mechanism in the process used to allocate investment funds to real capital investment projects. Securities markets help channel money to firms that can produce efficiently the goods and services consumers want to purchase. In order to obtain the most productive uses of the economy's investment dollars, securities markets must be efficient. Optimal allocation of financial resources requires two types of market efficiency: external and internal.

## External Efficiency

**External efficiency** is also called "pricing efficiency" and it exists when security prices fully reflect all available information about the economy, the industry, and the specific firm. Then, security prices reflect the consensus judgment of all investors about the future prospects of the firms. Any new information will very quickly be reflected in security prices. Investors are continually evaluating the firms' expected returns and risks. These returns and risk, in turn, depend on the real capital investment opportunities that the firms have available. Firms with good investment opportunities will have high security prices and firms with poorer investment opportunities will have lower prices. When a firm raises money by issuing new securities, the price it obtains for the securities depends on its investment opportunities. Through this process the allocation of financial resources to promising investment opportunities takes place.

From the perspective of the investor, an external efficient market is a fair game. In a **fair game** investors face a common set of rules and cannot expect to outperform each other by trading practices based on existing information. In Chapter 21, we will examine external efficiency in much more detail. We will conclude that the securities markets are fairly efficient. This implies that most of the investor's attention should be spent on managing portfolio risks, reducing taxes, and reducing transaction costs.

## *Internal Efficiency*

**Internal efficiency** exists if a market provides the means through which investors can buy and sell securities at prices as low as possible considering the costs of the services used by them. Internal efficiency is also referred to as "transactional" and "operating" efficiency. If commissions or market-making charges are too high, a market lacks internal efficiency. In order for investment resources to be properly allocated, both external and internal efficiency must exist. If transaction costs are too high, investors will not undertake the buying and selling necessary to establish prices that fully reflect the prospects of the firms. The national market system described in the next section is a legislative effort to improve the efficiency of the securities markets.

# *THE NATIONAL MARKET SYSTEM*

On May 17, 1792, 24 stockbrokers signed an agreement creating what became the NYSE. The agreement stated

> We, the subscribers, brokers for the purchase and sale of public stocks, do hereby solemnly promise and pledge ourselves to each other that we will not buy or sell from this date, for any person whatsoever, any kind of public stocks at a rate less than one-quarter of one percent commission on one specie value, and that we will give preference to each other in our negotiations.

It is ironic that the NYSE, a symbol of capitalism, was founded for two noncompetitive practices: to fix prices and limit access to the market.

Until 1975, NYSE rules fixed the commission rates member firms charged and forbade member firms to trade NYSE listed securities anywhere other than on the exchange. If by coincidence two customers entered an office of an NYSE member firm at the same time and one wanted to buy the exact stock that the other wanted to sell, the firm could not match the orders; both orders had to go to the exchange floor. The rule requiring all orders to come to the NYSE protected the exchange specialist from competing market makers. In the early 1970s, the growth of institutional investors and third and fourth markets created pressure for change.

### Top Ten Underwriters of U.S. Securities (1988)

| | Amount (In Billions) | Percent of Market Share |
|---|---|---|
| Merrill Lynch Capital Markets | 39.7 | 14.5 |
| Goldman, Sachs & Co. | 36.9 | 13.5 |
| Salomon Brothers Inc. | 33.9 | 12.4 |
| First Boston Corp. | 30.0 | 11.0 |
| Shearson Lehman Hutton Inc. | 25.7 | 9.3 |
| Morgan Stanley & Co. | 23.0 | 8.4 |
| Drexel Burnham Lambert Inc. | 20.9 | 7.7 |
| Prudential-Bache Capital Funding | 11.0 | 4.0 |
| Bear, Stearns & Co. | 9.1 | 3.4 |
| Kidder, Peabody & Co. | 7.1 | 2.6 |

## Objectives and Benefits

After extensive study and hearings, Congress passed a major piece of deregulation legislation, the Securities Act Amendments of 1975. Congress declared the securities markets an ''important national asset which must be preserved and strengthened.'' The amendments directed the SEC to foster a more competitive market for securities by developing a national market system. Although the exact form of the national market system was not detailed in the law, the objectives of the system were listed. The national market system was to assure

— Economically efficient securities transactions

— Fair competition among brokers, among dealers, and among exchanges and the OTC market

— The availability of transactions information

— The execution of investors' orders in the best market

— The opportunity to execute orders without the participation of dealers

The amendments directed the SEC ''to eliminate existing anticompetitive rules of stock exchanges'' and ''to require the development of national market system facilities.''

There were several expected benefits from the national market system. First, the whole market was to become a price-setting mechanism so that the investor would get the best price when buying or selling securities. Congress did not intend to eliminate distinctions among the exchanges and the OTC market; rather it intended to make them competing elements in the national market system. Second, Congress wanted a system that would minimize the investor's transaction costs, such as costs of information about the market, brokerage fees, and spreads between bid and ask prices. Third, Congress realized that competition would encourage advances in the systems and technology used in transacting security business.

## Eliminating Anticompetitive Rules

The three major SEC actions to end exchange anticompetitive practices are

— Forbidding fixed commission rates
— SEC rule 19c-1
— SEC rule 19c-3

SEC action to end fixed commission rates started before passage of the amendments in 1975. In April 1971, the commission on that part of an order exceeding $500,000 became negotiable between the customer and brokerage firm. In May 1972, the cutoff became $300,000. Finally, on May 1, 1975, all commission rates became negotiable between the customer and brokerage firm. Negotiable rates resulted in much lower commissions on the large orders of institutions and the development of discount brokerage firms to serve individuals.

SEC rule 19c-1 prohibits exchanges from requiring their members to bring all orders to the exchange floor. However, although exchange members acting as a customer's agent now can take the order to the market with the best price, they are not permitted to consummate the trade as a principal; that is, the member firms cannot buy securities from or sell them to the customer. Rule 19c-2 would have removed this last restriction. However, because of exchange opposition it never was put into effect.

Like the proposed rule 19c-2, rule 19c-3 removes off-exchange trading restrictions on exchange members. However, it applies only to stocks newly listed on the exchanges after April 26, 1979. Exchange member firms can buy and sell as principals (that is, make markets in) rule 19c-3 stocks.

## Development of Electronic Facilities

The SEC also was directed to require the development of electronic facilities which would support the objectives of the national market system. The most important electronic facilities are a composite tape, consolidated quotations, automatic execution of orders, and a consolidated limit order book.

***Composite Tape*** A composite tape consolidates reporting of the prices from trades of a security in all markets. An NYSE composite tape that reports the trading of NYSE listed stocks no matter in what market the trading takes place was developed in 1975. Trades of NYSE listed stocks that take place on the regional exchanges or in the OTC market are reported along with the NYSE trades. An AMEX composite tape that reports all the trading of AMEX listed stocks also is operational.

***Consolidated Quotations*** A system with consolidated quotations gives a broker the list of the bid and ask prices of all market makers for that security. In other words, the quotes of all exchange specialists and OTC dealers handling the security are available to the broker. The broker can then route the customer's order to the market with the best price.

The consolidated quotation service now available is the Intermarket Trading System (ITS) developed by the American, Boston, Midwest, New York, Pacific, and Philadelphia stock exchanges. The system displays the current quotes from the participating markets. A broker can use ITS to enter buy and sell orders to a specific market. Confirmation of the acceptance of the order is returned over ITS.

***Automatic Execution***   What is missing from ITS is automatic routing of orders to the market with the best price. If it existed, the broker could just enter the order and get the best price. Without it, he or she must go to the trouble of reviewing the available quotes and then choosing the best market for the order.

***Consolidated Limit Order Book***   At present, only the exchange specialist has access to the limit order book, and limit orders are executed only on the exchange where they were entered. It is possible that a market order could be executed by another market maker at a price inferior to a limit order on the specialist's book.

Proposals have been made for a consolidated limit order book so that any market maker could execute these orders. Specialists oppose these proposals because limit orders are profitable business for them; they do not want to share it with other market makers. Some consolidated limit order proosals would allow only market makers access to limit order information, while other proposals would make the lists of limit orders available to everyone. Knowing all the pending limit orders could influence the investor's decision to buy or sell at the current market price.

# SUMMARY

The primary market is where the first sale of a security takes place. Usually an investment banking firm assists the issuer in that initial sale. The investor does not pay a commission when buying a new issue of stock.

The secondary market is where previously issued securities are bought and sold. The secondary market consists of the organized exchanges and the over-the-counter market. Brokerage firms buy memberships on the organized exchanges so they can buy and sell for their customers the stocks listed on the exchange. Specialists are members of the exchange who provide a continuous, orderly market by buying and selling securities for their own account. The over-the-counter market does not have a specific location as do the organized exchanges. It depends on a modern communications system that allows a broker to send a customer's order to the dealer who offers the best price.

The third and fourth markets developed in the 1960s to serve institutional investors at a lower cost than exchange members would. The third market consists of OTC trading of securities that are listed on the exchanges. Brokers route the orders of the institutions to OTC market makers. The fourth market consists of direct trading of exchange listed securities by institutional investors without using brokers or dealers.

Our economic system requires security markets that allocate resources efficiently. External or pricing efficiency exists when security prices fully reflect all available information. Internal or operating efficiency exists if a market provides the means through which investors can buy and sell securities at prices as low as possible considering the costs of services used by them. The national market system mandated by Congress in 1975 is an effort to improve the efficiency of the securities markets.

## QUESTIONS

1. What is a securities market? What is the main difference between the money market and the capital market?

2. What is a stock exchange? Name the national exchanges and some of the regional ones.

3. What is the function of each class of NYSE membership?

4. How is an order for a stock traded on the NYSE transacted? What if it is a limit order?

5. When would you use a stop loss order? How does it work? What are the problems with stop loss orders?

6. How is the OTC market organized? If you place a purchase order for a stock traded in the market, how does the order get transacted?

7. What is the role of the National Association of Securities Dealers in the OTC market?

8. What are the third and fourth markets?

9. Differentiate between external and internal efficiency.

10. What are the objectives of the national market system?

11. Describe three major SEC actions to end exchange anticompetitive practices.

12. Describe some of the electronic facilities that are part of the development of the national market system.

## READINGS

Amihud, Yakov, Ho, Thomas, S. V., and Schuartz, Robert A. *Market Making and the Changing Structure of the Securities Industry.* Lexington, MA: Lexington Books, 1985.
> *The articles in this book assess major developments in the structure of the securities industry during the period from January 1977 to May 1984.*

Block, Ernest. *Inside Investment Banking.* Homewood, IL: Dow Jones-Irwin, 1986.
> *The major sections of this book cover the market-making functions in investment banking, the new issues process, the public policy issues regarding regulatory changes in the new issues process, and the investment management issues raised by the institutionalization of securities markets.*

Mayer, Martin. *Markets.* New York: W. W. Norton & Co., 1988.
> *This book describes how modern financial institutions and markets operate.*

National Association of Securities Dealers. *The NASDAQ Handbook: The Stock Market of Tomorrow—Today.* Chicago: Probus Publishing Company, 1987.
> *This is an extensive reference book for investors, researchers, and students of finance.*

# Participating in the Financial Markets

## OBJECTIVES

When you have finished studying this chapter, you should understand

1. The services that you should expect from a brokerage firm.

2. Buying on margin.

3. Selling short.

4. How to read stock and bond tables.

# 3

## *Electronic Trading Systems*

Modern computer-based communications systems are being used to perform some exchange functions. The NYSE *Fact Book* reports on the status of its SuperDot system.*

> SuperDot is an electronic order-routing system through which member firms transmit market and limit orders in NYSE-listed securities directly to the specialist post where the securities are traded or to the member firm's booth. After the order has been executed in the auction market, a report of execution is returned directly to the member firm office over the same electronic circuit that brought the order to the floor, and the execution is submitted directly to the comparison systems.
>
> *Opening Automated Report Service (OARS)* OARS, the opening feature of the SuperDot system, is designed to accept member firms' pre-opening market orders up to 5,099 shares for rapid, systematic execution and immediate reporting. OARS automatically and continuously pairs buy and sell orders and presents the imbalance to each specialist up to the opening of a stock, thus assisting the specialist as he determines the opening price. OARS is floorwide in all issues.
>
> *Market Order System* All SuperDot service features apply to post-opening market orders of up to 2,099 shares. However, SuperDot's post-opening market order system is designed to deliver member firms' post-opening market orders of up to 30,099 shares. The system guarantees that all execution reports will be returned within three minutes. And in 1987, 92% were executed and reported back to the originating member firm within two minutes.
>
> *Limit Order System* The limit order system electronically files orders which are to be executed when and if a specific price is reached. The system accepts limit orders up to 99,999 shares, appends a turnaround number and delivers printed orders to the trading post or the member firm's booth. Good-'til-canceled orders not executed on the day of submission are automatically stored until executed or cancelled.

---

*\*Fact Book 1988* (New York: New York Stock Exchange, 1988), p. 17.

# INTRODUCTION

In the previous chapter, we explained how the securities markets are organized and how orders are executed on the floors of the exchanges and in the OTC market. In this chapter, we explain how to open an account at a brokerage firm and what services can be expected from that firm. We discuss buying securities on margin (with borrowed money) and selling short (borrowing securities to sell and later buying back securities to replace those borrowed). In the last section, we will explain the information printed in the stock and bond tables in newspapers.

---

# BROKERAGE SERVICES

Brokerage firms can be grouped by size into national and regional firms. The national firms, such as Merrill Lynch and Dean Witter Reynolds, are the well-known ones which have branch offices in major cities across the nation. Their large staffs allow them to have experts in a wide range of investment instruments. Regional firms are smaller and, although they may not have experts in all the different investment instruments, they often have more expertise in regional investment opportunities.

## Opening an Account

Because most brokerage firms can meet the needs of most investors, it is more important that the investor find a suitable person in a firm (an account executive) than it is to pick the brokerage firm itself. "Account executives" are also called "brokers" and "registered representatives." If you call or visit a local office of a brokerage firm without an appointment, you will talk to an account executive assigned for that day to handle new customers. A better way to find an account executive is to take the recommendation of a friend or business associate or send the branch manager a letter outlining your investment objectives and requesting an account executive who best meets your needs. It is an industry fact, however, that good, well-established account executives have regular customers and do not seek new, small accounts. These accounts are assigned to the less experienced account executives.

Investors should be comfortable working with their account executive. The account executive's investment philosophy should be compatible with the customer's. Investors must remember that the account executive's earnings are based on volume of buying and selling, not on customers making a profit in the market. Therefore, investors must think about and communicate their trading frequency plans. If they are not satisfied with their account executive, they should discuss their problems with the manager. The manager may resolve the complaint by assigning a more compatible executive to an account. If a customer believes another firm can serve him or her better, the account executive of the new firm can easily transfer the securities in the old account to the new firm.

The minimum information required to open an account is

— basic personal and credit identification—address, social security number, employer, bank, and so on

—enough information about your financial status and objectives so the account executive will not encourage you to make inappropriate investments

Exhibit 3–1 is an example of the form to open a brokerage account.

---

**EXHIBIT 3–1    Form to Open a Brokerage Account**

Source: © 1988 Charles Schwab & Co., Inc. All Rights Reserved. Courtesy of Charles Schwab & Co., Inc.

## Full Service and Discount Brokers

Brokerage firms can be divided into two classes based on the services which they offer—full service and discount. A **full service broker** charges higher commissions and provides advice. When the investor opens an account, the account executive will inquire in more detail about his or her financial status, plans, and risk preferences. The account executive will suggest the most suitable strategies and investments. The full service brokerage firm has a research department that supplies the account executive with specific recommendations for investors. The account executive should keep in mind the stocks his or her customers own and their preferences, and should call them if there are new developments concerning a stock which they own or may want to buy.

**Discount brokerage firms** charge lower commissions because they do not give advice. The firms save the costs of well-paid account executives and of research departments. The employees' only job is to process buy and sell orders. The customer may not even talk regularly to the same person; often business is conducted by a toll-free number to a centralized office. Exhibit 3–2 is an advertisement for a discount broker.

Fortunately, full service brokers and discount brokers are straightforward about the differences between them. Each would say that if an investor wants the service that the other provides, the customer should take his business there. Therefore, investors have to decide if they want to pay for the advice and assistance provided by the full service firm. Exhibit 3–3 compares fees of typical discount and full service brokerage firms. The customer pays commissions when he or she both buys and sells stocks. The discount brokerage firm's commissions are less than half the full service brokerage firm's commissions.

To decide between a discount and full service brokerage firm, investors must estimate the interest, time, and knowledge they need to make wise decisions. Then they should estimate the total commission savings per year from using a discount broker. Of course, the more trading they do, the greater will be the total dollar savings per year from using a discount broker. However, if investors use the discount broker, they may need to pay other sources for advice and recommendations and do more detailed research themselves. If the full service broker's advice and time are worth the extra cost, customers should bring their business there; if not, they should use the discount brokerage firm. Some people enjoy doing the research and following their stocks. Others may not enjoy the work or have the time to do what is necessary to make wise decisions.

Both discount and full service brokerage firms will store securities, forward the reports sent by the issuing firms, and keep track of interest and dividends. If they store the securities, the securities will be kept in **street name;** that is, the name of the brokerage firm. Customers will receive a purchase confirmation and periodic statements showing what they own. They do not have to worry much about the brokerage firm failing or someone stealing the securities. Like accounts in depository institutions, accounts are insured by a government agency. The **Securities Investor Protection Corporation (SIPC)** insures an account for up to $500,000 in securities and cash.

---

**EXHIBIT 3–2** *Advertisement from a Discount Brokerage Firm*

# Buying stocks today? Call Schwab and save on commissions.

When you trade through Schwab, you can save up to 76% on brokerage commissions compared to the rates you've been paying full-commission brokers. At Schwab you can make your own investment decisions without any sales pressure, and with our 24-hour service, you can place your orders whenever it's convenient for you. For savings you can *count*—and service you can *count on:*

### Call toll free today
## 1-800-554-1700
Or mail this coupon.

Charles R. Schwab
Chairman
Charles Schwab & Co., Inc.

☐ **YES! Please send free discount brokerage information.**

Name_____
Please Print Clearly

Address_____

City_____

State/Zip_____

## Charles Schwab
*America's Largest Discount Broker*
Member SIPC/New York Stock Exchange, Inc.

**Three First National Plaza, Chicago, IL 60602**
*Over 100 offices to serve you including:*

| | | |
|---|---|---|
| • Cleveland | • Chicago (2) | • St. Louis |
| • Pittsburgh | • Northbrook | • Omaha |
| • Detroit | • Oakbrook | • Kansas City |
| • Southfield | • Schaumburg | • St. Paul |
| • Cincinnati | • Nashville | • Minneapolis |
| • Milwaukee | • Indianapolis | WMAN9 |

Source: © 1988 Charles Schwab & Co., Inc. All Rights Reserved. Courtesy of Charles Schwab & Co., Inc.

---

**EXHIBIT 3–3** *Comparison of Commissions for Full Service and Discount Brokerage Firms*

| Shares per Order | Price per Share | Commission | | |
|---|---|---|---|---|
| | | Full Service | Discount | Difference |
| 100 | $55 | $ 92.00 | $ 45.00 | $ 47.00 |
| 300 | 8 | 86.18 | 46.80 | 39.38 |
| 500 | 25 | 235.31 | 94.50 | 140.81 |
| 800 | 45 | 477.76 | 165.00 | 312.76 |
| 1,000 | 15 | 310.00 | 102.00 | 208.00 |
| 4,000 | 20 | 928.77 | 225.00 | 703.77 |

However, there is a $100,000 limit on the insurance for cash in the account. For larger accounts, many brokerage firms purchase additional coverage from private insurers. Unlike accounts in insured depository institutions, it sometimes takes months for customers to get their securities when a brokerage firm fails. During this time, they cannot sell them and prices could fall. The SPIC insures the securities, not their value.

In 1981, the typical services offered to brokerage firm account holders were greatly expanded when Merrill Lynch, Pierce, Fenner, & Smith, Incorporated, the nation's largest brokerage firm, offered their customers a new comprehensive asset management account. The new account links together (1) the customer's securities account, (2) a money market mutual fund, (3) a checking account, and (4) a bank card. It also permits customers to use the securities account as collateral to borrow money. Since 1982

---

**EXHIBIT 3–4   *Advertisement for a Comprehensive Asset Management Account***

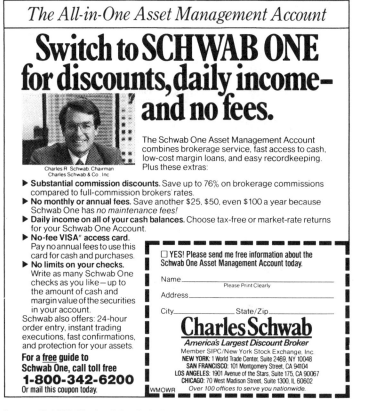

Source: © 1988 Charles Schwab & Co., Inc. All Rights Reserved. Courtesy of Charles Schwab & Co., Inc.

### Solving Problems

Unfortunately, you may experience problems with the service you receive from some people and firms in the securities business. Problems fall into three categories: fraud, unethical practices, and administrative errors.

Report any security fraud or fraud attempts immediately by phone to the local police or to your state's securities regulation agency. State agencies work with the Securities and Exchange Commission and the Commodity Futures Trading Commission on large, interstate frauds. Be prepared to give a full description of the scheme. Quick action by the authorities will help to recover any loss you might have had and prevent others from becoming victims.

Report in writing any unethical practices by securities industry personnel to the appropriate exchange or the NASD. Unethical practices include unsuitable advice, excessive trading, and bad order execution. Supply all the details. Member firms

of the exchanges and the NASD must submit to binding arbitration of customer complaints. There will be an investigation by the board, which will determine how to resolve the problem. The account agreement you signed when you opened the account may require you to take disputes to arbitration rather than to court.

For administrative errors, such as your not receiving money or securities due you, talk first to the firm's branch manager. If that does not resolve your complaint, write the firm's headquarters. If you are still not satisfied, write the appropriate exchange or NASD. Send a complete explanation of the problem and photocopies of any documents or statements.

Below are addresses to use for complaints. The agencies listed will forward your complaint to the proper organization if they cannot handle it.

—National Association of Securities Dealers
Customer Complaint Department
1735 K Street, N.W.
Washington, D.C. 20006 ·

—American Stock Exchange
Rulings and Inquiries Department
86 Trinity Place
New York, NY 10006

—New York Stock Exchange
Arbitration Director
11 Wall Street
New York, NY 10005

—Securities and Exchange Commission
Office of Consumer Affairs
450 Fifth Street, N.W.
Washington, D.C. 20549

—Commodity Futures Trading Commission
Enforcement Division
2033 K Street, N.W.
Washington, D.C. 20581

several other brokerage firms have offered similar accounts. Exhibit 3–4 is an advertisement for one of these comprehensive asset management accounts.

# BUYING ON MARGIN

Institutional arrangements exist that make it convenient to borrow money to buy securities. Borrowing a portion of money needed for the purchase of securities is called buying on **margin.** Buying securities on margin increases both potential returns and losses. When using margin, investors make a larger gain if the stock price goes up and suffer a larger loss if the price goes down than they would have without margin.

Before the Depression, investors were permitted to buy stock with as little as 10 percent down. This was wonderful in the early 1920s when stock prices were going up but disastrous during the market crash at the end of 1929. The Securities Exchange Act of 1934 made the Federal Reserve Board responsible for regulating the use of credit to buy securities. The board permits brokers to extend credit only to buy stocks and convertible bonds which are listed on the exchanges or on NASDAQ's National Market System or which are on an additional list of about 2,000 OTC stocks. The board sets initial margin requirements. The **initial margin requirement** limits the amount of money that can be borrowed to buy securities; it states the percentage of the price which must be paid by the account holder at the time of purchase. The board raises the requirement when it thinks there is excessive speculation and lowers it when it thinks more purchasing of securities would be good. The initial margin requirement is normally about 50 percent, although it has been as high as 100 percent and as low as 40 percent. Exchanges may have additional rules concerning margin accounts; for example, the NYSE states that no one may open a margin account with a member firm without depositing $2,000 in cash or securities with a loan value of $2,000 with the firm.

The money the investor borrows to buy securities on margin is loaned by the brokerage firm, which will, of course charge interest. The interest rate is based on the brokers' call loan rate and varies with conditions in the money market, but it is reasonable. From the brokerage firm's point of view, the loan is low risk because the firm is going to hold the securities purchased as collateral. As long as the market price of the securities does not fall, the firm is fully protected. If the price does fall significantly, the firm is going to demand that the investor put up more cash or securities. This demand is called a **margin call.**

Exhibit 3–5 demonstrates how the leverage provided by a margin account increases gains and losses. Notice that the indifference point between a cash and a margin account occurs where the percentage increase in the stock just equals the cost of borrowing (10 percent in this example). If the stock increases more than the cost of borrowing, the investor is better off using margin. If the percentage increase in the stock is less than the cost of borrowing, the investor is better off not using margin.

The power and risk of margin can be summarized by the margin magnification factor, which is the reciprocal of the margin requirement. For example,

| Margin Percentage | Magnification Factor |
|:---:|:---:|
| 100 | 1.00 |
| 80 | 1.25 |
| 60 | 1.67 |
| 50 | 2.00 |
| 40 | 2.50 |
| 33 | 3.00 |

---

**EXHIBIT 3–5  Margin Example**

*Example:*
Purchase 100 shares at $40 and sell one year later.

*No Margin*

|  |  |  |  |
|---|---|---|---|
| Selling Price | $   30 | $   44 | $   50 |
| Proceeds | 3,000 | 4,400 | 5,000 |
| Cost | −4,000 | −4,000 | 4,000 |
| Gain (Loss) | (1,000) | 400 | 1,000 |
| Equity | 4,000 | 4,000 | 4,000 |
| Return on Equity | (25%) | 10% | 25% |

*50% Margin*

|  |  |  |  |
|---|---|---|---|
| Selling Price | $   30 | $   44 | $   50 |
| Proceeds | 3,000 | 4,400 | 5,000 |
| Cost | −4,000 | −4,000 | −4,000 |
| Interest (10%) | −  200 | −  200 | −  200 |
| Gain (Loss) | (1,200) | 200 | 800 |
| Equity | 2,000 | 2,000 | 2,000 |
| Return on Equity | (60%) | 10% | 40% |

---

When commissions and interest are ignored, this factor can be multiplied by the percentage returns on a purchase not using margin to get the returns on a margin purchase.

Although these examples are based on owning only one security, margin requirements apply to an investor's total account. Therefore, he or she can use the securities already in the account (instead of cash) to meet the margin equity requirements. **Equity** is the market value of all the securities in the account minus the amount borrowed (debit balance). If the value of the securities goes up, the equity increases. If the value of the securities goes down, the equity decreases.

The initial margin requirement states what percentage of the total market value of the account must be equity (not borrowed) immediately after a purchase is made. For example, a 60 percent initial margin requirement means that immediately after a margin purchase, the equity in the account must be 60 percent of the total value of the account. In other words, the loan must be 40 percent or less of the total value of the account. If the value of the securities goes up, the investor could use the increased equity to purchase more securities. The account is said to have "buying power."

If the value of the securities declines so that the investor does not have enough equity to meet the initial margin requirement, the account is called a restricted account. A **restricted account** cannot make additional margin purchases without depositing more money or securities.

The **maintenance margin requirement** states the minimum percentage of equity to market value that must be maintained after the account is established. Margin calls are made to enforce this requirement. Maintenance margin requirements are set by the exchanges, not the Federal Reserve Board. Normally, the maintenance margin requirement is 25 percent; however, most brokerage firms are a little more strict, requiring perhaps 30 percent. If the maintenance margin requirement is 25 percent and the value of the equity falls to less than 25 percent of the value of the stock, the brokerage firm will demand that the investor put up more money, or the firm will sell some securities to bring the account up to the maintenance margin requirement.

When a margin call will occur can be computed using Equation 3–1

$$X = \text{loan} + (\text{maintenance margin \%})\, X \tag{3–1}$$

where $X$ equals market value of the account. In other words, a margin call occurs when the value of the account falls to an amount less than the loan balance plus the required equity.

---

| EXAMPLE |

Initial margin requirement is 50 percent and the maintenance margin requirement is 25 percent. You buy 200 shares when Ester is selling for $40 a share. This is the only security in your account. You put up $4,000 and the brokerage firm loans you $4,000. Your equity is $4,000 ($8,000 market price minus $4,000 loan). If the value of the stock falls, your account becomes restricted. You can compute when you will receive a margin call.

$$X = 4,000 + .25X$$
$$.75X = 4,000$$
$$X = \$5,333.30$$

You will receive the margin call when the value of your stock falls to $5,333.30, or $26.22 per share.                                                               □

In this section, we outlined general rules about margin accounts. The detailed rules are complex and vary with different brokerage firms. It also should be noted that if

---

### Borrowing from Your Broker

If you have a brokerage account and need to borrow money, the brokerage firm may offer better rates than other lenders. First, your account must be a margin account. Usually, it is easy to convert from a cash to a margin account; you just fill out the new account form for a margin account.

The interest rate varies. It is based on the brokers' call rate which is the rate big banks charge brokerage firms. The brokerage firm will charge you the brokers' call rate plus a 1 to 3 percent surcharge depending on the size of your account. The rate is variable, so using these loans for long-term purposes may not be wise, but they can be attractive for short-term purposes.

Margin requirements apply to your loan. Immediately after the loan, your account must meet the initial margin requirements. If the value of your securities falls a lot, you will get a margin call when the account approaches the maintenance margin requirement.

there is excess equity in a margin account, it can be withdrawn. The loan amount can be increased up to the initial margin requirements. In effect, money may be borrowed for other purposes using the securities as collateral.

# SHORT SELLING

**Short selling** is selling stock that the investor does not own but has borrowed. The most common motivation for selling short is that the investor hopes to profit from an expected price decline. The investor borrows the stock and sells it. If the price declines, the investor can purchase at the lower price the number of shares needed to replace what was borrowed. The difference between the selling and purchasing prices is the profit before commissions.

The investor's brokerage firm can usually arrange to borrow stock from its inventory or from the inventory of another brokerage firm. The brokerage firm will require a deposit from the short seller equal to the initial margin requirement. It will also hold the proceeds from the sale of the stock.

---

**EXAMPLE**

Ester is selling at $40 a share. You think that is too high and the stock will soon fall in price. You sell 100 shares short. If the initial margin requirement then in effect is 50 percent, you have to deposit $2,000 with the brokerage firm. The brokerage firm also holds the $4,000 from the sale. If the price fell and you purchased 100 shares of Ester at $32 to cover your short position, you would make $800 ($4,000 minus $3,200). ☐

---

The danger in selling short is that the stock can experience a sharp price rise. Then the investor must decide between buying at the higher price and taking a loss on the short sale or waiting longer. If he or she waits, the stock could go still higher. Since stock prices do not have any upper limit, the losses are theoretically unlimited. In practice, as the stock goes up and up, the brokerage firm enforces maintenance margin requirements; it will be demanding a greater deposit. If the short seller does not put up more money, the brokerage firm will buy the stock necessary to cover the short position.

The stock price at which the investor must put up more money can be computed using Equation 3–2.

$$X + (\text{maintenance margin }\%)\, X = \text{initial proceeds} + \text{initial margin (\$)}$$

$$(3\text{--}2)$$

where $X$ equals market value of the securities. In other words, a margin call occurs when the sum of the market value of the securities and the maintenance margin requirement times the market value equals the cash in the account.

| EXAMPLE | When you sold the 100 shares in the example above at $40, you had to deposit $2,000. Instead of falling, Ester's stock value has risen. When do you have to put up more margin if the maintenance margin requirement is 25 percent? |

$$X + .25X = 4,000 + 2,000$$
$$X = 4,800$$

You will receive a margin call when the value of the stock increases to $4,800, or $48 per share.                                                    □

Early drafts of the Securities Act of 1934 proposed forbidding short selling. The argument that short selling helps stock prices reflect "true values" by providing more sell orders for overpriced securities resulted in removing the provision before the law was passed.

Two important details of short selling need to be mentioned. First, if a stock is

### Arbitration of Disputes

In most, but not all, cases the forms used to open a brokerage account require that the customer take any dispute with the brokerage firm to an arbitration panel rather than to court. Arbitration panels are sponsored by the exchanges and the National Association of Securities Dealers.

In June 1987 in the case of *Shearson American Express v. McMahon,* the U.S. Supreme Court supported the enforceability of this contract provision. Eugene and Julia McMahon wanted to sue their broker and her employer, Shearson American Express. The McMahons, funeral directors, opened their account by signing, in a restaurant after cocktails, the usual forms. They turned over $500,000—their life savings and their employees' pension fund—to their new broker. They also gave her authorization to make trades for them at her discretion. In two years, they lost $300,000, while paying $200,000 in commissions. Their broker was later promoted to vice president. They wanted the court to let them sue. The court ruled they could not sue because when they opened the account they agreed to take disputes to arbitration instead.

Arbitration panels consist of three or five members who are officially impartial. However, critics claim proindustry biases because the panel members often have worked in the past for brokerage firms or law firms representing brokerage firms. Supporters of arbitration point out panel members know the securities business; therefore, time is not wasted explaining definitions and procedures.

Arbitration cases usually are heard within one year (versus four years for many court suits). Lawyers can represent the parties, but the panels do not have formal procedures. There are no rules of evidence and written opinions usually are not issued. There is no appeal.

Plaintiffs win something in about half of the cases. In these successful cases, awards average about 60 percent of the amount claimed. Most important, there are no awards for legal fees, travel costs, and other expenses; awards of punitive damages are very rare.

Source: "Sue Your Stockbroker? You Can't, You Know," *Business Week,* March 2, 1987, pp. 75–76. "Can't Sue Your Broker? It's No Big Loss," *Business Week,* June 22, 1987, p. 128.

sold short and the company pays a dividend, both the original owner of the stock and the person who purchased it from the short seller will expect to receive the dividend. The company will pay only the new owner—the one on its records. The short seller must pay the dividend to the person from whom he borrowed the stock. In other words, dividends are an expense when you sell short.

The second detail is that a short sale can be executed on the floor of the exchange only on an uptick (an increase in price over the last transaction) or a zero uptick (the price of this transaction is the same as the previous one, but the last price change to take place was an increase). This rule prevents short selling from accentuating price declines.

# READING STOCK TABLES

Major city newspapers, the *Wall Street Journal,* and *USA Today* report the stock trading of the day before. A standard format is used although some newspapers eliminate some columns to save space.

The *NYSE Composite Transaction* reports trading of the stocks listed on the NYSE, while the *AMEX Composite Transaction* reports trading of the stocks listed on the AMEX. In addition to the trading of these stocks on their respective exchanges, trading of them on other exchanges and OTC are included. The following listing for General Motors will be used for explanation.

| (1) 52 Week High | (2) Low | (3) Stock | (4) Divi- dend | (5) Yield | (6) P-E Ratio | (7) Sales 100s | (8) High | (9) Low | (10) Close | (11) Net Change |
|---|---|---|---|---|---|---|---|---|---|---|
| $77\frac{1}{2}$ | $41\frac{1}{8}$ | GMot | 2.40e | 3.5 | 11 | 6651 | $69\frac{1}{2}$ | $68\frac{1}{8}$ | $69\frac{3}{8}$ | $+\frac{3}{8}$ |
| $52\frac{1}{8}$ | $39\frac{1}{2}$ | GMot pf | 5 | 10 | | 4 | $49\frac{1}{2}$ | 49 | $49\frac{1}{2}$ | $-\frac{1}{8}$ |

The *first* column reports the highest price paid for the stock in the last 52 weeks including the current week but not the reported trading day. By tradition, stocks are bought and sold using an eighth of a dollar ($12\frac{1}{2}$ cents). The *second* column reports the lowest price paid for the stock in the same period. If the reported day's trading were to break one of these records, the stock would also be included in a separate new high or new low list. The *third* column identifies the stock issue. The first stock is General Motors common stock. The second is coded "pf" because it is General Motors preferred stock. If you could not recognize the name of the stock, you could check it in one of the investor information publications.

The *fourth* column lists the annual dollar amount of dividends paid based on the last dividend payment. General Motors pays a regular dividend on its common stock of $2.40 a year. The ''e'' denotes it also paid an extra dividend amount in the past 12 months. An explanation of the footnote codes is printed with the table.

The dividend yield in the *fifth* column is the percentage obtained by dividing the annual dividend by the closing price. For example, the 3.5 percent is $2.40 divided by $69.375. If a stock does not pay a dividend, both the dividend and the yield columns will be blank.

The price-to-earnings ratio in the *sixth* column is obtained by dividing the closing price by the company's earnings per share for the last year (not shown). The PE ratio reflects what investors are willing to pay for the stock based on its earnings. Reflected in the ratio are investors' opinions about the stability and growth of the earnings. Since preferred stockholders' dividends are based on the stated rate, a ratio of the preferred price to earnings is not very important and, therefore, is not reported.

The *seventh* column reports the number of round lots traded that day. If a round lot for a stock is 10 shares instead of 100, a footnote code letter will appear after the number. In the example, 400 shares of GM's preferred were traded and 665,100 shares of the common were traded.

The *eighth* column lists the highest price paid for a share of GM's stock that day. The *ninth* column reports the lowest price paid. The highest price for the common was $69.50 a share and the lowest was $68.125. A footnote code would indicate a new high or new low for the 52-week period.

The *tenth* column reports the price per share of the last round lot traded. The *eleventh* column compares this closing price to the closing price the day before. The last price for GM's common was $69.375. This was up $37\frac{1}{2}$ cents from the close the day before. Therefore, the close the day before must have been $69.

Some newspapers report the transactions of stocks listed on that area's regional exchange that are not also traded on the NYSE or AMEX. For OTC stocks, the NASDAQ system reports trading of the stocks on its National Market List using a format similar to the NYSE and AMEX. For a second list of OTC stocks it reports only the security name, dividend, volume of trading, bid and ask prices, and change in the bid price. For a list of less active OTC stocks, only bid and ask prices are reported.

# READING BOND TABLES

Although most bonds are traded in the OTC market, major newspapers report the trading of those bonds listed on the NYSE and AMEX. There are two important facts you need to know to interpret the bond tables.

1. The price applies to the principal only. Bonds sell on an accrued interest basis. This means the buyer pays the seller the interest that has accrued since the last interest payment by the issuer.

2. Bond prices are quoted as percent of face value. For example, a price quote of $72\frac{1}{8}$ for a $1,000 bond means the dollar price is $721.25 ($1,000 × 72.125%).

The bond quotes listed below provide instructive examples for explaining how to read the bond tables.

| (1) | (2) Current | (3) | (4) | (5) Net |
| --- | --- | --- | --- | --- |
| Bond | Yield | Volume | Close | Change |
| GnEl 7½ 96 | 10 | 10 | 72⅛ | +¼ |
| GnEl 8½ 04 | 11 | 10 | 77⅜ | +1⅜ |
| GTE 5 s 92 | cv | 6 | 98 | −3½ |

The *first* column identifies the bond by the name of the issuer, the coupon rate, and the year of maturity. The first bond was issued by General Electric, pays a coupon rate of 7½ percent and matures in 1996. Frequently, as in the case of the General Telephone bond, a small "s" is printed between the coupon rate and the maturity year. The "s," which is an abbreviation for "series," is not significant. If the same issuer had more than one bond issue with the same coupon rate and maturity year, the second issue would have a "B" printed after the maturity year, the third would have a "C," and so forth. An "f" after the year denotes that the bond is trading "flat," that is, without any accrued interest to be paid by the purchaser because the issuer is in default on the interest.

The current yield in the *second* column is the annual interest paid divided by the current price. Convertible bonds such as the General Telephone bond are coded "cv" in the current yield column.

The *third* column reports the number of bonds traded. The *next* column reports the last trade price. The *last* column reports the change in the close price from the previous trading day. Again, all the prices are in percentage of face value.

# SUMMARY

After the investor decides whether he or she wants the advice offered by a full service broker or the lower commission charges offered by a discount broker, it is easy to open an account with a brokerage firm. If you use a full service broker, it is important to discuss with the broker your goals and attitudes toward risk. Brokerage firms will store the securities for the customer. If the customer leaves the securities with a brokerage firm, they are insured by the Securities Investors Protection Corporation against theft or loss if the firm fails.

Aggressive purchasers can borrow money to use for securities purchases. This is called buying on margin and it increases the potential gains and losses. If an investor thinks a stock's price will decline, it is possible to borrow shares of the stock and sell them. When the price declines, the investor purchases the number of shares borrowed. This process of borrowing stock and selling it is called short selling.

# QUESTIONS

**1.** How would you pick a brokerage firm and account executive? Would you use a discount broker?

2. What protection does the Securities Investor Protection Corporation offer the investor? What are its limitations?

3. What services usually are provided by a brokerage firm to customers with a comprehensive asset management account?

4. What is buying on margin? How does it affect risk and potential return?

5. Who loans you the money when you buy on margin? Why is it so easy to borrow to buy on margin? What is the initial margin requirement? Who sets it? What is the maintenance margin requirement? Who sets it?

6. When would you sell a stock short? How does short selling work? Where does the borrowed stock come from? When you sell short do you get dividends? How risky is short selling?

7. Look up Ball Corporation on the NYSE table in the newspaper. Explain each entry in the listing.

8. Look up ATT on the N.Y. Bond Exchange. Pick one of its bonds and explain each entry in the listing.

## PROBLEMS

1. You buy 100 shares of Ester Electronics for $40 a share. At the same time, your friend, Mary, buys 200 shares putting up 50% margin.
   a. One year later you both sell when Ester's price is $45 a share. Ignoring commissions and assuming Mary must pay 12% interest on the borrowed money, how much in dollars and as a percentage return on equity do you and Mary each make?
   b. Instead of rising, Ester's stock falls to $30 a share one year later when you and Mary sell. How much in dollars and as a percentage return on equity do you and Mary lose?

2. You buy 100 shares of stock for $45 a share. At the same time, your friend buys 200 shares putting up 50% margin.
   a. One year later you both sell when the price is $50 a share. Ignoring commissions and assuming 10% interest on the borrowed money, how much in dollars and as a percentage return on equity do you each make?
   b. The stock falls to $35 a share when you both sell. How much in dollars and as a percentage return on equity do you each lose?

3. You purchase 100 shares of a stock selling at $50 using 50% margin. Your brokerage firm enforces a 30% maintenance margin. If the stock price starts to fall, at what price will you receive a margin call?

4. You purchase 200 shares of a stock selling at $30, borrowing 40% of the purchase price. Your brokerage firm enforces a 30% maintenance margin. If the stock price starts to fall, at what price will you receive a margin call?

5. You sell 100 shares of a stock short at $50. The initial margin requirement is 50% and the maintenance margin requirement is 30%. The stock price starts to rise. At what price will you have to put up more money?

6. You sell 100 shares of a stock short at $30. The initial margin requirement is 60% and the maintenance margin requirement is 30%. The stock price starts to rise. At what price will you get a margin call?

## CASE PROBLEM

Pretend you have $50,000 to invest. Invest in at least five securities on the day the assignment is given and sell them before the due date. Hand in

1. A list of the securities purchased, their prices, and amounts invested in each (including commission).

2. Prices and amounts received when sold (including commissions).

3. Profit or loss (including dividends).

## READINGS

"The Crash: Was Bloody Monday More a Correction Than a Catastrophe?" *Business Week* (April 18, 1988): 55–66.

> *This* Business Week *cover story takes an in-depth look at what the October 19, 1987, crash means to investors.*

Edgerton, Jerry. "Finding a Broker to Suit Your Taste," *Money* (September 1983): 72–74.

"Power Investors: How Wall Street Firms Want to Own the Company—Not Just Its Shares," *Business Week* (June 20, 1988): 116–130.

> *This* Business Week *cover story looks at the changes in investment banking and their implications for the investor and the economy.*

Saunders, Anthony, and White, Lawrence, ed. *Technology and the Regulation of Financial Markets.* Lexington, MA: Lexington Books, 1986.

> *The papers in this book, which were written by government regulators, representatives of the exchanges, individuals from the financial community, and academic researchers, examine how technology is changing the financial markets.*

Staff of the New York Institute of Finance. *How the Bond Market Works.* New York: New York Institute of Finance, 1988.

> *This book describes bonds and their markets.*

## APPENDIX 3A
## THE MONEY MARKET

The money market is an informal market where brokers and dealers buy and sell large denomination debt instruments with maturities of less than one year. The market has several sectors arranged according to the instruments traded: U.S. government securities, federal agency securities, negotiable certificates of deposit, commercial paper, bankers' acceptances, repurchase agreements, and federal funds. The market is informal in the sense that it does not operate in one location. it is a "telephone market" with its center in New York City. Its base is the large "money market banks" in New York and other financial centers, 43 primary and many more secondary government security dealers, about a dozen commercial paper dealers, a few bankers' acceptance dealers, and a few brokers who bring together large borrowers and lenders.

Dealers have inventories of securities and advertise the bid and ask prices at which they will buy and sell. Dealers do not charge commission; instead they make their money from the difference between the bid and ask prices—the spread. Dealers transact directly with customers and through brokers. Brokers do not maintain inventories but charge a commission for arranging transactions with the dealers. They keep track of the up-to-the-minute quotes of the dealers and can help get the best price available.

Most buyers and sellers of money market instruments place their orders with banks or brokerage firms which phone the orders to the money market dealers. Because trading in money market instruments is in large dollar amounts ($100,000 is a small transaction), most buyers and sellers are financial institutions, nonfinancial firms, and government units. However, individuals can participate in the money market mutual funds which are discussed later in the book.

## Treasury Security Dealers

In terms of dollar volume outstanding, U.S. Treasury bills are the most important money market instrument. Most Treasury bill dealers are units of large banks or brokerage firms, and they also handle Treasury notes and bonds. There are 43 primary dealers. These dealers register with the Federal Reserve Bank of New York and are the dealers with whom the bank buys and sells Treasury securities in order to influence the money supply and interest rates. There are hundreds of secondary dealers who trade Treasury securities but who do not trade with the Federal Reserve Bank. Until 1986, secondary dealers did not register with or report to any government agency. This, combined with their extensive use of borrowed money to finance their inventories, made some smaller dealers extremely vulnerable when interest rates changed. Following some spectacular failures in which customers lost large amounts, Congress passed the Government Securities Act of 1986 which regulates money market dealers.

## Repurchase Agreements

A *repurchase agreement* is the sale of securities and the seller's simultaneous agreement to repurchase them. Most repurchase agreements are for very short time periods—one to three days. The investor earns a return because the seller agrees to repurchase the securities at a higher price than at which they were sold. Usually, the securities sold are Treasury or government agency securities, although others, such as negotiable CDs and banker's acceptances, are sometimes used. The minimum size transaction is about $100,000 and most transactions are for $1 million or more. The term *reverse repurchase agreement* is used to describe a repurchase agreement from the view of the purchaser of the securities.

Government security dealers regularly raise funds using repurchase agreements. In effect, it is one method of financing their inventories of government securities. Government security dealers also act as brokers in matching a repurchase agreement with a reverse repurchase agreement at a higher rate. This occurs partly because the large, well-known dealers are able to get more favorable rates than smaller dealers or corporations.

Because they have large inventories of government securities and often seek funds, large banks regularly enter into repurchase agreements. Business firms and local governments, which temporarily have excess cash, find repurchase agreements low risk, highly liquid investments. Local governments are often constrained by law in how they can invest excess funds. Because repurchase agreements based on Treasury or government agency securities are technically purchases of these securities, the laws usually permit them.

## Short-Term Government Agencies Securities

In Chapter 6, we will discuss the debt securities issued by federally sponsored credit agencies. Several agencies issue notes with original maturities of less than one year. There is an established secondary market for these agency securities. Spreads are narrow and large transactions can be handled without upsetting the market. The yields on these securities fall above Treasury bills and below private sector money market instruments of similar maturity.

## Negotiable Certificates of Deposit

*Negotiable certificates of deposit* are large denomination (more than $100,000) time deposits in depository institutions. They are evidenced by a certificate which states the amount, maturity date, rate of interest, and how the interest is calculated. Banking regulations set the minimum maturity at 14 days. Typically, they are issued with maturities ranging up to a year. The average maturity of outstanding CDs is about three months. Although they can be registered in the name of the owner, the majority are bearer instruments. In fact, some banks do not classify registered CDs as negotiable even though they legally are.

Negotiable CDs can be classified into four types, domestic, Yankee, thrift, and Eurodollar: *domestic CDs* are issued by moneycenter banks and large regional banks; *Yankee CDs* are issued by U.S. branch offices of foreign banks; *thrift CDs* are issued by large savings and loans; *Eurodollar CDs* are dollar denominated time deposits in foreign banks and foreign branches of U.S. banks. The secondary market for Eurodollar CDs is centered in London. Some domestic dealers have London offices which handle Eurodollar CDs.

CDs can be issued directly to investors or through securities dealers. About 25 dealers make the secondary market in CDs. The minimum denomination traded in the secondary market is $1 million.

## Commercial Paper

*Commercial paper* is an unsecured short-term (270 days or less) promissory note sold by a large corporation on a discount basis. About 1,000 corporations issue commercial paper. Although the minimum denomination is $25,000, it is normally sold in multiples of $100,000. The average purchase is $2 million, and the average maturity on outstanding paper is 30 days. Issuers of commercial paper usually have backup lines of credit with banks in order to ensure that they will have the ability to redeem their paper.

Commercial paper is issued by finance companies, nonfinancial companies, and bank holding companies. Finance companies have sales personnel who sell the paper directly to investors. Nonfinancial companies and bank holding companies usually sell their paper using commercial paper dealers. There are six major commercial paper dealers. Investors usually hold commer-

---

**EXHIBIT 3A–1  Short-Term Interest Rates**

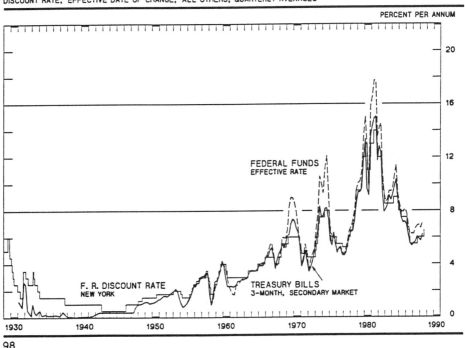

SHORT-TERM INTEREST RATES
MONEY MARKET
DISCOUNT RATE, EFFECTIVE DATE OF CHANGE; ALL OTHERS, QUARTERLY AVERAGES

98

Source: *1987 Historical Chart Book* (Washington, D.C.: Board of Governors of the Federal Reserve System, 1988), p. 98.

cial paper until maturity; secondary market trading is infrequent.

## Bankers' Acceptances

Bankers' acceptances have been a part of international trade for hundreds of years. They developed as a means to guarantee the purchaser's credit and the payment date when buyers and sellers are far apart. Bankers' acceptances are bills of exchange which have been guaranteed by a bank. A *bill of exchange* is a draft drawn by an exporter when goods are shipped. The bill of exchange orders the importer or its bank to pay a specific amount on a future date. When an individual, firm, or bank acknowledges the obligation to pay the draft by marking it "accepted," it becomes an acceptance. If it is accepted by a nonbank entity, it is a *trade acceptance*. If it is accepted by a bank, it is a *bankers' acceptance*. Large banks have departments that specialize in accepting drafts on behalf of their customers.

After the bill of exchange has been accepted by the bank and returned to the exporter, someone must hold it until the payment date, which is usually 30 to 180 days in the future. The exporter can hold it or sell it at a discount. Because the acceptance is now an obligation of the bank and, therefore, involves little default risk, a good secondary market exists. About 15 dealers make this secondary market.

## Federal Funds

*Federal funds* are short-term loans of immediately available funds between depository institutions. More particularly, the funds are deposits in Federal Reserve Banks and collected liabilities of commercial banks and other depository institutions. Most federal funds are lent out on one day and are repaid the following morning. However, a few loans are of longer maturity. Federal funds brokers earn a commission by matching lenders and borrowers. Transfers of funds are made by Federal Reserve wire services.

The federal funds market allows depository institutions to manage more actively the reserves they must maintain. Excess reserves can be lent at interest, and shortages can be borrowed. The interest rate on federal funds reflects the amount of available reserves in the banking system. Although only depository institutions buy and sell federal funds, they are an integral part of the money market. Any change in the Federal Reserve's monetary policy is immediately reflected in the federal funds rate. Other money market rates quickly adjust when the federal funds rate changes. Exhibit 3A–1 shows this relationship.

# Return and Risk Measurement

## OBJECTIVES

When you have finished studying this chapter, you should understand

1. Five measures of the rate of return and their advantages and disadvantages.

2. How to measure the riskiness of an investment.

3. The covariance and the correlation coefficient and how to compute them.

4. Alpha, beta, and the characteristic line.

5. The pattern of risk and return of financial instruments in the past.

**66**

## The Value of RJR Nabisco

RJR Nabisco Inc.'s stock was selling for $56 a share before the announcement of a buyout proposal on October 20, 1988. The proposed buyout was at $75 a share. Following the announcement, the market price jumped into the $80 range because investors expected higher competing buyout offers. In the following weeks, several competing offers were made, with a $109 offer being the top.

Were investors drastically undervaluing this stock before the first announcement? Management and some analysts argued that the market was overemphasizing the negatives associated with the tobacco industry. Although very profitable, the industry's growth was limited because of the health concerns related to cigarettes. Also, even though the industry had successfully defended itself in litigation, there was investor concern about potential liability in suits brought by smokers.

Some analysts believed RJR Nabisco would be worth more if it were divided up, with the pieces sold. One analyst thought its food division alone was worth more than the market value of the whole firm. Again, the argument was made that tobacco risks overwhelmed the high profits.

Another factor causing the different valuations could have been the firm's capital structure. A buyout would have resulted in a much higher debt-to-equity ratio. Perhaps, before the buyout RJR Nabisco had too much equity compared to debt. In other words, before the buyout, its capital structure was not optimal.

Other observers argue that the high fees paid to the investment banking firm that arranges the successful buyout encourages the payment of excessively high prices in circumstances such as these. They accuse investment bankers of putting their own interests ahead of those of the suppliers of the takeover capital. At such a high price, the long-term success of the restructured firm is questionable.

## INTRODUCTION

In this chapter, we learn how to compute the two most important measures of investment performance: rate of return and risk. In this process, we will see how the risk of an investment is conceptually different when it is viewed alone and when it is viewed as part of a portfolio. Additionally, we will examine historical return and risk performance of financial investments. This examination will show that investors have been rewarded for their risk taking and that the low correlations of rates of return on different financial instruments can make diversification advantageous.

---

# RATE OF RETURN

The rate of return on an investment is a measure of how much you receive from the investment compared to its cost. You can receive appreciation (the ending value of the investment minus the cost or beginning value), a cash flow, or both. Dividends from stock or interest from bonds are examples of cash flows.

The rate of return is the ratio of the appreciation plus the cash flows to the cost or beginning value.

$$\text{rate of return} = \frac{\text{ending value} - \text{beginning value} + \text{cash flows}}{\text{beginning value}} \qquad (4\text{--}1)$$

Although this is a simple concept, some questions make it more complex. For example, should you use the appreciation and cash flows from one month, one quarter, or one year? Another question is whether you should use the rate of return for one period, the arithmetic mean of the returns for many periods, or the geometric mean. Or should you use the internal rate of return for many periods? Also, how many periods should you choose to use? Each type of rate of return will be defined and discussed.

## Holding Period Return ($r_n$)

Even though common stock will be used as the example for the holding period return, the concept can be applied to any investment—bonds, diamonds, or real estate. Let

$P_0$ = the price at time zero (the beginning value)

$P_1$ = the price at the end of the first period

$P_2$ = the price at the end of the second period

$\vdots$

$P_n$ = the price at the end of the $n$th period

$D_0$ = the current dividend

$D_1$ = the dividend paid at the end of the first period

$D_2$ = the dividend paid at the end of the second period

$\vdots$

$D_n$ = the dividend paid at the end of the $n$th period

$r_1$ = the rate of return for the first period

$r_2$ = the rate of return for the second period

$\vdots$

$r_n$ = the rate of return for the $n$th period

Then the rate of return for period 1 is

$$r_1 = \frac{P_1 - P_0 + D_1}{P_0} \qquad (4\text{-}2)$$

The denominator represents the beginning value of the investment which is the price paid at the beginning of the period ($P_0$). The numerator represents the appreciation ($P_1 - P_0$) plus the cash flow ($D_1$) received at the end of the period. $P_1$ is the price the stock could be sold for at the end of period 1 and $D_1$ is the dividend received at the end of period 1.

The rate of return for period 2 is

$$r_2 = \frac{P_2 - P_1 + D_2}{P_1}$$

The rate of return for the $n$th period is

$$r_n = \frac{P_n - P_{n-1} + D_n}{P_{n-1}} \qquad (4\text{-}3)$$

This formula can be used for any length of period. You could choose the period to be a day, a month, a quarter, or a year. The choice of the length of period depends on the type of investment and why you are calculating the return.

---

**PRACTICE PROBLEM 1**  National Microwave was selling for $20 per share at the end of 1986 and at $30 per share at the end of 1987. During that year they paid $2 in dividends. What was the 1987 annual return?

*Solution*

$$r_1 = \frac{P_1 - P_0 + D_1}{P_0} = \frac{30 - 20 + 2}{20} = \frac{12}{20} = .600$$

**PRACTICE PROBLEM 2**  Prices for National Microwave at the end of the first, second, and third quarters of 1987 were $25, $22, and $28 respectively. They paid a $.50 dividend each quarter. Using the information in Practice Problem 1, compute the return for each quarter of 1987.

*Solution*

$$P_0 = \$20, P_1 = \$25, P_2 = \$22, P_3 = \$28, P_4 = \$30$$

$$D_1 = \$.50, D_2 = \$.50, D_3 = \$.50, D_4 = \$.50$$

$$r_1 = \frac{P_1 - P_0 + D_1}{P_0} = \frac{25 - 20 + .50}{20} = \frac{5.50}{20} = .275$$

$$r_2 = \frac{P_2 - P_1 + D_2}{P_1} = \frac{22 - 25 + .50}{25} = \frac{-2.50}{25} = -.100$$

$$r_3 = \frac{P_3 - P_2 + D_3}{P_2} = \frac{28 - 22 + .50}{22} = \frac{6.50}{22} = .295$$

$$r_4 = \frac{P_4 - P_3 + D_4}{P_3} = \frac{30 - 28 + .50}{28} = \frac{2.50}{28} = .089$$

The return can be stated as a decimal number or as a percentage. The magnitude of the rate of return is related to the size of the period (in the same way as interest rates). For instance, if the return is 1 percent every month, the return per quarter is 3 percent and the return per year is 12 percent. In Practice Problems 1 and 2, the return for the year was .600 which is a higher order of magnitude than the returns for the four quarters of .275, $-.100$, .295, and .089.

## Arithmetic Mean Return ($\bar{r}$)

If the rate of return is 1 percent each period, it is clear that the average or representative return is 1 percent per period. If, however, the returns are different each period, the average return can be found by taking the arithmetic mean of the returns of each period.

$$\bar{r} = \frac{r_1 + r_2 + r_3 + \ldots r_n}{n} \tag{4-4}$$

or

$$\bar{r} = \frac{\sum_{m=1}^{n} r_m}{n}$$

**PRACTICE PROBLEM 3**

Find the arithmetic mean return if $r_1 = .01, r_2 = .02, r_3 = .03, r_4 = .04$.

*Solution*

$$\bar{r} = \frac{.01 + .02 + .03 + .04}{4} = \frac{.10}{4} = .025$$

**PRACTICE PROBLEM 4**    Find the arithmetic mean of the returns in Practice Problem 2.

*Solution*

$$r_1 = .275, r_2 = -.100, r_3 = .295, r_4 = .089$$

$$\bar{r} = \frac{.275 - .100 + .295 + .089}{4} = \frac{.559}{4} = .140$$

The arithmetic mean return is not always, however, the best measure of the average of the returns. If there is a great variation in the returns, the arithmetic mean return can be upwardly biased.

**PRACTICE PROBLEM 5**    Find the arithmetic mean return if $P_0 = \$1$, $P_1 = \$2$, $P_2 = \$1$, $D_1 = 0$, $D_2 = 0$.

*Solution*

$$r_1 = \frac{P_1 - P_0 + D_1}{P_0} = \frac{2 - 1 + 0}{1} = \frac{1}{1} = 1 \text{ or } 100\%$$

$$r_2 = \frac{P_2 - P_1 + D_2}{P_1} = \frac{1 - 2 + 0}{2} = \frac{-1}{2} \text{ or } -50\%$$

$$\bar{r} = \frac{r_1 + r_2}{2} = \frac{100\% - 50\%}{2} = \frac{50\%}{2} = 25\%$$

In Practice Problem 5 the price rose from $1 to $2 in the first period and fell back to $1 at the end of the second period. Since there were no dividends, the return for two periods was zero. Yet, the arithmetic mean was 25%. While an average of 25% per period sounds good, in this case it was not. The geometric mean return provides a fairer measure of average return in such cases.

## Geometric Mean Return (G)

The geometric mean of the returns for many periods has some advantages over the arithmetic mean. Because it is derived in the same manner as compound interest, the geometric mean is not biased upwardly, and an ending value or future value of the investment can be computed which will be closer to the true value. The definition of the geometric mean ($G$) is

$$G + 1 = [(1 + r_1)(1 + r_2)(1 + r_3) \ . \ . \ . \ (1 + r_n)]^{1/n} \tag{4-5}$$

where $r_1, r_2, r_3 \ . \ . \ . \ r_n$ are the returns in periods 1 through $n$.

One is added to all of the returns including the geometric mean return so that the product will always be positive; and, therefore, the root will be positive.

**PRACTICE**   Find the geometric mean of the returns in Practice Problem 5.
**PROBLEM 6**
*Solution*

$$r_1 = 1, r_2 = -.5$$

$$G + 1 = [(1 + 1)(1 - .5)]^{1/2} = [(2)(.5)]^{1/2} = (1)^{1/2} = 1$$

$$G = 1 - 1 = 0$$

**PRACTICE**   Find the geometric mean of the returns in Practice Problem 2.
**PROBLEM 7**
*Solution*

$$r_1 = .275, r_2 = -.100, r_3 = .295, r_4 = .089$$

$$G + 1 = [(1 + .275)(1 - .100)(1 + .295)(1 + .089)]^{1/4}$$

$$= [(1.275)(.900)(1.295)(1.089)]^{1/4}$$

$$= [1.6182676]^{1/4} = 1.128$$

$$G = 1.128 - 1 = .128$$

**PRACTICE**   Use the data for National Microwave in Practice Problems 1, 2, 4, and 7 and calculate the ending
**PROBLEM 8**   value or future value by first using the arithmetic mean return and then the geometric mean
return. The present value is $P_0$. What can you conclude about the arithmetic mean return versus
the geometric mean return?

*Solution*

arithmetic mean return = .140

$PV = \$20, i = 14.0\%, n = 4, FV = ?$

$FV = \$33.78$

geometric mean return = .128

$PV = \$20, i = 12.8\%, n = 4, FV = ?$

$FV = \$32.38$

The arithmetic mean is higher than the geometric mean.

**PRACTICE**   Use the data of Practice Problems 5 and 6 and compute the ending value of the investment with
**PROBLEM 9**   both the arithmetic and geometric means.

*Solution*

arithmetic mean = 25%

$PV = \$1, i = 25\%, n = 2, FV = ?$

$FV = \$1.56$

geometric mean = 0

$PV = \$1, i = 0\%, n = 2, FV = ?$

$FV = \$1$

The geometric mean return gives the true ending value while the arithmetic mean gives a value which is too high. However, the geometric mean gives the exact ending value only when there are no dividends.

---

# Internal Rate of Return (i)

Another measure of return comes from the concept of the time value of money. The present value is the initial investment, the interest rate is the internal rate of return, and the payments are the cash flows received. Complications arise in the internal rate of return when payments received are not the same each period.

The internal rate of return is $i$ in Equation 4–6.

$$PV = \frac{PMT_1}{(1 + i)^1} + \frac{PMT_2}{(1 + i)^2} + \frac{PMT_3}{(1 + i)^3} + \cdots \frac{PMT_n}{(1 + i)^n} \qquad \textbf{(4–6)}$$

or

$$PV = \sum_{m=1}^{n} \frac{PMT_m}{(1 + i)^m}$$

where $PMT_1$, $PMT_2$, $PMT_3$, . . . $PMT_n$ are the payments in each period.

If there is only one payment or if all the payments are equal, the solution is easy. If, however, all the payments are different, the only way to solve the equation is to make successive approximations of $i$. Both methods will be illustrated.

---

**PRACTICE PROBLEM 10**   Using the data for National Microwave in Practice Problems 1 and 2, compute the internal rate of return.

*Solution*

$$P_0 = \$20, P_4 = \$30$$
$$D_1 = D_2 = D_3 = D_4 = \$.50$$

Using Equation 4–6 where $PV = P_0$, $PMT_1 = D_1$, $PMT_2 = D_2$, $PMT_3 = D_3$, and $PMT_4 = D_4 + P_4$

$$20 = \frac{.50}{(1 + i)^1} + \frac{.50}{(1 + i)^2} + \frac{.50}{(1 + i)^3} + \frac{30.50}{(1 + i)^4}$$

Solve by successive approximations of $i$. Let $i = 10\%$.

$$\frac{.50}{(1 + .1)^1} + \frac{.50}{(1 + .1)^2} + \frac{.50}{(1 + .1)^3} + \frac{30.50}{(1 + .1)^4} = 22.08$$

This is more than 20; therefore, the next estimate of $i$ should be higher than 10%. Let $i = 13\%$.

$$\frac{.50}{(1 + .13)^1} + \frac{.50}{(1 + .13)^2} + \frac{.50}{(1 + .13)^3} + \frac{30.50}{(1 + .13)^4} = 19.89$$

This is less than 20, therefore the next estimate of $i$ should be lower than 13%. Let $i = 12.9\%$.

$$\frac{.50}{(1 + .129)^1} + \frac{.50}{(1 + .129)^2} + \frac{.50}{(1 + .129)^3} + \frac{30.50}{(1 + .129)^4} = 19.95$$

This is still less than 20, therefore the next estimate of $i$ should be even lower than 12.9%. Let $i = 12.8\%$.

$$\frac{.50}{(1 + .128)^1} + \frac{.50}{(1 + .128)^2} + \frac{.50}{(1 + .128)^3} + \frac{30.50}{(1 + .128)^4} = 20.02$$

The internal rate of return is very close to 12.8% since 20.02 is very close to 20. A more accurate internal rate of return could be found by more successive approximations.

**PRACTICE PROBLEM 11**  Mr. Armstrong was contemplating an investment which would cost $10,000 and earn a return of $2,000 at the end of each of the next 8 years. What is the internal rate of return of this investment?

*Solution*

Since all the payments are equal and occur at the end of the periods, this is a regular annuity problem.

$$PV = \$10,000, \; PMT = \$2,000, \; n = 8, \; i = ?$$
$$i = 11.81\%$$

If you don't have a financial calculator, $i$ can be found by successive approximations.

---

The internal rate of return is a very good measure of return. It does, however, have some disadvantages, one of which is that it is difficult to calculate, although with the proliferation of computers and accompanying software, this is no longer a serious problem. Another disadvantage is that there may be more than one solution to the equation if in some periods there is additional investment in the project (since it is an equation of $n$ degrees). Therefore, you should always check your solution to make sure that it makes sense. The last disadvantage is that the formula assumes that each payment is reinvested at the internal rate of return. If it is not possible to reinvest the payments at that high a return, the amount of the internal rate of return may be overstated.

## Expected Value of Return [E(r)]

Another measure of return that is very useful is the expected value of the return. Up until now, we have been measuring rates of return which occurred in the past. Of more importance is the future rate of return. If we make an investment now, the rates of return which will affect us are the ones that occur in the future. Usually the future cannot be predicted with accuracy, but we can make some approximating forecasts. These forecasts are based on all the information we have of the past and the present. They usually take the form of a probability distribution. For instance, it is forecasted that XYZ stock will have a 30 percent probability of a rate of return of .10, a 40 percent probability of a rate of return of .15, and a 30 percent probability of a rate of return of .20.

The expected value of the return measures the central tendency of such a probability distribution. It is found by taking the weighted average of the expected returns weighted by the probability of each return.

If $r_1, r_2, \ldots r_n$ are the possible rates of return and $p_1$ is the probability of $r_1$ occurring, $p_2$ the probability of $r_2$, and $p_n$ the probability of $r_n$, then the expected value of the return, $E(r)$, is

$$E(r) = r_1 p_1 + r_2 p_2 + \ldots r_n p_n \tag{4-7}$$

or

$$E(r) = \sum_{i=1}^{n} r_i p_i$$

---

**PRACTICE PROBLEM 12**     Given the following returns and their probabilities, compute the expected value of return.

| Outcome | Return | Probability |
|---------|--------|-------------|
| 1 | $-.1$ | .1 |
| 2 | 0 | .2 |
| 3 | .1 | .3 |
| 4 | .2 | .3 |
| 5 | .3 | .1 |
|   |   | 1.0 |

*Solution*

$$E(r) = (-.1)(.1) + (0)(.2) + (.1)(.3) + (.2)(.3) + (.3)(.1)$$
$$= (-.01) + (0) + (.03) + (.06) + (.03)$$
$$= .11$$

---

# RISK

In order to make an investment decision, it is important to know not only the expected value of the return but also the dispersion around that expected value.

## Variance (One Investment)

Refer to Investments A and B in Exhibit 4–1. It is expected that Investment A will have a rate of return of zero for 30 percent of the time, a return of .2 for 40 percent of the time and a return of .4 for 30 percent of the time. The expected value of the return is .2 ($0 \times .3 + .2 \times .4 + .4 \times .3$).

It is expected that Investment B will have a rate of return of .1 for 30 percent of the time, a return of .2 for 40 percent of the time and a return of .3 for 30 percent of the time. The expected value of the return of Investment B is also .2 ($.1 \times .3 + .2 \times .4 + .3 \times .3$).

Both Investment A and B have the same expected return, but Investment A is riskier than Investment B. It is riskier because the lowest return is lower than for Investment B, and the highest return is higher than for Investment B. The wider the distribution of returns, the riskier the investment. In deciding which investment to choose, it is important to know the riskiness of the investment. Since more people are risk averse, they choose Investment B over Investment A because B is less risky but has the same expected return.

Since wideness of the distribution of returns is a measure of risk, variance is a proper measure of risk for one investment. The variance or its square root, the standard deviation ($\sigma$), measures how wide a distribution is. Either the variance or the standard deviation may be used. The standard deviation has the advantage that it is measured

---

**EXHIBIT 4–1  Investment Risk**

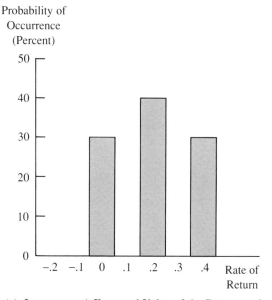

Probability of Occurrence (Percent)

(a) Investment A Expected Value of the Return = .2

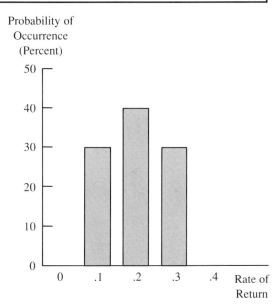

Probability of Occurrence (Percent)

(b) Investment B Expected Value of the Return = .2

in the same units as the rate of return, while the variance is measured in units of the rate of return squared (which does not make as much sense). On the other hand, variances can be summed but standard deviations are not additive.

Equation 4–8 is the formula for the variance. The terms in it have already been defined.

$$\text{var}(r) = \sum_{i=1}^{n} [r_i - E(r)]^2 P_i \tag{4–8}$$

---

**PRACTICE PROBLEM 13**

What are the variance and standard deviation of Investment A in Exhibit 4–1?

*Solution*

$$\text{var}(r) = [r_1 - E(r)]^2 p_1 + [r_2 - E(r)]^2 p_2 + [r_3 - E(r)]^2 p_3$$

$$= (0 - .2)^2 .3 + (.2 - .2)^2 .4 + (.4 - .2)^2 .3$$

$$= .012 + 0 + .012$$

$$= .024$$

$$\sigma = \sqrt{.024} = .155$$

**PRACTICE PROBLEM 14**

What are the variance and standard deviation of Investment B in Exhibit 4–1?

*Solution*

$$\text{var}(r) = (.1 - .2)^2 .3 + (.2 - .2)^2 .4 + (.3 - .2)^2 .3$$

$$= .003 + 0 + .003$$

$$= .006$$

$$\sigma = \sqrt{.006} = .077$$

---

Often the variance of historical returns is being computed. With historical returns there are not any probabilities. Therefore, Equation 4–9 is used to compute the variance.

$$\text{var}(r) = \frac{\sum_{i=1}^{n} (r_i - \bar{r})^2}{n} \tag{4–9}$$

where

$i =$ the period

$r_i =$ the return of Investment X in period $i$

$\bar{r} =$ the arithmetic mean of all the returns

$n =$ the total number of periods

**PRACTICE PROBLEM 15**   Find the variance and standard deviation of the following rates of return:

| Period | $r_i$ |
|--------|-------|
| 1 | −.11 |
| 2 | .22 |
| 3 | .14 |
| 4 | .17 |
| 5 | .21 |
| 6 | .07 |
| 7 | .08 |
| 8 | −.06 |
| 9 | .13 |
| 10 | .02 |
| 11 | .18 |
| 12 | .15 |

*Solution*

| Period | $r_i$ | $r_i - \bar{r}$ | $(r_i - \bar{r})^2$ |
|--------|-------|-----------------|----------------------|
| 1 | −.11 | −.21 | .0441 |
| 2 | .22 | .12 | .0144 |
| 3 | .14 | .04 | .0016 |
| 4 | .17 | .07 | .0049 |
| 5 | .21 | .11 | .0121 |
| 6 | .07 | −.03 | .0009 |
| 7 | .08 | −.02 | .0004 |
| 8 | −.06 | −.16 | .0256 |
| 9 | .13 | .03 | .0009 |
| 10 | .02 | −.08 | .0064 |
| 11 | .18 | .08 | .0064 |
| 12 | .15 | .05 | .0025 |
|   | 1.20 |   | .1202 |

$$\bar{r} = \frac{1.20}{12} = .10$$

$$\text{var}(r) = \frac{.1202}{12} = .0100$$

$$\sigma(r) = \sqrt{.0100} = .100$$

# Covariance and Correlation Coefficient (Two Investments)

If you own two or more investments, you have an investment portfolio. The dollar amount of the return of the portfolio is simply the sum of the dollar amount of the returns of each of the investments in the portfolio. The rate of return of the portfolio

**EXHIBIT 4–2  Portfolio of Two Stocks**

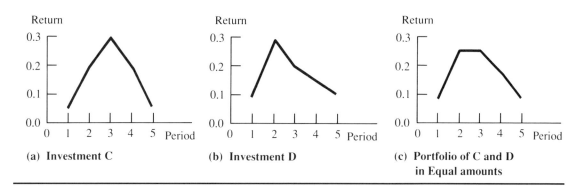

(a)  Investment C

(b)  Investment D

(c)  Portfolio of C and D
in Equal amounts

is the weighted average of the rate of return for each investment weighted by the proportion of the total portfolio value invested in that investment. The riskiness of the portfolio, however, can be less than the weighted average of the variances of each individual investment within the portfolio.

To illustrate why this is true, refer to Exhibit 4–2. The returns for periods one through five are graphed for Investments C and D. The returns for a portfolio of equal amounts of Investments C and D are also graphed. Note that when Investment D is added to the portfolio, the riskiness of the portfolio is less than the riskiness of Investment C alone.

If a second investment is added to a first investment and the second is not perfectly correlated with the first, then the resulting portfolio will have less risk than the weighted average of the risk of the individual securities.

If the second investment is negatively correlated with the first, then the risk of the portfolio is even lower. Exhibit 4–3 shows Investment E, which is negatively correlated to Investment C and the resulting portfolio of Investments C and E.

**EXHIBIT 4–3  Portfolio of Two Stocks with Negative Correlation**

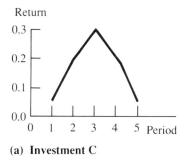 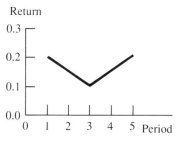 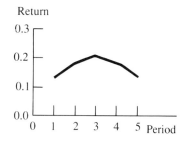

(a)  Investment C

(b)  Investment E

(c)  Portfolio of C and E
in Equal Amounts

If the returns of both investments move in the same direction (as Investments C and D), then they are positively correlated. If they move in opposite directions (like C and E), they are negatively correlated.

In order to measure the riskiness of a portfolio, it is necessary to be able to measure the correlation between every pair of investments. There are two measures of correlation: covariance and the correlation coefficient.

The formula for covariance of historical returns is similar to the variance except that it is between two different investments. The returns for the first investment in each period are $r_1, r_2, \ldots r_n$; the returns for the second investment are $R_1, R_2, \ldots R_n$; and $\bar{r}$ and $\bar{R}$ are the arithmetic means of the returns.

$$\text{cov}(r, R) = \frac{\sum_{i=1}^{n} (r_i - \bar{r})(R_i - \bar{R})}{n} \qquad (4\text{–}10)$$

**PRACTICE PROBLEM 16**    Given the following two sets of returns, calculate the covariance between them. (Note that the first set of returns is the same set as in Practice Problem 15.)

| Period | $r_i$ | $R_i$ |
|--------|-------|-------|
| 1 | −.11 | .05 |
| 2 | .22 | .15 |
| 3 | .14 | .17 |
| 4 | .17 | .20 |
| 5 | .21 | .18 |
| 6 | .07 | .15 |
| 7 | .08 | .12 |
| 8 | −.06 | .10 |
| 9 | .13 | .08 |
| 10 | .02 | .06 |
| 11 | .18 | .08 |
| 12 | .15 | .10 |

*Solution*

| Period | $r_i$ | $r_i - \bar{r}$ | $R_i$ | $R_i - \bar{R}$ | $(r_i - \bar{r})(R_i - \bar{R})$ |
|--------|-------|-----------------|-------|-----------------|----------------------------------|
| 1 | −.11 | −.21 | .05 | −.07 | .0147 |
| 2 | .22 | .12 | .15 | .03 | .0036 |
| 3 | .14 | .04 | .17 | .05 | .0020 |
| 4 | .17 | .07 | .20 | .08 | .0056 |
| 5 | .21 | .11 | .18 | .06 | .0066 |
| 6 | .07 | −.03 | .15 | .03 | −.0009 |
| 7 | .08 | −.02 | .12 | 0 | 0 |
| 8 | −.06 | −.16 | .10 | −.02 | .0032 |
| 9 | .13 | .03 | .08 | −.04 | −.0012 |
| 10 | .02 | −.08 | .06 | −.06 | .0048 |
| 11 | .18 | .08 | .08 | −.04 | −.0032 |
| 12 | .15 | .05 | .10 | −.02 | −.0010 |
|  | 1.20 |  | 1.44 |  | .0342 |

$$\bar{r} = \frac{1.20}{12} = .10, \bar{R} = \frac{1.44}{12} = .12$$

$$\text{cov}(r, R) = \frac{.0342}{12} = .00285$$

Like the variance, the covariance is measured in units of return squared, which does not make much sense. If the covariance is divided by the standard deviations of the returns of each of the two investments, the result is a number with no units which ranges between $-1$ and $+1$. It is called the correlation coefficient and measures the correlation between two variables.

If the correlation coefficient is $+1$, there is perfect correlation; if it is 0, there is no correlation; and if it is $-1$, there is perfect negative correlation.

$$\text{cor coef}(r, R) = \frac{\text{cov}(r, R)}{\sigma(r)\,\sigma(R)} \tag{4–11}$$

or

$$\text{cor coef}(r, R) = \frac{\sum_{i=1}^{n} (r_i - \bar{r})(R_i - \bar{R})}{\sqrt{\sum_{i=1}^{n} (r_i - \bar{r})^2} \sqrt{\sum_{i=1}^{n} (R_i - \bar{R})^2}} \tag{4–12}$$

**PRACTICE PROBLEM 17**   Calculate the correlation coefficient of the two sets of returns given in Practice Problem 16.

*Solution*

$$\text{cor coef}(r, R) = \frac{\text{cov}(r, R)}{\sigma(r)\,\sigma(R)}$$

Calculate the standard deviation of $R$.

$$\sigma(R) = .047$$

From Practice Problems 15 and 16,

$$\text{cov}(r, R) = .0031, \quad \sigma(r) = .100$$

$$\text{cor coef}(r, R) = \frac{.00285}{(.100)(.047)} = .606$$

# Beta

While the correlation coefficient measures the relationship between two investments, its use becomes very cumbersome in evaluating the relationships among the securities in a large portfolio. For a portfolio of 10 investments, 45 correlation coefficients could be computed. For a portfolio of 100 investments, 4,950 correlation coefficients could be computed. The solution to this problem is to compare the returns of each investment in the portfolio with the market.

The returns of all investments in the market would be impossible to calculate. Even calculating the returns of all stocks would be virtually impossible. However, the return for a large number of stocks would be easy. In fact, a number of organizations regularly calculate and publish the returns of a large number of stocks. For instance, Standard and Poors (S&P) publishes the returns of a sample of 500 stocks. Such an index is chosen as a surrogate for the stock market returns.

The returns of each investment in the portfolio are compared with the returns of the market as a whole. In practice, past returns are usually used and the assumption is made that the relationship that existed in the past between a stock and the market will hold in the future. Exhibit 4–4 provides the quarterly rates of return on the S&P 500, Ball Corporation, and Treasury bills for the years 1983 through 1986.

The Treasury bill rate is subtracted from the returns on the S&P 500 and the returns on Ball Corporation to obtain the excess returns on the index and Ball Corporation. Excess returns are compensation for bearing the risk of the index or stock as opposed to buying risk-free Treasury bills.

On a graph similar to Exhibit 4–5, the relationship between the excess returns on a security and the excess returns on the market can be displayed. Using least squares regression, a line which best fits the points can be found. This line is called the characteristic line for the individual investment.

The equation of the characteristic line is

$$r = \alpha + \beta R_m \qquad\qquad (4\text{--}13)$$

where

$r$ = the excess returns on the individual investment

$R_m$ = the excess returns on the market

$\alpha$ = the place where the characteristic line intercepts the excess returns axis

$\beta$ = the slope of the characteristics line

The equation for beta is

$$\beta = \frac{\operatorname{cov}(r, R_m)}{\operatorname{var}(R_m)} \qquad\qquad (4\text{--}14)$$

or

$$\beta = \frac{\displaystyle\sum_{i=1}^{n} (r_i - \bar{r})(R_{mi} - \bar{R}_m)}{\displaystyle\sum_{i=1}^{n} (R_{mi} - \bar{R})^2} \qquad\qquad (4\text{--}15)$$

The equation for alpha is

$$\alpha = \bar{r} - \beta \bar{R}_m \qquad\qquad (4\text{--}16)$$

## EXHIBIT 4–4  Quarterly Rates of Return Data

| Year–Quarter | Standard and Poors' 500 Index | | | | | | | Ball Corporation Common Stock | | | |
| --- | --- | --- | --- | --- | --- | --- | --- | --- | --- | --- | --- |
| | Price End of Quarter | Quarterly Dividend | Quarterly Return[a] | Annual T-Bill[b] | Quarterly T-Bill[c] | Excess Return[d] | | Price End of Quarter | Quarterly Dividend | Quarterly Return[a] | Excess Return[d] |
| 1982–4 | 140.64 | | | | | | | 14.313 | | | |
| 1983–1 | 152.96 | 1.73 | 0.0999 | 0.0836 | 0.0209 | 0.0790 | | 15.750 | 0.130 | 0.1095 | 0.0886 |
| 1983–2 | 168.11 | 1.74 | 0.1104 | 0.0882 | 0.0221 | 0.0884 | | 17.250 | 0.130 | 0.1035 | 0.0814 |
| 1983–3 | 166.07 | 1.75 | −0.0017 | 0.0905 | 0.0226 | −0.0244 | | 17.500 | 0.145 | 0.0229 | 0.0003 |
| 1983–4 | 164.93 | 1.77 | 0.0038 | 0.0896 | 0.0224 | −0.0186 | | 15.625 | 0.145 | −0.0989 | −0.1213 |
| 1984–1 | 159.18 | 1.80 | −0.0239 | 0.0944 | 0.0236 | −0.0475 | | 14.875 | 0.145 | −0.0387 | −0.0623 |
| 1984–2 | 153.18 | 1.83 | −0.0262 | 0.0994 | 0.0249 | −0.0510 | | 15.688 | 0.145 | 0.0644 | 0.0396 |
| 1984–3 | 166.10 | 1.85 | 0.0964 | 0.1041 | 0.0260 | 0.0704 | | 18.813 | 0.160 | 0.2045 | 0.1834 |
| 1984–4 | 167.24 | 1.88 | 0.0182 | 0.0816 | 0.0204 | −0.0022 | | 22.500 | 0.160 | 0.2095 | 0.1841 |
| 1985–1 | 180.66 | 1.92 | 0.0917 | 0.0857 | 0.0214 | 0.0703 | | 23.563 | 0.160 | 0.0544 | 0.0329 |
| 1985–2 | 191.85 | 1.94 | 0.0727 | 0.0701 | 0.0175 | 0.0552 | | 27.688 | 0.160 | 0.1819 | 0.1643 |
| 1985–3 | 182.08 | 1.96 | −0.0407 | 0.0708 | 0.0177 | −0.0584 | | 28.000 | 0.180 | 0.0178 | 0.0001 |
| 1985–4 | 211.28 | 1.98 | 0.1712 | 0.0707 | 0.0177 | 0.1536 | | 30.875 | 0.180 | 0.1091 | 0.0914 |
| 1986–1 | 238.90 | 2.01 | 0.1402 | 0.0659 | 0.0165 | 0.1238 | | 35.000 | 0.180 | 0.1394 | 0.1230 |
| 1986–2 | 250.84 | 2.03 | 0.0585 | 0.0621 | 0.0155 | 0.0430 | | 42.500 | 0.180 | 0.2194 | 0.2039 |
| 1986–3 | 231.32 | 2.06 | −0.0696 | 0.0519 | 0.0130 | −0.0826 | | 38.250 | 0.205 | −0.0952 | −0.1082 |
| 1986–4 | 242.17 | 2.07 | 0.0559 | 0.0549 | 0.0137 | 0.0421 | | 35.250 | 0.205 | −0.0731 | −0.0868 |
| Sum | | | 0.7567 | 1.2635 | 0.3159 | 0.4409 | | | | 1.1303 | 0.8144 |
| Average | | | 0.0473 | 0.0790 | 0.0197 | 0.0276 | | | | 0.0706 | 0.0509 |

[a] Quarterly return $= \dfrac{P_n - P_{n-1} + D_n}{P_{n-1}}$

[b] Treasury bill yields are the average rates on three-month bills issued in the last month of the quarter.

[c] Quarterly T-bill = annual T-bill ÷ 4.

[d] Excess return = quarterly return − quarterly T-bill rate.

**EXHIBIT 4–5  *Characteristic Line***

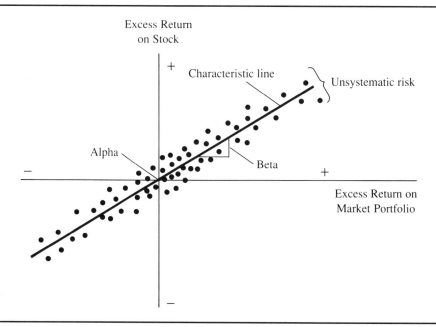

Beta is a measure of systematic risk. If beta equals 1, then the returns of the individual investment are perfectly correlated with the returns of the market. If beta equals −1, then the returns of the investment are perfectly negatively correlated. If beta equals 0, there is no correlation. If beta is greater than 1, then the individual investment is positively correlated with the market but is more volatile.

If the market is in equilibrium, alpha will equal zero. A positive alpha denotes returns greater than explained by the security's systematic risk. A negative alpha denotes returns less than explained by its systematic risk.

Since most investments are somewhat correlated with the market, one would choose an investment with a low beta to add to a portfolio in order to reduce the risk of the portfolio. This is because a low beta, having a low correlation with the market, would most likely also have a low correlation with the rest of the investments in the portfolio; therefore, by being included in the portfolio, it would reduce the risk of the portfolio as a whole.

**PRACTICE PROBLEM 18**

Using the data in Exhibit 4–4 compute the beta and alpha for Ball Corporation.

*Solution*

**Step 1** Using Equation 4–9, compute the variance of the excess returns on the S&P 500.

| $R_{mi}$ | $R_{mi} - \bar{R}_m$ | $(R_{mi} - \bar{R}_m)^2$ |
|---|---|---|
| 0.0790 | 0.0514 | 0.0026 |
| 0.0884 | 0.0608 | 0.0037 |
| −0.0244 | −0.0519 | 0.0027 |
| −0.0186 | −0.0462 | 0.0021 |
| −0.0475 | −0.0751 | 0.0056 |
| −0.0510 | −0.0786 | 0.0062 |
| 0.0704 | 0.0428 | 0.0018 |
| −0.0022 | −0.0298 | 0.0009 |
| 0.0703 | 0.0427 | 0.0018 |
| 0.0552 | 0.0276 | 0.0008 |
| −0.0584 | −0.0860 | 0.0074 |
| 0.1536 | 0.1260 | 0.0159 |
| 0.1238 | 0.0962 | 0.0093 |
| 0.0430 | 0.0154 | 0.0002 |
| −0.0826 | −0.1101 | 0.0121 |
| 0.0421 | 0.0146 | 0.0002 |
| 0.4409 | | 0.0734 |

$$\bar{R}_m = \frac{.4409}{16} = .0276$$

$$\text{var}(R_m) = \frac{.0734}{16} = .0046$$

**Step 2.** Using Equation 4–10, compute the covariance of the excess returns on Ball Corporation with excess returns on the S&P 500.

| $r_i$ | $r_i - \bar{r}$ | $(r_i - \bar{r})(R_m - \bar{R}_m)$ |
|---|---|---|
| 0.0886 | 0.0377 | 0.0019 |
| 0.0814 | 0.0305 | 0.0019 |
| 0.0003 | −0.0506 | 0.0026 |
| −0.1213 | −0.1722 | 0.0079 |
| −0.0623 | −0.1132 | 0.0085 |
| 0.0396 | −0.0113 | 0.0009 |
| 0.1834 | 0.1325 | 0.0057 |
| 0.1841 | 0.1332 | −0.0040 |
| 0.0329 | −0.0180 | −0.0008 |
| 0.1643 | 0.1134 | 0.0031 |
| 0.0001 | −0.0508 | 0.0044 |
| 0.0914 | 0.0405 | 0.0051 |
| 0.1230 | 0.0721 | 0.0069 |
| 0.2039 | 0.1530 | 0.0024 |
| −0.1082 | −0.1591 | 0.0175 |
| −0.0868 | −0.1377 | −0.0020 |
| 0.8144 | | 0.0621 |

$$\bar{r} = \frac{.8144}{16} = .0509$$

$$\text{cov}(r, R) = \frac{.0621}{16} = .0039$$

**Step 3.** Using Equation 4–14, compute beta.

$$\beta = \frac{.0039}{.0046} = .848$$

Ball Corporation has less systematic risk than the S&P 500.

**Step 4.** Using Equation 4–16, compute alpha.

$$\alpha = \bar{r} - \beta \bar{R}_m$$
$$= .0509 - (.848).0276$$
$$= .0275$$

The positive alpha indicates that during this period Ball Corporation had greater returns than explained by beta.

---

### Record Gains and Losses

Stock prices frequently are static for weeks or months. At other times, there can be drastic changes on one day. Listed here are the biggest one day gains and losses in the history of the Dow Jones Industrial Average (as of December 1987).

|  | | Gains | |
| --- | --- | --- | --- |
| Date | Close | Gain | Percent Change |
| Oct 21, 1987 | 2027.85 | 186.84 | 10.15 |
| Oct 20, 1987 | 1841.01 | 102.27 | 5.88 |
| Oct 29, 1987 | 1938.33 | 91.51 | 4.96 |
| Sept 22, 1987 | 2568.05 | 75.23 | 3.02 |
| April 3, 1987 | 2390.34 | 69.89 | 3.01 |

|  | | Losses | |
| --- | --- | --- | --- |
| Date | Close | Decline | Percent Change |
| Oct 19, 1987 | 1738.74 | 508.00 | −22.61 |
| Oct 26, 1987 | 1793.93 | 156.83 | −8.04 |
| Oct 16, 1987 | 2246.74 | 108.35 | −4.60 |
| Oct 14, 1987 | 2412.70 | 95.46 | −3.81 |
| Oct 6, 1987 | 2548.63 | 91.55 | −3.47 |

# HISTORICAL PERFORMANCE

Researchers have compiled evidence about the historical performance of different types of financial assets. When we look at historical performance, we are particularly interested in returns, risk, and the correlations among the returns of the different types of assets. While past performance is not an exact predictor of future performance, it provides some evidence of what we can expect from our investments. In any risky situation, we want to use all the evidence available to forecast outcomes. Past performance is one piece of information that can help us make predictions about the future performance of our investments.

When examining past performance, you want to look for underlying economic variables that influenced the performance. For example, in the 1970s, investment in housing provided high returns while common stocks performed poorly. In the early 1980s, common stocks performed well and housing prices remained about constant. Before projecting these returns into the future, you should ask what factors caused them. In the common stock and housing comparison, an important factor was the rate of inflation. In the inflationary 1970s, housing performed well. When people observed that housing prices were increasing while financial assets were performing poorly, they bid up housing prices even more. On the other hand, inflation caused high interest rates which drove down bond and stock prices. If you correctly forecasted that the inflation of the 1970s was not going to recur in the 1980s, you would not have expected the patterns from investment in housing and stocks to be similar in that decade.

A second reason to look at past performance is to test if the relationships we hypothesize hold. For example, we have said that the riskier an investment is, the higher its return should be. Past performance data allows us to examine if past riskier investments have paid higher returns. Likewise, later in the book, we will hypothesize that investors demand a liquidity premium; that is, they demand that the returns on long-term bonds be greater than the average of the expected short-term rates. With past performance data we can test this hypothesis.

## The Fisher and Lorie Study

Three major studies have looked at past performance of investment instruments. Fisher and Lorie looked at the performance of all the stocks listed on the NYSE during the period December 1925 through December 1976. They included every stock listed anytime during that period and were careful about handling of commissions, cash dividends, mergers, stock splits, and stock dividends. They computed returns for all the possible monthly holding periods within the 50-year period. The calculations were done with different assumptions concerning the amount invested in each stock (equally weighted investment and weights based on the total value of each stock outstanding), reinvestment of dividends, and investor tax rates.

Exhibit 4–6 summarizes important findings of the Fisher and Lorie study. The 9 percent figure in the first Equally Weighted column is the annual rate of return on an equally weighted portfolio of all stocks listed on the NYSE during the 50-year period. For the 20-year period ending December 1976 the annual rate of return was 9.6 percent,

**EXHIBIT 4–6   Rates of Return for Common Stocks Listed on the New York Stock Exchange**

| | 1926–1976 | | 1956–1976 | | 1966–1976 | |
|---|---|---|---|---|---|---|
| | Equally Weighted | Value Weighted | Equally Weighted | Value Weighted | Equally Weighted | Value Weighted |
| *Dividend Reinvested, Cash to Portfolio* | | | | | | |
| Tax exempt, current dollars | 9.0 | 9.1 | 9.6 | 8.5 | 8.4 | 7.4 |
| Tax exempt, deflated dollars | 6.5 | 6.6 | 5.6 | 4.5 | 2.4 | 1.4 |
| Lower tax rate, current dollars | 8.3 | 8.3 | 8.7 | 7.5 | 7.4 | 6.2 |
| Lower tax rate, deflated dollars | 5.8 | 5.9 | 4.7 | 3.6 | 1.5 | 0.3 |
| Higher tax rate, current dollars | 7.2 | 7.1 | 7.4 | 6.1 | 6.2 | 4.9 |
| Higher tax rate, deflated dollars | 4.7 | 4.7 | 3.5 | 2.2 | 0.4 | −0.9 |
| *Without Dividend Reinvested, Cash to Portfolio* | | | | | | |
| Tax exempt, current dollars | 7.3 | 7.9 | 9.9 | 8.6 | 8.4 | 7.1 |
| Tax exempt, deflated dollars | 5.8 | 6.7 | 6.4 | 5.1 | 2.5 | 1.3 |
| Lower tax rate, current dollars | 7.0 | N/A | 9.0 | N/A | 7.5 | N/A |
| Lower tax rate, deflated dollars | 5.4 | N/A | 5.4 | N/A | 1.6 | N/A |
| Higher tax rate, current dollars | 6.4 | 6.8 | 7.6 | 6.2 | 6.3 | 4.8 |
| Higher tax rate, deflated dollars | 4.6 | 5.3 | 3.9 | 2.6 | 0.4 | −0.9 |
| *Rates of Change in Prices, Cash to Portfolio* | | | | | | |
| Tax exempt, current dollars | 4.6 | 4.3 | 5.9 | 4.5 | 4.9 | 3.4 |
| Tax exempt, deflated dollars | 2.2 | 1.9 | 2.0 | 0.7 | −0.9 | −2.3 |

N/A   Not available.

Source: Constructed from data in Fisher, Lawrence, and Lorie, James H. *A Half Century of Returns on Stocks and Bonds* (Chicago: The University of Chicago Graduate School of Business, 1977).

and for the 10-year period ending the same date it was 8.4 percent. Value weighted portfolios give more importance to larger corporations when computing the overall return. For the 50-year period the annual rate of return for the value weighted portfolio is only slightly different from the equally weighted portfolio of all listed stocks. During the 10- and 20-year periods, the weaker performance of the larger companies caused the returns on the value weighted portfolios to be less than those on the equally weighted portfolios.

The next row of figures adjusts the returns for inflation. For the 50-year period the annual rate of return after adjustment for inflation on the equally weighted portfolio was 6.5 percent. The high inflation in the late 1960s and early 1970s caused the rates of return for the 20- and 10-year periods to be 5.6 and 2.4 percent respectively.

The next four rows compute the returns assuming the investor had to pay taxes. The calculations were done for both lower and higher tax rate investors. Notice how poor the rates of returns were during the 10-year period after adjusting for taxes and for inflation.

The middle section of the table redoes the calculations assuming the investor did not reinvest the dividends paid. The rates of return for the 50-year period were reduced. However, because of the market decline in the 1970s, the returns were higher if the investor did not reinvest dividends during the 20- and 10-year periods. The bottom section of the table ignores dividends and computes the rates of returns based on price changes only.

## The Ibbotson and Sinquefield Study

Exhibit 4–7 displays a summary of the results of the Ibbotson and Sinquefield study. In addition to common stocks, they computed returns on small firms stocks, long-term corporate bonds, long-term U.S. government bonds, U.S. Treasury bills, and consumer goods (a measure of inflation) over the period 1926 to 1987. From these basic series, they computed nine more series. The risk premiums on common stocks (equity risk premia) are computed by subtracting the risk-free returns on Treasury bills from the returns on common stock. This series measures what the market has paid for bearing the risk of common stock investment as compared to the risk-free alternative. The small stock premiums are computed by subtracting the returns on common stocks from the returns on small firms stocks. This series measures what the market paid for bearing the additional risk of investing in small firms. The maturity premiums on long-term government bonds (horizon premia) are computed by subtracting the returns on Treasury bills from the returns on long-term Treasury bonds. This series measures what the market has paid for investing in long-term rather than short-term, default-free securities. The default premiums on long-term corporate bonds are computed by subtracting the returns on Treasury bonds from the returns on corporate bonds. This series measures what the market has paid for bearing the default risk of these corporate bonds. The final five series are the first five adjusted for inflation.

Exhibit 4–7 gives two return measures for each series: the geometric mean and the arithmetic mean. As a risk measure, the exhibit presents the standard deviation of

**EXHIBIT 4–7 Rates of Return on Stocks, Bonds, and Bills, 1926–1987 (In Percentages)**

| Series | Annual Geometric Mean Rate of Return | Arithmetic Mean of Annual Returns | Standard Deviation of Annual Returns |
|---|---|---|---|
| Common Stocks | 9.9 | 12.0 | 21.1 |
| Small capitalization stocks | 12.1 | 17.7 | 35.9 |
| Long-term corporate bonds | 4.9 | 5.2 | 8.5 |
| Long-term government bonds | 4.3 | 4.6 | 8.5 |
| U.S. Treasury bills | 3.5 | 3.5 | 3.4 |
| Consumer price index | 3.0 | 3.2 | 4.8 |
| Equity risk premia | 6.2 | 8.3 | 21.1 |
| Small stock premia | 2.0 | 3.7 | 19.0 |
| Default premia | 0.6 | 0.7 | 3.0 |
| Horizon premia | 0.8 | 1.1 | 8.0 |
| Common stock (inflation adjusted) | 6.6 | 8.8 | 21.2 |
| Small capitalization stocks (inflation adjusted) | 8.8 | 14.2 | 35.2 |
| Long-term corporate bonds (inflation adjusted) | 1.8 | 2.3 | 10.0 |
| Long-term government bonds (inflation adjusted) | 1.2 | 1.7 | 10.2 |
| U.S. Treasury bills (inflation adjusted) | 0.4 | 0.5 | 4.4 |

Source: Ibbotson, Roger G., and Sinquefield, Rex A. *Stocks, Bonds, Bills, and Inflation* (SBBI), 1982, updated in *SBBI 1988 Yearbook* (Chicago: Ibbotson Associates).

**EXHIBIT 4–8 Rates of Return on Alternative Investment Media, 1949–1969**

| | Arithmetic Mean | Geometric Mean | Standard Deviation[a] | Coefficient of Variation[b] |
|---|---|---|---|---|
| S&P industrials | 12.97 | 11.63 | 17.55 | 1.51 |
| S&P utilities | 9.31 | 8.60 | 12.43 | 1.45 |
| Japanese stocks | 24.07 | 18.94 | 41.30 | 2.18 |
| Australian stocks | 7.80 | 6.82 | 14.22 | 2.09 |
| Treasury bill yields | 3.01 | 3.00 | 1.60 | 0.53 |
| U.S. government 2% bonds | 2.48 | 2.37 | 4.68 | 1.97 |
| Bethlehem Steel, 2¾% bonds (maturity 1970) | 2.06 | 2.00 | 3.40 | 1.70 |
| Canadian Pacific perpetual 4% bonds | 1.56 | 1.40 | 5.71 | 4.08 |
| Farm real estate | 9.56 | 9.47 | 4.50 | 0.48 |
| Cotton futures | 17.10 | 3.80 | 66.77 | 17.57 |
| Wheat futures | − 0.49 | − 22.88 | 64.07 | 2.80 |
| Copper futures | 121.02 | 26.60 | 244.02 | 9.17 |

[a] Standard deviation about geometric mean.

[b] Coefficient of variation = standard deviation ÷ geometric mean.

Source: Robichek, Alexander A., Cohn, Richard A., and Pringle, John J. "Returns on Alternative Investment Media and Implications for Portfolio Construction," *Journal of Business* 45 (July 1972): 432.

**EXHIBIT 4–9  Correlation Coefficients for Alternative Investment Media, 1949–1969**

| | S&P Industrial | S&P Utilities | U.S. Government | Bethlehem Steel | Canadian Pacific | Farm Real Estate | Cotton Futures | Wheat Futures | Copper Futures | Japanese Stocks | Australian Stocks |
|---|---|---|---|---|---|---|---|---|---|---|---|
| S&P utilities | .59[a] | — | | | | | | | | | |
| U.S. government 2% bonds 1970–65 | −.54[b] | −.17 | — | | | | | | | | |
| Bethlehem Steel 2¾% bonds 1970 | −.30 | −.08 | .81[a] | — | | | | | | | |
| Canadian Pacific perpetual 4% bonds | .23 | .34 | .02 | .10 | — | | | | | | |
| Farm real estate | −.13 | −.15 | −.19 | −.26 | −.13 | — | | | | | |
| Cotton futures | .29 | −.04 | −.21 | −.12 | −.01 | −.09 | — | | | | |
| Wheat futures | .29 | .06 | −.31 | −.41 | .14 | −.24 | .67[a] | — | | | |
| Copper futures | .32 | −.24 | −.20 | −.10 | .12 | −.21 | .23 | .38 | — | | |
| Japanese stocks | −.07 | .11 | −.21 | −.19 | .05 | .48[b] | −.31 | −.09 | −.13 | — | |
| Australian stocks | .22 | −.17 | −.28 | −.05 | −.44[b] | −.29 | .33 | .04 | .13 | −.15 | — |
| Treasury bill yields | −.55[a] | −.66[a] | .26 | .20 | −.40 | .06 | −.41 | −.35 | .05 | −.02 | .14 |

[a] Significant at the .01 level. Critical values and corresponding significance levels as follows: .55 (1%), .43 (5%), .37 (10%), and .29 (20%).

[b] Significant at the .05 level.

Source: Robichek, Alexander A., Cohn, Richard A. and Pringle, John J. ''Returns on Alternative Investment Media and Implications for Portfolio Considerations,'' *Journal of Business* 45 (July 1972): 433.

the annual returns. The figures in the exhibit should be studied. They are consistent with the Fisher and Lorie study and are what might have been expected.

## The Robichek, Cohen, and Pringle Study

In addition to stocks and bonds, the Robichek, Cohen, and Pringle study computes rates of returns for foreign stocks, farm real estate, and commodity futures. Exhibit 4–8 gives the exact categories and measures of return and variability for the 20-year period, 1949–1969. An important contribution of this study is Exhibit 4–9, which gives the correlation coefficients between the different series. The number of negative and low correlation coefficients points out how important and easy it is to diversify your investment portfolio. It also emphasizes the value foreign securities have in diversifying a portfolio.

# SUMMARY

Because return and risk are the most important features of an investment, the investor must understand their measurement. Holding period return is the ratio of the appreciation plus the cash flows to the amount invested. The arithmetic mean and geometric mean can be used to combine holding period returns. Of the two, the geometric mean is the better measure because changes in the amount invested over time will cause the arithmetic mean to overstate the true return.

The internal rate of return is a good measure of return except that it assumes any money returned during the life of the investment will be reinvested at the internal rate of return. If, when the cash flows are received, new investments are not available paying as high a return, the internal rate of return is not earned on all the money originally invested. If, when the cash flows are received, investments are available which pay a greater return, a higher rate of return is earned on the sum invested over the life of the investment.

Expected rate of return uses forecasted outcomes and probabilities to compute an expected value.

When viewing an investment in isolation, dispersion of outcomes measures risk. Variance and standard deviation measure this dispersion. With two investments, it is important to know the relationship between their return patterns. Combined risk can be reduced by choosing investments with low or negative correlation coefficients.

Beta measures the relationship between an investment and a market index. It is a measure of how systematic risk affects the investment.

Overall, the historical performance of the different types of financial assets is satisfying. The returns were adequate to compensate investors for the time value of their money and the risks undertaken. The inflation adjusted returns for the late 1960s and early 1970s show how damaging inflation can be to investors in financial assets. The low correlation coefficients for alternative investment media provide evidence of the benefits of both diversification across asset categories and into foreign securities.

The formulas below summarize the return measures developed in this chapter.

$$\text{rate of return} = \frac{\text{ending value} - \text{beginning value} + \text{cash flows}}{\text{beginning value}} \qquad \text{(4–1)}$$

One Period Return

$$r_1 = \frac{P_1 - P_0 + D_1}{P_0} \qquad \text{(4–2)}$$

$$r_n = \frac{P_n - P_{n-1} + D_n}{P_{n-1}} \qquad \text{(4–3)}$$

Arithmetic Mean Return ($\bar{r}$)

$$\bar{r} = \frac{r_1 + r_2 + r_3 + \ldots r_n}{n} \qquad \text{(4–4)}$$

Geometric Mean Return ($G$)

$$G + 1 = [(1 + r_1)(1 + r_2)(1 + r_3) \ldots (1 + r_n)]^{1/n} \qquad \text{(4–5)}$$

Internal Rate of Return ($i$)

$$PV = \frac{PMT_1}{(1 + i)^1} + \frac{PMT_2}{(1 + i)^2} + \frac{PMT_3}{(1 + i)^3} + \ldots \frac{PMT_n}{(1 + i)^n} \qquad \text{(4–6)}$$

Expected Value of Return [$E(r)$]

$$E(r) = r_1 p_1 + r_2 p_2 + \ldots r_n p_n \qquad \text{(4–7)}$$

The following formulas summarize the risk measures developed in this chapter.

Variance (One Investment)

$$\text{var}(r) = \sum_{i=1}^{n} (r_i - E(r))^2 p_i \qquad \text{(4–8)}$$

$$\text{var}(r) = \frac{\sum_{i=1}^{n} (r_i - \bar{r})^2}{n} \qquad \text{(4–9)}$$

Covariance and Correlation Coefficient (Two Investments)

$$\text{cov}(r, R) = \frac{\sum_{i=1}^{n} (r_i - \bar{r})(R_i - \bar{R})}{n} \tag{4-10}$$

$$\text{cor coef}(r, R) = \frac{\text{cov}(r, R)}{\sigma(r)\sigma(R)} \tag{4-11}$$

$$\text{cor coef}(r, R) = \frac{\sum_{i=1}^{n} (r_i - \bar{r})(R_i - \bar{R})}{\sqrt{\sum_{i=1}^{n} (r_i - \bar{r})^2} \sqrt{\sum_{i=1}^{n} (R_i - \bar{R})^2}} \tag{4-12}$$

Beta

$$r = \alpha + \beta R_m \tag{4-13}$$

$$\beta = \frac{\text{cov}(r, R_m)}{\text{var}(R_m)} \tag{4-14}$$

$$\beta = \frac{\sum_{i=1}^{n} (r_i - \bar{r})(R_{mi} - \bar{R}_m)}{\sum_{i=1}^{n} (R_{mi} - \bar{R}_m)^2} \tag{4-15}$$

$$\alpha = \bar{r} - \beta \bar{R}_m \tag{4-16}$$

## QUESTIONS

1. What does the rate of return measure?
2. Why is the geometric mean return a better measure than the arithmetic mean return?
3. List five methods for measuring the representative or "average" return. Describe their advantages and disadvantages.
4. When are variance, covariance, and beta used to measure risk?
5. What is the difference between the covariance and the correlation coefficient?
6. What does beta measure? Explain what the following values of beta mean: 1, .8, .2, 0, $-1$.
7. Summarize Fisher and Lorie's study of returns on stocks and bonds.
8. Summarize Ibbotson and Sinquefield's study of returns on stocks, bonds, bills, and inflation. Explain the significance of their derived series.
9. Summarize the Robichek, Cohn, and Pringle study of return on alternative investment media. What is the significance of this study for portfolio construction?

## PROBLEMS

1. Use the following price and dividend data for this problem.

| Period | $P_n$ | $D_n$ |
|--------|-------|-------|
| 0 | $20 | $1.00 |
| 1 | 21 | 1.25 |
| 2 | 22 | 1.30 |
| 3 | 21 | 1.30 |
| 4 | 19 | 1.10 |
| 5 | 21 | 1.15 |
| 6 | 22 | 1.20 |
| 7 | 23 | 1.25 |
| 8 | 22 | 1.25 |

   a. Calculate the rate of return for the eight periods.
   b. Calculate the arithmetic mean return for the eight periods.
   c. Calculate the geometric mean return for the eight periods. How does it compare with the arithmetic mean?

2. Use the following price and dividend data from IBM for this problem.

| Year–Quarter | Price | Dividend |
|--------------|-------|----------|
| 1985–2 | 123.75 | 1.10 |
| 1985–3 | 123.875 | 1.10 |
| 1985–4 | 155.50 | 1.10 |
| 1986–1 | 151.50 | 1.10 |
| 1986–2 | 146.50 | 1.10 |
| 1986–3 | 134.50 | 1.10 |
| 1986–4 | 120.00 | 1.10 |
| 1987–1 | 150.125 | 1.10 |
| 1987–2 | 162.50 | 1.10 |

   a. Calculate the rates of return for the periods 1985–3 through 1987–2.
   b. Calculate the arithmetic mean return for the eight periods.
   c. Calculate the geometric mean return for the eight periods. How does it compare with the arithmetic mean?

3. Karen bought 100 shares of stock for $25 per share. After five years she sold the stock for $35 per share. Each year the stock paid a $2 dividend. What was her annual internal rate of return?

4. David bought 100 shares of stock for $50 per share. After four years he sold the stock for $55 per share. Each year the stock paid a $4 dividend. What was his annual internal rate of return?

5. The following are the returns and their probabilities that are forecast for an investment. Compute the expected value and the variance of the return for this investment.

| Return | Probability |
|--------|-------------|
| − .05  | .10         |
| 0      | .10         |
| + .10  | .20         |
| + .15  | .30         |
| + .20  | .20         |
| + .25  | .10         |

6. The following are the returns and their probabilities that are forecast for an investment. Compute the expected value and the variance of the return for this investment.

| Return | Probability |
|--------|-------------|
| − .10  | .10         |
| − .05  | .10         |
| + .02  | .30         |
| + .05  | .20         |
| + .10  | .20         |
| + .15  | .10         |

7. Use the following data for this problem.

| Period | Returns of Investment A | Returns of Investment B |
|--------|-------------------------|-------------------------|
| 1      | .05                     | .17                     |
| 2      | − .02                   | .14                     |
| 3      | .07                     | .12                     |
| 4      | .11                     | .08                     |
| 5      | .14                     | .05                     |
| 6      | .19                     | .09                     |
| 7      | .18                     | .15                     |
| 8      | .16                     | .13                     |
| 9      | .17                     | .17                     |
| 10     | .15                     | .20                     |

   **a.** Graph the returns of Investments A and B against the period.
   **b.** Calculate the mean, variance, and standard deviation of the returns for both Investments A and B.
   **c.** Calculate the covariance and correlation coefficient between the returns for A and B.
8. Use the following data for this problem

| Year–Quarter | Returns on Digital Equipment | Returns on Ball Corp. |
|---|---|---|
| 1985–3 | .1545 | .0178 |
| 1985–4 | .2226 | .1091 |
| 1986–1 | .1906 | .1394 |
| 1986–2 | .0872 | .2194 |
| 1986–3 | .0481 | − .0952 |
| 1986–4 | .1655 | − .0731 |
| 1987–1 | .5525 | .1228 |
| 1987–2 | .0077 | .2179 |

  **a.** Graph the returns of both stocks against the period.
  **b.** Calculate the mean, variance, and standard deviation of the returns for both stocks.
  **c.** Calculate the covariance and correlation coefficient between the returns for the two stocks.

  **9.** Using the data for the S&P 500 and Treasury bills given in Exhibit 4–4 and these returns for Eli Lilly, compute beta and alpha.

| Year–Quarter | Returns |
|---|---|
| 1985–1 | .1902 |
| 1985–2 | .1228 |
| 1985–3 | .0092 |
| 1985–4 | .2994 |
| 1986–1 | .3444 |
| 1986–2 | .0916 |
| 1986–3 | − .1830 |
| 1986–4 | .1383 |

  **10.** Using the data for the S&P 500 and Treasury bills given in Exhibit 4–4 and these returns for Digital Equipment compute beta and alpha.

| Year–Quarter | Returns |
|---|---|
| 1985–1 | − .0609 |
| 1985–2 | − .0974 |
| 1985–3 | .1545 |
| 1985–4 | .2226 |
| 1986–1 | .1906 |
| 1986–2 | .0872 |
| 1986–3 | .0481 |
| 1986–4 | .1655 |

# READINGS

Brealey, Richard A. *An Introduction to Risk and Return from Common Stocks,* 2nd ed. Cambridge, MA: MIT Press, 1983.

    *This book provides a very complete analysis of the issues involved when computing risk and return.*

Brown, Stephen J., and Kritzman, Mark P., eds. *Quantitative Methods for Financial Analysis.* Homewood, IL: Dow Jones-Irwin, 1987.

> *This book is intended to motivate interest in the application of quantitative methods to financial analysis.*

Fisher, Lawrence, and Lorie, James H. *A Half Century of Returns on Stocks and Bonds.* Chicago, IL: The University of Chicago Graduate School of Business, 1977.

> *This book contains the report summarized in this chapter.*

Lakonishak, Josef, and Shapiro, Alan C. "Stock Returns, Beta, Variance and Size: An Empirical Analysis," *Financial Analysis Journal* 40 (July–August 1984): 36–41.

> *In this article, the authors examine the relationship among stock returns, systematic risk (beta), and total risk (variance).*

Robichek, Alexander A., Cohn, Richard A., and Pringle, John J. "Returns on Alternative Investment Media and Implications for Portfolio Construction," *Journal of Business* 45 (July 1972): 427–443.

> *This article contains the report summarized in this chapter.*

*Stocks, Bonds, Bills, and Inflation: 1988 Yearbook.* Chicago: Ibbotson Associates, 1988.

> *In addition to the historical returns data which are summarized in this chapter, this book presents the methodology used and much more detailed data.*

# Valuing Stocks and Bonds

## OUTLINE

## OBJECTIVES

When you have finished studying this chapter, you should understand

1.  The cost, market, and income approaches to valuation.

2.  The attributes of common stock, preferred stock, bonds, and warrants.

3.  How to compute the value of common stock, preferred stock, and bonds.

# 5

## *Investing for the Long Term*

Some corporate executives argue that investors put too great an emphasis on short-term profits, thereby forcing managers to emphasize the short term over the long term in their decision making. Although this argument has been voiced so many times that it usually is accepted without challenge, there is some evidence that investors do take a long-run view.

For example, many new common stock issues sell at high multiples of their current earnings. In fact, some new issues are made by firms that do not yet have any earnings. The prices of new issues demonstrate that investors are quite willing to invest in firms with strategies that emphasize long-term returns.

Even the prices of more established firms usually reflect a strong belief in long-term prospects. In November 1988, *Fortune* computed the present value of the next five years of forecasted dividends for each of the 20 largest publicly traded companies in the Fortune 500.* Next, *Fortune* compared this value to the price. Typically, only 15 to 30 percent of the market price was based on the next five years' dividends. In other words, 70 to 85 percent of what investors were buying was value based on long-term dividends.

---

*"Yes, You Can Manage Long Term," *Fortune*, November 21, 1988, pp. 64–76.

## INTRODUCTION

In this chapter, we introduce the types of securities issued by corporations: common stock, preferred stock, bonds, rights, and warrants. Although these instruments will be discussed in more detail later in the book, an introduction is appropriate here since they are mentioned in many of the following chapters. In this chapter, we describe the characteristics of each and apply to stocks and bonds models which value them based on the discounted cash flows expected by the security holder. However, before beginning the discussion of securities, we present different approaches to the valuation process.

Readers unfamiliar with time value of money computations should read Appendix A to this book before reading the chapter. Readers with good mathematical backgrounds will want to read Appendix B where the time value of money equations is derived.

---

# APPROACHES TO VALUATION

There are three basic approaches to the valuation of an asset: cost, market, and income. They are used to value many types of assets. For example, in addition to valuing securities, they are used in appraising real estate and in valuing farms and small businesses. Here they are discussed as they apply to common stock.

## Cost

The cost approach examines the value of the assets of the firm. The **book value** of a firm is computed from the firm's balance sheet accounts. Book value is the value of the assets minus the liabilities. By accounting definition this equals the stockholders' equity. Dividing the book value by the number of shares outstanding gives book value per share.

The difficulty with book value is that the balance sheet values of the assets might not reflect their market values. The depreciation that has been taken might not reflect actual wear of plant and equipment. Inflation could cause drastic differences between historical and current asset values. Intangible assets might not be carried at realistic values. Sometimes, analysts compute book value after adjusting for these factors. This adjusted book value better reflects the market value of the firm's assets. The notes to the financial statements contain information about depreciation, inflation, and intangible assets that help in computing an adjusted book value.

The stock of a firm can sell for more or less than its adjusted book value. If it sells for more, the firm has this extra value because of the success with which it is organized. If it sells for less than adjusted book value, consideration should be given to liquidating the firm. Book value is a more important valuation approach for firms that hold mostly financial assets (banks for example) than for manufacturing concerns where the assets are not as liquid.

## Market

The market value approach examines what the asset would sell for in a good market. The characteristics of good markets are: (1) there are many buyers and sellers; (2) no participant can significantly affect the market price; and (3) all participants have equal and good information. Stocks that trade on the exchanges or are actively traded in the OTC market have readily available market values. Privately held securities or very inactive OTC securities are at the other extreme and it is difficult to use the market value approach.

The market value approach examines the value of a stock relative to other stocks available in the market. Investors and security analysts who use this approach compare characteristics of a specific firm to those of others in the market in general and in the same industry in particular. They determine a value by comparing past, present, and future values of measures such as price-earnings ratios, return on stockholders' equity, growth, and dividend yield.

## *Income*

The income approach is based on the present value of the stream of future cash flows. In efficient markets, market value should equal income value. For securities the task of the investor or security analyst is to find overvalued or undervalued securities. An overvalued security is one whose price is more than it would be if other investors had the same perception of the firm. An undervalued security is one whose price is less than it would be if other investors had the same perception of the firm. To have a better perception of the firm the investor or analyst needs better information than other investors have or must do a better job of evaluating it. In this text the income approach will be emphasized in valuing securities.

# COMMON STOCK

The initial sale of common stock to a group of founders provides a corporation with its first assets. This initial equity financing is the foundation for all future equity and debt financing by the firm. Common stock represents ownership and has certain inherent characteristics, one of which is control. Stockholders adopt and amend the bylaws of the corporation. They elect the board of directors, which appoints the firm's officers. Each share of stock entitles the stockholder to one vote. Stockholders who cannot attend stockholder meetings may have other people vote their shares for them. A **proxy** is the legal instrument which allows another person to vote the shares of a stockholder. The management of a corporation routinely solicits the right to vote stockholders' shares by mailing them proxy forms for signatures. Exhibit 5–1 shows a stock certificate and Exhibit 5–2 shows a proxy form.

A second characteristic of common stock is that stockholders can obtain a financial return if the firm is successful. If the firm is profitable, the board of directors may declare a dividend, which will be paid for each share of stock. Legally, dividends can be paid only from current or past profits. Therefore, if a firm has never been profitable or if the total of past deficits is greater than the total of past profits, dividends cannot be paid. Even when the firm has profits from which dividends could be paid, the board of directors has to decide how much to pay out and how much to reinvest in the business. The reinvested profits should result in higher future profits and, therefore, more valuable stock.

A third characteristic of common stock is risk. If a firm does poorly, common stockholders will suffer. Dividends will decrease or stop, and the market value of the

**EXHIBIT 5–1 Sample Stock Certificate**

Source: Courtesy of Ball Corporation.

stock will decline. If the firm fails and is liquidated, stockholders will not receive any of their investment back until all creditors are paid in full. Frequently, when a large firm fails, some stockholders claim that they did not know their investment involved risk. Although the degree varies drastically, common stock is an investment with inherent risk.

Whenever a firm issues additional shares of common stock, a stockholder has a **preemptive right** which allows him or her to purchase enough additional shares to maintain the percentage control that he or she had before the issue of the additional stock. For example, if you owned 10 percent of the common stock of a firm, you could buy 10 percent of any additional shares issued so that you could maintain your 10 percent ownership.

If this preemptive right did not exist, new stock issues could shift control of the firm and dilute the value of existing stock. For example, without the preemptive right, the new stock might be sold to people who favored one stockholder faction. If the new stock were sold at too low a price, the value of existing shares would decline.

Exhibit 5–3 presents an example of dilution and how the preemptive right protects a stockholder. If a firm has 100,000 shares outstanding which are worth $30 each, the

---

**EXHIBIT 5–2  Sample Proxy Form**

---

# PROXY

**BALL CORPORATION**
345 South High Street, Muncie, Indiana 47305

**THIS PROXY IS SOLICITED ON BEHALF OF THE BOARD OF DIRECTORS**
The undersigned hereby appoints Edmund F. Ball, Alexander M. Bracken and John W. Fisher and each or any of them as Proxies, with full power of substitution, to vote all shares of Ball Corporation Common Stock entitled to be voted by the undersigned for the election of directors, on Proposals 2, 3, 4, 5 and 6 referred to on the reverse side of this Proxy Card and described in the Proxy Statement, and on any other business as may properly come before the Annual Meeting of Shareholders on April 26, 1988, or any adjournment thereof.

Please sign exactly as name appears at left. When signing as attorney, executor, administrator, trustee, or guardian, please give full title as such. If a corporation, please sign in full corporate name by President or other authorized officer. If a partnership, please sign in partnership name by authorized person.

DATED: _____ , 1988

PLEASE MARK, SIGN, DATE AND RETURN THE PROXY
CARD PROMPTLY USING THE ENCLOSED ENVELOPE

Signature _____

# SAMPLE

Signature _____

**(See other side for voting matters)**

---

This proxy when properly executed will be voted in the manner directed herein by the undersigned shareholder. If no direction is made, this proxy will be voted <u>FOR</u> Proposals 1, 2, 3, 4 and 5 and <u>AGAINST</u> Shareholder Proposal 6.

1. **ELECTION OF DIRECTORS:** (mark one) ☐ FOR all nominees listed below (except as written in to the contrary below)
☐ WITHHOLD AUTHORITY to vote for all nominees listed below

Nominees for three-year terms expiring at the 1991 Annual Meeting:
Thomas D. Bell, Jr., Howard M. Dean, Richard M. Gillett and Richard M. Ringoen

(INSTRUCTION: To withhold authority to vote for any individual nominee, write that nominee's name on the line provided below.)

_____

The **Board of Directors** recommends a vote **FOR:**

2. **PROPOSAL TO APPROVE THE APPOINTMENT OF PRICE WATERHOUSE**
as the independent public accountants of the Corporation                   ☐ FOR          ☐ AGAINST          ☐ ABSTAIN
3. **PROPOSAL TO AMEND THE AMENDED ARTICLES OF INCORPORATION**              ☐ FOR          ☐ AGAINST          ☐ ABSTAIN
4. **PROPOSAL TO ADOPT 1988 STOCK OPTION AND STOCK APPRECIATION RIGHTS PLAN**  ☐ FOR     ☐ AGAINST          ☐ ABSTAIN
5. **PROPOSAL TO ADOPT 1988 RESTRICTED STOCK PLAN**                          ☐ FOR          ☐ AGAINST          ☐ ABSTAIN

The **Board of Directors** recommends a vote **AGAINST:**

6. **SHAREHOLDER PROPOSAL** to adopt the MacBride Principles                 ☐ AGAINST      ☐ FOR              ☐ ABSTAIN
7. In their discretion, the Proxies are authorized to vote upon such other business as may properly come before the meeting.

**(Please date and sign on reverse side)**

---

Source: Courtesy of Ball Corporation.

---

total value of the stock is $3 million. If 100,000 additional shares were sold for $26 each, the total value of the stock would increase by $2.6 million to $5.6 million. Each of the 200,000 shares then outstanding would be worth $28. If an original shareholder did not purchase additional shares, the value of his or her investment would be diluted when the price fell to $28. On the other hand, if the stockholder purchased enough

---

**EXHIBIT 5–3   *Example of Dilution as the Result of the Issuance of Additional Stock***

|  | Number of Shares | Price ($) | Total Value ($) |
|---|---|---|---|
| *Firm's Position* |  |  |  |
| Existing shares | 100,000 | 30 | 3,000,000 |
| New shares | 100,000 | 26 | 2,600,000 |
| After new issue | 200,000 | 28 | 5,600,000 |
| *Stockholder's Position without Purchase of New Shares, Dilution Occurs* |  |  |  |
| Existing share | 10,000 | 30 | 300,000 |
| New shares | 0 | — | 0 |
| After new issue | 10,000 | 28 | 280,000 |
| *Stockholder's Position with Maintenance of Percentage Ownership, Dilution Does Not Occur* |  |  |  |
| Existing share | 10,000 | 30 | 300,000 |
| New shares | 10,000 | 26 | 260,000 |
| After new issue | 20,000 | 28 | 560,000 |

---

new shares to maintain the previous percentage of ownership, the value of the original stock plus the amount paid for the new stock would equal the value of the stockholder's ending position.

The preemptive right sometimes leads to a firm having a formal rights offering when it plans to sell more stock. In a rights offering, the firm mails **rights** to its shareholders which allow them to purchase the new stock at less than its market price. Because rights offerings are administratively burdensome, firms usually do not use them. When a firm sells new stock without a formal rights offering, courts will enforce the preemptive right if the stockholder can show that dilution or a shifting of control is taking place.

## Classified Common Stock

Usually only one class of common stock is issued by a corporation, and every share has the same rights. Occasionally, however, a corporation issues two or more forms of common stock. This is called **classified common stock.** Classified common stock is usually issued when certain investors want their shares to have priority over the founders' shares in the receipt of dividends. On the other hand, the founding group may want its shares to have more voting rights.

**EXAMPLE**

General Motors found a creative way to use classified common stock when it acquired Electronic Data System (EDS) in 1984. It issued a second class of GM common stock, dubbed Class E, to EDS shareholders and employees. Class E stock offered a dividend based on the earnings of GM's EDS subsidiary. The stock has voting and liquidation rights equal to half of those of regular GM common. GM hoped the use of classified common stock would provide

EDS employees with the financial rewards commonly found in high technology firms. □

## Valuing Common Stock

The value of a share of common stock is the present value of its future dividend payments. That is,

$$P_0 = \frac{D_1}{1 + r} + \frac{D_2}{(1 + r)^2} + \frac{D_3}{(1 + r)^3} \cdots \tag{5-1}$$

where

$P_0$ = the price of a share of stock at time 0

$D_1$ = the dividend expected at the end of period 1

$D_2$ = the dividend expected at the end of period 2

$D_3$ = the dividend expected at the end of period 3

$r$ = the risk-adjusted discount rate for stock of this risk class

In Equation 5–1, the dividends can change in any direction: they can rise, fall, remain constant, or fluctuate randomly. If a particular growth pattern is assumed, the formula can be simplified. Here we examine constant growth, zero growth, and supernormal growth.

### Leading Stocks in Market Value

The NYSE reported that at the end of 1987 the following were the leading stocks based on common stock market value.

| Company | Listed Shares (In Millions) | Market Value (In Millions) |
| --- | --- | --- |
| International Business Machines | 615.7 | $71,195 |
| Exxon Corp. | 1,812.8 | 69,338 |
| General Electric | 926.6 | 41,000 |
| American Telephone & Telegraph | 1,073.8 | 29,127 |
| Merck & Co. | 151.8 | 24,067 |
| du Pont de Nemours | 240.8 | 21,039 |
| Morris (Phillip) | 239.6 | 20,487 |
| General Motors | 320.5 | 19,668 |
| Dow Chemical | 216.1 | 19,503 |
| Ford Motor | 247.8 | 18,710 |

**Normal Growth**  If the dividends do not fluctuate but grow at a constant rate, $g$, the amount of the dividend each period will grow like an amount left in the bank which compounds interest. The dividend at the end of year 1, $D_1$, is the current dividend times $(1 + g)$, $D_0 (1 + g)$; the dividend at the end of year 2, $D_2$, is $D_1 (1 + g)$ or $D_0 (1 + g)^2$; the dividend at the end of year 3, $D_3$, is $D_2 (1 + g)$ or $D_0 (1 + g)^3$; and so on. Substituting into Equation 5–1 gives

$$P_0 = \frac{D_0 (1 + g)}{(1 + r)} + \frac{D_0 (1 + g)^2}{(1 + r)^2} + \frac{D_0 (1 + g)^3}{(1 + r)^3} + \cdots \qquad (5\text{–}2)$$

This equation simplifies (see Appendix B) to

$$P_0 = \frac{D_1}{r - g} \qquad (5\text{–}3)$$

Of course, Equation 5–3 cannot be used unless $r$ is greater than $g$, because it will not give a positive stock price for an answer. Normally, the appropriate discount rate, $r$, will be greater than the growth rate, $g$. The equation, however, will work with negative growth rates.

---

**PRACTICE PROBLEM 1**  Common Stock of Gemex Inc. is expected to pay a dividend of $2 at the end of next year. If investors in Gemex common stock require a return of 10%, what should be the value of Gemex common stock? Gemex dividends have been growing at a rate of 6% per year.

*Solution*

$$P_0 = \frac{D_1}{r - g}$$

$$D_1 = \$2, r = 10\%, g = 6\%, P_0 = ?$$

$$P_0 = \frac{\$2}{.10 - .06} = \frac{\$2}{.04} = \$50$$

**PRACTICE PROBLEM 2**  American Lighting Corporation paid a dividend of $1.50 at the end of last year. Its dividends have been growing at a rate of 8% per year and investors require a return of 11%. What should the value of this common stock be?

*Solution*

$$D_0 = \$1.50, r = 11\%, g = 8\%$$

$$D_1 = \$1.50 (1 + 8\%) = \$1.50 (1.08) = \$1.62$$

$$P_0 = \frac{\$1.62}{.11 - .08} = \frac{\$1.62}{.03} = \$54$$

---

***Zero Growth*** If dividends are not changing, $g$ equals zero and Equation 5–3 simplifies to

$$P_0 = \frac{D}{r} \tag{5–4}$$

**PRACTICE PROBLEM 3** American Iron is in a mature industry. It pays a dividend of $1.50 per year and expects this dividend to remain unchanged. Investors require a return of 11%. What is the value of a share of stock?

*Solution*

$$D = \$1.50, r = 11\%$$

$$P_0 = \frac{D}{r} = \frac{\$1.50}{.11} = \$13.64$$

***Supernormal Growth*** A firm might grow for several years at very high growth rate early in its life cycle. As the firm matures, its growth rate will fall to a more sustainable rate. In these cases, the value of the stock is the sum of: (1) the discounted value of the dividends during the supernormal growth period and (2) the value of the stock at the end of the supernormal growth period, discounted back to present. The value of the stock at the end of the supernormal growth period is computed using the constant growth model; that is,

$$P_n = \frac{D_{n+1}}{r - g} \tag{5–5}$$

where $P_n$ = the price at the end of the supernormal growth period and $D_{n+1}$ = the dividend at the end of the year following the end of the supernormal growth period.

**PRACTICE PROBLEM 4** High Technology Inc.'s last dividend was $2. The firm is expected to grow at 20% per year for the next three years. Then its growth rate will continue at 5% into the foreseeable future. If investors require a return of 11%, what is the value of this stock?

*Solution*

$$D_1 = \$2 (1.20) = \$2.40$$

$$D_2 = \$2 (1.20)^2 = \$2.88$$

$$D_3 = \$2 (1.20)^3 = \$3.46$$

$$D_4 = D_3 (1.05) = \$3.46 (1.05) = 3.63$$

$$P_3 = \frac{D_4}{r - g} = \frac{\$3.63}{.11 - .05} = \$60.50$$

$$P_0 = \frac{D_1}{(1 + r)} + \frac{D_2}{(1 + r)^2} + \frac{D_3}{(1 + r)^3} + \frac{P_3}{(1 + r)^3}$$

$$= \frac{\$2.40}{1.11} + \frac{\$2.88}{(1.11)^2} + \frac{\$3.46}{(1.11)^3} + \frac{\$60.50}{(1.11)^3}$$

$$= \$51.27$$

# PREFERRED STOCK

**Preferred stock** is favored, or preferred, in some way over common stock. Usually, preferred stock does not vote but comes ahead of common stock in the receipt of dividends and in return of capital if the firm is liquidated.

Usually, preferred stock has a par value upon which stated dividends and liquidation value are based. Preferred stock dividends are often stated as a percentage of the par value. For example, a preferred stock might have a stated dividend of 9 percent of its $100 par value or $9 per share per year. If the preferred stock is ever redeemed by the issuer, the par value must be paid for it. Sometimes common stock has a par value, but it has little significance because dividends or redemptive value are not based on it. A stated dividend on preferred stock conveys the intent of the firm to pay each share an annual dividend of this amount. Like dividends on common stock, most dividends on preferred stock are paid quarterly.

The preferred stock dividend still must be declared by the board of directors each quarter. If a board decides that the firm cannot pay the preferred dividend and does not declare it, the preferred stockholders cannot legally require payment. If it is **cumulative preferred stock,** then the preferred stockholders would be owed the missed dividend that would have to be paid before any common stock dividends were paid in subsequent quarters. If the preferred stock is noncumulative and the board does not declare the dividend one period, the preferred stockholders could never claim that last dividend. However, the preferred stockholders may be entitled to voting rights if this happens. Because most investors will not purchase noncumulative preferred stock, most preferred stock is cumulative.

Two provisions can be added to preferred stock to make it more attractive. First, the preferred stock can be convertible. A **convertible** security can be exchanged for, or converted into, common stock at the option of the preferred stockholder. Therefore, if the firm does well and the common stock increases greatly in price, the preferred stockholder can exchange the preferred stock for common stock. The exact conversion ratio between the preferred and the common stock is specified when the preferred stock is issued. It could be any ratio; for example, each share of preferred stock could be exchanged for two shares of common at any time desired by the investor. Many preferred stock issues are convertible.

A second provision, which allows an investor to share in the benefits if the firm is very successful, is that the preferred stock can be participating. **Participating preferred stock** can, under certain circumstances, receive more than the stated dividend.

In good years the stated dividend will be allocated to the preferred stock. Next, an equal dividend will be allocated to the common stock. Then, the preferred stock will participate with the common stock in receiving additional dividends. Most preferred stock issues are nonparticipating.

## Valuing Preferred Stock

The value of preferred stock is the present value of the preferred dividend payment where *n* is infinity and *r* is the yield required by investors of preferred stock of that particular risk.

$$\textbf{Preferred Stock: } Pfd = \sum_{m=1}^{\infty} \frac{D}{(1 + r)^m} \tag{5–6}$$

where

$Pfd$ = the value of preferred stock

$D$ = the preferred stock dividend

$r$ = the yield required by investors

This expression simplifies (see Appendix B) to

$$Pfd = \frac{D}{r} \tag{5–7}$$

---

**PRACTICE PROBLEM 5**  What is the value of a share of preferred stock which pays a preferred dividend of $3? Investors require a yield of 11% on that particular preferred stock issue.

*Solution*

$$Pfd = \frac{D}{r}$$

$$D = \$3, r = 11\%$$

$$Pfd = \frac{\$3}{.11} = \$27.27$$

---

# BONDS

A bond represents a debt contract between the issuer and the bondholder and states the amount to be repaid at maturity as well as the amount of interest to be paid. The amount to be repaid at maturity is called the principal, the face value, the maturity

---

**EXHIBIT 5–4  *Sample Corporate Bond***

Source: Courtesy of Union Electric Company.

---

value, or the par value. Most corporate bonds have a principal of $1,000 and pay interest every six months. Exhibit 5–4 shows a corporate bond.

In order to make bonds more attractive to investors, warrants are sometimes issued with the bonds. A **warrant** gives the holder the right to purchase one or more shares of common stock at a stated price. When the warrant is issued, the stated price is above the market price of the stock. If the market price increases to above the stated price, the warrant holder will profit. Most warrants have expiration dates, although a few are valid forever.

## Medium-Term Notes

Before the 1980s, borrowers usually issued only two types of debt securities; short-term notes and long-term bonds. In the early 1980s, many investors feared the return of high inflation and volatile interest rates. Therefore, they refused to purchase long-term bonds. At the same time, issuers hesitated to issue long-term bonds paying what were, by historical standards, unusually high rates. On the other hand, the issuers did not want to rely heavily on short-term borrowing because short-term rates fluctuate drastically. These forces led to the wide use of medium-term notes. **Medium-term notes** are unsecured promissory notes issued with maturities ranging from 9 months to 15 years, with most maturities ranging between 1 and 7 years. Each note usually has a maturity value of $1,000 and pays interest semiannually.

## Valuing a Bond

The value of a bond is the value of the discounted cash flows. Two kinds of payments are associated with a bond: interest payments, which are generally made twice a year, and the return of the face value (usually $1,000) to the investor when the bond matures. The interest payments are an annuity, while the return of the face value is a single cash flow. The value of a bond is the sum of the present value of the interest payments plus the present value of the final cash flow (the face value). The discount rate in the formula is the yield-to-maturity required by investors for bonds of that particular maturity and risk.

Value of bond = PV of interest payments + PV of face value

$$B = \sum_{m=1}^{n} \frac{I}{(1 + ytm)^m} + \frac{M}{(1 + ytm)^n} \tag{5–8}$$

where

$B$ = the value of the bond

$I$ = the interest payment

$n$ = number of periods to maturity of the bond

$ytm$ = the yield-to-maturity required by investors

$m$ = the counter for the summation sign

$M$ = the face value or maturity value of the bond

---

**PRACTICE PROBLEM 6** — Find the value of a bond with an 8% coupon rate with 16 years to maturity. The yield-to-maturity of similar bonds is presently 10%.

*Solution*

For a single bond, the face value is usually $1,000. If the coupon rate were 8% (quoted as an annual rate), the amount of interest paid each year would be $80 (8% × $1,000). Since bonds generally pay interest twice a year, each interest payment would be $40 ($80/2), the number of periods until maturity would be 32 (2 × 16), and the semiannual yield-to-maturity would be 5% (10/2).

$$B = \sum_{m=1}^{n} \frac{I}{(1 + ytm)^m} + \frac{M}{(1 + ytm)^n}$$

$I$ = $40, $n$ = 32, $ytm$ = 5%, $M$ = $1,000

$B$ = $632.107 + $209.866 = $841.97

---

# SUMMARY

This chapter introduces the securities issued by corporations. Common stock represents ownership. Common stockholders have voting rights and they hope to obtain a return on their investment but face risks. Stockholders have a preemptive right that allows them to buy a portion of any new stock issued by the corporation so that they can maintain their ownership percentage. Occasionally, a firm will issue more than one class of common stock; the classes usually vary in dividend and voting rights.

Preferred stock usually does not vote but is favored over common stock in the receipt of dividends and in liquidation. Preferred stock normally pays a stated dividend and is cumulative.

A bond represents a debt contract between the issuer and the bondholder. The principal is to be repaid at maturity and usually interest is paid every six months. Sometimes warrants are issued with bonds. A warrant gives the holder the right to purchase one or more shares of common stock at a stated price.

Common stock, preferred stock, and bonds are valued by finding the present value of the discounted cash flows expected by the investors.

The value of a share of common stock is given by

$$P_0 = \frac{D_1}{r - g} \tag{5-3}$$

The value of a share of preferred stock is given by

$$Pfd = \frac{D}{r} \tag{5-7}$$

The value of a bond is given by

$$B = \sum_{m=1}^{n} \frac{I}{(1 + ytm)^m} + \frac{M}{(1 + ytm)^n} \tag{5-8}$$

# QUESTIONS

1. Explain the three approaches to valuation.

2. What are the characteristics of common stock?

3. If a firm does not pay out as dividends all its profits, what does it do with the retained profits? Is this use of profits advantageous to the stockholder?

4. What is the purpose of the preemptive right of stockholders? Using an example, show how this right can prevent dilution of a stockholder's investment.

5. Why might a corporation issue both a Class A and a Class B common stock?

6. As a preferred stockholder, do you want your stock to be cumulative, participating, or convertible? Why?

7. Your wealthy friend is considering buying the $2.25 cumulative convertible stock of TWA which is selling for $25 per share. Explain the characteristics of this investment to him.

8. What are warrants? Why are they issued?

9. An investment alternative your friend has been offered is newly issued securities of International Mobile Machines Corporation. The securities are being sold in units by the investment banking firm. Each unit costs $1,000 and consists of: 40 shares of common stock—one cent par value, 100 shares of convertible preferred stock—ten cents par value, and 50 common stock purchase warrants. Explain this investment to him.

# PROBLEMS

1. Common stock of Huron Lumber Company is expected to pay a dividend of $2.50 at the end of this year. If Huron investors require a return of 12%, what should the value of Huron common stock be? Huron expects to grow at a rate of 8% per year.

2. Michigan Microwave, Inc., is expected to pay a dividend of $3 at the end of this year. It is expected that the dividend will grow at a rate of 6% per year. If investors require an 11% return on this stock, what should the value of Michigan Microwave's common stock be?

3. The common stock dividend of the Peach Software Co. was $1.75 at the end of last year and was expected to grow at a rate of 7% per year. If investors required a return of 10.5%, what should the price of Peach Software's common stock be?

4. U.S. Components, Inc.'s common dividends have been growing at a rate of 6.5% per year. At the end of last year, the company paid a dividend of $1. Investors require a return of 9%. What is the value of Components' common stock?

5. National Steel, which is in a mature industry, pays an annual dividend on its common stock of $2 per share. It does not expect this dividend to grow. Investors require a return of 9% on this stock. What is the value of a share of National Steel common stock?

6. The Wapahani Railroad pays a dividend of $1 each year. Since it is in a mature industry, it expects this dividend to remain unchanged. Investors require a return of 10.5%. What is the value of a share of common stock?

7. Innovative Computers Inc. is a young company in a growing field. It paid a dividend of $1.50 last year and expects to grow at a rate of 18% for the next five years. Then its growth rate will continue at a more moderate rate of 8% into the foreseeable future. If investors require a return of 10%, what is the value of their common stock?

8. Howard Inc. paid a dividend last year of $2.50. The firm is expected to grow at a rate of 15% for the next four years, then to level off at a growth rate of 7%. If investors require a return of 9%, what is the value of their common stock?

9. What is the value of a share of preferred stock which pays an annual dividend of $4 if investors require a yield of 10%?

10. American Manufacturing is planning to sell a preferred stock issue which will pay a dividend of $3. Similar preferred stock issues yield 8%. For what price should American Manufacturing's preferred stock sell?

11. Find the value of a $1,000 face value bond with 14 years to maturity and with a 10% coupon rate if the yield-to-maturity of similar bonds is 12%.

12. How much would you be willing to pay for a $1,000 face value bond with an 11% coupon rate and with 20 years to maturity? The yield-to-maturity of similar bonds is 8%.

13. Bob MacMillan bought a bond for $1,000 three years ago. It has a 20 year maturity and 12% coupon rate. Now he wishes to sell his bond to help finance a trip to Europe. If similar bonds currently have a yield-to-maturity of 13.5%, for how much will he be able to sell his bond?

14. If you had bought a bond for $1,000 two years ago, but now wished to sell it, what price would you be able to sell it for if it now has a 15 year maturity and a 10% coupon rate? Similar bonds currently have a yield-to-maturity of 12%.

# CASE PROBLEM

For each of five common stocks in which you are interested, forecast the annual dividends for each of the next five years. (*Value Line* makes these estimates.) Compute the present values of each stock's dividends discounted at 12 percent or at another rate if you feel this rate does not reflect investors' required rate of return for stocks of the risk you chose. For each stock, compare the present value figure to the price. Do you think investors are buying these stocks based on their long-term prospects?

# READINGS

Bhagat, Sanjai. "The Effect of Pre-emptive Right Amendment on Shareholder Wealth," *Journal of Financial Economics* 12 (November 1983): 289–310.
> *This paper investigates the effect on shareholder wealth of removing the preemptive right from corporate charters as 300 NYSE listed companies did between 1962–81.*

Koelman, Joe. "Revenge of the Nerds. Traditional Portfolio Strategists Beware: The Quants Advocating by-the-Computer Investing Are Moving Out of the Background," *Institutional Investor* 21 (September 1987): 84–88.
> *This article reports the growing influence of "quants," very mathematical analysts who apply complex dividend discount models.*

"Why 'One Share, One Vote' Is On Its Way Out," *Business Week* (July 21, 1986): 111–112.
> *This article reports on the NYSE's plan to throw out its long-standing ban on companies with multiple classes of common stock and unequal shareholder voting rights.*

# Government Securities

## OBJECTIVES

When you have finished studying this chapter, you should understand

1. The importance in the financial markets of Treasury, federal agency, and municipal securities.

2. The investment characteristics of Treasury bills, notes, and bonds.

3. The nature of government owned agencies and federally sponsored agencies.

4. The types and investment characteristics of securities issued by state and local governments.

# 6

## Inflation Indexed Government Bonds

Writing in a publication of the Federal Reserve Bank of Boston, economists Alicia H. Munnell and Joseph B. Grolnic made a strong case that the U.S. Treasury should issue bonds indexed for inflation. The principal and interest payments on the securities would be adjusted for inflation. Because these bonds would offer no risk of default as well as no risk of loss of purchasing power, they would be attractive to many investors, particularly retirees. No existing security provides such effective protection against loss. In addition, the U.S. Treasury would have an increased market for its debt. Great Britain has successfully issued inflation backed government bonds since 1981.

---

Source: Munnell, Alicia H., and Grolnic, Joseph B. "Should the U.S. Government Issue Index Bonds?" *New England Economic Review,* September–October 1986, pp. 3–21.

## INTRODUCTION

In the previous chapter we discussed the securities issued by corporations. In this chapter, we first will look at debt securities issued by the U.S. Treasury. Then we will learn about federal agencies and the securities they issue. Low risk and high marketability are among the features that make Treasury and agency securities attractive to many investors. Finally, we will examine what are called municipal securities. These are debt securities issued by state and local governments and their political subdivisions. The fact that interest earned on most of these securities is not taxed by the federal government makes them attractive to investors in higher tax brackets.

# TREASURY SECURITIES

Because the U.S. Treasury has borrowed more money than any other entity, it is by far the largest issuer of securities. Exhibit 6–1 shows the growth in Treasury debt in recent years. Treasury securities can be divided into two categories: nonmarketable and marketable.

## Nonmarketable Securities

About one-fourth of the Treasury debt is nonmarketable. **Nonmarketable Treasury securities** cannot be resold by the original purchaser to a third party. Nonmarketable debt is issued in specific series based on the type of purchaser. There are four major and some minor series. The largest series is sold to government trust funds such as social security and railroad retirement. The second largest series is U.S. savings bonds. The third largest series is sold to state and local governments. The fourth series is sold to foreign governments. We will discuss only the nonmarketable debt available to investors, U.S. savings bonds.

Savings bonds were referred to as Series E or Series H before 1980 and paid a fairly low rate of interest. After 1980 the names were changed to Series EE and Series HH, and the Treasury was permitted to change the interest rate every six months. Since November, 1982, EE bonds have paid a variable rate with a guaranteed minimum (currently 6 percent) if held longer than five years, and HH bonds have paid the guaranteed rate available on EE bonds. They both have a maturity period of ten years. Savings bonds are not negotiable, that is, they cannot be sold to another person. They can be purchased and redeemed at financial institutions, a Federal Reserve Bank (or

---

**EXHIBIT 6–1   *Treasury Debt Outstanding (Billions of Dollars)***

| Type | 1988 | 1980 | 1975 |
|---|---|---|---|
| *Marketable* | | | |
| Bills | 398 | 200 | 129 |
| Notes | 1,090 | 311 | 150 |
| Bonds | 300 | 84 | 37 |
| Subtotal | 1,788 | 595 | 316 |
| *Nonmarketable* | | | |
| Savings bonds | 106 | 73 | 65 |
| Foreign governments | 6 | 25 | 23 |
| Government trust funds | 536 | 190 | 124 |
| Other | 148 | 24 | 4 |
| Subtotal | 796 | 312 | 216 |
| *Total* | 2,584 | 906 | 532 |

Source: *Economic Report of the President* Washington, D.C.: U.S. Government Printing Office, 1989), Table B-84, p. 406.

branch), or the Treasury. No commission is charged. Savings bonds may not be redeemed until six months after the purchase date but they may be kept past the maturity date and will continue to earn interest for many years. They can be registered in individual or joint ownership form. If bonds are registered in joint ownership form, either owner may cash the bonds.

Series EE bonds are sold at a discount, while Series HH bonds are sold at face value. For example, for a $50 EE bond (the smallest one available) you pay $25. The face value is $50 and the purchase price ($25) is one-half the face value. Series EE bonds have face values ranging from $50 to $10,000. As shown in Exhibit 6–2, the purchase price is always one-half the face value. The difference between the purchase price and the amount you receive when you redeem your bond is the amount of interest you have earned. For Series EE bonds, you will not receive your interest until you cash in the bonds. Since the interest rate paid on EE bonds varies with a guaranteed minimum (if held longer than five years), the redemption value may be greater than the face value.

All EE bonds held five years will accrue interest at 85 percent of the average return of five-year Treasury securities during the five-year period with a guaranteed minimum (currently 6 percent). The interest will be compounded semiannually. After five years, the rate will be determined in the same manner for the period from issue date to the end of each additional six-month period. If the bond is redeemed before five years, it will earn less than the guaranteed minimum for the five-year holding period. If you hold an old Series E bond, you also earn the new rates if the bond has been held fewer than 40 years (currently the maximum amount of time a bond can earn interest).

Series HH savings bonds are sold at face values ranging from $500 to $10,000. Interest is paid to the owner twice a year. Series HH bonds can be purchased only in exchange for Series E or EE bonds held longer than six months. Series HH bonds are bought mainly by people who wish to use the interest as part of their income. Series

---

**EXHIBIT 6–2  U.S. Savings Bonds**

| Series EE | | Series HH | |
|---|---|---|---|
| *Purchase Price* | *Face Value* | *Denominations* | *Semiannual Interest Checks* |
| $    25.00 | $    50.00 | $    500.00 | $ 15.00 |
| 37.50 | 75.00 | 1,000.00 | 30.00 |
| 50.00 | 100.00 | 5,000.00 | 150.00 |
| 100.00 | 200.00 | 10,000.00 | 300.00 |
| 250.00 | 500.00 | | |
| 500.00 | 1,000.00 | | |
| 2,500.00 | 5,000.00 | | |
| 5,000.00 | 10,000.00 | | |

Source: Department of Treasury, U.S. Savings Bonds Division, ''Series EE and HH Savings Bonds (Washington, D.C.: U.S. Government Printing Office, December 1986).

### Tax-Free Education Savings

Beginning January 1, 1990, you will be able to purchase Series EE savings bonds that can provide tax-free earnings.

Here's how it works now. The IRS taxes interest earned on Series EE savings bonds. Taxes may be paid on an annual basis or deferred until redemption. Interest on federal government obligations may not be taxed by the states. Bonds purchased after January 1, 1990, that are redeemed and used for educational costs will result in tax-free interest.

The bonds must be recorded in the parent's name (or names). At the beginning of 1989, the Treasury had not issued final regulations concerning proof of using the bonds for educational purposes.

EE bonds are bought mainly by people who do not need the interest for their current income.

Series EE and E bonds have some attractive tax implications. You have the option of paying income tax on the interest earned either annually or at redemption. Taxes can be postponed even longer if you convert your Series EE or E bonds into Series HH bonds. The tax on the interest earned on the EE or E bonds before they were converted does not need to be paid for ten years, when the HH bonds mature. Federal income tax must be paid annually on the interest received from the HH bonds but state and local governments do not tax the interest earned on savings bonds.

If your bonds were lost, stolen, damaged, or destroyed, you could notify the Bureau of Public Debt for replacement. Since you would need to include the names, addresses, issue dates, and serial numbers of your bonds, it is important to keep a record of this information separate from the bonds.

## Marketable Securities

The U.S. Treasury issues marketable securities in four forms: Treasury bills, cash management bills, Treasury notes, and Treasury bonds. Treasury securities can be purchased without a service charge from a Federal Reserve Bank (or branch) or from the Treasury Department's Bureau of Public Debt. Purchasers of Treasury securities may submit either a competitive or noncompetitive bid. A competitive bid states the number of securities the investor wishes to buy and the offered purchase price. A noncompetitive bid states the number of securities the investor wishes to buy and agrees to pay the average price of the competitive bids accepted. Institutions make most of the competitive bids. Individuals usually make noncompetitive bids rather than risk paying too much or bidding too low and not having the bid accepted. After receiving the bids, the Federal Reserve uses the following priorities for allocation: (1) foreign official institutions, (2) Federal Reserve Banks to replace maturing issues they hold, (3) noncompetitive bids, and (4) competitive bids. Exhibit 6–3 displays the Treasury form used for bids.

**Treasury bills** are short-term debt of the U.S. government. Every week, new 91- and 182-day bills are sold. Every four weeks new 364-day bills are sold. The minimum

**EXHIBIT 6–3   Tender for Treasury Bills**

FORM PD 5176-3
(January 1986)

OMB No. 1535-0069
Expires: 01-31-89

TREASURY DIRECT

**TENDER FOR 52-WEEK TREASURY BILL**

**TENDER INFORMATION**

AMOUNT OF TENDER: $ _____

BID TYPE (Check One)  ☐ NONCOMPETITIVE  ☐ COMPETITIVE AT ____ . ____ %

**ACCOUNT NUMBER** _____

**INVESTOR INFORMATION**

ACCOUNT NAME

ADDRESS

CITY          STATE          ZIP CODE

**TAXPAYER IDENTIFICATION NUMBER**

1ST NAMED OWNER ____ - __ - ____    OR    __ - _____
SOCIAL SECURITY NUMBER          EMPLOYER IDENTIFICATION NUMBER

**TELEPHONE NUMBERS**

WORK ( ___ ) ___ - ____    HOME ( ___ ) ___ - ____

**PAYMENT ATTACHED**

TOTAL PAYMENT: $ _____

CASH (01): $ _____    CHECKS (02/03): $ _____

SECURITIES (05): $ _____    $ _____

OTHER (06): $ _____    $ _____

**DIRECT DEPOSIT INFORMATION**

ROUTING NUMBER

FINANCIAL INSTITUTION NAME

ACCOUNT NUMBER          ACCOUNT TYPE  ☐ CHECKING
(Check One)
ACCOUNT NAME          ☐ SAVINGS

**AUTOMATIC REINVESTMENT**

1   2          Circle the number of sequential 52-week reinvestments you want to schedule at this time

**AUTHORIZATION**

For the notice required under the Privacy and Paperwork Reduction Acts, see the accompanying instructions.

I submit this tender pursuant to the provisions of Department of the Treasury Circulars, Public Debt Series Nos. 1-86 and 2-86 and the public announcement issued by the Department of the Treasury

Under penalties of perjury, I certify that the number shown on this form is my correct taxpayer identification number and that I am not subject to backup withholding because (1) I have not been notified that I am subject to backup withholding as a result of a failure to report all interest or dividends, or (2) the Internal Revenue Service has notified me that I am no longer subject to backup withholding. I further certify that all other information provided on this form is true, correct and complete.

_____ SIGNATURE          _____ DATE

FOR DEPARTMENT USE

TENDER NUMBER
912794

CUSIP

ISSUE DATE

RECEIVED BY

DATE RECEIVED

EXT REG  ☐
FOREIGN  ☐
BACKUP  ☐
REVIEW  ☐

CLASS  ☐

NUMBERS

Source: Department of Treasury, Bureau of the Public Debt, Form PD 5176–3.

## U.S. Government Securities Quotes

About $100 billion of U.S. government securities are traded every business day by a relatively small group of major dealers. The bulk of these secondary market transactions in Treasury bills, notes and bonds is among banks, dealers and brokers which buy and sell securities after original issuance for their accounts or for customers.

A list of prices of marketable issues on the secondary market is published each afternoon by the Federal Reserve Bank of New York. It is called the "Composite Quotations for U.S. Government Securities" report.

The prices listed for the bills, bonds and notes are obtained from five securities dealers. From time to time, one or more of these dealers are changed. The New York Fed uses the most widely quoted price from the range of quotations received. Actual purchases or sales may have taken place at higher or lower prices.

These are six groups of numbers under five headings for each note and bond.

| Issue | Bid | Ask | Change | Yield |
|-------|-----|-----|--------|-------|
| 9¼ 8/15/98-N | 99.05 | 7 | +5 | 9.37 |

Numbers under the first heading identify the issue by interest rate (9¼ percent) and maturity date (Aug. 15, 1998). The "N" means the security is a note. In the market, this note is referred to as "9¼s of August 1998."

"Bid" is the price a buyer is willing to pay for the issue and "ask" is the price a seller is seeking. Both numbers are abbreviations.

Note and bond prices are quoted in 32nds of a point, so the bid quote of 99.05 means 99 plus 5/32 of a point or 99.15625 in decimal form. Therefore, for each $1,000 of face value of the note, the quote would be 10 times that or $991.5625. For each $1,000 of face value a full point equals $10 and a 32nd equals 31.25 cents (1,000 times 0.03125, the decimal equivalent of 1/32). For denominations other than $1,000, multiples of the quote for $1,000 are used.

The number "7" under "ask" is an abbreviation for the price sought by a seller. It also is expressed in 32nds of a point and in the above example stands for 99.07 or 99 and 7/32 or 99.21875. For a face value of $1,000, that figure is multiplied by 10 to obtain a quote of $992.1875.

Ask prices are always higher than bid prices for notes and bonds. If the ask price digits are lower than the numbers after the decimal in the bid, it indicates the next highest whole number must be used.

If, in the example above, the ask was "1", lower than the bid's "5", the ask price would be 100.01, not 1/32 more than 99.

Following the ask price is the difference between the current day's bid price and the listed bid price of the preceding business day. It, too, is a shorthand reference to the number after the decimal. In the example, it denotes an increase of 5/32 or $1.56 per $1,000 face value. Often, the bid and ask quotes change by the same amount from the previous day's levels.

A plus sign (+) may appear to the right of the price or its change, most frequently on the most active issues. It means dealers are quoting the issue in 64ths. A quote of 104.07 + means 104 and 7/32 plus 1/64, or 104 and 15/64.

The yield, 9.37 percent in the example, is the annualized percentage return an investor receives if the note is purchased on the day of the quotation at the ask price and held until maturity. However, when a security can be called in at a certain date before maturity and is quoted above par, the call date, rather than maturity date, is used to calculate the yield.

Bills are quoted differently from notes and bonds, since they do not pay a stated rate of interest. An investor's return on a bill is the difference between the purchase and subsequent sale price or, when held to maturity, the face value paid by the Treasury. Consequently, bills are quoted at a discount from face value, with the discount expressed as an annual rate based on 360 days.

Quotations of all bills are thereby comparable regardless of maturity.

As with notes and bonds, numbers on the report are abbreviated. But, Treasury bill numbers have different meanings than those for notes and bonds. For example,

| Issue | Bid | Ask | Change | Yield |
|-------|-----|-----|--------|-------|
| 8/03/89 | 7.73 | 7.71 | +.02 | 8.29 |

The first numbers refer to the bills's maturity date, August 8, 1989. For this example assume the current date is 55 days before the maturity date.

The bid, 7.73 percent is the return, on a discount basis, that the buyer would receive if a seller accepts the buyer's proposed price. In the example, to obtain a 7.73 percent annual return, the buyer is offering to pay $9,881.90 for a Treasury bill maturing in 55 days and with a face value of $10,000. When the bill is held to maturity the owner would receive $10,000 or $118.10 more than the purchase price. That $118.10 represents a 7.73 percent annualized return on a discount basis.

The ask quotation of 7.71 percent is the return the seller would like the buyer to accept on a discount basis. The seller always seeks a sale with a lower return (and thus a higher price) than the buyer wishes to pay. The buyer seeks a lower price (and thus a higher yield). Therefore, unlike the quotes on notes and bonds, bid quotes on bill are always higher than the ask quotes.

In the example, the seller would receive $9,882.21 for the $10,000 face value Treasury bill if the buyer agreed to accept the discount return of 7.71 percent (the ask quote). The return offered by the seller would give the seller 31 cents more than a transaction at the price the buyer is bidding (the difference between $9,882.21 and $9,881.90).

To determine bid and ask dollar prices for each $10,000 of face value, multiply the bid or ask return (excluding decimals) by the number of days to maturity and divide by 360 days. Subtract the result from the $10,000 face value. In the example, the bid dollar price per $10,000 face value would be

$$\$10,000 - \frac{(773 \times 55)}{360} = \$9,881.90$$

The ask dollar price would be

$$\$10,000 - \frac{(771 \times 55)}{360} = \$9,882.21$$

The "change" of plus .02 in the quotation is the change in the listed bid from the preceding day's bid in hundredths of a percentage point. Thus, the change in this example means the return on the previous day's bid was 7.71 percent. One hundredth of a percentage point is also called a "basis point."

Furthermore, since an increase in return indicates a drop in the price, this quote indicates that the market for this issue weakened from the previous day.

The yield is based on the ask rate and is the annualized rate of return if held to maturity. The yield is calculated on a coupon equivalent basis (the amount invested, not the face amount of the bill. See Fedpoints 28). In the example, the investor, receiving $117.79 more at maturity than the price he paid ($10,000 minus $9,882.21 equals $117.79), obtains a 8.29 percent annualized rate of return on the $9,882.21 he paid.

For additional information about Treasury bills, bonds and notes, see "Basic Information on Treasury Securities," available from the New York Fed.

---

Source: Reprinted from *Understanding U.S. Government Securities Quotes,* (New York: Federal Reserve Bank of New York) 1988.

denomination of Treasury bills is $10,000; after that, they are sold in $5,000 multiples. On an irregular schedule, the Treasury sells **cash management bills** which are short-term borrowings issued to adjust for the uneven flow of revenue from taxes. The maturities of cash management bills have ranged from 2 to 164 days and average about 50 days.

Yields on Treasury bills are quoted on a discount basis using a 360-day year. Under this procedure, the dollar amount of the discount is divided by the face value; then this percentage is annualized using a 360-day year.

$$\text{discount rate} = \frac{10,000 - \text{price}}{10,000} \times \frac{360}{\text{days to maturity}}$$

For example, a $10,000, 91-day bill which is auctioned for $9,629.50 will have a discounted yield of 14.657 percent.

$$\text{discount rate} = \frac{10,000 - 9,629.50}{10,000} \times \frac{360}{91}$$

$$= .14657$$

Computation of the true yield considers that the dollar amount of the discount should be divided by the cost, not the face value, and that there are 365 days in a year. That is:

$$\text{true yield} = \frac{10,000 - \text{price}}{\text{price}} \times \frac{365}{\text{days to maturity}}$$

In the above example, the true yield is 15.432 percent.

**Treasury notes** have maturities of one to ten years. Notes maturing in less than four years have a minimum denomination of $5,000 while notes maturing in four to ten years have a minimum denomination of $1,000. **Treasury bonds** have maturities of ten to thirty years and are issued with a minimum denomination of $1,000. Treasury notes and bonds pay interest twice a year. They do not earn interest after maturity. Exhibit 6–4 announces the features of a Treasury issue.

Most long-term bonds are issued with a call provision. The call provision allows the Treasury to redeem the bonds anytime within the five years before maturity. The Treasury has proposed issuing bonds with a call provision allowing them to be called for redemption anytime after five years from issue. At the time of this writing, bonds with this call feature have not been issued.

Treasury securities are issued only in **book-entry form.** This means ownership records are computerized; certificates are not issued. The Treasury's Bureau of Public Debt maintains two sets of computerized accounts for Treasury security owners. One set is the commercial book-entry system for securities owned by institutions; the other set is for securities owned by individuals. The Federal Reserve system operates a

**EXHIBIT 6–4 Features of a Treasury Note**

HIGHLIGHTS OF TREASURY OFFERING
TO THE PUBLIC OF 7-YEAR NOTES
TO BE ISSUED JANUARY 5, 1987

December 16, 1986

**Amount Offered:**

| | |
|---|---|
| To the public............................ | $7,250 million |

**Description of Security:**

| | |
|---|---|
| Term and type of security.................. | 7-year notes |
| Series and CUSIP designation............... | D-1994 |
| | (CUSIP No. 912827 UL 4) |
| Maturity date............................ | January 15, 1994 |
| Call Date.............................. | No provision |
| Interest rate............................ | To be determined based on the average of accepted bids |
| Investment yield......................... | To be determined at auction |
| Premium or discount...................... | To be determined after auction |
| Interest payment dates.................... | July 15 and January 15 (first payment on July 15, 1987) |
| Minimum denomination available........... | $1,000 |

**Terms of Sale:**

| | |
|---|---|
| Method of sale.......................... | Yield auction |
| Competitive tenders...................... | Must be expressed as an annual yield, with two decimals, e.g., 7.10% |
| Noncompetitive tenders................... | Accepted in full at the average price up to $1,000,000 |
| Accrued interest payable by investor........ | None |
| Payment by noninstitutional investors........ | Full payment to be submitted with tender |
| Payment through Treasury Tax and Loan (TT&L) Note Accounts.............. | Acceptable for TT&L Note Option Depositaries |
| Deposit guarantee by designated institutions.. | Acceptable |

**Key Dates:**

| | |
|---|---|
| Receipt of tenders........................ | Tuesday, December 30, 1986, prior to 1:00 p.m., EST |
| Settlement (final payment due from institutions) | |
| a) cash or Federal funds.................. | Monday, January 5, 1987 |
| b) readily-collectible check............... | Wednesday, December 31, 1986 |
| c) TREASURY DIRECT accounts.......... | Tuesday, December 30, 1986 |

Source: Department of Treasury, Bureau of Public Debt; ''Highlights of Treasury Offering'' (Washington, D.C.: U.S. Government Printing Office, December 16, 1986).

Commissioner of Public Debt wire transfer system to handle transfers of Treasury securities on the commercial book-entry system.

The Treasury security accounts for individuals are called **Treasury Direct accounts.** A person can open a Treasury Direct account in person or by mail at a Federal Reserve Bank (or branch) or at the Treasury Department's Bureau of Public Debt. All the Treasury securities owned by an individual are recorded in a single Treasury Direct account. This simplifies record keeping and offers built-in flexibility since changes to the details of the account information can be made very easily. When establishing a Treasury Direct account, the investor designates an account at a depository institution to which all payments from the Treasury account are electronically deposited. No checks are issued.

Treasury Direct accounts are designed primarily for those investors who plan to retain the securities to maturity. However, securities can be transferred to another account or to the commercial book-entry system. Automatic reinvestment of the proceeds from maturing Treasury bills can be arranged.

Instead of opening a Treasury Direct account, an investor can purchase Treasury securities at a depository institution or a brokerage firm. The Treasury's commercial book-entry system will show the institution owning the securities and the institution's records will show the individual owners. The advantage of an account at an institution is that sales of the securities are easier to make. Institutions handle buy and sell transactions for both new and previously issued securities. There will be a fee for their services.

Treasury based, zero coupon securities are created by brokerage firms from long-term Treasury bonds. The brokerage firm purchases many Treasury bonds, places them into a trust account, and sells new securities which have claims on the cash flows from the bonds. In particular, each newly created security has a claim on $1,000 of interest or principal payments due on a particular date. The new security is zero coupon; that is, it does not provide any return until that maturity date. It is priced at a deep discount from maturity value so that it can return a yield competitive with other securities.

Even though the owner does not receive any cash until maturity, the IRS taxes an ''imputed'' interest each year. This provision makes these securities unattractive to investors paying taxes. However, the securities are attractive for tax-deferred accounts such as pension funds, IRAs, and Keogh retirement plans. Another use is for parents to give their child Treasury-based, zero coupon securities which will mature when the child needs the money for college.

## Investment Considerations

The most attractive feature of Treasury securities is their safety—since they are backed by the full taxing power of the federal government, default risk is almost nonexistent. However, interest rate and purchasing power risks affect all fixed rate, long-term securities.

Interest earned on Treasury securities is exempt from state and local income taxes. This exemption also applies to earnings on Treasury-based, zero coupon securities. Interest is taxed, however, by the federal government.

Treasury securities are very liquid. More Treasury securities are resold daily than any other security. Any depository institution or brokerage firm can quickly sell a Treasury security for you. Mutual funds which purchase Treasury securities provide many convenient features.

# FEDERAL AGENCY SECURITIES

In addition to the Treasury, federal agencies issue debt. There are two types of federal agencies: government owned agencies and federally sponsored agencies. Exhibit 6–5 displays the amount of federal agency debt outstanding.

## Government Owned Agencies

Some agencies owned directly by the federal government formerly borrowed in the financial markets. Although their securities had the full backing of the Treasury, the different terms offered and the uncoordinated offering schedules resulted in the agencies having to pay higher interest than the Treasury paid when it borrowed. To reduce interest costs, Congress established the **Federal Financing Bank** in 1974 to issue securities or borrow from the Treasury and then loan the money to government owned agencies and other entities approved by law. The Federal Financing Bank's first public

---

**EXHIBIT 6–5  *Federal Agency Debt Outstanding (Billions of Dollars)***

| | *1986* | *1981* |
|---|---|---|
| *Federal Agencies* | | |
| Defense Department | .1 | .5 |
| Export-Import Bank | 14.2 | 13.3 |
| Federal Housing Administration | .1 | .4 |
| Government National Mortgage Association | 2.2 | 2.7 |
| Postal Service | 3.1 | 1.6 |
| Tennessee Valley Authority | 17.2 | 13.1 |
| U.S. Railroad Association | .1 | .2 |
| Subtotal | 37.0 | 31.8 |
| *Federally Sponsored Agencies* | | |
| Federal Home Loan Banks | 88.7 | 54.1 |
| Federal Home Loan Mortgage Corporation | 13.6 | 5.5 |
| Federal National Mortgage Association | 93.6 | 58.7 |
| Farm Credit Banks | 62.3 | 71.4 |
| Student Loan Marketing Association | 12.2 | .4 |
| Subtotal | 270.4 | 190.1 |
| *Total* | 307.4 | 221.9 |

Source: *Federal Reserve Bulletin* (Washington, D.C.: Board of Governors of the Federal Reserve System, March 1988), Table 1.44, p. A33.

offering was not received well by investors. Therefore, the bank has relied mainly on borrowing from the Treasury. Exhibit 6–5 lists government-owned agencies with outstanding debt.

## Federally Sponsored Agencies

Federally sponsored agencies are independent agencies established by the government to increase the flow of credit to desired activities, particularly agriculture, housing, and education. They are intermediaries which borrow money by selling debt securities in the financial markets and funnel it to appropriate credit institutions. Although these securities are not obligations of, or guaranteed by, the federal government, investors consider default risk to be very low. Let us briefly describe some of the issuers.

**Farm Credit Agencies**    Three sponsored agencies form what are collectively called the Farm Credit Banks. The Federal Land Banks make long-term loans to farmers. The Federal Intermediate Credit Banks provide loans to Production Credit Associations and other agricultural financing institutions which in turn lend to farmers, fishermen, and farm-related businesses. The Banks for Cooperatives lend to agricultural and aquatic marketing, supply, and business service cooperatives. In the past, each of these three agencies sold debt to raise funds. In recent years, their debt has been issued in the name of the Farm Credit Banks and is backed by all three agencies.

**Mortgage Credit Agencies**    Two federally sponsored agencies provide funds for housing. The Federal Home Loan Banks provide liquidity by making loans to savings and loan associations. The savings and loan associations in turn make home mortgage loans. The second agency, the Federal National Mortgage Association, provides funds for housing by borrowing money in the financial markets and using it to purchase mortgages from banks, savings and loan associations, mortgage bankers, and other organizations that meet its requirements.

**Student Loan Credit Agency**    The Student Loan Marketing Association borrows in the financial markets and uses the money to provide liquidity to lenders who make

### Rescuing the Farm Credit Banks

In 1987, Congress was considering proposals to rescue financially the federally sponsored Farm Credit Banks. The problems of the farm economy had led to the banks holding a record number of problem loans. Historically, the bonds issued by the Farm Credit Banks were considered a "moral obligation" of the federal government. With $62 billion of bonds outstanding and a crisis only months away, the strength of the government's commitment was being tested. Although most investors expected a government program to rescue the Farm Credit Banks, there were enough doubts that the bonds had fallen in price to the point that their yields were above those available on many corporate bonds.

student loans under the Federal Guaranteed Student Loan Program. Additionally, this agency can obtain money by borrowing from the Federal Financing Bank.

### Investment Considerations

Federal agency securities are close substitutes for Treasury securities. The interest on most (though not all) the securities is exempt from state and local income tax. The slightly higher yields on agency securities reflect slightly higher default risk and slightly lower liquidity. However, default risk is less than and liquidity higher than corporate bonds. Extensive secondary markets provide liquidity with low transactions costs. Usually, individuals purchase agency securities through depository institutions or brokerage firms.

# MORTGAGE-BACKED SECURITIES

The agencies discussed above issue their debt securities and in turn lend the money in order to encourage a desired activity. There is another way for agencies to provide funds for housing: the issue of **mortgage-backed securities.** Mortgage-backed securities represent pools of mortgages that have been packaged for sale by the agency. Interest and principal payments made on the mortgages are "passed through" monthly to the holder of the security. Three federal agencies issue mortgage-backed securities.

1. Ginnie Maes are issued by a government owned agency, the Government National Mortgage Association (GNMA). Monthly payments of the interest and principal due on these securities are guaranteed by the full faith and credit of the U.S. government.

2. Freddie Macs are issued by the Federal Home Loan Mortgage Corporation (FHLMC), which is owned by the Federal Home Loan Banks. The FHLMC buys home mortgages from savings and loan associations, forms pools, and issues securities backed by the pools. Monthly payments on these securities are guaranteed by the FHLMC, not the U.S. government.

3. Fannie Maes are issued by the Federal National Mortgage Association (FNMA). Monthly payments are guaranteed by it and not the U.S. government.

Interest rates on mortgage-backed securities range up to two percentage points more than Treasury bonds of similar maturities. If you invest in mortgage-backed securities, you will receive a check each month which represents interest and one repayment of principal. Although default risk is very low, these fixed income securities are subject to interest rate risk. When interest rates go up, the value of the outstanding mortgage-backed securities falls. The principal disadvantage of mortgage-backed securities is that when interest rates fall, homeowners refinance their mortgages. As a result, investors in mortgage-backed securities get repaid ahead of schedule when their only reinvestment alternatives offer low yields. Mutual funds which invest in mortgage-

backed securities provide convenience by allowing you to invest small amounts and
reinvest the monthly cash flows. They also simplify your record keeping for taxes.

# MUNICIPAL SECURITIES

**Municipal securities** are debt securities issued by state and local governments and
their political subdivisions. Municipal securities are issued by more than 30,000 governmental units, such as states, cities, towns, villages, counties, school boards, port
authorities, turnpike commissions, housing agencies, and government owned utilities.
Borrowing by local governments has been common practice in the United States since
the early 1800s. With only minor interruptions, the amount of debt outstanding has
been increasing steadily. Today there are over 1.2 million municipal security issues

---

**EXHIBIT 6–6    Tax-Exempt Municipal Debt Issued**

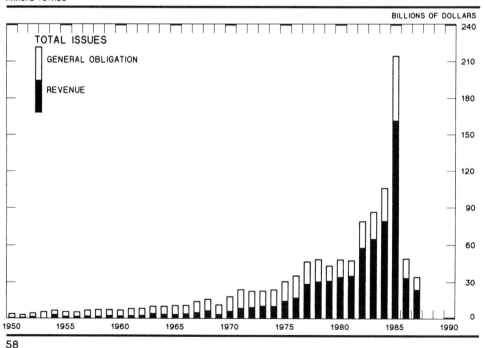

TAX-EXEMPT BOND ISSUES BY STATE AND LOCAL GOVERNMENTS
GROSS PROCEEDS
ANNUAL TOTALS

58

Source: *1988 Historical Chart Book*, (Washington, D.C.: Board of Governors of the Federal Reserve System,
1988) p. 58.

outstanding, ranging in size from $1 billion issues of large governmental units to $10,000 issues of local fire districts. Exhibit 6–6 shows the dollar amount of municipal debt issued in recent years.

Until the 1986 Tax Reform Act, the interest earned on almost all municipal bonds was exempt from federal income tax. The 1986 law, however, limited tax exemption to bonds used to finance traditional governmental functions and other specified activities such as airports, water supplies, and sewage systems. Tax-exempt bonds can no longer be used to finance pollution control facilities, sports stadiums, convention facilities, and parking facilities. Now, when the term "municipal bonds" is used, it usually connotes tax-exempt municipals, although taxable municipal bonds do exist. Usually, the investor need not worry about a municipal bond's tax status because it will be clearly identified as tax-exempt or taxable.

## Categories of Municipal Securities

There are several categories of municipal securities.

**1.** General obligation bonds are backed by the full faith, credit, and taxing power of the issuer.

**2.** Limited-tax bonds have only a portion of the issuer's taxing power backing them; this occurs when the taxing authority is limited by state constitution or statutes.

**3.** Special-tax bonds are backed by the proceeds of specific tax. Other tax revenue cannot be used to pay them. An example is highway bonds backed only by gasoline tax revenue.

**4.** Revenue bonds are issued to finance a revenue producing project and are backed only by the revenues of that project. If the project does not produce enough revenue to pay the interest and principal, tax revenue will not be used. Revenue bonds are issued to finance many projects including airports, toll roads and bridges, water and sewer constructions, health care facilities, and college dormitories.

**5.** Pollution control bonds are issued by a local government to finance pollution control equipment for a private firm. They are backed only by the revenues of that firm. This arrangement allows firms to finance this equipment at lower interest rates than if they issued the bonds directly. These bonds are taxable.

**6.** Industrial development bonds are issued by a local government to help finance the establishment or expansion of a private firm within the community. Usually the government unit uses the proceeds of the issue to build a plant which it leases to the firm. The lease payments will be enough to cover the principal and interest but will be lower than if the building were financed without using municipal securities. The bonds are backed only by the lease revenue. The federal government has detailed rules limiting the use by local governments of industrial development bonds. These bonds are taxable.

**7.** Short-term notes are issued by local governments to provide revenue for a period of between one month to two years. Usually, they are issued to provide temporary financing until other revenue is received. Tax anticipation notes provide financing until taxes are collected. Revenue anticipation notes provide financing until other revenue such as federal or state aid is received. Bond anticipation notes provide revenue until long term bonds are issued.

## Features of Municipal Securities

Most municipal bonds are issued with serial maturities. This means a portion of the issue matures each year. A municipal bond issue that has only one maturity is called a term bond.

Before bonds are issued, the issuer prepares an "official statement" for potential purchasers. This statement describes the bond issue and gives pertinent information about the issuer. Included in the statement is the bond counsel opinion, in which an independent law firm states it has made the proper examination, believes that the bonds are a legal and binding obligation of the issuer, and tells if the interest on the bonds is or is not exempt from federal income tax.

Most term bond issues require sinking funds. A sinking fund provision provides that the issuer regularly set aside money to redeem the bonds. Instead of just holding the sinking fund until maturity, some of the bonds can be redeemed early either through purchase in the market or through a call provision. If the bonds are selling for less than face value, buying them at that price in the market is most attractive. If they are selling for more than face value, a call provision is usually exercised.

Most term bonds are callable after ten years. If only a portion of the bonds is to be called, a lottery by serial number will be used to determine those called. If interest rates have fallen, the issuer might call the entire issue and sell new bonds at the lower rate.

In recent years municipal bond issues have tried many features to make their bonds more attractive to investors. Variable rate bonds have been issued, with the rates usually pegged to Treasury securities. Bonds have been issued with low coupon rates so that they sell at deep discounts from face value. Since call provisions are based on face value, these bonds provide the investor some protection from calls. Other issuers have tried **put bonds,** allowing the holder to redeem the bond at face value on certain dates before maturity. This provides the holder some protection against interest rate risk.

## Investment Considerations

The most important investment feature of tax-exempt municipal securities is that the interest earned on them is exempt from federal income tax. In addition, some states exempt the interest earned on municipal securities issued in that state from state and local income taxes. This feature makes these municipal securities very attractive to higher income investors.

Given your marginal tax rate—that is, the tax rate on the last dollar you earn—a simple formula permits you to compare tax-free rates of return to taxable rates of return.

$$TER = \frac{TFR}{1 - MTR}$$

where

TER = taxable equivalent rate of return

TFR = tax-free rate of return

MTR = marginal tax rate

For example, if your marginal tax rate is 33 percent, and a municipal security paying 9 percent is available, the rate of return on it is equivalent for you to a 13.43 percent taxable rate.

$$TER = \frac{TFR}{1 - MTR}$$
$$= \frac{.09}{1 - .33}$$
$$= .1343$$

Exhibit 6–7 uses this formula to convert tax-free rates to the taxable equivalent rate for several different marginal tax brackets.

Historically, market conditions have required municipal securities to pay interest at about two-thirds the rate on taxable securities of similar risk and maturity. This made them attractive to investors with marginal tax rates of 33 percent or more. However, in the 1980s, municipal securities have paid about 80 percent of the rate on similar taxable securities. This relationship makes them attractive to investors with marginal tax rates as low as 20 percent. The relationship between rates on municipal and taxable securities reflects the supply and risks of the different types of securities and relevant tax rates.

Overall, the default risk on municipal securities is low; however, the 1983 default of Washington Public Power Supply System and the financial difficulties of some large cities remind us that risk does exist. Major problems for an investor attempting to evaluate default risk are that financial reporting and auditing standards of state and local governments are inferior to those of private firms and that municipal securities offerings are exempt from review by the Securities and Exchange Commission. However, some help is provided by bond rating firms. In particular, Moody's Investors Service, Standard and Poors, and Fitch Investors Services grade the credit/worthiness of municipal issues.

To make their securities more attractive, some issuers buy default insurance. **Default insurance** pays the interest and principal if the issuer does not pay. Default insurance is issued by very financially stable insurance companies.

### Insuring Municipal Bonds

Municipal bonds contain a risk of default; that is, it is possible that the issuing governmental unit might not pay the principal or interest as promised. In the Depression of the 1930s, 16 percent of the municipal bond issues defaulted. In the mid-1970s, the financial difficulties of New York City caused municipal bond investors much worry. In 1983, the $2.25 billion Washington Public Power Supply System default caused serious losses for many of its investors.

In 1971, default insurance for municipal bonds was first issued. Its purpose is to assure the investor that the municipal bonds will pay their interest and principal as promised. The issuing government pays the insurance company a fee for its guarantee that investors will be paid. Because the insurance company has a better credit rating

than the issuing governmental unit the bonds can be sold at a lower interest rate, saving the governmental unit money. Notice of the insurance company's guarantee of payment is attached to the bond certificates. The guarantee is good for the life of the bond. If the governmental unit misses an interest or principal payment, the insurance company promises to make the payment to investors the next day. There is no deductible.

Insuring municipal bonds was a very profitable business in the late 1970s and early 1980s. That profitability led several insurance companies into the business. Although competition drove down the premium rates that the issuers had to pay, the business remained profitable because defaults were rare. In the mid-1980s about 20 percent of the municipal bonds issued were insured.

---

**EXHIBIT 6–7   Taxable Equivalent Rates**

*Taxable Equivalent Rates Based on Tax-Exempt Yield of:*

| Marginal Tax Bracket | 5% | 6% | 7% | 8% | 9% | 10% | 11% | 12% |
|---|---|---|---|---|---|---|---|---|
| 15% | 5.9% | 7.1% | 8.2% | 9.4% | 10.6% | 11.8% | 12.9% | 14.1% |
| 28 | 6.9 | 8.3 | 9.7 | 11.1 | 12.5 | 13.9 | 15.3 | 16.7 |
| 33 | 7.5 | 9.0 | 10.4 | 11.9 | 13.4 | 14.9 | 16.4 | 17.9 |

---

Most municipal bonds are liquid because a secondary market is made by municipal bond dealers who stand ready to buy and sell the bonds. However, the transaction costs on small trades can be high. Also, the normal denomination of a municipal bond is $5,000. To overcome these inconveniences, investors can invest in mutual funds which purchase municipal securities. The funds provide for smaller purchases and offer professional management and diversification. The tax law allows the tax-exempt feature to be passed through to the owners of the fund.

# SUMMARY

The dollar amount of securities issued by the Treasury, federal agencies, and state and local governments make them important forces in the financial markets. In addition, laws and regulations allow banks and other depository institutions to invest in and make markets in these securities. Therefore, the returns available on them greatly affect depository institutions and other securities.

Because they have almost no default risk, short-term Treasury securities are close to being a risk-free security. This makes them a close substitute for money and lowers the overall risk of portfolios consisting of them and other assets.

The exemption of interest earned on most municipal securities from federal income tax gives them a unique investment characteristic. Mutual funds which invest in Treasury securities or municipal securities provide many attractive features.

# QUESTIONS

1. What is nonmarketable Treasury debt? To whom is it sold?
2. Explain the investment characteristics of U.S. savings bonds (both Series EE and HH).
3. Describe Treasury bills, notes, and bonds. How do you purchase them?
4. What is the role of the Federal Financing Bank?
5. What are federally sponsored agencies? Give some examples.
6. Discuss the investment characteristics of federally sponsored agency securities.
7. What are mortgage backed securities? Is payment of the interest and principal guaranteed by the U.S. government?
8. What are municipal securities? Describe the categories of municipal securities.
9. Discuss the investment characteristics of municipal securities.

# PROBLEMS

1. What is the yield on a 182-day Treasury bill with a discounted yield of 7%?
2. What is the yield on a 91-day Treasury bill with a discounted yield of 8%?
3. A tax-exempt municipal bond pays 8.5% interest. If your marginal tax rate is 33%, what is the taxable equivalent rate of return?
4. A tax-exempt municipal bond pays 7.5% interest. If your marginal tax rate is 28%, what is the taxable equivalent rate of return?

# READINGS

Cooner, James J. *Investing in Municipal Bonds: Balancing Risks and Rewards.* New York: John Wiley & Sons, 1987.
> *This book reviews the different types of municipal bonds; it points out the advantages and disadvantages of each type.*

Fabozzi, Frank J., ed. *Mortgage-Backed Securities: New Strategies, Applications and Research.* Chicago: Probus Publishing, 1987.
> *This book provides the reader with a complete understanding of mortgage backed securities.*

Feldstein, Sylvan G., and Fabozzi, Frank J. *The Dow Jones-Irwin Guide to Municipal Bonds.* Homewood, IL: Dow Jones-Irwin, 1987.

> *This book provides descriptions of and conclusions about the critical points and questions regarding municipal bonds.*

Moran, Michael J. "The Federally Sponsored Credit Agencies: An Overview," *Federal Reserve Bulletin* 71 (June 1985): 373–388.

> *This article reviews the role of the federally sponsored credit agencies, including their growth over the long run and their effectiveness in channeling funds to their respective credit markets.*

Tucker, James F. *Buying Treasury Securities at Federal Reserve Banks.* Richmond: Federal Reserve Bank of Richmond, 1987.

> *This pamphlet explains how to buy Treasury bills, notes, and bonds.*

Walter, John R. "Short-term Municipal Securities," *Economic Review (Richmond)* 72 (November–December 1986): 25–34.

> *This article describes in depth short-term municipal securities.*

# *THE INVESTMENT SETTING*

# Sources of Investment Information

## OUTLINE

Introduction

The World Economy

The U.S. Economy
    The Financial Markets
    Particular Industries and Firms

Investment Information Services

Computerized Information Services

Investment Newsletters

Market Averages
    Uses of Market Averages
    Constructing Market Averages
    Major Market Averages

Summary

## OBJECTIVES

When you have finished studying this chapter, you should understand

1. That successful investing is based on anticipating future trends in the international and U.S. economies and in the financial markets.

2. The value of publications offered by investment information services such as Moody's, Standard & Poor's, and Value Line.

3. The value of computerized information services such as *Dow Jones News/Retrieval Service, The Source,* and *Compuserve.*

4. How market averages are constructed and used.

# 7

## *Investment Software*

Personal computers are changing the investment management and analysis process. Most of the available investment software (more than 500 packages) is designed to help the investor save time rather than be taught about investing. Investment software can be classified into three categories. Portfolio management software monitors the securities the investor owns or wants to follow. It keeps track of prices, interest and dividends, and margin arithmetic. Fundamental analysis software screens financial information by any criteria the investor chooses. Reports can be printed out or the selected data can be transferred to a spreadsheet program. Technical analysis software prints the graphs and charts discussed in Chapter 12.

## INTRODUCTION

The chances of your becoming a successful investor are enhanced if you can anticipate future developments in international and national economies. An understanding of the basic relationships between these economies offers some hope of anticipating the changes in the financial markets. After forecasting the long-term trends in the markets, investors can then turn their attention to investigating specific industries and companies. Therefore, the information an investor needs can be divided into five components: the world economy, the U.S. economy, the financial markets, specific industries, and specific firms.

An overwhelming amount of information exists to be examined, and the growth of computerized information services is rapidly expanding the amount of information you can access efficiently. In this chapter we present an overview of the sources of investment information.

# THE WORLD ECONOMY

Until the late 1960s, the strength of the U.S. economy and currency allowed it to dominate the world economy. At that time, the effects of other nations' economies on the United States were limited. This has changed drastically. The United States is now just one of many strong, interrelated economies. Today, almost all investments are at least slightly influenced by world conditions. Some corporations are very dependent on changes in the world economy. For example, foreign energy, autos, and steel have drastically affected the returns on many securities. Economically, nations continue to become more interdependent. Modern aircraft cross the oceans in a few hours; satellites allow instantaneous communications worldwide.

After the investor has obtained a basic understanding of the structure of the world economy, he or she needs to keep abreast of the changes taking place. News magazines such as *Time* and *Newsweek* report important world events weekly. Good libraries have international publications, such as the *Financial Times* and the *Economist,* which give a different perspective.

# THE U.S. ECONOMY

Once the investor has an understanding of the events taking place in the world, he or she must evaluate their significance in relationship to the changes taking place in the U.S. economy. Important changes in the U.S. economy are shaped by the attitudes of its population. First and most important, their buying decisions create profits for the suppliers of the goods and services. Changing lifestyles have greatly altered our expenditures patterns. Second, people's attitudes create the political and economic environments that affect the returns and risks of investments.

It is easy to collect information about changes taking place in the United States. We see them around us; we hear newscasts and read newspapers and magazines. The hard part is evaluating the trends and their significance for investments. A dedicated investor will carefully read and evaluate books about the future.

## The Financial Markets

Changes in important economic variables that influence the financial markets are well reported. Our government collects and disseminates an overwhelming array of numbers to help us evaluate present and future market conditions.

1. Monthly, the Department of Commerce, Bureau of Economic Analysis, issues its *Survey of Current Business,* which contains detailed information on prices, wages, employment, production, trade, and transportation.

2. The Bureau of Economic Analysis also publishes monthly the *Business Conditions Digest,* which can help you analyze the economy and future trends. Its charts provide 25 years of historical data on about 300 economic series. Included are the leading, coincident, and lagging economic indicators that help analyze economic cycles.

### Evaluating the Future: Helpful Books

Burnstein, Daniel. *Yen! Japan's New Financial Empire and Its Threat to America*. New York: Simon & Schuster, 1988.

    *This narrative presents a gloomy scenario in which Japan takes over the U.S. economy.*

Friedman, Benjamin M. *Day of Reckoning: The Consequences of American Economic Policy Under Reagan and After*. New York: Random House, 1988.

    *An economics professor examines how the budget deficit and the borrowing to finance it will affect the economy in the future.*

Goodman, George J. W. *The Roaring '80s* (by Adam Smith). New York: Summit Books, 1988, 303 pp.

    *This highly readable book introduces readers to the new world of high finance. It discusses takeover fights, budget officials, trade deficits, and the rise of Japanese firms.*

Hayes, Samuel L. III, ed. *Wall Street and Regulation*. Boston: Harvard Business School Press, 1987.

    *This book resulted from a research colloquium on the changes in the United States Financial Services Sector held by the Harvard Business School. In addition to the Introduction and Conclusions, the book contains five papers on aspects of the regulation of financial services.*

Ibbotson, Roger G., and Gary P. Brinson. *Investment Markets: Gaining the Performance Advantage*. New York: McGraw-Hill Book Company, 1987, 294 pp.

    *This book provides an analysis and history of capital markets throughout the world. The authors attempt to minimize the use of academic jargon, mathematical formulas, and statistical terms while still presenting a very thorough analysis.*

Kothin, Joel, and Yoriho Kishimoto. *The Third Century*. New York: Crown Publishers, 1988.

    *These authors explore the effects of the economic rise of Asia and the Pacific Rim. They believe that this changing geographic situation offers U.S. businesses abundant opportunities.*

    **3.** The Federal Trade Commission and the Securities and Exchange Commission jointly publish the *Quarterly Financial Report for Manufacturing Corporations* that reports information aggregated from the balance sheets and income statements of manufacturing corporations. Informative figures, such as "profits per dollar sales" and "annual rate of profit on stockholder's equity," are available by industry and firm size.

    **4.** The Federal Reserve System issues monthly the *Federal Reserve Bulletin* to report on the activities in the financial markets. It contains detailed information on interest rates of the different debt instruments.

    **5.** The Securities and Exchange Commission publishes a weekly *Statistical Bulletin* that reports such diverse information as the volume of securities trading, the number of new issues, expenditures for plant and equipment, and saving by individuals.

    Two magazines, *Business Week* and *Forbes,* do outstanding jobs of summarizing and evaluating economic and market conditions. In addition, they report in detail about the changes, strategies, and activities of particular industries and companies.

    Along with providing us news of the world and the nation, large city daily newspapers report in detail the economic and financial markets news and important events in business and finance. Two national papers have as their purpose reporting business and financial news. The *Wall Street Journal* is a daily that, in addition to reporting the news, has excellent feature articles and editorial comments. *Barrons* is a weekly that emphasizes current events in the financial markets. Both papers report the stock and bond trading on the major exchanges and in the OTC market. *USA Today* began publication in 1982 and has established a good reputation for daily coverage of both current events and business information.

## Particular Industries and Firms

After investors have analyzed world and national economic trends and the financial markets, they need detailed information about particular industries and companies. Some of the publications just mentioned help investors form projections of industry trends and the prospects for particular firms. Another source of information is the issuers of the securities. Annual reports are available in some libraries and some brokerage firm offices and can be obtained free from the company. Most firms whose stock is traded in the OTC market, and all firms whose stock is traded on the securities exchanges, must file annually a 10-K report with the SEC. These reports contain much more detailed information than the annual reports. Most companies will send you a copy of their 10-K report free or at the cost of copying it. Information services, which will quickly send you a copy of any 10-K report, regularly advertise in the financial press.

# INVESTMENT INFORMATION SERVICES

Three large investment information services provide data by industry and by firm: Standard & Poor's, Moody's, and Value Line. Their publications are somewhat expensive but are available in libraries.

Standard & Poor's (S&P) issues *Corporation Records*, which consists of six volumes containing background and financial information on over 5,900 corporations. Five days a week its *Daily News Section* updates *Corporation Records* with the latest developments. S&P's *Industry Surveys* provide economic and investment analyses of 65 industries. The *Industry Surveys* consists of an annual basic survey and three current surveys on each industry each year. A monthly trends and projections section forecasts industry and economic trends.

S&P's *Stock Reports* consists of three four-volume sets. One is for NYSE companies, one for AMEX companies, and one for nearly 1,100 OTC companies. Each company has a two-page report on its activities and financial position. Included are the latest price and current year's range, the price to earnings (PE) ratio, current earnings, and dividends. A report on Ball Corporation from S&P's *Stock Reports* is reproduced in Appendix Exhibit 7A–1.

S&P's also publishes monthly a *Stock Guide* and a *Bond Guide*. These 250 page pocket-size guides summarize investment data in a multi-column format. A sample page from S&P's *Bond Guide* is reproduced in Appendix Exhibit 7A–2.

Moody's best-known publication is *Handbook of Common Stocks*. It reports on individual stocks, giving the background of the corporation and any recent developments that have taken place. It also contains summarized financial statements of recent years along with historical stock price and volume data. Moody's also issues weekly a *Bond Survey* and a *Stock Survey* that contain buy and sell recommendations as well as information on new issues.

The *Value Line Investment Survey* reports on 1,700 stocks which include most of the stocks listed on the NYSE as well as some traded on the AMEX and OTC. Quarterly, it issues for each stock a detailed full-page report that contains past history and data as well as projections for the future. Unique to Value Line is that every week it ranks each stock for "probable market performance in the next twelve months." A report from Value Line's *Investment Survey* is reproduced in Appendix Exhibit 7A–3.

# COMPUTERIZED INFORMATION SERVICES

Computerized information services enable the investor to access by a personal computer a large body of information about the economy, particular industries, and specific firms. Software packages are available to aid the investor in efficiently sorting the information and data available. Although the prime benefit of a computerized information service is providing facts for better decision making, it also can help in investment portfolio record keeping. Software packages also are available to help analyze particular firms and securities.

Several competing investment information services are available to investors. Typically, they charge an annual fee of $40 to $100 plus per minute usage charges ranging from about $1.50 per minute during prime times to 10 cents per minute during nonprime times (usually 6 P.M. to 6 A.M.). After subscribing, an investor accesses the service using a personal computer with a modem. In most metropolitan areas, the investor does not have to pay long-distance phone charges because the companies have arranged local phone access to their systems.

To acquaint you with the breadth of the information available, we will discuss briefly three well-known services: *Dow Jones News/Retrieval Service, The Source,* and *Compuserve.*

The *Dow Jones News/Retrieval Service* is offered by Dow Jones, Inc., the publisher of the *Wall Street Journal* and *Barrons* (see Appendix Exhibit 7A–4). It offers general, business, and economic news; you can scan headlines and retrieve stories as recent as 90 seconds or as old as 90 days. You also can get sports, weather, and movie reviews. The full text of the *Wall Street Journal* is available. The current prices of stocks, bonds, options, and mutual funds are available. For common and preferred stocks, you can obtain daily prices for the past year, monthly prices back to 1979, and quarterly prices back to 1978. In addition to historical financial statement data on thousands of companies, forecasts of economic data and the earnings of 3,000 firms are available.

*The Source* is a product of Source Telecomputing Corporation, a subsidiary of The Readers' Digest Association, Inc. It provides access to the United Press International

Network; therefore, you can obtain up-to-the-second international, national, and local news. You can search this database using key words and then you can have specific articles printed on your screen. *The Source* also provides stock, precious metals, and foreign currency prices. Additionally, *The Source* has an arrangement with a discount brokerage firm which enables customers of the brokerage firm to maintain on-line accounts and enter transactions to buy and sell securities.

*Compuserve* offers Associated Press news and sports, *USA Today Update, The Washington Post, The St. Louis Dispatch,* and the NOAA weather wire. For investors, it provides over 11 years of daily historical information on over 50,000 stocks, bonds, mutual funds, options, and indexes. For commodities investors, it provides current prices of and news developments affecting commodity prices. Also provided is general commentary on energy, metals, and agricultural commodities. Through an arrangement with a discount brokerage firm, it offers on-line purchase and sale of securities, current stock and option prices, portfolio management, and tax record keeping.

# INVESTMENT NEWSLETTERS

Investment newsletters are publications that give advice about investing. Usually, they provide an analysis of both financial markets and specific investments. They are sold by subscription; costs and quality vary drastically. There are over 1,000 newsletters published; however, only about 100 are actively promoted. Examples of good quality newsletters are Standard & Poor's *Outlook* and Merrill Lynch's *Market Letter*. In a few pages, they analyze economic conditions, financial markets, and specific companies.

A newsletter should be registered with the Securities and Exchange Commission and should disclose the writers' credentials and investment philosophy. A good newsletter will disclose how *all* of its past recommendations turned out. Be cautious when subscribing to a newsletter. It can provide you with investment ideas, but its advice may not be worth the subscription cost. Of course, there are no guarantees; any money you lose following a newsletter's advice is your loss.

# MARKET AVERAGES

**Market averages** are summary measures of the movements of segments of the financial markets. Well-known examples are the Dow Jones Industrial Average and the Standard and Poor's 500. What are commonly called market averages should more correctly be called market indicator series or in many cases market indexes. For convenience, we will use the common term market average. Although stock market averages are what we first think of when we mention market averages, averages are computed for other markets such as bonds and futures. In this section, we will discuss the uses of market averages and the differences among them. Then, we will discuss some of the more commonly used averages.

## Uses of Market Averages

It is important for the investor to be familiar with market averages because they are used for several purposes. First, they summarize the movements of security prices. Investors cannot conveniently follow throughout the day the prices of securities they own; however, regular news reports that the market averages changed a certain amount can give you an indication of the movement of your securities. In a similar manner, a market average summarizes security prices. For example, researchers use a market average when they examine the relationship between stock prices and the money supply.

Second, an average provides a standard by which to measure the performance of a portfolio of securities. The portfolio could be one you chose or one put together by a professional money manager. One reason for studying the details of how market averages are computed is to make sure that an appropriate series is being used for these comparisons. For example, the performance of a portfolio of high technology stocks should not be compared to an average composed of blue chip stocks.

Third, an average is used as a proxy for the market when examining the historical relationship between the return on the market and the return on a specific security. In the chapter on portfolio theory, we will examine how measurement errors in the proxy used to measure the return on the market can influence how a security's or a portfolio's risk is measured.

Fourth, investors now can buy and sell futures contracts based on some of the stock market averages. We will discuss these futures contracts later in the book. Here, we want to point out that buyers and sellers of them need an understanding of the issues involved in constructing market averages.

Finally, averages are used heavily in technical analysis when looking for trends in the market and when comparing particular securities to the market. Having stressed why it is important to be familiar with market averages, we next look at their construction.

## Constructing Market Averages

Three factors are important in the construction of a market average: the selection of securities for inclusion, the weighting of the securities chosen, and the computational procedure used.

The first issue in the selection of the securities to be included is determining what population of securities the average is attempting to represent. For example, is the average to be a measure of the performance of the stocks of large firms (the S&P 500), of stocks listed on a particular exchange (the NYSE composite), or stocks traded in the OTC market (the NASDAQ composite index)? Once the population is identified, a choice has to be made between including all securities in the population or a sample of securities from the population. Before computers, the computational burden made it necessary to use a sample. For example, when the DJIA was originated in 1884, it included only 11 stocks. Today, the use of computers allows a market average to include all the securities in the population. For example, the NYSE composite includes all stocks listed on that exchange.

---

**EXHIBIT 7–1  Computation of a Price-Weighted Average**

| Stock | Beginning Price | After a 20 Percent Increase in A | After a 20 Percent Increase in C |
|-------|-----------------|----------------------------------|----------------------------------|
| A | 5 | 6 | 5 |
| B | 15 | 15 | 15 |
| C | 20 | 20 | 24 |
| Sum of price | 40 | 41 | 44 |
| Average price | 13.33 | 13.67 | 14.67 |
| Percent change | | 2.5 | 10 |

---

When using a sample, it is important that it represent the population from which it was chosen. Statistics teaches us that a small sample can do this if it is properly chosen. However, we also know it is easy accidentally to build a bias into the selection criteria for the sample. Some market averages are not carefully chosen to represent specific populations of securities.

The second issue is the weighting of the securities included in the average. Three weighting procedures are used: price-weighted, value-weighted, and equally weighted. In a price-weighted average, the importance of each security depends on its price. The prices of the securities are summed and divided by the number of securities. Exhibit 7–1 shows that under this procedure an increase of a given percentage in a high-priced stock will affect the average more than the same percentage increase in a low-priced stock. The only logic for using a price-weighted system is its ease of computation. The Dow Jones averages are price-weighted averages.

In a *value-weighted series,* each security's relative importance is determined by the total value of the security outstanding. This total value is obtained by multiplying the price by the number of shares outstanding. Exhibit 7–2 is an example of the

---

**EXHIBIT 7–2  Computation of a Value-Weighted Index**

| Stock | Beginning Price | × | Number of Shares | = | Market Value | New Price | × | Number of Shares | = | Market Value |
|-------|-----------------|---|------------------|---|--------------|-----------|---|------------------|---|--------------|
| A | 5 | | 2,000 | | 10,000 | 7 | | 2,000 | | 14,000 |
| B | 15 | | 2,500 | | 37,500 | 16 | | 2,500 | | 40,000 |
| C | 20 | | 1,800 | | 36,000 | 19 | | 1,800 | | 34,200 |
| Sum | | | | | 83,500 | | | | | 88,200 |

$$\frac{\text{current value}}{\text{base value}} \times \text{beginning index value} = \text{current index value}$$

$$\frac{88,200}{83,500} \times 50 = 52.81$$

---

---

**EXHIBIT 7–3  Computation of an Equally Weighted Index**

| Stock | Beginning Price | × | Number* of Shares | = | Market Value | New Price | × | Number of Shares | = | Market Value |
|-------|-----------------|---|-------------------|---|--------------|-----------|---|------------------|---|--------------|
| A | 5 | | 20 | | 100 | 7 | | 20 | | 140 |
| B | 15 | | 6.67 | | 100 | 16 | | 6.67 | | 106.67 |
| C | 20 | | 5 | | 100 | 19 | | 5 | | 95 |
| Sum | | | | | 300 | | | | | 341.67 |

$$\frac{\text{current value}}{\text{base value}} \times \text{beginning index value} = \text{current index value}$$

$$\frac{341.67}{300} \times 50 = 56.945$$

\* $100 is invested in each stock.

---

computation of a value-weighted series. A value-weighted series gives more influence to price changes of securities with high total market value than to securities with low total market value. A value-weighted series best represents the total movement of all the securities in the population. Therefore, a researcher doing a macroeconomic study of stock prices would want to use a value-weighted series. The Standard & Poor's indexes are value-weighted.

In an *equally weighted series,* each security is given the same importance. A given dollar amount is invested in each security. As shown in Exhibit 7–3, the number of shares involved depends on the price. In subsequent periods, the current price of each security is multiplied by the number of shares held, then these values are summed and compared to the beginning value. If you chose a portfolio by throwing darts at the stock table from a newspaper and invested $1,000 in each stock a dart hit, you would have an equally weighted portfolio.

The third issue in the construction of a market series is the computational procedure used. The procedure could be based on the arithmetic mean, the geometric mean, or an index. Computation of arithmetic and geometric means was discussed in chapter 4. Part B of Exhibits 7–2 and 7–3 show the computation of index numbers. The value of the portfolio at a given time becomes the base. The beginning index value, usually 10 or 50, is assigned to this base value. In the following periods, the new index value is obtained by dividing the current value of the portfolio by the base value and multiplying this ratio by the beginning index value.

# Major Market Averages

It is worthwhile to have a general knowledge of how the common market averages are constructed. We will summarize them here; more details can be found in the readings listed at the end of the chapter.

The Dow Jones averages are the best known market averages. Four series are reported: 30 industrials, 20 transportations, 15 utilities, and 65 stock composite. The Dow Jones averages are arithmetic averages of prices of the stock of large, well-known companies listed on the NYSE. Because they are price-weighted averages, a price change of a given percentage in a high-priced stock affects the average more than the same percentage change in a low-priced stock. To adjust for stock dividends and splits, the divisor used to compute the average is adjusted as shown in Exhibit 7–4.

The Dow Jones averages are criticized because they are price-weighted and based on a small sample. However, because the sample includes very large companies, the value of the stocks included represents a significant fraction of the total value of the stocks listed on the NYSE. In particular, the 30 industrials listed in Exhibit 7–5 constitute over 20 percent of the value of all NYSE stocks.

The next most widely known series is the Standard & Poor's 500. It is the composite of four subgroup indexes: 400 industrials, 20 transportations, 40 utilities, and 40 financials. Except for the financials, all the stocks include some OTC stocks. Advantages of the S & P indexes are that they are based on a large sample and are value-weighted. In their publication, *Outlook,* Standard & Poor's publishes a total of 90 individual industry series consisting of 3 to 11 companies each.

The NYSE composite consists of all the stocks listed on that exchange. The exchange also reports subgroup indexes for industrials, utilities, transportation, and finance. The indexes are value-weighted. The AMEX composite is a value-weighted index of all the stocks listed on that exchange. The AMEX also reports 8 industrial and 8 geographic subgroup indexes.

NASDAQ reports value-weighted indexes for the OTC market. All domestic stocks traded on the NASDAQ system are included in the OTC composite, which consists of six subgroups: industrials, insurance, banks, other finance, transportations, and utilities. It also reports composite and subgroup indexes for the National Market List.

Other stock market indexes are reported in the financial press. The Value Line composite average includes 1,700 stocks. It is an index using the geometric average

---

**EXHIBIT 7–4  *Procedure for Adjusting for Stock Dividends and Splits***

| Stock | Price Before Split | Price After Stock C Splits 2 for 1 |
|-------|--------------------|-----------------------------------|
| A | 5 | 5 |
| B | 15 | 15 |
| C | 12 | 6 |
| Sum | 32 | 26 |

Before split
Sum ÷ Divisor = Average
32 ÷      3   = 10.67

After split
sum ÷ New divisor  = Average before split
26 ÷ New divisor  = 10.67
New divisor        = 26 ÷ 10.67
New divisor        = 2.437

**EXHIBIT 7–5    Stocks in the Dow Jones Averages**

*30 Industrials*

| | | |
|---|---|---|
| Allied-Signal | Exxon | Philip Morris |
| Alcoa | General Electric | Primerica |
| Amer Express | General Motors | Procter & Gamble |
| Amer T & T | Goodyear | Sears Roebuck |
| Bethlehem Steel | IBM | Texaco |
| Boeing | Inter Paper | USX |
| Chevron | McDonalds | Union Carbide |
| Coca Cola | Merck | United Techn |
| DuPont | Minnesota M & M | Westinghouse |
| Eastman Kodak | Navistar Inter | Woolworth |

*20 Transportation*

| | | |
|---|---|---|
| AMR Corp | Consolid Rail | Piedmont Av |
| Allegis | CSX Corp | Syder Sys |
| Amer President | Delta Air | Santa Fe So Pac |
| Burlington North | Federal Express | TWA |
| Canadian Pacific | NWA Inc | Union Pac |
| Carolina Freight | Norfolk Stn | US Air Group |
| Consolid Freight | Pan Am Corp | |

*15 Utilities*

| | | |
|---|---|---|
| Am Elec Power | Consol Nat Gas | Panhandle Eastern |
| Centerior Energy | Detroit Edison | People Energy |
| Colum Gas Sys | Houston Indust | Phila Elec |
| Comwlth Edison | Niag Mohawk P | Pub Serv Enterp |
| Consol Edison | Pacific Gas & El | Son Cal Edison |

of price changes. The Wilshire 5,000 is a value weighted index of 5,000 stocks. It is the broadest index available; it includes all stocks on the NYSE, AMEX, and NASDAQ system. Two indexes, the *Financial Times* industrials and the Nikkei stock average, are composed of foreign securities.

For bonds, averages can be reported in either of two ways: by price or by yield. The Dow Jones bond averages—20 bonds, 10 utilities, and 10 industrials—are reported by price. When a bond average is reported by price, the stated price is a percentage of face value. For example, when the Dow Jones bond average of 20 bonds was reported at 78.96, the average price of a $1,000 bond was 78.96 percent of face value or $789.60. Instead of reporting prices, many sources compute and quote average bond yields. Normally, the average yield is computed for bonds of a particular class of issuer, quality, and maturity. Average yield reporting has the advantage of telling an investor the return that can be expected from a bond with certain characteristics.

# SUMMARY

You now know where to find the information needed for successful investing. You can obtain information about the world economy, the U.S. economy, the financial markets, specific industries, and specific firms by reading the publications described. Additionally, you can subscribe to a computerized information service or investment newsletters. Computerized information services provide large amounts of current information to their subscribers. Investment newsletters give advice on the financial markets and specific firms.

Basic background information which the investor needs includes an understanding of market averages. Market averages summarize security price changes. The averages differ because of the selection of securities for inclusion, the weighting of the securities chosen, and the computational procedure used.

# QUESTIONS

1. Where can an investor obtain information on the world economy, the U.S. economy, the financial markets, and particular industries and firms?

2. Describe some of the government publications that present information on economic trends.

3. Describe the major publications of Standard & Poor's, Moody's, and Value Line.

4. What are computerized information services? What types of information do they provide?

5. What should you check before subscribing to an investment newsletter?

6. For what purposes are market averages used?

7. What three factors are important in the construction of market averages?

8. Describe the Dow Jones averages, the Standard & Poor's indexes, the NYSE composite, the AMEX composite, and the NASDAQ indexes.

# PROBLEMS

1. Stock A sells for $10, Stock B for $15, and Stock C for $25.
   a. Compute their price-weighted average.
   b. Recompute it after a 10% increase in the price of Stock A.
   c. Recompute it after a 10% increase in the price of Stock C instead of Stock A.
   d. Compare the results obtained in b and c.

2. Stock A sells for $20, Stock B for $25, and Stock C for $50.
   a. Compute their price-weighted average.
   b. Recompute it after a 50% increase in the price of Stock A.
   c. Recompute it after a 50% increase in the price of Stock C instead of Stock A.

3. Stock A sells for $10 and 5 million shares are outstanding; Stock B sells for $15 and 7 million shares are outstanding; Stock C sells for $20 and 10 million shares are outstanding. After one month the prices of Stocks A, B and C are $12, $15, and $25 respectively.
   a. Compute a value-weighted index using the original data as the base.
   b. Compute an equally weighted index using the original data as the base.
   c. Why do the answers in a and b differ?

4. Stock A sells for $20 and 3 million shares are outstanding; Stock B sells for $25 and 5 million shares are outstanding; Stock C sells for $50 and 2 million shares are outstanding. After one month the prices of Stocks A, B, and C are $18, $20, and $55 respectively.
   a. Compute a value-weighted index using the original data as the base.
   b. Compute an equally weighted index using the original data as the base.
   c. Why do the answers in a and b differ?

5. Stock A sells for $12, Stock B for $20, and Stock C for $30.
   a. Compute their price-weighted average.
   b. If Stock C splits two for one, what new divisor should be used in computing the average?

6. Stock A sells for $16, Stock B for $30, and Stock C for $50.
   a. Compute their price-weighted average.
   b. If Stock C splits two for one, what new divisor should be used in computing the average?

## CASE PROBLEM

Go to the library and find information on a company that interests you as a potential investment. Summarize the information you find. Look up the firm's stock price in a major newspaper. Interpret everything reported in the stock table about that stock.

## READINGS

Butler, Hartman L., Jr., and De Mong, Richard F. "The Changing Dow Jones Industrial Averages," *Financial Analysts Journal* (July–August 1986): 59–62.
> *This article reviews the history of the DJIA, examines its economic sector representation, and makes suggestions for improving it.*

"Hangups with On-Line Data," *Changing Times* (November 1988): 89–98.
> *This article examines the services, costs, strengths, and weaknesses of seven computerized information services.*

Meyers, Thomas A. *The Dow Jones-Irwin Guide to Investment Software.* Homewood, IL: Dow Jones-Irwin, 1987.
> *This book teaches the reader how to use the three major types of investment software: portfolio management, fundamental analysis, and technical analysis.*

Reilly, Frank K. *Investment Analysis and Portfolio Management,* 2nd ed. Chicago: The Dryden Press, 1985, Chapter 5.
> *This chapter presents an in-depth discussion of market averages.*

Woodwell, Donald R. *Using and Applying the Dow Jones Information Services.* Homewood, IL: Dow Jones-Irwin, 1986.
> *In addition to explaining how to use Dow Jones' services, this book examines the electronic information explosion and its impact on society.*

**EXHIBIT 7A–1    Page from S & P's Stock Reports**

# Ball Corp.

272

NYSE Symbol BLL  In S&P 500

| Price | Range | P–E Ratio | Dividend | Yield | S&P Ranking | Beta |
|---|---|---|---|---|---|---|
| May 4'89 | 1989 | | | | | |
| 27⁷/₈ | 29–25¹/₄ | 23 | 1.08 | 3.9% | A | 0.98 |

## Summary

This company manufactures metal beverage containers and other packaging products, and has interests in aerospace and other technical fields. BLL has a 50% interest in Ball-Incon Glass Packaging, a joint venture with TBG Europe nv. Earnings in 1988 were impacted by lower margins in packaging products and an $18.6 million after tax charge, primarily to exit the blow molded plastic container business. Earnings in 1989 will continue to be affected by pricing pressures in the metal container business.

## Current Outlook

Earnings for 1989 may rise to about $1.60 a share from 1988's $1.40, which was after an $0.80 non-recurring charge.

Dividends should continue at $0.27 quarterly.

Sales of metal and glass containers in 1989 are expected to be flat as the substitution of plastic for glass and metal in beverage packages continues. Aggressive pricing policies and higher raw material costs could continue to penalize margins in packaging products. However, improved profits are likely at the aerospace and diversified products divisions, and 1988's $0.80 a share charge to exit the blow molded plastic container business will be absent.

## Net Sales (Million $)

| Quarter: | 1989 | 1988 | 1987 | 1986 |
|---|---|---|---|---|
| Mar. | 257 | 241 | 284 | 241 |
| Jun. | ... | 306 | 288 | 296 |
| Sep. | ... | 293 | 267 | 282 |
| Dec. | ... | 233 | 215 | 252 |
| | ... | 1,073 | 1,054 | 1,070 |

Sales for the quarter to April 2, 1989 rose 6.7%, year to year. Hurt by continued pricing pressures in packaging products, higher interest costs, and the absence of 1988's $5.9 million pretax gain ($0.16 a share after tax) on the sale of an investment, pretax income declined 41%. After taxes at 29.4%, against 34.4%, net income was down 37%, to $0.33 a share from $0.52, before a special credit of $0.77 in the 1988 period.

## Common Share Earnings ($)

| Quarter: | 1989 | 1988 | 1987 | 1986 |
|---|---|---|---|---|
| Mar. | 0.33 | 0.52 | 0.50 | 0.53 |
| Jun. | E0.45 | 0.73 | 0.96 | 0.81 |
| Sep. | E0.42 | 0.64 | 0.80 | 0.73 |
| Dec. | E0.40 | d0.49 | 0.54 | 0.49 |
| | E1.60 | 1.40 | 2.80 | 2.56 |

TRADING VOLUME
THOUSAND SHARES

1983 | 1984 | 1985 | 1986 | 1987 | 1988 | 1989

## Important Developments

**Apr. '89**— Earnings for the first quarter of 1989 were affected by continued pricing pressures in the packaging products segment and higher interest costs. The company said that price increases were implemented to reflect higher raw material costs. BLL stated that while it would not benefit from the full impact of the price increases this year, they were mandatory for the long-term health of the industry.

**Jan. '89**— In the fourth quarter of 1988 BLL recognized a $30 million ($18.6 million after tax, $0.80 per share) charge to exit the blow molded portion of the plastic container business and write off certain packaging products equipment removed from service as part of plant modernization programs.

**Next earnings report expected in late July.**

## Per Share Data ($)

| Yr. End Dec. 31 | 1988 | 1987 | 1986 | 1985 | 1984 | 1983 | 1982 | 1981 | ¹1980 | 1979 |
|---|---|---|---|---|---|---|---|---|---|---|
| Tangible Bk. Val. | 17.92 | 17.04 | 15.85 | 14.38 | 12.97 | 11.60 | 10.48 | 9.44 | 8.58 | 7.87 |
| Earnings² | 1.40 | 2.80 | 2.56 | 2.24 | 2.04 | 1.74 | 1.58 | 1.38 | 1.20 | 1.19 |
| Dividends | 1.02 | 0.89 | 0.77 | 0.68 | 0.61 | 0.55 | 0.48¹/₂ | 0.42¹/₂ | 0.37¹/₂ | 0.32¹/₂ |
| Payout Ratio | 73% | 31% | 30% | 31% | 30% | 32% | 31% | 31% | 31% | 28% |
| Prices—High | 35⁷/₈ | 48¹/₂ | 45¹/₂ | 32 | 22⁷/₈ | 18¹/₄ | 16 | 9 | 7³/₈ | 7¹/₄ |
| Low | 25⁵/₈ | 27¹/₄ | 26¹/₄ | 21³/₈ | 14³/₈ | 12³/₄ | 12³/₄ | 6¹/₄ | 4⁷/₈ | 5¹/₄ |
| P/E Ratio— | 26–18 | 17–10 | 18–10 | 14–10 | 11–7 | 10–7 | 10–5 | 7–4 | 6–4 | 6–4 |

Data as orig. reptd. Adj. for stk. div(s). of 100% Oct. 1985, 100% Oct. 1982. **1.** Reflects merger or acquisition. **2.** Before spec. item(s) of +0.77 in 1988. d·Deficit. E·Estimated.

## 272
### Ball Corporation

### Income Data (Million $)

| Year Ended Dec. 31 | Revs. | Oper. Inc. | % Oper. Inc. of Revs. | Cap. Exp. | Depr. | Int. Exp. | [3]Net Bef. Taxes | Eff. Tax Rate | [4]Net Inc. | % Net Inc. of Revs. |
|---|---|---|---|---|---|---|---|---|---|---|
| 1988 | 1,073 | 118 | 11.0 | 101 | 43.9 | 15.5 | 48 | 32.0% | 32.7 | 3.0 |
| 1987 | 1,054 | 160 | 15.2 | 124 | 41.3 | 9.2 | 114 | 41.6% | 66.3 | 6.3 |
| 1986 | 1,070 | 161 | 15.0 | 76 | 44.2 | 8.7 | 110 | 46.6% | 58.9 | 5.5 |
| 1985 | 1,106 | 141 | 12.7 | 72 | 39.2 | 11.6 | 93 | 44.7% | 51.2 | 4.6 |
| 1984 | 1,051 | 124 | 11.8 | 70 | 33.1 | 11.2 | 82 | 43.3% | 46.3 | 4.4 |
| 1983 | 910 | 115 | 12.6 | 41 | 30.9 | 13.1 | 72 | 45.8% | 39.0 | 4.3 |
| 1982 | 889 | 100 | 11.3 | 56 | 27.2 | 16.4 | 59 | 41.4% | 34.5 | 3.9 |
| 1981 | 815 | 86 | 10.5 | 60 | 23.8 | 16.6 | 48 | 39.3% | 29.2 | 3.6 |
| [1]1980 | 699 | 75 | 10.7 | 59 | 20.8 | 16.2 | 39 | 38.1% | 24.4 | 3.5 |
| 1979 | 555 | 65 | 11.7 | 58 | 15.1 | [2]12.2 | 40 | 40.3% | 23.7 | 4.3 |

### Balance Sheet Data (Million $)

| Dec. 31 | Cash | Curr. Assets | Curr. Liab. | Ratio | Total Assets | Ret. On Assets | Long Term Debt | Common Equity | Total Inv. Capital | % LT Debt of Cap. | Ret. On Equity |
|---|---|---|---|---|---|---|---|---|---|---|---|
| 1988 | 15.7 | 332 | 183 | 1.8 | 877 | 3.9% | 196 | 421 | 674 | 29.1 | 8.0% |
| 1987 | 16.6 | 316 | 203 | 1.6 | 795 | 8.6% | 101 | 397 | 575 | 17.5 | 17.3% |
| 1986 | 10.2 | 331 | 165 | 2.0 | 733 | 8.6% | 102 | 365 | 552 | 18.4 | 16.9% |
| 1985 | 15.0 | 265 | 136 | 2.0 | 642 | 8.1% | 90 | 331 | 493 | 18.3 | 16.3% |
| 1984 | 14.4 | 274 | 147 | 1.9 | 622 | 7.8% | 115 | 295 | 460 | 25.0 | 16.5% |
| 1983 | 23.5 | 254 | 134 | 1.9 | 559 | 7.2% | 109 | 262 | 415 | 26.1 | 15.6% |
| 1982 | 7.8 | 219 | 106 | 2.1 | 514 | 6.8% | 129 | 233 | 399 | 32.4 | 15.6% |
| 1981 | 6.4 | 220 | 104 | 2.1 | 482 | 6.3% | 141 | 204 | 369 | 38.1 | 15.1% |
| 1980 | 6.6 | 209 | 87 | 2.4 | 432 | 6.0% | 142 | 179 | 338 | 42.0 | 14.2% |
| 1979 | 9.3 | 179 | 88 | 2.0 | 374 | 6.6% | 108 | 159 | 281 | 38.3 | 15.7% |

Data as orig. reptd. 1. Reflects merger or acquisition. 2. Reflects accounting change. 3. Incl. equity in earns. of nonconsol. subs. 4. Bef. spec. item(s) in 1988.

### Business Summary

Ball is a large producer of metal containers and makes other packaging and diverse industrial items, and aerospace products. In mid-1987 it spun off commercial glass lines to a 50-50 joint venture with TBV Europe nv called Ball-Incon Glass Packaging. Results by business segment in 1988 were divided as follows:

| | Sales | Profits |
|---|---|---|
| Packaging products ........... | 62% | 63% |
| Aerospace products ........... | 24% | 22% |
| Diversified products ........... | 14% | 15% |

Food jars, freezer jars and jelly glasses are produced for the home food preservation market. Ball makes two-piece aluminum and steel beverage cans for beer and soft drinks firms. Over the past three years, beer and soft drink can and end sales accounted for about 50% of total sales. Sales to Anheuser Busch alone accounted for 21% of sales in 1988. Ball's share of the net income of the joint venture glass operations with TBV is included in profits of the packaging products segment.

Aerospace systems is comprised of five businesses: electro-optics/cryogenics, communications, space systems, time/frequency standards and systems engineering. Sales to agencies of the U.S. government accounted for some 25% of 1988 sales.

Diversified products include fabricated zinc for coin blanks, coextruded plastic sheet and associated containers, injection molded and extruded/thermoformed plastics and automated x-ray and vision inspection businesses. Light-gauge sheet metal is also cut, coated and lithographed.

### Dividend Data

Dividends have been paid since 1958. A dividend reinvestment plan is available. A "poison pill" stock purchase right was adopted in 1986.

| Amt. of Divd. $ | Date Decl. | Ex-divd. Date | Stock of Record | Payment Date |
|---|---|---|---|---|
| 0.27 | Jul. 26 | Aug. 26 | Sep. 1 | Sep. 15'88 |
| 0.27 | Oct. 25 | Nov. 25 | Dec. 1 | Dec. 15'88 |
| 0.27 | Jan. 24 | Feb. 21 | Feb. 27 | Mar. 15'89 |
| 0.27 | Apr. 25 | May 25 | Jun. 1 | Jun. 15'89 |

Next dividend meeting: Jul. 25'89.

### Capitalization

**Long Term Debt:** $196,300,000.

**Common Stock:** 23,557,516 shs. (no par). About 50% is closely held by Ball family members and others.
Shareholders of record: 10,103.

Office—345 South High St., Muncie, Ind. 47307. Tel—(317) 747-6100. Chrmn, Pres & CEO—R. M. Ringoen. VP-Secy—G. A. Sissel. VP-Treas—R. D. Hoover. Investor Contact—Larry Miller. Dirs—T. D. Bell, Jr., H. M. Dean, R. M. Gillett, H. C. Goodrich, J. F. Lehman, Jr., A. M. McVie, R. H. Mohlman, A. M. Owlsley, Jr., W. L. Peterson, R. M. Ringoen, D. C. Staley, W. P. Stiritz. Transfer Agent & Registrar—First National Bank, Chicago. Incorporated in Indiana in 1922. Empl—7,100.

Information has been obtained from sources believed to be reliable, but its accuracy and completeness are not guaranteed.      Joshua M. Harari

Source: Courtesy of Standard & Poor's Corporation.

## EXHIBIT 7A–2 Page from S & P's Bond Guide



| Title-Industry Code & Co. Finances (In Italics) | Ind | | Fixed Charge Coverage 1986 | 1987 | 1988 | Year End | Million $ Cash & Equiv. | Curr. Assets | Curr. Liab. | Balance Sheet Date | L. Term Debt (Mil $) | | Capital-ization (Mil $) | Total Debt % Capital | | | | | | |
|---|---|---|---|---|---|---|---|---|---|---|---|---|---|---|---|---|---|---|---|---|
| Individual Issue Statistics: Exchange | Interest Dates | S&P Debt Rating | Date of Last Rating Change | Prior Rating | Eligible | Bond Form | Redemption Provisions: Regular Price | Regular (Begins) Thru | Sinking Fund Price | Sinking Fund (Begins) Thru | Refund/Other Restriction Price | Refund/Other Restriction (Begins) Thru | Outst'g (Mil $) | Underwriting Firm | Underwriting Year | Price Range 1989 High | Price Range 1989 Low | Mo. End Price Sale(s) or Bid | Curr. Yield | Yield to Mat. |
| ***California Electric Power*** | ***72a*** | ***Now So'n Calif. Edison, see*** | | | | | | | | | | | | | | | | | | |
| 1st 5⅛s '90 | Mn | **AA** | 1/64 | A | X | CR | 100 | .... | □100 | .... | .... | .... | 12.0 | K1 | '60 | 96 | 94½ | 94⅞ | 5.40 | 10.23 |
| 1st 5s '91 | jJ | **AA** | 1/64 | A | X | CR | 100.42 | 6-30-89 | □100.20 | 6-30-89 | .... | .... | 8.00 | H1 | '61 | 92 | 89⅜ | 89½ | 5.59 | 10.34 |
| ***Calif Interstate Tel*** | ***67a*** | ***Now Cont'l Tel. of Cal., see*** | | | | | | | | | | | | | | | | | | |
| 1st A 4⅝s '89 | Mn | **A+** | 2/89 | A | X | CR | 100 | .... | □100 | .... | .... | .... | 4.00 | H1 | '64 | 99⅜ | 98¼ | 99⅜ | 4.65 | 11.97 |
| ***California Water Service*** | ***74*** | | ***3.82*** | ***4.20*** | .... | ***Dc*** | ***6.16*** | ***25.70*** | ***22.20*** | ***9-30-88*** | ***91.90*** | | ***200.0*** | ***46.0*** | | | | | | |
| 1st AA 12⅞s 2013 | mN | **AA+** | 2/86 | A+ | X | R | 108.941 | 10-31-89 | 100 | .... | ®105.961 | 10-31-93 | 35.0 | D3 | '83 | 111½ | 105⅛ | 106 | 12.15 | 12.10 |
| ***Calmar Spraying Systems,Inc*** | ***16d*** | | ***29.49*** | ***p0.26*** | .... | ***Dc*** | ***5.60*** | ***44.90*** | ***20.90*** | ***p11-06-88*** | ***★202.0*** | | ***232.0*** | ***87.6*** | | | | | | |
| Sr Sub[1]Disc Nts '99 | Fa15 | **B–** | | | Y | R | 108 | (2-15-92) | 100 | (2-15-97) | .... | .... | [2]150 | D9 | '89 | 66⅞ | 65¾ | 65¾ | .... | .... |
| ***Calton, Inc*** | ***38*** | | ***3.59*** | ***4.19*** | ***6.07*** | ***Nv*** | | | | ***11-30-88*** | ***87.40*** | | ***186.0*** | ***46.9*** | | | | | | |
| Sub Nts[3] 12⅝s '96 | Jd15 | **B+** | 10/88 | B– | | R | 105.44 | (6-15-91) | 100 | (6-15-92) | .... | .... | 41.5 | M3 | '86 | 91½ | 87 | 87 | 14.51 | 15.69 |
| ***Cambridge Electric Lt[4]*** | ***72a*** | | ***4.88*** | ***3.70*** | .... | ***Dc*** | ***0.20*** | ***14.00*** | ***26.20*** | ***9-30-88*** | ***20.60*** | | ***58.30*** | ***54.0*** | | | | | | |
| SF Nts C 6¼s '97 | Jd | **BBB+** | 6/87 | A | X | R | 102.48 | 5-31-89 | 101.37 | 6-1-89 | .... | .... | 4.90 | H1 | '67 | 80½ | 77¾ | 78½ | 7.96 | 10.19 |
| SF Nts D 7¾s 2002 | Jd | **BBB+** | 6/87 | A | X | R | 104.26 | 5-31-89 | 101.28 | 6-1-89 | .... | .... | 3.63 | M3 | '72 | 84¾ | 81¼ | 82¼ | 9.42 | 10.23 |
| ***Cameron Iron Works*** | ***44d*** | | ***1.38*** | ***d0.05*** | ***0.02*** | ***Je*** | ***41.90*** | ***458.0*** | ***190.0*** | ***12-31-88*** | ***121.0*** | | ***537.0*** | ***34.6*** | | | | | | |
| Nts 11½s '91 | Jd | **AAA** | 7/87 | BBB– | X | R | 100 | .... | .... | .... | .... | .... | [5]48.0 | F2 | '83 | 100⅛ | 98¾ | 99¼ | 11.59 | 11.88 |
| ***Canal Capital Corp[6]*** | ***62*** | | ***3.32*** | ***1.28*** | ***2.78*** | ***Oc*** | ***18.00*** | ***25.00*** | ***4.07*** | ***10-31-88*** | ***22.60*** | | ***47.80*** | ***47.9*** | | | | | | |
| • V/R[7]Mtg Nts 13.05s '93 | QMy15 | **NR** | | | | R | 105 | 5-14-89 | 100 | (5-15-90) | .... | .... | [2]20.0 | D9 | '85 | No Sale | | 90 | 14.50 | .... |
| ***Canal Electric[4]*** | ***72*** | | ***0.98*** | ***0.77*** | .... | ***Dc*** | ***0.10*** | ***22.40*** | ***116.0*** | ***6-30-88*** | ***52.70*** | | ***235.0*** | ***58.0*** | | | | | | |
| 1st A 7s '96 | aO | **BBB+** | 2/89 | BBB | X | R | 102.13 | 9-30-89 | ‡100.58 | 9-30-89 | .... | .... | 9.12 | F2 | '68 | 85 | 81⅝ | 82⅛ | 8.52 | 10.50 |
| 1st & Gen B 8.85s 2006 | Ms | **BBB+** | 2/89 | BBB | X | R | 105.81 | 8-31-89 | 100.90 | 8-31-89 | .... | .... | 34.7 | F2 | '76 | 90½ | 86½ | 87½ | 10.11 | 10.42 |
| ***Cannon Group*** | ***47*** | | ***0.35*** | ***d0.28*** | .... | ***Dc*** | ***31.10*** | | | ***7-02-88*** | ***493.0*** | | ***532.0*** | ***92.7*** | | | | | | |
| SrSubDeb 12⅞s 2001 | Ao15 | **NR** | 5/88 | D | | R | 112.45 | 4-14-90 | 100 | (4-15-96) | ®108.89 | 4-14-91 | 127 | D9 | '86 | 68½ | 54½ | 64½ | 19.96 | 21.09 |
| ***CapitalCities/ABCFinance*** | ***26*** | ***Gtd by Capital Cities/ABC Inc*** | | | | | | | | | | | | | | | | | | |
| Gtd Nts 8¼s '96 | Ms15 | **A+** | | | X | R | 100 | (3-15-93) | .... | .... | .... | .... | 200 | F2 | '86 | 92⅝ | 89⅝ | 90⅛ | 9.15 | 10.27 |
| GtdSFDeb 8¾s 2016 | Ms15 | **A+** | | | X | R | 106.937 | 3-14-90 | 100 | (3-15-97) | ®104.081 | 3-14-96 | 300 | F2 | '86 | 88¾ | 84¼ | 85¼ | 10.26 | 10.39 |
| ***[8]Capital Cities Commun*** | ***12*** | | ***3.09*** | ***4.12*** | .... | ***Dc*** | ***1089*** | ***2228*** | ***781.0*** | ***10-02-88*** | ***1692*** | | ***4632*** | ***36.6*** | | | | | | |
| SFDeb 11⅝s 2015 | fA15 | **A+** | | | X | R | 109.541 | 8-14-89 | 100 | (8-15-96) | ®105.613 | 8-14-95 | 300 | G2 | '85 | 110 | 107 | 107½ | 10.81 | 10.76 |
| Nts 10½s '97 | mS | **A+** | | | X | R | 100 | (9-1-92) | .... | .... | .... | .... | 200 | G2 | '85 | 101¾ | 99 | 99¾ | 10.53 | 10.54 |
| Sub SF Deb 11¾s 2013 | Jd15 | **A** | 7/85 | AA– | X | R | 108.4375 | 6-14-89 | 100 | (6-15-94) | ®105.625 | 6-14-93 | 200 | G2 | '83 | 109⅞ | 104¾ | 105⅝ | 11.12 | 11.07 |
| ***Capital Holding*** | ***35a*** | | ***6.15*** | ***6.24*** | .... | ***Dc*** | | | | ***9-30-88*** | ***288.0*** | | ***1491*** | ***19.3*** | | | | | | |
| • Deb A 12¾s 2006 | Jj15 | **AA** | | | X | R | 106.375 | (1-15-91) | 100 | (1-15-92) | .... | .... | 42.6 | Mgr | '80 | 111 | 107½ | s107½ | 11.86 | 11.71 |
| SF Deb 8¾s 2017 | Jj15 | **AA** | | | X | R | 107.875 | 1-14-90 | 100 | (1-15-98) | ®104.375 | 1-14-97 | 100 | G2 | '87 | 87⅝ | 83⅜ | 84⅜ | 10.37 | 10.49 |
| Nts 12s '90 | Jj15 | **AA** | | | X | R | 100 | .... | .... | .... | .... | .... | 25.0 | G2 | '84 | 101⅛ | 100¼ | 100½ | 11.94 | 11.27 |
| Nts 7.45s '91 | Jd15 | **AA** | | | X | R | NC | .... | .... | .... | .... | .... | 50.0 | G2 | '86 | 95⅛ | 92⅝ | 92¾ | 8.03 | 10.59 |
| Nts 12.15s '92 | Jj15 | **AA** | | | X | R | 100 | (1-15-90) | .... | .... | .... | .... | 25.0 | G2 | '84 | 103 | 101 | 101⅛ | 12.01 | 11.65 |
| Nts 7⅞s '93 | jD15 | **AA** | | | X | R | 100 | (12-15-91) | .... | .... | .... | .... | 50.0 | G2 | '86 | 93⅝ | 91⅜ | 91½ | 8.61 | 10.19 |
| ***Carborundum Co*** | ***1*** | ***Now Kennecott, see Kennecott Copper*** | | | | | | | | | | | | | | | | | | |
| SF Deb 9¼s 2000 | Mn15 | **AA** | 5/87 | AA– | X | R | 103.15 | 5-14-89 | 100 | .... | .... | .... | 40.0 | M6 | '75 | 96¼ | 92¼ | 93¼ | 9.92 | 10.28 |
| ***Care Enterprises*** | ***31*** | | ***1.06*** | ***d0.61*** | .... | ***Dc*** | ***Bankruptcy Chapt 11*** | | | | ***[9]197.0*** | | ***168.0*** | ***119.0*** | | | | | | |
| SrSubNts 16s '94 | §mS | **D** | 2/88 | CCC | Z | R | | | Default 3-1-88 int | | | | 16.0 | D9 | '84 | 34¼ | 33 | 34¼ | .... | Flat |
| ***Carlsberg Corp[10]*** | ***38*** | ***Subsid of Southmark Corp,see*** | | | | | | | | | | | | | | | | | | |
| Sub Nts 9⅜s '94 | Ms | **CC** | 12/88 | CCC | Y | R | 100 | .... | 100 | .... | .... | .... | [2]25.0 | D9 | '84 | 83⅛ | 81⅜ | 81⅝ | 11.49 | 14.75 |
| ***Carnation Co*** | ***27d*** | ***Guaranteed by Nestle SA*** | | | | | | | | | | | | | | | | | | |
| SF Deb 8½s '99 | Mn | **AAA** | | | X | R | 102.06 | 4-30-90 | 100 | .... | .... | .... | 24.7 | K1 | '74 | 94⅛ | 90⅛ | 91 | 9.34 | 9.93 |

**Uniform Footnote Explanations-See Page 1.** Other: [1] Int accr at 14% fr 2-15-92. [2] Incl disc. [3] Was 12.25% Sr Notes thru 3-21-89. [4] Subsid of Commonwealth Energy Sys. [5] Defeased,funds deposited with trustee. [6] Was United Stockyards. [7] Int thru 5-14-89,adj qtrly aft as defined. [8] Now Capital Cities/ABC Inc. [9] Incl Ch 11 liabs. [10] Now Southmark California.

Source: Courtesy of Standard & Poor's Corporation.

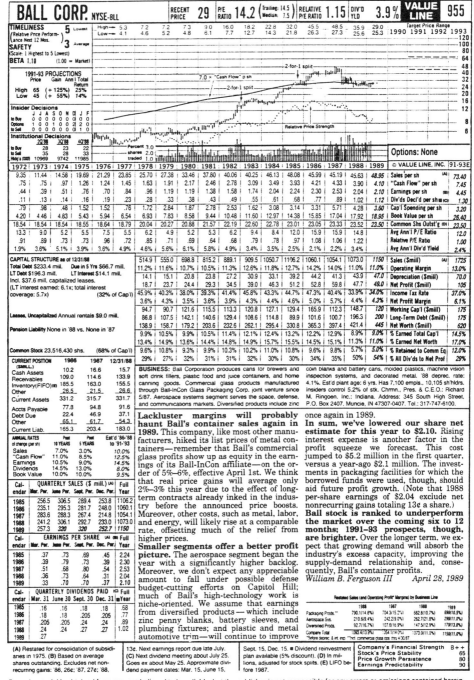

**BALL CORP.** NYSE-BLL | RECENT PRICE 29 | P/E RATIO 14.2 (Trailing: 14.5 Median: 7.5) | RELATIVE P/E RATIO 1.15 | DIV'D YLD 3.9% | VALUE LINE 955

**TIMELINESS** 5 Lowest
(Relative Price Performance Next 12 Mos.)
**SAFETY** 3 Average
(Scale: 1 Highest to 5 Lowest)
**BETA 1.10** (1.00 = Market)

**1991-93 PROJECTIONS**

| | Price | Gain | Ann'l Total Return |
|---|---|---|---|
| High | 65 | (+125%) | 25% |
| Low | 45 | (+55%) | 14% |

**Insider Decisions**

**Institutional Decisions**

**BUSINESS:** Ball Corporation produces cans for brewers and soft drink fillers, plastic food and juice containers, and home canning goods. Commercial glass products manufactured through Ball-InCon Glass Packaging Corp. joint venture since 5/87. Aerospace systems segment serves the space, defense, and communications markets. Diversified products include zinc coin blanks and battery cans, molded plastics, machine vision inspection systems, and decorated metal. '88 deprec. rate: 4.1%. Est'd plant age: 6 yrs. Has 7,100 empls., 10,105 sh'hldrs. Insiders control 5.2% of stk. Chrmn., Pres. & C.E.O.: Richard M. Ringoen, Inc.: Indiana. Address: 345 South High Street, P.O. Box 2407, Muncie, IN 47307-0407. Tel.: 317-747-6100.

**Lackluster margins will probably haunt Ball's container sales again in 1989.** This company, like most other manufacturers, hiked its list prices of metal containers—remember that Ball's commercial glass profits show up as equity in the earnings of its Ball-InCon affiliate—on the order of 5%–6%, effective April 1st. We think that real price gains will average only 2%–3% this year due to the effect of long-term contracts already inked in the industry before the announced price boosts. Moreover, other costs, such as metal, labor, and energy, will likely rise at a comparable rate, offsetting much of the relief from higher prices.

**Smaller segments offer a better profit picture.** The aerospace segment began the year with a significantly higher backlog. Moreover, we don't expect any appreciable amount to fall under possible defense budget-cutting efforts on Capitol Hill; much of Ball's high-technology work is niche-oriented. We assume that earnings from diversified products — which include zinc penny blanks, battery sleeves, and plumbing fixtures; and plastic and metal automotive trim—will continue to improve

once again in 1989. **In sum, we've lowered our share net estimate for this year to $2.10.** Rising interest expense is another factor in the profit squeeze we forecast. This cost jumped to $5.2 million in the first quarter, versus a year-ago $2.1 million. The investments in packaging facilities for which the borrowed funds were used, though, should aid future profit growth. (Note that 1988 per-share earnings of $2.04 exclude net nonrecurring gains totaling 13¢ a share.) **Ball stock is ranked to underperform the market over the coming six to 12 months; 1991–93 prospects, though, are brighter.** Over the longer term, we expect that growing demand will absorb the industry's excess capacity, improving the supply-demand relationship and, consequently, Ball's container profits.
*William B. Ferguson III* *April 28, 1989*

(A) Restated for consolidation of subsidiaries in 1975. (B) Based on average shares outstanding. Excludes net nonrecurring gains: '86, 26¢; '87, 27¢; '88.
13¢. Next earnings report due late July. (C) Next dividend meeting about July 25. Goes ex about May 25. Approximate dividend payment dates: Mar. 15, June 15.
Sept. 15, Dec. 15. ■ Dividend reinvestment plan available (5% discount). (D) In millions, adjusted for stock splits. (E) LIFO before 1987.

**Company's Financial Strength** B + +
**Stock's Price Stability** 65
**Price Growth Persistence** 80
**Earnings Predictability** 90

Factual material is obtained from sources believed to be reliable, but the publisher is not responsible for any errors or omissions contained herein.

# EXHIBIT 7A–4  Dow Jones News/Retrieval Databases

## Company/Industry News & Information

| Access Code | Additional Information |
|---|---|
| //DJNEWS | **Dow Jones℠ News:** Stories from The Wall Street Journal, Barron's and Dow Jones News Service as recent as 90 seconds, as far back as 90 days.<br><br>Terminal reads ENTER QUERY. Type a period, a stock symbol or news category symbol and press (Return). (See page 2 for a list of news category codes and industry symbols.) For example:<br><br>.UAL 01   headlines on United Airlines<br>.UAL      most recent story on United Airlines (UAL)<br>.//AIR 01  headlines on airlines (//AIR)<br>AE        type the two letter code preceding a headline to retrieve a story<br>01        return to headline list after viewing a story |
| //TEXT | **Text Search Services℠ :**Includes the following:<br><br>**The Wall Street Journal Full-Text Version:** All news articles published or scheduled to appear in The Wall Street Journal since January, 1984.<br><br>**Dow Jones News:** Selected stories from The Wall Street Journal, Barron's and the Dow Jones News Service since June, 1979.<br><br>**The Washington Post Full-Text Version:** Selected stories from The Washington Post since January, 1984.<br><br>**The Business Library:** The full text of the Public Relations Newswire plus selected articles from Forbes, Inc., Financial World and American Demographics. |
| //BUSINESS | **The Business and Finance Report:** Continuously updated business and financial news culled from The Dow Jones News Service, other newswires, and The Wall Street Journal. Detailed cross references to related information. |
| //QUICK | **Dow Jones℠ QuickSearch:** One command will generate a complete corporate report drawing information from multiple News/Retrieval sources. Covers latest news, current stock quotes, financial overview, market overview, earnings estimates, company vs. industry performance, income statements and more. |
| //MG | **Media General Financial Services:** Financial information on 4,300 companies and 170 industries. Includes revenue, earnings, dividends, volume, ratio, shareholdings and price changes. Compare company versus industry, company vs. company and industry vs. industry. For example:<br><br>KO    Detailed corporate financial information on Coca-Cola (KO) with comparative industry data on the same screen.   3 |

| Access Code | Additional Information |
|---|---|
| KO/TEP | Comparative corporate financial information on Coca-Cola (KO) and PepsiCo (PEP) on the same screen. |
| 332/400 | Comparative information on the soft drink industry and food chain industry. (MG industry numbers are found in //SYMBOL). |
| //EPS | **Zack's Corporate Earnings Estimator℠:** Consensus earnings per share estimates and P/E ratio forecasts for over 3,500 companies. Industries earnings estimates and lists of stocks outperforming or underperforming analysts forecasts. |
| //INVEST | **Investext®:** Full text of over 13,000 research reports on more than 3,000 U.S. and Canadian companies and 50 industries. |
| //DSCLO | **Disclosure® Online:** 10-K extracts, company profiles and other detailed data on over 10,000 publicly held companies from reports filed with the SEC. |
| //INSIDER | **Insider Trading Monitor:** Insider trading information on over 6,500 publicly held companies and 60,000 individuals (corporate directors,officers or shareholders with more than 10% ownership). Reports transactions of 100 shares or more. |
| //SP | **Standard & Poor's Online®:** Concise profiles of 4,600 companies containing current and historical earnings and estimates, dividend and market figures for the past four years. |
| //MMS | **Economic & Foreign Exchange Survey℠:** Weekly survey of U.S. money market and foreign exchange trends. Median forecasts of monetary and economic indicators. |
| //NEWS | **Dow Jones News/Retrieval World Report℠:** Continuously updated national and international news from the Associated Press, the Dow Jones News Service, and broadcast media. |
| //KYODO | **Japan Economic Daily®:** Same-day coverage of major business, financial and political news from the Kyodo News Service in Japan. |
| //WSW | **Wall Street Week℠ Online:** Transcripts of the public broadcasting program "Wall $treet Week." |
| //DEFINE | **Words of Wall Street℠:** Over 2,000 financial and investment terms defined. |

## Quotes & Market Averages

| Access Code | Additional Information |
|---|---|
| //CQE | **Enhanced Current Quotes:** Quotes on common and preferred stocks (with news alert feature), corporate and foreign bonds, mutual funds, U.S. Treasury Issues and Options. (Quotes minimum 15-minute delayed during market hours).  4 |

Source: Courtesy of Dow Jones News/Retrieval.

**Access Code** — **Additional Information**

Terminal reads ENTER QUERY. Type up to five stock symbols (hit space bar between symbols), and press (Return). Example:

| | |
|---|---|
| ROK | Rockwell International |
| ROK UTX LK GQ BA | Rockwell International, United Technologies, Lockheed Corp., Grumman Corp., Boeing Co. |

If current-day ticker news is available on a requested company, a message will appear. Type a period, the stock symbol, a space and 01 to see latest headlines.

**//RTQ** — **Real-Time Quotes:** Real-time stock quotes using the same commands as in //CQE. (Additional agreements must be completed for the use of Real-Time Quotes. Contact Customer Service for details.)

**//HQ** — **Historical Quotes:** Historical quotes for common and preferred stocks including daily quotes available for one year, monthly summaries back to 1979 and quarterly summaries back to 1978.

Terminal reads ENTER QUERY. Type a stock symbol, a space, trading period, instructions and press (Return). Example:

| | |
|---|---|
| KO 10/20/86 | quote for specific day on Coca-Cola (KO) |
| KO P1 | last 12 trading days |
| KO P2 | last 13-24 trading days |
| KO 79 M | monthly summary, 1979 |
| KO 78 Q | quarterly summary, 1978 |

**//FUTURES** — **Dow Jones Futures Quotes:** Current and historical quotes (10-30 minute delay) for over 80 contracts from the major exchanges. Updated continuously during market hours.

**//DJA** — **Historical Dow Jones Averages:** Historical averages including daily high, low, close and volume available for industrials, transportation, utilities and 65 stock composite indexes.

Terminal reads ENTER QUERY. Type one of the stock average's symbols below, a space, trading period and press (Return). For example:

| | |
|---|---|
| IND P1 | last 12 trading days on Industrial Averages |
| UTL P1 | last 12 trading days on Utilities Averages |
| TRN P2 | last 13-24 days on Transportation Average |
| 65 11/14/84 | specific day average for the 65 stock index |

**//TRACK** — **Tracking Service:** Create customized portfolios of up to 125 companies and automatically track news and quotes.

## Brokerage

**//FIDELITY** — **Fidelity Investor's Express:** Place trades online for listed securities; update and monitor your portfolio.

## General Services

**Access Code** — **Additional Information**

**//NEWS** — **Dow Jones News/Retrieval World Report™:** Continuously updated national and international news from the Associated Press, the Dow Jones News Service, and broadcast media.

**//OAG** — **Official Airline Guides™:** Airline schedules and fares; hotel/motel information. Make flight and hotel reservations online.

**//MCI** — **MCI Mail®:** Mail service for sending printed and electronic communications next door or world-wide.

**//AXP** — **American Express® Advance:** Statement information plus shopping and travel services from American Express.

**//ENCYC** — **Academic American Encyclopedia®:** Contains over 32,000 carefully researched and concisely written articles covering industry finance as well as academic subject areas.  Updated quarterly.

**//SCHOOL** — **Peterson's College Selection Service™:** Peterson's guide to two and four-year U.S. and Canadian colleges and universities.

**//STORE** — **Comp-u-store Online®:** An electronic shopping service of over 250,000 discounted brand-name products.

**//MOVIES** — **Cineman Movies Reviews:** Reviews of the latest releases as well as thousands of movies back to 1926.

**//BOOKS** — **Magill Book Reviews:** Reviews of many recent fiction and non-fiction works with new titles added weekly.

**//SPORTS** — **Dow Jones News/Retrieval Sports Report™:** Scores, stats, standings, schedules and stories for most major sports.

**//WTHR** — **Dow Jones News/Retrieval Weather Report™:** Three-day Accu-Weather® forecasts for over 100 U.S. and foreign cities.

## Using Dow Jones News/Retrieval

**//FYI** — **For Your Information:** FREE online newsletter covering database enhancements, new databases, rate changes, free-time offers and other important information. Check //FYI regularly for announcements.

**//MENU** — **Master Menu:** Complete listing of the information contained in the service, along with detailed access instructions.

**//SYMBOL** — **Dow Jones News/Retrieval Symbols Directory™:** A comprehensive online listing of the symbols and codes used within Dow Jones News/Retrieval databases. Updated daily.

# Security Laws and Ethics

## OBJECTIVES

When you have finished studying this chapter, you should understand

1. Why the federal government regulates securities trading and securities markets and institutions.

2. The provisions of the major securities laws.

3. The National Association of Securities Dealers' rules for fair dealing with customers.

4. The Institute of Chartered Financial Analysts's code of ethics and standards of professional conduct.

# 8

## Electronic Monitoring of Trading

The major stock exchanges search for securities law violations by electronically monitoring all trading. For example, the NYSE's Stock Watch System monitors every trade for price and volume abnormalities. Trades that are outside preset price and volume parameters are identified and examined. Of special interest are unusual trades *before* a major news announcement. Suspicious cases are then turned over to the SEC for futher investigation and possible prosecution.

In 1986, the NYSE identified 165 cases of unusual movement that could not be easily explained. Sixty of these cases were turned over to the SEC for investigation. The SEC does not report the status of these investigations, but in a normal year it takes action in only a few of the reported cases because insider trading is fairly difficult to prove.

The growth of futures and options trading has opened the door for more complex schemes. Therefore, in 1981 the exchanges formed the Intermarket Surveillance Group to monitor trading *across* markets in order to detect schemes using more than one exchange.

## INTRODUCTION

The United States has the world's most developed securities markets. These markets are an important national resource because they facilitate the efficient transfer of funds from savers to firms with profitable investment opportunities. Although huge amounts of money are involved, large-scale fraud and market collapse are relatively infrequent. Our securities laws and regulations and the people who enforce them deserve much of the credit for the prevention of shams and unscrupulous practices. Additionally, self-regulation by the exchanges, the National Association of Securities Dealers, and other securities industry groups has fostered honesty and ethical practices.

As an investor, you need to understand the provisions of the major securities laws. These laws provide you with some protection from deception and unscrupulous practices. Additionally, the laws require firms to provide investors with substantial amounts of information. This information provides the raw material for profitable investment decision making. Also, recent amendments to the security laws are helping to shape the securities markets in which you will buy and sell securities in the future.

# JUSTIFICATION FOR REGULATION

Although the securities markets in this country go back to the late 1700s, they were then subject to little governmental regulation. In the 1850s, Massachusetts passed the first state security law, and several other states followed with their own laws. On the national level, some regulation of securities came in the early 1900s with the Federal Trade Commission's enforcement of the antitrust laws. Although these early attempts at regulation set precedents, strong federal laws were not passed until the 1930s, thanks to the stock market crash in 1929, which began the Depression. The public needed to place blame for those horrible economic conditions and the securities industry became the scapegoat. In 1931, 1932, and 1933, congressional investigations and hearings concerning securities trading, the securities industry, and the market crash exposed numerous questionable practices. The hearings resulted in the laws that form the basic framework for today's governmental regulation of securities and their markets.

There are two major justifications for governmental regulation. The first one is to protect the investor from fraud and misrepresentation. Although the legal system puts primary responsibility on buyers or investors to protect themselves, analysis of securities is difficult and complex. Therefore the government aids investors by requiring the disclosure of certain information by the firms in order to prevent fraud. Because security investment is a long-term process, investors continue to need information after buying securities, in order to monitor their investments. Therefore, the law requires periodic reports and regular disclosures of information by the issuers of securities.

The second justification for securities regulation is that the nation requires efficient and stable markets. The economy would suffer greatly if large-scale security fraud and market collapse were frequent. People would not invest the money necessary for development of efficient businesses. Also, with the complexity and interrelationships in the economy, disruptions in the securities markets would spread to other segments of the economy. Because securities are used for collateral for loans and because much

### Parking Securities

In 1988, investigations and criminal charges showed that one of the most common illegal practices on Wall Street was "parking" of securities. The purpose of parking is to disguise ownership. An individual or firm (the parker) has another party buy the securities and hold them. The parker agrees to cover any losses the holder might suffer.

There are several possible motives for parking securities. Tax fraud, perhaps involving a phony sale from the parker to the holder, might be one purpose. On other occasions broker/dealer firms park securities with others because of rules limiting how much can be invested in securities given the amount of capital a firm has. Parking also often occurs in takeover attempts in order to hide a stock accumulator's position. However, the most offensive use of parking may be when it is used to manipulate prices by having others buy or sell stock for a party involved in a large transaction in the future.

Parking is hard to prosecute because often the crime is based on informal understandings rather than explicit statements. However in 1988 the firm of Drexel Burnham Lambert Inc. pleaded guilty to several felony counts involving parking of securities for its clients.

of the money invested in securities is borrowed, problems in the securities markets would affect financial institutions. In turn, the stress on the institutions would affect their lending. This would quickly influence the activities of consumers and other business firms.

# THE SECURITIES ACT OF 1933

The Securities Act of 1933 regulates the primary market. This act requires that a firm disclose important information by registering its securities with the Securities and Exchange Commission (SEC) before they are sold to the public. To register a security issue, a firm must submit a **registration statement** which describes the security, the company, its management, its financial position, the purpose for which the money will be used, and any potential conflicts of interest. Copies of the registration statement, which is a long, legal document, are available to the public. A 15 to 30 page pamphlet, called a **prospectus,** summarizing important information in the registration statement, is also prepared for potential investors. The salespeople for the investment banking firm must supply a copy of the prospectus to everyone they solicit to buy the securities. Exhibit 8–1 is the first page of a prospectus.

The Securities and Exchange Commission reviews the registration statement and the prospectus to make sure all the required information is disclosed. The SEC does not attempt to evaluate the securities as good or bad investments; it only checks that the required information is available for the investor's evaluation. Twenty days after filing, the registration statement becomes effective and the securities can be sold to the public. However, in the case of misrepresentation or omission of important information, the SEC can delay or stop the sale of the securities.

There are two classes of exceptions to the registration requirement: exempt securities and exempt transactions. Exempt securities are (1) short-term commercial paper, (2) securities of state and local governments, (3) securities of banks and savings and loan associations, (4) securities of not-for-profit charitable organizations, (5) securities of issuers where issuance is regulated by the Interstate Commerce Commission, (6) securities issued in bankruptcy or reorganization with court approval, (7) insurance policies and annuity contracts, (8) securities issued solely in exchange for existing securities, (9) securities sold intrastate, and (10) securities sold under Regulation A. Intrastate issues are exempt only when the issue is offered to and sold only to residents of the state where the issuer is registered and does most of its business. Regulation A permits an issuer to offer up to $1.5 million of securities in any 12-month period without registration. The issuer must prepare and provide an offering circular to all purchasers. This circular is much simpler and less detailed than a registration statement.

Exempt transactions include (1) limited offers not exceeding $500,000, (2) limited offers not exceeding $5 million, (3) private placements, and (4) limited offers solely to "accredited investors." The SEC's Rule 504 exempts from registration issues not exceeding $500,000 within 12 months provided the securities are sold without advertising, the issuer notifies the SEC of sales under the rule, and the issuer takes precautions against nonexempt, unregistered resales.

**EXHIBIT 8–1** *First Page of a Prospectus*

**PRELIMINARY PROSPECTUS DATED JULY 31, 1981**

**PROSPECTUS**

2,250,000 Shares

# DE LOREAN MOTORS
# HOLDING COMPANY
Common Stock
($.01 Par Value)

Prior to this offering, there has been no public market for the Common Stock. It is currently anticipated that the initial public offering price will be between $10 and $14 per share. For a discussion of factors considered in determining the initial public offering price, see "Underwriting".

Investment in the Common Stock involves a HIGH DEGREE OF RISK and should be considered only by those who can afford a total loss of their investment. See "High Risk Factors" for information with respect to product, market, production, finance and other matters.

THESE SECURITIES HAVE NOT BEEN APPROVED OR DISAPPROVED BY THE SECURITIES AND EXCHANGE COMMISSION NOR HAS THE COMMISSION PASSED UPON THE ACCURACY OR ADEQUACY OF THIS PROSPECTUS. ANY REPRESENTATION TO THE CONTRARY IS A CRIMINAL OFFENSE.

| | Price to Public | Underwriting Discounts and Commissions(1) | Proceeds to Company(2) |
|---|---|---|---|
| Per Share | $ | $ | $ |
| Total (3) | $ | $ | $ |

(1) The Company has agreed to indemnify the several Underwriters against certain liabilities, including liabilities under the Securities Act of 1933.

(2) Before deducting expenses payable by the Company estimated at $

(3) The Company has granted the several Underwriters an over-allotment option to purchase up to an additional 225,000 shares on the same terms as set forth above. (See "Underwriting".) If all 225,000 shares are purchased by the Underwriters, the total Price to Public will be $         , the total Underwriting Discounts and Commissions will be $         , and the total Proceeds to the Company will be $         (See "Underwriting".)

The shares are offered by the several Underwriters when, as and if issued by the Company and accepted by the Underwriters, subject to prior sale or withdrawal, cancellation or modification of the offer without notice. Delivery of the shares to the Underwriters is expected to be made on or about         , 1981 at the office of Bache Halsey Stuart Shields Incorporated, 100 Gold Street, New York, New York.

**BACHE HALSEY STUART SHIELDS**
INCORPORATED

1981

Source: Preliminary Prospectus, De Lorean Motors Holding Company

The SEC's Rule 505 exempts issues not exceeding $5 million within twelve months provided the securities are sold without advertising to an unlimited number of "accredited investors" and not more than 35 other purchasers. Accredited investors include banks, insurance companies, investment companies, officers and directors of the issuing firms, anyone who purchases at least $150,000 of the securities so long as the purchase does not exceed 20 percent of the investor's net worth, anyone whose net worth exceeds $1 million, and anyone whose income exceeds $200,000 per year. If the sale involves any nonaccredited investors, all purchasers must be provided information about the issuer, its business, and the securities. If all investors are accredited, there are no disclosure requirements.

The SEC's Rule 506 defines the private placement provisions of the law. It permits any size sale of securities, without advertising, to an unlimited number of accredited investors and not more than 35 other purchasers. If the sale involves any nonaccredited investors, all purchasers must be provided information about the issuer, its business, and the securities. If all investors are accredited, there are no disclosure requirements. A condition in this rule and not in Rule 505 is that if there are any nonaccredited investors, the issuer must believe that they or their representatives have the knowledge and experience in business matters to be able to evaluate the merits and risk of the investment.

In 1980 the law was amended to provide that if an issue not in excess of $5 million is sold only to accredited investors, without advertising, it does not need to be registered and no information is required. In general, securities issued under the exempt transaction

### Shelf Registration

Shelf registration allows corporations with over $150 million of publicly held stock outstanding to register new securities but with up to two years to offer them for sale.

Shelf registration is permitted by the SEC's Rule 415 under the Securities Act of 1933. First proposed in December 1980, this rule was adopted for a trial period on March 2, 1982, and became permanent at the beginning of 1984.

Shelf registration has become very popular with corporations. After registering the securities with the SEC, the issuing corporation can wait for the most favorable market conditions. At the time of sale, the issuer usually has investment banking firms submit competitive bids for the securities. This changes the traditional, negotiated price arrangement between an investment banking firm and the issuing firm, which tends to increase competition among investment banking firms. The issuer's flotation costs are thereby lowered.

Shelf registration also changes the nature of the "due diligence" investigation of the issuer by the investment banking firm. Last minute competitive bidding does not permit time for the traditional in-depth investigation. Because the SEC allows use of shelf registration only by corporations that already have securities outstanding, a great deal of information has already been released under the 1934 Act. The SEC's support of shelf registration reflects its belief that additional information from a more extensive investigation would not be that beneficial since market participants do a good job of analyzing the information already available.

provisions remain restricted securities which cannot be resold, without registration, except by means of another exempt transaction.

This law provides both criminal and civil penalties. It allows any purchaser to collect damages if he or she suffers a loss because of misrepresentation or material omissions. It also provides for severe penalties which may be imposed on the issuing firm, its officers, its directors, and any accountants, engineers, appraisers, underwriters, or other experts who participated in preparing the registration statement and prospectus. If sued, any defendant, other than the issuing firm, can assert a defense of due diligence. Due diligence requires the defendant to prove he or she made a reasonable investigation and that there was no reason to suspect misrepresentation or material omissions.

# THE SECURITIES EXCHANGE ACT OF 1934

While the 1933 law deals with the initial sale of securities in the primary market, the Securities Exchange Act of 1934 deals with the resale of securities in the secondary market. It requires the registration of all securities exchanges and provides for their regulation by the Securities and Exchange Commission. The exchanges, in turn, continue their historical practice of regulating their members. The act also requires companies whose securities are traded on the exchanges to disclose pertinent information in periodic reports.

In order to prevent people who have information not available to the general public from profiting at the expense of public investors, the law forbids security trading based on inside information. **Inside information** is information that is not available to the general public and which, therefore, could not be discovered if an investor searched for it. The law requires people who usually have inside information, such as officers, directors, and major stockholders, to report each month their trading in the stock of their company. Any profits they make on short-term trading must be turned over to the company. If an insider breaches his or her duty and provides inside information to an outsider, the outsider is forbidden to trade based on the information.

This law forbids several practices that were used to manipulate security prices. Included are pools, wash sales, and pegging prices. **Pools** are formed when individuals put together a large sum of money to buy stock and drive up its price. When others are buying at the new high price, the members of the pool sell. **Wash sales** are sales executed only to create the appearance of more sales activity in the stock. Wash sales combined with rumors deceive other investors into buying or selling. **Pegging prices** occurs when a powerful market participant buys whenever sell orders would force a stock below a certain price.

The Securities Exchange Act of 1934 directs the SEC to write regulations governing proxy solicitation. The SEC rules require a proxy solicitation to describe the issues to be voted on and to provide a proxy form on which the shareholder can vote for or against each proposal. Additionally, every shareholder has the right to communicate with other shareholders. Upon a shareholder's written request, the corporation must

## Insider Trading Scandals

The 1980s saw the growth of stock market arbitrageurs. Originally, arbitrageurs invested in companies after a merger was announced. They invested based on the relationship between the stock prices of the two firms involved and the probabilities that the merger would be completed. In the mid-1980s, arbitrageurs started investing in firms that *might* be candidates for mergers. They hoped to profit on the price increases at the time of announcement. Rumors of pending mergers were, therefore, very important to them.

The potential for abuse of confidential information arises because investment banking firms that employ arbitrageurs also advise the firms involved in mergers. To prevent arbitrageurs from obtaining nonpublic information, the firms enforce a "Chinese Wall" rule that forbids the mergers and acquisition specialists to talk business with their firm's stock traders. However, enforcement of the Chinese Wall rule was undermined by dishonest employees who bartered information about their firm's clients to employees of other firms in exchange for information about the other firms' clients. Thus, systems designed to monitor if employees bought or sold the stocks of their firm's clients could not catch illegal transactions.

A major Wall Street scandal started in May 1986 with a confidential tip from South America. An SEC investigation led to the arrest of Dennis Levine, a mergers and acquisitions specialist and a managing director at the Wall Street firm of Drexel Burnham Lambert. Levine was charged with using "material nonpublic information" in securities trading over a six-year period. The SEC accused him of using dummy Panamanian corporations and Bahamian banks to hide his trading. What immediately caught the SEC's attention was that many of the transactions involved inside information that had to have been leaked by employees of other firms.

In November 1986, Levine's cooperation with government investigators resulted in a felony guilty plea and cooperation from Wall Street's best known arbitrageur, Ivan F. Boesky. Boesky paid the largest fine in SEC history and received a jail sentence.

Information from Boesky led to SEC investigations of well-known Wall Street firms and their employees. In April 1987, the SEC arrested on related charges a senior executive at Goldman, Sachs & Co. and one present and one former executive at Kidder, Peabody & Co., two of Wall Street's most prestigious firms. The U.S. attorney said that these arrests were only the beginning "of a very long and substantial investigation."

No doubt by the time you read this it will be only the first part of a larger story. More arrests, congressional hearings, and new legislation are expected.

Source: "Are the 'Arbs' Too Cozy With Insiders," *Business Week*, June 16, 1986, pp. 32–34; "Suddenly the Fish Get Bigger," *Business Week*, March 2, 1987, pp. 28–35.

mail the shareholder's correspondence to the other shareholders or provide the shareholder with a list of names and addresses of the shareholders. An issuer who issues a false or misleading proxy statement is liable for any damages caused by it.

This law also limits the amount of money that can be borrowed to purchase securities. It directs the Federal Reserve Board to set initial margin requirements. Exhibit 8–2 shows that the board has set the requirement for stocks in a range of 40 to 100 percent equity. Margin requirements also apply to convertible bonds and short sales.

The 1934 act established the SEC as an independent, quasi-judicial agency to enforce the securities laws. The SEC is empowered to seek civil injunctions, to

---

**EXHIBIT 8–2   Historical Margin Requirements (Percent of Market Value)**

---

|  | Credit Extension Regulations[a] | | |
|---|---|---|---|
| Effective Date | Margin Stocks | Convertible Bonds | Short Sales[b] |
| 1934: Oct 1 | 25–45 | — | [c] |
| 1936: Feb 1 | 25–55 | — | [c] |
| Apr 1 | 55 | — | [c] |
| 1937: Nov 1 | 40 | — | 50 |
| 1945: Feb 5 | 50 | — | 50 |
| July 5 | 75 | — | 75 |
| 1946: Jan 21 | 100 | — | 100 |
| 1947: Feb 21 | 75 | — | 75 |
| 1949: Mar 3 | 50 | — | 50 |
| 1951: Jan 17 | 75 | — | 75 |
| 1953: Feb 20 | 50 | — | 50 |
| 1955: Jan 4 | 60 | — | 60 |
| Apr 23 | 70 | — | 70 |
| 1958: Jan 16 | 50 | — | 50 |
| Aug 5 | 70 | — | 70 |
| Oct 16 | 90 | — | 90 |
| 1960: July 28 | 70 | — | 70 |
| 1962: July 10 | 50 | — | 50 |
| 1963: Nov 6 | 70 | — | 70 |
| 1968: Mar 11 | 70 | 50 | 70 |
| Jun 8 | 80 | 60 | 80 |
| 1970: May 6 | 65 | 50 | 65 |
| 1971: Dec 6 | 55 | 50 | 55 |
| 1972: Nov 24 | 65 | 50 | 65 |
| 1974: Jan 3 | 50 | 50 | 50 |

[a] Regulations T (brokers and dealers), U (banks), G (others than brokers, dealers, or banks), and X (borrowers), adopted by the Board of Governors pursuant to the Securities Exchange Act of 1934, limit the amount of credit to purchase and carry ''margin securities'' and ''margin stock'' (as defined in the regulations) when such credit is collateralized by securities. Margin requirements are the difference between the market value (100 percent) and the maximum loan value of collateral as prescribed by the Board. Regulation T was adopted effective Oct. 15, 1934; Regulation U, effective May 1, 1936; Regulation G, effective Mar. 11, 1968; and Regulation X, effective Nov. 1, 1971.

[b] T only.

[c] The requirement was the margin ''customarily required'' by the brokers and dealers.

*Source*: *Annual Report 1987* (Washington, D.C.: Board of Governors of the Federal Reserve System) Table 12, p. 240.

### The Dismissal of the Junk Bond King

Michael R. Milken's MBA thesis examined the return-risk tradeoff on low-quality bonds. He found that the returns were very attractive even after adjusting for risk. After graduation, he joined the investment banking firm of Drexel Burnham Lambert Inc. and made it the leader in helping firms raise money by issuing low-quality (junk) bonds. His activities were so successful that well-known investment banking firms started underwriting junk bond issues for their clients.

In December 1988, the SEC was investigating if Drexel and Milken had violated securities laws. Under intense pressure from prosecutors, Drexel agreed to plead guilty. As part of that agreement, the firm denied Milken his bonus for his 1988 performance and dismissed him. These actions were demanded by the prosecutors before Milken was formally charged with any offense. Many observers thought this constituted punishment without trial. Milken promised that he would continue to fight for his rights.

recommend that the Justice Department bring criminal charges, and to suspend brokers and dealers. Until this law was passed, the Federal Trade Commission enforced the 1933 Act.

There have been numerous amendments to the Securities Exchange Act of 1934. Four of the additions are particularly significant: the Maloney Act of 1938, the Williams Act of 1968, the Securities Acts Amendments of 1975, and the Foreign Corrupt Practices Act of 1977.

## The Maloney Act of 1938

The 1934 act had provided for regulation of member firms by the exchanges. However, OTC dealers and brokers were not subject to any self-regulating association. Therefore, the Maloney Act of 1938 amended the 1934 act by authorizing the establishment of "national securities associations" which would register with the SEC and have rules "to prevent fraudulent and manipulative acts and practices [and] to promote just and equitable principles of trade" for the OTC market. The only association to register under this law is the National Association of Securities Dealers (NASD). Self-regulation of its members is based on its "Rules of Fair Practice." NASD's rules for fair dealings with customers are reprinted in Appendix 8A.

## The Williams Act of 1968

The 1934 act was amended by the Williams Act of 1968 to cover tender offers and other large block transactions. A **tender offer** is an invitation to stockholders to offer their shares for purchase at a specified price. Any person or group that makes a tender offer for or acquires more than 5 percent of a firm's stock must provide the SEC and the sellers with a statement containing (1) the tender offerer's background, (2) the source of the funds to be used, (3) the purpose of the acquisition, (4) the number of shares owned, and (5) any relevant contracts, arrangements, or understandings. Other provisions specify time limits under which a shareholder can withdraw his or her tender of shares and provide that if the offering price is increased, all tendering shareholders will get the higher price.

### The Securities Act Amendments of 1975

While the Securities Acts of 1933 and 1934 emphasized disclosure and fraud prevention, the Securities Acts Amendments of 1975 made the SEC responsible for the way the securities markets are organized. In particular, Congress directed the SEC "to facilitate the establishment of a national market system for securities."

Although specific details were not included in the law, Congress foresaw a strong central market system in which there would be more competition among market makers. All investors, all existing market institutions, and all qualified brokers and dealers were to have access to the central market system. To implement this national market goal, the amendments gave the SEC authority to establish a consolidated quotation system to reflect the bid and ask prices of all market makers in a security. The amendments also directed the SEC to amend any SEC or exchange rule "imposing a burden on competition which does not appear to the Commission to be necessary or appropriate in furtherance of the purpose of this title."

### The Foreign Corrupt Practices Act of 1977

Following public disclosure of several large bribes paid to foreign officials by U.S. firms, Congress amended the 1934 act by passing the Foreign Corrupt Practices Act of 1977. This act makes it unlawful for a firm or its agents to bribe any foreign official, political party, or political officer for the purpose of influencing actions or decisions. In order to prevent off-the-books slush funds from being used for bribes, the act requires strict record keeping and internal accounting controls. It also expands the disclosure requirements of the 1934 law.

## THE TRUST INDENTURE ACT OF 1939

An **indenture** is the contract detailing all the provisions of a bond issue. The Trust Indenture Act of 1939 provides bondholders protection by requiring that the indenture contain certain standard protective provisions and that essential provisions of the indenture be more fully disclosed.

The indenture normally provides for a trustee to represent the interest of the bondholders. This law requires that the trustee be a disinterested party, such as a financial institution, and that the corporation provide the trustee with periodic financial reports.

## THE INVESTMENT COMPANY ACT OF 1940

Investment companies, advisory services, insurance for brokerage accounts, and pension funds are discussed elsewhere in this book. However, in order to make this section on securities laws complete, the laws regulating them are described here even though the discussion overlaps other sections of the book. The Investment Company Act of 1940 and its 1970 amendments define what an investment company is and require investment companies to register with the SEC. The registration statement must give the fund's investment policy and other important information. A registered fund must also file annual reports with the SEC and maintain specified accounts and records. All securities owned by the fund must be in the custody of a bank or stock exchange member. An investment company cannot buy on margin or sell short.

The act has provisions to help insure that the fund has honest and unbiased management. The fund must publish semiannual financial reports. The act also limits the amount of money that can be charged when selling shares of the fund to the public.

# THE INVESTMENT ADVISORY ACT OF 1940

The Investment Advisory Act of 1940 requires individuals and firms that give advice for compensation about securities transactions to register with the SEC and conform their advice to SEC standards. Additionally, investment advisors must disclose their investment philosophy and any conflicts of interest. They also must maintain records in accordance with SEC rules. Registration may be denied or revoked by the SEC for fraud or violation of the securities laws.

# THE SECURITIES INVESTOR PROTECTION ACT OF 1970

Several brokerage firms failed in the late 1960s. In some of these failures, fraud or mismanagement was so extensive that the firm had not protected the cash and securities it held for customers. In order to provide investors protection in these cases, Congress passed the Securities Investor Protection Act of 1970. Following the pattern of the Federal Deposit Insurance Corporation, which protects bank depositors, the act established an insurance fund, the Securities Investor Protection Corporation (SIPC). If a brokerage firm fails and all the securities and cash owned by the customers are not available, the SIPC will pay each customer's loss up to a maximum of $500,000. A sublimit is that a customer's claim for cash held by the failed firm is limited to $100,000. This limit matches the insurance limits provided by the agencies which insure accounts in depository institutions, that is, the Federal Deposit Insurance Corporation (FDIC), the Federal Savings and Loan Insurance Corporation (FSLIC), and the National Credit Union Administration's (NCUA) share insurance program. SIPC protection applies to securities such as stocks, bonds, notes, and certificates of deposit. Not covered are unregistered investment contracts or any interest in a commodity, commodity contract, or commodity option.

All nonbank broker/dealers registered with the SEC are members of SIPC except for four kinds of firms. The exceptions are firms engaged exclusively in (1) the distribution of mutual fund shares, (2) the sale of variable annuities, (3) all aspects of the insurance business, or (4) furnishing investment advice to investment companies and insurance companies. Assessments on covered firms support the SIPC.

# THE EMPLOYEE RETIREMENT INCOME SECURITY ACT OF 1974

Congressional hearings in the early 1970s exposed many incidents in which retirees suffered greatly when they did not receive the pensions they thought they had earned or when the pensions were much smaller than expected. Often these hardships resulted from bad investment policies of the pension fund managers. To prevent similar abuses in the future, the Employee Retirement Income Security Act of 1974 (ERISA) brought pension fund managers under federal regulation. Most important, the "prudent investments" provision of the act required that fund managers not only protect the fund's principal but also invest the money so that it earns a reasonable return. Fund managers are made liable for any imprudent investments.

The word "prudent" was not precisely defined in the law. However, in practice, the returns on diversified portfolios such as the Standard and Poor's 500 composite stocks have become the standard. If a pension fund manager does not diversify or if he or she regularly underperforms the market averages, lawsuits are likely and defense will be difficult.

Another provision of ERISA defines and forbids conflicts of interest by pension fund managers. Other provisions address aspects of pension management other than investment practices. For example, ERISA sets standards for funding retirement plans and for determining worker eligibility.

# STATE REGULATION

When passing the 1933 and 1934 acts, Congress formally recognized the role of the states in securities regulation. A securities transaction is subject to state law in addition to federal law. State laws are known as *"blue sky laws"* after a 1917 court decision that recognized a state's right to prevent "speculative schemes which have no more basis than so many feet of blue sky." In most states, the laws provide for registration of securities, regulation of brokers and dealers, and fraud prevention. Although laws differ in many ways from one state to another, we will discuss the general structure of the laws in most states.

## Registration

There are three methods for state registration of securities. Most states provide for registration under "notification" and "qualification." Some states also provide for registration by "coordination" when an issue also is being registered with the SEC. Registration by notification is similar to the federal law registration provisions. Firms file a registration statement disclosing the required information and wait a specified number of days for it to become effective. The state officials check only that the required information is disclosed.

Under registration by qualification, firms must file a registration statement and wait for approval to sell the securities. While registration by disclosure centers on making information public and prevention of fraud, registration by qualification has a state official making a determination as to the value of the investment. The official determines if the offering is ''fair, just and equitable.'' In most states, firms that meet stated standards may register their offerings by registration while firms that do not meet the standards must register by qualification.

The states that have registration by coordination require only that documents required by federal law also be filed with the state.

## Summary of Securities Laws

| Act | Major Provisions |
|-----|------------------|
| Securities Act of 1933 | Regulates the primary market |
| | Requires registration statement and prospectus |
| Securities Exchange Act of 1934 | Regulates the secondary markets |
| | Provides for registration of exchanges |
| | Forbids trading based on inside information |
| | Outlaws pools, wash sales, and pegging prices |
| | Regulates proxy solicitation |
| | Establishes margin requirements |
| | Establishes the SEC |
| Major Amendments to the 1934 Act: | |
| Maloney Act of 1938 | Authorized a self-regulating organization for OTC brokers and dealers |
| Williams Act of 1968 | Regulates tender offers |
| Securities Acts Amendments of 1975 | Directs the SEC to facilitate establishment of a national market system |
| Foreign Corrupt Practices Act of 1977 | Outlaws bribes of foreign officials |
| | Requires strict internal accounting controls |
| Trust Indenture Act of 1939 | Requires protective provisions in bond indentures |
| | Provides for a disinterested trustee |
| Investment Company Act of 1940 | Requires registration of investment companies |
| | Requires honest fund management |
| | Limits selling charges on fund shares |
| Investment Advisory Act of 1940 | Requires registration of investment advisors |
| Securities Investor Protection Act of 1970 | Establishes an insurance fund for brokerage accounts |
| Employee Retirement Income Security Act of 1974 | Regulates investment practices of pension funds |

### Regulation of Brokers and Dealers

Almost every state requires brokers and dealers to register with it. Most states have standards of conduct and can deny or revoke registration in addition to imposing other sanctions.

### Fraud Prevention

Almost every state has a law defining securities fraud and providing for its enforcement by state securities officials. Some states actively enforce strong antifraud laws, while some are shockingly lax in both the writing and enforcement of the law.

## PROFESSIONAL ETHICS FOR FINANCIAL ANALYSTS

The Institute of Chartered Financial Analysts (ICFA) was founded in 1959 to enhance the professionalism of those involved in the investment decision-making process and to recognize those who achieve a high level of professionalism by the designation of "chartered financial analyst." As a self-regulated organization, the ICFA has adopted and enforces a code of ethics and standards of professional conduct, which are reprinted in Appendix 8A.

## SUMMARY

In this chapter, we summarize the security laws that protect the investor. These laws minimize fraud and dishonesty and provide for stable, efficient markets. The SEC and self-regulating securities industry organizations have provided a reasonable, safe mechanism for an efficient transfer of funds from savers to productive uses. The states continue their historical role in securities regulation by requiring registration of securities, regulating brokers and dealers, and preventing fraud.

## QUESTIONS

1. What justification is there for government regulation of securities and securities markets?
2. What is a registration statement? What does it contain? What is the SEC's role with it?
3. What securities are exempt from registration?
4. Describe the types of transactions that exempt securities from registration.
5. What is the purpose of the Securities Act of 1933? To whom does it apply?
6. What are the major provisions of the Securities Exchange Act of 1934?

7. How were pools, wash sales, and pegging prices used to manipulate securities prices?
8. Summarize the SEC rules concerning proxy solicitation.
9. What is the purpose of each of these amendments to the 1934 act: the Maloney Act of 1938, the Williams Act of 1968, the Securities Acts Amendments of 1975, and the Foreign Corrupt Practices Act of 1977?
10. Summarize NASD's "Rules of Fair Practice."
11. What are the main provisions of the Trust Indenture Act of 1939?
12. What are the main provisions of the Investment Company Act of 1940?
13. What does the Investment Advisory Act of 1940 require?
14. Describe the insurance provided by the Securities Investor Protection Corporation.
15. What are the main provisions of the Employee Retirement Income Security Act of 1974?
16. What is the role of the states in securities regulation?
17. Explain registration by notification, qualification, and coordination.
18. Summarize the Institute of Chartered Financial Analysts' code of ethics.
19. Summarize the Institute of Chartered Financial Analysts' standards of professional conduct.

# *READINGS*

Hayes, Samuel L., III, ed. *Wall Street and Regulation*. Boston: Harvard Business School Press, 1987.
>   *This book resulted from a research colloquium on the changes in the U.S. financial services sector held at the Harvard Business School. In addition to the Introduction and Conclusions, the book contains five papers on aspects of the regulation of financial services.*

The Institute of Chartered Financial Analysts, 2nd ed. *Standards of Practice Handbook*. Charlottesville, VA: The Institute of Chartered Financial Analysts, 1984.
>   *This book presents and explains the institute's code of ethics and standards of professional conduct.*

Phillips, Susan M., and Zecher, Richard J. *The SEC and the Public Interest*. Cambridge, MA: MIT Press, 1981.
>   *This book uses the tools of financial and regulatory economics to examine the costs and benefits of SEC programs.*

Ratner, David L. *Securities Regulation in a Nutshell*, 2nd ed. St. Paul, MN: West Publishing Co., 1982.
>   *This small book is a concise summary of the securities laws and regulations.*

Seligman, Joel. *The SEC and the Future of Finance*. New York: Praeger Publishers, 1985.
>   *A law professor analyzes several current securities and corporate law topics, including the national market systems, the options markets, the corporate disclosure debate, and the regulation of banks as they enter the securities and insurance fields.*

Seligman, Joel. *The Transformation of Wall Street*. Boston: Houghton Mifflin Co., 1982.
>   *A law professor presents a detailed history of the SEC from its beginning until 1977.*

# APPENDIX 8A
# INVESTOR PROTECTION

## NASD's Rules: Fair Dealing with Customers

Implicit in all member and registered representative relationships with customers and others is the fundamental responsibility for fair dealing. Sales efforts must therefore be undertaken only on a basis that can be judged as being within the ethical standards of the Association's rules, with particular emphasis on the requirement to deal fairly with the public.

This does not mean that legitimate sales efforts in the securities business are to be discouraged by requirements which do not take into account the variety of circumstances which can enter into the member-customer relationship. It does mean, however, that sales efforts must be judged on the basis of whether they can be reasonably said to represent fair treatment for the persons to whom the sales efforts are directed, rather than on the argument that they result in profits to customers.

District Business Conduct Committees and the Board of Governors have interpreted the Rules of Fair Practice, taken disciplinary action and imposed penalties in many situations where members' sales efforts have exceeded the reasonable grounds of fair dealing.

Some practices that have resulted in disciplinary action and that clearly violate this responsibility for fair dealing are set forth below, as a guide to members:

**1. Recommending Speculative Low-Priced Securities**  Recommending speculative low-priced securities to customers without knowledge of or attempt to obtain information concerning the customers' other securities holding, their financial situation and other necessary data. The principle here is that this practice, by its very nature, involves a high probability that the recommendation will not be suitable for at least some of the persons solicited. This has particular application to high pressure telephone sales campaigns.

**2. Excessive Trading Activity**  Excessive activity in a customer's account, often referred to as "churning" or "overtrading." There are no specific

standards to measure excessiveness of activity in customer accounts because this must be related to the objectives and financial situation of the customer involved.

**3. Trading in Mutual Fund Shares**  Trading in mutual fund shares, particularly on a short-term basis. It is clear that normally these securities are not proper trading vehicles and such activity on its face may raise the question of rule violation.

**4. Fraudulent Activity**  Numerous instances of fraudulent conduct have been acted upon by the Association and have resulted in penalties against members. Among some of these activities are

  **a.** Fictitious Accounts  Establishment of fictitious accounts in order to execute transactions which otherwise would be prohibited, such as the purchase of hot issues, or to disguise transactions which are against firm policy.

  **b.** Discretionary Accounts  Transactions in discretionary accounts in excess of or without actual authority from customers.

  **c.** Unauthorized Transactions  Causing the execution of transactions which are unauthorized by customers or the sending of confirmations in order to cause customers to accept transactions not actually agreed upon.

  **d.** Misuse of Customer's Funds or Securities  Unauthorized use or borrowing of customers' funds or securities.

In addition, other fraudulent activities, such as forgery, nondisclosure or misstatement of material facts, manipulations and various deceptions, have been found in violation of Association rules. These same activities are also subject to the civil and criminal laws and sanctions of Federal and State Governments.

**5. Recommending Purchases Beyond Customer Capability**  Recommending the purchase of securities or the continuing purchase of securities in amounts which are inconsistent with the reasonable expectation that the customer has the financial ability to meet such a commitment.

---

Source: *NASD Manual* (Washington, D.C.: National Association of Securities Dealers), 1988, pp. 2051–52.

While most members are fully aware of the fairness required in dealing with customers, it is anticipated that these enumerated practices, which are not all-inclusive, will be of future assistance in the training and education of new personnel.

The Securities and Exchange Commission has also recognized that brokers and dealers have an obligation of fair dealing in actions under the general antifraud provisions of the federal securities laws. The Commission bases this obligation on the principle that when a securities dealer opens his business he is, in effect, representing that he will deal fairly with the public. Certain of the Commission's cases on fair dealing involve practices not covered in the foregoing illustrations. Usually, any breach of the obligation of fair dealing as determined by the Commission under the antifraud provisions of the securities laws could be considered a violation of the Association's Rules of Fair Practice.

## Institute of Chartered Financial Analysts' Code of Ethics

A financial analyst should conduct himself* with integrity and dignity and act in an ethical manner in his dealings with the public, clients, customers, employers, employees, and fellow analysts.

A financial analyst should conduct himself and should encourage others to practice financial analysis in a professional and ethical manner that will reflect credit on himself and his profession.

A financial analyst should act with competence and should strive to maintain and improve his competence and that of others in the profession.

A financial analyst should use proper care and exercise independent professional judgment.

## Institute of Chartered Financial Analysts' Standards of Professional Conduct

### I. Obligation to Inform Employer of Code and Standards
The financial analyst shall inform his em-

---

* Masculine pronouns, used throughout the Code and Standards to simplify sentence structure, shall apply to all persons, regardless of sex.

*Source: Standards of Practice Handbook,* 4th ed. (Charlottesville, VA: The Institute of Chartered Financial Analysts), 1988, p. 2.

ployer, through his direct supervisor, that the analyst is obligated to comply with the Code of Ethics and Standards of Professional Conduct, and is subject to disciplinary sanctions for violations thereof. He shall deliver a copy of the code and standards to his employer if the employer does not have a copy.

### II. Compliance with Governing Laws and Regulations and the Code and Standards

**A.** Required Knowledge and Compliance   The financial analyst shall maintain knowledge of and shall comply with all applicable laws, rules, and regulations of any government, governmental agency, and regulatory organization governing his professional, financial, or business activities, as well as with these Standards of Professional Conduct and the accompanying Code of Ethics.

**B.** Prohibition Against Assisting Legal and Ethical Violations   The financial analyst shall not knowingly participate in, or assist, any acts in violation of any applicable law, rule, or regulation of any government, governmental agency, or regulatory organization governing his professional, financial, or business activities, nor any act which would violate any provision of these Standards of Professional Conduct or the accompanying Code of Ethics.

**C.** Prohibition Against Use of Material Nonpublic Information   The financial analyst shall comply with all laws and regulations relating to the use of material nonpublic information. (1) If the analyst acquires such information as a result of a special or confidential relationship with the issuer, he shall not communicate the information (other than within the relationship), or take investment action on the basis of such information, if it violates that relationship. (2) If the analyst is not in a special or confidential relationship with the issuer, he shall not communicate or act on material nonpublic information if he knows or should have known that such information was disclosed to him in breach of a duty. If such a breach exists, the analyst shall make reasonable efforts to achieve public dissemination of such information.

**D.** Responsibilities of Supervisors   A financial analyst with supervisory responsibility shall exercise reasonable supervision over those subordinate employees subject to his control, to prevent any violation by such persons of applicable statutes, regulations, or provisions of the code of Ethics or Standards of Professional Conduct. In so doing the financial analyst is entitled to rely upon reasonable procedures established by his employer.

### III. Research Reports, Investment Recommendations and Actions

**A.** Reasonable Basis and Representations
   1. The financial analyst shall exercise diligence and thoroughness in making an investment recommendation to others or in taking an investment action for others.
   2. The financial analyst shall have a reasonable and adequate basis for such recommendations and actions, supported by appropriate research and investigation.
   3. The financial analyst shall make reasonable and diligent efforts to avoid any material misrepresentation in any research report or investment recommendation.
   4. The financial analyst shall maintain appropriate records to support the reasonableness of such recommendations and actions.

**B.** Research Reports
   1. The financial analyst shall use reasonable judgment as to the inclusion of relevant factors in research reports.
   2. The financial analyst shall distinguish between facts and opinion in research reports.
   3. The financial analyst shall indicate the basic characteristics of the investment involved when preparing for general public distribution a research report that is not directly related to a specific portfolio or client.

**C.** Portfolio Investment Recommendations and Actions   The financial analyst shall, when making an investment recommendation or taking an investment action for a specific portfolio or client, consider its appropriateness and suitability for such portfolio or client. In considering such matters, the financial analyst shall take into account (1) the needs and circumstances of the client, (2) the basic characteristics of the investment involved, and (3) the basic characteristics of the total portfolio. The financial analyst shall use reasonable judgment to determine the applicable relevant factors. The fi-

nancial analyst shall distinguish between facts and opinion in the presentation of investment recommendations.

**D.** Prohibition Against Plagiarism   The financial analyst shall not, when presenting material to his employer, associates, customers, clients, or the general public, copy or use in substantially the same form, material prepared by other persons without acknowledging its use and identifying the name of the author or publisher of such material. The analyst may, however, use without acknowledgment factual information published by recognized financial and statistical reporting services or similar sources.

**E.** Prohibition Against Misrepresentation of Services   The financial analyst shall not make any statements, orally or in writing, which misrepresent (1) the services that the analyst or his firm is capable of performing for the client, (2) the qualifications of such analyst or his firm, (3) the investment performance that the analyst or his firm has accomplished or can reasonably be expected to achieve for the clients, or (4) the expected performance of any investment.
   The financial analyst shall not make, orally or in writing, explicitly or implicitly, any assurances about or guarantees of any investment or its return except communication of accurate information as to the terms of the investment instrument and the issuer's obligations under the instrument.

**F.** Fair Dealing With Customers and Clients   The financial analyst shall act in a manner consistent with his obligation to deal fairly with all customers and clients when (1) disseminating investment recommendations, (2) disseminating material changes in prior investment advice, and (3) taking investment action.

### IV. Priority of Transactions   The financial analyst shall conduct himself in such a manner that transactions for his customers, clients, and employer have priority over personal transactions, and so that his personal transactions do not operate adversely to their interests. If a financial analyst decides to make a recommendation about the purchase or sale of a security or other investment, he shall give his customers, clients, and employer adequate opportunity to act on this recommendation before acting on his own behalf.

**V. *Disclosure of Conflicts*** The financial analyst, when making investment recommendations, or taking investment actions, shall disclose to his customers and clients any material conflict of interest relating to him and any material beneficial ownership of the securities or other investments involved, which could reasonably be expected to impair his ability to render unbiased and objective advice.

The financial analyst shall disclose to his employer all matters which could reasonably be expected to interfere with his duty to the employer, or with his ability to render unbiased and objective advice.

The financial analyst shall also comply with all requirements as to disclosure of conflicts of interest imposed by law and by rules and regulations of organizations governing his activities and shall comply with any prohibitions on his activities if a conflict of interest exists.

**VI. *Compensation***

**A.** Disclosure of Additional Compensation Arrangements   The financial analyst shall inform his customers, clients, and employer of compensation or other benefit arrangements in connection with his services to them which are in addition to compensation from them for such services.

**B.** Disclosure of Referral Fees   The financial analyst shall make appropriate disclosure to a prospective client or customer of any consideration paid or other benefit delivered to others for recommending his services to that prospective client or customer.

**C.** Duty to Employer   The financial analyst shall not undertake independent practice for compensation or other benefit in competition with his employer unless he has received written consent from both his employer and the person for whom he undertakes independent employment.

**VII. *Relationships with Others***

**A.** Preservation of Confidentiality   A financial analyst shall preserve the confidentiality of information communicated by the client concerning matters within the scope of the confidential relationship, unless the financial analyst receives information concerning illegal activities on the part of the client.

**B.** Maintenance of Independence and Objectivity   The financial analyst, in relationships and contacts with an issuer of securities, whether individually or as a member of a group, shall use particular care and good judgment to achieve and maintain independence and objectivity.

**C.** Fiduciary Duties   The financial analyst, in relationships with clients, shall use particular care in determining applicable fiduciary duty and shall comply with such duty as to those persons and interests to whom it is owed.

**VIII. *Use of Professional Designation***

---
*FAF*
---

The financial analyst may use the professional designation ''Member of The Financial Analysts Federation,'' and is encouraged to do so, but only in a dignified and judicious manner. The use of the designation may be accompanied by an accurate explanation (1) of the requirements that have been met to obtain the designation and (2) of The Financial Analysts Federation.

---
*ICFA*
---

The Chartered Financial Analyst may use the professional designation Chartered Financial Analyst, or the abbreviation CFA, and is encouraged to do so, but only in a dignified and judicious manner. The use of the designation may be accompanied by an accurate explanation (1) of the requirements that have been met to obtain the designation and (2) of The Institute of Chartered Financial Analysts.

**IX. *Professional Misconduct*** The financial analyst shall not (1) commit a criminal act that upon conviction materially reflects adversely on his honesty, trustworthiness, or fitness as a financial analyst in other respects or (2) engage in conduct involving dishonesty, fraud, deceit, or misrepresentation.

---

*Source: Standards of Practice Handbook,* 4th ed. (Charlottesville, VA: The Institute of Chartered Financial Analysts), 1988, pp. 2–7.

# The Stock Market and the Economy

## OBJECTIVES

When you have finished studying this chapter, you should understand

1. How stock prices are affected by changes in earnings and price-to-earnings (PE) ratios.
2. How changes in earnings, dividends, dividends growth, and discount rates affect price-to-earnings ratios.
3. The relationship between stock prices and economic cycles.
4. How to determine the factors that are important when making an industry analysis.

# 9

## *Leaks of Economic Data*

On September 12, 1986, the *Wall Street Journal* attributed the previous day's fall in stock and bond prices to economic data rumored to have been leaked from the Commerce and Labor Departments. Inflation fears were kindled by the Commerce Department's retail sales report, which showed a strong increase, and the Labor Department's producer price index, which also showed an increase. Both leaked reports differed from investor expectations. The market was extremely sensitive to the reports because many economists had doubts about the future direction of the economy.

Government officials denied the leaks and suggested that skilled forecasters could predict their departments' releases of economic data. They also mentioned that in the past, government employees who leaked information had been fired.

## INTRODUCTION

The stock market provides a mechanism by which investors can profit from growth in the economy. When the economic outlook is promising, investors foresee increased corporate earnings and high returns from investment in stocks. When the economic outlook is dreary, however, investors expect reduced corporate earnings and hesitate to invest in stocks. Because investors are continually buying and selling stocks based on their updated economic forecasts, we expect stock prices to reflect a consensus view of the economic future and to lead economic cycles.

In this chapter, we will explore the determinants of the level of stock prices. Because the price-to-earnings ratio reflects investors' expectations about future stock performance, we will examine how this multiple changes drastically as investors' expectations change. Special attention will be given to the relationship between changes in the money supply and stock prices as well as to the relationship between inflation and stock prices. The correlation between stock prices and economic cycles will also be examined. In the final section of the chapter, we will outline issues to be addressed in an industry analysis.

# THE LEVEL OF STOCK PRICES

The first question to ask after deciding that common stocks belong in your portfolio is whether the market is going to go up or down. Although there are always some stocks which do well in a down market, your investment returns usually are much higher in a good market. Exhibit 9–1 is a graph of the Standard & Poor's 500 index which displays both long-term growth and drastic fluctuations. This section examines economic factors that relate to the level of stock prices.

Analysis of stock prices is facilitated if they are considered the product of two components: the earnings per share (EPS) and the price-to-earnings (PE) ratio. Exhibit 9–2 contains the S&P 500 prices, EPS, and PE ratios for the years 1966 to 1987. The annual percentage change in each variable is also given. Examination of this table

---

**EXHIBIT 9–1   Standard & Poor's Index**

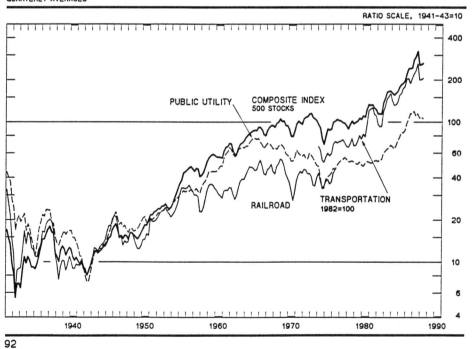

STOCK MARKET
STANDARD & POOR'S PRICE INDEX
QUARTERLY AVERAGES

Source: *1988 Historical Chart Book,* (Washington, D.C.: Board of Governors of the Federal Reserve System, 1988) p. 92.

---

**EXHIBIT 9–2    Standard & Poor's 500 prices, Earnings, and Price to Earnings Ratios**

| Year | Year-end Stock Prices | Percentage Change | Earnings per Share | Percentage Change | Price to Earnings Ratios | Percentage Change |
|------|------|------|------|------|------|------|
| 1966 | 80.33 | − 13.1 | 5.55 | 6.9 | 14.47 | − 18.8 |
| 1967 | 96.47 | 20.1 | 5.33 | − 4.0 | 18.10 | 25.1 |
| 1968 | 103.86 | 7.7 | 5.76 | 8.1 | 18.03 | − 0.4 |
| 1969 | 92.06 | − 11.4 | 5.78 | 0.3 | 15.93 | − 11.6 |
| 1970 | 92.15 | 0.1 | 5.13 | − 11.2 | 17.96 | 12.7 |
| 1971 | 102.09 | 10.8 | 5.70 | 11.1 | 17.91 | − 0.3 |
| 1972 | 118.05 | 15.6 | 6.42 | 12.6 | 18.39 | 2.7 |
| 1973 | 97.55 | − 17.4 | 8.16 | 27.1 | 11.95 | − 35.0 |
| 1974 | 68.56 | − 29.7 | 8.89 | 8.9 | 7.71 | − 35.5 |
| 1975 | 90.19 | 31.5 | 7.96 | − 10.5 | 11.33 | 46.6 |
| 1976 | 107.46 | 19.1 | 9.91 | 24.5 | 10.84 | − 4.3 |
| 1977 | 95.10 | − 11.5 | 10.89 | 9.9 | 8.70 | 19.7 |
| 1978 | 96.11 | 1.1 | 12.33 | 13.2 | 7.79 | − 10.5 |
| 1979 | 107.94 | 12.3 | 14.86 | 9.8 | 7.26 | − 6.8 |
| 1980 | 135.76 | 25.8 | 14.82 | − 0.3 | 9.16 | 26.2 |
| 1981 | 122.55 | − 9.7 | 15.36 | 3.6 | 8.12 | − 11.4 |
| 1982 | 140.64 | 14.8 | 12.64 | − 17.7 | 11.12 | 36.9 |
| 1983 | 164.93 | 17.3 | 14.03 | 11.0 | 11.76 | 5.8 |
| 1984 | 167.24 | 1.4 | 16.64 | 18.4 | 10.05 | − 14.5 |
| 1985 | 211.28 | 26.3 | 14.61 | − 12.2 | 14.46 | 43.9 |
| 1986 | 242.17 | 14.6 | 14.48 | − 0.9 | 16.72 | 15.6 |
| 1987 | 247.08 | 2.0 | 17.50 | 20.9 | 14.12 | − 15.6 |
| 1988 | 277.72 | 12.4 | 23.76 | 35.8 | 11.69 | − 17.2 |

Source: Compiled from data in *Security Price Index Record* (New York: Standard & Poor's Corporation, 1989).

---

shows that during these years EPS steadily increased with only temporary setbacks. However, PE ratios experienced drastic declines in some years. A cursory analysis shows that changes in the PE ratio accounted for most of the changes in the stock prices. Therefore, we begin the analysis of the level of stock prices by examining the determinants of PE ratios.

A PE ratio reflects the multiple investors are willing to pay for a dollar of earnings. It also can be thought of as the number of years' earnings necessary to recoup the price of the stock. The calculation of a stock's PE ratio usually is done using the past year's earning. However, using forecasted earnings is better because the investor is buying future, not past, earnings. Also, the PE ratio should be based on normalized earnings (earnings after unusual gains and losses have been removed).

In Chapter 5, we developed a model that valued a share of stock based on its discounted future dividends. In this section, we use that framework, Equation 9–1, to examine PE ratios.

$$P = \frac{D_1}{r - g} \tag{9-1}$$

where

$D_1$ = the dividend expected at the end of the first period

$r$ = the rate of return required by investors

$g$ = the dividend growth rate

Equation 9–1 can be related to PE ratios by dividing both sides of the equation by earnings ($E$) and obtaining Equation 9–2.

$$\frac{P}{E} = \frac{D_1/E}{r - g} \tag{9-2}$$

where $D_1/E$ is the dividend payout ratio.

In Chapter 1 we pointed out that the rate of return investors require is the sum of three variables: the risk-free rate ($R_F$), an inflation premium ($F$), and a risk premium ($R_p$).

$$r = R_F + F + R_p \tag{9-3}$$

Substituting 9–3 into 9–2 gives Equation 9–4, which relates the PE ratio to five variables: the dividend payout ratio ($D_1/E$), the risk-free rate ($R_F$), the inflation premium ($F$), the risk premium ($R_p$), and the dividend growth rate ($g$). We will analyze each variable.

$$\frac{P}{E} = \frac{D_1/E}{R_F + F + R_p - g} \tag{9-4}$$

## Earnings, Dividends, and Growth

Exhibit 9–3 compares after-tax profits and dividends over a 20-year period. The dividend column shows nearly continuous growth in dividends paid, while the growth of profits fluctuated from year to year. As a result of these profit fluctuations, the dividend payout percentage varied from 39 to 77 percent.

Since stock prices are the product of earnings per share multiplied by the PE ratio, we expect stock prices to increase when earnings increase. If dividends are not increased when earnings increase, the dividend payout ratio will fall but the growth rate will increase. The growth rate depends on the rate of return on equity earned by the firm and its earnings retention ratio. Since earnings must be either paid out or retained, the earnings retention ratio is equal to one minus the dividend payout ratio. Therefore,

**EXHIBIT 9–3  Corporate Profits and Dividends**

| Year | After-Tax Profits* Billions of Dollars | Percentage Change | Dividends Billions of Dollars | Percentage Change | Dividend Payout Percentage |
|------|------|------|------|------|------|
| 1968 | 51.4 | 0.0 | 22.0 | 8.9 | 43 |
| 1969 | 47.7 | − 7.2 | 22.5 | 2.3 | 47 |
| 1970 | 40.3 | − 15.5 | 22.5 | 0.0 | 56 |
| 1971 | 49.3 | 22.3 | 22.9 | 1.8 | 46 |
| 1972 | 58.8 | 19.2 | 24.4 | 6.6 | 41 |
| 1973 | 64.1 | 9.0 | 27.0 | 10.7 | 42 |
| 1974 | 49.9 | − 22.2 | 29.7 | 10.0 | 60 |
| 1975 | 66.7 | 33.7 | 29.6 | − 0.3 | 44 |
| 1976 | 81.0 | 21.4 | 34.6 | 16.9 | 43 |
| 1977 | 101.8 | 25.7 | 39.5 | 14.2 | 39 |
| 1978 | 113.7 | 11.7 | 44.7 | 13.2 | 39 |
| 1979 | 112.1 | − 1.4 | 50.1 | 12.1 | 45 |
| 1980 | 92.4 | − 17.6 | 54.7 | 9.2 | 59 |
| 1981 | 106.8 | 15.6 | 63.6 | 16.3 | 60 |
| 1982 | 86.9 | − 18.6 | 66.9 | 5.2 | 77 |
| 1983 | 136.5 | 57.1 | 71.5 | 6.9 | 52 |
| 1984 | 173.0 | 26.7 | 79.0 | 10.5 | 46 |
| 1985 | 185.9 | 7.5 | 83.3 | 5.4 | 45 |
| 1986 | 192.3 | 3.4 | 88.2 | 5.9 | 46 |
| 1987 | 176.6 | − 8.2 | 95.5 | 8.2 | 54 |

*After-tax profits with inventory valuation and capital consumption adjustments.

Source: Compiled from data in *Economic Report of the President* (Washington, D.C.: U.S. Government Printing Office, 1989), Table B-87, p. 409.

decreasing the dividend payout ratio will increase the earnings retention ratio and subsequently increase the growth rate.

A firm should reinvest its earnings rather than pay them out in dividends if it has investment opportunities that offer attractive risk-adjusted returns. On the other hand, if the firm does not have attractive investment opportunities, the earning should be paid out to stockholders so that they can reinvest them elsewhere.

## The Risk-Free Rate

Stocks compete with other financial assets for investors' money. The discount rate used by investors in evaluating stocks reflects the returns available on alternative

**EXHIBIT 9–4  Estimates of the Risk-Free Rate**

| Year | Yield on 91 Day Treasury Bills | Change in The CPI | Estimated Risk-Free Rate |
|------|------|------|------|
| 1968 | 5.5 | 4.7 | 0.8 |
| 1969 | 6.9 | 6.1 | 0.8 |
| 1970 | 6.7 | 5.5 | 1.2 |
| 1971 | 4.5 | 3.4 | 1.1 |
| 1972 | 4.2 | 3.4 | 0.8 |
| 1973 | 7.3 | 8.8 | −1.5 |
| 1974 | 8.2 | 12.2 | −4.0 |
| 1975 | 6.0 | 7.0 | −1.0 |
| 1976 | 5.1 | 4.8 | 0.3 |
| 1977 | 5.4 | 6.8 | −1.4 |
| 1978 | 7.5 | 9.0 | −1.5 |
| 1979 | 10.4 | 13.3 | −2.9 |
| 1980 | 12.0 | 12.4 | −0.4 |
| 1981 | 14.7 | 8.9 | 5.8 |
| 1982 | 11.1 | 3.9 | 7.2 |
| 1983 | 8.9 | 3.8 | 5.1 |
| 1984 | 10.0 | 4.0 | 6.0 |
| 1985 | 7.7 | 3.8 | 3.9 |
| 1986 | 6.2 | 1.1 | 5.1 |
| 1987 | 6.0 | 4.4 | 1.6 |

Source: Compiled from data in *Economic Report of the President* (Washington, D.C.: U.S. Government Printing Office, 1989), Tables B-61 and B-71, pp. 377 and 391.

investments. When interest rates are high, debt instruments attract investors away from equities. When interest rates are falling, investors find stocks more attractive.

**EXAMPLE**

On September 14, 1987, *Business Week* reported, "Now rising rates are trouble for stocks. In the last week of August the Dow fell 70 points as the rate on 30-year Treasury bonds vaulted the 9% barrier. Then, on September 1, the Dow plunged an additional 52 points—the fifth worst down day ever—as rates kept rising." [1]      □

The best proxy available for the real risk-free rate is the difference between 91-day Treasury bill yields and the inflation rate. Exhibit 9–4 displays these variables for

[1] "The Bull Market Takes a Hit," *Business Week,* September 14, 1987, p. 143.

## CPI Expenditure Categories

The Bureau of labor Statistics computes the Consumer Price Index (CPI) using 1982–84 as the base period. Each month the bureau measures prices in these categories of expenditures:

*Food and beverages*
Food
  Food at home: Cereals and bakery products; meats, poultry, fish, and eggs; dairy products; fruits and vegetables; other food at home, such as sugar and sweets, fats and oils, non-alcoholic beverages, other prepared food
  Food away from home
Alcoholic beverages

*Housing*
Shelter
  Renters' costs: Residential rent, other renters' costs
  Homeowners' costs: Owners' equivalent rent, household insurance
  Maintenance and Repairs: Maintenance and repair services, maintenance and repair commodities
Fuel and other utilities
  Fuels: Fuel oil and other household fuel commodities, gas (piped) and electricity
  Other utilities and public services
Household furnishings and operation: House furnishings, housekeeping supplies, housekeeping services

*Apparel and upkeep*
Apparel commodities: Men's and boys' apparel, women's and girls' apparel, infants' and toddlers' apparel, footwear, other apparel commodities
Apparel services

*Transportation*
Private transportation: New vehicles, new cars; used cars; motor fuel, gasoline; maintenance and repairs; other private transportation commodities and services
Public transportation

*Medical care*
Commodities
  Services: Professional medical services

*Entertainment*
Commodities
Services

*Other goods and services*
Tobacco and smoking products
Personal care: Toilet goods and personal care appliances; personal care services
Personal and educational expenses: School books and supplies, personal and educational services

a 20-year period. Notice the sharp rise in the risk-free rate in the early 1980s. That was when the Federal Reserve Board was maintaining a very tight monetary policy in order to slow down the double digit inflation of the late 1970s.

Numerous studies have been undertaken of the relationship between money supply and stock prices. Changes in the money supply affect (1) the amount of money available for investment in stocks, and (2) the amount and cost of funds available to corporations for investment in real assets. Therefore, you would expect decreases in the money supply to decrease stock prices and increases in the money supply to increase stock prices.

Empirical studies have confirmed that money supply does influence stock prices. However, there is no consistent time lag between changes in the money supply and changes in stock prices. Without knowing the time lag, it is difficult to predict future stock prices based on changes in the money supply. Also, market analysts continually watch for signs of change in monetary conditions and buy or sell at the first indication of change. This causes stock prices immediately to reflect the analysts' evaluations of indicators of change in the money supply.

## The Inflation Premium

Until the market performance of the 1970s proved them wrong, many securities and mutual fund salespeople argued that stocks were a good hedge against inflation. The usual argument was that stock ownership represented ownership of the plant, machinery, and other assets of the corporation and that these assets would increase in value in inflationary times. Basically, they assumed that stock values are determined by the value of a firm's assets.

However, the main determinant of a stock's value is the discounted future earnings of the company. Earnings of a corporation could increase as a result of inflation under any one of the following conditions:

1. The firm's prices rise before its labor costs rise.
2. The firm's prices rise before its raw materials costs rise.
3. The firm is a net debtor; that is, its financial liabilities are greater than its financial assets. Unanticipated inflation favors debtors over creditors.

Although any one of these conditions can occur in a specific firm or industry, empirical studies have disproved the first two for large samples of corporations. As for the third, empirical studies have shown that about one half of all firms are net debtors and the other half are net creditors. Therefore, this is not an important factor for the market as a whole.

Other empirical studies have compared stock market returns and inflation rates over long time periods, finding that the stock market does poorly in inflationary periods. During inflationary times, investors demand higher rates of return to compensate for inflation. As a result, the rate they use to discount future earnings is higher, thereby causing lower stock prices.

## The Risk Premium

The discount rate investors use contains a risk premium. The size of the premium they demand depends on two factors: the amount of risk involved and the price they demand for bearing that risk. Investors are continually evaluating international and national events to see if the risk of their investments is changing. For example, a market rise in November 1985 was attributed to better than expected results of the Reagan-Gorbachev summit.

The willingness of investors to bear risk also changes. Some analysts pay close attention to shifts in investors' moods. They see "investor psychology" as a major determinant of market prices.

# ECONOMIC CYCLES AND MARKET CYCLES

Historically, the level of activity in the economy has followed a cyclical pattern. The terms used to describe economic cycles are shown in Exhibit 9–5. The time of the lowest level of economic activity is called the trough, which is followed by economic expansion. The highest level of economic activity is called the peak, while decline from the peak to the next trough is a contraction.

Economic cycles continue to occur even though fiscal and monetary policies have shortened the contraction periods and lengthened the expansion periods. Exhibit 9–6 lists the dates and durations of the economic cycles in this century. At the bottom of the table, average durations of all cycles and all peacetime cycles are given. Notice that for peacetime cycles since World War II the average cycle lasts about four years with the contraction phase of it lasting less than a year.

## Leading, Lagging, and Coincident Indicators

The relationships between economic cycles and about 300 time series are analyzed by the Bureau of Economic Analysis of the Department of Commerce. These series measure many components of economic activity. They are grouped into seven broad categories: employment and unemployment; production and income; consumption, trade, orders, and deliveries; fixed capital investment; inventories and inventory investment; prices, costs, and profits; and money and credit.

The Bureau identifies the economic series that tend to lead, coincide with, or lag behind broad movements in aggregate economic activity. These series are called

---

**EXHIBIT 9–5   Economic Cycle**

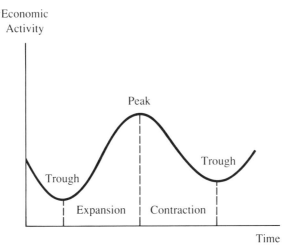

**EXHIBIT 9–6   Business Cycle Dates**

|  |  | Duration in Months | | | |
| --- | --- | --- | --- | --- | --- |
| *Trough* | *Peak* | *Contraction*[a] | *Expansion*[b] | *Trough to Trough Cycle* | *Peak to Peak Cycle* |
| Dec 1900 | Sep 1902 | 18 | 21 | 42 | 39 |
| Aug 1904 | May 1907 | 23 | 33 | 44 | 56 |
| Jun 1908 | Jan 1910 | 13 | 19 | 46 | 32 |
| Jan 1912 | Jan 1913 | 24 | 12 | 43 | 36 |
| Dec 1914 | Aug 1918 | 23 | <u>44</u> | 35 | <u>67</u> |
| Mar 1919 | Jan 1920 | <u>7</u> | 10 | <u>51</u> | 17 |
| Jul 1921 | May 1923 | 18 | 22 | 28 | 40 |
| Jul 1924 | Oct 1926 | 14 | 27 | 36 | 41 |
| Nov 1927 | Aug 1929 | 13 | 21 | 40 | 34 |
| Mar 1933 | May 1937 | 43 | 50 | 64 | 93 |
| Jun 1938 | Feb 1945 | 13 | <u>80</u> | 63 | <u>93</u> |
| Oct 1945 | Nov 1948 | <u>8</u> | 37 | <u>88</u> | 45 |
| Oct 1949 | Jul 1953 | 11 | <u>45</u> | 48 | <u>56</u> |
| May 1954 | Aug 1957 | <u>10</u> | 39 | <u>55</u> | 49 |
| Apr 1958 | Apr 1960 | 8 | 24 | 47 | 32 |
| Feb 1961 | Dec 1969 | 10 | <u>106</u> | 34 | <u>116</u> |
| Nov 1970 | Nov 1973 | <u>11</u> | 36 | <u>117</u> | 47 |
| Mar 1975 | Jan 1980 | 16 | 58 | 52 | 74 |
| Jul 1980 | Jul 1981 | 6 | 12 | 64 | 18 |
| Nov 1982 |  | 16 | · · · | 28 | · · · |
| Average, all cycles: |  |  |  |  |  |
| 1854–1982 (30 cycles) |  | 18 | 33 | 51 | 51 |
| 1854–1919 (16 cycles) |  | 22 | 27 | 48 | 49 |
| 1919–1945 (6 cycles) |  | 18 | 35 | 53 | 53 |
| 1945–1982 (8 cycles) |  | 11 | 45 | 56 | 55 |
| Average, peacetime cycles: |  |  |  |  |  |
| 1854–1982 (25 cycles) |  | 19 | 27 | 46 | 46 |
| 1954–1919 (14 cycles) |  | 22 | 24 | 46 | 47 |
| 1919–1945 (5 cycles) |  | 20 | 26 | 46 | 45 |
| 1945–1982 (6 cycles) |  | 11 | 34 | 46 | 44 |

Note: Underscored figures are the wartime expansions (World Wars I and II, Korean war, and Vietnam war), the postwar contractions, and the full cycles that include the wartime expansions.

[a] Peak to trough.

[b] Trough to peak.

Source: U.S. Department of Commerce, *Handbook of Cyclical Indicators* (Washington, D.C.: U.S. Government Printing Office, 1984), Table 10, p. 178.

---

**EXHIBIT 9–7   Composite Indexes**

*Leading Index Components*
Average weekly hours of production for nonsupervisory worker, manufacturing
Average weekly initial claims for unemployment insurance, state programs
Manufacturers' new orders in 1972 dollars, consumer goods and materials industries
Vendor performance, percent of companies receiving slower deliveries
Index of net business formation
Contracts and orders for plant and equipment in 1972 dollars
Index of new private housing units authorized by local building permits
Change in manufacturing and trade inventories on hand and on order in 1972 dollars, smoothed
Change in sensitive materials prices, smoothed
Index of stock prices, 500 common stocks
Money supply M2 in 1972 dollars
Change in business and consumer credit outstanding

*Coincident Index Components*
Employees on nonagricultural payrolls
Personal income less transfer payments in 1972 dollars
Index of industrial production
Manufacturing and trade sales in 1972 dollars

*Lagging Index Components*
Average duration of unemployment in weeks
Ratio, manufacturing and trade inventories to sales, in 1972 dollars
Index of labor cost per unit of output, manufacturing—actual data as a percent of trend
Average prime rate charged by banks
Commercial and industrial loans outstanding in 1972 dollars
Ratio, consumer installment credit outstanding to personal income

Source: U.S. Department of Commerce, *Handbook of Cyclical Indicators* (Washington, D.C.: U.S. Government Printing Office, 1984), Table 2, p. 67.

---

**cyclical indicators.** The Bureau constructs composite indexes of 12 leading, 4 coincident, and 6 lagging indicators. Exhibit 9–7 lists the series that are included in the composite indexes. Notice that stock prices are a leading indicator series.

## Stock Market Cycles

Having discussed economic cycles and the factors that determine the overall level of stock prices, the next questions are: "Is there a cyclical pattern in stock prices?" and "If a cyclical pattern exists, how is this pattern related to cyclical patterns of real economic variables?" A well-known study of stock market cycles was undertaken by Shiskin, who documented the existence of a cyclical pattern in stock prices and compared this pattern to the patterns of several economic variables, including employment, income, and production.[2] He found that the stock price pattern consistently leads the general economy. The Bureau of Economic Analysis reports that, on the average, stock prices peak nine months before the economy peaks. In the contraction phase stock prices hit bottom and start recovering four months before the economy. Unfortunately, the lead times vary greatly from cycle to cycle.

Shiskin's findings are what we expect if stock prices are determined by the discounted future earnings of firms. Investors are continually evaluating future economic conditions and assessing how these conditions will affect corporate earnings. If investors foresee improving economic conditions, they will buy stocks. If they foresee deteriorating conditions, they will sell stocks. One way to outperform the market is to do a better job than others in predicting the timing of economic cycles.

# INDUSTRY ANALYSIS

We recommend a three step approach to investment analysis. First, analyze the factors influencing the economy and the financial markets. Few stocks perform well in bad markets. Second, analyze how future economic conditions and trends will affect specific industries. Usually, it is better to own stock in a mediocre company in a prospering industry than in a strong company in a poor performance industry. When an industry is suffering decreasing demand or increasing costs, the pressures on the profits of most firms within the industry are intense. Third, examine specific firms.

Firms in an industry have their performance affected by common factors. Demand and supply forces affect the prices received by all producers. Usually, production technology, processes, and costs are similar and subject to the same pressures. Demographic, political, and international factor affect the entire industry.

## Support for Industry Analysis

Observation of the investment practices shows much support for industry analysis. Most brokerage firm analysts specialize by industry. Investors and mutual fund managers also believe that industry factors are important. Their belief is evidenced by the explosive growth in the 1980s in the number and size of mutual funds which specialize by industry.

Empirical studies have attempted to document the importance market and industry factors have on the returns of stocks. A study by King used stock price data from June 1927 to December 1960 to examine how much of the total price movement for a given stock over time was attributable to overall market influences, to industry influences,

---

[2] Julius Shiskin. "Systematic Aspects of Stock Price Fluctuations," in James Lorie and Richard Brealey, eds., *Modern Developments in Investment Management* (New York: Praeger Publishers, 1972), pp. 670–688.

and to factors unique to the firm.[3] He found that market influences explained about 50 percent of the price movements, the industry influences explained about 10 percent, and company factors accounted for the remaining 40 percent. He also noted that the importance of market factors declined over the time period and that the importance of market factors varied greatly from stock to stock.

Meyers enlarged King's sample and extended the analysis through December 1967.[4] While the results were consistent with the earlier study, they also showed that the influence of market factors declined from more than 55 percent prior to 1944 to less than 35 percent for the period 1952 to 1967. Also, after 1952 the influence of industry factors was declining.

In a study using data from January 1966 through June 1970, Livingston used a different methodology to examine the importance of market and industry factors.[5] He estimated that the market explained about 23 percent and the industry about 18 percent of the total variance in stock returns. Therefore, the industry influence was three-fourths as important as the market influence.

In summary, these three studies found that market and industry factors have an important influence on stock returns.

## Consistency of Industry Returns

A related question asks, "Does past industry performance predict future industry performance?" If it does, an investor could just invest in this year's high-return industries and have a profitable portfolio next year. Empirical studies have ranked industries each year by the performance of their firms' common stocks and examined the correlations among rankings from one year to the next. The correlations between one period's ranking and the next period's ranking are low. This means that past industry performance is not a good predictor of future industry performance.

Shifting emphasis from industry to firms, a related question asks, "Do past rankings by returns on common stock of the firms within an industry predict future rankings within an industry?" If they did, the investor could minimize the analysis of individual firms and just invest in the top performing firms in the industry. In doing empirical studies on this issue, researchers have ranked firms within an industry each year by returns on their common stocks and examined the correlations among rankings from one year to the next. Here again, the correlations between one period's rankings and the next period's are low. This means past stock performance within the industry is not a good predictor of future stock performance within the industry.

---

[3] Benjamin F. King. "Market and Industry Factors in Stock Price Behavior," *Journal of Business* 39 (January 1966), pp. 139–190.

[4] Stephen L. Meyers. "A Re-Examination of Market and Industry Factors in Stock Price Behavior," *Journal of Finance* 28 (June 1973), pp. 695–705.

[5] Miles Livingston. "Industry Movements of Common Stocks," *Journal of Finance* 32 (June 1977), pp. 861–874.

## Life Cycle of an Industry

An industry analysis begins with an examination of where the industry is in its life cycle, because the life cycle of an industry greatly influences the investment characteristics of firms within that industry. Exhibit 9–8 shows that the life cycle of an industry can be broken into four periods: experimentation, growth, maturity, and decline.

**Experimentation Period**   The experimentation period begins with the development of a new product upon which a new industry will be built. The firm which developed the product will have little competition as it markets the product and obtains initial sales. The initial financing of a new firm generally comes from the personal savings of the founders. If the market is large, the firm will need additional equity to finance its expansion. Because investment during this period is illiquid and very risky, venture capital firms are the main source of this equity financing.

**Growth Period**   The growth period will be characterized by wide acceptance of the product and, therefore, high sales growth. As soon as competitors see the market acceptance of the product and analyze their entry into the market as an attractive opportunity, the developing firm can expect competition. Competitors aggressively entering the market will cause a reshuffling of market participants. During this period, many firms will make initial public offering of stock. Investors will consider the stocks of the firms in the industry as speculative growth stocks.

---

**EXHIBIT 9–8   Life Cycle of an Industry**

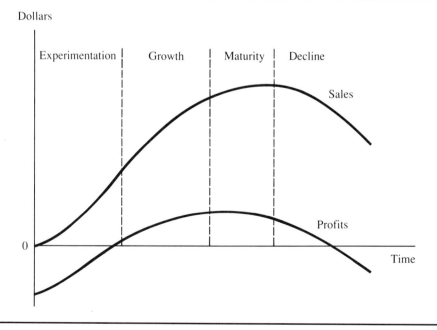

**Maturity Period**   During the maturity period, the growth in sales slows. The stocks of the firms in the industry shift from speculative growth firms to mature growth firms. Management attempts to prolong this period by extensive marketing efforts and development of new products. As the firms' growth and investment opportunities decline, they shift more of their earnings from reinvestment to dividends. Depending on industry characteristics, the stocks might be classified as income, cyclical, or defensive stocks.

**Decline Period**   The decline period is marked by a rate of sales growth less than the rate of growth of the GNP. At the beginning of the period, earning will be maintained and high dividends can be paid. However, when sales declines result in overcapacity in the industry, price cutting is likely to occur and profits and dividends could be reduced. Eventually, all industries face absolute market declines as technological advancement and consumption pattern changes occur. The firms in the dying industry must either move to products in other industries or fail.

## Related Industry Growth Considerations

The life cycle of an industry provides a framework in which to analyze specific questions about factors that influence industry growth. Several of the questions are listed here.

*Demand Growth*

- At what rate is demand growing?
- Can past growth rates be projected into the future?
- What is the total market?
- What percentage of the market has been penetrated?
- Is demand cyclical?
- Are prices stable?

*Nature of the Product*

- What is the life of the product?
- Are there other uses for it?

---

### The Graying of America

People over 65 years are the fastest growing segment of the population, increasing at more than twice the rate for the U.S. population. In the past 100 years the U.S. population has multiplied five times while the over 65 group has multiplied 15 times. Average life expectancy is over 75 years and still increasing. On July 1, 1983, for the first time the number of people in the United States over 65 surpassed the number under 25.

In contrast to the popular image, most older people have adequate to substantial wealth. Their household income on a per capita basis is greater than the national average. Therefore, the industries where older people spend their wealth may offer profitable investment opportunities. Examples are health care, drugs, travel, recreation, and financial services. As the population ages, these will be the growth industries.

- Will technological change make it obsolete?
- Will production methods change?

*Demographic and Social Change*

- How does the birth rate affect demand?
- How will the shifting age distribution of the population affect demand?
- Does the growth of nontraditional households influence demand?
- How will changing expenditure patterns affect demand?

*Political and International Factors*

- Do government expenditures affect demand?
- Do other government policies influence demand?
- Do import and export policies affect demand?
- Will there be increasing foreign competition?
- Is there an international market for the product?

# SUMMARY

Stock prices depend on the earnings of firms and the PE ratios investors assign to those earnings. The PE ratios are determined by the dividend payout, the risk-free rate, the inflation premium, the risk premium, and the dividend growth rate. Stock market cycles lead economic cycles.

The most common approach to investment analysis involves three steps: analysis of the economy, analysis of the industry, and analysis of specific firms. Industry analysis begins with an examination of the life cycle of the industry. The life cycle can be broken into four periods: experimentation, growth, maturity, and decline. The life cycle provides a framework for analyzing other factors that influence industry growth. These factors can be grouped into the categories of demand growth, nature of the product, demographic and social change, and political and international factors.

# QUESTIONS

1. Describe the historical relationships among stock prices, earnings, and PE ratios.
2. What variables influence PE ratios?
3. How do changes in the money supply affect stock prices? Can the investor profit from this relationship?
4. Are stocks good investments to hold during periods of unanticipated inflation?
5. On what two factors does the risk premium which investors demand depend?
6. Describe the relationship between stock market cycles and economic growth.
7. List some of the leading, lagging, and coincident economic indicators.

**8.** What are the three steps in investment analysis? What are the findings of empirical studies of the importance of the three steps?

**9.** Describe the four periods in the life cycle of an industry.

**10.** In addition to product life cycles, what are some of the other factors that influence product demand?

# READINGS

Arnott, Robert D., and Copeland, William A. "The Business Cycle and Security Selection," *Financial Analysts Journal* 41 (March–April 1985): 26–32.

> *This study tests multiple security selection models over time. It examines the performance of the models over the business cycle and during inflationary periods.*

Churchill, Neil C., and Lewis, Virginia L. "The Five Stages of Small Business Growth," *Harvard Business Review* 61 (May–June 1983): 30–50.

> *These authors build a framework consisting of five stages through which small companies pass. Assessing the stage at which a company is operating can help one better understand existing problems and anticipate future challenges.*

Peavy, John W., III, and Goodman, David A. "How Inflation, Risk and Corporate Profitability Affect Common Stock Returns," *Financial Analysts Journal* 41 (September–October 1985): 59–65.

> *This study examines these relationships using market data from 1966 to 1981.*

Porter, Michael E. "Industry Structure and Competitive Strategy," *Financial Analysts Journal* 36 (July–August 1980): 30–41.

> *This article presents a framework for analyzing industry competition.*

U.S. Department of Commerce. *Handbook of Cyclical Indicators.* Washington, D.C.: U.S. Government Printing Office, 1984.

> *This reference book describes the economic series and composite indexes published monthly in the* Business Conditions Digest. *It also contains historical data on the series and indexes.*

# CHOOSING INVESTMENTS

# Common Stock

## OUTLINE

## OBJECTIVES

When you have finished studying this chapter, you should understand

1. The sources of investment risk.

2. The categories used to describe the performance of common stocks under various conditions.

3. What stock dividends and stock splits are and how they affect the value of common stock.

4. The rights of stockholders and current issues in corporate control.

# 10

## *Future Stock Prices*

In his most famous book, *The General Theory of Employment, Interest, and Money,* John Maynard Keynes wrote

> Professional investment may be likened to those newspaper competitions in which the competitors have to pick out the six prettiest faces from a hundred photographs, the prize being awarded to the competitor whose choice most nearly corresponds to the average preferences of the competitors as a whole, so that each competitor has to pick, not those faces which he himself finds prettiest, but those which he thinks likeliest to catch the fancy of the other competitors, all of whom are looking at the problem from the same point of view. It is not a case of choosing those which, to the best of one's judgment, are really the prettiest, nor even those which average opinion genuinely thinks the prettiest. We have reached the third degree where we devote our intelligences to anticipating what average opinion expects the average opinion to be. And there are some, I believe, who practise the fourth, fifth and higher degrees.*

---

\* Keynes, John Maynard. *The General Theory of Employment, Interest, and Money* (New York: Harcourt Brace, 1936), p. 156.

## *INTRODUCTION*

An investor should choose common stocks based on the amount and the form of the expected returns as well as on the sources and amount of risk. A stockholder hopes to receive two forms of return from common stock: dividends and capital appreciation. Although firms vary drastically in the percentage of their earnings which they pay out in dividends, most of those which pay dividends try to declare at least the same dollar amount each year. Usually, therefore, an investor can easily approximate the return from dividends. The investor may receive additional return in the form of capital appreciation when he sells the stock. Estimating the return from capital appreciation is more difficult than estimating dividends because the future selling price depends on both market conditions and the prospects for the firm when the stock is sold.

In this chapter, we examine the sources of risk in securities and then the categories used to describe common stock performance. Next, we examine dividend payment procedures, stock dividends, and stock splits. Finally, we look at the rights of common stockholders and some of the current controversies relating to stockholder rights and institutional investors. In Chapter 11, we will introduce techniques to help the investor estimate corporate earnings and growth rates.

# SOURCES OF RISK

In order to do detailed analysis of the risk of an investment, the investor must examine the sources of risk in the expected return. These sources can be broken down for analysis into six categories: business risk, financial risk, management risk, market risk, interest rate risk, and purchasing power risk. Although this chapter is about common stock, the discussion of sources of risk applies to all securities.

## Business Risk

**Business risk** is the chance that the firm you invest in will not be as successful as planned. There are numerous causes for a firm's poor performance. Expected demand for its products may not materialize. Costs may increase drastically. Competitors may be more innovative or aggressive. Products may not perform as well as expected.

| EXAMPLE |

On April 10, 1987, Bic Corporation's common stock dropped 25 percent on reports that its disposable lighter was subject to many product liability lawsuits. Plaintiffs charged that when the lighters malfunction they can cause fires and injuries. The company argued that most accidents resulted from carelessness rather than defects in the lighter.                                                      □

## Financial Risk

**Financial risk** is the chance that the firm's use of debt financing will adversely affect the returns to its investors. Most firms borrow money to use in the business. These firms plan to gain by using the borrowed money to earn a return greater than the cost of the borrowed funds. If they successfully use the borrowed money, these firms will have additional profits. However, if they do not earn a return greater than the cost of the borrowed funds, the interest that must be paid becomes an additional burden that will lower the profits available to equity investors. An additional risk exists if the firm is unable to pay the interest or repay the principal when due. The lenders can go to court and force the firm out of business.

| EXAMPLE | In July 1983, Washington Public Power Supply System failed to make the interest payments on some of its bonds. The system had borrowed $2.25 billion in the 1970s to build five nuclear power plants. Because it experienced delays and high cost overruns, it was unable to complete four of the plants. Therefore, it was unable to earn the money necessary to pay the interest on the bonds. □ |

## Management Risk

**Management risk** is the chance that the managers of the firm will not perform as well as expected. They could fail in developing and carrying out a successful long-term strategy. They could make marketing, production, or financing mistakes. Fraud could possibly occur. As we will discuss later in this chapter, management might put its interests ahead of the stockholders' interests.

| EXAMPLE | In June 1983, Texas Instruments' stock fell drastically after the firm unexpectedly announced that it would have a large loss for the second quarter of the year. The loss resulted from problems in its home computer business. Texas Instruments had overestimated the demand for its model 99/4A home computer. It and other home computer manufacturers had accumulated large inventories and had to cut prices and offer large rebates in order to stimulate sales. □ |

| EXAMPLE | On April 19, 1987, Merrill Lynch & Co. announced that it had suffered the largest securities trading loss in history as a result of unauthorized mortgage-backed securities dealing by a senior trader. The $250 million loss occurred when a trader far exceeded his limits in acquiring securities. The value of the securities dropped when interest rates suddenly went up. Critics argued that Merrill Lynch lacked the internal controls to catch the unauthorized trading sooner. □ |

## Market Risk

While business, financial, and management risk are influenced by the specific firm's management, the three remaining sources of risk are not related to the management decisions of the particular firms. They are part of the economic environment and affect all securities.

**Market risk** is the chance that investors will become less willing to hold securities and, therefore, most securities will sell at lower prices. In other words, it is the risk that "the market will go down." Some analysts would explain market risk in terms of "investor psychology."

The factors that change the willingness of investors to purchase securities may be grouped into three broad categories. First, investors' expectations of returns may become lower because they fear worse economic conditions. Second, investors' willingness to purchase securities may decrease because social, political, and economic events make them view the securities as more risky. Third, even if investors' views of the future do not change, they (as a group) may become less willing to invest or to bear risk.

| EXAMPLE |

At the end of 1984 the price of the stocks in the S&P 500 was 10.07 times the earnings of these stocks. At the end of 1985, investors were willing to pay a price 14.46 times earnings. This increase in the price-to-earnings (PE) ratio reflects a drastic change in investors' willingness to invest in stocks. □

## Interest Rate Risk

**Interest rate risk** is the chance of decreases in the value of outstanding securities because interest rates throughout the economy rise. There is an inverse relationship between interest rates and security prices. If interest rates rise, investors will want to buy the new securities paying higher rates. The only way that previously outstanding securities paying lower rates can be sold is if the price of the securities is lowered.

| EXAMPLE |

In 1981, the Federal Reserve drastically decreased the rate of growth in the money supply in order to slow the rate of inflation. This caused record high interest rates and thereby lower stock and bond prices. In the second half of 1982 the Federal Reserve, in reaction to the severe recession and a lower rate of inflation, allowed the money supply to increase greatly. This caused stock and bond prices to rise correspondingly. □

| EXAMPLE |

During the last two weeks of April 1987, there was a substantial rise in long-term mortgage interest rates. Brokerage firms, mortgage bankers, and thrifts suffered huge losses as the value of their inventories of mortgage-backed securities dropped 7 to 9 percent. □

## Purchasing Power Risk

**Purchasing power risk** is the chance that the money returned on an investment will purchase less than expected because of inflation. Purchasing power risk is especially significant in investments such as bonds that promise a fixed amount of return. Investments with variable returns may have greater returns in inflationary times, but investments with fixed returns will not.

| EXAMPLE |

As a result of the high, unanticipated inflation of the late 1960s and the 1970s, most individuals who owned bonds were victims of purchasing power risk. A drastic example of an investment that suffered from purchasing power risk is American Telephone and Telegraph Company's 40-year debentures paying

$2\frac{7}{8}$ percent interest issued on June 1, 1947. The debenture issue was redeemed at maturity value on June 1, 1987. ☐

# PERFORMANCE UNDER VARIOUS CONDITIONS

To aid the investor in selecting them, stocks are commonly grouped into categories that reflect their expected return and risk characteristics. Although these categories are

## Dividend Payment Records

According to the NYSE, these stocks have been paying continuous dividends since the eighteenth and nineteenth centuries.

| Began | Stock | Began | Stock |
|---|---|---|---|
| 1784 | Bank of New York Co., Inc. | 1882 | Affiliated Pubs., Inc. |
| 1785 | Bank of Boston Corporation | 1882 | Bell Canada Enter., Inc. |
| 1791 | Fleet Financial Group, Inc. | 1883 | Carter-Wallace, Inc. |
| 1804 | Norstar Bancorp, Inc. | 1883 | Exxon Corporation |
| 1813 | Citicorp | 1885 | Consolidated Edison Co. |
| 1813 | First Fidelity Bancorp. | 1885 | Eli Lilly and Company |
| 1827 | Chemical New York Corp. | 1885 | UGI Corporation |
| 1840 | Morgan (J. P.) & Co., Inc. | 1886 | United Water Res., Inc. |
| 1841 | KeyCorp | 1889 | West Point–Pepperell, Inc. |
| 1848 | Chase Manhattan Corp. | 1890 | American Brands, Inc. |
| 1850 | Connecticut Energy Corp. | 1890 | Boston Edison Co. |
| 1851 | Connecticut Natural Gas Corp. | 1890 | Commonwealth Edison Co. |
| 1852 | Bay State Gas Co. | 1890 | Hydraulic Company |
| 1852 | Manufacturers Hanover Corp. | 1891 | Procter & Gamble Co. |
| 1852 | Washington Gas Light Co. | 1891 | South. New Engl. Telecomm |
| 1853 | Cincinnati Gas & Electric Co. | 1891 | Times Mirror Company |
| 1853 | Continental Corporation | 1892 | Westvaco Corporation |
| 1863 | Pennwalt Corporation | 1893 | Coca-Cola Co. |
| 1863 | Singer Company | 1894 | Amoco Corp. |
| 1865 | Irving Bank Corp. | 1895 | Colgate-Palmolive Co. |
| 1865 | PNC Financial Corp. | 1895 | Mellon Bank Corp. |
| 1866 | First Wachovia Corp. | 1895 | Unisys Corp. |
| 1866 | Travelers Corporation | 1896 | BET Public Limited Co. |
| 1867 | CIGNA Corporation | 1898 | General Mills, Inc. |
| 1868 | American Express Co. | 1898 | Shell Trans. & Trad., PLC |
| 1877 | Stanley Works | 1898 | Springs Industries, Inc. |
| 1879 | Cincinnati Bell, Inc. | 1899 | Borden, Inc. |
| 1881 | American Tel. & Tel. Co. | 1899 | General Electric Co. |
| 1881 | Corning Glass Works | 1899 | PPG Industries, Inc. |
| 1881 | Security Pacific Corp. | 1899 | Wash. Water Power Co. |

widely used, there are no universally accepted definitions of them. Therefore, the placement of a stock in one category or another is sometimes arbitrary. For our purposes, we will identify six categories of stocks.

**1. Income stocks** represent ownership of companies that pay high dividends and therefore give a high priority to maintaining their dividend records. Because these firms need stable revenue in order to pay stable dividends, they tend to be in mature, noncyclical industries. The stocks usually have betas of less than 1. Utility companies are the largest group in this category.

**2. Blue chip stocks** represent ownership of large, well-managed firms, which can be expected to grow as the economy grows. These firms have a history of consistent earnings and regular dividends. The betas of these stocks are around 1. General Electric and International Telephone and Telegraph are examples of blue chip stocks.

**3. Mature growth stocks** represent ownership of well-established firms in growth industries. The nature of their products, combined with aggressive management, should permit them to grow faster than the economy. Because they need most of their earnings to finance future growth, they tend to pay low dividends. The betas of their stocks are usually above 1. IBM, Litton Industries, and Xerox are examples of mature growth stocks.

**4. Speculative growth stocks** represent ownership of unproven young firms with the potential for spectacular growth. Investors buy the stock based on the promise of the future rather than on the firm's past record. Some of these stocks will provide fabulous returns, but most will perform poorly. The stocks of these firms often have high betas although factors unique to each firm are more important than their sensitivity to the market. Genentech, Inc., and Commodore International, Ltd., are examples of speculative growth stocks.

**5. Cyclical stocks** represent ownership of firms that are very sensitive to economic cycles and therefore tend to have high betas. Consumers buy the products of these firms in good times and put off their purchase in bad times. Cyclical companies are often in industries that require large amounts of expensive plant equipment. When volume of production is low, these fixed expenses cause large losses. Automobile companies, steel producers, and commercial airlines are examples of cyclical stocks.

**6. Defensive stocks** represent ownership in firms that continue to do well in bad economic times. Therefore, they have low or possibly negative betas. They are the opposite of cyclical firms in that we buy their products no matter what the economic conditions are. Cigarette, food, and beverage firms are the best examples.

# DIVIDEND PAYMENTS

Most corporations pay dividends quarterly. For example, Ball Corporation pays an annual dividend of 82 cents per share or 20.5 cents per share per quarter. The actual payment procedure is important to the investor. This procedure is also used for stock splits and rights offerings.

### Unbundled Stock Units

Common stock offers the investor dividend income, increases in dividend income, and capital gains. On December 5, 1988, four major companies—American Express Co., Dow Chemical Co., Pfizer Inc., and Sara Lee Corp.—announced plans to offer their shareholders the opportunity to exchange some of their common stock for a new type of security, unbundled stock units. Under the exchange plan, each share of common stock could be exchanged for (1) a 30-year bond that pays interest at the stock's current dividend rate, (2) preferred stock that initially pays no dividends but matches any dividend increases on the company's common stock during the 30 years, and (3) a security, similar to a warrant, that allows the owner to profit if the stock increases in value. Each of the three securities would trade independently after the exchange. Since the firms were offering to exchange from only 6.3 to 20 percent of their outstanding common stock, they would still have the traditional stock trading in the market.

The immediate question is whether the new securities should sell for more than the old common stock. One factor is that the interest on the new bond will be a tax deductible expense for the company while dividends are not deductible. This creates value for the firm—at the expense of the U.S. Treasury. A second factor is that the companies are exchanging some debt for equity. Observation of the financial markets in 1988 led many managers to believe investors wanted firms to use more debt financing. Moving toward the "optimal" capital structure would create value. A negative factor is that the markets for the securities would not be as liquid. Although the new securities were to be listed on the NYSE, they would not have nearly the volume of the common stock. On the day of the announcement, the prices of all four firms' common stock went up. The market believed the positives outweighed the negatives.

On March 28, 1989, Shearson announced that the unbundled stock unit concept was dead. The Securities and Exchange Commission's chief accountant had ruled that in calculating earnings per share these units must be counted as shares outstanding. This would result in lower earnings per share; therefore, the companies dropped the exchange proposal.

## Dividend Dates

Four dates are important in the payment procedure for corporate dividends: the declaration date, the **holder-of-record date,** the **ex dividend date,** and the payment date.

**1.** *Declaration date.* Dividends must be declared by the firm's board of directors. The declaration date is the day when the board formally decides to pay a dividend in the near future. On April 28, 1987, the directors of Ball Corporation declared a quarterly dividend of 20.5 cents per share payable June 15, 1987, to holders of record on June 1, 1987. The *Wall Street Journal* and other newspapers have a daily column that lists all dividend announcements.

In good years, cyclical stocks sometimes pay an annual extra dividend in addition to the regular quarterly dividends. The term extra dividend communicates to stockholders that the payment is the result of unusually good performance by the firm and that they should not expect the extra dividend every year.

**2.** *Holder-of-record date.* The firm must use its list of stockholders as of a particular date to pay dividends. Shareholders listed at the close of the corporate books on the holder-of-record date are the ones who will receive the dividends. Ball

Corporation mailed dividend checks to all stockholders on its books at the close of business on Monday, June 1, 1987.

**3.** *Ex dividend date.* The securities industry uses a five business-day settlement rule when stocks are bought and sold. If you purchase stock, you must pay within five business days. If you sell stock, you must deliver the certificates within five business days. To receive a dividend, you must own the stock five business days before the holder-of-record date. Therefore, the stock sells without its dividend, that is ex dividend, four business days before the holder-of-record date. If you buy the stock on the ex dividend date, you do not get the dividend; your name will not get on the company's books by the holder-of-record date. If nothing else happened to affect its value, the stock price would fall the amount of the dividend on the ex dividend date. Ball Corporation's stock went ex dividend on Tuesday, May 26, 1987. On the ex dividend date, an *x* is printed next to the volume figures in the stock tables in newspapers.

**4.** *Payment date.* The payment date is the day the firm actually mails out the dividend checks. Ball Corporation mailed out checks on June 15, 1987.

## Stock Dividends

In addition to, or instead of, paying cash dividends, a corporation sometimes gives its stockholders more stock in the corporation. This is referred to as a stock dividend. A stock dividend does not change any stockholder's proportional ownership in the firm. For example, if an investor owns 100,000 shares of the 400,000 shares outstanding (25 percent) of a company's stock and the company were to pay a 10 percent stock dividend, this investor would then own 110,000 shares out of the 440,000 shares outstanding, still 25 percent, of the company's stock. Because a stock's value is based on the firm's assets and the earning power of those assets and because a stock dividend does not increase assets or earning power, a stock dividend does not increase a stockholder's wealth. When there is a stock dividend, the market price per share falls to reflect the fact that each share now represents ownership of a smaller proportion of the firm.

## Stock Splits

While stock dividends increase the number of shares outstanding by a small percentage, usually 2 to 10 percent, stock splits increase the number of shares outstanding by much larger amounts, usually 25 to 400 percent. In a stock split, a larger number of new shares is issued to replace the old shares. For example, if an investor owns 100,000 shares of the 400,000 shares outstanding (25 percent) of a company's stock and the company were to declare a two for one stock split, this investor would then own 200,000 shares of the 800,000 shares outstanding, still 25 percent, of the company's stock. As with stock dividends, stock splits do not change a stockholder's proportional ownership of the firm, and the market price per share drops to reflect the lower proportional ownership of the firm. An investor whose 100,000 shares were worth $1,000,000 ($10 per share market price) when the stock split two for one would now own 200,000 shares worth $1,000,000 ($5 per share market price).

### Dividend Reinvestment Plans

Over 1,000 U.S. corporations have established procedures so that stockholders can automatically reinvest their dividends into the company's stock if they so desire. Usually, the money from the dividends is used to purchase stock in the market. Sometimes, however, the corporation issues new shares. In either case, the corporation normally pays all commissions and fees. A few corporations even allow the stock to be purchased at 3 to 5 percent discounts. Some plans even allow shareholders to invest up to an additional $5,000 or so per quarter in their stock commission free. Discounts on the additional investment amounts are rare.

If under the dividend reinvestment plan the same dollar amount is reinvested each quarter, dollar cost averaging occurs. That is, your average cost per share is lowered because you automatically purchase more shares when prices are low than you purchase when prices are high. On the negative side, the dividends are still taxable income even if reinvested, and keeping track of the cost of your stock holdings is a little more burdensome. On balance, however, dividend reinvestment plans are attractive for long-term investment in good companies.

An important question in a stock dividend or stock split is what is going to happen to the cash dividends. If a stockholder is going to receive a larger total amount of dividends after the stock dividend or split, the firm has in effect raised its dividends. For example, if there were a 5 percent stock dividend and the cash dividend per share remained $1, the shareholder would receive a larger total dividend in the future. However, if the stock were split four for one and the dividend per share were reduced from $1 to 25 cents, there would be no dividend increase. If a dividend increase reflects management's expectations of higher profits, it is good news for the stockholders.

---

**EXAMPLE**

On April 10, 1986, Ford Motor Co., citing improvement in its "underlying profitability," declared a 3 for 2 stock split and increased its quarterly cash dividend 18 percent to 82.5 cents from 70 cents on a presplit basis. That day the stock closed at $83.375, up $2.75. Most analysts would argue the stock went up because of the announcement of increased future profitability, not because of the stock split. ☐

There are several possible reasons a corporation might declare a stock dividend or split. Perhaps the board of directors believes that the shareholders will consider the stock split or stock dividend as good news. The directors might possibly desire to lower the price per share to a more affordable range. For example, a stock selling for $200 a share and split four for one would result in a new price of $50 which is in the more common range for a stock price. Investors who like to buy a certain number of shares, perhaps one hundred, of a stock may then be more likely to buy it. Occasionally, a stock's price becomes very low and the corporation declares a reverse split in order to raise it. In a reverse split, the outstanding shares are exchanged for a smaller number of new shares. For example, if a firm's stock were selling at 75 cents per share, a ten for one reverse split might be declared. In this case, stockholders would receive one new share worth about $7.50 for every ten old shares.

### Stock Repurchases

In the days following the market crash on October 19, 1987, more than 400 companies announced stock repurchase plans. Most of these firms were taking advantage of their high levels of liquidity after five years of economic expansion and the low prices of their shares after the crash. Many firms hoped that their repurchase announcements would stop the fall of their share prices.

A firm's repurchase of some of its outstanding stock may be viewed as a substitute to the payment of a large cash dividend. In both cases, money flows from the firm to its shareholders. Shareholders often find a stock repurchase attractive because the repurchase gives the shareholders flexibility in deciding how much income they want now from the corporation. They can consider their individual income and tax positions when making their decision. The firm's buying should help support the price of the shares not repurchased.

A firm can repurchase its shares in the open market over a period of time or by a tender offer. A tender offer invites shareholders to submit, or tender, their shares to the firm for an established price. The stock repurchase, of course, reduces a firm's equity and liquidity. The money used is not available to finance future investments by the firm.

Another reason a corporation might declare a stock dividend or split is to increase the number of shareholders. This increase does not take place immediately, but as the stock is resold, the larger number of shares will likely result in more stockholders. A larger number of stockholders will make it more difficult for a group hostile to management to purchase enough shares to take control of the corporation.

# STOCKHOLDER RIGHTS

The rights of common stockholders are established by the laws of the state in which the corporation is chartered and by the provisions of the corporate charter. These rights can be grouped into two categories: collective rights and individual stockholder rights.

## Collective Rights

Collective rights are given to the stockholders as a group. Although details vary from state to state, common stockholders usually have the collective right to

— Amend the corporate charter (with the approval of the state officials)

— Adopt and amend bylaws

— Elect the directors

— Authorize the sale of major assets

— Approve merger agreements

— Change the amount of authorized common stock

— Authorize the issue of preferred stock, bonds, and other securities

## *Individual Stockholder Rights*

Specific rights are given to the stockholders as individuals. Although their details also vary from state to state, individual stockholders usually have the right to

— Vote in the manner prescribed in the corporate charter

— Sell their stock whenever and to whomever they please

— Inspect the corporate books

— Receive dividends if and when declared by the board of directors

— Share in the residual assets of the corporation at the time of its liquidation

### *Master Limited Partnerships*

The number of master limited partnerships traded on the organized exchanges grew dramatically during the 1980s. At the beginning of the decade, master limited partnerships were rarely found outside the oil and gas industries. By the end of the decade they were being used by firms in many industries. Master limited partnerships combine features of corporations with those of partnerships.

A corporation is a legal entity chartered by the state government for the purpose of conducting a business. This form of organization provides several advantages to investors. First, the corporation has an unlimited life. It can continue even if the founders die or move on to other pursuits. Second, the owners of a corporation—stockholders—have limited liability. Therefore, the maximum that they can lose is the amount of their investment; they cannot be sued for the debts of the business. Third, stockholders in a corporation can sell their stock whenever and to whomever they desire. Finally, the corporation files its own income tax return. Stockholders report on their income tax return only any gains or losses on the sale of the stock and any dividends paid to them by the corporation.

A partnership is an association of two or more people for the purpose of conducting a business. Each partner has the authority to conduct business for the partnership, and each partner has unlimited liability for the debts of the partnership. The partnership ends with the death of any partner and it is difficult for a partner to sell his or her share.

Technically, if one partner dies or is selling out to another person, a completely new partnership has to be formed. For tax purposes, the partnership does not file a return; each partner reports his or her share of the profits or losses of the business on his or her personal income tax return.

Most investors do not want to be involved in running the business and most fear the liability feature of a partnership. Therefore, the law allows for the existence of a second type of partnership involving a limited partner. Limited partners invest money in the partnership, do not participate in the management, and have limited liability. Therefore, all they can lose is the amount they have invested. Most partnership agreements also make it easy for limited partners to transfer their interest to another party or to heirs.

Master limited partnerships provide for thousands of limited partnership shares. These securities are sold to the public by investment bankers and traded in the OTC market and on exchanges just like common stock. Because of the features of the tax law, a master limited partnership is an attractive form of organization for a firm that plans to pay out to investors most of its earnings. Only the investors, not the partnerships, will pay tax on those earnings. On the other hand, the corporate form is more attractive to growing firms that are reinvesting most of their earnings because investors do not want to pay taxes on earnings they do not receive.

## Stockholders Versus Managers

One corporation model, known as **contractual theory,** views the corporation as a set of explicit and implicit contracts among stockholders, debt holders, managers, and workers. These contracts define rights, obligations, and payoffs under alternative circumstances. Most parties opt for limited risk and fixed returns. Stockholders, however, have ultimate control, have a claim on the earnings and assets remaining after paying all other claims, and, therefore, bear the most risk.

Contracts reduce but do not eliminate the conflict between parties. In particular, some conflicts between stockholders and managers remain. Managers can be viewed as the agents of the shareholders. An **agency relationship** exists when one or more principals employ another person, the agent, to perform some service and delegate some authority to that agent. Conflicts arise when the goals of the agent clash with the goals of the principal.

In the case of managers, two areas of conflict are perquisites and risk preferences. First, managers may take excessive perquisites such as luxury offices, fancy executive dining rooms, chauffeured limousines, and expensive club memberships. The stockholders bear the cost of these benefits. Second, managers may avoid risky projects that diversified stockholders would want undertaken. If the projects did not work out and the firm failed, the managers would suffer the loss of their jobs. On the other hand, because most stockholders are diversified, they emphasize the returns and risk of their total portfolio and would be willing to undertake risky projects if the expected returns were high enough.

A drastic example of the conflict between managers and owners is a leveraged buyout of the firm by managers. In a leveraged buyout, managers arrange a legally complex loan backed by the assets of the firm. The money from the loan is used to purchase stock from the shareholders. The firm is then ''taken private'' by management instead of continuing as a publicly held corporation. Conflict exists because at the time of purchase, it is in the stockholders' interest that the stock price be high while it is in the managers' interest that it be low.

One check on management is the possibility that it will be ousted as the result of a proxy fight or hostile takeover. A proxy fight involves stockholders soliciting proxy votes for candidates for directorships who are running against the nominees supported by management. A hostile takeover involves an attempt to buy enough stock to take control of the firm. Both proxy fights and hostile takeovers are most likely to occur when a firm's stock price is depressed relative to its potential. The best way for management to avoid proxy fights and hostile takeover attempts is to keep the stock price high. More questionable ways to fight hostile takeovers are poison pills and greenmail.

A **poison pill** is an agreement that destroys the value of the firm if a hostile takeover occurs. One example is debt contracts that make the firm's debts payable immediately if management changes. Another is an employment contract that gives huge retirement bonuses to managers if the firm is taken over. These retirement bonuses, which will take a large portion of the firm's assets, are called golden parachutes.

**Greenmail** is paid when a potential acquirer buys a large amount of stock and management fears a hostile takeover. Management has the firm repurchase the stock

## The Battle for control of CBS

The September 1986 change of management at CBS resulted from a very public battle for control. The main players were:

Thomas Wyman, chairman and chief executive

William Paley, age 84, CBS founder and director

Laurence Tisch, chairman of Loews Corporation and one of the richest men in the United States

In 1985, Senator Jesse Helms suggested conservatives buy up CBS shares in the hope of becoming "Dan Rather's boss." The effort failed, but it was followed by a takeover attempt by Ted Turner of cable TV. Turner offered to buy the CBS stock with low-quality bonds. Wyman fought off Turner but CBS took on a lot of debt in doing so. At the time of the Turner takeover attempt, Tisch bought more than 5 percent of the CBS stock and

was elected a director. He allied himself with Wyman in opposing Turner.

By the September 17, 1986, board of director's meeting, Tisch had become dissatisfied with CBS performance. Competition from cable and independent TV stations was increasing, advertising revenue was declining, and costs were rising. CBS reported its first quarterly loss ever and was laying off employees. By this date, Tisch owned 24.9 percent of the CBS stock and Paley owned 8.1 percent of the stock.

The 14 CBS directors met for over nine hours. At the end of the meeting, it was announced that Wyman had resigned, Tisch was appointed chief executive, and Paley was appointed acting chairman. Control of CBS had been transferred.

Source: "Civil War at CBS," *Newsweek*, September 15, 1986, pp. 46–54; and "Corporate Shoot-out at Black Rock," *Time*, September 22, 1986, pp. 68–72.

## Greenmail

Greenmail is the repurchase by the corporation of its stock from a potential acquirer of control. This opportunity is not offered to the other shareholders. Therefore, greenmail creates disillusionment and resentment in individual investors who see it as favoring big shareholders over them. They also

realize it involves management putting their job security ahead of the stockholders' interests. In recent years, some companies have put antigreenmail provisions in their corporate charters and congress is considering laws limiting it.

Here are some examples of greenmail.

### WHO HAS PAID GREENMAIL LATELY

|  | Goodyear Tire & Rubber | CPC International | Federated Department Stores | Gillette |
|---|---|---|---|---|
| Investor | James Goldsmith | Ronald Perelman | Haft Family | Ronald Perelman |
| Buyout price per share | $49.50 | $88.50 | $88.88 | $59.50 |
| Previous close | $41.75 | $84.13 | $86.63 | $56.63 |
| Price 11/15/86 | $42.88 | $77.13 | $86.13 | $47.00 |

Source: Reprinted from December 8, 1986 issue of *Business Week* by special permission, copyright © 1986 by McGraw-Hill, Inc.

### The Institutional Investor and Corporate Control

As institutions become the largest owners of corporate stock, they are becoming more active in corporate governance issues. Pension funds are leading the movement. In 1965, pension funds owned 6 percent of all corporate stock; in 1986, they owned 25 percent. The Federal Reserve Board estimates pension funds will own 50 percent by the year 2000. The funds argue that they must be more active investors because their size prevents them from continuing the old practice of just selling the stock if they are dissatisfied with management.

Angry about companies paying green mail, adopting poison pills, approving golden parachutes, and changing the traditional one share–one vote rule, the public pension funds formed the Council of Institutional Investors, which now represents over 50 funds controlling $200 billion worth of investments. The Council has adopted a "Shareholders Bill of Rights," which demands stockholder approval of significant corporate actions. Examples are issuing stock that would dilute voting powers of existing shares by 20 percent or more, selling 20 percent or more of the corporate assets to hostile bidders, paying greenmail, or adopting poison pills. In Spring 1987, pension funds led proxy fights against antitakeover measures in about 40 stockholder meetings including those of International Paper Co., United Technologies, Control Data, and J.C. Penney.

Source: "And Now, Proxy Power," *Time*, April 21, 1986, p. 62; and "The Battle for Corporate Control," *Business Week*, May 18, 1987, pp. 102–109.

from the aggressor at a price above the current market price without offering to purchase the stock of other owners at this price. Often the stock price declines after the payment of greenmail because stockholders know the takeover attempt from which they might have benefitted is over.

## SUMMARY

The return on an investment in common stock is affected by business risk, financial risk, management risk, market risk, interest rate risk, and purchasing power risk. To help explain their performance under various conditions, stocks can be grouped into six categories: income stocks, blue chip stocks, mature growth stocks, speculative growth stocks, cyclical stocks, and defensive stocks.

Dividends must be declared by the board of directors. The directors establish a holder-of-record date. A stock goes ex dividend four business days before the holder-of-record date. Stock dividends and stock splits do not increase a shareholder's wealth because a stock's value depends on the future earnings of the firm. A stockholder's percentage ownership of those future earnings does not change as the result of a stock dividend or stock split.

Stockholders have collective and individual rights under state law and corporate charters. Recently, practices such as poison pills, greenmail, and golden parachutes have made pension funds much more active investors. Public pension funds have formed the Council of Institutional Investors which has adopted a "Shareholders Bill of Rights."

# QUESTIONS

1. In what forms might a stockholder receive returns from common stock? Which form of return is more difficult to predict in dollar amounts? Why?

2. Define the six sources of risk that affect investments. Which are specific to the firm and which affect all securities?

3. What are the long-run factors that influence interest rates? What are the short-run factors?

4. Define each of the categories into which stocks are commonly grouped.

5. Explain the dividend payment dates.

6. What is the difference between a stock dividend and a stock split? Why do they not increase the stockholder's wealth? Why do firms have them?

7. List the collective rights and individual rights of common stockholders.

8. How do contractual theory and agency theory relate to common stockholders?

9. Do you believe it is wrong for corporations to pay greenmail, to approve poison pills, and to provide golden parachutes? Why or why not?

# READINGS

Barnea, Amir, Haugen, Robert A., and Sembet, Lemma W. "Market Imperfections, Agency Problems, and Capital Structure: A Review," *Financial Management* 10 (Summer 1981): 7–22.

> *This article is a good summary and integration of the literature on agency problems and capital structure.*

Diamond, Stephen C. *Leveraged Buyouts.* Homewood, IL: Dow Jones-Irwin, 1985.

> *This book explores all aspects of leveraged buyouts including key financial and technical issues.*

Miller, Robert E., and Reilly, Frank K. "An Examination of Mispricing, Returns, and Uncertainty for Initial Public Offerings," *Financial Management* 16 (Summer 1987): 33–38.

> *This article examines the returns on 510 new issues of common stock.*

# Analyzing the Firm

## OUTLINE

## OBJECTIVES

When you have finished studying this chapter, you should understand

1. The importance of evaluating the firm's strategic plan, its market and products, its management, and its workers.

2. The important factors to examine in an income statement, a balance sheet, a statement of stockholders' equity, a statement of cash flows, and the notes to financial statements.

3. The concept of earnings quality.

4. The factors that limit the sustainable growth rate of the firm.

# 11

## *Intangible Assets*

In 1986, the investment firm of Kohlberg Kravis Roberts & Co. (KKR) purchased Beatrice Cos. for $8.2 billion. KKR put up $417 million in equity, borrowed $5.8 million, and assumed $2 billion in Beatrice debt in what at that time was the largest leveraged buyout ever. KKR planned to earn profits many times its equity investment by breaking Beatrice up and selling the pieces. Parts of it sold quickly, but others did not. Although there were tax advantages in selling the remaining pieces as a going concern, an analysis of the company's balance sheet gives some evidence of why this was very difficult.

For years Beatrice had been purchasing firms and using the "pooling of interest" method to account for the excess of the value of the common stock it issued for the purchase over the book value of the assets it obtained. This excess was entered on its books as goodwill and slowly depreciated. Over the years, Beatrice had issued common stock with a market value of $440 million to purchase assets with a book value of $204 million. That resulted in goodwill of $236 million.

After the KKR purchase, when Beatrice sold off parts of itself, the goodwill remained on its books as other assets decreased. Therefore, goodwill became a larger percentage of total assets and the depreciation of it each year became a larger percentage of income. In fact, on August 31, 1988, intangible assets, mostly goodwill, exceeded stockholders' equity by $1.2 billion. Hence, the difficulty in selling Beatrice.

## INTRODUCTION

The basis of an evaluation of any equity investment is a thorough analysis of the future prospects of the firm. The investor must forecast the future performance of the firm. The objectives of the forecast are accurate estimates of future earnings and their probable growth as well as the risks the firm faces. Financial statements provide historical information that helps predict future performance; however, the dynamics of the firm are more important as well as more difficult to evaluate.

# DYNAMICS OF THE FIRM

In examining the dynamics of the firm, the investor must evaluate its strategic plan, its market and products, its management, and its workers.

## Strategic Plan

A formal long-range plan is necessary for the success of a business enterprise in today's complex environment. Along with knowing the outline of this long-range plan, the investor should evaluate management's planning skills and its ability to execute the plan. The plan should identify which market needs the firm's products fulfill, and its strengths and weaknesses should be noted. The long-range plan is the basis for the firm's short-range plans and its forecasted financial performance.

For competitive reasons, a firm cannot make public its plans and forecasts but it can communicate its general thrust. Articles in the business and trade press describe firms' long-range plans and problems. The investor should carefully read annual reports and other corporate releases in order to appraise firms' strategies.

## Market and Products

The investor must understand the firm's products and its markets. Products should be developed in order to fulfill market needs rather than as an extension of new technology that does not focus on the market demand for them. Extensive market evaluations should be the basis for the sales forecast. The stage of development and the life cycle of each product must be known. The firm should have product diversification; that is, it needs several successful products along with several new ones under development. Profit margins must provide reasonable returns, and production capacity must relate to sales forecasts.

The number and strength of the firm's competitors must be analyzed. What are this firm's advantages over manufacturers of similar products? Advantages could be a technological lead, an overlooked segment of the market, or lower production costs. Perhaps the market is big enough or expanding rapidly enough to absorb sufficient sales volume from all producers for several years. The analyst should estimate the breakeven volume and the profits and losses that come from operating above or below it.

## Management

Because people will be the main determinant of the success of the firm, an evaluation of the quality of the management and workers must be made. Management should consist of a team rather than being based on one person. That team should have successful in-depth experience in the firm's industry in the areas of management, production, finance, marketing, and research and development.

The investor should look also at the board of directors. Is the board controlled by outsiders who represent the stockholders or by the firm's management? Outside directors should be of such stature that they can be an important source of independent advice.

## Workers

The firm should hire good people, train them well, and provide a positive environment. Employment contracts must be fair to both the firm and the workers. The effects of any labor problems, including any chance of a strike, must be evaluated fully. After the investor understands the dynamics of the firm, more information can be obtained by analyzing its financial statements.

# ANALYSIS OF FINANCIAL STATEMENTS

The firm's financial statements provide the basic information for evaluating the firm's securities. Although financial statements report data from the past, analysis of them can help predict future cash flows because the basic revenue and cost relationships displayed in the statements usually will exist in the future. Likewise, financial statements provide information about management's performance. Management's degree of success in the past helps in predicting its future performance.

The four basic financial statements are

— The income statement

— The balance sheet

— The statement of stockholders' equity

— The statement of cash flows

Exhibit 11–1 shows the relationships among the financial statements. The financial position at the beginning of the period is shown by its beginning balance sheet. Changes

---

**EXHIBIT 11–1   Relationships Among Financial Statements**

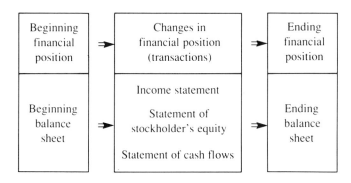

that take place during the period are reflected in the income statement, the statement of stockholders' equity, and the statement of cash flows. These three statements measure performance during the period and show how the firm obtained its ending financial position as reflected in its ending balance sheet.

# Income Statement

Because of the importance of future earnings in security valuation, the income statement is the most important statement for financial analysts. The income statement, which reports financial performance during the period, can be divided into four major sections as shown in Exhibit 11–2.

**1.** Revenues and expenses from operations indicate how successful the company is at its primary business activities. This section results in the figure for income from operations.

**2.** Other revenues and other expenses are related to the secondary activities of the firm. Examples are interest, dividends, rents received, gains or losses on the sale of investments or equipment, and interest expense. This section results in the figure for income before taxes and extraordinary items.

---

**EXHIBIT 11–2   Model of an Income Statement**

*XYZ Corporation*
*Income Statement*
*For the Year Ending December 31, 1989*

| | | |
|---|---:|---:|
| Net sales | | $570,000 |
| Cost of goods sold | | 330,000 |
| Gross margin | | 240,000 |
| Operating expenses: | | |
|   Selling expenses | $73,000 | |
|   General and administrative expenses | 30,000 | |
|   Depreciation expenses | 34,500 | |
|   Total operating expenses | | 137,500 |
| Income from operations | | 102,500 |
| Other revenues | | 21,000 |
| Other expenses | | 19,500 |
| Income before taxes and extraordinary items | | 104,000 |
| Income tax expense | | 33,600 |
| Income before extraordinary items | | 70,400 |
| Extraordinary items (after tax) | | (24,000) |
| Net income | | $ 46,400 |
| Per share of common stock | | |
|   Income before extraordinary items | | $1.40 |
|   Extraordinary items | | (.48) |
|   Net income | | .92 |

**3.** Next, income tax expense is shown and the income before extraordinary items is computed. This income figure is the one most emphasized in financial analysis.

**4.** Extraordinary gains and losses result from infrequent occurrences of an unusual nature. Examples are damages from rare storms or earthquakes and losses from governmental expropriation.

Exhibit 11–3 displays the income statement of Ball Corporation. Like most corporations, it also prints financial information from previous years for comparison purposes. Ball Corporation's activities were such that it did not require the extraordinary items section listed above. Analysis of this income statement and the applicable notes shows that net income is growing, although sales declined from the previous year. The ratio of costs and expenses to sales improved. In particular, sales decreased 3.2 percent while net income increased 15 percent in 1986, while cost and expenses decreased to 89.7 percent of sales. Nothing on the statement or in the notes requires the analyst to make substantial adjustments or to worry about future earnings.

## Balance Sheet

The balance sheet is the statement of the firm's financial position at the end of the period. It reports the firm's account balances as of the date of the statement. The balance sheet reports stocks while the income statement reports flows. The three major sections of a balance sheet—assets, liabilities, and owners' equity—are shown in Exhibit 11–4.

---

**EXHIBIT 11–3  Ball Corporation's Income Statement**

| | Year Ended December 31 | | |
| --- | --- | --- | --- |
| | **1986** | 1985 | 1984 |
| Net sales* | **$1,070.3** | $1,106.2 | $1,050.7 |
| Costs and expenses | | | |
| Cost of sales | **872.5** | 921.5 | 876.6 |
| Selling, general and administrative expenses | **81.2** | 83.2 | 83.1 |
| Interest expense | **6.3** | 8.9 | 9.3 |
| | **960.0** | 1,013.6 | 969.0 |
| Income before taxes on income | **110.3** | 92.6 | 81.7 |
| Provision for taxes on income | **51.4** | 41.4 | 35.4 |
| Net income | **$   58.9** | $   51.2 | $   46.3 |
| Net income per share of common stock | **$   2.56** | $   2.24 | $   2.04 |

* Dollars in millions except per share amounts.

Source: Courtesy of Ball Corporation.

---

---

**EXHIBIT 11–4   *Model of a Balance Sheet***

---

*XYZ Corporation*
*Balance Sheet*
*December 31, 1989*

*Assets*
Current assets
  Cash                                                           $ 22,500
  Marketable securities                                            40,000
  Accounts receivable                                              76,500
  Inventory                                                        35,000
  Prepaid expenses                                                 10,000
    Total current assets                                                $184,000
Investments and funds
  Land held for future plant                                       56,800
  Plant expansion fund                                             48,700
    Total investments and funds                                          105,500
Property, plant, and equipment
  Land                                                             22,000
  Building                               $100,000
  Less: accumulated depreciation           30,000                  70,000
  Equipment                                80,000
  Less: accumulated depreciation           20,000                  60,000
    Total property, plant, and equipment                                 152,000
Intangible assets
  Goodwill                                                                      38,500
Other assets
  Bond issue costs                                                              10,000
Total assets                                                                    $490,000

*Liabilities and Stockholders' Equity*
Current liabilities                                              $40,400
  Notes payable                                                    12,000
  Interest payable                                                  4,200
  Income tax payable                                                6,400
    Total current liabilities                                           $ 63,000
Long-term liabilities
  Bonds payable                                                                 80,000
    Total liabilities                                                    143,000
Stockholders' equity
  Common stock                                                     70,000
  Additional paid-in capital                                      200,000
  Retained earnings                                                77,000
    Total stockholders' equity                                           347,000
Total liabilities and stockholders' equity                                      $490,000

The assets are subdivided into current and noncurrent assets. Current assets are to be sold or consumed during the normal operating cycle of the business or within one year, whichever is longer. They are listed on the balance sheet in the order of their liquidity: cash, short-term investments, receivables, inventories, and prepaid expenses.

Noncurrent asset categories are investments and funds; plant, property, and equipment; intangible assets; and other assets. Investments and funds report the various types of investments and funds that are not used in the business operations. Property, plant, and equipment are tangible and long-lived assets. Except for land, they are depreciated or depleted over their expected lives. Their cost, accumulated depreciation or depletion, and book value are shown. Intangible assets are long-lived resources that lack physical substance and are used in the business operations. They have value because they convey certain rights and privileges to the business. Examples are patents, copyrights, goodwill, trademarks, franchises, and organizational costs. Amortization allocates over time the benefits of an intangible asset. Because intangible assets are reported on the balance sheet at cost minus amortization and because so many factors affect their true value, the financial analyst should examine them very closely. Their actual value to the firm could be much greater or much less than the reported value. The other assets category contains assets that do not fit conveniently into one of the other categories. Examples are machinery rearrangement costs, bond issue costs, long-term rental prepayments, and prepaid income tax resulting from the application of interperiod tax allocation.

The liabilities are divided into current and long-term liabilities. Current liabilities are obligations that will require the use of current assets or the creation of other current liabilities to liquidate. Examples are accounts payable, wages payable, commissions payable, income tax payable, short-term notes payable, and the currently maturing portion of long-term debt. Long-term liabilities are obligations that will not require the use of current assets or the creation of current liabilities. Examples are bonds payable, long-term notes payable, deferred income tax, long-term obligations under warranty contracts, obligations under capital leases, and pension obligations.

Owners' equity is a measure of the owners' interests in the business. It is computed as the residual obtained from subtracting liabilities from assets. The two major subcategories are paid-in capital and retained earnings. The paid-in capital consists of the capital stock account and the additional paid-in capital account. Retained earnings equal the firm's accumulated earnings less its dividends.

Exhibit 11–5 is a balance sheet of Ball Corporation. In 1986, total current assets increased because accounts receivable, inventories, and prepaid expenses were more than in 1985. Additional investments were made in land, buildings, and plant and equipment while other assets were reduced. Both current and long-term liabilities were increased.

Computation of some ratios aids in the analysis of a balance sheet. A firm's ratios can be compared to its ratios in past years and to other firms in its industry. The liquidity available to meet short-term obligations is revealed by the current ratio.

$$\text{current ratio} = \frac{\text{current assets}}{\text{current liabilities}}$$

---

**EXHIBIT 11–5   Ball Corporation's Balance Sheet**

|  | *December 31,* | |
| --- | ---: | ---: |
|  | **1986** | 1985 |
| *Assets* | | |
| Current assets* | | |
|   Cash and temporary investments | **$ 10.2** | $ 15.0 |
|   Accounts receivable, less allowance for doubtful accounts | | |
|     of $1.2 in 1986 and $1.1 in 1985 | **109.0** | 98.8 |
|   Inventories | | |
|     Raw materials and supplies | **79.0** | 68.3 |
|     Work in process and finished goods | **106.5** | 78.9 |
|   Prepaid expenses | **26.5** | 3.9 |
|   Total current assets | **331.2** | 264.9 |
| Property, plant and equipment, at cost | | |
|   Land | **11.9** | 10.5 |
|   Buildings | **128.8** | 125.9 |
|   Machinery and equipment | **486.6** | 432.6 |
| | **627.3** | 569.0 |
|   Less accumulated depreciation | **261.3** | 231.7 |
| | **366.0** | 337.3 |
| Other assets | **35.5** | 39.5 |
| Total assets | **$732.7** | $641.7 |
| *Liabilities and Shareholders' Equity* | | |
| Current liabilities | | |
|   Short-term borrowings | **$ 9.1** | $ — |
|   Current portion of long-term obligations | **13.3** | 8.0 |
|   Accounts payable | **77.8** | 63.5 |
|   Pension costs and other employee benefits | **20.9** | 25.5 |
|   Salaries and wages | **15.2** | 12.4 |
|   Current and current deferred taxes on income | **9.8** | 9.9 |
|   Other current liabilities | **19.2** | 16.2 |
|   Total current liabilities | **165.3** | 135.5 |
| Long-term obligations | **101.6** | 89.9 |
| Deferred taxes on income | **85.2** | 71.9 |
| Deferred compensation and other | **15.3** | 13.6 |
| Shareholders' equity | | |
|   Common stock | **37.2** | 41.6 |
|   Retained earnings | **332.3** | 291.5 |
| | **369.5** | 333.1 |
|   Less treasury stock, at cost | **4.2** | 2.3 |
| | **365.3** | 330.8 |
| Total liabilities and shareholders' equity | **$732.7** | $641.7 |

* Dollars in millions.

Source: Courtesy of Ball Corporation.

Ball Corporation's current ratio at the end of 1986 was 2.0 (331.2/165.3). This is slightly higher than 1985's current ratio of 1.95 and is adequate liquidity. Adequate liquidity is confirmed by computation of the quick ratio.

$$\text{quick ratio (acid test)} = \frac{\text{current assets } - \text{ inventories } - \text{ prepaid expenses}}{\text{current liabilities}}$$

Ball Corporation's quick ratio is

$$\frac{331.2 - 185.5 - 26.5}{165.3} = .72$$

The total debt to total assets ratio is a measure of financial leverage. The use of debt financing increases risk and potential returns. Firms with high debt ratios may face problems in bad economic times while firms with low debt ratio have the safety provided by the additional equity. Ball Corporation's 1986 and 1985 total debt to total asset ratios were .50 (367.4/732.7) and .48 (310.9/641.7). This level of debt financing is safe for a diversified manufacturer serving the packaging, industrial, and high technology markets.

The balance sheet reports that the stockholders' equity is $365.3 million. A note tells us that there were 23,052,435 common shares outstanding at the end of the year. Therefore, the stockholders' equity (book value) per share was $15.85. Book value is a cost approach to valuation. If a corporation functions efficiently, its market value should be at least as great as its book value. The market value to book value ratio compares the market's valuation of the firm's future to the historical costs of its assets. Ball Corporation's closing stock price at the end of 1986 was $35.25. Therefore, the market to book value ratio was 2.22 (35.25/15.85). The market thinks Ball Corporation is going to use its assets very efficiently.

## Statement of Changes in Stockholders' Equity

The statement of changes in stockholders' equity has two purposes. First, it describes the changes in a company's retained earnings account during the period and thereby relates the income statement to the balance sheet. Second, it shows the changes in the components of stockholders' equity that result from capital stock transactions such as selling additional stock and buying and selling treasury stock. If the firm does not have any capital stock transactions, it will issue only a statement of changes in retained earnings.

Exhibit 11–6 is the statement of changes in stockholders' equity from Ball Corporation. In addition to the dividends paid, it shows the results of an acquisition paid for by common stock, share repurchases, stock option plan, and dividend reinvestment plan.

## Statement of Cash Flows

The Financial Accounting Standards Board now requires, as part of the full set of financial statements, a statement of cash flows instead of the old working capital-based

**EXHIBIT 11-6  Ball Corporation's Statement of Stockholders' Equity**

| | Common Stock | | Treasury Stock | | Retained Earnings |
|---|---|---|---|---|---|
| | Shares | Amount | Shares | Amount | |
| Balance December 31, 1983* | 22,668,522 | $40.7 | (72,200) | $ (1.2) | $222.6 |
| Net income for the year | | | | | 46.3 |
| Dividends paid | | | | | (13.9) |
| Shares reacquired | | | (436,158) | (7.5) | |
| Shares issued for stock options and other employee and shareholder stock plans less shares exchanged | 116,178 | (.1) | 502,454 | 8.6 | |
| Current foreign currency translation adjustment | | | | | (.1) |
| Balance December 31, 1984 | 22,784,700 | $40.6 | (5,904) | $ (.1) | $254.9 |
| Net income for the year | | | | | 51.2 |
| Dividends paid | | | | | (15.6) |
| Acquisition of business | 76,202 | | | | .6 |
| Shares reacquired | | | (489,354) | (11.9) | |
| Shares issued for stock options and other employee and shareholder stock plans less shares exchanged | 224,551 | 1.0 | 417,603 | 9.7 | |
| Current foreign currency translation adjustment | | | | | .4 |
| Balance December 31, 1985 | 23,085,453 | $41.6 | (77,655) | $ (2.3) | $291.5 |
| Net income for the year | | | | | 58.9 |
| Dividends paid | | | | | (17.8) |
| Purchase of business | 40,414 | 1.5 | | | |
| Shares reacquired | | | (569,683) | (21.1) | |
| Shares issued for stock options and other employee and shareholder stock plans less shares exchanged | 37,178 | (5.9) | 536,728 | 19.2 | |
| Current foreign currency translation adjustment | | | | | (.3) |
| Balance December 31, 1986 | 23,163,045 | $37.2 | (110,610) | $ (4.2) | $332.3 |

Dollars in millions.

Source: Courtesy of Ball Corporation.

---

**EXHIBIT 11–7   Model of a Statement of Cash Flows**

ABC Corporation
Statement of Cash Flows
For the Year Ending December 31, 1989

| | | |
|---|---:|---:|
| *Cash Flows from Operating Activities* | | |
| Cash received from customers | $334,500 | |
| Interest income | 500 | |
| Cash provided by operating activities | | $335,000 |
| Cash paid for merchandise | 190,000 | |
| Cash paid to suppliers and employees | 50,000 | |
| Interest paid | 9,000 | |
| Taxes paid | 52,000 | |
| Cash disbursed for operating activities | | 301,000 |
| Net cash flow from operating activities | | 34,000 |
| *Cash Flows from Investing Activities* | | |
| Purchase of equipment | (90,000) | |
| Proceeds from sale of equipment | 27,000 | |
| Sales of investments | 2,000 | |
| Net cash flow from investing activities | | (61,000) |
| *Cash Flows from Financing Activities* | | |
| Stock sale | 44,000 | |
| Dividends | (27,000) | |
| Net cash flow from financing activities | | 17,000 |
| *Net Increase (Decrease) in Cash* | | ($10,000) |
| *Schedule of Non-Cash Investing and* | | None |
| *Financing Activities* | | |

---

statement of changes in financial position. The statement of cash flows converts accrual based financial statements to a cash basis. In it, cash flows are categorized into cash from operating activities, from investing activities, and from financing activities. Investing activities, such as the purchase of plant and machinery, are uses of funds. Financing activities, such as the sale of securities, are sources of funds.

Exhibit 11–7 shows the format for a statement of cash flows. Disclosure of all significant financing and investing activities that did not affect cash is required in either a separate schedule or within the statement itself. Besides providing information on actual cash flows, this statement helps assess future cash flows and evaluate the availability of cash for dividends and investment.

## Notes to Financial Statements

The accompanying notes to the financial statements are an important step in the analysis process. They must be read carefully. The notes have several purposes. Some notes summarize significant accounting policies: they state the choices made among acceptable accounting alternatives, any unusual application of accounting principles, and any accounting practices peculiar to the firm's industry. Some notes report important subsequent events: events that occurred between the date on the balance sheet and the date on which the financial statements were issued. Examples are the purchase of a business, the sale of a stock or bond issue, and the loss of assets due to a casualty. Some notes disclose contingent liabilities, such as a pending lawsuit. Some notes give details of major contracts such as leases and pension plans. Other notes detail the data summarized in the financial statements. Examples are information by operating division, detailed interest costs, detailed inventory information, and inflation adjustments.

# EARNINGS QUALITY

**Economic earnings** are the maximum amount of wealth that can be consumed by the owners of the firm in any period without decreasing future consumption opportunities. This means all the firm's economic earnings could be paid out in dividends at the end of the period; then the firm's value after the dividend, based on discounted future earnings, would equal the firm's value at the beginning of the period. Because financial statements report earnings as determined by accounting principles instead of economic earnings, the quality of the reported earnings must be examined.

There are no absolute standards for earnings quality. However, earnings should have integrity, in the sense that they are not the result of accounting or management manipulation designed purely to make them look better. Likewise, earnings should be reliable, in the sense that they are a good indication of the firm's earning power. The concept of earnings quality looks at the comparative integrity and reliability of reported earnings.

Earnings quality varies because of the accounting methods selected. Conservatively computed earnings have more quality than those computed using more liberal choices. Important quality issues are inventory method used, depreciation method and asset lives used, and how pension costs and leases are handled. An analyst also should examine closely the effect on earnings quality of any change in accounting methods.

## Ten Most Active Stocks

The stocks listed below were the ten most actively traded on the NYSE in 1987.

| | |
|---|---|
| American Telephone & Telegraph | Navistar International |
| International Business Machines | USX Corporation |
| General Electric | Exxon Corporation |
| American Express | General Motors |
| Texaco Inc. | Eastman Kodak |

Business choices also influence earnings quality. Management makes choices between long-run and short-run earnings. Emphasizing short-run earnings lowers earnings quality. The analyst must examine the level of expenditures for human resources, research and development, advertising, and maintenance. Standards for comparison are the expenditures of other firms in the industry and past practices of the firm being analyzed.

# SUSTAINABLE GROWTH

While quality of earnings was concerned with the integrity and reliability of the reported earnings, this section identifies important variables for a more detailed analysis of performance and estimates the future growth potential of the earnings stream. This analysis uses financial ratios which reflect different components of earnings performance.

Return on equity is the rate of return of most concern to the common stock owners. It is earnings after tax divided by the common equity and is the product of four components: sales margin, asset turnover, financial leverage, and a tax adjustment.

Sales margin is the ratio of earnings before tax to revenue. It reflects the sales level, pricing decisions, and expense and cost control. Competition keeps pressure on the sales margin. Ball Corporation's sales margin is 10.31 percent.

$$\text{sales margin} = \frac{\text{earnings before tax}}{\text{revenue}}$$

$$= \frac{110.3}{1070.3}$$

$$= .1031$$

Asset turnover is revenue divided by total assets. It reflects the firm's capacity and efficiency in using its assets and it is greatly influenced by the state of technology of the industry. For example, heavy industries such as steel and electrical utilities must have huge investments in plant and equipment in comparison to revenue. On the other hand, most retailers of perishable goods have high turnover. Ball Corporation's asset turnover ratio is 1.461.

$$\text{asset turnover} = \frac{\text{revenue}}{\text{total assets}}$$

$$= \frac{1070.3}{732.7}$$

$$= 1.461$$

The leverage ratio that is most convenient to use in analyzing the components of return on equity is total assets divided by net worth. The leverage available to a firm is limited by the increase in risk that can be accepted and by the willingness of lenders to supply additional funds on favorable terms. For Ball Corporation the leverage ratio is 2.006.

$$\text{leverage} = \frac{\text{total assets}}{\text{net worth}}$$

$$= \frac{732.7}{365.3}$$

$$= 2.006$$

Return on equity (ROE) is measured after taxes while sales margin was computed using earnings before tax. Therefore, a tax adjustment is necessary. Although a firm's control over taxes paid is limited, computing this factor emphasizes the effect taxes have on ROE.

The most useful form of the tax adjustment factor is given by

$$\text{tax adjustment} = 1 - \text{average tax rate}$$

$$= 1 - \frac{\text{taxes on income}}{\text{income before tax}}$$

For Ball Corporation the tax adjustment factor is .534.

$$\text{tax adjustment} = \frac{51.4}{110.3}$$

$$= .534$$

Having computed these four components, they can be multiplied to obtain ROE. For Ball Corporation, the ROE is 16.14 percent.

$$\text{ROE} = \text{margin} \times \text{turnover} \times \text{leverage} \times \text{tax adjustment}$$

$$= .1031 \times 1.461 \times 2.006 \times .534$$

$$= .1614$$

The level of sustainable growth is computed based on the current levels of ROE and earnings retention. The sustainable growth figure computed assumes that there will be no additional equity financing and that ROE cannot be increased by improving one or more of its components. Therefore, growth is limited to that supported by the equity retained after dividends are paid out of earnings. This maximum rate of growth can be computed with the following relationship:

$$g = \text{ROE} \times \left(1 - \frac{D}{E}\right)$$

where

$g$ = the sustainable growth rate of earnings

$D$ = the dividends paid

$E$ = the earnings of the firm

For Ball Corporation the growth rate is limited to 11.26 percent unless new equity is obtained or one of the components of ROE improves.

$$g = .1614 \times \left(1 - \frac{17.8}{58.9}\right)$$

$$= .1126$$

# SUMMARY

Analysis of a firm is undertaken to access the return-risk tradeoff its securities offer. The investor analyzes the firm to determine its value. The security's value per share is then compared to its price per share in order to determine if it is over- or underpriced. The future earnings of the firm depend on its strategic plan, its market and products, its management, and its workers. The firm's financial statements provide the investor with information about its past performance and present position. This information helps the investor evaluate the future prospects of the firm.

The quality of the earnings reported in the financial statements depends on past accounting and management decisions. Therefore, the integrity and reliability of the reported earnings must be examined. The sustainable growth rate of a firm depends on its sales margin, its asset turnover, its leverage ratio, its average tax rate, and its dividend payout ratio.

## QUESTIONS

1. What issues should an investor examine when assessing the dynamics of a firm?
2. Name the four basic financial statements and describe the relationships among them.
3. What should the investor look for when examining the firm's income statement?
4. What should the investor look for when examining the firm's balance sheet?
5. What does the statement of stockholders' equity reveal?
6. What should an investor look for in a statement of cash flows?
7. What information is contained in the notes to financial statements?
8. What are economic earnings? How does the concept of earnings quality relate to economic earnings?
9. Explain the concept of sustainable growth. What variables determine the sustainable growth rate?

# PROBLEMS

1. IBM's 1985 return on equity was 20.5%. Its dividends per share were $4.40 and its earnings per share were $10.67. Using the sustainable growth model, compute its maximum growth rate.

2. Lilly's 1986 return on equity was 20.4%. Its dividends per share were $1.80 and its earnings per share were $4.01. Using the sustainable growth model, compute its maximum growth rate.

3. The following figures are from the 1985 financial statements of Celanese Corporation. What is its maximum sustainable growth? If it wants to grow more than this, what are its options?

   — Revenue: $3,046 million

   — Income before tax: $240 million

   — Income tax: $60 million

   — Total assets: $2,809 million

   — Net worth: $1,017 million

   — Dividends: $61 million

4. The following figures are from the 1985 financial statements of Brunswick Corporation. What is its maximum sustainable growth? If it wants to grow more than this, what are its options?

   — Revenue: $1,538,538,000

   — Income before tax: $117,129,000

   — Income tax: $51,000,000

   — Total assets: $1,002,172,000

   — Net worth: $523,186,000

   — Dividends: $12,201,000

# READINGS

Babcock, Guilford C. "The Concept of Sustainable Growth," *Financial Analysts Journal* 26 (May–June 1970): 108–114.

*This article is an analysis of the basic elements of stock price appreciation.*

Bernstein, Leopold A., and Siegel, Joel G. "The Concept of Earnings Quality," *Financial Analysts Journal* 35 (July–August 1979): 72–75.

*The authors are accountants who describe for financial analysts some of the issues involved in earnings quality evaluation.*

Craig, Darryl, Johnson, Glen, and Joy, Maurice. "Accounting Methods and P/E Ratios," *Financial Analysts Journal* 43 (March–April, 1987): 41–45.

*The authors examined the relationship between a company's P/E ratio and its method of accounting for inventory, depreciation, and investment tax credit.*

Gibson, Charles. "How Chartered Financial Analysts View Financial Ratios," *Financial Analysts Journal* 43 (May–June, 1987): 74–76.

*This article reports the results of a survey of CFAs which asked which ratios they view primarily as measures of liquidity, long-term debt-paying ability, and profitability. It also reports the CFAs' opinions of the relative importance of specific financial ratios.*

Hoban, James P., Jr. ''Characteristics of Venture Capital Investments,'' *American Journal of Small Business* 6 (Fall, 1981): 3–12.

> *This article reports on an attempt to quantify the dynamics of 50 new firms in which venture capitalists made investments. The study tested a model in which success was a function of a set of independent variables which measured the firm's management, products, market, and financing.*

Pratt, Shannon. *Valuing a Business: The Analysis and Appraisal of Closely Held Companies.* Homewood, IL: Dow Jones-Irwin, 1986.

> *This book discusses gathering data, analyzing financial statements, presenting the report, and using evaluations for such purposes as estate planning, tax valuations, and buy/sell agreements.*

# Technical Analysis

## OUTLINE

## OBJECTIVES

When you have finished studying this chapter, you should understand

1. The philosophy of technical analysts.

2. How to make line charts, bar charts, and point and figure charts.

3. How sentiment for individual stocks and for the market is measured.

4. How well technical indicators have performed.

**234**

# 12

## *Technical Analysis Advertisements*

These quotes were taken from current advertisements for publications based on technical analysis.

> 250 pages of strategies, charts, info to help U swim in crisis waters and make money from them.

> We ''read'' each stock to determine where, in our opinion, it stands in the four-stage cycle all stocks must go through: (1) the Basing area, (2) Advancing stage, (3) Top area, and (4) Declining stage.

> Don't be scared away by the old wives' tale that there's something particularly dangerous about short selling. When proper precautions are taken and the major trend is bearish (as is the case now), short selling can offer you far less risk than going against the trend, as well as an excellent opportunity to increase your capital.

> I do not predict stock market changes. Rather, I let the market itself tell me what it is doing . . . through my indicators.

## INTRODUCTION

So far in this book we have discussed security analysis in terms of fundamental analysis. Fundamental analysts attempt to determine the value of a security by analyzing the economy, the industry, and the firm. Their emphasis is on estimating future earnings, growth rates, and discount rates. Their basic data consist of financial statements and economic indicator series.

In contrast, technical analysts study only market generated data, such as prices and volume. Technical analysts use these data to forecast the performance of the market as a whole as well as individual securities. Although **technical analysis** is explained in this chapter using stock market examples, technical analysts also analyze other markets and the securities traded in them. In particular, technical analysis is widely used to forecast commodity prices.

# FOUNDATIONS OF TECHNICAL ANALYSIS

Technical analysts believe that a security's price captures all of its supply and demand forces. They emphasize that security prices and other transactional data are quickly reported and easily analyzed. In comparison, technical analysts argue that although fundamental analysts have large quantities of financial and economic data, fundamental analysis is limited by a lack of all the pertinent information and by slowness in processing and assessing the available information. They also point out that past financial performance is a poor predictor of future stock prices. To summarize the contrast, technical analysts believe that their tools are more efficient than those used by fundamental analysts.

Technical analysts do not care which fundamental factors are changing a stock's price. They believe that the buy and sell orders reflect the evaluation of new information that has not been made public and is being used by insiders. A very important assumption is that new information enters the market slowly. Therefore, prices move in trends that persist for appreciable lengths of time. When prices are graphed, these trends form recognizable price patterns which recur over time. Comparison of a current pattern with similar past patterns allows the technical analyst to predict future prices.

Technical analysts do not argue that any one of their indicators is 100 percent reliable; therefore, they use several indicators and personal judgment when analyzing patterns. Additionally, they are not much concerned with why the indicators work. If the indicators have worked in the past, technical analysts will continue to use them even though there is no theoretical justification for them.

The tools of technical analysis can be divided into two broad categories: price patterns and sentiment indicators. We will briefly present some of the techniques from each category. Because technical analysis keeps getting more sophisticated, entire books on technical analysis are available that contain more elaborate tools than those presented here.

# PRICE PATTERN CHARTS

Technical analysts are also called chartists because of their extensive use of price charts. The three most common types of charts are line charts, bar charts, and point and figure charts.

## Line Charts

To make a line chart, each day you plot the closing price of the market index or stock you are following. Then you connect the points. Exhibit 12–1 is an example.

The Dow theory is an example of a technical analysis tool which uses line charts. In the 1890s, the Dow theory was formulated by Charles Henry Dow, a founder of Dow Jones Company and the first editor of the *Wall Street Journal*. Its greatest triumph

---

**EXHIBIT 12–1  Line Chart Dow Theory**

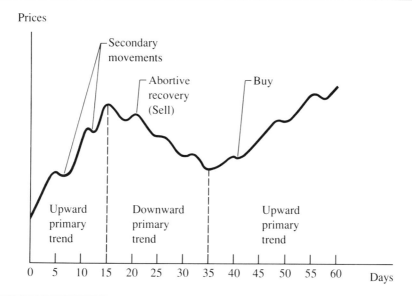

was predicting the market crash in 1929. On October 23, 1929, the *Wall Street Journal* contained an editorial based on the Dow theory which said that the bull market was over and a bear market was beginning.

The Dow theory is usually used on market averages to analyze trends in the market. Many versions and refinements exist. It is based on the belief that there are three components to market prices: daily fluctuations, secondary movements, and primary trends. By using a line chart, daily fluctuations are deemphasized. The line chart is used to display the secondary movements and primary trends.

The line chart in Exhibit 12–1 begins with an upward trend interrupted by two downward secondary movements. However, on day 20 the attempt to recover from a secondary movement fails when the price climb does not match the previous high (day 15). This is an abortive recovery, the sell signal. From then until day 35 the market follows a primary downward trend with a few secondary movement recovery attempts. On day 40 the decline, following a recovery attempt, is stopped before it goes below the previous low. This is the buy signal for a new primary upward trend.

Dow theory users also commonly follow a second market average such as the transportations and seek confirmation of major market turns in the price pattern of that average.

## Bar Charts

To make a bar chart you plot the high, low, and closing price for each day. Then, you draw a line connecting each day's high and low and put a dash at the closing price. Exhibit 12–2 is a bar chart.

---

**EXHIBIT 12–2   Bar Chart Showing Head and Shoulders Pattern**

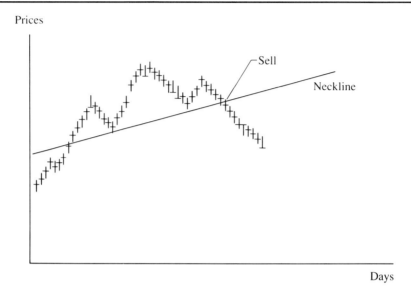

---

Technical analysts search for familiar price patterns in the bar chart. Some common patterns are head and shoulders, channels, triangles, pennants, rectangles, double tops, triple tops, wedges, and diamonds. Exhibit 12–2 displays a head and shoulders pattern. You can see the left shoulder, head, and right shoulder. A neckline has been drawn tangent to the left and right shoulders. In this example, the price dropped through the neckline (a sell signal).

We do not have enough space in this book to explain the other price patterns. However, all involve searching for a signal of change in the market's supply and demand forces. Usually the signal involves penetration of a support or resistance level. A **support level** is the price where a decline is expected to stop because of buying forces. A **resistance level** is the price where a rise is expected to stop because of selling forces.

## Point and Figure Charts

A point and figure chart emphasizes price changes and price pattern reversals. The vertical axis is scaled in dollars. An *X* is placed on the chart when the price rises by some arbitrary amount, usually $1 for a low priced stock and $2 for a high priced one. An *O* is placed on the chart when the price falls that arbitrary amount. The horizontal axis is not scaled in units of time. Instead, a new column is started each time prices reverse direction by some predetermined amount—perhaps three dollars. Price reversals are not recorded unless they are as large as the predetermined amount.

**EXHIBIT 12–3   Point and Figure Chart for Eli Lilly & Co., 1987**

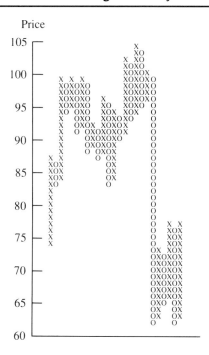

Note: This is a four-point reversal chart. Four dollars of price change are necessary before moving to the next column.

In Exhibit 12–3 a point and figure chart is drawn. Point and figure charts enable the viewer to see trends, resistance levels, and support levels without any distortion because of time.

# SENTIMENT INDICATORS

Technical analysts examine other market generated data which they believe reflect the strength of the supply and demand forces. Some sentiment indicators are used to measure the forces affecting individual securities, some are used to measure the forces affecting broad market movements, and some are used for both purposes.

## Volume

When following individual stocks and market averages, chartists pay close attention to volume of trading figures. Often they graph volume on the bottom of their price charts. This enables them to see trends in prices and volume at the same time.

If prices are up or down on heavy volume, they weigh the significance of the price changes more heavily than if they occurred with low volume. There are two exceptions to this general rule. Bull markets sometimes end in a **speculative blowoff,** where prices go up on very heavy volume just before a long-term price decline starts. Likewise, bear markets sometimes end in a **selling climax,** where prices go down in very heavy volume just before the market starts recovering.

## Moving Averages

Moving average analysis enables the chartist to compare easily the recent price to the trend in prices. Moving average analysis is used on both individual securities and market averages. The period for which the moving average is computed varies; however, a 200-day moving average is most commonly used. To compute it, each day the average closing price for the past 200 days is figured and graphed.

Chartists see buy and sell signals in the relationship between the current price and the moving average. Many consider the following to be buy signals:

1. The moving average graph line flattens out and the current price moves above it.
2. The current price falls below a rising moving average line.
3. The current price is above the moving average line; the price falls some but turns higher before reaching the moving average line.

Many chartists consider the following to be sell signals:

1. The moving average graph line flattens out and the current price moves below it.
2. The current price rises above a falling moving average line.
3. The current price is below the moving average line; the price rises some but turns lower before reaching the moving average line.

## Insider Transactions

Although corporate insiders such as officers, directors, and large stockholders cannot legally use nonpublic information for stock trading, they can and frequently do buy and sell stock of the firm in which they are involved. Even if they are not using nonpublic information, they should have an accurate view of the firm's prospects. Technical analysts assume insiders buy when the prospects are good and sell when the prospects are bad. Buying and selling of stock by corporate insiders must be reported to the SEC, which makes this information public. Some analysts follow the example of the corporate insiders in their buying and selling decisions.

## Short Sales

The exchanges report the number of short sales by individual security. Technical analysts interpret short selling volume figures in two conflicting ways. Some analysts believe high volume is a bearish sign because most short sellers are sophisticated investors. These analysts recommend selling a stock when there has been a lot of short selling. On the other hand, some analysts stress that because short sellers will have to purchase the stock in the future to cover their short positions, this future demand for the stock is a bullish force. These analysts recommend buying the stock when the amount sold short is significant in comparison to normal trading volume.

## Odd Lot Trading

We now look at four indicators used to measure sentiment toward stocks in general: odd lot trading, the advance-decline line, the confidence index, and mutual fund liquidity.

Most buying and selling of odd lots is undertaken by individuals rather than institutional investors. The volume of odd lot sales and purchases is reported daily in the financial press. Analysts who watch odd lot trading believe that individual investors tend to buy and sell at the wrong times in the market cycle. They believe individual investors become overly optimistic and invest heavily just before the market peaks and become overly pessimistic and sell just before the market reaches bottom. Therefore, the analysts compare the odd lot purchase volume with the odd lot sale volume and then do the opposite of the majority of the odd lot investors.

## Advance-Decline Line

The advance-decline line is used to measure the underlying strength of market advances or declines. Each day the NYSE reports the number of stocks that advanced and the number that declined. In order to compute the cumulative net advances and declines, analysts each day subtract the declines from the advances and add this difference to the previous cumulative net advance-decline figure.

| Day | Advances | − Declines | = Net Change | Cumulative |
|---|---|---|---|---|
| Monday | 801 | 837 | − 36 | − 36 |
| Tuesday | 646 | 940 | − 294 | − 330 |
| Wednesday | 982 | 627 | 355 | 25 |
| Thursday | 704 | 821 | − 117 | − 92 |
| Friday | 775 | 793 | − 18 | − 110 |
| Monday | 1,130 | 468 | 662 | 552 |
| Tuesday | 947 | 638 | 309 | 861 |
| Wednesday | 918 | 643 | 275 | 1,136 |

Analysts consider it very significant when the direction of prices and the advance-decline line diverge. That is, the market averages keep increasing while the advance-decline line falls (sell signal), or the market averages keep decreasing while the advance-decline line rises (buy signal).

## Confidence Index

The confidence index measures the sentiment of managers of bond portfolios. When they are optimistic about the economy, they tend to buy lower-quality bonds. When they are pessimistic about the economy, they move to higher-quality bonds. Their optimism or pessimism will be reflected in the yields available on high-grade bonds in comparison to low-grade ones. The confidence index measures this sentiment; it is the ratio of high-grade bond yields to low-grade bond yields.

$$\text{confidence index} = \frac{\text{average yield on high-grade bonds}}{\text{average yield on low-grade bonds}}$$

If institutional investors are optimistic, the ratio goes up (approaches one) because they are buying more low-grade bonds which drives their prices up and yields down. *Barron's* computes and reports a confidence index each week. Some analysts make a point and figure chart of the confidence index.

## Mutual Fund Liquidity

Because large institutional investors are becoming much more important in determining market prices, one factor in estimating future stock demand is the amount of cash institutions hold. If the institutions hold a large amount of cash and stock prices start rallying, the institutions could quickly invest large amounts of cash and thereby drive price up even more.

Mutual funds, one type of institution, have to make public their portfolio positions. Therefore, analysts monitor the amount of cash held by mutual funds in order to predict future stock prices.

# PERFORMANCE OF TECHNICAL INDICATORS

Technical analysis appeals to many investors who accept the premises of slow market adjustment to new information and recurring patterns. In the last 30 years, advances in statistics and in computers have enabled researchers to test the performance of some of the technical analysts' tools and techniques. As explained in more detail in Chapter 21, there are two approaches to these tests. The first approach is to search for correlations in stock prices over time. If past price patterns predict future prices, correlation among the prices must exist. Researchers have not found the correlations among prices that would have to be there if price patterns recurred.

The second testing approach is to convert the technical analyst's decision rules into a computer program and then test the profitability of the decision rules using past stock price data. These tests have not revealed any set of decision rules which beat, after commissions, a long-term buy and hold strategy.

Technical analysts refute this evidence by arguing that technical analysis is an art and not a science. They argue that their decision rules are too complex to be easily tested and that experience teaches them how to interpret unique situations. They also argue that computers are not good at recognizing patterns; if there are small abnormalities, the computer will not recognize the pattern. Computers cannot match the performance of the human eye at this task.

We should point out that an investor should not expect a simple technical tool to be profitable. If a particular tool worked and its success were commonly known, it would self-destruct as a profitable trading tool. Users of it would seek greater profits by buying and selling in anticipation of the signal. As other investors sought more profits by acting before these investors, prices would adjust sooner. Before long this process would smooth out the price patterns.

# SUMMARY

Technical analysts work with market generated data, believing that new information slowly enters the market and causes recurring price patterns. They use line charts, bar charts, and point and figure charts to try to discover the patterns. Important in interpreting the charts are trends and support and resistance levels. Technical analysts use several measures of investor sentiment. In this chapter, we presented a sampling of these indicators: volume, moving averages, insider transactions, short sales, odd lot trading, advance-decline line, confidence index, and mutual fund liquidity.

Many research studies fail to substantiate the profitability of common technical tools. As more complex trading tools are tested, even more complex ones are developed. Researchers argue that under scientific testing the tools of the technical analyst fail. Technical analysts argue that statistics and computers cannot adequately test their art.

# QUESTIONS

1. Why do technical analysts prefer their approach to that of fundamental analysts?
2. Demonstrate how line charts, bar charts, and point and figure charts are drawn.
3. Explain a speculative blowoff and a selling climax.
4. How are moving averages used in technical analysis?
5. If corporate insiders are buying more of the company's stock than they are selling, would you follow their example? Why or why not?
6. Explain the two conflicting ways in which technical analysts might interpret short selling.
7. Why do technical analysts compare odd lot sales to odd lot purchases and then do the opposite of the majority of odd lot traders?
8. How is the advance-decline line calculated?

9. This week *Barron's* confidence index was .85. A month ago it was .81. What does this mean?

10. At present, the percentage of the portfolios of mutual funds held in cash is abnormally low. Interpret this measure.

11. What is the relationship between technical analysis and correlation among prices?

12. What arguments do technical analysts use to defend their methods from criticism?

## CASE PROBLEMS

1. Using daily high, low, and closing prices, make bar charts for a stock and for a market index. Compare the charts and look for price patterns. (You need at least 60 days of prices.)

2. Make a point and figure chart based on a stock's daily closing prices. (You need at least six months of prices.)

## READINGS

Bookstaber, Richard. *The Complete Investment Book.* Glenview IL: Scott, Foresman and Company, 1985.
   *Chapters 14 through 20 explain and have computer programs written in Basic for technical analysis.*

Colburn, Hardy C. *Investor's Guide to Technical Analysis.* New York: McGraw-Hill, 1978.
   *This book explains how to use technical analysis.*

Levy, Robert A. "Conceptual Foundations of Technical Analysis," *Financial Analysts Journal* 22 (July–August, 1966): 83.
   *This article presents well the basic philosophy and assumptions of technical analysis.*

Pring, Martin J. *Technical Analysis Explained.* New York: McGraw-Hill, 1985.
   *This book shows how technical analysis is being used in the 1980s.*

# Bonds

## OUTLINE

## OBJECTIVES

When you have finished studying this chapter, you should understand

1. The types of assets that can be pledged as security for a bond issue.

2. How to calculate the coupon rate, current yield, and the yield to maturity on a bond.

3. How interest rate risk, purchasing power risk, and default risk influence the returns offered on bonds.

4. The unique features recently offered on some bond issues.

5. The features of income bonds.

*246*

# 13

## *Bondholders and Leveraged Buyouts*

On October 20, 1988, RJR Nabisco Inc.'s president announced a plan under which management would buy all the publicly owned stock and take the company private. Such a transaction is called a leveraged buyout because it involves issuing bonds to obtain the money to buy the stock. The bonds are backed by the future earnings and the assets of the corporation.

This announcement caused the prices of the firm's publicly traded debt to fall drastically, as much as $150 per $1,000 bond. Prices fell because bond investors believed that the new debt would make the existing bonds riskier. In addition to RJR Nabisco's bonds, prices of other higher-quality corporate bonds fell, as investors realized that other large corporations could be targets of leveraged buyouts and takeovers.

Two large institutional owners of RJR Nabisco's bonds filed suit. ITT Corp. argued that federal disclosure laws were broken because RJR Nabisco did not disclose that it was considering a leveraged buyout when it sold bonds to ITT Hartford insurance units the previous April. Metropolitan Life Insurance Co. argued that as a bondholder it was owed a "continuing duty of good faith and fair dealing" and that issuing so much new debt violated that obligation.

## INTRODUCTION

In the past 20 years bonds have become a much more timely topic in investments courses. The amount of money invested in bonds has always been large; more money is invested in bonds than in stocks. In recent years, however, high and variable interest rates have made efficient bond portfolio management of critical importance. In this chapter, we examine the features of bonds and the risks associated with bond ownership. We will also look at some of the new features that bond issuers are offering in their attempt to make bonds more attractive to investors.

# BOND FEATURES

Bonds provide return in two forms: periodic interest payments and capital appreciation on sale or redemption. The periodic interest payments are usually fixed for the life of the bond. There have been some exceptions to this in recent years, as some bonds have been issued which pay variable amounts of interest; their interest rates are based on some measure of market interest rates (such as Treasury bill rates). Bonds are issued with original maturities of from 10 to 30 years. In recent years many issuers have been offering medium-term notes which have maturities of from 9 months to 15 years. Most of the discussion about bonds in this chapter also applies to medium-term notes.

The amount of the interest payments, the redemption date, and the redemption value are stated in the bond **indenture,** which is the contract on which the bond is based. This contract states the rights and responsibilities of the issuer, the bondholders, and the trustee. The **trustee** is a financial institution which has the responsibility of representing the bondholders and enforcing the indenture agreement. If the issuer violates a provision of the indenture, the trustee will initiate a lawsuit.

## Secured Bonds

The bond indenture also states whether an asset is pledged as security for the bond. A **secured bond** has a specific asset pledged in addition to the pledge of the general credit of the issuer. An unsecured bond is backed only by the pledge of the general credit of the issuer.

Secured bonds can be categorized into several different types based on the type of asset pledged. **Mortgage bonds** pledge land and/or buildings as security. Senior or first mortgage bonds have first claim on the asset. Junior or second mortgage bonds have a claim on any remaining value of the asset after the senior mortgage bondholders have been paid in full. **Equipment trust certificates** are bonds issued to finance the purchase of equipment, and title to that equipment is held by the bond trustee. These bonds are widely used to finance railroad cars and engines, commercial aircraft, and

### Asset-Backed Securities

In the 1970s, mortgage-backed securities became popular investment vehicles. Mortgages were purchased from lenders and pooled into a trust which then issued debt securities backed by the mortgages. As property owners make their mortgage payments, security holders receive the principal and interest payments.

In the 1980s, the same arrangement was used to create securities backed by auto loans. A lender such as General Motors Acceptance Corporation (GMAC) would create a trust. The trust's property would be a pool of retail installment sales contracts secured by new automobiles and light trucks. Certificates of ownership in the trust were sold to the public. As the vehicle owners made their payments, the principal and interest were passed on to the certificate owners. The trust paid GMAC a fee for servicing the sale contracts.

The same principle can be used to create trusts of other consumer debt such as boat loans and vacation time share notes. Even outstanding bank card balances became an asset to be pooled into a trust. The first deal was a $50 million offering from Ohio's BancOne Corporation.

trucking fleets. **Collateral trust bonds** have stocks or bonds of other firms pledged as security. Usually they involve a holding company pledging the stocks or bonds of its subsidiaries.

## Unsecured Bonds

Unsecured bonds, called **debentures,** are bonds secured only by the general credit of the issuer; there is no pledge of a specific asset. Debentures are issued either by firms with such good credit ratings that they do not need to pledge any specific asset or by firms that have borrowed so much that they have already pledged all their assets to other lenders. **Subordinate debentures** have a claim on earnings and assets which ranks after secured debt, debentures, and sometimes general creditors.

The importance of security in a bond issue is demonstrated by the market prices of the bonds of People Express Airline when it was in serious financial trouble in September 1986. Between December 1983 and April 1986, $540 million of People Express bonds were sold to the public. Of the $465 million outstanding in September 1986, $165 million of the bonds were secured by airplanes; the other $300 million were debentures. At their low point, the secured bonds sold for 70 percent of face value while the debentures plunged to 35 percent of face value.

## Provisions for Paying Off Bonds

Most corporate bonds are **term bonds.** A term bond has one maturity date for the entire issue. This is in contrast to **serial bonds,** where the issue contains bonds with different maturity dates—perhaps one-seventh of the issue matures each year for the last seven years of the life of the issue. Equipment trust certificates are usually issued as serial bonds. That way, the amount of the outstanding bonds will decrease as the value of the equipment decreases.

Bond indentures may contain a **call provision** which gives the issuer the right to redeem the bonds early. This is an advantage to the issuer and a disadvantage to the bondholder because the issuer will probably call the bonds only if interest rates in the economy go down or if the firm's financial position improves enough so that it can issue new bonds paying lower interest rates.

The details of any call provision are specified when the bond is issued. An important provision is the amount of the call premium. A **call premium** is an amount in addition to the principal that an issuer is required to pay the bondholder if the bonds are called. Call premiums are usually 5 to 10 percent of the face value of the bond. For example, a call premium of 6 percent would require the issuer to pay $1,060 per $1,000 bond if it wanted to redeem the bonds early. Some issuers agree not to call the bonds during their first three or five years of existence. Also, call premiums sometimes decrease as maturity approaches. For example, a bond maturing in 1998 might have a 10 percent call premium through 1990, a 9 percent premium in 1991, an 8 percent premium in 1989, and so on.

Some bonds are convertible into common stock at the option of the bondholder. The conversion provision is also detailed in the indenture. It specifies either a conversion ratio or a conversion price. A conversion ratio states the number of shares into which the bond can be converted. For example, each $1,000 bond could be exchanged for 40 shares of common stock. Another way of stating the same thing is to say that the common stock has a conversion price of $25. If the conversion price of the stock is $25, each $1,000 bond will purchase 40 shares of common stock.

The bond indenture may contain a sinking fund provision which requires the issuer to pay the trustee a certain portion of the principal each year. The trustee then randomly selects by serial number specific bonds to be called for redemption. The issuer commonly has the option of going into the market and repurchasing bonds to retire instead of making a cash sinking fund payment to the trustee. The issuer will repurchase bonds in the market when the bonds are selling for less than face value.

From the bondholders' point of view, a sinking fund provision reduces the risk of default at maturity. For the issuer to make periodic payments instead of having to redeem all the bonds at once reduces the probability of a crisis at maturity. The disadvantage, however, is that your bond might be called for redemption when interest rates are low and it is selling at a premium.

# BOND YIELDS

Bond investors want to be able to calculate the return available on bonds being offered in the market. Investors commonly refer to three measurements of return on bonds: the coupon rate, the current yield, and the yield to maturity.

## Coupon Rate

The **coupon rate** is the amount of interest that a bond promises to pay annually divided by the face value of the bond. Normally the interest is paid semiannually. For example, if the coupon rate on a $1,000 bond is 10 percent, each bond pays $100 interest per year ($50 semiannually).

The term "coupon rate" developed from an old method of paying bond interest. To save the trouble of keeping track of the bond owners and of mailing out interest checks, bonds were issued "payable to the bearer" (called bearer bonds) and had interest coupons attached to them. Each coupon contained the name of the issuer, an interest payment date, and the amount of interest payable. On the interest payment date, the bondholder cut off the appropriate coupon and took it to a brokerage firm or bank in order to receive the interest. Hence, the terms coupon interest and coupon rate developed.

Most bonds issued in the last 30 years and all bonds issued after July 1, 1983, have the name of the owner recorded on the certificate. The issuer keeps track of the owners of these registered bonds. When a bond is sold, the bondholder signs the back of the bond and relinquishes possession. A new certificate is issued to the new owner. Interest payments are mailed by the issuer directly to the bondholders.

In recent years, some bonds have been issued with low or zero coupon rates. Of course, they sell at large discounts from maturity value. Investors who do not need current income but who want to buy bonds find them attractive investments. As time passes to maturity, the value of the bond increases (the discount decreases). At maturity, they are redeemed at face value.

## Current Yield

When investors purchase a bond, they also want to know both the current return on the bond and the rate of return they will earn if they hold the bond to maturity. The current rate of return is called the **current yield** on the bond. It is computed by dividing the annual coupon interest by the current price of the bond.

---

| EXAMPLE | A bond pays $100 interest per year and sells for $885. The current yield is 11.3% (100/885). □ |

## Yield to Maturity

Yield to maturity considers the coupon interest and any discount or premium. If bondholders buy the bond at face value, the yield to maturity equals the coupon rate. If they buy the bond at a discount (less than face value) and hold it until it is redeemed at face value at maturity, they earn the coupon interest plus the amount of the discount. Therefore, the yield to maturity is greater than the coupon rate. If they buy the bond at a premium (more than face value) and hold it until it is redeemed at maturity, they will earn the coupon interest less the amount of the premium. Therefore, the yield to maturity is less than the coupon rate.

In Chapter 5, we used Equation 13–1 to value a bond based on the present value of its promised future cash flows.

$$ B = \sum_{m=1}^{n} \frac{I}{(1 + ytm)^m} + \frac{M}{(1 + ytm)^n} $$

where

$B$ = the value of the bond

$I$ = the interest payment

$ytm$ = the yield to maturity required by investors

$n$ = the number of periods to maturity

$M$ = the maturity value of the bond

This equation can also be used to find the yield to maturity if the price of the bond is known. The yield to maturity is the discount rate that equates the price of the bond to the discounted interest payments plus the discounted maturity value.

**PRACTICE**   Find the yield to maturity on a $1,000 bond which is selling for $885.30. The bond has a coupon
**PROBLEM 1**   rate of 10% ($50 semiannually) and has 10 years to maturity.

*Solution*

$$885.30 = \sum_{m=1}^{20} \frac{50}{(1 + ytm)^m} + \frac{1,000}{(1 + ytm)^{20}}$$

$B = PV = 885.30; I = 50; n = 20; M = 1,000; ytm = ?$

$ytm = 6\%$ (semiannually)

$ytm = 12\%$ (annually)

Notice that the bond sells at a discount and its yield to maturity is greater than its coupon rate.

**PRACTICE**   Find the yield to maturity if the bond described above is selling for $1,135.90.
**PROBLEM 2**
$$1135.90 = \sum_{m=1}^{20} \frac{50}{(1 + ytm)^m} + \frac{1,000}{(1 + ytm)^{20}}$$

$B = PV = 1,135.90; I = 50; n = 20; M = 1,000; ytm = ?$

$ytm = 4\%$ (semiannually)

$ytm = 8\%$ (annually)

Notice that the bond sells at a premium and its yield to maturity is less than its coupon rate.

# CHOOSING BONDS

Like most investments, a bond offers the buyer a risk-return tradeoff. In this section
we examine the main determinants of that tradeoff: interest rate risk, purchasing power
risk, and default risk. We will also examine some marketability issues. These factors
greatly influence the yield to maturity which investors demand from a bond.

## Interest Rate Risk

If investors plan to hold a bond to maturity, they are not very concerned about interest
rate risk. However, if they plan to sell the bond before maturity, the price received
will depend on the level of interest rates at that time. If interest rates are high compared
to the coupon rate on the bond being sold, investors will prefer to buy other bonds.
To sell the bond, the holder will have to accept a price below face value.

**PRACTICE**   What is the price of a $1,000 face value bond with a 10% coupon rate ($50 semiannually) when
**PROBLEM 3**   the current market rate for bond of this quality and maturity is 12% (6% semiannually)? The
bond has 3 years left to maturity.

*Solution*

$$B = \sum_{m=1}^{6} \frac{50}{(1 + .06)^m} + \frac{1,000}{(1 + .06)^{20}}$$

$I = 50; n = 6; M = 1,000; ytm = 6\%; B = ?$

$B = \$950.83$

**PRACTICE PROBLEM 4**
What is the value of a bond similar to the one above but with 20 years to maturity?

*Solution*

$I = 50; n = 40; M = 1,000; ytm = 6\%; B = ?$

$B = \$849.53$

Notice that the value of the long-term bond was much less than the short-term bond.

---

If interest rates are low compared to the coupon rate when the bondholder wants to sell, investors will prefer this bond to others in the market. Thus, they will pay more than face value for it. If interest rates fell to 8 percent, the 3-year bond above would sell for $1,052.42. The 20-year bond would sell for $1,197.93. Notice that the premium on the long-term bond is greater than that on the short-term bond.

The above example demonstrates two very important relationships between bond prices and interest rates.

---

**THEOREM 1**
There is an inverse relationship between bond prices and interest rates.

**THEOREM 2**
The longer the time to maturity, the more the price of a bond will change for a given change in interest rates.

---

If two bonds with different coupon rates have the same maturity and yield to maturity, the price of the one with the lower coupon rate will change more when interest rates change because most of the dollars being returned are farther away and, therefore, affected more by discounting at the new rate.

---

**THEOREM 3**
For a given maturity, the lower the coupon rate, the greater will be the percentage change in price for a given change in interest rates.

---

In Appendix 13B we will cover duration. **Duration** is a measure of a bond's term to maturity. It considers the amount and timing of all the cash flows (interest and principal). The concept of duration will allow us to understand better and state more exactly these theorems.

### Guessing Wrong on Interest Rates

In June 1984, the nation's largest insurance broker, Marsh & McLennan Cos., fired its treasurer and several of his subordinates. The firm had lost $155 million in its government bond portfolio between April 1983 and April 1984. In particular, it had purchased long-term bonds on margin. As interest rates moved up and losses were incurred, it made additional purchases with the expectation that interest rates would fall and the entire portfolio would rise in value. Interest rates continued to go up.

Several factors contributed to the bad investment decisions made at Marsh & McLennan. The firm may have encouraged excess risk taking in cash management by making the cash management function a profit center. Also the firm did not have a formal written investment policy. Finally, a faulty record keeping system prevented auditors from uncovering the situation sooner.

Postscript: If the firm had held its position in long-term bonds during the following year, it would have been very profitable when interest rates fell.

_____

Source: "Big Insurer Fires Treasurer for Part in Bond Debacle," *The Wall Street Journal* (June 11, 1984): 4.

**Reinvestment Rate Risk**   There is another risk factor to consider in connection with interest rate changes. The computation of yield to maturity assumes that coupon interest payments are reinvested at the yield to maturity. If interest rates fall, reinvestment at this rate will not be possible. The risk of not being able to reinvest interest payment at the bond's yield to maturity rate is **reinvestment rate risk.** Exhibit 13–1 illustrates the effect of different reinvestment rates on a 20 year, 10 percent bond. Described in Appendix 13B is immunization, a technique that can be used to manage reinvestment rate risk.

---

**EXHIBIT 13–1   *Effects of Different Reinvestment Rates (20 Year, 10 Percent Bond)***

| Reinvestment Rate | Future Value of the Reinvested Interest Payments[a] | Future Value of the Reinvested Payments Plus the Principal Repayment | Realized Compound Yield[b] |
|---|---|---|---|
| 0% | $2,000 | $ 3,000 | 5.57% |
| 6 | 3,770 | 4,770 | 7.97 |
| 8 | 4,751 | 5,751 | 8.94 |
| 10 | 6,040 | 7,040 | 10.00 |
| 12 | 7,738 | 8,738 | 11.14 |
| 14 | 9,982 | 10,982 | 12.35 |

[a] $PMT = 50$, $n = 40$, $i$ = reinvestment rate/2, find $FV$.

[b] $FV$ = future value of the reinvested payments plus the principal repayment, $n = 40$, $PV = 1000$, find $i$, yield = $i \times 2$.

## Purchasing Power Risk

Because most bonds are dollar denominated and have fixed interest payments, inflation erodes the purchasing power of the promised cash flows. Because market interest rates contain a premium for anticipated inflation, the price of the bond and/or its coupon interest rate are based on expected inflation. It is unanticipated inflation that harms the bondholder the most. The unanticipated inflation of the 1970s was disastrous for bond prices while the unexpected low inflation in 1984, 1985, and 1986 resulted in high (25–35 percent) gains for bondholders.

## Default Risk

Default is the failure by the issuer to meet a provision of the bond indenture. Most often, it is the failure to make an interest or principal payment on the prescribed date. The seriousness of a bond default depends on its cause. On one extreme, default might be caused by a temporary cash flow problem which can be corrected in a few days. At the other extreme, default might be the result of serious problems which could lead a firm to bankruptcy.

The investor's task of estimating the probability of default is greatly reduced because bond rating agencies estimate it and publish their opinions. There are two well-known rating agencies—Moody's and Standard & Poor's—and two smaller agencies—Fitch's Rating Service and Duff and Phelps, Inc.

By doing fundamental analysis of the bond issuer, the bond rating agencies estimate the likelihood of a default on a bond issue. This task is easier than fundamental analysis of a stock because it involves only an investigation of the issuer's ability to meet the contractual obligation for the life of the bond issue. Since rating agencies do a thorough job, most investors rely on agency opinions and do not do their own fundamental analysis of bond issuers.

The two most important factors in determining a bond's rating are the firm's financial condition and the provisions of the bond indenture. Financial ratios are used to analyze the firm's financial position. Particularly important are interest coverage ratios, financial leverage ratios, liquidity ratios, turnover ratios, and profitability ratios. Important provisions of the bond indenture are the collateral, any sinking fund provision, and other provisions such as sale of asset restrictions, additional debt restrictions, and negative pledge clauses. Negative pledge clauses prohibit using assets as security for new loans. A rating agency might also obtain nonpublic information from issuers. For competitive reasons the information might be confidential but the issuers are willing to disclose it to the rating agencies in order to obtain better ratings. In summary, it is more efficient for the specialists at the rating agency to undertake bond evaluations and sell their ratings than it is for individual investors to undertake this analysis.

Bond ratings are printed in Standard & Poor's *Bond Guide* and Moody's *Bond Record*. Exhibit 13–2 shows the definitions of each firm's rating categories. The first three ratings, AAA, AA, and A are considered good investment quality. BBBs are considered medium investment quality. BBs and below are speculative. In the 1980s, several investment banking firms started underwriting newly issued speculative bonds.

---

**EXHIBIT 13–2   Bond Rating Definitions**

| | Moody's | Standard & Poor's | Definition |
|---|---|---|---|
| High grade | Aaa | AAA | The highest quality rating assigned to bonds. Interest and principal payments are well-protected. Bonds in this category are called "gilt edge" securities. |
| | Aa | AA | This high-quality rating is assigned to bonds which have only slightly less protection than Aaa or AAA. |
| Medium grade | A | A | These bonds have many favorable investment characteristics but elements exist which make them more susceptible to adverse circumstances and economic conditions. |
| | Baa | BBB | These bonds are of medium grade. Interest payments are secure at present, but protective provisions for the future are lacking. |
| Speculative | Ba | BB | These bonds have speculative elements and their future cannot be considered assured. Protection of interest and principal is moderate. |
| | B | B | These bonds lack desirable characteristics. There is little assurance of interest and principal over long periods of time. |
| Default | Caa | CCC | These bonds are of poor standing. They may be in default or elements of danger are present. |
| | Ca | CC | These bonds are highly speculative. They are in default or have other shortcomings. |
| | C | | Moody's lowest bond rating. These issues have extremely poor prospects. |
| | | C | This rating is reserved for income bonds on which interest is not being paid. |
| | | D | These bonds are in default. Payment of interest or repayment or principal is in arrears. |

Note: S&P's uses plus or minus to show relative strength within categories AA to B. Moody's uses the numbers 1, 2, and 3 to indicate strength within categories Aa to B.

---

These bonds, called **junk bonds,** offered the buyer higher returns and higher risk than better-quality bonds. Default rates were low until 1985 and 1986 when several large issuers defaulted on their junk bonds. The Peoples Express Airline bonds described earlier were junk bonds.

Usually, Standard and Poor's and Moody's give a bond the same rating. When they give a bond different ratings, the bond is said to have a **split rating.** Bonds are

---

**EXHIBIT 13–3   Yield Spreads**

| | | Industrial Bonds By Quality | | | |
|---|---|---|---|---|---|
| Date[a] | Treasuries | AAA—T[b] | AA—T | A—T | BBB—T |
| Mar 1975 (trough) | 8.05% | .36% | .56% | 1.03% | 1.34% |
| Jan 1980 (peak) | 10.53 | .34 | .60 | .85 | 1.24 |
| Jul 1980 (trough) | 10.21 | .31 | .51 | .94 | 1.46 |
| Jul 1981 (peak) | 13.37 | .60 | .84 | 1.18 | 1.86 |
| Nov 1982 (trough) | 10.30 | .40 | .82 | 1.55 | 3.30 |
| Dec 1987 | 9.24 | .51 | .89 | 1.65 | 2.10 |

[a] First five dates are peaks and troughs of economic cycles.

[b] Yields on AAA industrials minus (−) yields on long-term Treasuries.

Source: Compiled from data in *Standard & Poor's Security Price Index Record* (New York: Standard & Poor's Corporation), 1988.

---

rated at the time of initial issue and these ratings are reviewed regularly. Most bonds carry the same rating for many years. However, on occasion, a review will result in a rating being revised upward or downward.

**Yield spreads** are the differences between yields on bonds of different quality. Usually, yield spreads are measured between bonds of given quality and a Treasury security of the same maturity. The yield spreads reflect the risk premiums offered by the lower-quality bonds. Exhibit 13–3 shows the yield spreads on different quality bonds in recent years. Yield spreads change over the economic cycle. During bad economic times they usually are greater, particularly on lower-quality bonds. There are two reasons why investors demand larger risk premiums in bad times. First, sales, profits, and cash flows decline for most firms. Therefore, default and bankruptcy are more likely. Second, most investors are more averse to risk during recessions because they worry more about the stability of their own job and investment income.

## Marketability Factors

An investor can buy new bonds in the primary market or buy outstanding bonds in the secondary market. The investor does not pay a commission on new issues and may get a slightly higher interest rate than available on a comparable issue in the secondary market. On the other hand, the selection of new issues is limited while the selection of outstanding bonds is large. Particular maturities and features may not be available in the primary market.

If bondholders are not going to hold the bonds until maturity, they must be concerned about marketability. Some bond issues are listed on the exchanges, but the majority are traded in the OTC market. For some OTC bonds, the spreads between the bid and asked prices are large. In these cases the investor should use limit orders when buying and selling. Bond yields are influenced slightly by the marketability of the bond.

### Ten Most Active Bonds

The ten most actively traded bonds on the NYSE
in 1987 are listed below.

1. International Business Machines                    cv7 7/8S '04
2. Public Serive Company of New Hampshire            17 1/2S '04
3. Bethlehem Steel Corporation                       8.45s '05
4. Merrill Lynch                                     cv zero coupon '06
5. Occidental Petroleum                              9.65s '94
6. National Gypsum Company                           zero coupon '94
7. Marathon Oil Company                              9 1/2S '94
8. Pan American World Airways                        15s '94
9. Texaco Capital Incorporated                       13s '91
10. American Telephone & Telegraph                   8 3/4S '00

Note: cv = convertible bond
7⅞s = 7⅞% coupon rate ($78.75 interest per year)
04 = bond matures in the year 2004

# UNIQUE BOND FEATURES

In order to make their bonds more attractive to specific classes of purchasers, issuers sometimes offer bonds with unique features. Occasionally, these features are beneficial to both the issuer and the bondholder, but in most cases the firm is accepting an unwanted feature in order to obtain a lower interest rate on the bonds.

## Original Issue Deep Discount Bonds

Original issue deep discount bonds have abnormally low coupon rates, usually 0 to 7 percent. Depending on their quality and maturity, they sell for 25 to 40 percent of face value. They are attractive to the investor who does not want current income but prefers the risk-return tradeoff offered on bonds. Remember, however, that for a given maturity, the lower a bond's coupon rate, the more its price will change when interest rates change. Therefore, these bonds are very sensitive to interest rate risk with the zero coupon bonds being the most sensitive. On the other hand, reinvestment rate risk is less on low coupon bonds and nonexistent on zero coupon ones.

| EXAMPLE |

The first original issue deep discount bond issued by a large U.S. corporation was Martin Marietta Corporation's $175 million of 7 percent, 30-year debentures sold in March 1981. At a price of $538.35, its yield to maturity was 13.25 percent.                                                                 ☐

| EXAMPLE | On April 22, 1981, the J.C. Penney Company issued $200 million of zero coupon notes due May 1, 1989. At a price of $334.27, its yield to maturity was 14.25 percent. □ |
|---|---|

Original issue deep discount bonds are not attractive investments for the investor who pays income tax. The tax law requires amortization of the discount over the life of the bond. Because each year's portion is considered taxable income for that year, income tax must be paid even though no cash is received! Because of this tax law provision, most zero coupon bonds are purchased by nontax-paying investors.

## Floating Rate Notes

Floating rate notes originated in Europe and were first offered in the United States by Citicorp in 1974. Although these securities are called notes, maturities of up to 20 years occur. The coupon interest on a floating rate note changes with interest rate changes on a specified base series, such as Treasury securities. For example, a good quality floating rate note might pay 1.5 percent above the six-month Treasury bill rate. The interest sensitivity of their assets makes financial institutions more frequent issuers of floating rate notes than industrial firms. Floating rate notes are often convertible into fixed rate long-term debt at the holder's option. Notice that this is a case of a debt security being convertible into another debt security instead of equity securities. Note also that this is an example of a case where the feature is beneficial to the purchaser, but not to the issuer because the purchaser will convert to fixed rate long-term debt when interest rates are high. Floating rate notes shift interest rate risk from the holder to the issuer.

## Put Bonds

**Put bonds** allow the holder to redeem them before maturity at an agreed upon price, which is usually par value. Put bonds reduce the bondholder's interest rate risk. If interest rates go up, the bondholder can redeem the bond and invest the money at the higher rates. Actually, put bonds shift interest rate risk back to the issuer, who will be forced to redeem the bonds and perhaps issue new debt if interest rates move up. The floating rate notes described above often have a put feature.

## Commodity Backed Bonds

Commodity backed bonds promise to pay at maturity the greater of the par value or the dollar value of a given quantity of a commodity. These bonds offer the bondholder some protection from purchasing power risk. Because the bond issuers normally are in the business of producing the commodity which backs their bonds, they are attractive securities for the issuers. Issuers get low-cost financing at the time of issue, and financing gets more expensive only if the price of their product goes up.

| EXAMPLE | On June 23, 1986, the Standard Oil Company issued $37.5 million of oil indexed notes due in 1990 and another $37.5 million due in 1992.        ☐ |

| EXAMPLE | On September 26, 1986, Echo Bay Mines Ltd. used bonds with warrants to achieve a similar result. The bonds were sold with warrants attached that permitted the holder to buy gold from Echo Bay Mines at a set price.        ☐ |

## Stock Index Bonds

**Stock index bonds** promise to pay at maturity the greater of the par value or a dollar amount based on a stock index. For example, a bond that is issued when the S&P 500 index is at 250 might promise at maturity to repay the greater of $1,000 or four times the S&P 500 index. If the S&P went to 350, the bondholder would get $1,400.

| EXAMPLE | In August 1986, Solomon Brothers issued four year notes tied to the S&P 500 index. They referred to them as SPINs, an acronym for Standard & Poor's 500 Index Subordinated Notes.        ☐ |

## Guaranteed Bonds

A **guaranteed bond** has its interest and/or principal payments guaranteed by another corporation. The default risk and rating of the bond then depends on the financial strength of both the issuer and the guarantor. A guaranteed bond may have more than one guarantor, in which case each guarantor may be responsible for either a pro rata share or for the entire amount of the issue.

# INCOME BONDS

Income bonds are a very unattractive security for the investor. **Income bonds** have to pay interest only if the firm has enough earnings to cover the interest payment. If the firm does not have sufficient earnings, the interest will not be paid and does not become a future obligation. The bondholder loses the interest forever.

Income bonds are usually issued only when a firm has failed and is being reorganized under the bankruptcy laws. Usually when firms fail, they are liquidated; that is, the firm goes out of business and all its assets are sold to pay debts. However, sometimes the corporation may petition the court for the right to reorganize. The court may agree that it is in the best interest of all parties to keep the firm in business because the firm is worth more as a going concern than it would be if it were liquidated. This is referred to as a Chapter 11 bankruptcy. In a reorganization, stockholders and bondholders of the failed firm may be given income bonds to replace their other securities.

# SUMMARY

Bonds are securities based on a debt contract that exists between the issuer and investors. Bondholders have loaned the issuer money in return for the promise of periodic interest payment and repayment of the principal at maturity. Important aspects of any bond issue are the coupon rate, the maturity, any security behind the issue, and the repayment provisions.

Bondholders face interest rate risk, reinvestment rate risk, purchasing power risk, and default risk. Bond rating services publish their estimates of default risk. Unique bond features that have been offered recently by issuers include original issue deep discount bonds, floating rate notes, put bonds, commodity backed bonds, and stock index bonds. Income bonds are bonds that pay interest only when the firm makes a profit.

# QUESTIONS

1. In what forms might a bondholder receive returns? For which form of return is it more difficult to predict the dollar amount? Why?

2. What is the difference between a coupon bond and a registered bond?

3. What is the difference between a secured and an unsecured bond? What are some different types of secured bonds?

4. Why might a bond sell at a discount or premium? Explain the relationship between discounts and premiums and coupon yields and market interest rates.

5. Define interest rate risk. Do long-term or short-term bonds have more interest rate risk? Do high or low coupon rate bonds have more risk? How does duration relate to interest rate risk?

6. Define reinvestment rate risk. How does immunization relate to reinvestment rate risk?

7. How do anticipated and unanticipated inflation affect bond returns?

8. Exactly what do bond rating agencies do? Name four of them. Explain their rating systems. How do their ratings affect the yields on bonds?

9. Define and give examples of the following unique bond features: original issue deep discount bonds, floating rate notes, put bonds, commodity backed bonds, and stock index bonds.

10. Why are income bonds unattractive investments? When are income bonds normally issued?

# PROBLEMS

1. A bond with a face value of $1,000 pays $40 interest semiannually. The bond currently sells for $900.
   a. What is the bond's coupon rate?
   b. What is the bond's current yield?

2. A bond currently selling for $1,210 pays $50 interest semiannually. The bond has a face value of $1,000.

    **a.** What is the bond's coupon rate?

    **b.** What is the bond's current yield?

**3.** Karen bought a $1,000 bond with a 9% coupon rate several years ago. It now has a 12 year maturity and other bonds with similar risk characteristics have yields to maturity of 12%.

    **a.** What is the bond's semiannual interest payment?

    **b.** What is the current value of this bond?

**4.** A bond has an 11% coupon rate, a face value of $1,000, and a 15 year maturity. The current market rate for bonds of this quality and maturity is 8%.

    **a.** What is the bond's semiannual interest payment?

    **b.** What is the price of this bond?

**5.** A $1,000 bond with a coupon rate of 9% is currently selling for $1,100. The bond matures in 15 years.

    **a.** What is the bond's semiannual interest payment?

    **b.** What is the bond's current yield?

    **c.** What is the bond's yield to maturity?

**6.** A $1,000 bond with 18 years to maturity is currently selling at $850. With a coupon rate of 12%,

    **a.** What is the bond's semiannual interest payment?

    **b.** What is the bond's current yield?

    **c.** What is the bond's yield to maturity?

**7.** A zero coupon bond with a 20-year maturity sold for $300. If it has a $1,000 face value, what is its yield to maturity?

**8.** If a zero coupon bond with an 18-year maturity and a $1,000 face value sold for $400, what would be its yield to maturity?

**9.** A $1,000 face value bond has a 9% coupon rate. The current market rate for bonds of this quality and maturity is 11%.

    **a.** What is the price of this bond if the bond has four years to maturity?

    **b.** What is the price of this bond if it has 18 years to maturity?

    **c.** Which theorem of interest rate risk does this problem illustrate?

**10.** A bond has coupon rate of 7% and a $1,000 face value. Bonds of similar risk characteristics have a yield to maturity of 10%.

    **a.** What is the current value of the bond if it has 2 years to maturity?

    **b.** What is the current value of the bond if it has 20 years to maturity?

    **c.** What principle of interest rate risk does this problem illustrate?

**11.** A $1,000 face value bond has 10% coupon rate with 20 years to maturity.

    **a.** If bonds with similar risk characteristics have a yield to maturity of 12%, what is the price of this bond?

    **b.** If bonds with similar risk characteristics have a yield to maturity of 7%, what is the price of this bond?

    **c.** What principle of interest rate risk does this problem illustrate?

**12.** A bond with a $1,000 face value and an 8% coupon rate has 18 years to maturity.

    **a.** If the current market rate for bonds of this quality and maturity is 6%, what is the current value of this bond?

    **b.** If the current market rate for bonds of this quality and maturity is 11%, what is the current value of this bond?

    **c.** Which theorem of interest rate risk does this problem illustrate?

13. A bond with a $1,000 face value matures in 18 years.
    a. If the bond has a 10% coupon rate, what percent will the price of the bond change when interest rates on similar bonds change from 6% to 8%?
    b. If the bond has a 4% coupon rate, what percent will the price of the bond change when interest rates on similar bonds change from 6% to 8%?
    c. Which theorem of interest rate risk does this problem illustrate?

14. A bond which matures in 15 years has a face value of $1,000.
    a. If the bond has an 8% coupon rate, what percent will the value of the bond change when the yield to maturity on similar bonds changes from 10% to 12%?
    b. If the bond has a 5% coupon rate, what percent will the value of the bond change when the yield to maturity on similar bonds changes from 10% to 12%?
    c. What principle of interest rate risk does this problem illustrate?

15. Mr. Bradford bought a 20-year bond with a face value of $1,000 and a coupon rate of 8% for a price of $1,000. However, he found that the semiannual interest payments could be reinvested at only 6%.
    a. What is the future value of the reinvested interest payments?
    b. What is the future value of the reinvested payments plus the principal repayment?
    c. What is Mr. Bradford's realized compound yield if he holds the bond to maturity?

16. Professor Plum found that he could reinvest the interest payments from a National Clue Co. bond he bought at 8%. He bought the $1,000 face value 12% coupon bond for $800. It matures in 15 years.
    a. What is the future value of the reinvested interest payments?
    b. What is the future value of the reinvested payments plus the principal repayment?
    c. What is Professor Plum's realized compound yield if he holds the bond to maturity?

17. Mr. Apple paid $700 for an AAA rated bond with a $1,000 face value, a coupon rate of 11%, and a maturity of 18 years. Mr. Apple intended to hold this bond to maturity.
    a. If interest rates declined to 7%, what would be Mr. Apple's realized compound yield?
    b. If interest rates declined to 6%, what would be Mr. Apple's realized compound yield?

18. Abe bought for a price of $1,000 a 20 year $1,000 bond with a 12% coupon yield. He intended to hold the bond to maturity, but since interest rates had gone down right after he bought it, he knew his yield to maturity would be lower than 12%.
    a. What would Abe's realized compound yield be if he can reinvest at 10%?
    b. What would Abe's realized compound yield be if he can reinvest at 8%?

# READINGS

*Credit Overview, Corporate and International Ratings.* New York: Standard and Poor's Corporation, 1982.
   *This book highlights the major aspects of Standard and Poor's rating process, methodology, and organization. It also discusses a number of credit-related subjects that shed light on the rating process.*

Ederington, Louis H. "Why Split Ratings Occur," *Financial Management* 15 (Spring 1986): 37–47.
   *This paper explores the possible reasons for split ratings on new issues of corporate bonds.*

Fabozzi, Frank J., and Fabozzi, T. Dessa. *Bond Markets, Analysis, and Strategies.* Englewood Cliffs, NJ: Prentice Hall, 1989.

> *The objective of this book is to provide an overview of the fixed income market. It covers Treasury securities, agency securities, corporate bonds, municipal bonds, international bonds, mortgages, and mortgage-backed securities.*

Hsueh, L. Paul, and Kidwell, David S. ''Bond Ratings: Are Two Better Than One?'' *Financial Management* 17 (Spring 1988): 46–53.

> *This study examines why borrowers obtain more than one credit rating for their bond issues, and what is the impact on the net borrowing cost of a second credit rating?*

Stigum, Marcia, and Fabozzi, Frank J. *The Dow Jones-Irwin Guide to Bond and Money Market Investments.* Homewood, IL: Dow Jones-Irwin, 1987.

> *This book describes Treasury, municipal, and corporate debt securities.*

# APPENDIX 13A —————————————————————————————
# THE TERM STRUCTURE OF INTEREST RATES

This appendix explores the role of a security's time to maturity in determining the interest rate demanded by market participants. The framework for this analysis is the term structure of interest rates, which is the pattern of interest rates on securities identical in all respects except time to maturity. This requirement of identicalness is best met by Treasury notes and bonds; therefore, these securities usually are used to illustrate the term structure of interest rates. Examination of why Treasury securities of different maturities offer the investor different yields to maturity will demonstrate the importance of liquidity and expected inflation in determining interest rates.

The term structure of interest rates does not address other factors important in determining interest rates. The level of interest rates was discussed in Chapter 1 and the relationship among securities with different default risk was discussed in Chapter 13. Here the question is limited to ''What determines the relationship among interest rates on securities of different maturities?'' A narrower statement of the question is ''What is the relationship between long and short-term interest rates?''

The yields available on Treasury securities with different maturity dates are reported daily in the financial sections of newspapers under a heading such as ''Treasury bonds and notes.'' For each security, the yield and time to maturity can be plotted on a graph. The line which fits these points is called the yield curve. The **yield curve** reflects interest rates available on securities of different maturities. Here we ask, ''What

determines the shape of the yield curve?'' and ''Why does its shape change?''

In Exhibit 13A–1 the yield curves that existed for Treasury securities on three specific dates are shown. On May 29, 1981, short-term yields were above 15 percent while long-term yields were about 13 percent. This is a downward sloping yield curve; short-term rates are higher than long-term rates. Three months earlier on March 31, 1981, Treasury securities of all maturities were yielding about 13 percent. The yield curve was flat (horizontal). By September 30, 1985, short-term yields had fallen to below 8 percent while long-term yields were less than 11 percent. The yield curve was upward sloping; short-term rates were lower than long-term rates.

Three theories exist to explain the shape of the yield curve. Each has some evidence supporting it. The three theories are the expectations theory, the liquidity premium theory, and the market segmentation theory.

## Expectations Theory

The expectations theory states that long-term interest rates are the geometric mean of the consecutive expected short-term interest rates over the period. Supporters of the expectation theory argue that an investor can buy a long-term security or a series of short-term securities. If the returns are not equal, buying and selling pressures will force equilibrium. For example, if a five year bond yields 8 percent but investors except five one-year bonds purchased consecutively to return an average yield of

---

**EXHIBIT 13A–1  Yield Curves**

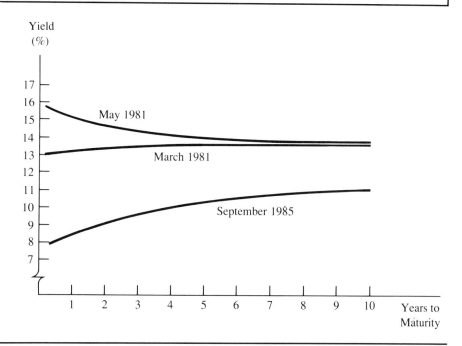

---

9 percent, they will purchase the one-year bonds. Because bond yields are readily available information, markets will adjust prices quickly.

By definition interest rates expected to be available in the future cannot be observed now. This is what makes the testing of term structure theories difficult. However, forward rates that exist now can be computed from the yield curve. The $n$ period forward rate is the yield to maturity which is fixed today on a $T$ year bond from year $T - n$ to year $T$. To keep things as simple as possible we will work only with one year forward rates. Equation 13A–1 related yield to maturity to forward rates.

$$(1 + R_T) = (1 + {}_0r_1)(1 + {}_1f_2)$$
$$(1 + {}_2f_3) \cdots (1 + {}_{T-1}f_T)$$
$$\textbf{(13A–1)}$$

where

$R_T$ = the yield for a $T$ year bond

${}_0r_1$ = the yield that exists now for a 1-year bond

${}_1f_2$ = the 1-year forward rate from year 1 to year 2

${}_2f_3$ = the 1-year forward rate from year 2 to year 3

${}_{T-1}f_T$ = the 1-year forward rate from year $T - 1$ to year $T$

This relationship can be used to compute forward rates from the data available in the yield curve. For example, if observation of the yield curve shows 1, 2, and 3 year bonds yielding 7, 8, and 9 percent respectively, we can compute the forward rates for the second and third years. (The rate for the first year is observable, 7 percent.)

To compute the forward rate for the second year, we use

$$(1 + R_2)^2 = (1 + {}_0r_1)(1 + {}_1f_2) \qquad \textbf{(13A–2)}$$

or
$$1 + {}_1f_2 = \frac{(1 + R_2)^2}{1 + {}_0r_1}$$

$$1 + {}_1f_2 = \frac{(1 + .08)^2}{1 + .07} = \frac{1.1664}{1.07} = 1.09$$

$${}_1f_2 = 9\%$$

Nine percent is the one-year rate for the second year.

To compute the forward rate for the third year, we use

$$(1 + R_3)^3$$
$$= (1 + {}_0r_1)(1 + {}_1f_2)(1 + {}_2f_3) \qquad \textbf{(13A–3)}$$

or
$$1 + {}_2f_3 = \frac{(1 + R_3)^3}{(1 + {}_0r_1)(1 + {}_1f_2)}$$
$$= \frac{(1 + R_3)^3}{(1 + R_2)^2} \qquad \textbf{(See 13A–2)}$$

Eleven percent is the one-year rate for the third year.

The expectations theory says that the shape of the yield curve depends on expected short-term rates and that forward rates equal the expected short-term rates. Therefore, an upward sloping yield curve implies that investors anticipate a rise in interest rates and a downward sloping yield curve implies that investors anticipate a fall in interest rates. Remember that inflation is a major determinant of nominal interest rates. Expected inflation rates are strongly correlated with expected interest rates. Therefore, the term structure of interest rates provides information about expected future inflation rates.

## Liquidity Premium Theory

The liquidity premium theory states that long-term interest rates are the geometric mean of the consecutive expected short-term interest rates plus a liquidity premium. It is based on the fact that interest rate risk is a function of time to maturity. Therefore, investors are not indifferent between a long-term bond and a series of short-term ones. If expected returns are equal on the two alternatives, investors will choose the series of

short-term bonds and avoid the interest rate risk. Investors must be paid a premium to hold the long-term security. Additionally, most borrowers prefer to borrow long-term. Then, they do not have to refinance. They are assured of the money and its cost over the life of their projects. The liquidity preference theory concludes that the normal shape of the yield curve is upward sloping.

## Market Segmentation Theory

The market segmentation theory states that the shape of the yield curve at a particular time reflects the supply and demand forces for particular maturities. Its supporters believe that securities of different maturities are poor substitutes for each other. They argue that each market participant has a particular preferred holding period. For example, because of their liquidity requirements, commercial banks want to hold short-term Treasury securities. On the other hand, life insurance companies and pension funds want to make long-term investments.

In general, however, more lenders prefer to lend short-term and more borrowers prefer to borrow long-term. Therefore, supporters of the market segmentation theory believe that the normal shape of the yield curve is upward sloping.

## Empirical Evidence

Each theory has some validity. Expectations of future short-term rates do influence the long-term rates. This can be seen during periods of high interest rates when the yield curve is downward sloping because rates are expected to fall. During these time periods many lenders want to lend long-term in the hopes of capital gains when rates fall. At the same time borrowers prefer to borrow short-term and later refinance at the lower long-term rates. These forces are reflected in the downward sloping yield curve.

When market participants do not expect rates to change, the yield curve is upward sloping because of liquidity preferences. This supports the liquidity preference theory. Finally, at other times, the yield curve changes because of supply and demand conditions for particular maturities. This supports the market segmentation theory.

## Uses of the Yield Curve

The yield curve is important to investors for several reasons. First, the yield curve is an important forecasting tool. The future short-term rates for any period can be computed as was demonstrated in the expectations theory discussion above.

Second, the yield curve provides information when deciding on which maturity bonds to invest. An investor might even try to outguess the yield curve. That is, the investor could believe that the expectations reflected in the slope of the yield curve are not the best estimates of the future.

Third, the yield curve can be used when searching for over- or underpriced bonds. Bond yields can be plotted and the yield curve drawn. Then bonds plotted above the yield curve should be examined. Unless unique features exist, they are underpriced and should be purchased. In contrast, bonds plotted below the yield curve may be overpriced.

Fourth, some investors attempt to ride the yield curve. Riding the yield curve requires an upward sloping yield curve and the belief that its shape will not change. It involves buying a long-term bond, holding it until it becomes a shorter-term, lower-yielding bond, and then selling it at the higher price that goes with its new lower yield. The result is a capital gain in addition to the interest during the holding period.

## QUESTIONS

1. Explain the expectations theory for the term structure of interest rates.

2. Explain the liquidity premium theory for the term structure of interest rates.

3. Explain the market segmentation theory for the term structure of interest rates.

4. In what four ways can an investor use the yield curve?

## PROBLEMS

1. Observation of the yield for Treasury securities shows that 1, 2, and 3 year bonds are yielding 7, 9, and 10%, respectively. Compute the one-year forward rates for the second and third years.

2. Observation of the yield curve for Treasury securities shows that 1, 2, and 3 year bonds are yielding 8, 10, and 10%, respectively. Compute the one-year forward rates for the second and third years.

## CASE PROBLEM

Graph the yield curve that exists today on Treasury securities. What does its shape imply about interest rates in the future? Compute the one-year rate that is expected to exist one year from now.

# APPENDIX 13B————
# DURATION AND IMMUNIZATION

In this chapter, we discussed the relationship between a bond's maturity and interest rate risk. The concept of duration allows one to specify more exactly the amount of interest rate risk a bond faces. After exploring this relationship between duration and interest rate risk, this appendix presents the concept of immunization as a tool for managing this risk.

## Duration

Duration measures a bond's average term to maturity. It considers the timing and amount of each cash flow from the bond. **Duration** is the weighted average number of years until a bond's cash flows occur. The weights used to compute the average are the relative present values of each payment. Mathematically,

$$Dur = \frac{\sum_{t=1}^{n} t\left[\frac{I_t}{(1 + ytm)^t}\right] + n\left[\frac{M}{(1 + ytm)^n}\right]}{B}$$

(13B–1)

where

$t$ = the time period when a cash flow occurs

$I_t$ = the cash flow at the end of period $t$

$M$ = the face value

$ytm$ = the going yield to maturity

$n$ = the time to maturity

$B$ = the bond's market value

For example, a $1,000 bond with 5 years to maturity has a coupon rate of 8%. The yield to maturity for bonds of this maturity and quality is 10%. The bond's duration, assuming annual coupon payments, is computed in Exhibit 13B–1. The duration of this bond is 4.28 years. For bonds making semiannual payments, discount at the semiannual rate and divide the duration computed using semiannual periods by two.

Duration will always be less than or equal to a bond's years to maturity. It will be equal to the years to maturity in the case of a zero coupon bond. If a bond makes coupon payments, its duration will be less than the years to maturity and the higher the coupon the shorter the duration. A rise in market interest rates also shortens a bond's duration.

In summary, a bond's duration is a better measure of its time structure than just the length of time until the last payment is made, because duration takes into account the amount of each payment and its timing.

## Interest Rate Elasticity

A bond's interest rate elasticity measures the percentage change in its price which occurs for a given percentage change in market interest rates. Interest rate elasticity ($IE$) is the ratio of the percentage change in price to the percentage change in the yield to maturity.

$$IE = \frac{\dfrac{\Delta B}{B}}{\dfrac{\Delta ytm}{ytm}}$$

(13B–2)

A bond's interest rate elasticity will always be a negative number because bond prices and yields to maturity move inversely. For example, if yields to maturity increase from 10 to 12% and a bond's price falls 7.4%, its interest rate elasticity is −.37.

$$IE = \frac{-.074}{.20}$$
$$= -.37$$

A bond's interest rate elasticity applies to any percentage change in yields. In the above example, if interest rates had increased 40 percent, the bond's price would have fallen 14.8%, (−.37 × .40).

There is a mathematical relationship between a bond's interest rate elasticity and its duration.

---

### EXHIBIT 13B–1   Computation of a Bond's Duration

| $t$ | Cash Flow | PV of Cash Flow | PV as % of Price | t × PV as % of Price |
|---|---|---|---|---|
| 1 | 80 | 72.73 | .0787 | .0787 |
| 2 | 80 | 66.12 | .0715 | .1430 |
| 3 | 80 | 60.11 | .0650 | .1950 |
| 4 | 80 | 54.64 | .0591 | .2364 |
| 5 | 1080 | 670.59 | .7256 | 3.6265 |
| | | 924.19 | 1 | 4.2796 |

$$(-1)IE = Dur\left(\frac{ytm}{1 + ytm}\right) \qquad \text{(13B–3)}$$

Equation 13B–3 shows that interest rate elasticity is directly related to duration. Anything which increases a bond's duration (such as longer to maturity or a lower coupon rate) increases its interest rate elasticity.

In summary, interest rate elasticity is a measure of a bond's interest rate risk. Therefore, Equation 13B–3 shows the relationship between duration and interest rate risk.

## Bond Immunization

An investor in bonds faces two risks in connection with interest rate changes: interest rate risk (price risk) and reinvestment rate risk. When interest rates rise, the investor suffers a decline in a bond's market value. At the same time, the investor gains because the coupon payments from the bond can be reinvested at the new higher rates. When interest rates fall the opposite happens.

The return an investor earns over the life of a bond is the weighted average of the yield to maturity and the reinvestment rate.

$$RY = \left(\frac{d}{H}\right)ytm + \left(1 - \frac{d}{H}\right)RR \qquad \text{(13B–4)}$$

where

$RY$ = the realized yield
$ytm$ = yield to maturity
$RR$ = reinvestment rate (average)
$d$ = duration of the bond
$H$ = holding period

Examination of Equation 13B–4 shows that the realized yield will equal the yield to maturity when the duration of the bond equals the holding period.

The key to immunization is for the investor to have a definite holding period in mind and to buy a bond whose duration equals that holding period. Immunization locks in the expected rate of return if there is an immediate one-time change in market interest rates. When the holding period equals the duration, the lost accumulation from the coupon reinvestment is exactly offset by the bond's price gain and vice versa.

## Bond Portfolio Immunization

In practice, bond immunization usually is applied to a portfolio of bonds. The duration of a bond portfolio is the weighted average of the durations of the bonds in the portfolio where the weights are the proportions of the total portfolio invested in each bond.

To build an immunized bond portfolio, the portfolio manager would select bonds with maturities equal to or greater than the expected holding period. The bonds would be of the type and quality that meet the investors' preferences. The proportions of the portfolio invested in each bond would be determined in such a way as to maximize return subject to the immunization restriction. Linear programming can be used to construct the optimal portfolio.

Although the mathematics of portfolio immunization are straightforward, difficulties arise when applying it.

1. Most portfolio managers are not given a single exact holding period requirement. The proceeds from the portfolio may be required over a period of years and the dates may be uncertain.

2. Given the type and quality of restrictions, there may not be many bonds with long enough durations available.

3. When interest rates change, the durations of the bonds change and the portfolio is no longer immunized. Frequent reimmunization may be required.

4. There is not a one-to-one relationship between the passage of time and the decline in a bond's duration. For example, when one month passes, the duration of a bond has not shortened exactly one month. Occasional reimmunization is necessary.

These factors make it difficult to maintain a completely immunized portfolio. However, even though perfect immunization may not be possible, immunization is a valuable tool for handling interest rate risk.

## QUESTIONS

1. What is the duration of a bond?
2. What does a bond's interest rate elasticity measure?
3. What is the relationship between a bond's inter-

est rate elasticity and its duration? What is the significance of this relationship?

**4.** What risks are offset with bond immunization?

**5.** How does the duration of a bond portfolio relate to the durations of the bonds in it?

**6.** What are four of the difficulties that arise when immunizing a bond portfolio?

## PROBLEMS

**1.** Compute the duration of a $1,000 bond with four years to maturity and a coupon rate of 9%. The yield to maturity for bonds of this maturity and quality is 10%. Assume annual coupon payments.

**2.** Compute the duration of a $1,000 bond with four years to maturity and a coupon rate of 9%. The yield to maturity for bonds of this maturity and quality is 12%. Assume annual coupon payments.

**3.** If yields to maturity increase from 8 to 10% and a bond's price falls 9%, what is its interest rate

elasticity? How much would its price have fallen if interest rates had risen from 8 to 12%?

**4.** If yields to maturity increase from 10 to 11% and a bond's price falls 5%, what is its interest rate elasticity? How much would its price have fallen if interest rates had risen from 10 to 12%?

## READINGS

McEnally, Richard W. "How to Neutralize Reinvestment Rate Risk," *Journal of Portfolio Management* 6 (Spring, 1980): 59–63.

> This article discusses in detail the tradeoff between interest rate risk and reinvestment rate risk.

Reilly, Frank R., and Sidhu, Rupinder S. "The Many Uses of Bond Duration," *Financial Analysts Journal* 36 (July–August 1980): 58–72.

> This article discusses how duration is affected by maturity, coupon rate, and market yield. It then considers the main uses of duration in bond analysis and in bond portfolio management.

# Convertible Securities, Warrants, and Rights

## OBJECTIVES

When you have finished studying this chapter, you should understand

1. The features of convertible bonds and how to value them.

2. The features of convertible preferred stocks and how to value them.

3. What warrants are and how to value them.

4. Why rights are issued and the choices available to the investor who receives them.

# 14

## Too Much Debt Financing?

The use of debt financing by a firm increases its potential returns and its risk. When deciding how much debt to use, the firm's management faces return-risk tradeoff which depends on its view of future economic conditions and on its risk preferences. If economic conditions deteriorate, the interest expense on the debt may be greater than the firm's cash flow. In 1988, corporations had taken on so much debt that total corporate interest payments reached 32 percent of total corporate cash flow and many people worried that corporations had taken on excessive debt. A record number of large leveraged buyouts added to their concerns.

The risk premium that lenders require for holding lower quality (higher risk) debt depends on investors' view of future economic conditions and their risk preferences. Many analysts believe that several years of economic expansion make lenders too willing to buy risky debt which, in turn, leads to a deterioration of credit quality throughout the economy. Of course, it is always difficult to decide when the amount of credit available is excessive and when, therefore, greater caution is justified.

Business cycles researcher Geoffrey Moore has identified five signals of credit excesses within an economy.

- A rapid increase in the volume of debt
- A rapid, speculative increase in the prices of the assets that are bought with the rapidly increasing credit, such as real estate, common stocks, or commodities
- Vigorous competition among lenders for new business
- Relaxation of credit terms and lending standards
- A reduction in the risk premiums sought or obtained by lenders

Source: Geoffrey H. Moore, "The Quality of Credit in Booms and Depressions," *Journal of Finance* 11 (May 1956): 288–300.

## INTRODUCTION

So far in this book, we have emphasized stocks and bonds. In this chapter we examine convertible bonds, convertible preferred stocks, warrants, and rights. These four types of securities are issued by corporations and offer the investor unique features.

Convertible bonds and convertible preferred stocks have a fixed conversion price at which they can be exchanged for common stock. Warrants and rights have fixed exercise prices at which common stock can be purchased with them. If the common stock performs well, the owners of convertible securities, warrants, and rights can make large profits. On the other hand, potential losses are limited because the convertibles have value as bonds or preferred stocks and the warrants and rights have low prices compared to the underlying common stock. Therefore, the securities discussed in this chapter offer risk-return combinations that are attractive to many investors. In this chapter, we explore the characteristics and valuation of these securities.

# CONVERTIBLE BONDS

Convertible securities are bonds or preferred stocks that are exchangeable into another security (usually common stock) at the option of the investor under specified terms and conditions. Many features of convertible bonds are also found in convertible preferred stocks. We will describe convertible bonds first.

Convertibility is an advantage for the security holder and a disadvantage for the issuing firm. Issuers offer a convertibility feature as a sweetener when selling debt. In return, they get fewer restrictions in the indenture or a lower interest rate than would be the case with nonconvertible debt. A convertible bond offers the investor the fixed interest payments and prior claims of debt securities along with the growth potential or equity.

Exhibit 14–1 gives examples that illustrate some important features of convertible bonds. Column 1 identifies the issuing company. Because many firms issue convertible debt, an investor has a large selection of issues with a wide choice of coupon rates.

---

**EXHIBIT 14–1   Examples of Convertible Bonds**

| *1* | *2* | *3* | *4* | *5* | *6* | *7* |
|---|---|---|---|---|---|---|
| *Issue* | *Rating* | *Conversion Ratio* | *Common Stock Price* | *Conversion Value* | *Price of Bond* | *Call Price* |
| Alaska Airlines, 9%, 2003 | BBB | 55.172 | $18.00 | $   993.10 | $1,122.50 | $1,072.00 |
| Atlantic Research, 8%, 2008 | NR | 33.579 | 23.00 | 772.30 | 980.00 | 1,056.00 |
| COMPAQ Computer, 9.25%, 2005 | B | 86.957 | 15.375 | 1,336.96 | 1,440.00 | 1,083.30 |
| Oak Industries, 10.5%, 2002 | CC | 29.740 | 1.25 | 37.20 | 762.50 | 1,094.50 |
| Union Carbide, 10%, 2006 | B | 45.537 | 20.50 | 933.51 | 1,100.00 | 1,075.00 |
| Wang Labs, 7.75%, 2008 | BBB | 19.171 | 12.875 | 246.80 | 905.00 | 1,077.50 |
| Zenith, 6.25%, 2011 | BBB | 32.000 | 19.875 | 636.00 | 950.00 | 1,062.50 |

Source: Various financial publications as of September 30, 1986.

---

The major determinant of the coupon rates is the level of interest rates when the bonds are issued. The maturity dates also vary greatly. Like nonconvertible bonds, the original maturities usually are from 10 to 30 years.

Column 2 gives the bond rating by Standard & Poor's. Most convertible bonds are rated by the bond rating services, although Atlantic Research is not rated. Since convertible bonds usually are subordinate debentures and since the issuers have offered a convertible bond because of the firms' speculative prospects, the ratings tend to be low. Therefore, when comparing yields on convertible and nonconvertible bonds, it is necessary to adjust for quality differences.

Column 3 is the conversion ratio that states the number of shares obtainable by converting the bond. Dividing the $1,000 face value of a bond by the conversion ratio gives the conversion price. The indenture may provide for a conversion ratio that changes (usually declines) over the life of the bond. Convertible securities usually are protected by antidilution clauses that state that events such as stock dividends, stock splits, and issuing new shares at below the conversion price will result in adjustment of the conversion ratio.

Column 4 reports the market price of the common stock on a given day. The conversion ratio times the price of the common stock gives the conversion value (column 5). This is the value of the common stock investors would receive if they convert on this day. The conversion values range from $37.20 for the Oak Industries bond to $1,336.96 for the COMPAQ Computer bond.

Column 6 shows the market price of the bond. The market price is at least as great as the conversion value and if the conversion value is very low (such as Oak Industries) the market price is much greater. We will explore these value relationships below.

Column 7 is the call price, which is the face value plus the call premium. Most convertible bonds are callable because the call provision enables the issuer to force the bondholders to convert. Since the market price of the bond is always at least as great as its conversion value, bondholders do not have any incentive to convert. If the bond is called and if the conversion value is greater than the call price, the informed investor will convert. The firm is said to force conversion if it calls the bond at a time when the conversion value is greater than the call price.

## Valuation of Convertible Bonds

The process of valuing a convertible bond starts with the computation of its value as if it were not convertible. This value is often referred to as the bond's straight value. It is the present value of the bond's interest and principal payments. The discount rate used reflects the level of interest rates in the economy and the quality of the bond. Over time the straight value will change if the discount rate changes.

---

**EXAMPLE**

Union Carbide has nonconvertible bonds outstanding. Comparing their ratings and maturities to Union Carbide's convertible bond in Exhibit 14–1, we estimate that the market would demand a yield to maturity of 11 percent if this bond were not convertible. By discounting the interest and principal payments

**EXHIBIT 14–2    *Valuation of a Convertible Bond (Union Carbide's 10%, 2006)***

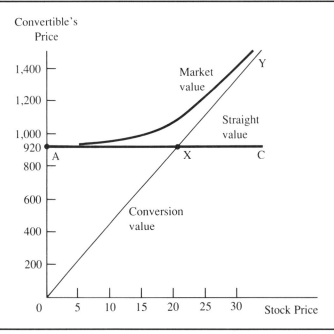

using this rate, we find that on September 30, 1986, the bond's straight value is $920.36 ($FV = 1{,}000$, $PMT = 50$, $n = 39$, $i = 5.5$, $B = \text{?}$). This value is graphed in Exhibit 14–2.                                                       ☐

The conversion value is the current value of the stock into which the bond could be converted. A convertible bond will always be worth at least the greater of its straight value or its conversion value.

**EXAMPLE**    The Union Carbide bond's conversion ratio is 45.537. Its conversion value is line 0XY in Exhibit 14–2. The bond's minimum price is reflected by line AXY.                                                       ☐

Most convertible bonds sell at premiums over their minimum values. When the stock price is low, a premium over straight value exists because investors know there is some probability that the stock price will rise and the conversion value of the bond will be more than its straight value. On the other hand, when the conversion value is greater than the straight value, the bond will sell at a premium because the straight value provides a floor if the stock price falls. The holder of the convertible is in a better position than a stockholder because the convertible's value will not fall below its straight value.

| EXAMPLE | The market value line in Exhibit 14–2 estimates what the actual price of Union Carbide bond will be at different stock prices. Remember, however, if interest rates change, the straight value and actual price of the bond will change. □ |
|---|---|

## Determinants of Convertible Bond Premiums

The premium that investors are willing to pay over the minimum value of a convertible security is influenced by several factors.

***Growth Potential*** The most important factor is the growth potential of the common stock. The greater the potential of the common stock, the greater the premium investors are willing to pay. In Exhibit 14–1 the prices of the Alaska Airlines, COMPAQ Computer, and Union Carbide bonds reflect optimistic outlooks for the common stock.

***Current Yield Differences*** A holder of a convertible security will compare the current yield on the bond to the dividend yield on the stock. This comparison is particularly important when the investor is considering conversion. A high bond yield compared to the stock yield will encourage holding the bond and will add to the premium over conversion value. The holder of the Union Carbide bond receives $100 interest per year; the holder of 45.537 shares of common stock receives dividends of $68.30 ($1.50 per share).

***Transaction Costs*** Investors who are considering buying a convertible bond or converting one they already own to stock, which they soon might sell, should consider the differences in transaction costs between bonds and stocks. The commission on a bond purchase or sale is about $10 while the commission on a $1,000 stock transaction is about $40. However, for small transactions, the bond trade probably is subject to a minimum fee of about $35. In general, commission rates favor bonds over stock; therefore, the convertible bond should sell for a slight premium over its conversion value.

***Terms of the Convertible*** Several factors concerning the terms of conversion affect the premium. The first is the number of years in which the conversion can take place. The longer the period, the more likely that the stock price will increase and, therefore, the higher the premium. Any change in the conversion ratio also will affect the premium. If this ratio declines over time, the conversion feature is of less value. Finally, the protection against dilution should be complete. Sometimes the conversion ratio is not adjusted for small stock dividends. This incomplete dilution protection negatively influences the premium.

## Call Provisions

Convertible bonds are usually callable. Normally, they are callable any time after issue and until maturity. The call provision usually requires that the bondholders be given

30-days notice so that they can convert the bond if the conversion value is above the call price. The call provision enables the firm to force bondholders to convert.

| EXAMPLE |

Exhibit 14–1 shows that the COMPAQ Computer bond has a price of $1,440.00, a conversion value of $1,336.96, and a call price of $1,083.30. If COMPAQ called the bond, bondholders would take the stock worth $1,336.96 rather than the $1,083.30 call price. COMPAQ would have forced conversion. □

When a bond is called, its market price will fall to the higher of the conversion value or call price. If the call price is below the conversion value, any premium over conversion value will disappear. The premium exists because investors do not expect the firm to call the bond now. The more likely a call the less the premium will be.

| EXAMPLE |

The market price of the COMPAQ bond would fall to its conversion value of $1,336.96 when a call is announced. The premium of $103.04 would be gone. An investor who bought the bond the day before the call would have an immediate loss. □

Analysis of a convertible bond must include an estimation of the probability of a call. The investor has to evaluate the firm's position in regard to the bond. The first question is "Why did the firm issue convertible debt?" Sometimes convertible bonds are issued when the firm wants permanent debt financing but has to add the convertible feature as a "sweetener." This firm will not be anxious to force conversion. In other cases, the firm wants equity financing but issues convertible debt because it believes its stock price is temporarily depressed. If the stock price increases, this firm is likely to force conversion.

The second question is "Do any future financing needs encourage the firm to force conversion of this issue?" Perhaps it wants a better debt to equity mix before approaching the market with another debt issue. A third question is, "How does the interest on this debt issue compare to other outstanding issues and to current rates?" If interest rates are down, the firm might pay off this issue with the proceeds of a new issue.

## Investing in Convertible Bonds

Some investors view convertible bonds as a fixed income investment. Bonds with low conversion values appeal to them. They get the interest and have the bonus of a small chance of the conversion feature having value in the future. In Exhibit 14–1, the Wang Labs bond has a low conversion value and, therefore, is selling at a price near its straight value. So is the Oak Industries bond, but note its low rating; it is very speculative.

Other investors view convertible bonds as a common stock substitute. Bonds with high conversion values appeal to them. They may prefer the convertible to the common stock because it offers greater current income or because of the lower downside risk provided by its debt features. In Exhibit 14–1, Alaska Airline, COMPAQ Computer, and Union Carbide bonds would appeal to these investors.

| EXHIBIT 14–3 Examples of Convertible Preferred Stocks | | | | | | |
|---|---|---|---|---|---|---|
| *1* | *2* | *3* | *4* | *5* | *6* | *7* |
| | *Stated* | *Conversion* | *Common* | *Conversion* | *Preferred* | *Call* |
| *Issue* | *Dividend* | *Ratio* | *Stock Price* | *Value* | *Stock Price* | *Price* |
| American Motors | $2.375 | 8.333 | $ 3.00 | $ 25.00 | $ 25.75 | $ 27.50 |
| American Sav. & Loan (Fla) | 2.19 | .874 | 16.50 | 14.40 | 21.00 | 26.53 |
| Navistar Intl. | 5.76 | 1.33 | 7.125 | 9.47 | 57.50 | 52.88 |
| Owens-Illinois | 4.75 | 6.00 | 41.50 | 249.00 | 249.00 | 100.00 |
| Reynolds Metals | 4.50 | 2.13 | 46.00 | 97.98 | 97.875 | 100.00 |

Source: Various financial publications as of October 31, 1986.

# CONVERTIBLE PREFERRED STOCK

A good selection of convertible preferred stocks is available. Exhibit 14–3 gives some examples of these. Column 1 lists the issuing firms. Column 2 gives the stated dividend. Dividing it by the price in column 6 shows that a wide selection of dividend yields is also available. The stated dividend yield is strongly influenced by the level of interest rates at the time of the preferred stock issue. Column 3 is the conversion ratio, which is multiplied by the common stock price (column 4) to compute the conversion value (column 5). Column 7 lists the call price of the preferred stock. Like convertible bonds, most convertible preferred stock is callable so that the issuer can force conversion.

## Valuation of Preferred Stock

The process of valuing a convertible preferred stock is similar to valuing a convertible bond. A convertible preferred stock has a straight value, which is its value without the conversion feature. The straight value is the present value of the stated dividends where the discount rate reflects the level of interest rates and the risk of the preferred stock. Because there is no maturity date, the present value calculation is the present value of the perpetual preferred dividend discounted at the appropriate rate.

The second step in valuing a convertible preferred stock is to compute its conversion value. The minimum value of a preferred issue will always be the larger of its straight or conversion value.

| EXAMPLE |
|---|

In Exhibit 14–3, the Navistar International preferred is selling for $57.50, which is only slightly more than its straight value. It provides a dividend yield of about 10 percent while its conversion value is only $9.47. There is only a slight chance that the conversion value will be greater than its straight value in the next few years.

The American Motors issue sells at a premium over its conversion value. Its conversion value ($25) is only a little above its straight value (about $23).

Therefore, the floor provided by the straight value makes the preferred more attractive than owning the common stock. □

Because preferred stock is technically equity and because it does not have any maturity date, there is little motivation for the firm to force conversion. Therefore, conversion values can be very high. In these cases there will not be much, if any, premium over conversion value because investors do not expect the stock price to fall so far that the floor provided by the straight value will be important.

| EXAMPLE | The Owens-Illinois preferred is selling at exactly its conversion value. Because prices are quoted in eighths, the price of the Reynolds Metals issue is slightly below its conversion value. □

## Investing in Preferred Stock

Like convertible bonds, convertible preferred stocks appeal to two classes of investors: those who want the fixed income feature of the stated dividend will buy those preferreds selling near their straight values; those who want a substitute for the common stock will buy the preferreds with high conversion values.

# WARRANTS

A **warrant** is a security that gives the holder the option of purchasing from the issuing company a given number of shares of a specified security at a stated price for a specified time period. Exhibit 14–4 has examples of warrants.

Column 1 shows the issuing company. Most warrants are issued as a sweetener with a bond issue. They allow the bond purchaser to take an equity position if the firm

---

**EXHIBIT 14–4   Examples of Warrants**

| 1 Company | 2 Number of Shares | 3 Expiration Date | 4 Exercise Price | 5 Stock Price | 6 Warrant Price |
|---|---|---|---|---|---|
| American General | 1 | 1/5/89 | $24.25 | $38.50 | $17.125 |
| Lilly | 1 | 3/31/91 | 75.98 | 65.375 | 18.50 |
| McDermott Intl. | 1 | 4/1/90 | 25.00* | 20.25 | 3.125 |
| McLean | 1 | 7/15/90 | 11.20 | 4.125 | .625 |
| Pan American | 1 | 5/1/93 | 8.00* | 5.375 | 1.375 |

*CD warrants: The issuing firm has outstanding a debenture that will be accepted at face value in payment of the exercise price.

Source: Various financial publications as of October 31, 1986.

does well. Although the warrants and the bonds originally are issued as a unit, the warrants usually are "detachable"; that is, they can be resold separately from the bond.

Column 2 shows the number of shares that can be purchased with each warrant. Most warrants are for the purchase of common stock, although it is possible for the specified security to be preferred stock or a bond. The number of shares each warrant is worth can vary from a fraction of a share to thousands of shares. In Exhibit 14–4 every warrant is for one share of common stock.

Column 3 is the expiration date of the warrant. Although any expiration date is possible, most warrants are issued with lives of two to ten years. Some warrants do not have expiration dates; they can be exercised anytime.

Column 4 lists the exercise price at which shares can be purchased with the warrant. The asterisk indicates a CD warrant. CD stands for cash or debenture. These warrants permit a specific debenture issue of the firm to be used at par value to pay the exercise price. This is a very valuable feature if interest rates have risen and the debentures are selling at a discount.

Column 5 gives the price of the common stock while column 6 gives the price of the warrant. Warrants are much less expensive.

## Valuation of Warrants

The value of a warrant is the sum of two elements: a mathematical value and a speculative premium. The mathematical value (also called theoretical value) is the difference between the market price of the common stock and the exercise price of the warrant. If the warrant is for other than one share, this difference is multiplied by the number of shares each warrant will purchase. If this difference is negative, the mathematical value is zero.

The speculative premium results from the attractiveness of the leverage inherent in warrants. Because of the fixed exercise price, a change in the price of the common stock will result in a larger percentage change in the price of the warrant.

| **EXAMPLE** | The American General warrant in Exhibit 14–4 has a mathematical value of $14.25 ($38.50 − $24.25). Its speculative premium, therefore, is $2.875. Because the exercise prices of the other warrants in the table are greater than their stock prices, their mathematical values are zero. These warrant prices are based completely on the speculative premiums. ☐ |

The size of the speculative premium depends on several factors. The most important is investors' expectations about the future price of the stock and its relationship to the exercise price. The better the stock's outlook, the higher the price of the warrant. Also, the longer the remaining life of the warrant, the more valuable it is. Minor influences on the speculative premiums are the stock's dividend yield and the secondary market for the warrant. Stocks that reinvest all or most of their earnings can be expected to have higher future prices than do high dividend stocks. Therefore, warrant holders prefer warrants on low dividend stocks. Additionally, investors prefer warrants traded on the organized exchanges. Because warrants have low prices, the spreads between bid and ask prices in the OTC market can be high percentages of the price.

## Investing in Warrants

Because of the leverage provided by the fixed exercise price, warrants are great when the common stock is going up. On the other hand, they are bad when the stock price is going down.

**EXAMPLE**  On April 30, 1986, the prices of the Lilly common stock and warrants were $67.375 and $16.125 respectively. On June 30, 1986, they were $80.875 and $27.875. The common stock price had increased 20 percent while the warrant had increased 72 percent. By September 30, 1986, the stock price was down to $65.375 and the warrant price down to $18.50. The stock had decreased 19 percent and the warrant had decreased 34 percent.  □

Disadvantages of warrants are that they do not receive dividends or interest, they have no claim on assets, and they have no voting rights. Because they do not have voting rights, warrant holders are often treated poorly in mergers. The merger agreement may redeem the warrants at mathematical value, in which case the speculative premium is lost.

# RIGHTS

A **preemptive right** allows a shareholder to maintain a given percentage ownership of the corporation when new shares are issued. The preemptive right prevents control of a corporation from being shifted by the selling of new stock to certain investors. It also prevents present stockholders from suffering dilution of the value of their investment because new stock is sold at too low a price. If an investor buys enough of the new shares to maintain the same percentage ownership, dilution of his or her investment does not occur.

Some states require corporations chartered in that state to have a formal rights offering when additional shares are sold. In states that do not require it, some corporate charters require the formal rights offering but, for most corporations, a formal rights offering is not required before selling additional stock. However, if a voting control shift or dilution is taking place when additional stock is issued, shareholders can sue to protect their ownership position.

The preemptive right leads to the issuing of rights when a corporation plans to sell new stock. A **right** is a security issued by a corporation to its stockholders. A right gives its holder the option to buy a certain number of common shares at a specified subscription price. At the time of issue the subscription price is usually 10 to 20 percent below the market price of the common stock. Rights expire about 30 days after issue.

Each stockholder receives one right for each share of stock owned. Because the number of new shares the corporation is issuing is usually less than the number of existing shares, several rights are needed to purchase a new share at the subscription price. On occasion, however, the number of new shares to be issued is greater than the number of existing shares and, therefore, a right allows the purchase of more than one share. In this case, if the number of shares that can be purchased with a right is not in whole numbers (say, 1.3 shares), trading in rights will take place in such a manner that only whole new shares will be purchased by the exercise of the rights.

## Valuation of Rights

A right has value because it provides for buying a share of stock for less than its market price. The value of a right can easily be computed. Like a dividend payment, a rights issue has a holder of record date. Because of the five-day settlement rule used in the securities industry, to be on the corporate record of shareholders a purchaser needs to own the stock five business days before the holder of record date. Therefore, the stock goes ex rights four business days before the holder of record date. We compute the value of a right before and after the ex rights date.

**Rights On** Equation 14–1 gives the value of a right when the stock is selling with the rights attached, that is, rights on.

$$R = \frac{P_{\text{on}} - P^s}{N + 1} \qquad (14\text{–}1)$$

where

$P_{\text{on}}$ = the price of a share of stock selling rights on

$P^s$ = the subscription price of a new share

$N$ = the number of rights required to purchase a new share

| EXAMPLE | XYZ Corporation has announced a rights offering. With eight rights a shareholder can purchase a new share for \$80. The market price of the stock is \$100. What is the value of a right? |

$$R = \frac{\$100 - \$80}{8 + 1} = \$2.22$$

If nothing else changes when the stock goes ex rights, its price should drop to \$97.78, and the rights should sell for \$2.22 each. ☐

**Ex Rights** Equation 14–2 gives the value of a right when the stock is selling ex rights.

$$R = \frac{P_{ex} - P^s}{N} \qquad\qquad\qquad (14\text{--}2)$$

where $P_{ex}$ = the price of a share of stock selling ex rights.

**EXAMPLE**    The value of the rights described above after the stock goes ex rights is

$$R = \frac{\$97.78 - \$80}{8} = \$2.22 \qquad\qquad \square$$

In the past it was believed that selling more stock through a rights offering put downward pressure on the stock price. However, the empirical studies of stock price behavior during rights offerings are inconclusive. The important factor is how successfully the firm is expected to invest the additional money raised. If its investment opportunities are promising, the stock price should increase with a successful equity offering.

## Investing in Rights

A stockholder who receives rights has three choices

— Exercise them
— Sell them
— Let them expire

Letting them expire is dumb: they have value before the expiration date but none after it. The choice between exercising and selling the rights depends on the investor's desire to invest more money in this stock. Wealth position will be the same if the investor exercises the rights or sells them.

**EXAMPLE**    An owner of eight shares of XYZ Corporation receives eight rights and exercises them. Before the rights offering, he owned $800 worth of stock and had $80 cash. After exercising the rights, he has stock worth $880 (nine shares at $97.78 each).

If he had sold the rights for their value of $2.22 each, his ending position would have been stock worth $782.24 and cash of $97.76 ($17.76 from the rights sale plus his original $80).    $\square$

Rights are traded in the secondary market where participants sell rights they received and do not want to exercise or buy rights they intend to exercise. The fixed subscription price makes rights a high leverage security. Small percentage changes in the value of the stock price result in large percentage changes in the value of the rights. However, because rights have short lives and commissions are high as a percentage of price, they do not appeal to most investors.

# SUMMARY

Corporations issue convertible securities, warrants, and rights, which offer features that are attractive to some investors. Convertible securities combine the feature of fixed annual income with the right to convert to common stock if the firm does well. A call provision permits the issuing firm to force investors to convert.

A warrant is another method of allowing a bondholder to share in the rewards if a firm does well. If warrants are sold with a bond issue the holder will be able to purchase stock at a fixed exercise price with the warrants. The value of a warrant is the sum of its mathematical value and its speculative premium. The size of the speculative premium depends on investors' expectations about the future price of the stock and its relationship to the exercise price, the stock's dividend yield, and the warrant's marketability.

A preemptive right allows a shareholder to maintain a given percentage ownership when new shares are issued. A right gives its holder the option to buy a certain number of common shares at a specified subscription price.

## QUESTIONS

1. What is a convertible bond? Why do corporations issue them? Why do they appeal to investors?

2. Why are the bond ratings assigned to convertible bonds so low?

3. Define the straight value and the conversion value of a convertible bond. How does the price of the bond relate to them?

4. Discuss the factors that determine convertible bond premiums.

5. How does an issuer force conversion of a convertible security?

6. How do you value convertible preferred stock?

7. What types of investors are attracted by convertible preferred stocks?

8. What is a warrant? Why do corporations issue them? Why do they appeal to investors?

9. What is a CD warrant?

10. How do you value a warrant?

11. What factors influence the size of a warrant's speculative premium?

12. What is the purpose of a stockholder's preemptive right?

13. What is a right? Why does a right have value?

14. If you are a stockholder who receives rights, is it better for you to exercise or sell them?

## PROBLEMS

1. An 8% convertible subordinate debenture matures in 10 years. It can be converted into 25 shares of common stock. The common stock's price is $45 per share and the going rate for nonconvertible bonds of this quality is 9%. What is the bond's minimum price?

2. A 10% convertible subordinate debenture matures in 12 years. It can be converted into 20.5 shares of common stock. The common stock's price is $50 a share and the going rate for nonconvertible bonds of this quality is 11%. What is the bond's minimum price?

3.  On November 30, 1986, Amax Incorporated has outstanding a $3.00 cumulative preferred stock, which was selling for $35.50 a share. It was convertible into 1.31 shares of common stock. The common stock was selling for $13.125 a share and the going rate for nonconvertible preferreds of this quality was 10%. What are the straight value and the conversion value of this preferred? Why does it sell at a premium?

4.  On November 30, 1986, Bell and Howell had outstanding a $0.60 cumulative preferred stock, which was selling for $38 a share. It was convertible into one share of common stock. The common stock was selling for $37.75 a share and the going rate for nonconvertible preferreds of this quality was 10%. What are the straight value and the conversion value of this preferred? Why does it sell at so small a premium?

5.  On March 31, 1987, Lilly's warrant to purchase one share of common stock at $75.98 was selling for $37.375. The common stock price was $91.50. Divide the price of the warrant into its mathematical value and speculative premium.

6.  On April 21, 1987, McDermott International's warrant to purchase one share of common stock at $25 was selling for $6.625. The common stock price was $29.125. Divide the price of the warrant into its mathematical value and speculative premium.

7.  ABC Corporation's stock is selling for $50 a share. It announces a rights offering. With 4 rights you can buy a new share for $45. What is the value of a right? What will the stock price be when it sells ex rights?

8.  CBA Corporation's stock is selling for $35 a share. It announces a rights offering. With 4 rights you can buy a new share for $30. What is the value of a right? What will the stock price be when it sells ex rights?

9.  You own 100 shares of ABC Corporation. Your mail brings you 100 rights. With each 4 rights you can buy a new share for $45. The newspaper reports the stock is selling for $49. What is the value of each right? Show that your ending wealth will be the same if you exercise or sell your rights (ignore commissions).

10. You own 100 shares of CBA Corporation. Your mail brings you 100 rights. With each 4 rights you can buy a new share for $30. The newspaper reports the stock is selling for $34. What is the value of each right? Show that your ending wealth will be the same if you exercise or sell your rights (ignore commissions).

# *READINGS*

Brigham, Eugene F. "An Analysis of Convertible Debentures," *Journal of Finance* 21 (March 1966): 35–54.

>   *This paper develops and tests a theoretical framework for analyzing the nature of convertible securities.*

Galai, Jan, and Schneller, Meir I. "Pricing of Warrants and the Value of the Firm," *Journal of Finance* 33 (December 1978): 1333–1342.

>   *This article derives the value of the warrant and the value of the firm that issues warrants.*

Heinkel, Robert, and Schwartz, Eduardo S. "Rights versus Underwritten Offerings: An Asymetric Information Approach," *Journal of Finance* 41 (March 1986): 1–18.

>   *This article examines why most firms selling new equity use the more costly underwriting rather than the less costly rights offer.*

# Part IV

# OTHER INVESTMENT VEHICLES

# Investment Companies

## OBJECTIVES

When you have finished studying this chapter, you should understand

1. The advantages offered to investors by investment companies.
2. How investment companies are organized.
3. The classification of investment companies by investment objectives.
4. How investment companies have performed.
5. The similarities and differences among investment companies, commingled funds, and investment clubs.

# 15

## "Socially Responsible" Mutual Funds

In the 1970s and 1980s, several mutual funds were started that invested only in "socially responsible" companies. Examples are the Parnassus Fund, the Calvert Group's Social Investment Fund, the Pax World Fund, and the Dreyfus Corp.'s Third Century Funds.

Definitions of "socially responsible" differ greatly among the funds. Some emphasize issues such as equal employment opportunities and employee and community relations; others emphasize workplace and product safety; still others are environmentally oriented. Some are antinuclear power or antidefensive contractor based. Unfortunately, investments that meet everyone's definition of "socially responsible" are very rare. For example, some funds that use the criteria above invest in companies that do business in South Africa. In the mid-1980s, when opposition to investment in South Africa became a popular issue, some funds made it the major criterion when deciding if a company was "socially responsible."

As one might expect, the performance of "socially responsible" funds is mixed. Some have outperformed market averages; others have not. Because many are conservative in choosing companies to invest in, some analysts expect them to perform less well in up markets but better than average in down markets.

## INTRODUCTION

If you do not want to devote your spare time to analyzing individual securities, investment companies will be attractive to you. An investment company is a financial intermediary operating for the purpose of investing mainly in securities. The Investment Company Act of 1940 defines an investment company as a firm with over 40 percent of its assets in securities other than U.S. government obligations or majority owned subsidiaries. The Securities and Exchange Commission, which enforces the 1940 law, reports that there were over 3,300 active investment companies in 1987.

Investment companies originated in Europe in the 1800s and became popular in England and Scotland in the 1870s. The first investment companies in the United States to offer their shares to the public were founded in 1924, and by 1929 about 150 such companies had been chartered. However, because these investment companies were very speculative and used margin heavily, their performances were disastrous when the market crashed in 1929. Abuses by the companies' management in these years led to a very detailed law (the Investment Company Act of 1940) to regulate investment companies.

After the 1940 Act, investment companies started slowly to regain some of their popularity. Because most companies invested in stocks, the good stock market years of the 1960s accelerated growth, while the declining stock prices in the 1970s caused a decline. As interest rates increased in the late 1970s, investors turned to bonds, money market securities, and tax-free municipal securities. Investment companies provided a means for investors with limited funds to invest in these securities. When stock prices boomed in the mid-1980s, investment companies prospered, with records being set in the number of investment companies and the dollar amount invested in them. Today investment companies have assets of over $700 billion with more than 25 million investors. Exhibit 15–1 shows the growth in mutual fund accounts and assets.

# WHY INVEST USING INVESTMENT COMPANIES?

Investment companies offer you several advantages over direct investment in securities. The most important advantages are convenience, diversification, and professional management.

## Convenience

It is convenient to utilize the services of an investment company because it can save you the work of choosing and monitoring individual securities. After you choose an investment company, whose investment objectives match yours and whose past performance is good, you can spend your time in pursuits other than managing your investments.

Many investment companies also provide the convenience of enabling you to invest small amounts at regular intervals, for example $75 per month. Additionally, your investment is very liquid; you can quickly sell your shares. Investment companies provide a vehicle by which anyone who wants to and has the funds can invest in securities. Without investment companies, the number of people allocating money to and benefiting from ownership of stocks and bonds would be smaller.

## Diversification

An investment company provides you with the risk-reducing benefit of diversification—allowing you to buy stocks of different types of industries. Investment companies commonly invest in 30 to 80 different securities. Therefore, the overall value of the

---

**EXHIBIT 15–1 Mutual Fund Growth**

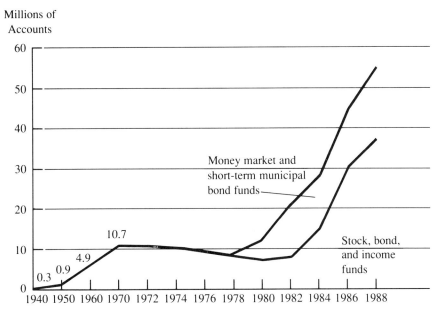

(a) **Mutual Fund Shareholder Accounts**

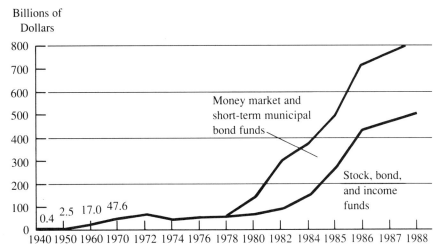

(b) **Assets of Mutual Funds**

Source: Investment Company Institute, *1989 Mutual Fund Fact Book* (Washington, D.C.: Investment Company Institute, 1989), p. 15. Reprinted with permission from Investment Company Institute, Washington, D.C.

portfolio of the investment company does not suffer much because of a few bad investments. If you have only a few thousand dollars to invest, you cannot obtain adequate diversification when buying securities. If you attempt to spread your money among enough different securities to be diversified, you will find that the commission charges on the small purchases take a high percentage of your investment.

### Professional Management

Investment companies have well-qualified personnel working full-time at the task of seeking out and evaluating investment opportunities and information. Because the companies are managing large amounts of money, they can afford the analysts, publications, computers, software, and data bases necessary for top quality research. Because they place large buy and sell orders, brokerage firms supply them with research reports and recommendations and allow them to talk directly to the brokerage firm's researchers. This timely, in-depth information should give investment companies the opportunity to perform well in their investment decisions.

# HOW INVESTMENT COMPANIES ARE ORGANIZED

An investment company has a board of directors, which hires a management company to run the investment company. The management company makes buy and sell decisions for the investment company's portfolio and performs administrative duties, such as issuing investment company shares and handling redemptions and dividends. In practice, a management company starts an investment company and nominates board members who will hire the management company. Management companies usually manage several investment companies with different portfolio objectives. Management companies are paid management fees by the investment company. The fee is usually stated as a percentage of the value of the fund. A fee of one-half percent per year is common.

The board of directors will also hire a bank or brokerage firm to be the custodian of the securities of the fund. Just as individuals do, investment companies pay commissions when buying or selling securities. Frequent buying and selling, called high turnover, will result in high total commissions being paid by the fund. High turnover is justified only if it results in better performance by the fund.

The 1940 law defined three main types of investment companies: open-end investment companies, closed-end investment companies, and unit trusts.

### Mutual Funds

**Open-end investment companies (mutual funds)** sell new shares to any interested person and repurchase their outstanding shares when requested by the shareholder. Thus the number of shares outstanding can change daily. The basis of the price at which sales and redemptions take place is net asset value (NAV) per share. This is computed daily using the following equation.

$$\frac{\text{net asset value}}{\text{per share}} = \frac{\text{market value of the fund's assets} - \text{the fund's liabilities}}{\text{number of shares outstanding}}$$

In other words, NAV per share is computed by subtracting the fund's liabilities from the value of the fund's assets and then dividing this difference by the number of shares the fund has outstanding.

We said that this is the "basis" for the price because there may also be a sales charge and a small redemption charge. If the fund has a sales charge, it is called a load fund. If it does not have a sales charge, it is called a no-load fund. Among the load funds, the amounts of the sales charges (loads) vary; however, they are usually based on a sliding scale that provides lower percentage charges for large purchasers. Exhibit 15–2 is an example of sliding scale load charges.

As this example shows, sales charges are usually stated as a percentage of the offering price. For example, with a $1,000 investment and a 5.5 percent sales charge, $55 would go for the load (sales commission) and $945 would be invested in the fund. As a percentage of the actual amount invested, the sales charge would be 5.82 percent ($55/$945).

No-load funds do not have sales charges. Because there is no commission to pay a salesperson, no one is going to explain a particular no-load fund to you personally. To purchase a no-load fund, you write or call the fund and ask for a prospectus. Exhibit 15–3 is an example of an advertisement that gives the address and phone number of a no-load fund. These advertisements appear in the business sections of major newspapers. To purchase shares of the fund, you complete the purchase form that comes with the prospectus and mail the form and your check to the fund.

The traditional distinction between load and no-load funds is being blurred by new ways of charging sales fees. One trend is toward lower front end load charges combined with redemption fees, called back load fees. Often redemption fees are on a sliding

---

**EXHIBIT 15–2  Example of Sliding Scale Load Charges**

| Amount of Single Transaction | Sales Charge | |
| --- | --- | --- |
| | Percentage of Public Offering Price | Approximate Percentage of Amount Invested |
| Less than $25,000 | 5.50% | 5.82% |
| $ 25,000 but less than $ 50,000 | 5.00 | 5.26 |
| $ 50,000 but less than $100,000 | 4.25 | 4.44 |
| $100,000 but less than $250,000 | 3.25 | 3.36 |
| $250,000 but less than $500,000 | 2.50 | 2.56 |
| $500,000 and over | 1.75 | 1.78 |

---

**EXHIBIT 15–3    Advertisement from a No-Load Fund**

---

# How to keep your money in play until you're sure of your next move.

**SteinRoe Cash Reserves** gives you a secure position for planning your investment strategy. As a money market fund, SteinRoe Cash Reserves offers liquidity, safety and income through changing market conditions.

SteinRoe Cash Reserves earns you a competitive money market return every day. So your money is always hard at work.

### Keep your money in a strong position.

But just as important, SteinRoe Cash Reserves gives you the instant flexibility to move your money into any of the other no-load funds in the SteinRoe family. With no sales charges, commissions or withdrawal penalties of any kind. You can take advantage of market changes with the speed of a phone call.

So when you're ready to get back

into the market, our nine growth-oriented funds give you a variety of investment avenues. And if your investment objectives include high income, you can select from our taxable *and* tax-free bond funds.

### Move to sound money management by SteinRoe.

These are the kind of diversified opportunities you'd expect from Stein Roe & Farnham. We're one of the nation's largest investment managers, with 56 years of professional experience.

You can open your Cash Reserves account for only $1,000. And you'll enjoy round-the-clock access to your money with free checkwriting. What's more, you can call us toll-free anytime for the Fund's current yield.

Call 1-800-338-2550 for a prospectus today. It's a safe way to

keep your money in the game while you plan your next move.

### Call 1-800-338-2550

Please send me a prospectus containing more complete information, including management fees and expenses, on SteinRoe Cash Reserves. I will read it carefully before I invest or send money.

Name_____

Address_____

City_____

State_____ZIP_____
Daytime
Phone (_____)

SteinRoe Mutual Funds
P.O. Box 1143 · Chicago, IL 60690

**SteinRoe**
*CASH RESERVES*

© 1988, Stein Roe & Farnham Incorporated
Liberty Securities Corporation, Distributor

---

Source: Courtesy of Stein Roe & Farnham Incorporated.

scale starting as high as 5 percent if redeemed in the first year and declining to zero after a five-year holding period. Sometimes there is a lower front end load charge combined with an annual charge of 1 or 2 percent to pay for advertising and similar selling expenses. These fund expenses are called 12b-1 charges after the 1980 SEC rule that permits them.

Since there is no evidence that the performance of load funds is better than no-load funds, you should decide between them after you have evaluated the services that the salesperson provides you with the load funds. If that person provides you with comprehensive financial planning assistance, valuable financial advice, or retirement and estate planning help, the load fund may be worth the commission charges to you. If the salesperson does not provide services you need and want, it is better to buy a no-load fund and save the load charge.

***Classification by Investment Objectives*** The most important factor in picking an investment company is that its objectives should be compatible with yours. The prospectus that the company must give you before you invest will clearly state the fund's objectives. These objectives should include statements about current income in contrast to long-term gains, risk level, and type of securities to be included in its portfolio. The fund's risk-return tradeoff is determined by the securities in which the fund invests. The following are the most common classes of mutual funds based on their portfolios.

Common stock funds invest almost completely in common stocks. Funds can specialize in income stocks, blue chip stocks, mature growth stocks, aggressive growth stocks, cyclical stocks, or defensive stocks.

Specialized stock funds invest only in stocks of young companies, companies in specific industries, or companies in specific regions of the country. In the mid-1980s specific industry funds, called sector funds, boomed. They concentrate their investments in a specialized sector of the market, such as energy, health care, high technology, aerospace, financial services, leisure, or utilities. Some investors purchase sector funds

***Fidelity Select Portfolios***

Fidelity Investments manages a group of 35 single industry funds, called Fidelity Select Portfolios. Popular industry funds include health care, leisure, retailing, utilities, and financial services. A shareholder may switch funds for a $10 per switch fee. In order to facilitate switching, Fidelity computes the value of these sector funds hourly instead of just at the closing of the market. This allows investors to switch immediately by phone if they believe they can profit from short-term market fluctuations. Investors can also switch to a money market fund if they anticipate a market decline.

Fidelity points out that these funds are not diversified and are targeted to investors willing to accept greater share price volatility. Fidelity argues that these funds are managed by industry experts who know both their specialized sectors and the market. Independent newsletters, which cost $100 to $200 per year, advise Fidelity shareholders on what funds to switch into or out of.

Fidelity charges a 2 percent load on the initial purchase of a sector fund and a 1 percent redemption fee. There is no load or redemption fee on switches between sector funds.

because of the long-term prospects for the industry. Other investors buy and sell frequently as the prospects for a given industry change. Companies that manage sector funds allow a shareholder to transfer investments by telephone to other funds it manages.

**International funds** invest in the securities of foreign companies. A segment of the international fund category, **global funds,** also invests in U.S. securities. International funds often specialize in a particular country or region of the world. The comparative values of international currencies greatly affect the performance of international funds.

Bond and preferred stock funds, which often appeal to retired people, seek high dividends and lower risk than provided by common stock funds. Funds that invest in bonds and preferred stocks often meet these objectives. These funds, however, differ greatly in risk. Some funds give up some return in order to reduce risk, buying only high-quality securities. Other funds attempt to earn greater return by holding higher risk securities. In bad economic times, many of these lower-quality securities could stop paying interest and dividends. An important caution on bond and preferred stock funds is that their portfolios, and thereby their own shares, are very sensitive to interest rate risk. If interest rates go up, the value of the fund's shares will go down. Although the fund will continue to pay high dividends, this decline will be important to the investor who has to sell his shares.

Balanced funds buy common stocks, preferred stocks, and bonds. While providing high current dividends, they attempt to reduce risk by diversifying among the different types of securities.

U.S. government bond funds buy only bonds and notes issued by the federal government. Except for interest rate risk, these funds are very low risk.

Ginnie Mae funds invest the majority of their portfolios in mortgage securities backed by the Government National Mortgage Association (GNMA). The federal government guarantees that the mortgages' principal and interest will be paid on time.

Municipal bond funds buy only state and local bonds. These funds are attractive to high-income investors because the federal tax law allows the tax-free status of the interest on these bonds to apply to the dividends of the funds. There are also single state municipal bond funds that invest only in state and local securities issued in one state. In most states the income from these funds is free of both federal and state taxes.

Money market funds invest in the short-term debt instruments traded in the money market. These funds had fantastic growth in the late 1970s when money market interest rates were above 10 percent while depository institutions were paying around 5 percent on short-term deposits. Money market funds allow withdrawals by check (usually a $500 minimum) and by wire transfers to the investor's bank. This feature, combined with high interest rates and low risk, makes them attractive to many people. Tax-exempt money market funds invest in short-term municipal securities. Exhibit 15–4 shows the growth of money market funds.

**Index funds** attempt to match the performance of a popular stock market index. Instead of spending money on analysts, researchers, and commissions for frequent buying and selling, they buy a diversified portfolio of the stocks of well-established companies and hold it.

Option/income funds seek a high level of current income by investing in dividend-paying stocks on which call options can be written. Their high current return consists

| EXHIBIT 15-4   Money Market Funds, 1974-1987 (in Millions of Dollars) | | | | | | | |

| Year End | Total Sales | Total Redemptions | Net Sales | Number of Funds | Total Accounts Outstanding | Average Maturity (Days) | Total Net Assets |
|---|---|---|---|---|---|---|---|
| 1974 | $ 2,232.0 | $ 556.0 | $ 1,676.0 | 15 | n.a. | n.a. | $ 1,715.1 |
| 1975 | 6,748.7 | 5,883.9 | 864.0 | 36 | 208,777 | 93 | 3,695.7 |
| 1976 | 9,360.9 | 9,609.2 | (248.3) | 48 | 180,676 | 110 | 3,685.8 |
| 1977 | 10,673.0 | 10,662.7 | 10.3 | 50 | 177,522 | 76 | 3,887.7 |
| 1978 | 30,452.2 | 24,294.5 | 6,157.8 | 61 | 467,803 | 42 | 10,858.0 |
| 1979 | 111,855.1 | 78,363.4 | 33,491.7 | 76 | 2,307,852 | 34 | 45,214.2 |
| 1980 | 232,172.8 | 204,068.5 | 28,104.5 | 96 | 4,745,572 | 24 | 74,447.7 |
| 1981 | 451,889.5 | 346,701.5 | 105,188.0 | 159 | 10,282,095 | 34 | 181,910.4 |
| 1982 | 581,758.9 | 559,581.1 | 22,177.8 | 281 | 13,101,347 | 37 | 206,607.5 |
| 1983 | 462,978.7 | 508,729.9 | (45,751.2) | 307 | 12,276,639 | 37 | 162,549.5 |
| 1984 | 571,959.3 | 531,050.9 | 40,908.4 | 329 | 13,556,180 | 43 | 209,731.9 |
| 1985 | 730,073.8 | 732,343.0 | (2,269.2) | 348 | 14,435,386 | 37 | 207,535.3 |
| 1986 | 792,349.1 | 776,303.2 | 16,045.9 | 360 | 15,653,595 | 40 | 228,345.8 |
| 1987 | 869,099.1 | 865,668.4 | 3,430.7 | 389 | 16,832,666 | 31 | 254,676.4 |
| 1988 | 903,425.9 | 899,397.3 | 4,028.6 | 432 | 17,800,097 | 28 | 272,296.3 |

Source: *1989 Mutual Fund Fact Book* (Washington, D.C.: Investment Company Institute, 1989), p. 87. Reprinted with permission from Investment Company Institute, Washington, D.C.

of dividends, premiums from writing call options, and any gains from the sales of portfolio securities.

Precious metal funds invest in the stocks of gold mining companies and other companies in the precious metals business.

***Convenient Features of Mutual Funds***   The most attractive feature of mutual funds is the affordable entry into a diversified investment vehicle. The majority of funds allow you to open an account with between $250 and $1,000. Afterwards, additional investments can be made at the convenience of the shareholder. Many funds have programs where additional investments can be made through payroll deduction plans.

Frequently, an investor signs a letter indicating an intention to invest a certain amount in the fund over a given period. This letter does not legally bind the investor to follow through with the stated plans, but it usually entitles the investor to a lower commission rate, one based on the total planned investment. If the investor does not follow through with the additional investment, the commission fees will be adjusted to reflect the actual total purchase amount.

Dividends and capital gains distributions can be paid to you or automatically reinvested. If they are reinvested, there usually is no sales fee. Shares can automatically be redeemed so that investors receive a check of a requested amount at regular intervals, for example $300 a month. If a firm manages more than one fund, investors can usually switch their investment to one of the firm's funds with different objectives for only a small administrative charge, perhaps $10. The switch can usually be done by phone. Note that a switch is treated as a sale and a purchase under income tax regulations. Capital gains (losses) will have to be reported on the sale.

# Closed-End Investment Companies

**Closed-end investment companies** are structured like other corporations—they have a fixed number of common shares, which are originally sold through investment banking firms. Purchasers resell the shares in the secondary market in the same manner as any other stock. Some closed-end investment companies have their stock listed on the organized exchanges but usually the stock is traded in the OTC market.

Like other stocks, the price of the shares of closed-end investment companies is determined by supply and demand in the market. The stock's price is not tied to the company's NAV. It may sell for more (a premium) or less (a discount). Closed-end investment companies may also issue preferred stocks and bonds.

***Classification by Investment Objectives***   The classification of closed-end funds by investment objectives overlaps the classification for mutual funds. There are common stock funds, specialized stock funds, international and global funds, bond and preferred stock funds, and precious metal funds. Two classes of funds are available only as closed-end funds: SBIC funds and dual-purpose funds.

SBIC funds invest in the securities of small firms. The Small Business Investment Act of 1958 authorized the Small Business Administration to license firms as Small Business Investment Companies (SBICs). In order to stimulate equity investment in small business, the law provides SBICs with tax advantages and the right to issue government guaranteed debt securities.

Dual-purpose funds issue two classes of stock: capital shares and income shares. Capital shares receive all the capital appreciation earned by the fund while the income shares receive all the dividend income minus fund expenses. Dual-purpose funds are liquidated after a limited life of usually 10 to 15 years. Dual-purpose funds provide income seekers with attractive periodic returns and capital seekers with the potential for large long-term gains (and losses). Because dual-purpose funds are popular in good market periods, several existed during the 1960s. They almost disappeared in the 1970s and made a comeback in the mid-1980s.

# Unit Trusts

Unit trusts are the third type of investment company defined under the 1940 law. **Unit trusts** are much like mutual funds in that the investor owns shares, called units, in a diversified portfolio of securities. However, the difference is that a unit trust is composed of a fixed portfolio of securities; it is not actively managed. After the money is raised through the sale of the investment trust units, the trust purchases securities that are held by a bank trustee. An investment trust has a limited life because its securities are sold after the prescribed number of years if they have not already matured. The life of a trust can be from 6 months to 20 years depending on the type of securities it holds.

Usually, unit trusts are sponsored by a brokerage firm. In most circumstances, the units are originally sold for $1,000 each; this includes a sales charge of 2 to 5 percent depending on the type of trust. Unit trusts do not have management fees since the fixed portfolios do not require management or trading. The sponsoring brokerage firm usually provides liquidity by making a secondary market in the units of the trust.

Unit trusts are available to match the objectives of many investors. Most popular are trusts that buy and hold debt securities: U.S. government securities trusts, tax-exempt municipal securities trusts, and corporate bond trusts. These trusts buy bonds that match their prescribed lives.

A recent trend is equity investment trusts, which originate when brokerage firms put together trusts based on the growth stocks that their research departments recommend highly. These trusts allow investors to own high-risk growth stocks and yet be diversified in their holding so that if there are a few losers, the winners will compensate for them. These equity trusts usually have short lives, one to three years. In order to have a good return after a 4 percent sales charge, the funds must have a very good performance in this short period of time.

# RELATED INVESTMENT VEHICLES

Some other investment vehicles provide the investor some of the benefits provided by investment companies. Here we describe the features of commingled funds, real estate investment trusts, and investment clubs.

## Commingled Funds

Many banks have trust departments that manage retirement funds and personal trust accounts. Although their larger accounts are handled individually, it is much more efficient to combine smaller accounts with similar objectives. Although these commingled funds are not legally mutual funds, in practice they are very similar. They have investment units that are valued at net asset value. Usually, a bank will manage several commingled funds with different objectives.

## Real Estate Investment Trusts

Real Estate Investment Trusts (REITs) are not classified as investment companies but operate like closed-end investment companies. REITs are corporations that invest in real estate and/or mortgages. They offer investors in real estate the advantages offered by investment companies: convenience, diversification, and professional management.

REITs provide the investor a convenient way to diversify into real estate. Because REITs do not have to pay taxes if they pay out in dividends more than 90 percent of their earnings, most REITs pay high dividends. They are, however, subject to interest rate risk and the cycles in commercial real estate profitability. REITs are discussed in more detail in Chapter 19.

## Investment Clubs

Investment clubs offer the small investor two of the advantages of investment companies: a convenient method to invest regularly small amounts and diversification. Investment clubs also provide socializing and exchange of investment ideas with club members. There are about 25,000 investment clubs in the United States. The typical club has about 15 members and meets once a month. Usually, each member contributes about $50 per month. Most clubs select stocks based on fundamental analysis of their prospects and avoid trying to outguess market cycles. They stay fully invested for long-term growth. When members quit, they receive a cash distribution representing their share of the club's portfolio.

# PERFORMANCE OF INVESTMENT COMPANIES

Because of the growth and influence of institutional investors, several studies of their performance have been undertaken in the past 25 years. Because mutual funds must publish semiannual reports on their portfolios, they are the subject of most of these studies. In this section we review three of the better known studies and then summarize mutual fund performance.

Friend, Blume, and Crockett examined the performance of 136 funds over the period January 1960 through June 1968.[1] They grouped the funds according to risk and compared fund performance to equally weighted and value weighted averages of NYSE stocks. Exhibit 15–5 summarizes some of their many findings.

Overall the funds had an average annual return of 10.7 percent for the period. This figure reflects all capital gains and dividends and is based on equal weighting of the funds. During the same time period an equal investment in each of the NYSE stocks would have yielded an annual return of 12.4 percent. Weighting the NYSE stocks according to their market value would have yielded an annual return of 9.9 percent. Thus, the funds performed worse than the equally weighted portfolio and better than the value weighted portfolio of NYSE stocks.

Dividing the funds and NYSE stocks into three risk classes based on beta, we find

1. High-risk funds outperformed the value weighted high-risk stocks
2. Medium-risk funds did a little better than the value weighted medium-risk stocks

---

[1] Friend, Irwin, Blume, Marshall, and Crockett, Jean. *Mutual Funds and Other Institutional Investors: A New Perspective* (New York: McGraw-Hill, 1970), pp. 50–68.

---

**EXHIBIT 15–5   Mutual Fund Performance for 136 Funds, January 1960–June 1968**

| | Mean Return | | |
| --- | --- | --- | --- |
| Risk Class (Beta) | Mutual Funds (%) | Equally Weighted NYSE Portfolio (%) | Value Weighted NYSE Portfolio (%) |
| All | 10.7 | 12.4 | 9.9 |
| Low risk ($\beta$ = .5–.7) | 9.1 | 12.8 | 11.6 |
| Medium risk ($\beta$ = .7–.9) | 10.6 | 13.1 | 9.7 |
| High risk ($\beta$ = .9–1.1) | 13.5 | 13.7 | 10.3 |

Source: Compiled from data in Friend, Irwin, Blume, Marshall, and Crockett, Jean. *Mutual Funds and Other Institutional Investors: A New Perspective* (New York: McGraw-Hill, 1970), pp. 53–56, 150.

---

**3.** Low-risk funds did worse than the value weighted low-risk stocks

**4.** All three groups did worse than the comparable unweighted average

In summary, the funds did about the same as the standard—a risk-adjusted randomly selected portfolio. Additional analysis found that return was not related to nonrisk factors such as new sales, size, management fees, load fees, and turnover.

Sharpe measured the performance of 34 funds over the period 1954–1963. He adjusted each fund's return for its risk as measured by the standard deviation of its returns. Before considering management fees, 19 of the 34 funds outperformed the DJIA. After considering management fees, 11 of the 34 outperformed the DJIA. Sharpe concluded

> It appears that the average mutual fund manager selects a portfolio at least as good as the Dow-Jones Industrials, but that the results actually obtained by the holder of mutual fund shares (after the costs associated with the operations of the fund have been deducted) fall somewhat short of those from the Dow-Jones Industrials.[2]

McDonald examined the objectives and performance of 123 mutual funds using monthly data from 1960–1969. He found that most funds had risk levels consistent with their stated objectives. Updating Sharpe's study, he found that only 39 of 123 funds outperformed the market. He also updated an earlier study by Treynor that measured return adjusted for risk as measured by beta. Using Treynor's measure, he found 67 of the 123 funds outperformed the market. He concluded

---

[2] Sharpe, William F. "Mutual Fund Performance," *Journal of Business* 39 (January 1966): 137.

For the mutual fund sample as a whole, the data clearly show neither significantly "superior" nor "inferior" performance over the decade 1960–1969.[3]

## Performance Summary

The returns that the funds earn are about what would be achieved with a portfolio of securities randomly selected from a population of appropriate risk. There is no evidence that fund managers excel at security selection or market timing. Individual funds do not have above average returns consistently year after year. That is, performance rank in past years does not predict performance rank in the future.

The good news is that mutual funds invest according to their stated objectives. That is, funds that say they will invest in low-risk securities do so; those that say they will take on more risk do so. There is the expected positive relationship between return and risk. Also, the funds do hold well-diversified portfolios. These findings and the convenient features the funds offer make them very attractive to investors with limited resources.

# SUMMARY

Investment companies provide the investor with convenience, diversification, and professional management. Mutual funds sell new shares at an offering price that may or may not include a sales charge. They stand ready to repurchase their shares at a bid price that equals the net asset value per share. Mutual funds exist that match most investors' objectives. Empirical studies of past performance have found that although mutual funds do not outperform the market if you adjust for risk, they do invest according to their objectives and do achieve good diversification.

Closed-end investment companies have a fixed number of shares that are originally sold through an initial public offering. Purchasers resell their shares in the same way as the shares of industrial firms. The shares may sell for a premium above or a discount from net asset value. Closed-end funds that have SBIC licenses invest in the securities of small firms. Dual-purpose funds issue two classes of stock: capital shares and income shares.

Unit trusts are investment companies that do not have active management. When the trust is established, the sponsoring brokerage firm puts together a portfolio of securities that will be held until the end of the trust. Although not legally investment companies, commingled funds of bank trust departments, real estate investment trusts, and investment clubs have some similarities to investment companies.

# QUESTIONS

1. What advantages do investment companies offer the investor?
2. How are investment companies organized?

---

[3] McDonald, John G. "Objectives and Performance of Mutual Funds, 1960–1969," *Journal of Financial and Quantitative Analysis* 9 (June 1974): 331.

3. How do open-end and closed-end investment companies differ?

4. What is the difference between a load and no-load mutual fund? Would you buy a load fund? Why or why not?

5. Based on their portfolios, what are some of the types of mutual funds?

6. Describe SBICs and dual-purpose funds.

7. How does a unit trust differ from a mutual fund?

8. What is a commingled fund?

9. What is a real estate investment trust (REIT)? What are the risks in REITs?

10. How does an investment club work?

11. Summarize the studies of the performance of mutual funds.

## PROBLEMS

1. On September 30, 1988, the assets of Dreyfus A Bonds Plus Fund were $287,868,580. The fund's liabilities were $3,375,648. There were 21,008,391 shares outstanding. This is a no-load fund.
   a. What is the net asset value per share?
   b. On September 30, 1988, how many shares could you purchase for $5,000?

2. On November 30, 1983, the assets of Fidelity High Yield Municipals Fund were $820,627,864. The fund's liabilities were $10,542,734. There were 67,163,572 shares outstanding. This is a no-load fund.
   a. What is the net asset value per share?
   b. On November 30, 1983, how many shares could you purchase for $5,000?

3. You write a check for $10,000 to purchase shares of Templeton Growth Fund. The net asset value per share is $13.68; the offering price is $14.95.
   a. How many shares do you buy?
   b. What is the effective commission rate?
   c. The next day the net asset value per share increases 12 cents. What is the new value of your holdings?

4. You write a check for $5,000 to purchase shares of Franklin Gold Fund. The net asset value per share is $10.99; the offering price is $11.45.
   a. How many shares do you buy?
   b. What is the effective commission rate?
   c. The next day the net asset value per share decreases three cents. What is the value of your holdings?

## CASE PROBLEM

Find an advertisement for a mutual fund. Call or send for a prospectus. Summarize the objectives of the fund and analyze its past performance.

## READINGS

Haslem, John A. *The Investor's Guide to Mutual Funds*. Englewood Cliffs, N.J.: Prentice Hall, 1988.

*This book explains the nature of mutual funds and advises the individual investor on how to select them.*

Investment Company Institute. *Mutual Fund Handbook*. Washington, D.C.: Investment Company Institute, annual.

*This book discusses trends in the mutual fund industry and presents much statistical data.*

Lehmann, Bruce N., and Modest, David M. "Mutual Fund Performance Evaluation: A Comparison of Benchmarks and Benchmark Comparisons," *Journal of Finance* 42 (June 1987): 233–265.

*This study finds that mutual fund performance rankings are very sensitive to the model chosen to measure performance.*

Maginn, John L., and Tuttle, Donald L. *Managing Investment Portfolios, A Dynamic Process*. Boston: Warren, Gorham and Lamont, 1983.

*This book documents the portfolio management process. It blends academic theory with the experience of practitioners.*

Rugg, Donald D. *The Dow Jones-Irwin Guide to Mutual Funds,* 3rd ed. Homewood, IL: Dow Jones-Irwin, 1986.

*This author attempts to show the investor how to set up an investment program, how to select investment objectives, how to pick no-load mutual funds, and how to time the market.*

Wiesenberger Investment Company Services. *Investment Companies*. Boston: Wiesenberger Investment Company Service, annual.

*This book contains statistics on 600 mutual funds. For each fund it presents a brief history, investment objectives, portfolio analysis, special services available, and sales charges. A hypothetical $10,000 investment is charted over ten years for major funds.*

# Options

## OUTLINE

## OBJECTIVES

When you have finished studying this chapter, you should understand

1. What put and call options are and how they originate.

2. The functions of the Options Clearing Corporation.

3. Standardized contract features necessary for a smooth functioning options market.

4. The variables that are important in determining the value of a call option.

5. The features of stock options, bond options, stock index options, and foreign currency options.

# 16

## Options, Futures, and the Public Interest

In 1984, Nobel prize winning economist James Tobin wrote:

> The new options and futures contracts do not stretch very far into the future. They serve mainly to allow greater leverage to short-term speculators and arbitrageurs, and to limit losses in one direction or the other. Collectively, they contain considerable redundancy. Every financial market absorbs private resources to operate and government resources to police. The country cannot afford all the markets that enthusiasts may dream up. In deciding whether to approve proposed contracts for trading, the authorities should consider whether they really fill gaps in the menu . . . not just opportunities for speculation and financial arbitrage.*

*Tobin, James. "On the Efficiency of the Financial System," Fred Hirsch Memorial Lecture (May 15, 1984). Published in *Lloyds Bank Review* (July 1984): 10.

## INTRODUCTION

Before 1973, options were traded only in the over-the-counter market. In 1973, the Chicago Board of Trade (CBOT) began trading options on the exchange. The CBOT was successful in options trading because of its experience in futures trading. Many of the mechanisms used to expedite future trading were adopted for options trading. The CBOT was so successful in options trading that it organized, in 1985, a separate organization, the Chicago Board Options Exchange (CBOE), to take over options trading. Today the CBOE trades more options contracts than any other exchange and is the only exchange that trades only options.

In addition to the CBOE, options are traded domestically on the American Stock Exchange, the Coffee, Sugar and Cocoa Exchange, the New York Stock Exchange, the Pacific Stock Exchange, the Philadelphia Board of Trade, the Philadelphia Stock Exchange, and in the OTC market. Options are also traded on nine foreign exchanges.

Many other exchanges trade options on futures. Growth in the number of option contracts traded has been explosive as more and more investors are participating in the market. Formal trading now takes place in stock options, stock index options, debt instrument options, foreign currency options, and futures options. The development of these new options is creating close links among stock, options, and futures trading.

---

# DEFINITIONS

An **option** is a contract that allows its holder to buy or sell a specified security at an established exercise price anytime before the expiration date. A **call option** allows its holder to buy; a **put option** allows its holder to sell. The contract is between two parties, the seller who ''writes'' the contract and the holder who ''buys'' it. When the contract is originated, the buyer pays the seller an agreed upon amount of money, called the **option premium.** If the contract is ''exercised'' by the holder, the underlying security and the exercise price are exchanged. If the contract is not exercised by the holder by its expiration date, no securities are transferred and the seller has profits in the amount of the option premium paid.

The above definition is for an **American option,** which can be exercised anytime before expiration. A **European option** can be exercised only on the expiration date. Most options traded in the United States are American options.

## The Options Clearing Corporation

The Options Clearing Corporation (OCC) serves as a clearing agency by interposing itself between the buyer and the seller of the option. After the buyer and seller agree on the option premium, two contracts are originated: one between the OCC and the seller and the other between the OCC and the buyer. This arrangement provides the buyer and seller with two important features.

1. The buyer does not need to be concerned with the ability of the seller to meet the contractual commitment. The credit of the OCC is behind the contract.
2. A buyer or seller can cancel a contract by taking the opposite side of a new contract. The OCC will cancel the individual's two offsetting contracts.

When an option holder decides to exercise the option, the party who originally sold the option is usually not the one who delivers the security (call option) or buys the security (put option). The original seller may have closed out his or her position by buying a similar contract. Therefore, upon exercise by the contract holder, the OCC randomly selects from among the clearing member accounts with outstanding options with the exact features as the one being exercised. The clearing member, in turn, selects from among its clients with outstanding obligations on the option being exercised.

The option contract writer chosen must deliver the securities in the case of a call or buy them in the case of a put.

## Standardized Contracts

Option trading takes place efficiently because the exchanges have standardized option contracts. Three provisions of the contract needed to be standardized: the underlying security, the exercise price, and the expiration date.

**Underlying Security**   The stock option contract is based on 100 shares of the common stock.

**Exercise Price (Striking Price)**   It is established before trading of the option begins. Usually, two different contracts with different striking prices will be available. If the stock price is less than $50, there will be a $5 interval between the two exercise prices. If the stock price is from $50 to $200, there will be a $10 interval between the exercise prices. If the stock price is greater than $200, there will be a $20 interval between exercise prices. As stock prices move up or down, the exchanges establish trading in contracts with different exercise prices. Therefore, a choice of contracts with several different exercise prices often is available to market participants.

**Expiration Date**   The exchanges have established expiration dates for stock options on three-month cycles. The longest expiration date is nine months. After three months have passed and the option now expires in six months, trading in a new nine-month contract begins. After another three months have passed and the existing options now expire in three or six months, trading in a new nine-month contract begins. Options for some stocks are on the January, April, July, and October cycle; others are on the February, May, August, and November cycle; the remaining are on the March, June, September, and December cycle. Stock options expire on the Saturday following the third Friday of the expiration month. However, the holder must direct his or her broker to give exercise instructions to the OCC no later than the last business day before expiration.

## Reading Option Quotations

Exhibit 16–1 can help you understand these features and teach you to read the stock option table in the newspaper.

**EXHIBIT 16–1   Option Quotations, April 29, 1986**

| Option and Close | Strike Price | Calls–Last | | | Puts–Last | | |
|---|---|---|---|---|---|---|---|
| | | Jun | Sep | Dec | Jun | Sep | Dec |
| Ford | 75 | $6\frac{1}{2}$ | $8\frac{1}{2}$ | $10\frac{1}{8}$ | $1\frac{1}{4}$ | $3\frac{1}{2}$ | $4\frac{3}{8}$ |
| $79\frac{1}{4}$ | 80 | $3\frac{1}{2}$ | $6\frac{1}{8}$ | r | $3\frac{3}{8}$ | $5\frac{7}{8}$ | r |
| | 85 | $1\frac{3}{4}$ | $4\frac{1}{8}$ | 6 | 7 | $9\frac{1}{2}$ | $9\frac{3}{4}$ |

The first column of the table identifies the underlying stock and gives its closing price. Ford stock had closed at $79.25 on the NYSE. The second column gives the striking (exercise) price of the option. Options with striking prices of $75, $80, and $85 are available. The next three columns list the last price (per share) for call options expiring in the respective months. The last three columns list the last price for put options expiring in the respective months. The letter "r" means the option did not trade; "s" means that option is not available. Note that this table lists nine different call option contracts and nine different put option contracts.

## Market Terminology

A call option is in-the-money when the market price of the stock is more than the striking price. In Exhibit 16–1, the call option that allows the holder to buy Ford at $75 per share when the market price per share is $79.25 is in-the-money. The more the market price of the stock exceeds the striking price, the deeper in-the-money the option is.

A put option is in-the-money when the striking is above the market price of the stock. In Exhibit 16–1, the put option that allows the holder to sell Ford at $85 per share when the market price per share is $79.25 is in-the-money. The more the striking price exceeds the market price, the deeper in-the-money the option is.

An option is at-the-money when the striking price is equal to the market price of the stock. An option is close-to-the-money when the striking price is near the market price. In Exhibit 16–1 both the call and the put options with the $80 striking price are close-to-the-money.

A call option is out-of-the-money when the market price of the stock is less than the striking price. It would not make sense to exercise the option. The call option that allows the holder to buy Ford at $85 per share when the market price is $79.25 is out-of-the-money.

A put option is out-of-the-money when the market price of the stock is greater than the striking price. The put option that allows the holder to sell Ford at $75 per share when the market price is $79.25 is out-of-the-money. Out-of-the-money options are least expensive.

# CALL OPTIONS

A call option is a contract that allows its holder to buy a specified security at an established price anytime before the expiration date. You buy a call option when you expect the price of the underlying security to go up. Call options offer the holder the potential for high returns on a small investment. Additionally, losses are limited to the cost of the option.

| EXAMPLE | On April 29, 1986, the stock of Ford Motor Company was selling for $79.25 per share. On that day, you could have purchased a call option for $175 that gave you the right to buy 100 shares of Ford at $85 per share anytime before |

June 21, 1986. If Ford's stock went above $85, you could exercise your option to buy the stock at $85 and immediately resell the stock at the market price. If the market price never reached $85, you would just let your option expire and you would have lost only $175.

Assume Ford's stock went from its current price of $79.25 to $90 per share. Ignoring commissions, if you owned the stock, you would have made about 13.5 percent ($10.75 ÷ $79.25). If you had purchased the option and exercised it, you would have made 186 percent. The computations on a per share basis are

| | |
|---|---|
| $ 90 | market price |
| − 85 | striking price |
| − 1.75 | option cost |
| 3.25 | profit |
| ÷ 1.75 | investment |
| 186% | return |

Call option holders have another choice besides exercising the option or letting it expire. They could sell a similar option contract and thereby close out their position. The price of the call option moves up when the price of the underlying security moves up and vice versa.

For each call option buyer, there has to be an option writer (seller). When the option writer owns the underlying security, he or she is a covered option writer. When the option writer does not own the underlying security, he or she is a naked option writer.

Writing covered call options is conservative. The covered writer is earning the option premiums the buyer is paying (less commissions) and giving up potential gains should the stock rise significantly.

---

**EXAMPLE**

A covered writer of the Ford option in the example above gets the $175 premium. If the stock price does not go above $85, the option holder will not exercise it. If the stock price goes above $85, the option will be exercised and the writer sells the underlying stock for $85.

Writing naked call options is very risky since the stock price could go up a lot. The option would be exercised and the writer would have to buy the stock at the high price and deliver it at the striking price.

## Determinants of Call Option Premiums

Exhibit 16–2 graphs the relationship between a stock's price and the price of call options with different periods to maturity. The two most important determinants of call option premiums are reflected in the graph: the price of the stock and the life of the option.

The market price of the stock greatly influences the call premium. A call option will never be worth more than the stock. Line OB in the exhibit reflects this maximum

---

**EXHIBIT 16–2   Call Option Premiums**

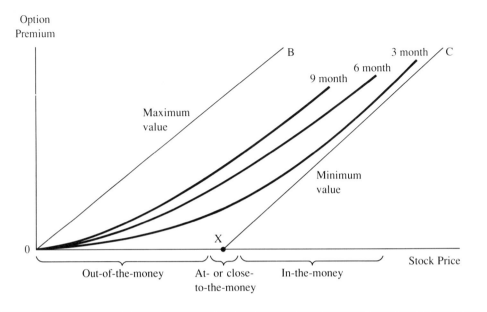

value. The minimum value of a call option is the stock price minus the striking price. Line XC reflects this minimum value. An option can never have a negative market value.

The longer the life of the option the more valuable it is. The longer life gives a greater probability that the stock will increase in value enough to allow a gain on the option. Exhibit 16–2 shows that longer maturity options have higher prices.

Another important determinant of the call option premium is the volatility of the stock. The greater the volatility, the more likely it is that the stock price will move up to where the option is profitable. The volatility of an option premium is greater than that of the underlying stock price because of the leverage offered by the option. However, the further in-the-money the option is, the more consistent its volatility is with that of the stock.

A less important determinant of the call option premium is the level of interest rates. If nothing else changes, when interest rates are rising, option prices tend to move upward; when interest rates are falling, option prices move downward.

# PUT OPTIONS

A put option is a contract that allows its holder to sell a specified security at an established price anytime before the expiration date. You buy a put option when you expect the price of the underlying security to go down. Like call options, put options offer the holder the potential for high returns on a small investment. Losses are limited to the cost of the option.

| EXAMPLE | Exhibit 16–1 shows that on April 29, 1986, you could have purchased for $125 a June put option giving you the right to sell 100 shares of Ford at $75 per share. If the stock price fell to $70, you would make a 300 percent return. The details on a per share basis are |

$ 70 cost of the stock
<u>75</u> exercise the put
5 difference
<u>− 1.25</u> cost of the put
3.75 profit
<u>÷ 1.25</u> investment
300% return ☐

Sometimes owners of stocks buy puts in order to limit their losses should the stock price fall. Of course, they pay the amount of the option premium for this loss protection.

The writer of a put option earns the option premium but runs the risk of having to buy the stock at the exercise price if the market price goes down. Writing put options is risky, but not as risky as writing naked call options. In the case of the put option, the worst outcome is that the stock price falls to zero and the writer must pay the exercise price for worthless stock.

# THE UNDERLYING SECURITIES

The exchanges sponsor trading in options on five types of underlying securities: stocks, debt instruments, stock indexes, foreign currencies, and futures. Options on futures are discussed in Chapter 17. Here we present the features of the other types.

## Stock Options

Options are available on hundreds of exchange listed stocks and a few OTC stocks. The important features of stock options were covered above.

## Debt (Interest Rate) Options

Put and call options can be written on debt instruments. Debt options are similar to stock options and trade in the same manner. Because of the inverse relationship between the prices of debt instruments and interest rates, these options allow holders to take option positions that reduce the interest rate risk that they might face from other business transactions.

Call options become more valuable as the underlying security prices rise and put options become more valuable as underlying security prices fall. Therefore, the relationship between interest rates, debt security prices, and debt options is

$$\text{interest rates fall } = \text{ prices rise } = \begin{cases} \text{call options rise} \\ \text{put options fall} \end{cases}$$

$$\text{interest rates rise } = \text{ prices fall } = \begin{cases} \text{call options fall} \\ \text{put options rise} \end{cases}$$

At the time of this writing, the markets for debt options are just developing; the only debt securities on which options are available are Treasury bills, notes, and bonds. The bill options cover $1,000,000 principal amount of 13-week bills. In case of exercise by the holder, the deliverable security is not a specific issue of Treasury bills with a predetermined maturity date but rather a ''current'' bill with a full 13 weeks remaining to maturity. Exercise prices for Treasury bill options are based on annualized discount rates. However, exercise prices are expressed as complements of discount rates (100 minus the annualized discount rate) for the sake of consistency with other kinds of options, where the higher exercise price means payment of a higher dollar price in the event of exercise.

Treasury note and bond options cover $100,000 principal amount. Upon exercise, the specified issue of Treasury notes or bonds must be delivered. Exercise prices for Treasury note and bond options are expressed in the same way as prices for the bonds; that is, as a percentage of face value. Upon exercise, accrued interest from the last interest payment date through the exercise settlement date must be paid in addition to the exercise price.

## Index Options

**Index options** give the holder the right to buy and sell the cash value of a stock market index at the exercise price in the contract. Notice that the contract is based on the cash value of the index; settlement is made in cash rather than securities. Most of the contracts are for one, two, or three months and they expire on the Saturday following the third Friday of the month.

A stock market index may represent the stock market as a whole, a particular market (NYSE), a broad market sector (industrials), or a particular industry (electronics). Exhibit 16–3 lists some of the index options available.

In general, index options are similar to stock options but some differences should be noted. Most important, upon exercise the option writer pays the holder an amount equal to the difference between the level of the index and the exercise price multiplied by a specified index ''multiplier.'' The multiplier is a fixed feature of the option contract for a particular index. It determines the value of each point of the index.

---

**EXHIBIT 16–3  Index Options**

| Market | Description |
| --- | --- |
| AMEX | Major Market Index |
| AMEX | Institutional Index[a] |
| AMEX | Oil Index |
| AMEX | Computer Technology Index |
| CBOE | Standard & Poor's 100 Index |
| CBOE | Standard & Poor's 500 Index |
| CBOE | U.S. 30-Year Treasury Bond Index |
| CBOE | U.S. 5-Year Treasury Note Index |
| NYSE | NYSE Composite Index |
| PSE | *Financial News* Composite Index |
| PHLX | Gold/Silver Index |
| PHLX | Value Line Composite Index[b] |
| PHLX | National OTC Index |
| PHLX | Utilities Index |

[a] Traded in the European style.

[b] Traded in both the American and European style

---

**EXAMPLE**

The holder of a call option on XYZ index exercises it when the index is at 85. The exercise price of the option is 80. If the multiplier for XYZ index options is 100, the writer would have to pay the holder $500. □

Because index options are settled in cash, a call option writer cannot buy securities in advance to deliver in case of exercise by the holder. The writer might try to reduce his or her risk exposure by buying and holding all the stock in the index and then selling the stocks if and when the option is exercised. As a practical matter, the large investment required and the transactions costs prevent most investors from doing this. Some large institutions do take positions involving index options and the underlying securities. Because settlement of the options is at closing index prices, these institutions often try to buy or sell the securities in an index just before the market closes on the day the options are expiring. This can cause stock prices to change dramatically in the last few minutes of the trading day.

## Foreign Currency Options

Foreign currency exchange rates are very volatile. In a single day, the German Deutsche mark may fluctuate 3 percent relative to the U.S. dollar. Between September 1984 and March 1985, the dollar rose 25 percent relative to the British pound. During the next four months the dollar declined by 35 percent relative to the pound. Foreign currency options allow businesses and financial institutions to hedge the foreign currency risk they face.

### Writing Put Options

On October 19, 1987, the market declined drastically in the heaviest trading volume in history. The Dow Jones Industrial Average was down 508 points. The fall in stock prices caused hundreds of millions of dollars in losses to investors who had written put options on stocks or stock indexes. Their option contracts required them to buy the underlying stock or the value of the index at a set price. When the holders of the options exercised them, the writers were required to pay the set price which was much more than the reduced value of the securities. To make matters worse, many of the option writers had used margin heavily and did not have the money to purchase the securities. When the option writers defaulted, the brokerage firms were responsible for fulfilling the option contracts.

H. B. Shaine & Co. of Grand Rapids, Michigan, an NYSER member firm, could not meet the obligations on which its customers defaulted. The customers, in turn, argued that they did not fully understand the risks of writing "naked put options."

The national discount brokerage firm of Charles Schwab Corp. lost $17 million on one customer's account. Days before the crash, the customer began writing, using margin, put options on stock market indexes. His losses on October 19 were $84 million. When he could not meet his margin calls, he declared bankruptcy. Charles Schwab settled the $84 million obligation for a $67 million payment. Charles Schwab Corp. stated it would never allow another customer to have so large a position.

The drastic market decline on October 19 brought demands for more regulation of stock index futures and options. Proponents of new regulations demanded margin requirement on stock index futures and options be equal to the higher margin requirements on stock purchases.

Foreign currency options allow the holder to buy or sell a foreign currency for a set dollar amount anytime before the expiration date. The option premiums are expressed in terms of U.S. cents per unit of foreign currency. For example, if an option covering 62,500 Swiss francs is purchased at a premium of .81, the cost of the option will be $.0081 times 62,500 or $506.25. Exhibit 16–4 describes the features of foreign currency options traded on the Philadelphia Stock Exchange.

# OPTIONS TRADING

Options trading strategies run from simple, low-risk ones, such as writing covered calls, to complex and/or high-risk ones. In this section, we give you a better understanding of options trading.

## Commissions and Taxes

The returns from options trading are greatly affected by commissions and taxes. Commission costs on options as a percentage of the option premiums are much greater than commissions on stocks and bonds. Options also have short lives, so commissions are paid frequently. Commissions are especially significant in options trading strategies calling for multiple purchases and sales.

Tax rules for options are too complex for us to cover in this book. The rules vary depending on the underlying security. They are different for puts and calls. Also,

---

**EXHIBIT 16–4**  *Foreign Currency Options Contract Features*

| Currency | Contract Size (*Units of Currency*) | *Exercise Price Interval (per Unit of Currency)* |
|---|---|---|
| German mark | 62,500 | 1 cent |
| Swiss franc | 62,500 | 1 cent |
| French franc | 125,000 | ½ cent |
| Canadian dollar | 50,000 | ½ cent |
| British pound | 31,250 | 2½ cents |
| Japanese yen | 6,250,000 | 1/100 cent |
| Australian dollar | 50,000 | 1 cent |
| European currency unit | 62,500 | 8 cents |

Notes: *Expiration months:*   Five expirations at any given time: the two nearest months plus three from the March/June/September/December cycle. More frequent expirations offer more flexibility in hedging near-term currency risks.

*Exercise price:*   At least three exercise prices will be available for each expiration month. Exercise prices will bracket spot and forward prices.

---

ownership of the underlying security can change the tax treatment of both the option and the underlying security. Brokerage firms have pamphlets explaining the details of the tax rules. Understand the tax consequences before trading options!

## Margin Requirements

In the stock market, margin refers to buying stocks with borrowed money. Options cannot be bought on credit. In the options market, margin refers to the cash or securities that must be deposited by the option writer with his or her broker to ensure fulfillment of the contract if it is exercised. Because the buyer of the option cannot lose more than the option premium already paid, he or she is not required to put up any margin.

For option writers, margin requirements are set by individual brokerage firms, subject to minimum requirements imposed by stock exchanges and by other self-regulatory organizations. If market prices move against them, uncovered option writers may have to meet calls for substantial additional margin. Option writers must understand the complex margin requirements, which vary from broker to broker, and must have sufficient liquid assets to meet margin requirements. Margin requirements substantially affect an option writer's risk and return position.

## Option Strategies

Strategies for profiting using options vary from use of a single call or put to complex combinations using puts and calls and the underlying securities. There is an almost

**EXHIBIT 16–5   *Profit Profile for a Straddle (Exercise Price is $60)***

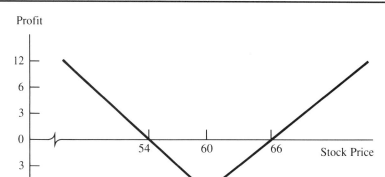

endless list of option strategies. Here we discuss three examples: straddles, straps, and strips.

A straddle is a combination containing a put and a call with the same striking price and maturity. The straddle holder expects the security price to move away from the exercise price but does not know whether it will go up or down. The holder will profit on the call if the price of the underlying security increases and on the put if it decreases. Of course, the straddle buyer has to pay the premiums for both the put and call. Therefore, the underlying security price must move above or below the exercise price enough to cover these costs. The straddle holder suffers the maximum loss if the stock price stays at the exercise price.

Exhibit 16–5 is the profit profile for a straddle with an exercise price of $60 and a combined premium of $6. The straddle holder breaks even if the stock moves $6 either way from the exercise price. The farther the stock moves, the greater the holder's profit.

The writer of a straddle receives the option premiums from the put and the call. He or she profits the most if the price of the underlying security does not move away from the exercise price and suffers a loss if the price of the security moves up or down by an amount greater than the premium amounts received. In analyzing spreads, do not forget that option premiums are greater when the underlying security is more volatile and when the option maturities are longer. A straddle writer earns higher premiums but takes more risk by writing longer-term options on volatile securities.

If an option buyer thought that there was a greater chance of a security going up but still wanted to profit if it fell substantially, he or she would purchase a strap instead of a straddle. A strap consists of two calls and one put, all with the same exercise price and time to expiration.

---

**EXHIBIT 16–6   Option Strategies**

| Strategy | Action |
|---|---|
| Straddle | Buy a call and a put with the same exercise price |
| Short straddle | Write a call and a put with the same exercise price |
| Strap | Buy two calls and one put, all with the same exercise price and time to expiration |
| Strip | Buy two puts and one call, all with the same exercise price and time to expiration |
| Strangle | Buy a call with an exercise price above the stock price; buy a put with an exercise price an equal distance below the stock price |
| Time spread | Buy an option with a longer time to expiration; write an option with a shorter time to expiration |
| Back spread | Buy an option with a shorter time to expiration; write an option with a longer time to expiration |
| Bull spread | Buy a call with a lower exercise price; write a call with a higher exercise price |
| Bear spread | Buy a call with a higher exercise price; write a call with a lower exercise price |
| Butterfly spread | Buy a call with a high exercise price; buy a call with a low exercise price; and write two calls with an exercise price in between the high and low exercise prices, with all options having the same expiration date |

---

If an option buyer thought that there was a greater chance of a security going down but still wanted to profit if it went up substantially, he or she would purchase a strip. A strip consists of two puts and one call, all with the same exercise price and time to expiration. Exhibit 16–6 lists more option strategies.

# SUMMARY

A call option is a contract that allows its holder to buy a specified security at an established price before the expiration date. A put option is a contract that allows its holder to sell a specified security at an established price before the expiration date. Standardization by exchanges of the features of option contracts has permitted efficient trading. The OCC enhances this process by guaranteeing fulfillment of the contract upon exercise and by allowing market participants to liquidate their positions by entering an offsetting contract.

Options present the investor with an additional investment vehicle. They can be used by both conservative and aggressive investors. The growth and continuous development of options trading show that they fulfill a need of investors. In addition to stocks, options are traded on bonds, stock indexes, foreign currencies, and futures.

The value of an option depends on the price of the underlying security, the time to maturity, the volatility of the underlying security, and the level of interest rates.

Option valuation models relate these factors to option premiums and allow investors to search for mispriced options. The relationship between the values of options and their underlying securities encourages many investors to take positions in both options and the underlying securities. These investors link together the markets for the options and the underlying securities.

# QUESTIONS

1. What is the difference between an American and a European option?

2. Describe the functions of the Options Clearing Corporation.

3. What provisions of option contracts must be standardized so that they can trade efficiently?

4. When is a call option in-the-money, at-the-money, and out-of-the-money? When is a put option in-the-money, at-the-money, and out-of-the-money? Give examples.

5. Why is writing naked call options very risky?

6. List four important factors in determining the value of a call option.

7. Describe the relationship between the premiums on Treasury bond call options and interest rates. Do the same for put options.

8. Describe the features of stock index options.

9. Describe the features of foreign currency options.

10. What is margin in reference to options? Who must deposit it?

11. What is the strategy of a straddle holder?

# PROBLEMS

1. On March 16, 1988, Chrysler is selling for $24 a share. You purchase a July call option with a strike price of $25 for $2 per share. How much do you make if in July Chrysler sells for $25? For $26? For $30? How much does the writer make in each case?

2. On March 16, 1988, GTE is selling for $38.50 a share. You purchase a June call option with a strike price of $40 for $1 per share. How much do you make if in June GTE sells for $38? For $42? For $45? How much does the writer make in each case?

3. On March 16, 1988, Litton is selling for $84.75 a share. You purchase a June put option with a strike price of $85 for $4 per share. How much do you make if in June Litton sells for $80? For $83? For $88? How much does the writer make in each case?

4. On March 16, 1988, IBM is selling for $115 a share. You purchase a July put option with a strike price of $120 for $9.50 per share. How much do you make if in July, IBM sells for $115? For $118? For $123? How much does the writer make in each case?

# READINGS

Bookstaber, Richard. *Option Pricing and Strategies in Investing.* Reading, Mass: Addison-Wesley, 1981.
   *Chapters 7, 8, and 9 present advanced strategies using options in combinations.*

Brill, Edward A., and Harriff, Richard B. "Pricing American Options: Managing Risk with Early Exercise," *Financial Analysts Journal* 42 (November–December 1986): 48–55.

> *This article discusses the relationship between options and futures options and quantifies the differences between European options, American spot options, and American futures options.*

Cox, John C., and Rubinstein, Mark. *Options Markets*. Englewood Cliffs, NJ: Prentice Hall, 1985.

> *This book provides a detailed discussion of institutional developments in and academic studies of stock options.*

Kolb, Robert W., and Gay, Gerald D. *Interest Rate and Stock Index Futures and Options: Characteristics, Valuation and Portfolio Strategies*. Charlottesville, VA: Financial Analysts Research Foundation, 1985.

> *This book shows how to hedge interest rate and stock price risk.*

Whaley, Robert E. "On Valuing American Futures Options," *Financial Analysts Journal* 42 (May–June 1986): 49–59.

> *This article clarifies the principles and intuition underlying European futures option pricing and extends these principles and intuition to American futures option pricing.*

# APPENDIX 16A
## The Black–Scholes Call Valuation Model

The most widely known call valuation model was developed by Black and Scholes.[1] This model and models which are extensions and refinements of it are widely used by participants in the options market. Software programs that compute the value of an option using these models are also widely used. Here we will not get into the mathematics but will look at the approach used, the assumption necessary, the input variables required and the valuation formula.

The Black–Scholes model is based on a riskless hedged position created by owning the underlying security and writing a call option. If the price of the security goes up, that gain offsets the loss on the call option. If the price of the security goes down, that loss is offset by the gain on the call option. The buying and selling of market participants will price the option so that this riskless hedged position returns the risk-free rate of return.

The assumptions listed here were used in developing the original valuation model. Advanced versions of the model make modifications of these assumptions in order to obtain better results. The assumptions of the Black–Scholes models are

1. The short-term interest rate is known and constant.

2. The stock price follows a random walk in continuous time with a variance proportional to the square of the stock price. Thus, the distribution of possible stock prices at the end of any finite interval is log normal. The variance of the return is constant.

3. The stock pays no dividends.

4. Only European options are considered.

5. There are no transaction costs.

6. Market participants can borrow or lend at the short-term interest rate.

7. There are no restrictions on short selling.

The following input variables are required to compute the value of an option:

> The current stock price
>
> The yield on a Treasury bill with a maturity equal to the option's expiration date
>
> The option's exercise price and term to expiration

---

[1] Black, Fischer, and Scholes, Myron. "The Pricing of Options and Corporate Liabilities, *Journal of Political Economy* 81 (May–June 1973): 637–654.

The variance of the rate of return on the stock

Given the assumptions above, the value of an option, $V_o$, that entitles the holder to buy one share of stock is:

$$V_o = V_s N(d_1) - \frac{E}{e^{rt}} N(d_2)$$

where

$V_s$ = the current price of the stock

$E$ = the exercise price of the option

$e$ = 2.71828

$r$ = the short-term annual interest rate continuously compounded

$t$ = the length of time in years to the expiration of the option

$N(d)$ = The value of the cumulative normal density function

$d_1 = \{\ln(V_s/E) + [r + (\frac{1}{2})(\sigma^2)]t\}/\sigma\sqrt{t}$

$d_2 = \{\ln(V_s/E) + [r - (\frac{1}{2})(\sigma^2)]t\}/\sigma\sqrt{t}$

$\ln$ = the natural logarithm

$\sigma$ = the standard deviation of the annual rate of return on the stock continuously compounded

# Futures Trading

## OUTLINE

## OBJECTIVES

When you have finished studying this chapter, you should understand

1. What future contracts are and which ones are available.
2. How a futures market operates.
3. The uses of financial futures in hedging.
4. What options on futures are.

# 17

## *Inflation Protection*

Buying commodity contracts has been viewed by some investors as a way of protecting themselves, or even profiting, from unanticipated inflation. Until recently, however, a particular commodity future had to be chosen, and the price increase in that commodity might not reflect the overall increases in commodity prices. Now, the New York Futures Exchange offers CRB Index Futures—future contracts based on the prices of many commodities: live cattle, cocoa, coffee, copper, corn, cotton, crude oil, gold, heating oil, hogs, lumber, oats, orange juice, platinum, pork bellies, silver, soybeans, soybean meal, soybean oil, sugar, and CBT wheat. CRB Index Futures provide an opportunity to hedge against inflation in these commodity prices or to speculate that their price trend is predictable.

## INTRODUCTION

By 1848 Chicago was the largest market for farm products in the Midwest. However, it was a chaotic scene of feast and famine cycles. At harvest time, when farmers transported their products to Chicago, there was a glut on the market, but transportation to other parts of the country was poor, partly due to undeveloped harbor facilities. Also, there was a lack of storage facilities. Therefore, the Chicago packers, millers, and other users of farm products would, in the face of such supply, bid down the price. At times, in fact, farmers dumped grain on the street, rather than transport it back home, because absolutely no market existed.

On the other side of the cycle, users bid the prices very high when the supply of farm products was low. The price fluctuations dictated by this supply and demand cycle were violent.

On April 3, 1848, some Chicago businessmen, realizing the plight of both the buyers and sellers of grain, organized the Chicago Board of Trade. At first, the Chicago Board of Trade was an exchange for members to make cash contracts for the sale of agricultural products and to alleviate the problems of excess supply or demand by addressing the problems of storing and transporting grain and livestock.

Some forward contracts were entered into also. Eventually, the Chicago Board of Trade evolved into an institution that provided a place where futures contracts could be bought and sold. Although most of the records were lost in the Great Chicago Fire of 1871, it is believed that due to the impetus of demand during the Civil War, most of the elements of the futures contract were in place by the 1860s.

# CASH, FORWARD, AND FUTURES CONTRACTS

In order to understand futures contracts, it is necessary to understand cash contracts, forward contracts, and the differences between them.

A **cash contract** is a contract between a buyer and a seller of a product where the product is delivered immediately and payment is received immediately. The product, its quality, quantity, and price are all negotiated components of the contract.

A **forward contract** is a contract between a buyer and a seller of a product for delivery and payment at some specified future date. The product, its quality, quantity, price, and future delivery and payment date are all negotiated elements of the contract.

A **futures contract** is a contract to buy or sell a product and to make payment or delivery at some specified future date.

What, then, is the difference between a forward contract and a futures contract? A futures contract can be entered into only on an organized futures exchange, but any buyer and seller can enter into a forward contract anywhere. The parties of a forward contract negotiate the terms: product quality, quantity, price, and delivery and payment date. The terms of a futures contract are standardized by the futures exchange. The futures contract for each product at each futures exchange is for a standard quantity, a standard grade of the product, and standard delivery dates. Only the price varies from contract to contract.

At the Chicago Board of Trade, for instance, futures contracts for corn are for 5,000 bushels and delivery months are March, May, July, September, and December. At the Chicago Mercantile Exchange, futures contracts for live hogs are for 30,000 pounds and the delivery months are February, April, June, July, August, October, and December. See Exhibit 17–1 for contracts specifications of other commodities.

For each futures exchange, a clearing house, which stands between the buyers and sellers, guarantees the contract. The clearing house is the buyer to every seller and the seller to every buyer. This means that in reality there are two types of futures contracts: a contract to buy in the future (or take a long position) where the clearing house is the seller, and a contract to sell in the future (or take a short position) where the clearing house is the buyer. Since all contracts for a particular product and delivery date are standardized, all contracts to sell the same product in the same delivery month are identical and all contracts to buy the same product in the same delivery month are identical. Therefore, if you have entered into one contract to sell September corn, you

---

**EXHIBIT 17–1   Futures Contracts for Selected Commodities**

| Commodity | Contract Months | Contract Size | Exchange Where Traded* |
|---|---|---|---|
| Corn | Mar/May/Jul/Sep/Dec | 5,000 bu. | CBT |
| Oats | Mar/May/Jul/Sep/Dec | 5,000 bu. | CBT |
| Wheat (soft winter) | Mar/May/Jul/Sep/Dec | 5,000 bu. | CBT |
| Wheat (hard red winter) | Mar/May/Jul/Sep/Dec | 5,000 bu. | KCBT |
| Wheat (hard red spring) | Mar/May/Jul/Sep/Dec | 5,000 bu. | MGE |
| Hogs, live | Feb/Apr/Jun/Jul/Aug/Oct/Dec | 30,000 lb. | CME |
| Orange juice | Jan/Mar/May/Jul | 15,000 lb. | Citrus Associates of NYCE |
| Gold | Current month, next two months, plus Feb/Apr/Jun/Aug/Oct/Dec | 100 troy oz. | COMEX |
| Heating Oil | All months | 42,000 gal. | NYME |
| Unleaded Gasoline | All months | 42,000 gal. | NYME |

* See Exhibit 17–6 for a list of domestic exchanges.

---

can liquidate your position by entering into one contract to buy September corn. As a matter of fact, it is seldom that a delivery is made; only about 3 percent of futures contracts result in delivery. The remainder are liquidated because the original seller enters into the opposite contract to buy or the original buyer enters into the opposite contract to sell.

It eventually became apparent that with the ability to liquidate a position came the ability to hedge or speculate. **Hedging** is a strategy whereby prospective buyers or sellers of a product can buy or sell futures contracts to reduce their risk of price fluctuations. **Speculating** is a strategy of taking risk in the hopes of making a profit. Hedging and speculating without taking or making delivery are the main reasons why the futures markets exist today. Hedging and speculating have become more important than the delivery of and payment for a product. Most of the actual delivery and payment occurs today in the cash or spot market.

# THE FUTURES MARKET TODAY

Today there are 12 futures exchanges in the United States and 19 in foreign countries. On these exchanges, futures contracts of many products are bought and sold. The products can be divided into two main categories: commodities and financials.

**Commodities** are homogeneous raw materials and farm products which include agricultural products like grains and livestock, metals like gold and silver, and energy products like crude oil and gasoline. See Exhibit 17–2.

**Financial futures** include interest rate sensitive financial instruments like U.S. Treasury bills, U.S. Treasury bonds, and commercial paper; indexes like the Major

---

**EXHIBIT 17–2   *Futures***

---

   I. Commodities
     A. Agricultural
     B. Metal
     C. Energy
  II. Financials
     A. Financial instruments
     B. Currencies
     C. Indexes
       1. Stock
       2. Bond
       3. Other
 III. Options on futures
     A. Commodities
     B. Financials

---

Market index (MMI) or the S&P 500; and currencies like the Deutsche mark and the Japanese yen. Exhibits 17–3 and 17–4 list the commodities and financial futures contracts traded in the United States.

Options on futures contracts are also traded on futures exchanges. Options on both commodity and financial futures are traded. Examples of options on financials are options on U.S. Treasury bond futures and options on the New York Stock Exchange (NYSE) Composite Index futures. Examples of options on commodity futures are soybeans, live hogs, and copper. Exhibit 17–5 lists the options on futures contracts that are traded in the United States.

Futures exchanges tend to specialize in the types of futures contracts they trade. For instance, the Chicago Board of Trade, the world's largest futures exchange, trades futures contracts in grain products, long-term financial instruments, the Major Market index (MMI), gold, silver, and options contracts on some of their futures contracts. The Chicago Mercantile Exchange trades futures contracts in livestock products, lumber, foreign currencies, short-term financial instruments, Standard & Poor's indexes, and also options contracts on some of their futures contracts. The Commodity Exchange (COMEX) in New York trades futures contracts only in metals and options contracts on some metal futures contracts. The MidAmerica Commodity Exchange, an affiliate of the Chicago Board of Trade, offers smaller-sized versions of contracts traded elsewhere. With few exceptions, each product is represented on only one futures exchange in the United States unless a smaller version is also traded on the MidAmerica Commodity Exchange. Exhibit 17–6 lists all the U.S. futures exchanges and the type of contracts offered by each. Exhibit 17–7 lists the foreign exchanges.

The futures market is a market of rapid innovations and changes. Futures contracts on new products are frequently added; unpopular contracts are dropped. For instance, the New York Mercantile Exchange, founded in 1972, discontinued trading potato futures in May 1987. At one time potato futures had been the exchange's most actively

**EXHIBIT 17–3   Commodity Futures Contracts Traded in the United States**

| Contract | Exchange Where Traded |
|---|---|
| *Agriculture* | |
| Corn | CBT, MidAm |
| Oats | CBT, MidAm |
| Soybeans | CBT, MidAm |
| Soybean oil | CBT |
| Soybean meal | CBT, MidAm |
| Wheat | CBT, KCBT, MidAm, MGE |
| Cattle | CME, MidAm |
| Hogs | CME, MidAm |
| Pork bellies | CME |
| Lumber | CME |
| Rough rice | CRCE |
| Cotton | NYCE |
| Cocoa | CSCE |
| Coffee | CSCE |
| Sugar | CSCE |
| Orange juice | NYCE |
| *Metals* | |
| Gold | CBT, COMEX, MidAm |
| Silver | CBT, COMEX, MidAm |
| Aluminum | COMEX |
| Copper | COMEX |
| Palladium | NYMEX |
| Platinum | NYMEX, MidAm |
| *Energy* | |
| Propane gas | NYMEX |
| No. 2 heating oil | NYMEX |
| Crude oil | NYMEX |
| Unleaded gasoline | NYMEX |

traded contract. Examples of innovations that were extremely successful are the introduction of financial futures in 1975 by the Chicago Board of Trade and the introduction of index futures in February 1982 by the Kansas City Board of Trade.

A more recent innovation is the opening of futures trading during evening hours. The Chicago Board of Trade opened evening trading on U.S. Treasury bond and note futures and options on futures contracts on April 30, 1987, to solve several problems. At that time Far Eastern interests held about one-fifth the total U.S. debt. They needed the depth and liquidity of a futures market that was open during their business hours. Also, there was great volatility in overnight Treasury bond prices. So evening trading was beneficial to domestic parties as well. The evening trading hours were so successful

---

**EXHIBIT 17–4**   *Financial Futures Contracts Traded in the United States*

| *Contract* | *Exchange Where Traded* |
|---|---|
| *Financial Securities* | |
| U.S. Treasury bonds | CBT, MidAm |
| U.S. Treasury notes ($6\frac{1}{2}$–10 yr) | CBT, MidAm |
| U.S. Treasury bills (90 day) | CME, MidAm |
| Eurodollar time deposit (3 month) | CME |
| Five year Treasury note | FINEX |
| *Currencies* | |
| Deutsche mark | CME, MidAm, PBT |
| Canadian dollar | CME, MidAm, PBT |
| Swiss franc | CME, MidAm, PBT |
| British pound | CME, MidAm, PBT |
| Japanese yen | CME, MidAm, PBT |
| Australian dollar | CME, PBT |
| *Indexes* | |
| Major Market Index–Maxi | CBT |
| Municipal Bond Index | CBT |
| Standard & Poor's 500 Stock Index | CME |
| Value Line Stock Index | KCBT |
| Mini Value Line Stock Index | KCBT |
| U.S. Dollar Index | FINEX |
| NYSE Composite Stock Index | NYFE |
| CRB Futures Price Index | NYFE |

---

that on September 13, 1987, trading was opened on Sunday evening also. This corresponds to Monday morning in Japan.

### The Commodity Futures Trading Commission

The futures market is regulated like the stock market with a governmental commission, the **Commodity Futures Trading Commission (CFTC).** The commission is empowered to approve exchange trading rules and contract terms, to review exchange actions denying membership, to establish fitness requirements for such persons as floor brokers, to establish minimum financial requirements for futures commission merchants, and to require exchanges to maintain daily trading records containing information about the day's trade.

# PARTICIPATING IN THE FUTURES MARKETS

The futures exchange is a place where traders can meet to buy or sell futures contracts. It is an auction market of open outcry, where traders cry out and simultaneously use

---

**EXHIBIT 17–5   *Options on Futures Contracts Traded in the United States***

| *Contract* | *Exchange Where Traded* |
|---|---|
| *Commodity* | |
| Agricultural | |
|   Wheat | CBT, KCBT, MidAm, MGE |
|   Soybeans | CBT, MidAm |
|   Soybean meal | CBT |
|   Soybean oil | CBT |
|   Corn | CBT |
|   Cattle, live | CME |
|   Cattle, feeder | CME |
|   Hogs, live | CME |
|   Pork bellies | CME |
|   Lumber | CME |
|   Cocoa | CSCE |
|   Sugar | CSCE |
|   Coffee | CSCE |
|   Cotton | NYCE |
| Energy | |
|   Crude oil | NYMEX |
|   Heating oil | NYMEX |
|   Gasoline | NYMEX |
| Metal | |
|   Silver | CBT, COMEX |
|   Copper | COMEX |
|   Gold | COMEX, MidAm |
| *Financial* | |
| Financial instruments | |
|   U.S. Treasury bonds | CBT |
|   Treasury notes | CBT |
|   Eurodollar time deposit (3 month) | CME |
| Currencies | |
|   Deutsche mark | CME |
|   Swiss franc | CME |
|   British pound | CME |
|   Japanese yen | CME |
|   Canadian dollar | CME |
| Indexes | |
|   Municipal Bond Index | CBT |
|   S&P 500 Stock Index | CME |
|   U.S. Dollar Index | NYCE |
|   NYSE Composite Stock Index | NYFE |

**EXHIBIT 17–6   U.S. Futures Exchanges**

| | Agricultural | Metal | Energy | Financial Instruments | Currencies | Indexes | Options on Futures, Commodities | Options on Futures, Financials |
|---|---|---|---|---|---|---|---|---|
| Chicago Board of Trade (CBT) Chicago, Illinois | X | X | | X | | X | X | X |
| Chicago Mercantile Exchange (CME) Chicago, Illinois | X | | | X | X | X | X | X |
| Chicago Rice & Cotton Exchange (CRCE) Chicago, Illinois | X | | | | | | | |
| Coffee, Sugar & Cocoa Exchange (CSCE) New York, New York | X | | | | | X | X | |
| Commodity Exchange, Inc. (COMEX) New York, New York | | X | | | | | X | |
| Kansas City Board of Trade (KCBT) Kansas City, Missouri | X | | | | | X | X | |
| MidAmerican Commodity Exchange (MidAm) Chicago, Illinois | X | X | | X | X | | X | |
| Minneapolis Grain Exchange (MGE) Minneapolis, Minnesota | X | | | | | | X | |
| New York Cotton Exchange (NYCE) New York, New York | X | | | X | | X | X | X |
| New York Futures Exchange (NYFE) New York, New York | | | | | | X | | X |
| New York Mercantile Exchange (NYMEX) New York, New York | | X | X | | | | X | |
| Philadelphia Board of Trade (PBT) Philadelphia, Pennsylvania | | | | | X | X | | |

Source: Compiled from data in ''1988 Reference Guide to Futures/Options Markets,'' *Futures*. Published by Oster Communications.

**EXHIBIT 17–7  Foreign Futures Exchanges**

| | Agricultural | Metal | Energy | Financial Instruments | Currencies | Indexes | Options on Futures, Commodities | Options on Futures, Financials |
|---|---|---|---|---|---|---|---|---|
| Toronto Futures Exchange, Toronto, Ontario, Canada | | | | X | X | X | | |
| Winnipeg Commodity Exchange, Winnipeg, Manitoba, Canada | X | X | | | | | | |
| Baltic Futures Exchange (BFE), London, England | X | | | | | X | | |
| International Petroleum Exchange of London Ltd., London, England | | | X | | | | X | |
| London Futures and Options Exchange (FOX), London, England | X | | | | | | X | |
| London International Financial Futures Exchange, Ltd., London, England | | | | X | X | X | | X |
| London Metal Exchange, London, England | | X | | | | | X | |
| London Grain Futures Market, London, England | | | | | | | X | |
| London Potato Futures Market, London, England | | | | | | | | X |
| Brazilian Futures Exchange, Rio de Janeiro, Brazil | | X | | X | X | X | | |
| Sao Paulo Commodities Exchange, Sao Paulo, Brazil | X | X | | X | X | | | |
| Bolsa Mercantile & de Futuros (BM&F), Sao Paulo, Brazil | X | X | | | X | X | X | |
| Financiele Termijnmarket Amsterdam N.V. (FTA), Amsterdam, The Netherlands | | | | | | X | | |
| Hong Kong Futures Exchange Ltd., Hong Kong | X | | X | | | X | | |
| International Futures Exchange Ltd. (INTEX), Hamilton, Bermuda | | | | | | X | | |
| Kuala Lumpur Commodity Exchange, Kuala Lumpur, Malaysia | X | | | | | | | |
| Marche a Terme des Instruments Financiers de Paris (MATIF), Paris, France | | X | | | | | | X |

(*continued*)

---

**EXHIBIT 17–7   Foreign Futures Exchanges (continued)**

| | Agricultural | Metal | Energy | Financial Instruments | Currencies | Indexes | Options on Futures, Commodities | Options on Futures, Financials |
|---|---|---|---|---|---|---|---|---|
| New Zealand Futures Exchange<br>Auckland, New Zealand | X | X | | | X | X | | |
| Osaka Securities Exchange<br>Osaka, Japan | | | | | | X | | |
| Paris Futures Exchange<br>Paris, France | X | | | | | | | |
| Singapore International Monetary Exchange (SIMEX)<br>Singapore | | X | X | | X | X | | X |
| Stockholm Options Market (OM)<br>Stockholm, Sweden | | | | | | X | | |
| Swedish Options and Futures Exchange (SOFE)<br>Stockholm, Sweden | | | | | | X | | |
| Sydney Futures Exchange Ltd.<br>Sydney, Australia | X | X | X | | X | X | | X |
| Tokyo Stock Exchange<br>Tokyo, Japan | | X | | | | | | |

Source: Compiled from data in ''1988 Reference Guide to Futures/Options Markets,'' *Futures*. Published by Oster Communications.

---

hand signals. Hands signal the price bid, the quantity, and whether the contract is a buy or sell. Palms away from the trader signal ''sell''; palms toward the trader signal ''buy.''

## Participants

Only members of the exchange can trade on the floor. If a person or institution who is not a member wishes to trade, the trade must be placed with a brokerage house or commission house that is a member.

The two types of traders on the floor of the exchange are commission brokers (floor brokers) and locals. Commission brokers may fill orders for commission houses who are not members, or they may be employees of commission houses who are members. **Locals** are members who buy and sell for their own account.

---

### Electronic Futures Trading

In February 1989, the Commodity Futures Trading Commission approved the Chicago Mercantile Exchange's plan for electronic futures trading. The system, called Globex, was envisioned as a worldwide commodities trading arrangement. The Sydney Futures Exchange was the first foreign exchange to join Globex. Japanese exchanges were considering joining.

Globex was scheduled to begin trading in October 1989. Its original contracts would be currency futures. Other contracts would be added later.

After announcement of approval of the Mercantile Exchange's Globex system, the Chicago Board of Trade began working on a competing electronic trading system. Previously, the Board of Trade had favored meeting the demand of international traders by evening trading on its trading floor. (Six P.M. in Chicago is nine A.M. in Tokyo.) In fact, it had formally opposed approval of the Globex system.

---

Local are speculators because they trade in the hopes of making a profit. The futures market would not exist without them because they are willing to assume price risk in pursuit of the profit opportunity. Hedgers, on the other hand, use the futures markets in order to reduce their risk. Customers who buy and sell futures contracts can be either hedgers or speculators.

## Executing a Trade

Let us follow the path of an order. A customer places an order with a broker who is a member of the exchange. The broker communicates the order to the floor of the exchange by teletype or phone. Around the edge of the floor of the exchange are many booths with teletypes and phones. The broker's clerk receives the order and hands it to a runner. The runner takes the order to the broker's trader who is standing in the pit.

On the floor of the exchange are a number of pits. The pits have steps that descend to a center. Each product is traded in a different pit. The trader cries out the order while using hand signals. After completing the trade, the trader notes the price and identity of the trader taking the opposite side of the trade on the order form. An exchange employee at the pit, called a recorder, also notes the transaction, which is then flashed onto an electronic board high on the wall around the room. The runner returns the form to the clerk who communicates the trade to the broker who then calls the originator of the order.

## Margin

Before placing an order in the futures market, it is necessary for a customer to make a margin deposit with a broker. Margin does not represent a down payment in the futures market as it does in the stock market. Rather, it represents earnest money or a commitment to perform on the contract. Therefore, both the buyer and seller of futures contracts must make a margin deposit. The buyer has a commitment to make a payment in the future while the seller has a commitment to make a delivery in the future.

Initial margin requirements and maintenance margin requirements are set by the exchange for each contract it trades. More stringent margins may be required by individual brokers. If market prices move against a customer's position, the account is reduced by the price change. When the account falls below the required minimal level, the customer will receive a margin call from his or her broker.

## The Role of the Clearing House

Every futures contract to buy or sell is made with the clearing house. Because the clearing house stands between the buyer and seller, it is able to accomplish three important objectives.

First, the clearing house guarantees every contract. Second, because of the guarantee, the buyer does not need to perform a credit check on the seller, or vice versa. Third, it makes it possible for a person who enters into a futures contract to liquidate his or her position by entering into the opposite futures contract.

### Fraud in the Futures Pits

In January 1989, the *Chicago Tribune* learned from Washington sources that a large-scale FBI probe of the Chicago Board of Trade and the Chicago Mercantile Exchange had been underway for over two years. The FBI was using undercover agents posing as floor traders. The agents had observed daily activities in the pits and had tape recorded hundreds of conversations.

After the *Tribune* broke the story, several traders sold their exchange memberships. A federal grand jury issued over 200 subpoenas to futures traders, brokers, and firms. It was alleged that dozens of dishonest brokers had cheated futures customers out of millions of dollars by executing orders at arranged prices. Brokers working with other traders would execute buy orders at too high a price and sell orders at too low a price. Later, the conspirators would split the illegal gains. They avoided being caught by keeping the false prices within the range of market prices. The exchanges' open outcry system left an incomplete record of prices at a particular time. On a per contract basis the amount of fraud was small, but the large volume of trading made the total gains huge. Phony trades also were arranged in order to help people cheat on taxes.

The public and investor reactions to the scandal were strong. Fraud on this scale showed that self-regulation by the exchanges had failed to protect the public. The personal integrity necessary for the honest operation of an open outcry market was lacking.

Some long-time exchange procedures would have to change. Strongly criticized was the practice of "dual trading," which allowed a member to trade both for his customers and himself. Critics argued that brokers sometimes put their own interests ahead of their customers' interests. Also, there were calls for more electronic monitoring of trading to provide a more complete record of trading.

In addition to the exchanges, the Commodities Futures Trading Commission was strongly criticized for the fact that extensive fraud was taking place in the markets it regulated. From a broader perspective, the growth and development of futures markets were damaged because of a decrease in investor confidence. This blow to the U.S. futures markets took place just as competition from European and Asian markets was increasing. At the same time, the movement in Congress for greater regulation of financial markets and institutions gained momentum.

At the end of every trading day the clearing house matches up the trades. For instance, if Trader A reports he sold three contracts of September corn at a particular price to Trader B, this is matched with Trader B's report of buying three contracts of September corn at that particular price from Trader A. If any of the pieces of information—the trader, the number of contracts, the price, the delivery month, identity of the trader taking the opposite side of the trade, or whether it is a buy or sell—do not match up, it is called an out-trade. Because traders are human, there are usually quite a few out-trades. Most of the mistakes are easily resolved, because the trader just put down the wrong number or letter. However, sometimes a costly mistake is made (that is, the selling trader thought he sold many more contracts than the buying trader thought he bought). If it is clear which trader made the mistake, he pays the cost to make good on the contract. If it is not clear who made the mistake, the two traders must split the cost of the mistake. Most likely the customer who sent in the order never knows there has been an out-trade. His transactions are guaranteed. As a matter of fact, the Board of Trade Clearing Corporation, established in 1925, is justly proud of the fact that no customer has ever suffered a financial loss due to a default on a Chicago Board of Trade futures contract.

At the end of every trading day, the clearing house marks to market: the account of every clearing member (both individuals and brokerage houses) is credited or debited to reflect the settlement price (the price at the end of the day). Every brokerage house also marks to market the account of each of its customers. If credited, this amount can be used to buy additional contracts based on the "paper" profit.

# COMMODITY FUTURES

Agricultural futures were the earliest futures contracts traded. Both producers and users of agricultural commodities can use futures contracts to hedge against adverse price movements. Farmers who are planting their crops in May may sell December futures contracts. In this way, they can lock in the price that they will get for their crops. If in the meantime prices go down, they still will get the previously agreed upon price. If, on the other hand, prices go up, they will not make as much profit as they might have. However, the hedge in the futures market will have removed the risk of a price decrease.

Users of agricultural commodities, like millers and cereal manufacturers, can buy commodity futures contracts in order to reduce their risk of a price increase. Cereal manufacturers may buy May futures contracts in November. Then they have locked in the cost of raw materials. Knowing these costs ahead of time helps to plan ahead. If the price rises in the meantime, they will have saved money by entering into the futures market. If prices decrease, they will not have saved money, but will have had the certain knowledge of costs to enable them to plan ahead.

Today most hedgers do not actually deliver or accept delivery on a futures contract. Rather, they liquidate their position and buy or sell the actual commodity in the cash market. Also, a farmer usually will hedge only part of his entire crop. Likewise, a user of commodities will not hedge the entire amount he or she intends to buy, but rather a portion of it.

# FINANCIAL FUTURES

The reason for the creation of financial futures is the same as the reason behind the creation of commodity futures. It allows participants in financial markets to hedge against price risk in the underlying instrument. Buyers and sellers of short-term financial instruments can hedge by buying or selling U.S. Treasury bill futures. Buyers and sellers of long-term financial instruments like corporate bonds can hedge by buying or selling U.S. Treasury bond futures. Participants in the stock market can use stock index futures to hedge. Importers and exporters can hedge against changes in currency values with foreign currency futures.

The main impetus to trading financial futures came in the middle to late 1970s with the gargantuan fluctuations in interest rate levels. Exhibit 17–8 illustrates the wide swings in interest rates by showing the history of prime rates. Note that the level of the prime rate changed three times in 1966, going from 5.5 percent to 6.0 percent. In 1980, however, the prime rate changed 42 times and the level went from 11 percent to 21.5 percent. With such wide swings in interest rate levels, many people soon found that they could reduce their interest rate risk by hedging in financial futures.

The Chicago Board of Trade (CBT) introduced in 1975 the first financial futures contract. It was based on Government National Mortgage Association (GNMA) certificates. In 1977 they introduced futures contracts based on U.S. Treasury bonds and 90-day commercial paper but abandoned the commercial paper soon after. In 1979, the 4–6 year Treasury notes were introduced. Meanwhile, the Chicago Mercantile Exchange (CME) introduced financial future contracts on 90-day Treasury bills in 1976, 1-year Treasury bills in 1978, and 4-year Treasury notes in 1979. In 1980 the New York Stock Exchange organized the New York Futures Exchange (NYFE). It now trades a stock index, a futures price index and a beta index. In 1982 trading began in stock index futures. A municipal bond index was also introduced by the Chicago Board of Trade. In 1982 options on futures contracts started trading. Every year new futures contracts are introduced to meet the needs of participants in the financial community.

## U.S. Treasury Bonds

In order to explore the facets of the financial futures market, we are going to use the U.S. Treasury bond future contract as our example. One of the reasons for picking this contract is that it has been the most popular financial future traded. Exhibit 17–9 shows the growth of the U.S. Treasury bond futures trading volume.

The standardized contract for U.S. Treasury bonds is for $100,000 face value, 8 percent coupon rate, and 20-year maturity with delivery in March, June, September, and December. Note that the futures contract has a standard quantity of $100,000, and standard grade of 8 percent coupon rate, 20-year U.S. Treasury bond. Only the price is allowed to vary.

---

**EXHIBIT 17–8   *History of Prime Rates, 1965–1987***

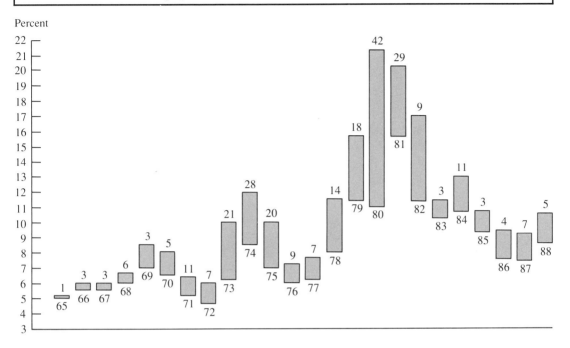

Note: Length of bar shows yearly range. The value above the bars is the number of times the rate changed during the course of the year.

Source: Compiled from data in *Federal Reserve Bulletin* (Washington, D.C.: Board of Governors of the Federal Reserve System), various issues.

---

One would naturally question where it would be possible to find an 8 percent coupon rate, 20-year Treasury bond to deliver in a futures contract. It is unlikely that any exist. However, very few financial futures contracts result in delivery. Most participants in the market liquidate their position by making an offsetting trade. Only about one-half of one percent of the financial futures contracts result in delivery. When a delivery actually occurs, any U.S. Treasury bond with at least 15 years to call or maturity can be delivered. The actual price paid on delivery is adjusted based on the delivered bond's coupon rate and maturity.

***Delivery Invoice Price***   The actual price paid on delivery, the invoice price, is equal to the price originally bid for the standard U.S. Treasury bond futures contract adjusted by a conversion factor.

---

**EXHIBIT 17–9   U.S. Treasury Bond Futures Contract Trading Volume**

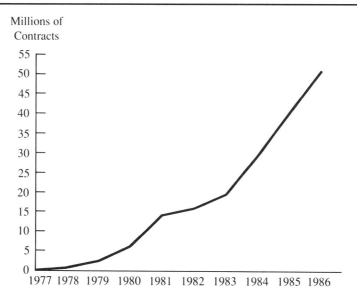

Source: *The Financial Futures Professional,* Vol. ii, No. 8 (August 1987), p. 2. Published by the Chicago Board of Trade.

---

invoice price = price × conversion factor

The conversion factor is the price per dollar of bond face value at which the delivered issue will yield 8 percent at its current time to maturity.

---

**PRACTICE PROBLEM 1**   If the price to be paid for a standard U.S. Treasury bond futures contract is $83,500, what will be the actual invoice price if bonds with a 7% coupon rate and an 18-year maturity are delivered?

*Solution*

To compute the conversion factor find the present value of a $1 bond with a 7% coupon rate, an 18-year maturity, and an 8% yield to maturity.

$$\text{semiannual interest payment} = \$.07/2 = \$.035$$

$$\text{semiannual yield to maturity} = 8\%/2 = 4\%$$

$$\text{number of periods} = 2 \times 18 = 36$$

$$\frac{\text{conversion}}{\text{factor}} = .035 \sum_{t=1}^{36} \frac{1}{(1 + 4\%)^t} + \frac{1}{(1 + 4\%)^{36}}$$

$$= .661789 + .243668 = .9055$$

$$\text{invoice price} = \text{price} \times \text{conversion factor}$$

$$= \$83,500 \times .9055 = \$75,609.25$$

Note in Practice Problem 1 that a person had agreed to buy $100,000 of face value of 8 percent, 20-year U.S. Treasury bonds for $83,500. Since 7 percent, 18-year bonds were delivered, he actually paid only $75,609.25. If the delivered bonds had a coupon rate higher than 8 percent, the invoice price would have been more than the original bid price. See Practice Problem 2.

---

**PRACTICE PROBLEM 2**

If the bid price to be paid for a standard U.S. Treasury bond futures contract is $83,500, what will be the actual invoice price if bonds with a 10% coupon rate and an 18-year maturity are delivered?

*Solution*

$$\text{semiannual interest payment} = \$.10/2 = \$.05$$

$$\text{semiannual yield to maturity} = 8\%/2 = 4\%$$

$$\text{number of periods} = 2 \times 18 = 36$$

$$\frac{\text{conversion}}{\text{factor}} = .05 \sum_{t=1}^{36} \frac{1}{(1 + 4\%)^t} + \frac{1}{(1 + 4\%)^{36}}$$

$$= .945414 + .243669$$

$$= 1.1891$$

$$\text{invoice price} = \text{price} \times \text{conversion factor}$$

$$= \$83,500 \times 1.1891$$

$$= \$99,289.85$$

---

**Bid Price**   Bond prices in the futures market and in the cash market are quoted in points, where one point is one percent of the bond face value. Fractions of one percent are quoted in thirty-seconds of one percent. A bond futures contract price of "83–16" means 83 16/32% of $100,000 or $83,500. A price of "105–12" means 105 12/32% of $100,000 or $105,375.

The bid price of the futures contract is the present value of the $100,000 face value, 8 percent coupon rate, 20-year maturity bond discounted at the yield to maturity that the buyer and seller of the futures contract feel is appropriate.

---

**PRACTICE PROBLEM 3**

What should you bid for a U.S. Treasury bond futures contract if you feel that an 11½% yield is appropriate?

*Solution*

Find the present value of a $100,000 face value, 8% coupon rate, 20-year maturity bond with a yield to maturity of 11½%.

$$PMT = \frac{8\% \times \$100,000}{2} = \$4,000$$

$$N = 2 \times 20 = 40$$

$$\%i = \frac{11\frac{1}{2}\%}{2} = 5.75\%$$

$$FV = \$100,000$$

$$PV = \$4,000 \sum_{t=1}^{40} \frac{1}{(1 + 5.75\%)^t} + \frac{\$100,000}{(1 + 5.75\%)^{40}}$$

$$PV = \$62,132.00 + \$10,685.26 = \$72,817.26$$

But prices are quoted as a percent of the $100,000 face value and fractions of a percent are quoted in thirty-seconds.

$$\$72,817.26 = 72.81726\% \text{ of } \$100,000$$

$$.81726 = \frac{x}{32}$$

$$x = (.81726)(32) = 26.15232$$

Rounding off to the closest thirty-second, bid price = 72 26/32% of $100,000 or 72–26.

---

Since the yield to maturity in Practice Problem 3 is greater than 8 percent (the coupon rate), the bid price is lower than $100,000 (the face value). If the yield to maturity is less than 8 percent, the bid price is higher than $100,000. This is illustrated in Practice Problem 4.

---

**PRACTICE PROBLEM 4**

What should you bid for a U.S. Treasury bond futures contract if you feel that 7% is an appropriate yield to maturity?

*Solution*

Find the present value of a $100,000 face value, 8% coupon rate, 20-year maturity bond with a yield to maturity of 7%.

$$PMT = \$4,000$$

$$N = 40$$

$$\%i = \frac{7\%}{2} = 3.5\%$$

$$FV = \$100,000$$

$$PV = ?$$

$$PV = \$110,677.5362$$

bid price $= 110.6775362\%$ of $\$100,000$

$$.677536 = \frac{x}{32}$$

$$x = (.677536)(32) = 21.68$$

Rounding off, bid price $= 110$–$22$.

**PRACTICE PROBLEM 5**  If 83–26 is the bid price of a U.S. Treasury bond futures contract, what do the seller and buyer feel is the appropriate yield to maturity?

*Solution*

$$83\text{–}26 \text{ means } 83 \ 26/32\% \times \$100,000 = \$83,812.50$$

Find the yield to maturity of a $\$100,000$ face value, 8% coupon rate, 20-year maturity bond with a price of $\$83,812.50$.

$$PV = \$83,812.50$$

$$PMT = \$4,000$$

$$N = 40$$

$$FV = \$100,000$$

$$\%i = ?$$

$$\%i = 4.935\% \text{ (semiannual rate)}$$

yield to maturity (annual) $= 2 \times 4.935\% = 9.87\%$

## Index Futures

Before the advent of stock index futures, if traders believed the stock market would move up, they would buy a sample of stocks in order to take advantage of their opinion. If they were right about the movement of the stock market as a whole, they could still be wrong about the movement of the particular stocks in their sample. Now, with stock index futures, it is possible to translate stock market opinion into action by buying broad-based stock index futures contracts.

Since the first stock index futures contract was introduced in 1982, the stock market has been very volatile. This volatility has fueled the rapid expansion of the stock index futures market not only in terms of trading volume, but in the number of different types of contracts. Now, many indexes form the basis for both futures contracts and options contracts.

Some stock index futures contracts are based on broad indexes like Standard & Poor's 500 and Value Line 100, NYSE Composite Stock and the AMEX Major Market

Indexes. In order to give players in other markets the opportunity to hedge or speculate there are even index futures based on a municipal bond index, a U.S. Dollar Index, a U.S. Treasury Index, and a futures price index.

The purpose of all types of futures contracts including index futures is to provide an opportunity for speculating and hedging. A speculator in stock index futures hopes to profit on gains (or losses) in the overall stock market without buying (or selling short) a large portfolio. A hedger in stock index futures hopes to reduce risk.

There are two kinds of risk in a stock portfolio: systematic and unsystematic. Unsystematic risk can be reduced by diversification. Systematic risk can be reduced by using stock index futures to hedge. By holding the proper number of stock index futures contracts, a portfolio manager can reduce systematic risk because the loss in the stock portfolio will be approximately offset by gains in the index futures market.

The Kansas City Board of Trade was the first exchange to offer an index futures contract. In February 1982, they introduced the Value Line Stock Index futures contract. The size of the contract is $500 times the Value Line Stock Index. Later the Kansas City Board of Trade introduced the Mini Value Line Stock Index, which is only $100 times the index.

The Chicago Board of Trade has a stock index futures contract based on the American Stock Exchange's Major Market Index (MMI) of 20 stocks. The contract size of the Major Market Index–Maxi is $250 times the value of the index. The Major Market Index has great appeal because it has had, at least in the recent past, a correlation of 97 percent with the Dow Jones Industrial Average. This is not surprising, however, since 15 of the stocks in the Major Market Index are the same as 15 of the 30 stocks in the Dow Jones Industrial Average.

Index futures differ from other futures contracts in that they are not based on any underlying commodity or financial instrument that can be delivered; therefore, there is no cash market associated with them. In fact, a trader of stock index futures is placing a bet on the direction of the stock market. A trader of Consumer Price Index futures is betting on how the Consumer Price Index will move. As in other types of futures markets, most traders liquidate their position by an offsetting trade. However, there is a delivery mechanism. A buyer who has not offset his or her position will receive a settlement in cash from the seller based on the current value of the index on the delivery date.

# HEDGING

Hedging is a means of reducing price risk. Just as the grain farmer and the grain user can use grain futures contracts to hedge grain prices, so can participants in the financial market use financial futures to hedge.

There are two kinds of hedges: a long hedge (buying hedge) and a short hedge (selling hedge). A long or buying hedge is for those who are planning to buy a product. It is a hedge against a possible price increase. A short or selling hedge is for those who are planning to sell or borrow. It is a hedge against a price decrease. In order to explain hedging in detail we will continue to use the U.S. Treasury bond futures contract as our example.

# Long Hedge

The long hedge or buying hedge is not used as often as the short hedge, but is easier to understand, so we will present it first in Practice Problem 6.

---

***PRACTICE PROBLEM 6***    Max Hershey, a financial manager of a corporation, expects to receive $1 million in September as payment for completion of a construction project. The financial manager plans to buy $1 million of U.S. Treasury bonds. It is now March and while he can buy $7\frac{1}{4}\%$, 27-year U.S. Treasury bonds (yielding 11.96%) for 62–10, he feels that the price will rise before September (i.e., interest rates will decline). If prices were to rise to 72–10, this would be an opportunity loss of $100,000 (72–10 minus 62–10 equals 10; 10% of $1 million equals $100,000) because he does not have the cash to buy now.

Construct a long hedge for Mr. Hershey showing the results if he can buy September U.S. Treasury bond futures contracts in March for 60–30 and sell them in September for 73–08. Mr. Hershey was correct in his forecast because the cash price for $7\frac{1}{4}\%$ U.S. Treasury bonds (now yielding 9.81%) is 75–28 in September.

*Solution*

Mr. Hershey intends to buy $1,000,000 of U.S. Treasury bonds in September. Therefore, he buys ten September U.S. Treasury bond futures contracts (10 × $100,000 = $1,000.000). In September he sells his ten futures contracts and buys $1,000,000 of U.S. Treasury bonds in the cash market. These transactions are illustrated below.

| *Cash Market* | *Price* | *Futures Market* | *Price* |
|---|---|---|---|
| *March* | | | |
| Current U.S. Treasury bonds | 62–10 | Buy 10 September bond futures | 60–30 |
| *September* | | | |
| Buy $1 million U.S. Treasury bonds | 75–28 | Sell 10 September bond futures | 73–08 |
| Opportunity loss | 13–18 | Actual gain | 12–10 |

overall gain or loss per contract = gain minus loss

$$= \text{12–10 minus 13–18}$$

$$= \text{1–8 overall loss}$$

Overall loss on $1 million of 1–08 means overall loss of 1 8/32% × $1 million or $12,500.

Note that while his opportunity loss was $135,625 (13 18/32% × $1,000,000), he almost made up for it by making an actual gain of $123,125 (12 10/32% × $1,000,000) through his transaction in the futures market.

## Short Hedge

The short hedge or selling hedge is used by those who are planning to sell or borrow a product. For instance, a corporation may be planning to borrow by selling corporate bonds.

**PRACTICE PROBLEM 7**  An institutional investor owns $1 million of U.S. Treasury bonds which she plans to sell in December. It is now June and she fears that interest rates will rise, causing the price of her bonds to decline. Construct a short hedge for the investor given the information below.

The June cash price for $9\frac{1}{8}$%, 20-year U.S. Treasury bonds yielding 10% is 92–16, while December futures are 90–19. The December cash price for the bonds now yielding 11.61% is 80–27, while December futures are 76–23.

| Cash Market | Price | Futures Market | Price |
|---|---|---|---|
| *June* | | | |
| Current U.S. Treasury bonds | 92–16 | Sell 10 U.S. Treasury bond contracts | 90–19 |
| *December* | | | |
| Sell $1 million U.S. Treasury bonds | 80–27 | Buy 10 U.S. Treasury bond contracts | 76–23 |
| Opportunity loss | 11–21 | Actual gain | 13–26 |

overall gain or loss per contract = 13–16 minus 11–21 = 2–05 gain

overall gain on $1 million = 2 5/32% × 1,000,000

= $21,562.50

Most hedges are not perfect hedges, where the opportunity loss is exactly offset by the actual gain made in the futures market. In Practice Problem 6 on a long hedge the opportunity loss was more than the actual gain. In Practice Problem 7 the opportunity loss was less than the actual gain. Notice that the hedges in the foregoing problems do not really hedge the entire million dollars because the bonds were selling at a discount from their face value. A more sophisticated solution to these examples would adjust the number of futures contracts bought and sold to account for this.

## Basis

The **basis** is defined as the cash price minus the futures price of a particular product at a certain point in time. The basis tends not to vary as much as either the cash prices

**EXHIBIT 17–10  Hedging Activities**

| | Long Hedge | Short Hedge |
|---|:---:|:---:|
| *Use* | | |
| Planning to | | |
|   Buy | X | |
|   Sell or borrow | | X |
| Hedging against | | |
|   Price increase | X | |
|   Price decrease | | X |
|   Interest rate rise | | X |
|   Interest rate decline | X | |
| Transacting in futures market | | |
|   Buy then sell | X | |
|   Sell then buy | | X |
| *Result* | | |
| Overall gain | | |
|   Basis moves down | X | |
|   Basis moves up | | X |

or futures prices because the cash prices and futures prices tend to move together. In Practice Problem 6 the basis in March was 1–12 (62–10 minus 60–30) while the basis in September was 2–08 (75–28 minus 73–08). If the basis had remained constant, the hedge of Practice Problem 6 would have been a perfect hedge. However, the basis moved in the wrong direction and so the opportunity loss was greater than the actual gain. The basis in Practice Problem 7 moved also, but in the direction to make the actual gain larger than the opportunity loss. Exhibit 17–10 summarizes hedging.

# OPTIONS ON FUTURES

Options on stocks have been around for a long time. Options on futures contracts were first introduced by the Chicago Board of Trade. In 1982 they opened trading on options on U.S. Treasury bond futures. Since then options have traded on futures contracts based on other financial instruments, on currencies, and on indexes. Also, exchanges have offered options contracts on commodity futures—agricultural, metal, and energy. At least 10 domestic exchanges and 12 foreign exchanges now trade options on futures contracts. A list of options on futures contracts traded in the United States is shown in Exhibit 17–5.

## Definition of Options on Futures

Options on actuals are defined as contracts that allow the holder to buy or sell the actual underlying security, index, currency, or metal at an established exercise price anytime before the expiration date. Options on futures are defined as contracts that allow (but do not obligate) the holder to buy or sell an underlying futures contract at an established exercise price anytime before the expiration date. If the option is not exercised by the expiration date, it ceases to exist. Call options on futures contracts allow the holder to take a long position in the futures market (enter into a futures contract to buy a product) at an established exercise price anytime before the expiration date. Put options on futures contracts allow the holder to take a short position in the futures market (enter into a futures contract to sell a product) at an established price anytime before the expiration date.

## Margin Requirements

A holder of a call option or put option on a futures contract pays a premium for the option but may let the option expire. Therefore, the risk of the holder is limited to the premium paid. Because there is no contractual obligation for the holder to pay anymore than the premium, there is no requirement for the holder of an option on futures to pay margin.

On the other hand, the writer of a put option or a call option faces a great risk and is, therefore, required to maintain a certain margin requirement. At the end of every trading day options on futures are marked to market and writers of options on futures could receive a margin call.

## Risk

Options on futures allow participants in the commodities and financial markets to reduce their risk. They also allow speculators to assume risks in hopes of making a profit.

Market participants can use many strategies in the options on futures markets in order to reduce their risk. Many strategies involve taking positions in the futures market or actual market as well as a position in the options on futures market.

## Clearing House

The clearing house functions in the options on futures market just as it does in the futures market. It is the buyer to every seller (writer of options) and the seller to every buyer (holder of options). It ensures performance on all options sold.

## Offsetting Transactions

Because of the function of the clearing house, buyers or sellers can offset their transactions and liquidate their option positions. As a matter of fact, most traders do offset their positions before the options expire.

A buyer (holder) of a call option can offset his or her position by selling (writing) calls with the same exercise price and the same expiration date. Likewise, a buyer (holder) of a put option can offset his or her position by selling (writing) calls with the same exercise price and the same expiration date. The profit or loss on this transaction is the difference between the premium received when selling (writing) and the premium paid when buying.

In like manner, the seller (writer) of a put or call option can offset his or her position by buying puts or calls with the same exercise price and expiration date. Again, the profit or loss is the difference between the premium received and the premium paid.

# Options on U.S. Treasury Bond Futures

Since the U.S. Treasury bond futures contract was used as an in-depth example of futures contracts, we will use the option on a U.S. Treasury bond futures contract as our example of options on futures.

**Definition**   The trading unit of one option on U.S. Treasury bond futures is one $100,000 face value CBT U.S. Treasury bond futures contract of a specified contract month. The delivery months are the same as for the Treasury bonds futures: March, June, September, and December.

The Treasury bond futures contract is for $100,000 of U.S. Treasury bonds. Prices are quoted in terms of points and thirty-seconds where one point is one percent of $100,000 or $1,000 and each thirty-seconds of a point is worth $31.25. Options on Treasury bond futures are quoted in points and sixty-fourths of a point. Each sixty-fourth is equal to $15.625. Therefore, a premium quoted as 2–01 would be two points and 1/64 of a point or $2015.625. A premium of 2–02 would be $2031.25.

The exercise prices for options on Treasury bonds are in integral multiples of two points ($2,000) per Treasury bond futures contract (that is, 86, 88, 90).

**Options on Futures vs. Options on Actuals**   U.S. Treasury bonds are traded in the cash market. Options on actual U.S. Treasury bonds are traded at the Chicago Board Options Exchange. U.S. Treasury bond futures are traded at the Chicago Board of Trade. Options on U.S. Treasury bond futures are traded also at the Chicago Board of Trade.

What is the interrelationship between all these markets? The Treasury bond futures market could not function without the existence of the underlying Treasury bond security and its cash market. Also, the market for options on actual Treasury bonds could not function without the underlying Treasury bond and its market. The market for options on Treasury bond futures could not function without the existence of the underlying Treasury bond futures contract and its market.

Options on Treasury bond futures have some advantages over options on actual Treasury bonds. Two advantages occur because of the differences in the underlying markets: first, the Treasury bond futures market is extremely liquid; second, trading occurs on one centralized exchange. On the other hand, the market for actual Treasury bonds is not always very liquid and trading is accomplished by dealers over the phone. Another advantage also is the fact that exercising an option on Treasury bond futures requires a margin that is only a fraction of the price of a bond, while exercising an option on actual Treasury bonds requires payment of the full market price of the bond in cash. Also, Treasury bond futures and options on Treasury bond futures are traded on the same floor and are processed by the same clearing house.

# SUMMARY

A cash contract is a contract between a buyer and a seller of a product for immediate delivery and immediate payment. The product, quality, quantity, and price are negotiated. A futures contract is a contract to buy or sell a product and to make payment or delivery at some specified future date. It can only be entered into on an organized futures exchange and all elements of the contract except price are standardized by the exchange.

Participants in the futures market can be classified as hedgers or speculators. Hedgers use the futures market to reduce their risk by using either a long hedge or short hedge. Speculators use the futures market to assume risk in pursuit of the profit motive. Both buyers and sellers are required to make a margin deposit to ensure performance on the contract in the future.

The clearing house guarantees every contract. It is the buyer to every seller and the seller to every buyer. Because of the function of the clearing house it is possible to liquidate one's position by an offsetting trade. Most participants do liquidate their positions. Thus, there are few actual deliveries. The futures trading industry is regulated by the Commodity Futures Trading Commission.

Commodities are homogeneous raw materials and farm products. Commodities currently traded on futures exchanges include agricultural products, metals, and energy products.

Financial futures traded on exchanges include futures contracts where the underlying product is a debt instrument, a currency, or an index. Index futures are an interesting breed of futures contracts. It is impossible to deliver an underlying product. Therefore, a cash delivery is provided.

Options on futures are contracts that allow the holder to buy or sell an underlying futures contract at an established price anytime before the expiration date. Only the writers of options on futures are required to maintain a margin account. Options on futures allow participants in commodity and financial markets to reduce their risk. Writers of options on futures can liquidate their position by buying an offsetting option. Likewise, buyers can also liquidate their position by writing an offsetting option. Options on futures have some advantages to options on actuals because of the efficiency of the futures markets.

## QUESTIONS

1. Differentiate cash contracts, forward contracts, and future contracts.

2. What are commodities? List some of the commodity futures contracts traded in the United States.

3. What are financial futures? List some of the financial futures contracts traded in the United States.

4. What is the Commodity Futures Trading Commission? What are its duties?

5. What are the two types of traders on the floor of the exchange?

6. How is a trade executed on a commodities exchange?

7. What is margin in commodities trading?

8. Explain the role of the clearing house.

9. How are commodities futures used to reduce risk?

10. How are financial futures used to reduce risk?

11. Explain some of the features of the U.S. Treasury bond futures contract.

12. Explain long and short hedges.

13. What is the basis?

14. How do options on futures work?

15. Which participants in the options on futures market pay margin and which do not? Why?

16. Explain how to offset your position in the options on futures market.

17. Explain the difference between options on actual Treasury bonds and options on Treasury bond futures. What are the advantages of options on Treasury bond futures?

## *PROBLEMS*

1. If the price paid for a standard U.S. Treasury bond futures contract is $87,000, what will the actual invoice price be if bonds with a 6.5% coupon rate and a 17-year maturity are delivered?

2. If the bid price to be paid for a standard U.S. Teasury bond futures contract is $92,000, what will the actual invoice price be if bonds with a 7% coupon rate and a 20-year maturity are delivered?

3. If the bid price for a Treasury bond futures contract is $75,000, what will be the actual invoice price if bonds with a 9% coupon rate and a 19-year maturity are delivered?

4. If the price to be paid for a Treasury bond futures contract is $108,000, what will be the actual invoice price if bonds with an 8.5% coupon rate and an 18-year maturity are delivered?

5. What should you bid for a U.S. Treasury bond futures contract if you feel that a 9% yield is appropriate?

6. What should you bid for a Treasury bond futures contract if a 10% yield is the appropriate yield to maturity?

7. If you feel that 6.5% is the appropriate yield, what would you bid for a Treasury bond futures contract?

8. What should you bid for a Treasury bond futures contract if a 7.2% yield to maturity is the appropriate yield?

9. If 76–20 is the bid price of a U.S. Treasury bond futures contract, what do the buyer and seller feel is the appropriate yield to maturity?

10. Find the yield to maturity if a U.S. Treasury bond futures contract has a price of 92–30.

11. Find the yield to maturity if a U.S. Treasury bond futures contract has a price of 104–10.

12. If 110–08 is the bid price of a Treasury bond futures contract, what do the buyer and seller feel is the appropriate yield to maturity?

13. A financial manager expects to receive $1 million in December as payment for completion of a contract. He plans to buy $1 million of U.S. Treasury bonds with this money. It is now April and while he can buy 7%, 18-year U.S. Treasury bonds in the cash market for 70–22, he feels that the price will rise before December (i.e., that interest rates will decline). Construct a hedge for this manager showing the results if he can buy December U.S. Treasury bond futures in April for 71–06 and sell them in December for 85–10. The manager was correct in his forecast because the cash price for a 7% U.S. Treasury bond is 87–14 in December.

14. The financial manager for Housewares, Inc., Mr. Baker, expects to receive a payment of $1 million in March for goods recently shipped. He plans to invest that money in U.S. Treasury bonds. It is now October. Currently, he can buy 9%, 17-year U.S. Treasury bonds in the cash market for 92–10, but he feels that the price will rise before next March (i.e., that interest rates will decline).

    Construct a hedge for Mr. Baker showing the results if he can buy March Treasury bond futures in October for 84–16 and sell them in March for 97–22. The manager was correct in his forecast because the cash price for the 9% Treasury bonds is 103–04 in March.

15. A pension fund owns $1 million of U.S. Treasury bonds. The pension fund manager plans to sell the bonds in June. It is now January. The pension fund manager predicts a decline in bond prices (because of an interest rate rise) by June. He wishes to take advantage of the current high price of bonds. Construct a hedge for him given the information below. In January the cash price for 8.5%, 16-year U.S. Treasury Bonds is 112–18 while June futures are 115–10. In June the cash price for 8.5% bonds is 98–12 while June futures are 101–30.

16. A mutual fund manager has $1 million of U.S. Treasury bonds which he plans to sell in September. It is now February and he fears that interest rates will rise, causing the price of his bonds to decline. Construct a hedge for the manager given the information below. The February cash price for 9%, 18-year U.S. Treasury bonds is 83–14 while September futures are 85–12. The September cash price is 76–19 while December futures are 74–16.

## *READINGS*

*Commodity Trading Manual*. Chicago: Board of Trade of the City of Chicago, 1985.
> *This book provides a history of futures trading, information on all futures exchanges and futures contracts traded in 1985, and a description of how the futures markets work.*

*The Delivery Process in Brief: Treasury Bond and Treasury Note Futures*. Chicago: Board of Trade of the City of Chicago, 1987.
> *This booklet can be obtained free of charge by writing to the Chicago Board of Trade. It provides a detailed description of the delivery process for Treasury bonds and Treasury note futures.*

*A Guide to Financial Futures at the Chicago Board of Trade*. Chicago: Board of Trade of the City of Chicago, 1987.

*This booklet can be obtained free of charge by writing the Chicago Board of Trade. It provides a very good introduction to trading and hedging with financial futures.*

Markham, Jerry W. *The History of Commodity Futures Trading and Its Regulation.* New York: Praeger, 1987.

*This book traces the beginnings of futures trading in the U.S., describes the problems that engendered a call for federal regulation, and traces the history of that regulation.*

Murphy, John J. *Technical Analysis of the Futures Markets.* New York: New York Institute of Finance, 1986.

*This book covers the most important areas of technical analysis as they are applied to the futures market.*

Schwarz, Edward W., Hill, Joanne M., and Schneeiveis, Thomas. *Financial Futures: Fundamentals, Strategies, and Applications.* Homewood, IL: Irwin, 1986.

*The purpose of this book is to provide a source of information on the theories, applications, and strategic uses of financial futures.*

# APPENDIX 17A
# PROGRAMMED TRADING

Programmed trading is the use of computers to place buy or sell orders for securities. Usually, orders for thousands of shares can be executed in minutes. The exchanges' computer systems, such as the NYSE's designated order turnaround (DOT) systems, receive these orders and execute them without human intervention at the specialists' posts on the exchanges. There are three major uses of computers for programmed trading: portfolio trading, portfolio insurance, and stock index futures arbitrage.

## Portfolio Trading

Computers can be programmed to buy or sell stock when a predetermined price or other signal is reached. The programs and signals range from very simple to very complex. Particular securities or entire portfolios can be bought or sold on signal. Portfolio trading does not involve futures or options.

## Portfolio Insurance

Portfolio insurance is a portfolio management tool that protects a stock portfolio in market declines. It usually involves the use of futures or options contracts that will increase in value when the market falls. A portfolio manager who wants to maximize return subject to a limit on portfolio losses will use portfolio insurance. Because someone in the market has to provide the in-

surance, it has a cost; the marketplace charges for assuming the portfolio insurance risk. From the portfolio manager's viewpoint, the cost of the insurance is giving up some of the profit if the market goes up. Investment consulting services arrange portfolio insurance for institutional investors.

In its simplest form, portfolio insurance can be provided by buying put options that give the portfolio manager the right to sell at established prices all the stocks in the portfolio. If the market goes up, the manager just lets the options expire and has the gain on the portfolio. Of course, the cost of the puts reduces the portfolio's return from what it would have been if the portfolio had not been insured. On the other hand, if the market goes down, the portfolio manager exercises the puts in order to protect the original value of the portfolio.

Any level of protection can be purchased with portfolio insurance. It is possible to insure against any loss, although this is expensive. For a lower cost the portfolio could be insured against losses of more than 5 or 10 percent of its value.

Instead of put options on individual stocks, futures or put options on market indexes usually would be used. In a down market the gains on the futures or put options could offset the losses on the portfolio. In practice, portfolio insurance is a dynamic process in which services of futures or options contracts are used. Also, shifting some of the portfolio from stocks to cash at the appropriate time will help in the insurance process. Therefore, the value of the portfolio and the securities used to insure it will be constantly monitored by computer. Purchases and sales of stocks and the insuring securities will be made when the market reaches predetermined levels.

## Stock Index Futures Arbitrage

Arbitrage is the simultaneous purchase and sale of the same or substitute goods in two markets in order to profit from market pricing discrepancies. Arbitrage opportunities sometimes exist using stock index futures and the stocks included in the index. At these times, the futures prices and the stock prices are out of line with one another and a profit based on these price discrepancies can be locked in. Because arbitrage requires quick purchases and sales of futures and of the stocks included in the index, computers are programmed to initiate the orders upon prearranged signal. Because the dollar amounts involved are huge, stock index futures arbitrage is a major form of programmed trading.

Equation 17A–1 gives the basic relationship between stock index futures and the underlying stock prices.

$$F = S (1 + r - d) \qquad \textbf{(17A–1)}$$

where

$F =$ the price of an equity futures contract

$S =$ the underlying stock price index

$r =$ the riskless rate of interest over the life of the futures contract

$d =$ the rate at which dividend income is expected to accrue on an investment in the underlying index over the contract life

To understand the logic of Equation 17A–1, let an investor buy the underlying stocks, $S$, with money borrowed at the riskless rate, $r$. The investor also sells short the stock index futures contract, $F$. At time period $t$, the investor has the value of the stocks in the index, $S_t$, and the dividends received, $Sd$. He owes a loan

balance of $S (1 + r)$ and a settlement on the futures of $S_t - F$. Putting these together, his wealth position is

$$S_t + Sd - S (1 + r)$$
$$- (S_t - F) \qquad \textbf{(17A–2)}$$

When it is set equal to zero, Equation 17A–2 simplifies to Equation 17A–1.

If Equation 17A–1 does not hold, an arbitrage opportunity exists. If $F$ is greater than $S (1 + r - d)$, a long arbitrage opportunity exists. The investor will make a riskless profit if he uses the proceeds from borrowing to buy the index stocks and sell the futures.

If $F$ is less than $S (1 + r - d)$, a short arbitrage opportunity exists. The investor should sell the index stocks, put the money into the riskless asset, and buy the futures. He will make a riskless profit.

Long arbitrage is attractive to institutions that have a low cost of funds. They come closest to being able to borrow at the riskless rate. Short arbitrage requires selling the underlying stocks short. Because the investor must be able to borrow the stock for the short sales, and short sales can be executed only when the last price change was an up-tick, the short sales might be delayed. Therefore, short arbitrage opportunities are most attractive to institutions that already own the stock. They can sell the stock, put the proceeds in debt instruments, and replace the stock with the futures contract. The payoff is the same but the transaction costs are lower. Arbitrage is attractive to large institutions rather than individual investors because transaction costs are high. These costs involve commissions and bid-ask spreads in both the stock and futures markets. Even on large transactions, round trip transaction costs can be one-half to three-fourths percent. Also, arbitrage opportunities disappear quickly. Several arbitrageurs are going to act on the same signal; price discrepancies will not remain for long. In practice, arbitrage requires continuous computer monitoring of prices and an investment of at least $3 million. It is a major source of programmed trading.

## Effects of Programmed Trading

Programmed trading became very controversial with the huge market drop in massive volume on Monday, October 19, 1987. On the following morning, the NYSE suspended its members' use of programmed trading and exchange officials talked of the possibility of it causing a "meltdown" of the stock market.

Because programmed trading was undertaken by large institutions and was not understood by the public, it received much criticism. Regulators and congressional investigators undertook extensive studies of its effect on the markets. Initial analysis of programmed trading's role in the market decline indicated most of the trading that day resulted from the portfolio insurance program. It appeared that massive selling under these programs contributed to the speed of the fall, which, in turn, damaged the effectiveness of the insurance. The market decline might have happened anyway but programmed trading did speed it up drastically.

## Exchange Specialists and Futures Markets

As the volume of stock index futures trading has grown, questions arise about how futures trading affects the exchange specialists' market-making capabilities. When stock prices are falling, specialists have a duty to maintain continuous and orderly markets. While they try to slow the price declines by buying stocks, futures markets operate by open outcry of prices with no one responsible for maintaining an orderly price decline. Because the prices of the futures and the underlying stocks are related, the specialists might have an impossible task. They can spend great amounts of their capital buying stocks but the quickly falling prices in the futures markets are going to bring the stock prices down very soon. The problems the specialists had during the drastic decline on October 19, 1987, suggested that the procedures of the futures markets and stock exchanges might be incompatible and that the underlying market systems might need changing.

## READINGS

Garcia, C. B., and Gould, F. J. "An Empirical Study of Portfolio Insurance," *Financial Analysts Journal* 43 (July–August 1987): 44–54.

    This article reviews different approaches to portfolio insurance and measures its cost compared to alternative portfolio management strategies.

Rendleman, Richard J., Jr., and McEnally, Richard W. "Assessing the Costs of Portfolio Insurance," *Financial Analysts Journal* 43 (May–June 1987): 27–37.

    This study measures the costs of portfolio insurance in terms of foregone returns.

Rubinstein, Mark. "Alternative Paths to Portfolio Insurance," *Financial Analysts Journal* 41 (July–August 1985): 42–52.

    This article outlines different approaches to insuring a portfolio.

Stall, Hans R., and Whaley, Robert E. "Program Trading and Expiration—Day Effects," *Financial Analysts Journal* 43 (March–April 1987): 16–28.

    After explaining index futures arbitrage, this article examines what happens to the prices of the underlying stocks on the day the futures expire.

# International Investing

## OUTLINE

## OBJECTIVES

When you have finished studying this chapter, you should understand

1. The structure and role of international securities markets.
2. The advantages international investment offers the U.S. investor.
3. The ways in which foreign investments can be made.

# *18*

## *Global Markets*

Large brokerage firms employ stock traders in the world's major financial cities. A firm's worldwide trading units keep in close contact with each other, especially when markets in one country are opening or closing. They allow the firm to trade securities almost 24 hours a day and help in tracking rumors and financial news. A change in a major country's fiscal policy, economic growth, interest rates, or currency value will quickly be reflected in stock prices worldwide.

The 508-point plunge of the Dow Jones Industrial Average on October 19, 1987, sent shock waves around the world. Within hours of the NYSE close, Tokyo prices were down 14 percent, the Sydney market was down 25 percent, and the Hong Kong market closed. A few hours later, European markets opened and joined the fall. During the past decade, a world market for equities has developed; on October 19 and 20, 1987, its drawbacks were seen.

## INTRODUCTION

In recent years, U.S. investor interest in foreign investment has increased dramatically. Both individual and institutional investors have decided not to limit their investment opportunities to U.S. securities. International investing can provide the investor with higher returns as specific foreign stocks, or even specific foreign markets, outperform alternatives available in the domestic market. International investing also can diversify the investor's portfolio because the returns in foreign stock markets are not perfectly correlated with the returns in the U.S. stock market. In this chapter, we outline the advantages and disadvantages of foreign investment and discuss the various forms of foreign investment.

# THE ROLE OF FOREIGN INVESTMENT

In the 1800s, investment by British, French, and German citizens paid for the building of U.S. railroads, canals, and utilities. The United States was rich in natural resources but it was underdeveloped. It offered European investors higher returns than available in their own countries. In addition to their security holdings, foreign investors owned nearly 35 million acres of U.S. real estate (roughly the size of Illinois) just prior to World War I. Until then U.S. citizens had invested minimally in foreign countries thus making the United States a debtor nation.

World War I changed the creditor-debtor status of Western nations. Europeans needed money for the war so they sold their U.S. investments to Americans, often at low prices. In addition, foreign countries borrowed heavily from U.S. citizens. By the end of the war, the United States had become a net creditor nation, a status it maintained until 1985.

After World War II, foreign investment by Americans increased. The Marshall plan sent $13 billion in aid to Europe and was followed by large amounts of private investment.

During the 1960s, U.S. multinational corporations, such as Exxon and Texaco, proliferated. A **multinational corporation** is a company headquartered in one country with operating affiliates elsewhere; it conducts business on a global scale. The economic power of multinational corporations gives them important roles in the economies in which they operate. As U.S. multinationals grew, there was criticism from both Western European and developing countries that these firms were hurting their economies and colonizing them.

In 1960, 42 of the world's 100 largest corporations were headquartered in the United States. In 1985, only 22 were. As foreign based multinational corporations have grown, Americans have made some of the same complaints against them as foreigners had against the U.S. multinationals.

## Globalization of Financial Markets

The globalization of financial markets started in the 1960s when U.S. banks developed worldwide branch networks. Then, in the 1970s, U.S. securities firms built up their foreign operations. At the same time, foreign banks and securities firms expanded into the United States.

In the 1970s, foreign exchange markets were globalized with major banks dealing from their offices in the Far East, the Middle East, Europe, and North America. In the 1980s, the market in U.S. government securities became global with market makers operating in Tokyo, London, New York, and other cities. In the 1980s, stock markets have been globalized with large companies listing their stock on exchanges around the world. For example, U.S. stocks are listed on the Tokyo exchange and Japanese stocks are listed on U.S. exchanges. (See Exhibit 18–1.)

## Foreign Stock Markets

Exhibit 18–2 is an estimate of the size of the world equity and bond markets. The total value of the bonds is slightly more than the value of the equities. U.S. stocks represent

**EXHIBIT 18–1 Foreign Stock Listed on the New York Stock Exchange, December 31, 1987**

| Country | Company | Industry |
|---|---|---|
| Australia | Broken Hill Proprietary Co. Ltd.* | Petroleum; minerals; steel |
| | News Corporation Ltd.* | Publishing; broadcasting |
| British W.I. | Club Med, Inc. | Hotel, resort operator |
| Canada | Abitibi-Price Inc. | Newsprint, uncoated papers |
| | Alcan-Aluminium Ltd. | Aluminum producer |
| | AMCA International Limited | Industrial prods.; construct. services |
| | American Barrick Resources Corporation | Gold mining |
| | Bell Canada Enterprises Inc. | Holding co.—telecommunications services |
| | Campbell Resources Inc. | Holding co.—diversified natural resources |
| | Canadian Pacific Limited | Transportation; telecom.; oil; mining |
| | Cineplex Odeon Corporation | Motion pictures theatres operator |
| | Domtar Inc. | Pulp, paper, packaging; construction prods. |
| | Inco Ltd. | Nickel, copper producer |
| | LAC Minerals Ltd. | Gold mining |
| | McIntyre Mines Ltd. | Coal mining |
| | Mitel Corporation | Telecommunications equip. manufacturer |
| | Moore Corporation Ltd. | Business forms manufacturer |
| | Northern Telecom Ltd. | Telecommunications equip. manufacturer |
| | Northgate Exploration Limited | Holding co.—metal producer |
| | Placer Dome Inc. | Gold, silver, copper mining |
| | Ranger Oil Limited | Oil and gas exploration, production |
| | Seagram Co. Ltd. | Distilled spirits producer |
| | TransCanada PipeLines Ltd. | Natural gas transmission |
| | Varity Corporation (2 issues) | Farm equipment producer |
| | Westcoast Transmission Co., Ltd. | Natural gas distributor |
| Denmark | Novo Industri A/S* | Industrial enzymes; pharmaceuticals |
| England | Barclays PLC* | Holding co.—bank |
| | BET Public Limited Company* | Industrial; transport; construction servs. |
| | British Airways PLC* | Passenger airline |
| | British Gas PLC* | Natural gas distributor |
| | British Petroleum Company Ltd.* (2 issues) | Holding co.—integrated int'l oil co. |
| | British Telecommunications PLC* | Telecommunications services and products |
| | Dee Corporation PLC* | Food; sporting goods retailer |
| | Dixons Group PLC* | Consumer electronics, appliances retailer |
| | Glaxo Holdings PLC* | Pharmaceuticals |
| | Hanson Trust PLC* | Consumer goods; building products |
| | Imperial Chemical Industries PLC* | Diversified chemical producer |
| | National Westminster Bank PLC* | Holding co.—bank |
| | Plessey Company Ltd.* | Telecommunications and electronic equip. |
| | Saatchi & Saatchi Company PLC* | Advertising; consulting |
| | "Shell" Transport and Trading Co., PLC* | Holding co.—integrated int'l oil co. |
| | Tricentrol PLC* | Oil and gas production, oil trading |
| | Unilever PLC* | Holding co.—branded foods |
| Hong Kong | Universal Matchbox Group Ltd. Inc. | Designs and manufacturers toys |

---

**EXHIBIT 18–1   *Foreign Stock Listed on the New York Stock Exchange, December 31, 1987 (continued)***

---

| Country | Company | Industry |
|---|---|---|
| Israel | Elscint Ltd. | Diagnostic medical imaging equipment |
| Italy | Montedison S.p.A.* (2 issues) | Diversified chemicals |
| Japan | Hitachi, Ltd.* | Electronic equip.; machinery; consumer prods. |
| | Honda Motor Co., Ltd.* | Motor vehicle manufacturer |
| | Kubota, Ltd.* | Agricultural equipment; pipe manufacturer |
| | Kyocera Corp.* | Ceramic products; electronic equipment |
| | Matsushita Electric Industrial Co., Ltd.* | Consumer electronic manufacturer |
| | Pioneer Electronic Corporation* | Consumer electronic manufacturer |
| | Sony Corporation* | Consumer electronic manufacturer |
| | TDK Corporation* | Electronic comp.; magnetic tape producer |
| Netherlands | Ausimont N.V. | Chemicals |
| | KLM Royal Dutch Airlines** | Air transportation |
| | Philips N.V.** | Electronics, applicances; professional prods. |
| | Royal Dutch Petroleum Co.** | Holding co.—integrated int'l oil co. |
| | Unilever N.V.** | Holding co.—branded foods |
| Netherlands | Erbamont N.V. | Pharmaceuticals |
| Antilles | Schlumberger Limited | Oilfield services; electronics |
| Norway | Norsk Hydro a.s.* | Agriculture; oil and gas |
| Philippines | Benguet Corporation | Mining; industrial construction |
| South Africa | ASA Limited | Closed-end inv. co.—gold mining |
| Spain | Banco Central, S.A.* | Holding co.—bank |
| | Banco de Santander, Sociedad Anonima de Credito* | Banking, financial services |
| | Compania Telefonica Nacional de Espana, S.A.* | Telephone service—Spain |

* American depository receipts/shares.

** N.Y. shares and/or guilder shares.

Source: *Fact Book* (New York: New York Stock Exchange, 1988), pp. 26–27.

---

over half of the world equities, while U.S. bonds are less than half of the world bonds.

Exhibit 18–3 shows the market value by country of the non-U.S. equities. Japan has by far the most equities, with the United Kingdom and Canada ranked second and third respectively.

Like the United States, other developed capitalistic countries tend to have one dominant stock exchange and several smaller ones. The Japanese, Canadian, and Swiss markets are dominated by the Tokyo, Toronto, and Zurich exchanges, respectively. Frankfurt is the largest of eight West German exchanges and Sydney is the largest of six Australian exchanges. The exception to this pattern is in the United Kingdom where a 1973 merger of the London exchange and six others formed the Stock Exchange. (See Exhibit 18–4.)

> **EXHIBIT 18–2   Size of World Equity and Bond Markets at the End of 1980 in Billions of U.S. Dollars (World Total = $5,289.9 Billion)**

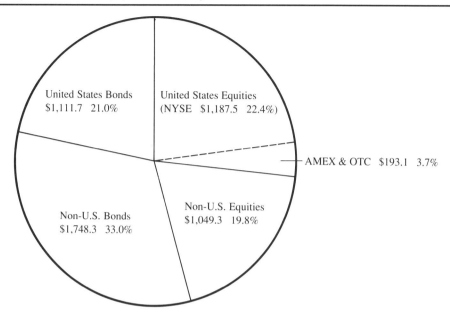

United States Bonds
$1,111.7   21.0%

United States Equities
(NYSE  $1,187.5   22.4%)

AMEX & OTC  $193.1   3.7%

Non-U.S. Bonds
$1,748.3   33.0%

Non-U.S. Equities
$1,049.3   19.8%

Source: Roger G. Ibbotson, Richard C. Carr, and Anthony W. Robinson, "International Equity and Bond Returns," *Financial Analysts Journal* 38 (July–August 1982), p. 62.

# ADVANTAGES AND DISADVANTAGES OF INTERNATIONAL INVESTING

The advantages of international investing are increased returns and reduced risk through diversification.

## Increased Returns

Exhibit 18–5 presents country-by-country returns on equity for the 21-year period 1960–1980. While returns from the European group were slightly less than the U.S. returns, the Asian equities far outperformed U.S. equities. The bottom three rows of the table show that the market-value-weighted portfolio of non-U.S. equities outperformed the U.S. equities portfolio. Therefore, the world equities portfolio also outperformed the U.S. equities portfolio. One dollar invested in non-U.S. equities would have grown to $8.23 in the 21-year period, while one dollar invested in U.S. equities would have grown to $5.78 and one dollar invested in the world equities portfolio would have grown to $6.47.

**EXHIBIT 18–3   Market Value of Non–U.S. Equities at the End of 1980 in Billions of U.S. Dollars (Non–U.S. Equity Total = $1,049.3 Billion)**

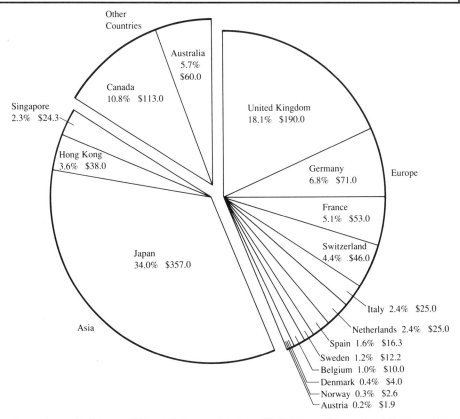

Source: Roger G. Ibbotson, Richard C. Carr, and Anthony W. Robinson, "International Equity and Bond Returns," *Financial Analysts Journal* 38 (July–August 1982), p. 63.

**EXHIBIT 18–4   Stock Price Indexes of Major Foreign Stock Exchanges**

ANP-CBS General Index (Amsterdam)         *Financial Times* Ordinary Share Index (U.K.)
Australian Share Price Index               Japo Industrial (Sweden)
CAC General Index (France)                 MIB Historical Index (Milan)
Faz (W. Germany)                           TSE Stock Price Index (Tokyo)

Source: *Fact Book* (New York: New York Stock Exchange, 1988), p. 69.

**EXHIBIT 18–5   World Equities Summary Statistics for 1960–1980**

| Asset | Annual Returns in U.S. Dollars | | | Year-End Wealth Index 1959 = 1.00 | 1980 Year-End Value in Billions U.S. $ |
| | Compound Return (%) | Arithmetic Mean (%) | Standard Deviation (%) | | |
|---|---|---|---|---|---|
| *Non-U.S. Equities* | | | | | |
| Europe | | | | | |
| Austria | 9.1 | 10.3 | 16.9 | 6.23 | 1.9 |
| Belgium | 9.2 | 10.1 | 13.8 | 6.39 | 10.0 |
| Denmark | 9.5 | 11.4 | 24.2 | 6.72 | 4.0 |
| France | 6.2 | 8.1 | 21.4 | 3.56 | 53.0 |
| Germany | 8.3 | 10.1 | 19.9 | 5.32 | 71.0 |
| Italy | 2.4 | 5.6 | 27.2 | 1.63 | 25.0 |
| Netherlands | 9.3 | 10.7 | 17.8 | 6.45 | 25.0 |
| Norway | 10.3 | 17.4 | 49.0 | 7.81 | 2.6 |
| Spain | 8.4 | 10.4 | 19.8 | 5.49 | 16.3 |
| Sweden | 8.4 | 9.7 | 16.7 | 5.40 | 12.2 |
| Switzerland | 10.2 | 12.5 | 22.9 | 7.74 | 46.0 |
| United Kingdom | 10.0 | 14.7 | 33.6 | 7.39 | 190.0 |
| Europe Total | 8.4 | 9.6 | 16.2 | 5.47 | 457.0 |
| Asia | | | | | |
| Hong Kong* | 24.6 | 40.3 | 61.3 | 11.24 | 38.0 |
| Japan | 15.6 | 19.0 | 31.4 | 20.86 | 357.0 |
| Singapore* | 23.2 | 37.0 | 66.1 | 9.96 | 24.3 |
| Asia Total | 15.9 | 19.7 | 33.0 | 22.29 | 419.3 |
| Other | | | | | |
| Australia | 9.8 | 12.2 | 22.8 | 7.12 | 60.0 |
| Canada | 10.7 | 12.1 | 17.5 | 8.47 | 113.0 |
| Other Total | 10.6 | 11.9 | 17.1 | 8.24 | 173.0 |
| *Non-U.S. Total Equities* | 10.6 | 11.8 | 16.3 | 8.23 | 1049.3 |
| *U.S. Total Equities* | 8.7 | 10.2 | 17.7 | 5.78 | 1380.6 |
| *World Total Equities* | 9.3 | 10.5 | 15.8 | 6.47 | 2429.9 |

* 1970–1980.

Source: Roger G. Ibbotson, Richard C. Carr, and Anthony W. Robinson. "International Equity and Bond Returns," *Financial Analysts Journal* 38 (July–August 1982), p. 65.

## Reduced Risk

The standard deviation column in Exhibit 18–5 provides a measure of the risk of foreign investment. While the standard deviations of returns for many countries are greater than the standard deviation of returns for U.S. equities, the standard deviation of the portfolio of non-U.S. equities is lower. Therefore, the non-U.S. equities offered a

**EXHIBIT 18–6    International Diversification**

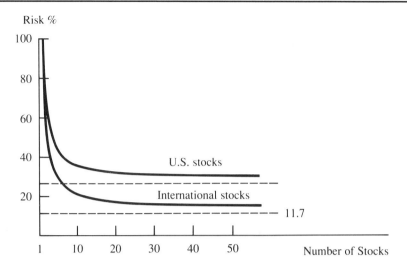

Source: Bruno H. Solmik, ''Why Not Diversify Internationally Rather Than Domestically,'' *Financial Analysts Journal* 30 (July–August 1974), p. 51.

better return-risk combination than the U.S. equities. Because of the low correlations among returns from different markets, the world equities portfolio offers a very attractive return-risk combination.

Exhibit 18–6 summarizes the diversification advantage of international investing. For a given number of securities, an internationally well-diversified portfolio is about half as risky as a well-diversified portfolio of U.S. securities.

## Additional Risks and Problems

Foreign securities present the investor with additional risks and problems. The risks result from exchange rate variations, exchange controls, and country-specific risks. Exchange rate variations strongly influence the returns earned on foreign securities. If the dollar increases in value relative to the foreign currency, the returns to the U.S. investor decrease, and vice versa. See Exhibit 18–7. However, **exchange controls** can be even more damaging. A government might place restrictions on converting its currency to dollars, thus preventing the investor from repatriating dividends and liquidating investments. Country-specific risks include expropriation, war and government instability.

Problems may arise from low financial reporting requirements and foreign tax laws. Financial reporting requirements vary from country to country, but nowhere is release of information as complete and quick as in U.S. markets. Canada, Japan, and the United Kingdom are the most stringent of the foreign countries. At the other extreme

---

**EXHIBIT 18–7   Changes in the Value of the Dollar**

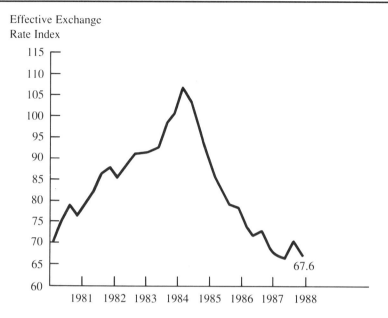

Source: Federal Reserve Bank of St. Louis, *International Economic Conditions,* April 1989, p. 2.

---

among the European countries, information on West German and Swiss companies is limited (trading on inside information is not even illegal in West Germany).

The investor in foreign securities becomes subject to foreign tax laws, which vary drastically from country to country, but which likely will include foreign withholding on dividends and the proceeds from sales.

# FORMS OF FOREIGN INVESTMENT

Foreign investment consists of two categories: direct investment and portfolio investment. **Direct foreign investment** is the ownership of foreign real assets such as land and factories. **Portfolio foreign investment** is the ownership of foreign financial assets such as stocks, bonds, and bank accounts.

## Direct Investment

Direct investment in foreign countries usually is undertaken by firms that plan foreign production. The firms probably are seeking increased sales or lower production costs. Producing in a foreign country ensures access to that country's markets. Therefore, direct investment can be a means of overcoming a country's import quotas and tariffs.

## Foreign Investment in the United States

Foreign investment in the United States is more than $1.5 trillion, about 10 percent of the economy. However, in certain industries and in certain parts of the country, foreign investment is even more important. Some 40 percent of the cement industry is foreign owned and a large percentage of the new jobs in the Southeast are in foreign firms.

Foreign investment in the United States comes in two forms: foreign direct investment and foreign portfolio investment. Although it is less than 25 percent of the total foreign investment, the direct investment is most controversial. The U.S. government defines foreign direct investment as ownership of 10 percent or more of a company's equity. The government assumes 10 percent ownership gives the foreign owner some control. Foreign direct investment includes complete acquisition of one company by another, purchase of part of one company by another, startup of a new subsidiary, and formation of a joint venture. The major investors are British, Canadian, Japanese, Dutch, West German, Swiss, and French companies.

Foreign direct investment implies a long-term commitment by the investors and provides access to U.S. markets. Depending on relative currency values, U.S. production might be less expensive. U.S. workers are well-educated, well-trained, and in many cases, are less expensive and more flexible than foreign workers. Many state and local governments aggressively seek foreign investment because of the jobs it provides.

Less visible but five times greater than foreign direct investment is foreign portfolio investment, which includes foreign purchase of financial assets such as stocks and bonds as well as bank deposits. Portfolio investment involves only a short-term commitment. Foreign investors are attracted by the returns and low risk of U.S. securities. In recent years, the Japanese have been buying as much as 25 percent of the new Treasury securities. Without foreign portfolio investment, U.S. interest rates would be higher and stock prices lower. On the negative side, however, economists worry about the disruption of the financial markets that could result if foreigners suddenly decide to sell their securities and withdraw their bank deposits.

Lower-cost production is possible if raw materials or labor is cheaper than in the home country. Goods produced in the foreign country will often be exported back to the firm's home country.

Direct foreign investment has all the risks of any large capital expenditure project. In particular, accurate estimates of future revenue and costs are critical. Additional risks result from cultural differences and foreign governmental relations.

The investor can participate in the benefits of direct foreign investment by buying the stocks of the domestic multinational firms undertaking the direct investment. Investment in domestic multinational firms is convenient for the investor. He or she does not have to worry about unfamiliar procedures, exchange rates, and foreign taxes. Although exchange rates and foreign taxes affect the investor's return, the multinational firm handles them internally.

There are disadvantages, however, in investing in multinational corporations: foreign governments may limit profits the firm can repatriate; foreign holdings could be expropriated without adequate compensation; and, most important, empirical studies indicate that investing in U.S. multinational companies does not provide the diversification benefits of owning foreign securities. The stock returns from domestic multinational corporations are too heavily influenced by systematic forces in the domestic financial markets.

## Portfolio Investment

Foreign securities can be purchased directly but this involves the administrative and tax problems discussed above. Fortunately, there are more convenient methods of foreign investments.

**American Depository Receipts (ADRs)** represent ownership of foreign securities that have been deposited with a bank custodian. The ADRs are bought and sold using the procedures that apply to U.S. stocks. Some ADRs are listed on the exchanges but most are traded in the OTC market. Some well-known foreign companies that have ADRs traded in the United States are Sony, Hitachi, Honda Motor, and Club Med.

Investment companies provide another convenient way to invest in foreign securities. Both open-end and closed-end investment companies invest in foreign securities. **Global funds** invest in both U.S. and foreign securities. **International funds** invest in only foreign securities. Some international funds specialize in particular geographic areas (such as the Pacific Basin) or specific countries (such as Japan). Exhibit 18–8 lists some global and international funds.

---

**EXHIBIT 18–8  Global and International Funds**

| Global | International |
|---|---|
| Dean Witter World Wide | Alliance International |
| First Investors International | Canadian Fund |
| Massachusetts Financial International Trust | Europacific Growth |
| Merrill Lynch International Holdings | Fidelity Overseas |
| New Perspective Fund | Financial Port Pacific |
| Oppenheimer AIM | FT International |
| Paine Webber Atlas | GAM International |
| Principal World | GT Europe Growth |
| Prudential-Bache Global | GT International Growth |
| Putnam International Equities | GT Japan Growth |
| Shearson Global | GT Pacific Growth Fund |
| Templeton Global | IDS International |
| Templeton Growth | Kemper International |
| Templeton World | Keystone International |
| | Merrill Lynch Pacific |
| | Newport Far East |
| | Nomura Pacific Basin |
| | Scudder International |
| | Sigma World |
| | Stragegic Israeli |
| | Templeton Foreign |
| | Transatlantic Fund |
| | T Rowe Price International Fund |
| | Trustee Commingled International |
| | United International Growth |

# SUMMARY

In the 1960s, U.S. banks opened branches worldwide. In the 1970s, the large U.S. securities firms expanded internationally. Today, foreign currencies, U.S. Treasury securities, and the stocks and bonds of large corporations are traded in Tokyo, London, New York, and other financial centers.

Empirical studies show global investing has provided higher returns than U.S. investing. Because different growth factors and risks affect foreign securities, investors can reduce risk by diversifying internationally. However, foreign securities have additional risks (exchange rate variations, exchange controls, expropriation, war, and government instability) and additional problems (low financial reporting requirements and foreign tax laws).

Direct investment in foreign countries involves owning foreign real assets. An investor can participate in direct foreign investment by purchasing the stock of U.S. multinational corporations. Portfolio investment is the ownership of foreign financial assets such as stocks, bonds, and bank accounts. The most convenient ways to invest in foreign securities are to buy American Depository Receipts or shares of global or international investment companies. Global funds invest in U.S. and foreign securities while international funds invest in only foreign securities.

# QUESTIONS

1. What is a multinational corporation? Are most of the large ones headquartered in the United States?

2. When did large-scale international expansion of U.S. banks and securities firms start? Which financial assets now have international markets?

3. Worldwide are there more stocks or bonds? What proportion of the world equities are United States? What proportion of the world bonds are United States? What non-U.S. countries have the most equities?

4. Explain the advantages of international investing.

5. What are some risks and problems in international investing?

6. Define the two categories of foreign investment.

7. What are the advantages and disadvantages of investing in multinational firms?

8. What are American Depository Receipts (ADRs)?

9. What is the difference between global and international funds?

# READINGS

Abrams, Richard K., and Kimball, Donald V. "U.S. Investment in Foreign Equity Markets," *Economic Review* (Federal Reserve Bank of Kansas City) 66 (April 1981): 17–31.
   *This paper provides an overview of investment in foreign equity markets from the perspective of the individual U.S. investor. The stock market in Australia, Canada, Japan, Switzerland, the United Kingdom, and West Germany are examined.*

Errunza, Vihang. "Emerging Markets: A New Opportunity for Improving Global Portfolio Performance," *Financial Analysts Journal* 39 (September–October 1983): 51–58.

>*This paper argues that diversification into emerging stock markets can offer substantial investment gains.*

Ibbotson, Roger G., and Brinson, Gary P. *Investment Markets: Gaining the Performance Advantage.* New York: McGraw-Hill Book Company, 1987.

>*This book provides an analysis and history of the world's capital markets.*

Ibbotson, Roger G., Carr, Richard C., and Robinson, Anthony W. "International Equity and Bond Returns," *Financial Analysis Journal* 38 (July–August 1982): 61–80.

>*This study examines the returns on equities and bonds of the United States and 17 foreign countries and finds foreign stocks and bonds generally outperform U.S. securities.*

Officer, Dennis T., and Hoffmeister, J. Ronald. "ADRs: A Substitute for the Real Thing?" *Journal of Portfolio Management* 13 (Winter 1987): 61–65.

>*This paper examines the investment characteristics of ADRs.*

Pardee, Scott E. "Internationalization of Financial Markets," *Economic Review* (Federal Reserve Bank of Kansas City) 72 (May 1987): 3–7.

>*This article examines three aspects of the internationalization of financial markets: the globalization of financial markets, new types of securities, and the diminishing distinctions between banks and brokers.*

Solnick, Bruno H. "Why Not Diversify Internationally Rather Than Domestically?" *Financial Analysts Journal* 30 (July–August 1974): 48–54.

>*This article shows that substantial advantages in risk reduction can be attained through portfolio diversification into foreign securities.*

# Real Estate

## OBJECTIVES

When you have finished studying this chapter, you should understand

1. The most common reasons for purchasing real estate as an investment.

2. Types of real estate investments that are most likely to be purchased by the individual investor.

3. Costs that are usually involved in owning real estate.

4. The tax implications of real estate ownership as an investment.

# 19

## *Real Estate Prices in Japan*

According to Japan's National Land Agency, land prices rose dramatically in that country during 1987. Residential property increased in value approximately 68.5 percent. In contrast, Salomon Brothers Inc. reported that housing in the United States rose in value 6.8 percent during this period.

If you are in the market for a choice piece of commercial real estate in downtown Tokyo, you can expect to pay about $6.7 billion per acre! That's $153,811 per square foot.

## INTRODUCTION

In this chapter, we examine why people invest in real estate, the different types of real estate investments, risk and return tradeoffs, costs of ownership, and types of ownership.

Owning real estate has often been touted as an investment where the investor cannot lose. While this is not necessarily true, over the long run investments in real estate have tended to be profitable for most people.

# WHY OWN REAL ESTATE?

The most common reasons given for investing in real estate are summarized below.

## Appreciation

The buyer of real estate expects the value of the property to increase over time. The amount of **appreciation** may be affected by the national real estate market in general or by the demand for real estate in a particular geographical location. Appreciation may also be affected by interest rates, which will have a bearing on the number of people able to purchase property at a given time. A further determinant of real estate appreciation may be whether the property in question is urban or rural. Rural property may be bought with the intention of farming, or with the expectation of platting the land and selling building lots (subject to zoning regulations). Occasionally land on the outskirts of a city is purchased with the hope that the city will be expanding in that direction, thereby increasing its value. In some periods, real estate appreciation may be very rapid. During the mid and late 1970s, for example, many people who bought residential property were able to sell it for a substantial profit a few months later. During the first part of the 1980s, however, real estate prices began to stagnate in most of the country and even to drop in many communities. Farmland prices in the Corn Belt dropped year after year. According to information from the U.S. Department of Agriculture, between the 1981 peak and 1986, the value of farm acreage in the Midwest dropped an average of 45.8 percent. Iowa led the list with a drop of 59 percent, from an average of $2,147 per acre to less than $1,000 per acre. Farmers did not want (or could not afford) to buy additional land because the prices of the commodities that could be produced were extremely low. Foreclosures by lending agencies also dumped large amounts of land on the market, depressing prices even more.

## Current Income

Real estate may produce **current income** from renting the property owned: houses or apartments can be rented to tenants, commercial structures can be rented to various business enterprises, farmland can be rented or farmed by the owner. The investor, of course, hopes that the income produced will be greater than the expenses involved in producing the crops or in preparing and maintaining the building for rental.

## Tax Shelter

Because of losses incurred in owning real estate, other taxable income is reduced. Farmland often produces such a loss. Extensive renovation of rental units may also result in a net operating loss for some years. Some real estate units for sale have been developed with the sole intent of serving as tax shelters. Tax reforms of 1986 demand that the owner of income-producing property be an active participant in its management before losses can be deducted from earnings from other sources. Tax reform is explored more fully later in Chapter 24.

## Leverage

Using real estate for **leverage** means using property that is already owned as collateral for loans that will be used for additional financing of investments—real estate or otherwise. During the 1970s, when farmland values were soaring, many farmers (as well as nonfarm investors) used Farm A as collateral to secure a no down-payment mortgage to buy Farm B. When Farm B had appreciated somewhat in value, it was in turn used as collateral to buy Farm C. This arrangement began to fall apart as the market value of Farm A and Farm B declined and lenders asked for repayment of the loans or for additional collateral. While leverage with real estate can be profitable, it can also be risky.

# REAL ESTATE POSSIBILITIES

There are several ways in which to invest in real estate. We will discuss the main features of some of them here.

## Personal Residence

For tax purposes, your **principal residence** is usually the house, mobile home, condominium, or cooperative apartment in which you live. For most people, a home is the largest financial commitment they will make in their lifetimes. For some individuals, this is really the only investment they have when they reach retirement. For others, it is simply one aspect of their investment portfolios. The personal home can be used to store value. As each payment is made on the mortgage, the amount of equity in the home increases. In addition, during most economic cycles, inflation is giving additional equity. When the house is sold at some point in the future, the owner will have funds to use to purchase a replacement house, to meet current living expenses, or to make other investments.

Real estate taxes, interest on the mortgage, and a portion of uninsured or under-insured casualty losses are deductible when itemizing (Schedule A) on federal income taxes. (These deductions are limited after 1986 to a principal residence and one second home. A third vacation property would no longer generate allowable deductions.) In addition, some local taxing units will give you a break on property taxes when you have an outstanding mortgage.

***Capital Gains and Losses*** Property held for personal use or for investment use is a capital asset. Gain from a sale of a personal capital asset results in a taxable capital gain, but losses from a sale of personal property are not deductible. Gains from a sale of investment property are taxable, and losses on such sales may be treated as capital losses.

A **capital gain (loss)** is the difference between the selling price of the property and its basis. **Basis** is a way to measure your investment in property for tax purposes. It is usually the purchase price. An adjusted basis must be computed at the time of a sale to determine gain or loss. For example, original basis plus capital improvements (remodeling or expanding, not repairs) less any **depreciation** claimed (if the property had been used as a rental or for business purposes) equals the adjusted basis.

If you change your principal residence into a rental unit or a business, depreciation will be based on the fair market value of the house or its adjusted basis, whichever is less.

Until the end of the 1986 tax year, capital gains (losses) were classified as long or short-term, depending on the length of time the property was held. Property sold within six months of its purchase resulted in a short-term gain or loss. Short-term gains and losses were fully taxable or deductible. Property held for more than six months resulted in a long-term gain or loss with only 40 percent of a long-term gain considered as taxable income. Beginning with the 1987 tax year, property held for any length of time results in a fully taxable gain. Gains and losses are reported and explained on Schedule D.

---

| EXAMPLE |

(1986 and before.) Your rental unit was purchased for $100,000 and sold for $125,000. If you had sold four months after purchase, you would have had $25,000 of taxable income. If you had sold seven months after the purchase, you would have had $10,000 taxable income ($25,000 × 40%).

(1987 and thereafter.) You will have $25,000 of taxable income in either instance. □

---

| EXAMPLE |

The above rental unit had to be sold for $75,000. The capital loss would be $25,000. This $25,000 loss must first be subtracted from other capital gains realized the same tax year. If you had sold another rental unit this year on which you realized a $15,000 capital gain, the tax computation would be: $15,000 gain minus the $25,000 loss leaves a $10,000 loss to be applied against other income. However, there is a yearly loss limit of $3,000 that can be applied against other income. If your deductible loss is more than that, you may carry over the unused part to the next tax year. If you cannot use all the carried over portion the second year, you may continue to carry the loss forward from year to year.

In our example, $3,000 could be deducted this tax year, with $7,000 carried forward to be used in subsequent years

— Year 2—deduct $3,000 loss, $4,000 balance
— Year 3—deduct $3,000 loss, $1,000 balance

The final carried forward loss would be $1,000 in the fourth year. This assumes, of course, no additional gains or losses in future years. □

**Principal Residence Tax Break**    If you invest the entire amount of money realized from the sale of your personal residence into another personal residence within a 24-

month period (this 24 months may be either before or after the sale of the property), you will not have to pay taxes on the capital gains at the time of the sale. Note that this is a **tax deferment,** not an exclusion. Form 2119, Sale or Exchange of Principal Residence, is to be filed for the year the sale is made. You can continue to defer taxation indefinitely as you move from one home to another. Both the house you buy and the house you sell must qualify as your principal residence, not a vacation home.

The IRS enforces the 24-month period very stringently. The only acceptable reasons for extending this time are active duty in the armed forces within the United States (48-months maximum), active duty with the armed forces outside the United States, being required to live in on-base housing (96-months maximum), or having your tax home (as a civilian) be located outside the United States (48-months maximum). The 24-month limitation applies even if you are kept from moving into your new house by conditions beyond your control. Suppose that 20 months after selling House A, you are preparing to move into House B when it is rendered uninhabitable by a tornado. Repairs are not completed until six months after the disaster. You have missed the 24-month deadline and may not defer taxes on the capital gains from House A.

| EXAMPLE | You sold your first house for $60,000 (purchased for $40,000) and bought a second home for $75,000. You may defer any taxes based on the $20,000 gain from the sale of the first house. However, if your second house had cost $50,000, you would have to pay taxes on part of the profit realized from the sale of the first house since you did not roll over the entire $60,000. □ |
| --- | --- |

Any gain not taxed at the time of sale will be subtracted from the cost of your new home to determine its basis. This will give you a lower basis for the new home than if you merely considered the purchase price. For example, Home A (in the example above) was bought for $40,000 and sold for $60,000. You bought Home B for $75,000, qualifying yourself for the deferment. However, the basis of your new home will be $55,000 (purchase price minus the $20,000 deferred gain). If you later sell Home B for $85,000, you will have a $30,000 gain for tax purposes.

If you are aged 55 or older, you may choose to use the once-in-a-lifetime **tax exclusion** which allows you to exclude from taxation the first $125,000 of capital gains from a sale of your principal residence. You must have lived in this property for three of the five years prior to the date of the sale. This exclusion applies to your personal residence only, not to vacation homes or to investment property. The exclusion may be used only once, and using a portion of the $125,000 actually means that the entire amount has been used. Say you bought your home some time ago for $40,000. Today you sold it for $90,000. Since you are 59, you elect to use the exclusion. Excluding the $50,000 gain now will not result in a $75,000 balance to be used at some later date. In effect, any use of the exclusion results in the total use of it. If you are single, you are allowed an exclusion of $125,000. If you are married, the two of you are allowed the same total exclusion (or $62,500 each if filing separate tax returns). Using the exclusion with one spouse will prohibit your using it with another spouse at some later date, even if the second spouse has never been a party to an exclusion. The second spouse could use her/his exclusion only if it were exercised before the marriage vows were taken.

A capital loss on personal residential property is not deductible for tax purposes.

Under some conditions, you may rent out all or part of your personal residence to produce income. Your home is considered to be your residence if you live there more than 14 days in a given year or more than 10 percent of the number of days during the year that you rented it, whichever is greater. This ruling enables you to claim a vacation home as a personal residence, which allows you to claim deductions for mortgage interest and property taxes.

If you use the property as a dwelling (see above) and rent it, the money received must be reported as income, and allowable expenses (interest, property taxes, operating expenses, depreciation) may not exceed rent received (see IRS Schedule E). Mortgage interest and property taxes that apply to the time you occupy the premises may be deducted on Schedule A. If the property is not used as a dwelling, all expenses may be deducted, even if a negative income is produced. The 1987 tax year brought some limitations on tax losses relating to rental property. Individuals with adjusted gross incomes under $100,000 may claim up to $25,000 a year in losses. This ceiling is reduced for those earning between $100,000 and $150,000. Anyone earning over $150,000 may not claim any tax losses. After a four-year phase out period, this rule will be fully implemented in 1991. Sale of a residence that has been used both as a rental and an occupied dwelling may result in a more complicated tax picture since depreciation taken as a rent expense will change the basis of the house. Temporary renting of your house for a couple of months while you are trying to sell it will normally not affect the capital gains issue.

Property used partly as a home and partly as a business (for example, living on a farm or having your business clients come to your office in one or two rooms of your home) will result in a pro-rated tax situation. A division of expenses must be made for the property. Only those that relate to the business may be deducted (on Schedule C, Schedule E, Schedule F). When the property is sold, only the capital gains that apply to the living quarters may be deferred or excluded.

## Vacation Homes

The majority of individuals who own vacation property do not inhabit it year round. They usually occupy the premises during the prime vacation periods. The remainder of the year the property may sit vacant, or the owner may choose to rent the property to others who wish to vacation in that particular location.

While the tax law concerning rental of vacation homes is somewhat confusing, one basic rule is often called the 14-day rule. If you use the property yourself for more than 14 days or more than 10 percent of the total days it was rented, the vacation property will be considered a personal residence. If your personal use is below this, the IRS considers the vacation property to be a business.

The distinction is important in determining how (if) to deduct expenses for mortgage interest, property taxes, and depreciation. The new "passive income" rule enters the picture also, should you determine a loss occurred on the rental.

You should keep careful records of occupancy and rental income and consult a tax expert before filling your return.

When vacation property is sold, any capital gain is taxable at the time of sale; deferment or exclusion is allowed only on a principal residence. While a capital gain is taxable, a capital loss is not deductible.

A variation of owning vacation property in total is the ownership of a **time share** in a vacation condominium. Under this arrangement, you own the right to spend a specified period of time during the year in the property; for example, you might have the right to occupy the premises for the first two weeks in March.

There are two basic time share arrangements. One is direct ownership of a specified property for a specific time each year. You will receive a deed to this property, and mortgage interest and any property taxes paid will be deductible when you itemize taxes if this property is your one allowable vacation home. This ownership is for life or until you sell the time share. The second arrangement does not include any ownership of property. This is simply a "right to use" agreement that enables you to occupy the premises for a specified time share of the year, usually for a specified number of years rather than for life.

In addition to the purchase price, you will usually be charged for your share of insurance and property taxes. Maintenance fees and recreational fees will most likely be your responsibility. In addition, any special assessments for major expenditures will be pro-rated among the owners. If you cannot occupy your space during the time indicated, you may have the option to rent this time to others. In fact, the ability to rent the space to others is often used as a selling feature by those attempting to sell time shares. Some individuals have purchased time shares with the total intention of renting rather than occupying.

Some organizations in the United States will help time share owners find each other if they are interested in trading locations. For example, you "own" the first two weeks in March in a Miami condo, but you would like to go to Scotsdale this year. The organization will attempt to match you with someone in Scotsdale who wants to come to Miami this Spring. Some sellers of time shares include this service in their sales package.

When you get ready to sell your time share, you are likely to find the going a little more difficult than selling your personal residence (or a vacation cottage on the lake). Local real estate agents may not have the market range necessary to find buyers. Again, some of the original sellers of time shares will promise to find you a buyer when the time comes; these promises are not always fulfilled. For most time share owners, the advantages of the arrangement have been that space is available at a given time each year for vacation enjoyment. There seems to have been little or no investment advantage. As previously mentioned, capital losses on personally held real estate are not deductible.

## Building Lots

Residential building lots in platted developments are another real estate possibility. In some areas of the country, the value of such lots has increased tremendously. Generally speaking, however, they increase in value slowly. Ownership requires that property taxes be paid (which are tax deductible). Owners may also carry liability insurance to cover damages incurred by those who may be on the property. In some instances, even those people who are trespassing may be able to recover for their damages. The IRS usually treats lot ownership as property held for personal use, disallowing any claimed capital loss. Furthermore, the 1986 tax reform considers the interest paid on a loan to acquire the lot to be consumer interest, which is no longer fully deductible and will be phased out completely by 1991.

## Rental Property

You may choose to purchase real estate with an eye to increasing your income. The first idea that usually comes to mind is the purchase of houses or apartment buildings to rent to others. You might choose to buy a duplex, triplex, or apartment building and rent the part of the building you are not occupying. If you do occupy part of a rental building, you must pro-rate all expenses (interest, taxes, insurance, and so on) and deduct as rental expenses only that portion that applies to the rented section of the building. Interest and property taxes that apply to the portion you occupy can be deducted on your Schedule A. Insurance and depreciation on your occupied portion cannot be deducted. Let us explore some of the advantages and disadvantages of being a landlord.

Successful landlords have carefully assessed the rental market in their community. What types of property are in demand? Are there numerous unoccupied rental units? What types of people in this community are likely to become tenants—college students, young singles, retired people? A community that already has a large number of un-occupied rental units and a great many unsold houses on the market is not likely to provide a good income for the prospective landlord.

The landlord must also realize that being successful entails a great deal of time to check units, make repairs, pacify tenants, collect rents, and secure tenants for unoccupied units. He or she must be a person who can get along with people and who does not mind interrupted evenings and weekends. An alternative is to hire a manager.

Rental income (loss) is reported on Schedule E, with the bottom line being reported on Form 1040. Schedule E provides for a listing of income produced during the year, the rent paid by tenants. Rent received in advance is taxable in the year when received. It may not be reduced by anticipated expenses. Damage deposits do not count as income if they are accepted with the intention of returning them to the tenant at the expiration of the lease (subject, of course, to deductions for damage done). Deposits taken with the intention of applying them to the final rent, due when notice has been given that the tenant is leaving, are treated as advance rental payments and are considered to be income when received.

The landlord may deduct expenses for mortgage interest, property taxes paid, insurance, repairs (not remodeling), legal fees, utilities, fees paid to others for collecting rent or managing the building, and advertising. In addition, the building (whether a house or an apartment building) may be depreciated over its lifetime. The IRS has specific regulations concerning depreciation schedules. These depend on when the property was purchased and whether or not the landlord is also occupying the premises. Remodeling expenses are treated as capital expenditures and are to be depreciated rather than being taken in full when incurred. Since the rental business is operated (usually) with the intent to make a profit, losses that exceed the rental income may be carried forward to Form 1040 to reduce taxable income from other sources as long as the landlord was actively rather than passively managing the property. If the property is rented with no intent to make a profit, allowable expenses are limited to rent received.

When the rental property is sold, any gain will be considered as capital gains and will be taxable; the gain may not be deferred or excluded. Losses (if any) may be taken as deductible capital losses since this is considered to be investment property. Property that was formerly your personal residence and is now used as rental property (except on a temporary basis) will not be allowed the tax deferment or exclusion. Gain will depend on selling price compared to purchase price less depreciation (adjusted basis).

You might choose to acquire commercial property rather than residential property when you become a landlord. Here the major problem is high vacancy rates. It usually takes much more time to fill commercial property than it does to fill residential property. Many prospective landlords have unrealistic projections of how business will grow in a particular location. Overbuilding in many locations has resulted in many empty stores and offices. Commercial real estate tends to be highly illiquid.

Farmland is another rental possibility. For this discussion, we are talking about unimproved land (without buildings). Land may be rented for growing crops or for pasturing livestock. When the prices of livestock and crops are good, rents will increase to reflect this profitability. When the prices of livestock and crops decline, however, farmers are not interested in renting extra land; if already renting, they may request lowered rental costs. Cropland can also produce income on a ''sharecrop'' basis. This arrangement allows the landowner and the farmer to split the expenses involved with raising the crop—seed, fertilizer, herbicides, and so on. The farmer is usually responsible for planting and harvesting expenses while the landlord is responsible for paying property taxes and mortgage interest. When the crop is sold, the money is divided between the landowner and the crop producer. In this way, both parties share in the good and bad times.

## Urban Development

Land may be purchased with the anticipation that the nearby community will be moving in a certain direction. The owner may or may not use the land to produce income while the hoped-for movement is taking place. He or she expects that businesses, factories, or builders will be interested in purchasing the land in the future, hopefully at a large profit. Capital gains on this property will be taxable. Capital losses are deductible only if the landowner can prove to the IRS that the land was bought as an investment (which did not pan out). Sometimes this is difficult.

## Real Estate Limited Partnerships (RELPs)

If you do not have sufficient funds or knowledge to invest directly in residential or commercial real estate, you might consider joining with other individuals to make the purchase. One arrangement is called a **real estate limited partnership (RELP).** A RELP consists of (1) general partner(s)—the firm or individual who packages and manages the deal, and (2) limited partners—the individuals who put up most of the money.

For as little as $5,000 ($2,000 in the case of an IRA), you may purchase units or shares in funds that are backed by a mix of commercial or residential property that might include office buildings, warehouses, shopping centers, apartments, condominiums, or land. These are called equity RELPs. Mortgage funds make or acquire loans on various types of real estate. Limited partners can claim tax deductions for depreciation, property taxes, interest on loans, and various other expenses.

Some RELPs have been marketed as tax shelters, promising large deductions in the early years to offset income from other sources. The typical limited partner does not participate in the management of the partnership's assets. Limited partners share in the profits from income-producing property or from payments made on mortgages. The general manager, who manages the fund and makes the decisions concerning the property, may take 15 or more percent of the earnings. Limited partners have limited liability; they can lose no more than their investment.

Tax reform 1986 has made some drastic changes that will affect investors in RELPs that produce negative incomes. No longer can the "passive investor" use such losses to offset income such as wages, interest, dividends, stock capital gains, and so on. These changes apply to individuals who put money into a business and then play a "passive" role in the business operation. In order to deduct losses from other income, taxpayers must be involved in the operations of the activity on a "regular, continuous, and substantial basis." Occasional or even periodic consultation on general management decisions does not appear sufficient to meet these criteria. Deductions may still be taken from income produced by the particular RELP or from income produced by another RELP. Some rehabilitation projects may qualify for state or federal tax credits. After 5 to 12 years, tax benefits diminish, and the property is usually sold or refinanced with profit from the sale being distributed to the limited partners. Partners may continue to receive periodic payments in the form of interest if a mortgage is taken on the property when it is sold.

RELPs may be public offerings, in which case they should be registered with the Securities and Exchange Commission. Materials explaining the fund should be readily available for examination. Private RELPs are usually offered to people in a given community and are often involved in the purchase of a single property. Private funds generally require a much larger investment ($25,000 to $100,000) from each partner.

There has been a great deal of increased activity in these funds over the past few years. In 1980 investors put $1.9 billion into public RELPs; by 1984, the figure had risen to $6 billion, with another $4.7 billion going into private funds. In a few instances, this increased growth meant that a few groups had difficulty finding property to buy and therefore purchased some properties that were difficult to sell when the fund was to be liquidated. Nearly half the funds are sold as tax shelters, but, as noted, changing tax regulations have already eroded and will probably continue to erode many of the tax benefits. The IRS requires most promoters to register with it and to turn over names and addresses of investors if requested. Most experts feel that tax benefits should be considered to be secondary to sound economic potential.

If you are interested in investing in a limited partnership, investigate thoroughly. You should have information about:

- The experience of the general partner.
- Fees that will be charged. Many partnerships have so many fees and commissions attached that it is difficult to tell how much of your investment is actually going into the property. Some investors have reported being charged as much as 40 percent of their investment. A few funds (such as T. Rowe Price Realty Income Fund) operate as no-load funds.
- Valuation of assets held by the partnership and how this figure was determined. It is difficult to compare this investment with others because in many cases property is not acquired until after the money is received from the investors.
- Realistic appreciation prospects. Total return to investors cannot be determined until the assets are liquidated. Furthermore, when researching a RELP, remember that rate of return records compiled during the ''roaring'' 1970 real estate markets are not relevant to the 1980s.

Partnerships have an uneven record, with some making tremendous profits for their investors while others have barely kept pace with the Consumer Price Index. There seems to be no real evidence that RELPs have performed any better than such investments as money market funds or insured savings certificates. Overbuilding in various areas, high vacancy rates, or a recession could greatly hurt most RELPs, while an increase in the rate of inflation might help others.

A RELP investment should be considered as long-term. There is no major resale market in case you want out early. A few organizations such as Liquidity Fund Investment Corporation in Emeryville, CA, MacKenzie Securities in San Francisco, and National Partnership Exchange in St. Petersburg, FL, *may* offer to buy your shares, at a deep discount, and on only a limited number of RELPs currently in existence.

## Real Estate Investment Trusts (REITs)

Another form of investment in real estate is the **real estate investment trust (REIT).** REITs pool investors' dollars to assemble portfolios of properties, mortgages, or both. Trusts are managed by professionals and a board of trustees elected by shareholders.

REITs were established by Congress in 1960 as a way for smaller investors to participate in capital appreciation and other income benefits of real estate ownership. REITs grew steadily during the 1960s, fell into disfavor during the 1970s, but appear to be growing in the 1980s.

One major advantage of REITs over RELPs is that they can be traded like stock, on the major exchanges or over the counter. REIT shares can sell for as little as $25. Their comparative safety is an important factor for many conservative investors. By law they must keep at least 75 percent of their assets in real estate investments and hold each investment for several years. This latter requirement curtails short-term speculation. REITs must also distribute most of their income to shareholders.

REITs usually do not begin to pay back investors immediately. Some analysts believe that a REIT investment should be at least a 10-year commitment for the investor, although some REITs may break even after two or three years.

REITs come in three basic forms:

1. Equity REITs own a selection of hard assets such as office buildings, shopping malls, or apartment complexes. Income is earned both from rents and from the purchase and sale of properties.

2. Mortgage REITs put their money into construction loans and mortgages. These tend to be more inclined toward high risk and income than the equity REITs.

3. Hybrid REITs include both types of investments in their portfolios.

Some REITs may start out as mortgage or equity and then change to the other form in a few years. Today's market shows a 60/40 split between equity and mortgage holdings.

A blind pool REIT does not own any properties at the time it is offered. When sufficient funds have been gathered, the managers will then begin investing. Most advisers recommend avoiding these.

A self-liquidating REIT (sometimes called a FREIT or finite real estate investment trust) has a predetermined lifespan. After the property has been held for the specified number of years, the trust is liquidated and profits are returned to investors. A perpetual REIT is open-ended and can buy and sell property indefinitely.

Anyone interested in becoming an investor in a REIT should check out the following factors.

1. Portfolio diversification. Those REITs that limit portfolios to one type of property or certain geographical areas tend to be more subject to market swings.

2. Quality properties that are fully leased. In some parts of the country, overbuilding makes it difficult for managers to fill real estate space; consequently, profits decline.

3. Low debt ratios. Investors should take a look at the short-term debt load of the REIT. The norm is considered to be a one-to-one debt/equity ratio.

4. Experienced management. Managers with several years of experience usually show REITs with the greatest profitability.

REITs do not offer the same tax benefits of RELPs. The main income is the receipt of dividends, taxed at ordinary income tax rates. Profits on the sale of shares will result in a capital gain tax. When a REIT is dissolved (either because it was self-liquidating or has simply been sold), cash distributions to stockholders in excess of original investment are treated as capital gains.

# RISK AND RETURN

Many of the risks involved in owning real estate are not controllable by the individual. The prospective owner can reduce the risk to some extent by careful investigation of the property in mind. As mentioned in the opening of this chapter, land and/or property values go down as well as up. This undulation may be on a nationwide basis, or it may be totally localized. For example, if a major employer leaves an area, many real estate units may go on the market at once, depressing the market for all sellers. The upward or downward trend may continue for a short time or for several years. If you are interested in purchasing farmland, you must have some knowledge about the expected income to be realized from the production of crops or livestock. Interest rates play a big part in a prospective owner's ability to secure the property (and subsequently pay for it).

Most real estate has a relatively low degree of liquidity. Weeks or months may be needed to find a buyer. Even if you sell the property immediately, it will probably take at least a month before the sale is closed and the money is in your hands. If a buyers' market exists when you want to sell, you will find there are few buyers who wish to take the property at the price for which you are willing to sell. In the past couple of years, foreclosure of property due to nonpayment of loans has put a lot of land and houses on the market in various locations.

In cities, declining neighborhoods will produce negative effects on your property, even though your particular house may be well-maintained. The prospective buyer is looking at the total picture and sees a deteriorating area. Of course, if the blight is beginning to recede and buyers are coming in to pick up property to rehabilitate and sell at a profit, you may be able to get your money (and more) back.

Careful review of the movement of urban development can minimize the losses if you are buying in anticipation of selling property when the city comes to your doorstep. However, there are no guarantees. Sometimes cities stop moving in one direction, for no apparent reason, and go the other way. You may be left with several lots just outside the city that cannot be sold for the anticipated profit. Plans for highways, apartment buildings, hospitals, and schools are often scrapped. Sometimes these changes are due to budgetary restraints; sometimes they are due to population patterns that were not apparent when the original plans were made.

A further risk arises for the landlord with several properties, either residential or commercial. Tenants, even carefully chosen tenants, may not fulfill their leases, leaving unoccupied and/or damaged units. Time and money will be required to correct the problems. Just a few months of unoccupancy or a very few damages can erode all the profit for the year. Expenses for carrying the property—utilities, insurance, taxes, interest—go on whether or not the units are producing any income. Some landlords find that the personal contacts with many tenants are a drain they had not anticipated. Neighborhood decline may mean that the rental units are no longer attractive to the tenant market. Such a decline may also mean that the units are not marketable, either as units for someone else to rent or for people to buy as their own personal residences.

# COSTS OF OWNERSHIP

Costs of ownership include coming up with a down payment on the property at the time it is purchased, finding enough money each month to meet the mortgage payment, being able to keep the property insured, making sure the property taxes are paid when due, and keeping the property in good repair, both to ensure that it can be rented and that it retains value for resale.

You have to remember that putting a large amount of money into a real estate down payment effectively removes that money from other investment possibilities.

Landlords may have management fees if they are unable to take care of all their units themselves.

# TYPES OF OWNERSHIP

Property can be owned in several ways:

**1.** Single (often called severalty). The owner has all rights and responsibilities in the property. He can sell it, give it away, or will it to anyone without regard to the wishes of others. If there are mortgages or other liens attached, they must be satisfied at the time of a transfer.

**2.** Joint tenancy—with the right of survivorship—called tenancy of the entirety for husband/wife ownership in some states. This stipulates that should one of the parties die, his/her share of the property will go to the survivor. Passage of title moves smoothly and quickly. It is a right that cannot be negated by a will entry. For example, Sam and Sally own property with the right of survivorship. Even though Sam has an entry in his will that his half of the property should pass to Margaret, this entry will not be honored. The ownership with survivorship takes precedence.

**3.** Joint tenancy—tenants in common. Here, two or more people own property, usually in equal shares. Each person has the right to do with his share of the property as he pleases. He can, therefore, write a valid will entry to dispose of his share. If Sam and Sally own property as tenants in common, Sam's will entry to leave his half of the property to Margaret will be honored. Unfortunately, there may be some conflicts now between Sally and Margaret. Tenants in common should make some arrangements about what rights (if any) the survivor(s) may have. For example, there could be an agreement that Margaret must offer her half of the property to Sally at a price to be determined by a fair appraisal. This way, Sally's enjoyment of the property is protected.

**4.** Partnership. This involves two or more people, with the property owned by the partnership. The arrangement must include guidelines as to what will happen should one of the partners die. The partnership could have life insurance payable to the partnership, which would provide sufficient money to pay the deceased's heirs for his or her fair share of the property. This way, a new partnership would not have to include the heirs. Partnerships will be considered equal unless some indication to the contrary is mentioned in the partnership agreement. While it is possible to form and carry on a partnership with an oral agreement, the prudent person puts a partnership in writing, with the advice of an attorney.

# SUMMARY

If you are considering real estate as a possible investment, you should generally expect to treat it as long-term ownership in order to be able to realize the best gains. Real estate may be purchased for appreciation, current income, as a tax shelter, or to use as leverage.

You might invest money in your personal residence, commercial or residential rental units, farmland, or building lots. If you do not want to or do not have enough money to invest on your own, you might choose to buy into a RELP or REIT.

All real estate ownership will involve risks, some of which can be avoided or minimized by careful investigation of your investment choice. Most real estate investments will result in low to moderate liquidity.

Various tax breaks are available for the owner of real estate, whether it is the ownership of your personal residence or investment property. All aspects of any real estate purchase should be investigated and evaluated thoroughly before making any financial commitment.

# QUESTIONS

1. Give three reasons for owning real estate. Indicate which of these you feel would be most important to you now. Would a change in your position in the life cycle make a difference in how you feel? Explain.

2. What local factors could affect the appreciation of real estate you had purchased as an investment?

3. What types of real estate could produce a current income? During which periods of your life would a current income be more important than appreciation?

4. Why do you think the IRS keeps such a close eye on investments that are sold as tax shelters?

5. What is meant by using real estate for leverage? What problems can result from a high use of leverage?

6. Describe the various tax breaks available for the homeowner: (a) when filing an annual return, (b) when selling a personal residence.

7. How does the capital gain (loss) treatment differ concerning a personal use asset and an investment asset?

8. What is meant by basis when discussing real estate and taxes?

9. Is there any tax difference between a long-term capital gain (loss) and a short-term gain (loss)?

10. How could the length of time I rent out my vacation home affect my tax situation?

11. Explain a time share ownership. What advantages and disadvantages can you think of for this type of vacation possibility?

12. What are the two basic time share arrangements?

13. Several years ago you purchased a building lot in a subdivision on which you expected to build a home. Now you have sold the property, resulting in a loss of $1,000. Is this loss tax deductible? Explain.

14. List three questions that you would want to ask before deciding to become a landlord.

15. How would being a commercial landlord differ from being a residential landlord?

16. Will the IRS allow you to report a negative rental income? Explain.

17. What problems could you foresee with being a landlord of farm property?

18. Explain the basic structure of a Real Estate Limited Partnership.

19. What is the difference between an equity RELP and a mortgage RELP?

20. Why is it difficult to determine up front what your return will be from a RELP?

21. List three questions you would want to have answered when considering a RELP investment.

22. List several ways you could reduce your risk with an investment in real estate.

23. Real estate has a fairly low degree of liquidity. What does that mean?

24. List four costs that will be involved with owning most real estate.

25. What is the major difference between joint ownership with survivorship and joint ownership as tenants in common?

26. List three possible areas you would want to have covered in a partnership agreement concerning real estate.


# CASE PROBLEMS

1. You have $25,000 available to invest in real estate. Explain which type of real estate you will purchase:
   a. Rental property—residential or commercial,
   b. Farmland—to rent or farm or wait for urban development (or a combination of these), or
   c. RELP or REIT—public/private, equity/mortgage.

   Explain why you made this choice. Be sure to consider liquidity, income (current or capital gains), management costs (in time and dollars), other costs of ownership, and tax implications (current and future).

2. Would your choice have been different if you had had $50,000 to invest? Why or why not?


# READINGS

"Cut the Risks of Going Commercial," *Changing Times* (September 1985): 73–77.
   *This article outlines cautions necessary for the commercial investor.*

"Land Prices Hurt by Low Inflation, Poor Earnings," *Prairie Farmer* (February 16, 1985): 67.
   *This article, in a farm magazine, shows declining land and commodity prices in the Midwest.*

Smith, Halbert C., and Corgel, John B. *Real Estate Perspectives*. Homewood, Ill.: Richard D. Irwin, Inc., 1987.
> *This principles textbook views real estate from four perspectives: legal, economic, financial, and business.*

"A Way to Play the Rebound," *Changing Times* (March 1988): 71–75.
> *This article reviews the history of REITs and discusses advantages they offer the investor today.*

# Precious Metals and Collectibles

## OUTLINE

Introduction

Precious Metals
- Gold
- Silver
- Platinum
- Jewelry

Collectibles
- Stamps
- Gems

Currently Manufactured Collectibles

Summary

## OBJECTIVES

When you have finished studying this chapter, you should understand

1. The advantages and disadvantages of owning precious metals as investments.
2. Some items that are considered to be collectibles and the problems associated with investing in collectibles.

# 20

## *Collectibles*

If you get tired of all the hoopla generated every four years by presidential campaigns, remember that political memorabilia is a favorite of collectors.

The American Political Items Collectors has 25 chapters in the United States, publishes a newsletter, and provides an appraisal service. Items given out by the losers are also collectible; save your Gary Hart buttons!

It is remarkable that even your old credit cards may have some value. Few old ones are in existence since owners tend to destroy expired cards as new ones arrive. According to the "Credit Card Collector," a Diners Club booklet card from 1950 is now worth about $100 retail.

## INTRODUCTION

In this chapter, we examine the benefits, risks, and the basic rules for investment in some of the nonfinancial assets that can be included in an investment portfolio. We will examine first precious metals and then collectibles. The most common precious metal investments are in gold, silver, and platinum. There are numerous collectibles, the most common being stamps, artwork, and gems. In the final section of this chapter, we look at currently manufactured collectibles.

# PRECIOUS METALS

For thousands of years, people have been fascinated with gold, silver, and platinum. Precious metals have been used throughout history as decoration for powerful leaders and as a storehouse of value for the commoner. Countries sent expeditions around the world, into the unknown, in search of them. The Spaniards virtually destroyed the Inca civilization in their zeal to acquire gold. Alchemists spent countless hours trying to find the magic formula to turn base metals into gold. Precious metals are generally impervious to destruction from time or the elements, as evidenced by items found in the tombs of the pharaohs and in shipwrecks on the bottom of the ocean. Gold items purchased today may be made from recycled metal, originally mined centuries ago.

During almost any economic cycle, some financial experts advocate holding precious metals as a part of the investment portfolio; others do not. Since predicting the future is an inexact science, you take your choice of forecasts and chances in the market. Those interested in "survivalism" recommend the acquisition of some gold and/or silver to be used as a trading medium in case of disaster.

## Gold

January 1, 1975, marked the beginning of a new financial era in the United States—the legalization of investing in gold for the first time since 1934. It was the effective birth of the U.S. gold market.

Many predicted at that time that gold would soon take its place beside stocks and bonds as an essential part of an investment portfolio. Since that optimistic beginning, the market has grown—but much more slowly than originally predicted. In 1975, contracts representing 86.7 million ounces of gold were traded. This increased to 1.1 trillion ounces in 1984, which, however, was down some 22 percent from the peak year of 1982.

One reason for this slow growth is that purchasing gold for most investors serves as an anti-inflation hedge. This means the item must be kept for a relatively long time in order to realize a profit. During the past few years, the inflation rate in the United States has been low—somewhat less than 5 percent per year. Consequently, interest in gold has waned compared to the double digit inflation years of the 1970s.

A major problem with gold is that it produces no income while being held. Income will not result until the item is sold. A capital gain then results in taxable income while a capital investment loss may be deducted from other investment gains or partially from other income. Many investors cannot afford to hold investments for long periods of nonproductive time.

There are, of course, no guarantees that the price of gold will increase. When the gold market opened in 1975, gold was selling for about $175/ounce. The low for the modern market was $104 in August 1976. The peak price, $850, was reached on January 11, 1980, equalled later that year, and followed by a rather rapid decline. During the past couple of years, the price has fluctuated between $350 and $475 (May 1989, $378), with no clear upward or downward trend. World events have a tremendous impact on gold prices.

If you are convinced that gold should be included in your investment strategy, several considerations follow. The first distinction for new investors is between the physical gold—coins and bars (bullion)—and financial instruments backed by or denominated in gold. These include certificates, warehouse receipts, shares in gold mutual funds and/or mining companies, options, futures contracts, and contracts that involve buying gold on credit.

The Commodity Futures Trading Commission (CFTC) oversees trading in gold futures and leveraged contracts. However, no federal authority has primary responsibility for dealers who do not perform as contracted or for firms that go bankrupt. Since gold is not considered a security, the Securities and Exchange Commission (SEC) has no jurisdiction over the way in which coins and ingots are packaged or promoted and sold. By the same token, the Securities Investor Protection Corporation (SIPC) cannot help to recover lost, undelivered, or stolen gold.

You can avoid some potential problems by

**1.** Buying only from companies or people you know. Anyone can open an office, make a few calls identifying himself as a broker for an international gold exchange, and sell gold. Someone always buys!

It is not difficult to find qualified sellers. Banks and coin dealers sell coins, wafers, and ingots. Brokerage firms may also become involved in these sales. For most investors, coins are more practical. They are fairly simple to store, and a partial liquidation is possible. It is impossible to shave gold off a bar; it is fairly easy to sell one coin from your holdings.

**2.** Buying in person. This eliminates the problem of dealers defaulting on contracts. If you must deal over the phone or through the mail, make sure you are dealing with reputable people. Ask for and check references. You may have to pay for the items you are purchasing in cash, especially if you are dealing with a small concern. Larger firms will take personal checks or major credit cards. You may also request that the seller deliver gold to a middleman, the bank, for example. After you have examined and approved the purchase, the bank can make arrangements for payment.

**3.** Arranging for storage yourself. One of the easiest ways to store small amounts of gold is to place it in a financial institution safe deposit box. The cost of the storage is partially tax deductible (with some new limitations imposed in 1987). Insurance will not be provided by the bank, but you can usually add an endorsement to your Homeowners policy, or you can purchase a special policy for this purpose.

If you have no wish to store the gold yourself, check storage possibilities with the dealer, although this could result in difficulty in getting your gold if the dealer runs into financial problems. If all assets of the business—your gold and company assets—are commingled, you should refuse to have your gold stored with the dealer. Make sure you know the name and address of the company that is handling the storage; it may be different from the broker/dealer who made the arrangements.

**4.** Being sure you understand prices. Retail gold prices include a commission on top of a wholesale markup over and above the posted world price. These extra charges may account for an additional 5 to 20 percent, with 8 percent being the most common. In addition, you may have to pay sales tax.

The dealer may also have a minimum order that he or she will ship. For example, most coin dealers prefer to send at least ten coins (ten ounces). If you are interested in smaller purchases, you will have to shop around for a dealer who is willing to accommodate you (usually for an extra fee).

Remember also that the prices quoted for the "weight" coins will be based on the gold market price while dated coins of some numismatic importance will have prices based on the demand by collectors. Numismatics is the study or collection of coins and/or medals. Medals might include the Olympic "coins" minted and sold by the U.S. government in commemoration of the 1984 games. The minimum prices of collector coins, however, would be based on their weight and the current world price.

Investors should note that while the 1984 Olympic coins helped the U.S. Olympic teams and made a good souvenir, most were probably a poor investment. Their value as collector's items should be low because of the large number that were minted. The 1984 Olympic silver coins had a face value of $1 but sold for $38, while the gold coins had a $10 face and sold for $376.

On the other hand, South Korea used the 1988 Olympics as an opportunity to mint the first one-ounce Olympic gold coins. Only 120,000 were planned, and this small number should ensure an increase in value over time.

***Coins***   The most commonly purchased "weight" coins are

- South African Krugerrand (politically unpopular; import to the United States banned in 1986)
- Canadian Maple Leaf (considered by most to be the highest quality coins)
- Mexican 50 Peso (contains approximately 1.2 ounces gold)
- Austrian 100 Corona (contains .98 troy ounce)
- Chinese Panda (also available in $\frac{1}{20}$ ounce)
- Australian Nugget (introduced in the United States in May 1987)
- American Golden Eagle (put on the market October 20, 1986)

The American Eagles are legal U.S. tender and have the following face values: 1 oz.—$50; $\frac{1}{2}$ oz.—$25; $\frac{1}{4}$ oz.—$10; $\frac{1}{10}$ oz.—$5). Exhibit 20–1 shows an advertisement by the U.S. Treasury.

The value of most of these coins as collectibles is small since so many are available. The Chinese Panda is an exception. The design changes each year (with the year of issue stamped on the coin), and the number of coins struck each year is limited.

There was an interesting development in the marketing of the Golden Eagle early in 1987. By law, the one-ounce coins, which Congress believed would be purchased by investors, must weigh exactly one ounce. In contrast, the U.S. Mint felt that the fractional coins would be purchased mainly for souvenirs, jewelry, or gifts. Therefore, their standards were much more lax, and coins were allowed to be both underweight

---

**EXHIBIT 20–1    American Eagle Coins**

## American Eagles. An investment you can actually hold.

In a world of electronic funds, computerized puts and calls and paper profits and losses, it's good to know there's an investment you can see and touch. An investment that actually feels good to hold on to.

That investment is American Eagle Gold Bullion Coins.

You know what you're getting when you get American Eagles. Because they're the only gold bullion coins to

have their content and weight backed by the United States Government.

American Eagle Gold Coins come in one ounce, ½, ¼, ¹⁄₁₀ oz. sizes; a one ounce American Eagle Silver Coin is also available. You can buy them at participating banks, brokers, coin and precious metals dealers. Their price, of course, will fluctuate with the metals market.

So consider American Eagle Gold Coins. One investment you can actually get your hands on.

## AMERICAN EAGLE GOLD & SILVER BULLION COINS ⊚

Source: Department of Treasury, U.S. Mint.

---

and overweight. After complaints from both the U.S. and foreign investment market, the Mint began to produce the fractional coins to exact standards also.

If you prefer to own coins of collection value, be aware that **appreciation** varies tremendously from period to period. For example, between 1975 and 1984, the average annual appreciation of rare coins was 20.4 percent. However, during the period 1980 to 1984, the return was only .1 percent.

Value is determined by the demand for a fixed supply of rare coins. Experts indicate you should buy high-quality coins and expect to hold them for a minimum of three to five years. Your best bet for appreciation will be with high-quality, high-priced coins. You should have money that can be tied up, and you must be willing to take the time to learn about the coins and the market in order to do well.

Dealer markups in the rare coin market may amount to 10 to 30 percent. Therefore, your investments will have to appreciate a great deal before the profit exceeds the transaction costs.

Coin dealers and collectors may have access to the services of the Professional Coin Grading Service, an agency that works to standardize grading of investment coins. Generally speaking, the more perfect a coin (uncirculated, for example), the higher the value.

**Other Gold Investments**   The Commodity Exchange (COMEX) in New York City is the largest precious metals futures market and is a leading market for gold options, which give you a right (not an obligation) to buy or sell gold at a given strike price before the option expires. Options are written on futures.

European government bonds are available that will repay the principal either in local currency or in gold.

Depository certificates for either gold or silver prove ownership of bullion stored and insured by such providers as the Deak-Perara Group or Dreyfus Gold Deposits.

You can also buy gold denominated certificates, most commonly issued by investment firms.

Mutual funds are available that specialize in shares of companies that mine gold or silver, or you can buy stock directly in companies that mine metals. Mining company stock tends to fluctuate a great deal. Some possible investments include American Barrick Resources, Newmont Gold, Agnico Eagle, Pegasus Gold, Newmont Mining, Lec Minerals, and Echo Bay Mines. All these represent mines in North America. Stock offerings are also available in foreign mines. Examples of gold mutual fund are United Services and New Prospects.

## Silver

Owning silver presents many of the same problems as owning gold. One major difference is that the price per ounce of silver is much lower than the price of gold. The record for silver was set in January 1980, when the price reached $50/ounce. Prices in early 1987 were in the $7 to $7.50 range (May 1989, $5.64). Since the world supply of silver is quite large, it is considered unlikely by most experts that large price increases can be anticipated.

You may purchase silver as bullion; silver bars weigh between 1 and 1,000 troy ounces. Bars should be marked with a recognizable refinery label, which ensures that you are getting what you are paying for. Such a mark also makes the resale of your silver easier. You may also purchase silver in bags of coins that weigh about 50 pounds and cost about $6,000. These bags have usually had the really rare coins removed.

It is more difficult to find stock market offerings in silver. The metals mutual funds traditionally emphasize gold. Hecla Mining, Sunshine Mining, Couer D'Alene, and Dome Mines are some publicly traded silver companies, but the list of such companies is much shorter than it is for gold mining stocks. The only pure silver mutual fund is Strategic Silver.

## Platinum

One metal that is frequently considered more valuable than gold is platinum, primarily because of its limited availability. Since 1974, when catalytic converters for pollution control became standard for the United States auto industry, demand has grown steadily. Emission standards are now being phased in by the European Economic Community.

Between 1982 and 1986, the sale of platinum increased from 45,000 ounces to 390,000 ounces. Most platinum is sold in small bars—1, 5, or 10 ounces—but 50 ounce bars are also available. Purchases can be made from major brokerage houses or some coin dealers. There is a one-ounce platinum coin, the Noble, from England.

The record price for platinum was reached in February 1980, when it reached $1,050 per ounce. Prices during 1986 ranged from $350 to $650.

Since the world's major supply comes from South Africa, the volatile political situation there can have a sudden and major influence on world availability. Small amounts of buying or selling can create very large price moves.

## Jewelry

A word needs to be said about the purchase of jewelry made from precious metals. Frequently the collector believes he or she is buying items that will hold their value quite well and will, in addition, respond to increases in the world market price of the metal.

Jewelry is priced according to the intricacy of the design, the reputation of the designer/artist, and the metal content (usually small). You will buy at retail prices, including a markup for the seller. When the time comes to sell the item, you will be offered wholesale prices. If the designer is an unknown (which is usually the case), there will be no premium offered. In other words, the chances of recovering your money from the sale of metal jewelry is slim. The best advice here (which is true for almost every other area of collecting) is that you buy something that you like and can continue to enjoy because the chances of your making a great deal of money on the transaction are almost zero.

# COLLECTIBLES

A collectible can be anything. While stamp, doll, and baseball card collecting have many participants, people also collect Elvis Presley memorabilia and Mickey Mouse watches. Men of all ages are fond of antique cars, either in original or "hotrod" condition. You may pick up matchbook covers or sugar sacks at every opportunity. Hopefully (from an investor's standpoint), there will be other people interested in the same items you are when it comes time to liquidate. From a financial standpoint, collectibles do not seem to be what they once were. During the inflationary 1970s, demand soared for almost anything with some aesthetic and scarcity value; paintings, coins, stamps, old cars, and comic books were eagerly sought after. When the double digit inflation cooled to an annual rate of less than 5 percent, the market quickly dried up.

Salomon Brothers calculates that for the period 1980 through 1985, stamps and coins rose just .1 percent a year in value, Old Masters paintings rose 1.5 percent, and Chinese ceramics increased 1 percent. An ordinary passbook savings account would have earned more.

Figures cannot measure the rewards that a few lucky people received because they had the items that for some difficult to determine reason appealed to a great many potential buyers. Figures also do not attempt to measure the personal rewards that motivate many buyers of collectibles no matter what economic conditions prevail.

Many financial experts agree that the main lesson of the past few years is that if you go in search of easy money in collectibles, you will most likely be disappointed. Ownership of such items offers beauty to the eye of the beholder and a pride of ownership that is difficult to get from a bank account. Owning a collectible may result in a negative cash flow since you will have expenses for appraisals, insurance, storage, and other measures to keep the item's condition from deteriorating.

Some items that are extremely rare and/or unusual may reduce the threat of theft since the market for them may be almost totally illiquid!

Since there are not many experts in many speciality areas, it is difficult to determine that an unusual item is indeed authentic. If you are buying something unusual from someone who knows more about the market than you do, you are at his or her mercy. Pricing is difficult even when the item is authentic.

Insurance may present a problem since the company and you may not agree on the value of a particular item. Insurance may not be available or may be extremely expensive.

If you want to collect art, gemstones, antiques, rare coins, or stamps, keep in mind their drawbacks as investments. You will receive no current income. You will be subject to changing fashions. Insurance and security costs can be very high. There are few resale markets, and if you sell through dealers or auction houses, transaction fees will be high. Short-term gains are generally small and unpredictable. However, over the long run, most experts believe that most collectibles will increase in value.

Whatever you are collecting—silver, antique furniture, or Tiffany lamps—generally speaking a collection of a number of related pieces will be more valuable than a random selection of things. Most experts believe you should specialize by period or artist or item. Estimating the worth of collectibles is difficult. You can obtain appraisals, but be prepared for a shock. What a dealer will pay for an item is usually much lower than the original price you paid—you paid retail but the dealer will pay you wholesale.

Let us discuss a few of the most common collectibles available.

## *Stamps*

Philately is the collection and/or study of postage and imprinted stamps. The first adhesive postage stamp appeared in 1840, issued by Great Britain and called the Penny

Black because of its color and price. Stamp collecting is said to be the world's most popular hobby, with an estimated 22 million collectors in the United States and 50 million worldwide.

In 1980, $935,000 was paid for a one-cent British Guiana stamp, the one-cent Magenta, that had sold for about $45,000 in 1940. Rare stamps are like any choice collectible—people who want them badly enough will pay anything. Over time, prices for highly prized stamps tend to rise as the collecting population increases while the number of desirable stamps does not.

Most experts believe that if money is the most important aspect of your collecting, you should stay away from stamps. They feel stamps should be purchased as a hobby for enjoyment rather than as an investment. However, if you have the time and effort and cash to invest in stamps, then you may make a modest return. There is a great deal of written material available, but serious collecting will require years of study to become informed about quality, grading, and supply/demand. You must learn how to determine authenticity, store the stamps, buy at auction, and do business with a dealer.

A dealer can be a prime source of information as well as a source of stamps, usually a better source of stamps for the novice than an auction. Always buy the best looking and soundest stamps available. You cannot improve a defective, torn stamp.

A major disadvantage of owning stamps as an investment is that they pay no interest or dividends. There is no payback until and unless stamps are sold. Time is required to sell. You are likely to find that the market is fickle since stamps have value only in the amount that an interested buyer is willing to pay. The stamps ''in fashion'' change from year to year. Two stamps from the same issue can differ greatly in value depending on the quality of the ink or glue or general condition.

Insurance against fire or theft is a must, but you cannot buy insurance against damage caused by wear and tear. Safekeeping can be expensive and time consuming, but it is mandatory since even a tiny tear can reduce the value of a stamp considerably.

In the past, the value of holdings has been primarily determined by dealers, auctions, and catalogs. In March 1987, Coach Investments, Inc., International Stamp Exchange Corp., was begun to serve as a stamp clearing house. Those with access to the exchange computer can find information about one million stamps. Sellers may present their stamps to the exchange for grading and insuring. They are then stored in a vault pending their sale. Sellers set ask prices; buyers may submit bid prices. When a sale is finalized, the exchange receives about 3 percent commission from buyers and 6 percent from sellers. Most auctions collect about 10 percent from each party.

Since buying stamps sight unseen can be bad for your collecting health, the exchange will allow buyers to back out during the ten days following the purchase. Buyers are also given a lifetime guarantee that they can get their money back if the stamp has been misgraded. During its first six months of operation, the exchange handled about $1 million in transactions.

One advantage of such a clearing house is that it can provide up-to-date prices. Catalogs that are commonly used as a source for price information become outdated shortly after their issuance.

Once a year, Salomon Brothers, the investment banking house, checks prices of 14 kinds of assets, including stocks, bonds, Treasury bills, and leading tangibles. Yields from income and/or changes in price are calculated, and assets are ranked according to how well they performed for various periods.

According to their interpretation, compound annual return for stamps over the past 15 years was 14.3 percent. However, philatelists point out that this return is based on prices quoted in various catalogs. Since prices actually received by sellers are generally much lower than those quoted in the catalogs, the actual rate of return is less. Experts note that most stamps trade for between 50 and 85 percent of their catalog value, and some stamps may trade as low as 10 percent. Looking at auction prices or dealer prices will give you a more realistic indication of value increases.

Linn's U.S. Stamp Market Index is plotted from dealer and auction sales. This index is a weighted average of U.S. selling prices of 47 of the most widely owned and actively traded issues of typical quality stamps. Prices shot up in the late 1970s, peaked in 1981, and then began falling. In 1987 they were about where they were in 1978. The rapid increase was due to high inflation and uncertainty over the economy. Investors were apprehensive over the more common types of investments and put their money into all kinds of tangibles, stamps included. When inflation abated, prices declined. Stamps historically have moved slowly but steadily upward, just a little over the inflation rate. There is no guarantee that you can get from a stamp what you have paid for it.

Once you have determined the type(s) of stamps you are interested in, the American Stamp Dealers Association can send you a list of member dealers who handle the kinds of stamps you are interested in.

The Philatelic Foundation or the American Philatelic Society (see Exhibit 20–2 for addresses) can provide appraisals of your stamps for a fee.

## Gems

Diamonds may be a girl's best friend but gems are not always an investor's best friend. Amateurs are frequently dazzled by anything that glitters. Experts caution that not every red stone is a ruby, not every green stone is an emerald, and not everything that looks like a diamond is.

The value of stones is determined by several variables. One is color. The United States uses a grading system that ranges from D to Z with D being perfectly colorless. The grade of the jewel is determined by its clarity and absence of flaws; many flaws cannot be seen with the naked eye.

The cut, done by hand, will also determine value. The appraiser will note the faceting and proportioning to see how they have affected the brilliance of the stone.

The gem will be weighed. As carat weight increases, the cost per carat increases. A qualified gemologist will give you this information in writing about a stone in which you are interested. You can verify the credentials of the gemologist through such organizations as Gemological Institute of America, American Gem Society, American Society of Appraisers, Jewelers of America, International Society of Appraisers, or Accredited Gemologists Association. Addresses can be found at your local library or local jeweler.

---

**EXHIBIT 20–2    *Addresses of Selected Appraisers and Collector Societies***

Professional Coin Grading Service
P.O. Box 9458-B
Newport Beach, CA 92658

Coach Investments, Inc. (stamps)
International Stamp Exchange Corp.
310 Arthur Godfrey Road
Miami Beach, FL 33140

National Depression Glass Association
P.O. Box 11123
Springfield, MO 65808

Baseball Card News
700 East State Street
Iola, WI 54990

Royal Doulton International Collectors Club
P.O. Box 1815
Somerset, NJ 08873

Dolls—The Collector Magazine
1910 Bisque Lane
P.O. Box 1972
Marion, OH 43305

Doorknob Collector
4125 Colfax Avenue, South
Minneapolis, MN 55409

Antique Radio Club of America
81 Steeplechase Road
Devon, PA 19333

Cookie Cutters Collectors Club
5426 27th Street, NW
Washington, DC 20015

Coca Cola Collectors Club International
Route 4, Box 2
Kutztown, PA 19530

American Political Items Collectors
P.O. Box 340339
San Antonio, TX 78234

American Stamp Dealers Association
Five Dakota Drive
Suite 102
Lake Success, NY 11042

Philatelic Foundation
270 Madison Avenue
New York, NY 10016

American Philatelic Society
P.O. Box 8000
State College, PA 16803

Jewelers Vigilance Committee, Inc.
1180 Avenue of the Americas
New York, NY 10036

---

If you have purchased a stone that turns out to have been fraudulently represented, your recourse may have to be in court. The Jewelers Vigilance Committee, Inc. (address in Exhibit 20–2) can advise consumers on their options and can provide a letter stating its findings to aid you in proving your case.

Sometimes, the cut, clarity, and weight of gems and jewelry are not the most important consideration in determining value. In April 1987, the jewels of the Duchess of Windsor were sold at auction. The auction house, Sotheby's, expected the collection to bring $7.5 million. When the last "sold" had resounded, buyers from around the world had paid some $50.3 million to acquire a piece of history.

Exhibit 20–2 gives the addresses of some collectibles appraisers and several national collector societies in the United States. It is certainly not a complete listing. There are also many local and state clubs.

# CURRENTLY MANUFACTURED COLLECTIBLES

Many items, ranging from plates and bells to miniature silver cars and chess pieces, are manufactured currently and are marketed as "collectibles."

Many collectibles take advantage of a particular event. For example, in April 1987, after Indiana University won the NCAA basketball tourney, fans and collectors were inundated with offers. One of them was for a "limited edition silver commemorative coin." These coins, which contained one troy ounce of .999 fine silver, were made available for $25, plus shipping. The price of silver during this time was about $7 per ounce.

These items are sold at retail prices, which contain a large markup. There is nothing to guarantee that any of them will have lasting interest for collectors. The number of items produced will also have some effect on future prices. Perhaps you may be lucky enough to buy a *Gone with the Wind* plate and find a willing buyer down the road, but usually the person is not available when you want to sell. The manufacturer does not promise to serve as a clearing house when you want to sell.

# SUMMARY

Precious metals have always been a part of some people's investment portfolios. The main advantage of metals is their continuing value. They serve as a hedge against inflation. Their main disadvantage is that there is no return on an investment until a sale occurs. If you want to invest in metals, you have a wide choice of investment possibilities ranging from acquiring the metal itself to buying mining stocks.

Collectibles also produce no current income and may have liquidity problems. In addition, they sometimes present storage and insurance problems. Unless you have sufficient time to research the market carefully, most experts advise you to purchase items you can enjoy rather than hope to make a killing in the market. You will probably be happier with that philosophy.

# QUESTIONS

1. Why has the U.S. gold market not grown as rapidly since 1975 as was originally predicted when gold ownership was opened to Americans?

2. What is the main reason most investors buy gold or other precious metals?

3. What is the main disadvantage of owning metals?

4. What was the price of gold when the U.S. market opened in 1975? What was the peak price? What is the current price?

5. What steps should you take to ensure that your entry into the metals market will be advantageous to you?

6. What is the difference between buying weight coins and coins of numismatic value?

7. How would you go about buying and selling numismatic coins?

8. If you did not wish to buy bullion, how else could you invest in gold?

9. How is owning silver similar and dissimilar to owning gold?

10. What is the main use for platinum in the world today?

11. Why is owning jewelry not the best way to invest in metals?

12. What is a collectible?

13. List five commonly held collectibles. Why would you personally want or not want to invest in each of these?

14. What problems might you have in buying insurance for your collectibles? Choose a collectible and check with an insurance agent about the cost of protection and any special requirements that would be made by the insurance company.

15. What is a major problem with currently manufactured collectibles?

# READINGS

"Collectibles—What's Hot, What's Not," *Changing Times* (November 1987): 123–128.

> *This article, in addition to outlining which collectibles are currently in favor, also gives some information about the Salomon Brothers indexes as they relate to some collectibles.*

Eckardt, Walter L. Jr., and Bargomery, Bruce D. "Numismatic Investments: an Examination of Intramarket and Intermarket Diversification Effects upon Portfolio Risk," *Journal of the Midwest Finance Asssociation* (1982): 1–24.

> *This article shows the returns, variability, and diversification benefits of coin investments.*

"How Not to Take a Licking in Stamps," *Changing Times* (November 1986): 77–82.

> *This article outlines basics for investing in stamps.*

"How to Sell Any Collectible," *Changing Times* (March 1988): 62–66.

> *This article outlines possible ways to sell collectibles of various types.*

"Investing in Nostalgia," *U.S. News and World Report* (April 4, 1988): 73.

> *A chart shows values of some selected collectibles for 1958–1988.*

# PORTFOLIO CONSIDERATIONS

# Market Efficiency

## OBJECTIVES

When you have finished studying this chapter, you should understand

1. The weak, semistrong, and strong forms of the efficient markets hypothesis.

2. The empirical evidence supporting each form.

3. The implications for investors of each form.

# *21*

## *How Rational Is the Stock Market?*

The October 19, 1987, drastic fall in stock prices makes observers question how rational the pricing of securities is. Prices are supposed to reflect underlying investment values, based on future prospects for the economy in general and companies in particular. Could these underlying values have changed 18 percent in one day?

Those who believe strongly that the market sets prices in a rational manner point out that in the week before the fall there were several pieces of bad economic news that could have been indicators of serious economic problems to come. Congress was discussing tax law changes that would have made corporate takeovers less attractive. The trade deficit was larger than expected. Interest rates were up: long-term Treasury bond yields went above 10 percent and banks raised their prime interest rates. The Treasury secretary was publicly arguing with West Germany over the value of the dollar. Some analysts argue that these events were enough to decrease the value of stocks, based on their future earnings, by the $500 billion that was lost on October 19.

Other observers argue that the events mentioned above were not important enough to cause such a large drop in underlying values and that investors are not as rational as some would like to believe. They point to psychological research that shows that people overemphasize recent news when making decisions. They believe that on October 19 investors overreacted to bad news and to other investors' emotions. Some academic research supports this view by demonstrating that historically the volatility of stock prices is excessive.

## INTRODUCTION

In this chapter, we examine the efficient markets hypothesis, the empirical studies of it, and implications that can be drawn from these studies. The efficient markets hypothesis holds that security prices reflect all available information. After examining the empirical evidence, we will conclude that the capital markets are very efficient, although not perfectly so.

There are two reasons for studying market efficiency. First, the financial markets allocate scarce economic resources. In the financial markets, investors allocate their funds to the securities offering the highest returns adjusted for risk. In order for resources to be allocated most productively, security prices must accurately reflect the expected returns and risk of the investment projects that the firms are undertaking. If security prices do not properly reflect return and risk characteristics, investors' money will not be put to the most productive uses.

Second, investors need to know about the environment in which they are making their investment decisions. In particular, before committing large amounts of time or money to the process of security analysis, an investor should be aware of the payback to be expected from these efforts. The studies of market efficiency demonstrate that identifying mispriced securities is a very difficult task and therefore the ability to outperform the market consistently is rare.

# THE EFFICIENT MARKETS HYPOTHESIS

Capital markets are perfectly efficient when security prices reflect all available information about the economy, the financial markets, and specific firms. If all available information is to be reflected in the price of a security, there must be very quick price adjustment when new information becomes available. Therefore, an investor cannot earn abnormal returns by using old information to predict security prices.

Security prices result from investors' buy and sell decisions. Prices reflect their consensus judgment of the future potential of the securities. If investors search out and properly evaluate all information about securities and can buy and sell with low transactions costs, the securities will be properly priced. Markets are efficient because investors and analysts are continually seeking out, anticipating, and correctly evaluating information that affects value.

Said more formally, perfectly efficient capital markets will exist if the following three conditions hold:

1. There are no transactions costs in securities trading.
2. All information is available at no cost to all market participants.
3. All market participants agree on the implications of the available information.

These conditions do not exist fully in the real world; there are some transactions costs when buying and selling securities, information is not available at no cost to everyone, and investors make different judgments using the same information. The existence of these real-world frictions does not void the efficient markets hypothesis, but they are potential sources of inefficiency. The purpose of the empirical studies discussed below is to measure how efficient the markets are.

The studies of capital markets efficiency are called tests of the efficient markets hypothesis. Studies can be classified into three categories or tests of subhypotheses based on the categories of information reflected in the market prices. There are tests of the weak form of the efficient markets hypothesis, the semistrong form of the efficient markets hypothesis, and the strong form of the efficient markets hypothesis.

## The Weak Form of the Hypothesis

The weak form of the efficient markets hypothesis states that all historical price information is reflected in the current market price. Therefore, past price patterns do not provide any information about future prices (which would allow an investor to earn abnormal returns). What developed into the weak form of the efficient market hypothesis was first referred to as the random walk hypothesis. The mathematical term **random walk** is used to describe a price series in which each price change is independent of the price pattern that occurred previously.

***Early Development*** Statistical investigation into securities prices began before any hypothesis was developed. Although his work was ignored for sixty years, in 1900 the French mathematician Bachelier developed a theory of speculative prices and tested it on the French government bond market.[1] He found that prices followed what later would be called a random walk. In the 1930s, Working, a pioneer in the statistical study of price movements in the commodities markets, found that commodity prices followed a random walk.[2]

In 1953, the British statistician Kendall examined 19 indexes of British weekly stock prices as well as weekly prices for cotton (New York market) and for wheat (Chicago market). He found that, ''The series looks like a 'wandering' one, almost as if once a week the Demon of Chance drew a random number from a symmetrical population of fixed dispersion and added it to the current price to determine the next week's price.''[3]

***Statistical Independence*** Modern studies into the behavior of stock prices began in 1959 with the publication of articles by Roberts and Osborne. Roberts demonstrated that patterns generated using random numbers look very much like actual stock market price patterns. Exhibits 21–1 and 21–2 are reprinted from Roberts' article. Exhibit 21–1 graphs the actual Friday closing levels of the Dow Jones Industrial Average from December 30, 1955, to December 28, 1956. The graph in Exhibit 21–2 was generated using random numbers. In both graphs, we see several of the familiar patterns used

---

[1] Bachelier, Louis, *Theorie de la Speculation* (Paris: Gauthier-Villars, 1900), trans. in Paul Cootner, ed. *The Random Character of Stock Market Prices* (Cambridge: M.I.T., 1964), pp. 17–18.

[2] Working, Holbrook, ''A Random Difference Series for Use in the Analysis of Time Series,'' *Journal of the American Statistical Association* 29 (March 1934): 11–24.

[3] Kendall, Maurice G., ''The Analysis of Economic Time Series, Part I: Prices,'' *Journal of the Royal Statistical Society* 96 (1953): 13.

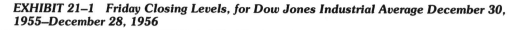

**EXHIBIT 21–1   *Friday Closing Levels, for Dow Jones Industrial Average December 30, 1955–December 28, 1956***

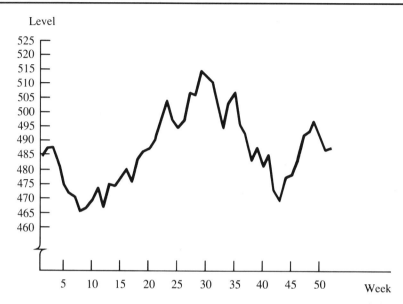

Source: Harry V. Roberts, "Stock Market 'Patterns' and Financial Analysis," *Journal of Finance* 14 (March 1959), p. 6.

by technical analysts. Roberts suggested that "the patterns of technical analysis may be little, if anything, more than a statistical artifact."[4]

Osborne's paper argued that not absolute price changes but rather changes in the logarithm of prices are independent of one another. This would be consistent with investor behavior that indicated an interest in proportionate changes in prices rather than absolute dollar changes. Osborne foresaw major advances in financial theory and research when he suggested studying the variance of price changes and the relationship of individual stocks to the general market.[5]

In the 1960s, increases in the capabilities of computers enabled researchers to undertake larger studies into the behavior of stock prices. The work of Fama serves as an example of the studies that tested for statistical independence of changes in stock prices.[6] Fama tested for serial correlation using daily price changes of the 30 stocks

---

[4] Roberts, Harry V., "Stock Market 'Patterns' and Financial Analysis: Methodological Suggests," *Journal of Finance* 14 (March 1959): 1.

[5] Osborne, M. E. M., "Brownian Motions in the Stock Market," *Operations Research* 7 (March–April 1959): 145–173.

[6] Fama, Eugene F., "The Behavior of Stock Market Prices," *Journal of Business* 38 (January 1965): 34–105.

**EXHIBIT 21–2   Simulated Market Levels for 52 Weeks**

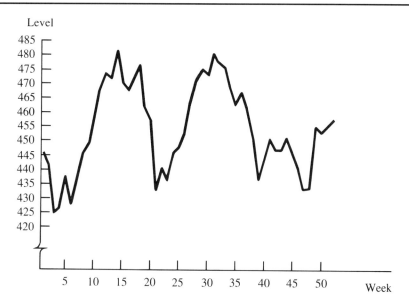

Source: Harry V. Roberts, "Stock Market 'Patterns' and Financial Analysis," *Journal of Finance* 14 (March 1959), p. 5.

in the Dow Jones Industrial Average for the five-year period ending in 1962. He examined successive price changes over intervals of one, four, nine, and sixteen days. Some evidence of serial correlations was found in the lagged price changes. However, these small levels of correlation would not allow one to build a trading system based on them that would be profitable after transaction costs.

Because a few extreme observations can dominate correlation coefficients, Fama performed a runs test. A runs test ignores the size of successive price changes and looks only at their signs. Daily price changes are coded as positive, negative, or zero. A sequence of $+ + 0 - - - + +$ consists of four runs of the same sign. If price trends exist, the number of runs would be less than if the series were random. Fama found that the number of runs was close to what would be expected in a random series.

***Filter Rules***   The weak form can be examined by testing the profitability of mechanical trading rules. An example is this filter rule: if the price of a security moves up at least $y$ percent, buy and hold the security until its price moves down at least $y$ percent from the subsequent high, at which time simultaneously sell and go short. Maintain the short position until the price rises at least $y$ percent from the subsequent low. Then cover the short position and buy the security.

Alexander tested this filter rule using daily data on price indexes from 1897 to

1959 and filters from 1 to 50 percent.[7] He found that some very small filters were profitable before transactions costs. However, they required very frequent trading and after transactions costs could not beat the return earned with a buy and hold strategy.

***Anomalous Evidence***   Some evidence contradicts the weak form of the hypothesis. A small but statistically significant weekend effect has been discovered. Prices tend to rise all week long and to peak on Friday. On Monday the prices are lower and begin another week's climb. The weekend effect is so small that a trader who buys stocks on Monday and sells them on Friday cannot make money after commissions. However, if an investor were making buy and sell decisions for other reasons, it would be wise to sell on Fridays and buy on Mondays.

There is also evidence of a seasonal effect in stock prices. Prices fall in late December and then rise in early January. This seasonal pattern is especially important in the stocks of small firms. At first, taxes were suspected as the cause of the seasonal effect. However, studies have not been able to document that the seasonal effect is caused by tax selling. Other studies indicate that the seasonal effect is worldwide, not just a phenomenon of U.S. markets and tax laws. Another possible cause could be the cash flow and liquidity patterns of pension funds and other investors.

In summary, the tests of the weak form of the efficient markets hypothesis have found a definite weekend effect, a definite seasonal effect, some evidence of serial correlation in stock price changes, and some filter rules that were profitable before transactions costs. However, the correlations and filter rules would not allow an investor to beat a buy and hold strategy after transaction costs are considered. Therefore, we conclude that historical prices provide limited information about future prices that would allow an investor to earn abnormal returns. However, the weak relationships that do exist tend to give hope to those searching for a profitable trading system based on past price patterns.

## The Semistrong Form of the Hypothesis

The semistrong form of the efficient markets hypothesis states that all available public information is quickly reflected in security prices. The weak form would have to hold for the semistrong form to hold because past price patterns are public information. The semistrong form considers prices to be summaries of the evaluations of public information by thousands of analysts and investors. Public information is so quickly and thoroughly appraised by so many knowledgeable evaluators that an investor cannot earn abnormal returns by using "old" public information.

Testing of the semistrong form investigates how quickly prices adjust to new information. If there were time delays as price slowly adjusted to new information, an investor could earn abnormal returns by using that information. This would refute

---

[7] Alexander, Sidney S., "Price Movements in Speculative Markets: Trends or Random Walks, No. 2," *Industrial Management Review* 5 (Spring 1964): 25–46.

the hypothesis. Researchers have studied the speed of price adjustment to several types of new public information. Four examples are corporate earnings announcements, Federal Reserve discount rate changes, stock split announcements, and large secondary offerings.

### Corporate Earnings Announcements

In 1966, Ball and Brown reported the first large-scale study of the effect that corporate earnings announcements have on stock prices.[8] Their data consisted of the annual earnings announcements of 261 firms over a 20-year period. Earnings were classified as either worse or better than expected. After adjusting for movement of the market as a whole, they found that prices adjusted months before the earnings were announced. On the average, only about 10 percent of the price adjustment occurred after the earnings were announced. This was not enough to earn abnormal returns after transaction costs.

Several subsequent studies examined the adjustment of stock prices to quarterly earnings announcements using improved methodology. Most found that prices adjusted before or at the time of the announcement. This is consistent with semistrong form efficiency.

However, in a 1982 study Rendleman, Jones, and Latané analyzed stock price adjustment to quarterly earnings announcements using improved methodology, a very large sample, and daily return data.[9] They estimated expected earnings on the basis of historical data. Then they computed unexpected earnings by comparing the actual earnings for the quarter to the expected earnings. They found that adjustment of prices starts 20 days before the earnings announcements, and much adjustment takes place at the time of the announcement. Most important, they found that roughly 50 percent of the adjustment of stock returns to unexpected quarterly earnings occurs over a 90-day period following the announcement. This would allow abnormal returns to be earned based on investment after the public announcement of the unexpected quarterly earnings. This is evidence against the semistrong form of the hypothesis.

### Federal Reserve Discount Rate Changes

We have learned that interest rate changes affect stock prices and that the Federal Reserve attempts to influence interest rates. One of its tools is changes in the discount rate. These changes are announced when the market is closed and receive extensive coverage in the financial press.

Waud examined the effects discount rate changes had on stock prices.[10] He found that the discount rate changes were anticipated; stock prices changed before the announcement. The very small price change on the first trading day following the discount

---

[8] Ball, Ray, and Brown, Philip, "An Empirical Evaluation of Accounting Income Numbers," *Journal of Accounting Research* 6 (Autumn 1968): 159–178.

[9] Rendleman, Jr., Richard J., Jones, Charles P., and Latané, Henry A., "Empirical Anomalies on Unexpected Earnings and the Importance of Risk Adjustments," *Journal of Financial Economies* 11 (November 1982): 269–287.

[10] Waud, Roger N., "Public Interpretation of Federal Reserve Discount Rate Changes: Evidence of the 'Announcement Effect,' " *Econometrica* 38 (March 1970): 231–250.

rate announcement was not enough to provide the investor with abnormal returns after transaction costs.

***Stock Split Announcements***    Many market advisors believe that abnormal profits can be earned by investing in stocks that are about to split. Some have even argued that abnormal price increases follow split announcements. If true, this would be strong evidence against the semistrong form, because splits in themselves provide no new information about the future earnings of the firm.

A study by Fama, Fisher, Jensen, and Roll examined all the 940 stock splits of NYSE listed stocks from 1927–1959.[11] Using monthly data, they examined market adjusted returns of each stock for the 29 months before and 30 months after the split. They found positive residual returns in each of the 29 months before the split. Because this is long before stock splits are announced, they believed that this was evidence that firms experiencing abnormally good returns are the ones that have stock splits. After the split month, positive residual returns were not found, even though 71.5 percent of the firms experienced greater percentage dividend increases in the year after the split than the average for NYSE listed companies. The authors suggest that when a split is announced, the market interprets it as a signal that the company is confident that future earnings will be sufficient to maintain the higher dividends. Thus, the price increases in the months before the split reflect the market's evolution of future earnings— not the effects of the split. They conclude that the market efficiently adjusts to new information.

Reilly and Drzycimski examined stock splits using price and volume data for 36 trading days: 15 trading days prior to the announcement of the split, the day of the announcement, and the 20 days following the announcement.[12] For each day, the analysis considered the closing price for the split stock relative to the closing price for the S&P 500 Index and the volume of trading for the split stock relative to total trading volume of the NYSE. Their sample consisted of 130 NYSE listed stocks that split two-for-one during the 13-year period 1964–1976. They found that stock splits provided no benefits to stockholders. The stock prices adjusted prior to or very shortly after the public announcement of stock splits. Their results indicate that abnormal profits were not available to investors who had to pay normal transactions costs. Therefore, the study supports the semistrong form.

***Large Secondary Offerings***    Observation of the market reveals that there is a price decline when there is a large secondary offering of a stock. Some observers believe the decline is a temporary inducement to get the large blocks of stock sold quickly.

---

[11] Fama, Eugene F., Fisher, Lawrence, Jensen, Michael, and Roll, Richard, "The Adjustment of Stock Prices to New Information," *International Economic Review* 10 (February 1969): 1–21.

[12] Reilly, Frank K., and Drzycimski, Eugene F., "Short-Run Profits for Stock Splits," *Financial Management* (Summer 1981): 64–74.

They believe the price later recovers. If the price decline were significant compared to transactions costs and if the price recovery were slow, this would be evidence of market inefficiency. Other observers believe the price decline is permanent. They see the decline as an immediate reaction to new information. The new information is that a large investor's view of the future prospects for the firm is less favorable than previously.

Scholes examined the price effects of large block sales of outstanding stock using daily closing prices.[13] He found that when block sales took place, there was an average price decline of from 1 to 10 percent. The decline was permanent and not the result of temporary price pressures. Further evidence that large block sales were an informational event was provided by an examination of the relationship between the price declines and the type of seller. Sales by corporate insiders, as well as investment companies, are likely to be seen as conveying more negative information than sales by estates and trusts. Empirical evidence shows that price declines are greater when corporate insiders and investment companies are the sellers. Scholes' finding of rapid, permanent adjustment to the new information provided by large secondary offerings supports the semistrong form.

Kraus and Stoll used intraday prices to undertake a much more detailed examination of the price effects of large secondary offerings.[14] They found a permanent price decline after some price recovery on the day of the block sale. Dann, Mayers, and Rabb used intraday prices to undertake the most extensive study of large block sales.[15] They were very careful to consider the actual mechanics of tradings and all transaction costs. They found that prices adjusted within 15 minutes of the block transaction. An NYSE nonmember could not earn abnormal profits after transactions costs by trading during the 15-minute period.

***Anomalous Evidence*** In addition to the Rendleman, Jones, and Latané study of quarterly earnings announcements, two important phenomena contradict the semistrong form of the hypothesis. One is called the *size effect*. Empirical studies have found that on a risk-adjusted basis the common stocks of small firms earn significantly higher rates of return than do the stocks of medium and large corporations. It also has been found that this size effect is related to the seasonal effect; most of the extra return is earned in the first few days of January.

It also has been documented that stocks with *low price-earnings (PE) ratios* earn additional risk-adjusted returns. The PE ratio—or perhaps the underlying variables for

---

[13] Scholes, Myron S., "The Market for Securities: Substitution versus Price Pressure and the Effects of Information on Share Prices," *Journal of Business* 45 (April 1972): 179–211.

[14] Kraus, Alan, and Stoll, Hans R., "Price Impacts of Block Trading on the New York Stock Exchange," *Journal of Finance* 27 (June 1972): 569–88.

[15] Dann, Larry Y., Mayers, David, and Rabb, Jr., Robert J., "Trading Rules, Large Blocks and the Speed of Price Adjustment," *Journal of Financial Economics* 4 (January 1977): 3–22.

which the PE ratio is a proxy—can explain a considerable portion of the variation in stock returns.

When evaluating the significance of the excess risk-adjusted returns from the size effect and the price-earnings effect, the question arises if risk is properly measured. Perhaps these phenomena are evidence of the weakness of the risk measurement developed from the portfolio theory discussed in the next chapter, rather than evidence against the semistrong form of the efficient markets hypothesis. At this time, we do not know if there are risk measurement problems or market inefficiencies. However, pending further analysis, these phenomena must be reported as exceptions to the efficient markets hypothesis.

In summary, most empirical tests uphold the semistrong form of the efficient markets hypothesis. Usually, prices adjust so quickly to new information that an investor cannot earn abnormal returns trading on that information. However, the Rendleman, Jones, and Latané study of quarterly earnings announcements, the weekend effect, and the price-earnings effect provide some counterevidence.

## The Strong Form of the Hypothesis

The strong form of the efficient markets hypothesis states that all public and private information is reflected quickly in security prices. This is stronger than the semistrong form because it argues that prices also reflect information not available to the public. In other words, it argues that even private information is so quickly reflected in security prices that abnormal profits cannot be made using it.

No one says that the strong form completely and accurately describes the capital markets. Studies of the semistrong form suggest some parties are profiting from the use of private information. When prices adjust before an announcement, it is very likely that either corporate insiders are trading on the information or it has been leaked to a few individuals who use it. The empirical question examines how extensive the deviation from strong form efficiency is.

Testings of the strong form investigate the returns earned by those who have monopolistic access to information. Because the use of this monopolistic information would subject the users to strong criticism and in some cases criminal prosecution, no one profiting from monopolistic access to information is going to supply data for a study and thereby make public his or her unfair advantage. Therefore, testing of the strong form is limited.

***Mutual Fund Studies***    One group that does have to make public its investment record is mutual funds. If one assumes that the managers and analysts employed by mutual funds have the contacts in the business and financial communities to obtain private information, studies of mutual fund performance are a test of strong form efficiency. If one assumes that the managers and analysts have access only to public information, studies of mutual fund performance are a test of semistrong form efficiency.

In Chapter 15, we discussed the performance of mutual funds. The conclusions were that, as a group, mutual funds do not earn abnormal profits, and no individual funds consistently earn abnormal profits. Therefore, the mutual fund performance studies provide evidence that strong form inefficiency is not widespread.

**Corporate Insiders**    A direct test of the strong form was undertaken by Jaffe.[16] Corporate insiders must report their trading to the SEC, and it is made public in the *Official Summary of Insider Trading*. Jaffe analyzed the trading reported therein and concluded that insiders earn abnormal returns. These abnormal returns earned by corporate insiders are evidence against the strong form of the hypothesis.

**Specialists**    The book of limit orders provides the exchange specialist with monopolistic information. Niederhoffer and Osborne found that specialists earn monopoly profits from trading on this information.[17] Of course, specialists perform a valuable economic function, and these profits might be considered payment for their market-making activity. In any case, their profits should be considered evidence against strong form efficiency.

In summary, the strong form of the efficient markets hypothesis should be rejected. Insiders and specialists earn abnormal returns using private information. However, the performance of mutual funds suggests that the opportunities available to profit from private information are very limited.

## Implications of the Hypothesis

Empirical testing has shown that the weak and semistrong forms of the efficient markets hypothesis provide a fairly good description of how effectively the market values securities. The testing of the strong form indicates that investors can profit from the use of private information, but that valuable private information is available to only a few market participants. The implications of these findings will be discussed under three topics: economic implications, security analysis, and portfolio management.

**Economic Implications**    The finding that capital markets are fairly efficient is good economic news. It means the markets are fulfilling their function of allocating scarce resources effectively. If prices reflect all relevant information about the discounted future earnings of the firm, investment money will flow to the firms having the most promising opportunities. If capital markets were inefficient, invesment funds would not be allocated optimally.

The finding of efficient markets is also good news for the investor. The individual investor can buy securities at fair prices; the resources of the large institutions do not give them great advantages. The results of all their research efforts are reflected in the

---

[16] Jaffe, Jeffrey, "The Effect of Regulation Changes on Insider Trading," *Bell Journal of Economics and Management Science* (Spring 1974): 93–121.

[17] Niederhoffer Victor, and Osborne, M. F. M., "Market Making and Reversal on the Stock Exchanges," *Journal of the American Statistical Association* 61 (December 1966): 897–916.

prices the individual investor pays. Investment in securities involves risk, but the source of most of the risk is unexpected future events rather than advantages other market participants may have.

**Security Analysis**    Studies of the weak form of the efficient markets hypothesis show that technical analysis based on past price patterns does not beat a buy and hold strategy. If one analyzes technical analysis, this is not a surprising finding. If price patterns recurred regularly, many technical analysts would be trying to anticipate the forming of the patterns and the buy and sell signals. Because each analyst would try to act before the others, prices would adjust before the signal became evident. The result is that competition among analysts would destroy the recurring pattern. There would be no hope of obtaining valuable information by the time a subscriber received the ''old'' technical information contained in a market advisory letter.

The studies of the semistrong form show that fundamental analysis using public information is unlikely to uncover mispriced securities. When identifying mispriced securities using fundamental analysis, you must ask why your evaluation varies from the market's evaluation. Having information not available to others might be the reason. This, however, is a rare occurrence. The more likely reason is that you did a better job of evaluating the available information. There are thousands of very good fundamental analysts; it is an unusual individual who consistently does a better job of evaluating investment information.

The individual investor should expect little, if any, extra return from studying information from advisory services, market letters, or annual reports. It is unlikely that subscribing to advisory services and market letters will result in extra profit after paying for the subscriptions.

**Portfolio Management**    Belief in efficient markets shifts some of the emphasis in portfolio management from security selection to risk management, tax management, and reducing transaction costs. In efficient markets, the source of higher returns is bearing more risk. You need to ensure that the risk level of your portfolio matches your risk preference. For the institutional portfolio, this means making sure the risk level of the portfolio meets the stated objectives.

Belief in efficient markets promotes a buy and hold strategy. If you cannot identify mispriced securities, there is no reason to buy and sell frequently. Most buying and selling will be for cash flow purposes or tax management. (Taxes are discussed in Chapter 24.) Most important, however, the investor will trade securities so that gains and losses are recognized in the most advantageous tax years. Additionally, a portfolio manager should be very concerned about research and transactions costs. If better performance does not result from these expenditures, they are not justified.

The evidence that some anomalies exist has developed a trend toward computer based, quantitative portfolio management. Some portfolio managers use computers and giant data bases to search for formulas that will help them exploit market inefficiencies and thereby outperform the market. The complex models that they develop allow them to select securities by screening sequentially on important characteristics. For example,

### Indexing Pension Funds

In the mid-1980s, many large pension funds began indexing a large portion of their portfolios. The indexed portion should match the return on the index chosen, most likely the S&P 500. As pension funds become large, indexing is almost a necessity. There is no use trying to beat the market when a fund is so large it has to invest in most of the large stocks. Small stocks do not provide large pension funds enough liquidity for them to invest large amounts.

Most funds are not completely indexed, however. Often 10 to 20 percent of the portfolio is actively managed. Part of this portion may be designated for investment in smaller companies or foreign issues.

the first screen could be on PE ratios, the second on growth rates of earnings, the third on size, and so on. Stocks passing all screening criteria would then be added to the portfolio. Related screening criteria would be developed for deciding when to sell.

# SUMMARY

We study market efficiency to learn how well the capital markets allocate financial resources and to learn about the investment environment. Capital markets are perfectly efficient when security prices reflect all available information about the economy, the financial markets, and specific firms. The studies of market efficiency are classified as tests of three subhypotheses based on the categories of information reflected in the prices.

The weak form of the efficient markets hypothesis states that all historical price information is reflected in the current market price. This means that past price patterns do not provide any valuable information about future prices. Tests of the weak form test for statistical dependence in price patterns and profitability of mechanical trading rules. The correlations and trading rules will not provide the investor with abnormal returns after transaction costs are considered.

The semistrong form of the efficient markets hypothesis states that all public information is quickly reflected in security prices. Testing of the semistrong form examines how quickly prices adjust to new information, such as corporate earnings announcements, Federal Reserve discount rate changes, stock split announcements, and large secondary offerings. Most tests find that prices adjust so quickly to new information that abnormal returns cannot be made trading on that information.

The strong form of the efficient markets hypothesis states that all public and private information is quickly reflected in security prices. Testing of the strong form is limited. Studies of mutual fund performance show that they do not profit from private information. However, studies of corporate insiders and specialists show these groups do profit from private information. The strong form of the hypothesis is rejected; however, only a few market participants have access to valuable private information.

## QUESTIONS

1. What are two reasons for studying market efficiency?

2. Describe perfectly efficient capital markets. What three conditions will produce perfectly efficient markets?

3. Define the weak, semistrong, and strong forms of the efficient markets hypothesis.

4. Summarize the evidence concerning the weak form of the hypothesis.

5. Summarize the evidence concerning the semistrong form of the hypothesis.

6. What are the implications of the efficient markets hypothesis?

## READINGS

Cootner, Paul H., ed. *The Random Character of Stock Market Prices,* Rev. ed. Cambridge, MA: M.I.T. Press, 1964.
   *This book contains many of the early studies into market efficiency.*

Fama, Eugene F. ''Efficient Capital Markets: A Review of Theory and Empirical Work,'' *Journal of Finance* 25 (May 1970): 383–417.
   *This article is the best summary of the efficient markets research undertaken before 1970.*

Gropper, Diane L. ''Mining the Market's Inefficiencies,'' *Institutional Investor* 19 (July 1985): 81–91.
   *This article reports how money managers use complex computer models to profit from market inefficiencies. It is a companion article to the Rohrer article listed below.*

Haugen, Robert A. *Modern Investment Theory.* Englewood Cliffs, N.J.: Prentice-Hall, 1986.
   *Chapter 22 contains a summary of the recent tests of market efficiency.*

Keane, Simon M. ''The Efficient Market Hypothesis on Trial,'' *Financial Analysts Journal* 42 (March–April 1986): 58–63.
   *This article discusses the implications of the evidence that conflicts with the efficient markets hypothesis.*

Lorie, James H., Dodd, Peter, and Kimpton, Mary Hamilton. *The Stock Market: Theories and Evidence,* 2d ed. Homewood, IL: Richard D. Irwin, Inc., 1985.
   *Chapter 4 summarizes the efficient markets hypothesis and the testing of it. Chapter 5 discusses the implications of the efficient markets hypothesis.*

Rohrer, Julie. ''Ferment in Academia,'' *Institutional Investor* 19 (July 1985): 69–78.
   *This article reports on some anomalies in stock market prices and on their implications.*

# *Portfolio Theory*

## OUTLINE

Introduction

Portfolio Return

Portfolio Risk
    Covariance and Correlation Coefficent
    Portfolio Standard Deviation

Portfolio Opportunities

Investor Utility Preferences
    The Utility Function
    Indifference Curves

Portfolio Selection
    The Role of the Risk-Free Security
    The Capital Market Line
    The Separation Theorem

The Capital Asset Pricing Model
    The Security Market Line
    Empirical Tests

Arbitrage Pricing Theory

Summary

## OBJECTIVES

When you have finished studying this chapter, you should understand

1. The measurement of portfolio return and risk and the risk reduction power of diversification.

2. The effect that an investor's utility preferences have on portfolio selection.

3. The capital asset pricing model's and the arbitrage pricing theory's approaches to security valuation.

# 22

## *Asset Allocation*

Asset allocation is an investor's game plan to diversify his or her assets among categories such as stocks, bonds, money market securities, real estate, and precious metals. Many financial planners believe the asset allocation decision is more important than the securities selection decision because most of the returns an investor earns depend on how well the categories do. Individual securities tend to follow the performance of all assets in their category. When stocks and bonds are not performing well, real estate and precious metals might be, and vice versa.

Strategic (long-term) asset allocation became popular in the mid 1980s. It addresses the question of what proportion of an investor's wealth should be in each of the categories. As the investor progresses through life, the allocations are changed to reflect new circumstances and economic conditions.

In the late 1980s, some money managers began offering tactical (short-term) asset allocation plans to pension funds. These plans move money back and forth among stocks, bonds, and money market securities in anticipation of market trends. They are usually based on very quantitative, computerized models, and they readjust the allocations as frequently as every month.

## INTRODUCTION

A portfolio is a combination of investments. Because most investors own more than one security, they are more interested in the performance of their total portfolio than in the performance of the individual securities. Although the return from a portfolio is the sum of the returns from the securities in it, portfolios have an advantage over single security investment holdings in that some of the risk can be diversified away.

In this chapter, we examine the return and risk of portfolios and the selection of the optimal portfolio for the investor. An important aspect of the discussion is how each security affects the total risk of the portfolio. The important measure of a security's risk will not be the dispersion of its returns but rather how the security contributes to the dispersion of the portfolio's expected returns. This will lead us to examine the relationship between a security's expected return and its risk. During the development of these topics, we will look at the measurement of an investor's return and risk preferences.

---

# PORTFOLIO RETURN

The first thing an investor will want to know about an investment portfolio is its expected return. The dollar amount of the expected return from the portfolio is simply the sum of the dollar amounts of the expected returns from each investment in the portfolio. The expected rate of return on a portfolio is the weighted average of the expected rates of return on the investments in the portfolio. The weights used are the proportions of the total portfolio value invested in each security. This relationship is put in the form of Equation 22–1.

$$E(R_p) = \sum_{i=1}^{n} w_i \, E(r_i) \tag{22–1}$$

where:

$E(R_p)$ = the expected return on the portfolio

$w_i$ = the portion of the portfolio invested in security $i$

$E(r_i)$ = the expected return on security $i$

$n$ = the total number of securities in the portfolio

Exhibit 22–1 displays forecasted returns on two investments. In order to keep this example manageable, we assume that there are only five possible outcomes for the economy. These states of nature and the probabilities of their occurring are listed in columns 1 and 2. Columns 3 and 4 list the projected rates of return on Investments A and B for the different states of nature. Also shown are the expected values and the standard deviations of these returns. We will discuss columns 5, 6, and 7 soon.

Using Equation 22–1 and the data in the table, we compute that the expected return on a portfolio with half the money in Investment A and the other half in Investment B is 18 percent.

$$E(R_p) = W_A E(r_A) + W_B E(r_B)$$
$$= .5\,(.21) + .5\,(.15)$$
$$= .18$$

## EXHIBIT 22–1  Covariance Example

| 1 State of Nature | 2 Probability | 3 Return on Investment A | 4 Return on Investment B | 5 $R_{Ai} - E(r_A)$ | 6 $R_{Bi} - E(r_B)$ | 7 $p_i[r_{Ai} - E(r_A)][r_{Bi} - E(r_B)]$ |
|---|---|---|---|---|---|---|
| Very poor | .1 | .10 | .18 | −.11 | .03 | .1(−.11)(.03) = −.00033 |
| Poor | .2 | .16 | .17 | −.05 | .02 | .2(−.05)(.02) = −.0002 |
| Average | .4 | .22 | .15 | .01 | 0 | .4(.01)(0) = 0 |
| Good | .2 | .25 | .13 | .04 | −.02 | .2(.04)(−.02) = −.00016 |
| Very good | .1 | .30 | .12 | .09 | −.03 | .1(.09)(−.03) = −.00027 |
|  | 1.0 |  |  |  |  | −.00096 |
| $E(r)$ |  | .21 | .15 |  |  |  |
| $\sigma^2$ |  | .00288 | .00034 |  |  |  |
| $\sigma$ |  | .05366 | .01844 |  |  |  |

# PORTFOLIO RISK

The risk of a portfolio is measured by its standard deviation. However, in order to compute the standard deviation of a portfolio, the covariance between the returns of each pair of securities in the portfolio must be known. Therefore, we must learn to compute and interpret the covariance before proceeding with computation of the portfolio standard deviation.

## Covariance and Correlation Coefficient

The covariance measure is similar to the variance except that it involves two different investments. The covariance measures to what extent the two investments vary together. A positive covariance will exist when one investment's return is usually above its mean when the second investment's return is above its mean. A negative covariance will exist when one investment's return is usually below its mean when the second investment's return is above its mean.

The returns forecast on Investment A are $r_{A1}, r_{A2} \ldots r_{An}$; the returns forecast on Investment B are $r_{B1}, r_{B2} \ldots r_{Bn}$; and $E(r_A)$ and $E(r_B)$ are the expected returns on Investments A and B. Using this notation, Equation 22–2 gives the formula for the covariance.

$$\text{cov}\,(r_A, r_B) = \sum_{i=1}^{n} p_i\,[r_{Ai} - E(r_A)][r_{Bi} - E(r_B)] \qquad (22–2)$$

In columns 5, 6, and 7 of Exhibit 22–1 this formula is used to compute the covariance between Investments A and B.

Like the variance, the covariance is measured in units of return squared, which does not have much intuitive attractiveness. However, if the covariance is divided by the product of the standard deviations of the returns of each of the two investments, the result is a number with no units, which ranges between $-1$ and $+1$. This number is called the correlation coefficient, and it measures the correlation between two variables. Equation 22–3 is the formula for the correlation coefficient ($\rho$)

$$\rho_{AB} = \frac{\text{cov}\,(r_A, r_B)}{(\sigma_A)(\sigma_B)} \qquad (22–3)$$

Using this equation, we find that the correlation coefficient between Investments A and B is $-.97$.

$$\rho_{AB} = \frac{-.00096}{(.05366)(.01844)}$$
$$= -.97$$

If the correlation coefficient is $+1$, there is perfect correlation; if it is 0, there is no correlation; and if it is $-1$, there is perfect negative correlation. Examination of the returns in columns 3 and 4 of Exhibit 22–1 shows that Investment A does better in good economic times while Investment B does worse.

Multiplying both sides of Equation 22–3 by the product of the standard deviations will give Equation 22–4.

$$\text{cov}(r_A, r_B) = \rho_{AB}\, \sigma_A\, \sigma_B \qquad (22\text{--}4)$$

## Portfolio Standard Deviation

Equation 22–5 is the formula for the variance of a portfolio.

$$\sigma_p^2 = \sum_{i=1}^{n} \sum_{j=1}^{n} w_i\, w_j\, \text{cov}\,(r_i,\, r_j) \qquad (22\text{--}5)$$

This equation shows that the variance of the portfolio depends on the covariance of each pair of securities in the portfolio and on the weight of each security in the portfolio. Because a portfolio may be comprised of many securities, the securities are numbered 1, 2, 3 . . . $n$ to keep track of them. The weight of security $i$ ($w_i$) equals the amount invested in $i$ divided by the total amount invested in the portfolio. If you invest \$1,000 in each of three investments, then the weight of each investment is $\frac{1}{3}$. If, on the other hand, you invest \$1,000 in one investment and \$500 in two other investments, then the weights of the investments are $\frac{1}{2}$, $\frac{1}{4}$, and $\frac{1}{4}$, respectively.

By the definition of the covariance, the cov ($r_i$, $r_j$) equals cov ($r_j$, $r_i$). The cov ($r_i$, $r_i$) is the covariance between investment $i$ and itself, which (as can be seen by the defining equation) is the same as the variance of investment $i$.

For a portfolio of two investments, 1 and 2, the variance of the portfolio is

$$\sigma_p^2 = w_1 w_1\, \text{cov}(r_1, r_1) + w_2 w_2\, \text{cov}\,(r_2, r_2) + 2\, w_1 w_2\, \text{cov}\,(r_1, r_2)$$

For a portfolio of three investments, 1, 2, and 3, the variance of the portfolio is

$$\sigma_p^2 = w_1 w_1\, \text{cov}(r_1, r_1) + w_2 w_2\, \text{cov}\,(r_2, r_2) + w_3 w_3\, \text{cov}\,(r_3, r_3)$$
$$+ 2\, w_1 w_2\, \text{cov}(r_1, r_2) + 2\, w_1 w_3\, \text{cov}\,(r_1, r_3) + 2\, w_2 w_3\, \text{cov}\,(r_2, r_3)$$

For large portfolios the computation of the variance is very cumbersome. For a portfolio of 10 investments, it has 55 terms; for a portfolio of 100, it has 5,050 terms. The standard deviation of a portfolio is simply the square root of the variance.

---

***PRACTICE*** Calculate the variance and standard deviation of a portfolio formed by the two investments whose
***PROBLEM 1*** returns are given in Exhibit 22–1. The portfolio was formed by equal investment in each security.

*Solution*

Let Investment 1 be A and Investment 2 be B.

$$w_1 = .5; w_2 = .5$$

$$\text{cov } (r_1,r_1) = \text{variance } (r_1) = .00288$$

$$\text{cov } (r_2,r_2) = \text{variance } (r_2) = .00034$$

$$\text{cov } (r_1,r_2) = -.00096$$

$$\sigma_p^2 = w_1 w_1 \text{ cov } (r_1,r_1) + w_2 w_2 \text{ cov } (r_2,r_2) + 2 w_1 w_2 \text{ cov } (r_1,r_2)$$

$$= (.5)(.5)(.00288) + (.5)(.5)(.00034) + 2(.5)(.5)(-.00096)$$

$$= .00072 + .000085 - .00048$$

$$= .000325$$

$$\sigma_p = \sqrt{.000325} = .01803$$

**PRACTICE PROBLEM 2** Calculate the variance and standard deviation of a portfolio formed by the two investments whose returns are given in Exhibit 22–1. However, this time weigh Investment A as .25 and Investment B as .75.

*Solution*

$$\sigma_p^2 = w_1 w_1 \text{ cov } (r_1,r_1) + w_2 w_2 \text{ cov } (r_2,r_2) + 2 w_1 w_2 \text{ cov } (r_1,r_2)$$

$$= (.25)(.25)(.00288) + (.75)(.75)(.00034) + 2(.25)(.75)(-.00096)$$

$$= .00018 + .000191 - .00036$$

$$= .000011$$

$$\sigma_p = \sqrt{.000011} = .00332$$

Exhibit 22–2 summarizes the results of the practice problems we have been doing. It shows the expected return and risk on five different portfolios obtained by changing the proportions of the portfolio invested in Securities A and B. Portfolio 1 was 100

**EXHIBIT 22–2  Return and Risk of a Two Security Portfolio**

| Portfolio Number | Percent in Security A | Percent in Security B | $E(r_p)$ | $\sigma_p$ |
|---|---|---|---|---|
| 1 | 100 | 0 | .21 | .05366 |
| 2 | 75 | 25 | .195 | .03579 |
| 3 | 50 | 50 | .18 | .01803 |
| 4 | 25 | 75 | .165 | .00332 |
| 5 | 0 | 100 | .15 | .01844 |

percent investment in Security A while Portfolio 5 was 100 percent investment in Security B. The other three portfolios were obtained by investing in both securities. Notice that Portfolios 3 and 4 would be preferred to 5 because they offer more return and less risk. In fact, because the two investments have negative correlation between them, Portfolio 4 has very little risk. If the investments had been positively, but not perfectly, correlated, risk reduction through diversification would still have been possible, but it would not have been as dramatic. In the case of perfect correlation, diversification does not reduce portfolio risk.

# PORTFOLIO OPPORTUNITIES

We have learned that the expected return and standard deviation of a portfolio can be computed if the securities' expected returns, variances, and covariances are known. Because a large number of securities are available and because different portfolios result from changing the portions of the portfolio invested in different securities, a huge number of portfolios is available to the investor.

In Exhibit 22–3, portfolios are graphed in $E(R_p)$ and $\sigma_p$ space. Each dot represents a portfolio with a particular risk-return combination. The portfolio **opportunity set** is composed of all the available portfolios. It is the shaded area in the figure.

In some cases, the choice between two portfolios in the opportunity set is easy because some portfolios dominate others. A **dominant portfolio** offers a higher return and the same risk as the other portfolio or it offers less risk and the same return. The investor would not choose a portfolio dominated by another portfolio choice.

**EXHIBIT 22–3  Portfolio Opportunities**

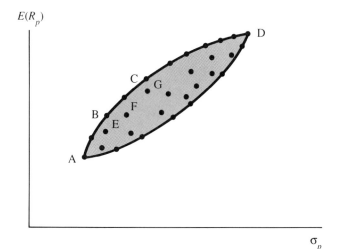

Examine Portfolios B and F. B dominates F because it offers less risk and the same return. Given the choice between Portfolios B and F, the investor would choose B. Examine Portfolios C and G. C dominates G because it offers more return and the same risk. Given the choice between C and G, the investor would choose C. A careful analysis of Exhibit 22–3 will show that any portfolio in the interior of the opportunity set is dominated by one on the upper edge of the opportunity set. The portfolios on the upper edge of the opportunity set, on line ABCD, are efficient portfolios. **Efficient portfolios** offer the maximum return for a given amount of risk or the least risk for a given amount of return. The efficient set is the collection of all the efficient portfolios. The efficient set is the efficient frontier of the opportunity set.

# INVESTOR UTILITY PREFERENCES

In order to know which portfolio from the efficient set an investor will choose, we must know about the investor's preferences toward the risk-return tradeoff. Utility theory helps us understand investor choice.

Investors strive to maximize the utility (satisfaction) they receive from present and future consumption. Utility maximization involves two decisions: the consumption-investment tradeoff and the return-risk tradeoff. Each period, investors must decide what portion of their wealth to consume. This division of wealth will depend on the return expected on the wealth invested. However, because we live in an uncertain world, the future wealth obtained from investment is not definitely known. Therefore, risk in addition to expected return affects the investor's utility.

---

**EXHIBIT 22–4   An Investor's Utility Function**

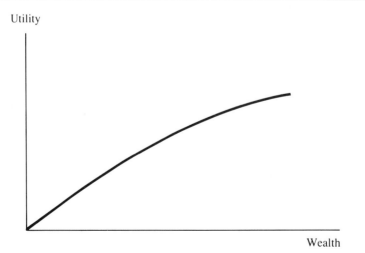

---

## The Utility Function

Utility is measured in units called utiles. Exhibit 22–4 reflects an investor's utility for different amounts of wealth. The utility function is drawn concave to the origin. This concavity reflects that marginal utility is a decreasing function of wealth. An investor who is averse to risk has a concave utility function. Appendix 22A shows how a particular investor's utility function can be obtained.

## Indifference Curves

An investor's utility function reflects the tradeoff that the investor makes between expected return and risk. These preferences can be displayed by indifference curves graphed in expected return and standard deviation space. Exhibit 22–5 reflects the indifference curves of a typical investor.

The figure shows that the investor is indifferent among Portfolios A, B, and C. The additional return on Portfolio B is just enough to compensate the investor for the additional risk that it has over Portfolio A. The additional return on Portfolio C is just enough to compensate the investor for the additional risk it has over Portfolio B. The investor will choose a portfolio on the highest possible indifference curve. For this reason, Portfolio D is preferred over A, B, and C. Likewise, Portfolio E is preferred over D.

The slope of the indifference curve reflects the investor's risk-return tradeoff. Exhibit 22–6 shows the indifference curves of a very risk-averse investor while Exhibit 22–7 shows the indifference curves of an aggressive investor.

---

**EXHIBIT 22–5   *Indifference Curves***

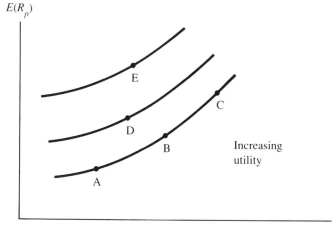

**EXHIBIT 22–6** **Indifference Curves of a Very Risk Averse Investor**

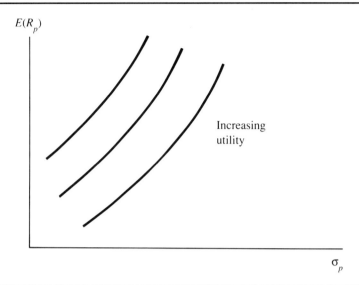

**EXHIBIT 22–7** **Indifference Curves of an Aggressive Investor**

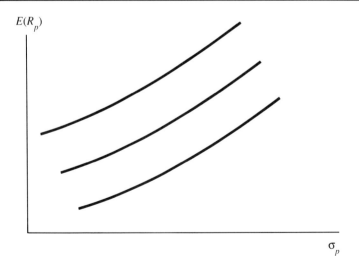

# PORTFOLIO SELECTION

Which portfolio the investor chooses depends on the portfolios that are available and the investor's indifference curves. Exhibit 22–8 brings together the portfolio opportunity set from Exhibit 22–3 and the investor's indifference curves from Exhibit 22–5. The investor wants to choose the portfolio offering the best return-risk tradeoff. Graphically, the investor will choose the portfolio represented by the point tangent to the highest indifference curve and the efficient frontier of the opportunity set.

In Exhibit 22–8 Portfolio A would be selected by the investor with these indifference curves. A more or less risk-averse investor would have indifference curves with different slopes and therefore would pick a different portfolio from the efficient frontier. Portfolio B might be tangent to the highest obtainable indifference curve of a more risk-averse investor while Portfolio C might be tangent to the highest obtainable indifference curve of a less risk-averse investor.

## The Role of the Risk-Free Security

The analysis of portfolio selection changes when we assume one can invest in a risk-free security. In practice, buying short-maturity Treasury bills is a good proxy for investing in a risk-free security. In order to simplify the analysis, we also want to assume the investor can lend at the risk-free rate. One cannot get a rate that low, but

---

**EXHIBIT 22–8  *Portfolio Opportunity Set and Indifference Curves***

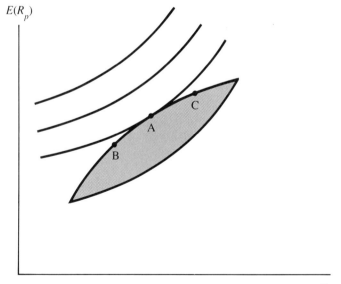

**EXHIBIT 22–9   Capital Market Line**

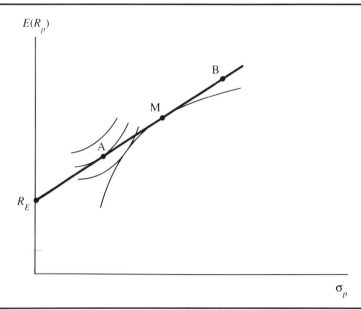

some forms of borrowing, such as margin accounts, have rates near the Treasury bill rate.

In Exhibit 22–9 a line is drawn from the point on the vertical axis that depicts the return on the risk-free security through the point of tangency, M, on the efficient frontier. Point M represents the return and risk tradeoff available in what is called the market portfolio. An investor can achieve any return-risk combination on this line. Points on the line segment $R_F$M are achieved by the investor putting part of his or her wealth in the risk-free security and the other part in Portfolio M. Points on the line beyond point M are achieved by the investor borrowing at the risk-free rate and investing original wealth and the borrowed money in portfolio M. The expected return of a portfolio where both borrowing and lending at the risk-free rate are possible is shown in Equation 22–6.

$$E(R_p) = wR_F + (1 - w) E(R_M) \tag{22–6}$$

where:

> $w$ = the proportion of the wealth invested in the risk-free security (if instead of investing at the risk-free rate the investor is borrowing, $w$ is negative)
>
> $E(R_M)$ = the expected return on the market portfolio

Because by definition the standard deviation of the risk-free security is zero, the standard deviation of a portfolio where both borrowing and lending at the risk-free rate is possible is given by Equation 22–7.

$$\sigma_p = (1 - w)\,\sigma_M \qquad\qquad (22\text{–}7)$$

The return-risk combinations on the line from $R_F$ through M now dominate all portfolios of the old efficient frontier except Portfolio M. An examination of Exhibit 22–9 shows the investor can achieve the return-risk combination depicted by point A and move to a higher indifference curve than could be reached without bringing the risk-free security into the analysis. An aggressive investor might borrow and invest in Portfolio M and achieve the return-risk combination depicted by point B. This would put him or her on a higher indifference curve than was possible to obtain before borrowing was brought into the analysis.

## The Capital Market Line

The line from the risk-free return through the point of tangency with the efficient frontier is called the capital market line. The **capital market line** describes the tradeoff between expected return and risk for various efficient portfolios. Equation 22–8 algebraically represents the capital market line.

$$E(R_p) = R_F + \left[\frac{E(R_M) - R_F}{\sigma_M}\right]\sigma_p \qquad\qquad (22\text{–}8)$$

where:

$E(R_M)$ = the expected return on Portfolio M

$\sigma_M$ = the standard deviation of Portfolio M

The term in brackets in Equation 22–8 is the slope of the capital market line. It represents the price the market pays for bearing risk.

In words, Equation 22–8 states that the expected return on an efficient portfolio equals the risk-free rate of return plus a risk premium. The risk premium is the product of the market price for risk bearing and the standard deviation of the portfolio.

## The Separation Theorem

The market portfolio has a unique status. It is the only portfolio of risky assets that investors will purchase; all other portfolios in the opportunity set are dominated by the capital market line. Therefore, every security will be priced based on how it fits into the market portfolio. The market portfolio will contain every outstanding security.

Investing can now be separated into two independent decisions.

1. Selecting securities for the market portfolio. This selection does not depend on the risk preferences of the investor.

2. Dividing the investor's wealth between the risk-free security and the market portfolio. An aggressive investor will borrow and put these proceeds into the market portfolio in addition to his or her other wealth. The division between the risk-free security and the market portfolio will depend on the risk preferences of the investor.

The separation theorem can be applied to practical investment decisions. Instead of trying to pick securities to meet risk preferences, an investor can divide money between an index fund and a money market fund. An aggressive investor can borrow to obtain extra money to put into the index fund.

# THE CAPITAL ASSET PRICING MODEL

The capital asset pricing model (CAPM) uses this portfolio selection model to value individual securities. Like every model, the CAPM was developed based on certain assumptions. Remember that the value of a model is based on the empirical testing of it, not the validity of its assumptions. The assumptions necessary for derivation of the CAPM are:

1. Efficient capital markets exist where all securities are infinitely divisible with no investor large enough to affect price; there are no transactions costs or taxes.

2. Investors are well-informed and have similar expectations about the returns and risks of securities.

3. Investors base their expectations on a common holding period, perhaps one year.

The CAPM describes the relationship between expected return and risk for a security. The important issue for a security is how it will affect the risk of the market portfolio.

The total risk of a security can be divided into two components: systematic and unsystematic risk. **Systematic risk** measures the relationship between the security's returns and the market portfolio's returns. Beta ($\beta$) is an index of systematic risk. **Unsystematic risk** is return dispersion that is unique to the firm. Unsystematic risk can be eliminated through diversification. Equation 22–9 summarizes the relationship among total, systematic, and unsystematic risk.

$$\sigma_i^2 = \beta_i^2 \, \sigma_M^2 + \sigma_\epsilon^2 \tag{22–9}$$

where:

$\sigma_i^2 =$ the variance of the rates of return on the security (total risk)

$\beta_i^2 \sigma_M^2 =$ systematic risk

$\sigma_\epsilon^2 =$ unsystematic risk

For a typical stock about 70 percent of the total risk is due to unsystematic factors; the remaining 30 percent is systematic risk. Various empirical studies have shown that a randomly chosen portfolio of about 15 securities eliminates most of the unsystematic risk. Enough unexpected good things happen to offset the unexpected bad things. Investors who own less than 15 securities are not fully diversified. Investors with small amounts to invest should achieve diversification by investing in a mutual fund. On the other end of the spectrum, there is little advantage to be obtained from diversification beyond 15 securities.

## The Security Market Line

The **security market line** (SML) describes the relationship between a security's expected return and its systematic risk. Exhibit 22–10 graphs the SML and Equation 22–10 gives the equation for it.

$$E(r_i) = R_F + [E(R_M) - R_F] \beta_i \qquad \qquad (22\text{--}10)$$

This equation states that the expected return on a security is equal to the expected excess returns on the market $[E(R_M) - R_F]$ times $\beta_i$, the index of the security's systematic risk.

Frequently, after stock analysts have predicted the returns and betas of stocks, the points that represent the stocks are graphed with the SML. Securities above the SML offer more return than justified by their systematic risk; they are underpriced. Securities below the SML do not offer the return justified by their systematic risk; they are overpriced.

---

**EXHIBIT 22–10  Security Market Line**

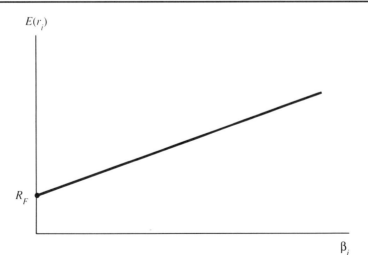

The market is expected to return 17 percent. The risk-free rate is 7 percent. The following investments are available.

| Security | Predicted Return (in Percent) | Beta |
|----------|-------------------------------|------|
| ABC | 18 | 1.1 |
| DEF | 20 | 1.2 |
| GHI | 14 | .8 |

Which securities are over- or underpriced?

*Solution*

$$SML: E(r_i) = R_F + [E(R_M) - R_F]\beta_i$$

$$= .07 + [.17 - .07]\beta_i$$

$$ABC: E(r_i) = .07 + [.17 - .07]1.1$$

$$= .18$$

The return justified by the SML (.18) equals the predicted return (.18). ABC is properly priced.

$$DEF: E(r_i) = .07 + [.17 - .07]1.2$$

$$= .19$$

The return justified by the SML (.19) is less than the forecasted return (.20). DEF is underpriced.

$$GHI: E(r_i) = .07 + [.17 - .07].8$$

$$= .15$$

The return justified by the SML (.15) is more than the forecasted return (.14). GHI is overpriced.

## Empirical Tests

There have been many empirical tests of how well the CAPM describes stock returns. The basic methodology of the empirical tests involves four steps.

1. Estimate securities' betas from past performance data.
2. Group the securities into portfolios based on the size of their betas. For example, the 10 percent of the securities with the lowest betas form Portfolio A, the 10 percent with the next lowest betas form Portfolio B, and so on.
3. Measure the performance of the portfolios by computing the return on each portfolio in a subsequent period.
4. Regress the portfolio returns on the portfolio betas.

The evidence confirms a positive linear relationship between return and beta; that is, the higher beta portfolios have higher returns. However, the intercept of the SML is higher than the risk-free rate and the slope is less than predicted. This means that the extra return on high versus low beta stocks is not as great as the CAPM predicts.

***Empirical Difficulties***   There are other empirical problems with security betas.

1. Security betas are unstable over time. They drift toward 1. That is, high beta stocks tend to become less risky and low beta stocks tend to become more risky as time passes.
2. A security's beta will vary depending on the unit of time used to compute it. That is, betas are different if they are computed using weekly, monthly, and quarterly returns.
3. Betas depend on the proxy used to measure the market returns when they are computed. Use of different market indexes, for example the NYSE composite instead of the S&P 500, can result in a different security beta.

***Betas in Practice***   Market advisory publications have different procedures for computing beta. Merrill Lynch betas are computed using security and market returns that consider only price changes, not dividends. Merrill Lynch uses the S&P 500 for the market portfolio and bases the computation on 60 monthly observations. It uses Equation 22–11 to adjust for the bias discussed above.

$$\beta_{ML} = .33743 + .66257\beta \qquad\qquad (22\text{--}11)$$

Value Line betas also are computed using only price changes and not dividends. For the market portfolio, Value Line uses the NYSE Composite. It bases the computations on 260 weekly observations. It uses Equation 22–12 to adjust for bias.

$$\beta_{VL} = .35 + .67\beta \qquad\qquad (22\text{--}12)$$

# ARBITRAGE PRICING THEORY

**Arbitrage pricing theory** (APT) is a more complex model than the CAPM. While the CAPM attempts to explain security returns based only on the security's systematic risk, APT explains security returns by using more than one causal factor. APT states the market equilibrium will be characterized by a linear relationship between each security's expected return and its loadings on several factors common to the returns of all securities. Equation 22–13 describes this relationship.

$$\bar{r}_i = E(r_i) + b_{i1}\,F_1 + b_{i2}\,F_2 + \ldots + b_{in}\,F_n + \epsilon_i \qquad\qquad (22\text{--}13)$$

where:

$\bar{r}$ = the stochastic rate of return on security $i$

$E(r_i)$ = the expected return on security $i$

$F_1, F_2 \ldots F_n$ = return generating factors common to all securities

$b_{i1}, b_{i2} \ldots b_{in}$ = the sensitivity of security $i$'s returns to the movement of the common factors

$\epsilon_i$ = an unsystematic risk component

The attractiveness of APT is based on its assumptions, which are less stringent and more plausible than those of the CAPM, and its ability to explain security return. APT requires no utility assumptions beyond monotonicity and concavity. It is a multiperiod model. Importantly, APT does not require the assumption of the existence of a market portfolio; therefore, in testing it one does not need to decide on the "best" proxy for the market portfolio.

In testing APT, factor analysis is used to identify the factors common to all security returns. Research by Roll and Ross has identified four underlying factors:

1. Changes in the expected level of industrial production
2. Changes in a default risk premium (measured by the differences in promised yields to maturity on AAA versus Baa corporate bonds)
3. Twists in the yield curve (measured by the differences in promised yields to maturity on long- and short-term government bonds)
4. Unanticipated inflation[1]

An important question in testing APT is whether it explains security returns better than the CAPM. The results of different studies conflict. Some find no improvement over CAPM when using APT. Others find APT better. APT is an improvement over CAPM particularly when the security returns contain some CAPM anomaly, such as the size effect (the CAPM does not adequately explain the returns of the stocks of small firms). More empirical evidence is necessary before the multifactor APT replaces the single factor as the major model used to explain security returns.

# SUMMARY

Most investors own a portfolio of securities and therefore are interested in the portfolio return and risk. The rate of return on the portfolio is the weighted average of the rates of return on individual securities in the portfolio. However, portfolio risk can be reduced by combining securities with less than perfect positive correlation.

---

[1] Roll, Richard W., and Ross, Stephen A., "The Arbitrage Pricing Theory Approach to Strategic Portfolio Planning," *Financial Analysts Journal* 40 (May–June 1984): 14–26.

The portfolios that offer the most return for a given amount of risk or offer the least risk for a given amount of return are efficient portfolios. The capital market line describes the relationship between portfolio return and portfolio risk. The security market line describes the relationship between security returns and beta. Arbitrage pricing theory relates security returns to more than one factor.

# QUESTIONS

1. What is the relationship between the rates of return on a portfolio and the rates of return on the securities in the portfolio?

2. Describe the relationship between the risk of a portfolio and the risk of the securities in the portfolio.

3. What does the covariance measure? How is it related to the correlation coefficient?

4. When does a portfolio dominate another portfolio? What is an efficient portfolio?

5. Name two decisions an individual needs to make in the utility maximization process.

6. Describe the utility function of a risk-averse individual.

7. What do an investor's indifference curves indicate? Describe the indifference curves of an aggressive investor and of a risk-averse investor.

8. Given the opportunity set, what portfolio will an investor choose? How does being able to lend and borrow at the risk-free rate change the portfolio selection process?

9. What is the capital market line? What does its slope represent?

10. What is the market portfolio?

11. What is the separation theorem?

12. List the assumptions of the capital asset pricing model. What does it describe?

13. What is the security market line? How is it used in security selection?

14. Describe the procedure for testing the CAPM. What are the results of the empirical tests?

15. What are the empirical difficulties with beta? How do market advisory services adjust for them?

16. What is arbitrage pricing theory? List its advantages over the CAPM. What factors have been identified in the empirical studies using it?

# PROBLEMS

1. The expected return on Stock A is 10%; the expected return on Stock B is 8%. If you put 80% of your investment money in Stock A and 20% in Stock B, what is your expected return?

2. The expected return on Stock A is 12%; the expected return on Stock B is 16%. If you put 25% of your investment money in Stock A and 75% in Stock B, what is your expected return?

3. You own five stocks. The expected return on each and the proportion of your money invested in each are given.

| Stock | Proportion | Expected Return |
|-------|------------|-----------------|
| A | .2 | .12 |
| B | .1 | .08 |
| C | .3 | .15 |
| D | .3 | .14 |
| E | .1 | .09 |

What is the expected return on your portfolio?

4. You own four stocks. The expected return on each and the proportion of your money invested in each are given.

| Stock | Proportion | Expected Return |
|-------|------------|-----------------|
| A | .3 | .06 |
| B | .3 | .08 |
| C | .2 | .05 |
| D | .2 | .04 |

What is the expected return on your portfolio?

5. Compute the standard deviation of a portfolio of two stocks using the following data.

$$w_1 = .7 \qquad \text{var}(r_1) = .03 \qquad \text{cov}(r_1, r_2) = -.02$$
$$w_2 = .3 \qquad \text{var}(r_2) = .06$$

6. Compute the standard deviation of a portfolio of two stocks using the following data.

$$w_1 = .6 \qquad \text{var}(r_1) = .06 \qquad \text{cov}(r_1, r_2) = .04$$
$$w_2 = .4 \qquad \text{var}(r_2) = .05$$

7. Compute the standard deviation of a portfolio of three stocks using the following data.

$$w_1 = .5 \qquad \text{var}(r_1) = .04 \qquad \text{cov}(r_1, r_2) = .04$$
$$w_2 = .25 \qquad \text{var}(r_2) = .06 \qquad \text{cov}(r_1, r_3) = .03$$
$$w_3 = .25 \qquad \text{var}(r_3) = .09 \qquad \text{cov}(r_2, r_3) = .07$$

8. Compute the standard deviation of a portfolio of three stocks using the following data.

$$w_1 = .4 \qquad \text{var}(r_1) = .08 \qquad \text{cov}(r_1, r_2) = .05$$
$$w_2 = .3 \qquad \text{var}(r_2) = .05 \qquad \text{cov}(r_1, r_3) = .04$$
$$w_3 = .3 \qquad \text{var}(r_3) = .04 \qquad \text{cov}(r_2, r_3) = .03$$

9. A research firm's economists predict five possible states of the economy and the probabilities of these states occurring. The firm's security analysts have predicted the rates of return of Stocks A and B for each state of the economy. Here are the predictions.

| State of the Economy | Probability | Return on Stock A | Return on Stock B |
|---|---|---|---|
| Very poor | .1 | .00 | .05 |
| Poor | .2 | .06 | .06 |
| Average | .4 | .10 | .08 |
| Good | .2 | .14 | .09 |
| Very good | .1 | .20 | .13 |

   **a.** Compute the expected returns and variances of the two stocks.

   **b.** Compute the return of portfolios with 80%, 60%, 40%, and 20% invested in Stock A. In each case the remainder of the portfolio is invested in Stock B.

   **c.** Compute the correlation coefficient between Stocks A and B.

   **d.** Compute the standard deviations of portfolios with 80%, 60%, 40%, and 20% invested in Stock A. In each case the remainder of the portfolio is invested in Stock B.

**10.** A research firm's economists predict five possible states of the economy and the probabilities of these states occurring. The firm's security analysts have predicted the rates of return of Stocks A and B for each state of the economy. Here are the predictions.

| State of the Economy | Probability | Return on Stock A | Return on Stock B |
|---|---|---|---|
| Very poor | .1 | −.10 | .06 |
| Poor | .2 | .00 | .07 |
| Average | .3 | .10 | .08 |
| Good | .3 | .20 | .10 |
| Very good | .1 | .30 | .12 |

   **a.** Compute the expected returns and variances of the two stocks.

   **b.** Compute the return of portfolios with 80%, 60%, 40%, and 20% invested in Stock A. In each case the remainder of the portfolio is invested in Stock B.

   **c.** Compute the correlation coefficient between Stocks A and B.

   **d.** Compute the standard deviations of portfolios with 80%, 60%, 40%, and 20% invested in Stock A. In each case the remainder of the portfolio is invested in Stock B.

# *READINGS*

Chen, Nai-Fu. "Some Empirical Tests of the Theory of Arbitrage Pricing," *Journal of Finance* 38 (December 1983): 1393–1414.

   *This paper compares the empirical performance of the APT with that of the CAPM. It also tests whether the APT can explain some of the empirical anomalies related to the CAPM.*

Elton, Edwin J., and Gruber, Martin J. *Modern Portfolio Theory and Investment Analysis*, 3rd. ed. New York: John Wiley & Sons, 1987.

   *This book presents a detailed presentation of the theory of modern portfolio analysis.*

Keim, Donald B. "The CAPM and Equity Return Regularities," *Financial Analysts Journal* 42 (May–June 1986): 19–34.

> *This article summarizes and evaluates all of the recent evidence which conflicts with the CAPM and the efficient markets hypothesis. The article is easy to read, but has 79 references to help in deeper investigation by the reader.*

Roll, Richard, and Ross, Stephen A. "The Arbitrage Pricing Theory Approach to Strategic Portfolio Planning," *Financial Analysts Journal* 40 (May–June 1984): 14–26.

> *This article provides an intuitive description of APT and discusses its merits for portfolio management.*

# APPENDIX 22A ─────────────────────
# *INVESTOR UTILITY PREFERENCES*

Utility theory argues that for a particular investor the relationship between utility and wealth can be quantified. Utility theory measures in units called utiles the satisfaction the investor obtains from varying amounts of wealth. The utility function quantifies the return-risk tradeoff inherent in an investor's preferences.

## *Axioms of Rational Behavior*

In order to quantify utility four axioms which describe rational behavior must hold.

1. Ranking. Investors must be able to rank alternatives. Given a choice between alternatives A and B the investor must say, "I prefer A to B," "I prefer B to A," or "I am indifferent between A and B."

2. Transitivity. The investor's preferences must be transitive. That is, if A is preferred to B, and if B is preferred to C, A must be preferred to C.

3. Independence. Various alternatives must be independent in the mind of the investor. Therefore, the ranking of two alternatives is unchanged when they are combined with a third alternative. That is, if A is preferred to B, A plus C must be preferred to B plus C. This is a strong assumption; in effect, it denies that goods can complement or substitute for one another.

4. Certainty equivalent. For any gamble, a certainty equivalent exists in the mind of the investor. A certainty equivalent is an amount between that amount and the gamble the investor is indifferent.

## *Derivation of a Utility Function*

If the investor's decision making conforms to these axioms, the utility function can be obtained by posing a series of gambles and having the investor specify a certainty equivalent for each of them. The process follows these steps.

1. Arbitrarily assign utiles to two dollar amounts. The amounts should be within the investor's normal decision-making range. For example, let 0 utiles equal $0, and let 1 utile equal $100,000.

2. Offer the investor a gamble involving these two dollar amounts in order to determine the certainty equivalent at which the investor is indifferent between that sum and the gamble. For example, "How much would you pay to play a lottery with a 50 percent chance of $0 and a 50 percent chance of $100,000?" Suppose the investor answers $35,000.

3. Compute the utile value of the dollar answer given. For example, this investor said that he was indifferent between the utility he receives from $35,000 and the utility of the gamble. That is,

$$U(\$35,000) = .5[U(\$0)] + .5[U(\$100,000)]$$

Substitute 0 utiles for U($0) and 1 utile for U($100,000) and obtain

$$U(\$35,000) = .5(0) + .5(1)$$
$$= .5 \text{ utiles}$$

We now know that the utility of $35,000 equals .5 utiles.

**4.** Offer the investor a new lottery using two of the dollar amounts with known utile values. For example, "How much would you pay to play a lottery with a 50 percent chance of $35,000 and a 50 percent chance of $100,000?"

**5.** Compute the utile value of the dollar answer given. For example, this investor said he was indifferent between the utility he receives from $55,000 and the utility of the gamble. That is,

$$U(\$55,000) = .5[U(\$35,000)]$$
$$+ .5[U(\$100,000)]$$

Substitute .5 utiles for $U(\$35,000)$ and 1 utile for $U(\$100,000)$ and obtain

$$U(\$55,000) = .5(.5) + .5(1)$$
$$= .75 \text{ utiles}$$

We now have the utile value of a fourth dollar amount.

**6.** Continue to offer the investor gambles involving two of the dollar amounts with known utile values. Compute the utile value of the answer. Have some gambles that check for consistency with earlier answers.

**7.** Plot the utile values with the dollar amounts. The utility function is the curve that fits the points.

In this example all the gambles were presented as having 50–50 chances. Although this is the easiest type of gamble for the investor to evaluate, the probabilities are unimportant. Other percentages such as 30–70 and 40–60 could be used.

## The Shape of the Utility Function

The above investor is risk-averse. Every time he gave a certainty equivalent it was less than the expected dollar value of the gamble. This tells us that he does not like to gamble. Risk-averse investors have concave utility functions. With a concave utility function, marginal utility is a decreasing function of wealth. See Exhibit 22A–1.

If the investor had been risk-neutral or risk-indifferent, his certainty equivalents would have equalled the expected dollar values of the gambles. The risk-neutral investor has a linear utility function. With a linear utility function, marginal utility bears a constant relationship to wealth.

If the investor had been a risk-seeker, his certainty equivalents would have been greater than the expected dollar values of the gambles. The risk-seeking investor

---

**EXHIBIT 22A–1   *Utility Functions***

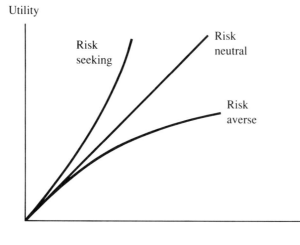

has a convex utility function. With a convex utility function, marginal utility is an increasing function of wealth.

Observation of human behavior and common financial contracts indicates that most investors are risk-averse. Many financial arrangements exist for the purpose of transferring risk, such as insurance, limited liability of common stock, cost plus contracts, options, and futures. Portfolio theory is based on the assumption that most investors have concave utility functions.

## An Application of Expected Utility

An investor will make investment decisions that maximize expected utility, not the expected dollar amounts. Let us illustrate the difference with a simple example. The investor whose utility function we derived is faced with two investment alternatives. These are the possible outcomes and their probabilities:

*Investment A*

| Outcome | Probability |
| --- | --- |
| $0 | .3 |
| $35,000 | .3 |
| $100,000 | .4 |

*Investment B*

| Outcome | Probability |
| --- | --- |
| $35,000 | .35 |
| $55,000 | .65 |

First, we compute the expected dollar value of each investment.

$$\text{expected value of A} = .3(\$0) + .3(\$35,000)$$
$$+ .4(\$100,000)$$
$$= 0 + 10,500 + 40,000$$
$$= \$50,500$$

$$\text{expected value of B} = .35(\$35,000) + .65(\$55,000)$$
$$= 12,250 + 35,750$$
$$= \$48,000$$

Investment A has a higher expected value than B.

Now we substitute utiles for dollar amounts in order to compute the expected utility that each investment has for this investor.

$$\text{expected utility of A} = .3[U(\$0) + .3[U(\$35,000)]$$
$$+ .4[U(\$100,000)]$$
$$= .3(0) + .3(.5) + .4(1)$$
$$= .65 \text{ utiles}$$

$$\text{expected utility of B} = .35[U(\$35,000)]$$
$$+ .65[U(\$55,000)]$$
$$= .35(.5) + .65(.75)$$
$$= .6625 \text{ utiles}$$

For this investor the expected utility of Investment B is greater. The rankings of the two investments were different under the expected dollar value and the expected utility criteria. This risk-averse investor preferred Investment B.

### Reading

Swalm, Ralph O. "Utility Theory—Insights into Risk Taking," *Harvard Business Review* 44 (November–December 1966): 123–136.
The purpose of this article is to explain utility theory to businesspeople. Although it looks at business peoples' attitudes toward return and risk, the article helps us understand the value of utility theory in investments.

### Case Problem

Derive your own utility function.

# Part VI

# *INDIVIDUAL PORTFOLIOS OF WEALTH*

# *Financial Planning*

## OUTLINE

## OBJECTIVES

When you have finished studying this chapter, you should understand

1. Why financial planning is important.
2. How to set up a financial plan that will work for you.
3. How your position in the life cycle affects your financial planning.
4. How a professional financial planner can help you.

**446**

# *23*

## *Financial Planners*

According to a recent study by the Securities and Exchange Commission, you may not receive what you expect with a professional financial planner.

If a financial planner indicates that he or she is a Certified Financial Planner or a Chartered Financial Consultant, you will at least know that your planner has done enough studying to pass a series of exams. Otherwise, anyone can claim to be a financial planner. The SEC study described the profession of financial planning as being a relatively well-educated industry. However, it found that clients tended to have more education than their planners! One very surprising finding was that 6 percent of the planners were not high school graduates (compared to only 1 percent of the clients). A large number of planners had less than ten years experience in the field, not surprising since financial planning is one of the fastest growing service industries in the country.

Knowing how the planner will be compensated is important. The study found that some 85 percent were selling financial products, but only 47 percent of the planners made this clear to their clients. Fee-only planners were generally given higher marks for consumer satisfaction than those working on commissions. According to Mary Malgoire, chairman of the National Association of Personal Financial Advisors, a group of fee-only planners, your total bill for financial planning should not exceed 2 percent of your investment base.

## INTRODUCTION

During your lifetime, you will earn thousands of dollars. You may choose to spend these dollars on current wants and needs or to put some of them aside for the future. The investments you choose to make now should enhance future spending. Your earnings and your position in the life cycle will be the main determinants of your choices to spend now or later.

A life cycle is progress through life, from birth to death. Your life cycle will be unique to you, although some aspects of yours will probably resemble others. Elements of financial planning need to be addressed at each stage of this cycle, including writing a will, buying life insurance, deciding on a place to live, putting money aside for emergencies, taking care of current wants and needs, and planning for retirement. In this chapter, we will explore all of these.

# FINANCIAL PLANNING NECESSITIES

## Writing a Will

Everyone who has reached the age of majority (usually 18 or 21, depending on the state) can write a legally binding will indicating how his or her property, both personal and real, should be divided upon death. Dying **intestate,** without a valid will in existence, means that state laws will determine the disposition of your property, with no regard to your wishes. With or without a will, you are going to die, and someone is going to get your property. Exhibit 23–1 shows the **law of descent** in many states (check with an attorney for the exact law in your state).

---

**EXHIBIT 23–1    *Partial Examples of Typical Law of Descent***

*One Marriage*
Survivors:  Husband or wife
                 No children
Inheritance:  Entire estate to survivor

Survivors:  Husband or wife
                 No children
                 Parents of deceased
Inheritance:  $^3/_4$ to spouse; $^1/_4$ to parents

Survivors:  Husband or wife
                 One child
Inheritance:  $^1/_2$ to spouse; $^1/_2$ to child

Survivors:  Husband or wife
                 Two or more children
Inheritance:  $^1/_3$ to spouse; $^2/_3$ to children

*Two Marriages*
Survivors:  Husband or wife
                 No children this marriage
                 One or more children of first marriage
Inheritance:  $^1/_3$ personal property to spouse; $^2/_3$ to children
                 $^1/_3$ life interest in real estate to spouse, which will pass at death to surviving
                 children; $^2/_3$ to children

Survivors:  Neither spouse
                 Children
Inheritance:  Equal shares to children; children of a deceased child will take their deceased
                 parent's share

Survivors:  Neither spouse or parents
                 No children
                 Brothers and sisters of deceased
Inheritance:  Equal shares to brothers and sisters; children of a deceased sibling will take
                 their deceased parent's share

Survivors:  None
Inheritance:  All to the state

---

A will does not have to be long or elaborate. Legal assistance is not mandatory, but a lawyer can make sure that the correct form is used and that all wording and witnessing have been done to meet state laws. Wills should be revised periodically.

## *Buying Life Insurance*

Since the primary purpose of life insurance is to provide financial protection for those who are dependent on you, some individuals have no need for this insurance. Ask the question, "If I died now, would anyone suffer financially?" If the answer is yes, then you must make an attempt to determine the amount of life insurance necessary to ease the financial burden of your survivors. This is not an easy job. Furthermore, you will have to sort through a myriad of policies available to find one that fits your needs and pocketbook. Life insurance should be purchased after careful thought and shopping; it should not be purchased because a salesman has indicated that you need insurance. A brief description of the most common types of life insurance follows. This is not all inclusive, and your agent will be able to give you more complete and up-to-date information.

**Term insurance** is designed to provide protection for a prestated period of time. The most common terms covered are one year, five years, and twenty years. Mortgage insurance that runs for the duration of the mortgage is term insurance. If death occurs during the specified term, the beneficiary will receive the face value of the policy. If the term expires before death occurs, there is no cash value (savings) for the insured. Term insurance provides the most protection per dollar of insurance premium. During the years when large amounts of life insurance are needed and money for premiums may be limited (when children are at home, for example), term insurance may be the best protection available.

**Permanent life insurance** provides protection for the entire lifetime of the insured. A straight life or ordinary life policy requires that premiums be paid from the time of the policy inception until death or until the policy is dropped. Straight life is the least expensive permanent life insurance. Part of the premiums charged in the early years is not needed to provide death benefits; they will build up cash values, the living benefits mentioned by insurance companies. If you live beyond the time when financial protection is needed for your family, you may choose to drop this policy and take the cash value.

Straight life insurance may present a budgetary problem at some point in your life. For example, when income drops at retirement, paying a life insurance premium may be difficult. The life insurance industry has responded to this potential problem by providing for some **limited payment insurance** programs. Under these programs, the insured makes premium payments for a limited period of time. "Twenty pay life" (premiums are paid for 20 years) and "paid up at age 65" are the most popular programs, but other limited payment policies are available. After the payment period has passed, the insured does not make further premium payments but protection will continue until death. A limited payment policy will build cash values somewhat faster than a straight life policy because of the higher annual premiums.

In addition to these standard policies, insurance companies in the past few years have introduced **variable life insurance** policies, which usually have the final face value tied to the performance of a stock portfolio. The insurance company will guarantee that a minimum amount will be paid to the beneficiary. The actual amount paid will be determined by how well the investments made by the insurance company perform.

**Universal life** is also a recent development from the insurance industry. With such a policy, you have the opportunity to make changes as they are needed to meet your financial needs. For example, most of these policies will allow you to make extra premium payments if you wish. The additional money is put into the investment aspect of your policy. If necessary, you may skip a premium payment or two, with perhaps a resulting decrease in coverage. Additional coverage may be acquired upon proof of insurability. There are several variables in these plans; careful comparison is advised.

## Deciding on a Place to Live

Deciding whether to rent or own a home may be determined by your current job status, geographical location, and position in the life cycle. For most people, the purchase of a residence is the largest financial commitment made during their lifetimes. Buying property usually requires the previous accumulation of some funds for down payment, closing fees, moving costs, and house furnishings. Having sufficient money available to meet the monthly expenses of living requires careful planning. An overcommitment to a mortgage payment or rent payment can make meeting other living expenses difficult.

## Putting Money aside for Emergencies

All rational people know that some emergencies are going to befall them; they just don't know when. In order to take care of emergencies, you will need to have some money that is readily available (liquid), adequate insurance (auto, homeowners, health, life), and/or a ready line of credit (cash advances on credit cards or small loans available for the asking at financial institutions).

## Taking Care of Current Wants and Needs

Financial planning ensures that there is sufficient cash flow to take care of day-to-day living expenses. There are periods in almost everyone's life when it is a struggle just to cover the needs, and wants must be postponed. Having more money does not necessarily make spending decisions easier; there are just more decisions to be made.

## Planning for Retirement

Retirement is looked forward to by many and dreaded by some. In order for retirement to be pleasant, you must plan how you will handle your drop in earnings. You cannot live comfortably on Social Security. It was never meant to be more than a safety net to keep you from being totally destitute. You will need additional funds. Review coverage of all employer-provided pensions so that you know exactly what will be available.

In addition to your own rights under your pension plan, your spouse will have some rights granted by federal law. The Employment Retirement Income Security Act

(ERISA) of 1974 provided that the normal form of retirement benefits for a married couple would be a joint-and-survivor annuity, which would pay pension benefits to a retired worker's surviving spouse. A worker was allowed under the original law to decide whether he or she wanted benefits to be paid in that manner, in a lump sum, or in the form of a single life pension. The last choice provided for higher monthly retirement payments while the worker was alive but meant that when the worker died, pension benefits would end. Since male pension participants tended to choose the higher paying single annuity, ERISA has given protection to widows.

The **Retirement Equity Act of 1984** (effective January 1, 1985) granted automatic rights for a spouse to share in the distribution of funds from pension and profit-sharing plans. Only if a spouse agrees in writing to waive these rights can a worker decide to whom and in what form the retirement benefits will be distributed. This law also provides that pension benefits may be divided at the time of a divorce with payments to the divorced partner starting the first day that the working spouse reaches the minimum retirement age—whether or not he or she chooses to retire at that time and receive benefits himself or herself.

You may need to set up your own pension plan in the form of **Individual Retirement Accounts (IRAs)** or **Keogh Plans** (for the self-employed). Some groups of employees may be able to contribute to annuity plans during their earning years.

As mentioned in Chapter 1, all of us are risk-averse to some degree. In order for a financial plan to work successfully, you must know yourself. A professional financial planner should ask you many questions designed to determine your beliefs and feelings in this regard. He or she will use this information when making suggestions concerning the programs to be implemented.

# LIFE CYCLE

Since you are a unique individual, your life cycle will not be exactly like anyone else's. However, we can review the stages that the majority of us will pass through during our lifetimes.

## Single

Everyone is single at some time during life. Some of you will remain single for your entire lifetimes (statistically a small minority). Current indications are that men and women are remaining single until later in life, as the average age for getting married moves to the mid twenties. According to the Census Bureau Population Profile (1983–1984), the average age for marriage in 1984 was 25.4 for men and 23 for women. Some people will become single again through the death of a spouse or a divorce.

Those of you who are single will make financial decisions based on your own wants and needs; no one else is financially dependent on you. Sometimes the single person feels very little urgency to plan, since there is only one paycheck and no one to share it. However, sloppy planning or no planning will result in a great deal of wasted money wherever you are in the life cycle.

Becoming single again because of a divorce or the death of a spouse will be much different from the first single experience. If you have parents or children to support, you will, of course, be making different decisions than the single person who has no other responsibilities.

| EXAMPLE | Allison is single, aged 45, with an annual income of $35,000. She does not expect to marry. Since she has no financial obligations other than herself, she is able to set aside a large portion of her current income in anticipation of early retirement. She wants to earn as much as possible on her investments while being reasonably certain that her initial investment will remain intact. With this in mind, she is putting $5,000 each year into a money market mutual fund and another $5,000 into a local real estate syndicate, which buys apartment buildings and renovates them for resale. Allison expects to retire in five years. (Her employer has attractive arrangements for early retirement.) She expects to use the earnings from the money market fund and real estate holdings for her retirement living expenses. She also contributes the annual maximum to a self-directed IRA, counting on the tax deferment on earnings to add to her retirement income. Her will directs her estate to be divided among surviving nieces and nephews. |

| EXAMPLE | At age 65, Angela is single because of a divorce ten years ago. Her main assets are $20,000 in an IRA, $5,000 in a regular savings account, and a house worth $75,000. She expects to work part-time for the next few years at the library, a job that pays her $5,000 annually. She feels preservation is of prime importance now. She plans to sell her house (taking the once-in-a-lifetime exclusion for gains on the sale of personal residence real estate), take the proceeds plus the IRA funds and invest the total in an annuity which will guarantee her monthly payments for life. Since she wants to be free from investment decisions, Angela believes this to be the best program for her. Because she has only distant relatives, her will provides for bequests to her alma mater and the local hospital. |

## Married without Children

Statistics indicate that you will marry at least once during your lifetime. For many couples, one of the most difficult problems of marriage is the merging of incomes and financial philosophies. Will earnings go into a common pot with all expenses paid from it? Will each partner handle some expenses himself or herself? Sometimes couples decide to use one income for living expenses and the other for savings and investments. If the marriage partners have diametrically opposed ideas about investing, some compromises will have to be made. If she wants to put money into speculative stocks while he prefers money market funds, both will be called on to recognize the differences of opinion (not right or wrong, just different) and to figure out some way to keep the peace. Frequently, each person decides to make some individual investments, without advice or recrimination from the spouse.

Couples need to bring wills up to date in order to include spouses. In most states, spouses not mentioned in a will are entitled to a portion of the deceased's estate, unless there was a differing prenuptial agreement. Life insurance may not be necessary if the couple does not have large debts for which they are jointly liable and the survivor could still support himself or herself.

| EXAMPLE | Bill and Judy are 25; both are working at jobs they consider important; they earn about $22,000 each. They are able to save a large portion of their combined incomes. They do not anticipate the arrival of children within the next few years. Their debt load consists of a $50,000 house mortgage and a $5,000 car loan. They have mortgage life insurance that will pay this debt in the event of either's death. Since Bill is basically conservative in his investment thinking, he puts his half of the investment funds into money market funds and Blue Chip stocks where he can be somewhat assured of steady earnings and moderate increases in value. Judy is willing to take a few more chances, and she invests in financial futures where increases or decreases in value may occur rapidly. She finds it necessary to spend more time than Bill in reviewing her holdings. Their combined investment earnings, either appreciation or dividends, will be used for setting up their IRAs. □ |

| EXAMPLE | Libby and Herb are 45 and have never had children. They have accumulated a large stock portfolio, and they own several real estate units in their hometown. Libby recently retired from teaching to devote herself full-time to renovating and acting as rental agent for the houses and apartment buildings they own. After paying herself a salary, earnings from these units are used for further real estate acquisitions. Libby and Herb expect to retire in ten years and hire a manager to handle the real estate for them. They believe that good management can ensure them a steady income for the remainder of their lives. □ |

## Married with Children

In today's world, child-bearing decisions are frequently financial decisions. Family patterns in the past couple of generations show that families have gotten smaller. The average family size in 1984 was 3.24 people, somewhat down from the 1970 figure of 3.58. Only children are much more common, and there are more couples who indicate that they are childless by choice. Furthermore, the birth of the first (and sometimes only) child has been coming later in the marriage, as both mother and father take time to become established in their careers. In 1984, 22 percent of all births were to women aged 30 or older. In 1970, only 18 percent of babies had been born to women over 30.

When children arrive (and the majority of couples do plan to have at least one child), there will be some disruption in the family's financial picture. Frequently, because of lack of planning, this disruption may cover a long period of time and may be difficult to overcome.

There will, with few exceptions, be some interruption of income from one spouse upon the birth of the child. Many companies will provide for an unpaid maternity leave with the promise of reinstating her job when a mother returns to the labor force. These agreements rarely cover more than a year and frequently cover only a few months. Some companies provide that either mother or father may take a leave. Of course, mother will have to deliver the child, but many fathers are choosing to stay home for a few months with the newborn while mother returns immediately to the workplace. Few employers will provide a paid paternity leave. Unlike many foreign countries, there is no legal requirement for U.S. companies to provide either unpaid or paid maternity leaves. If a mother or father stays out of the job market for a number of years, she or he will frequently need some job retraining.

The cost of raising children may mean that investments get put on the back burner for awhile. Morally and legally, your first obligation is to your children.

Wills are extremely important during this period. Guardians for the children should be specified in case both parents die. (Please ask a potential guardian before putting a name in your will; this is not a surprise to give anyone.) Many people assume that a surviving spouse will get everything when one spouse dies, but you will remember from Exhibit 23–1 that this is not necessarily true. When a portion of the estate is given to a minor child(ren), a guardian must be appointed by the court to supervise this share until the child reaches adulthood. Most courts would appoint the surviving parent as the guardian, but there is no legal obligation to do so. This parent (guardian) usually must make annual reports to the court concerning the managing of the child's estate. There have been a few successful lawsuits by children against their surviving parents charging that the parent did not handle the estate wisely during the years preceding the reaching of majority.

Life insurance is mandatory for the family with young children. Even though a surviving spouse would no doubt be earning money, it would probably be too little to raise the children as you would have wanted. Since the years of greatest need for life insurance commonly coincide with the years when the least money is available for its purchase, careful shopping is a must to secure the most protection per premium dollar.

Residential real estate holdings usually expand at this time simply because more people require more space. More money is necessary for house support, maintenance, and utilities when there are children present.

---

**EXAMPLE**

At age 27 Niclas and Hilda have two children, aged 2 and 4. Their main investment now is their personal home. They will use it as a tax shelter and for the accumulation of equity. When their children have left, they can use the savings in their home to relocate or to make other investments. Safety of their investments is extremely important now since there is little available extra money. They do try to make annual payments into their IRAs. In addition, they are making regular payments into accounts for the children's education.

As the balances grow, they are transferred from regular savings accounts to CDs or money market funds. This saving now will enable the children to finance their educations without having to borrow or without their parents having to come up with large sums of money during the college years.  ☐

| EXAMPLE | Niclas and Hilda are now 45, and the children are about ready to leave home. With the college years mostly behind them, the parents will make a review of their life insurance, housing requirements, and wills. They can devote more time and money to their investment programs with the idea that retirement is only 15 to 20 years away. Money not now needed for the children will be put into the stock market or mutual funds. While 20 years is not a great deal of time to accumulate money for retirement, many people find this period is all that is available when they have been raising children.  ☐

## Empty Nest

When the last child has left home, the financial burden eases. Earning power is still increasing for most families, and these are the years when retirement programs must expand.

During the past few years, studies have shown that the empty nest is coming at a later age. Children are staying at home after graduation from both high school and college (with mixed feelings from their parents). Census information from 1984 showed that 52 percent of men ages 20–24 and 32 percent of women in that age bracket lived with their parents. In 1970, 42 percent of men and 27 percent of women in these brackets were at home.

Wills should be revised to remove guardianships for the children. Perhaps you would like to leave some portion of your estate to organizations or individuals other than your adult, financially independent children. You may do this with a will.

Life insurance programs must be reviewed. Coverage can frequently be lowered since there is no longer any obligation to raise the children. The reduction of large debts (house mortgage) is another reason for dropping some coverage.

Personal real estate holdings are often changed during this period. Many couples no longer want or need the space that was necessary when children were home. You may choose to move to a different neighborhood, or you may acquire a vacation home that could at some point in the future be transformed into a retirement home.

There may still be a few years when funds may be used for somewhat speculative investments. You must remember, however, that time is finite, and losses occurring now must be made up in a shorter and shorter time. Since retirement is rapidly approaching, all investment and pension holdings must be accurately reviewed and changes made to ensure that the retirement years will not be financially difficult.

| EXAMPLE | Nora and Max, aged 52, have seen the last of their three children leave home. They have put their large house on the market and plan to move into a small condominium, which they believe will relieve them of many of the chores

and finances required by the large house. Life insurance has been cut in half since there is no longer any need to provide for the children, and both Nora and Max could meet their own living expenses from their earnings if necessary. The life insurance that continues could be used for final expenses and paying off the remainder of the mortgage. For the next ten years, they plan to put as much as possible into a growth mutual fund, with extra dollars earmarked for a money market fund that will give them liquidity if needed.    □

---

**EXAMPLE**    Maxine and George are 64 and are planning to retire next year. While they did not exchange homes when their children left, they plan to do so after retirement. They have spent time in several parts of the United States to determine if a major relocation would suit them. At this time, they have decided to remain in their hometown in a smaller house with the possibility of spending the winter months in the South. Pensions plans have been reviewed for retirement benefits, and they know how much money will be needed to supplement pension and Social Security payments. They are working this year to consolidate their stock and mutual fund holdings into a more easily managed portfolio. Safety of their investments and a reliable income are the most important investment qualities at this time. They will begin to withdraw funds from their IRAs as needed. Maxine and George have been especially careful to check the health insurance coverage that will be provided as a retirement benefit and to search for supplemental policies that will help them with the expected increase in health care costs as they grow older.    □

## Retired

Retirement comes sooner or later to most people, with the most common age being about 65. Many companies have programs for early retirement, and some make this option very attractive. In some cases, especially when you are self-employed, you may choose to continue working until the end of your life. Working beyond the usual retirement age may be done because the individual chooses to work—he cannot imagine doing anything else—or because resources are so limited that working is a necessity for economic survival. Some employers will require that you retire by a specified age. However, for most jobs, federal law prevents mandatory retirement before age 70 of workers able to perform their jobs.

Retirement normally results in less available money and more time. How well you handle either of these problems will depend on advance planning. You cannot have a successful retirement by simply waking up one morning and realizing, "Tomorrow I will be retired. What will I do?"

Your financial planning needs to be carefully reviewed in anticipation of retirement. What additional amounts, after Social Security benefits and pension payments, will be needed to meet your living needs? Dropping or switching life insurance coverage may result in some cash values becoming available. Often a personal residence is too large and time consuming to be functional at retirement. Surplus money derived from selling or exchanging the property can be used for income producing investments. Retirement years are not the time to be speculative with investments since there will usually not be sufficient income to make up losses. Unfortunately there are individuals who prey on retirees with stories of large riches to be gained from their investment programs.

At retirement, investment goals may have to be changed. You may, for example, sell growth stock and buy income stock. You could take an IRA accumulation and buy an annuity. You may sell nonincome producing collections and put the money into interest-bearing CDs. Whatever you do should be done only after careful thought about the current and long-range implications.

Some thought should be given to where you will spend your retirement years. Do you want to stay where you are, move to a retirement community, or spend part of the year in the North and part in the South? What would be your wishes if medical problems make it impossible for you to continue living as you do now? Thinking about these potential problems in advance, and thinking about the potential cost of these moves, can save you and your family from having to make decisions on a "crisis" basis.

**EXAMPLE**

Maxine and George are now 68 and have been retired for about three years. They receive money from employer provided pensions plans and are drawing Social Security benefits. In addition to these funds, they have periodically withdrawn money from their IRAs. They have now decided to spend the next two or three years traveling around the United States. In order to do this, they will need additional money. They have, therefore, decided to sell their home and invest this money in a money market fund. This fund will provide them with a steady income and will allow them to write checks and make withdrawals if necessary. Thus, the fund will provide the liquidity that may be necessary as they proceed with their travel plans. After their travel lust is satisfied, they expect to rent a small apartment. ☐

**EXAMPLE**

Alice and Ben are both 75. The past ten years of retirement have not been easy. Both have developed costly health problems. Their medical bills have used up their limited savings, and now they are being forced to sell their home in order to have sufficient funds to meet daily living expenses. Since this sale will not come at a good time in the real estate market, they will not realize the same profits that could have been made only a couple of years ago. This family had no savings built up in anticipation of retirement. They expected the "good" pension from their employers and Social Security to provide much more than has been forthcoming. They will probably be forced to ask their children for financial assistance if their medical problems continue. ☐

## Widowed

If you lose a spouse through death, one of the biggest problems is that decisions often have to be made when emotions are raw. Well-meaning friends and relatives give tremendous amounts of advice. If the deceased has made wishes known concerning funeral arrangements and disposal of property, things are made much easier for the survivor. Counselors who work with bereaved family members urge that major decisions be postponed if possible, knowing that not everyone will have the luxury of time. Time allows the spirit to heal; it allows an individual to get advice from experts (not just relatives); it allows him to make decisions based on his head rather than his heart.

When you lose a spouse, you must look at the disposition of the property when your own death will occur. A will written to leave everything to your spouse must be changed. Life insurance with the spouse as beneficiary needs to be dropped or beneficiaries changed. Real estate holdings may be changed. It is time for the survivor to get his own financial life in order.

If the spouse dies at an early age, financial affairs tend not to be in order. The survivor often feels angry and deserted because the young are not supposed to die. Often the inability to continue making the mortgage payments alone may force a change in residence.

When an elderly spouse dies, there may be anger, but the family usually sees the death as a natural progression—the culmination of a life well lived. Older people tend to be more realistic about their mortality and have made arrangements for handling the financial affairs they will leave behind. There are, of course, some people who refuse to accept the fact that death is inevitable and refuse to write wills or disclose the location of important documents—life insurance policies, stock certificates, property deeds.

Death is not an "if I die" proposition; it is a "when I die" proposition. Failure to face your own mortality, admittedly not easy, may result in your leaving your finances in total chaos for others.

---

**EXAMPLE**  Becky Jones, ages 35, died yesterday, leaving her husband Pete and a seven-year old daughter. Since, like most people, she believed that death was only for the elderly, she had no will. Property jointly held with her husband will pass to him as the survivor. Her savings accounts and other property, which she held in sole ownership, will be divided according to the laws in her state. In this case, her husband will receive half and her daughter will receive half. Because the child is a minor, Pete will be appointed guardian to control these assets for the next 11 years. The laws of intestacy will not take into account the fact that Becky wanted everything to go to her husband.

Although her pension fund and IRA do list her husband as the beneficiary, an old life insurance policy naming her parents as beneficiaries will cause some trouble. Morally perhaps, but not legally, the parents have an obligation to release the money to their son-in-law and granddaughter.

Pete will find his contributions to investing will be curtailed for some time as he struggles to find the necessary money to support a household that was formerly supported by two wage earners. For a few years, his daughter will require large amounts of child-care money.                                    □

| EXAMPLE | Bert, aged 79, died after a long illness. He is survived by a wife and two adult children. His will provided for the major portion of his estate to pass to his wife, with small bequests to charities that were important to him. Now his widow must determine how she wishes to dispose of her estate. She must decide whether she can live comfortably on the earnings of the estate or whether she will have to liquidate some of her holdings. Some of these decisions will be determined by her state of health and the number of years she outlives her husband. ☐ |

## Divorced

Statistics do not paint a very optimistic picture concerning marriage. Almost half the marriages in the United States will be dissolved; most of the people involved will then remarry, which in itself presents some interesting financial problems. A divorce requires that the financial assets of the partners be divided in some manner. State laws differ concerning the ownership of both real and personal property acquired during the marriage years. Usually, property owned prior to the marriage will remain the property of the individual. Dividing the marital property may be difficult and emotionally draining. The court will usually have to approve the property settlement and may, in some cases, decree how it will be done.

If there are children involved, arrangements must be made for their custody and support. Although the courts are beginning to take more time to come to custodial decisions, the majority of children will live with their mothers when a marriage is ended. While the financial responsibility for the children is to be shared by both parents, the noncustodial parent frequently makes little or no contribution to the expenses of raising the children.

Merging families makes for both financial and emotional decisions. Arrangements must be made for the caring and nurturing of the first family, the step-family, and the half-family. As the age of the marriage partners increases, adult children become involved. Often a bride and groom will draw up prenuptial agreements, providing for the children to the exclusion of the current spouse. These arrangements are legal and binding, but they must be handled carefully. Legal advice is imperative.

| EXAMPLE | Marie and Jason are both 32, have two children each, and are entering their second marriages. Jason has custody of his son and daughter, while Marie's former husband has custody of her daughters. Marie must pay $50 weekly child support. She also has a court mandated life insurance policy with her daughters named as beneficiaries. If she should die while the girls are young, the insurance will be put into an insurance trust in their behalf. The financial support obligations for Marie will continue until the girls have graduated from college, marry, or reach the age of 22. |

Marie and Jason's initial problem will be to make sure that the financial commitments for both families are understood and met. They must also make decisions concerning the costs of maintaining their home (with Jason's children in attendance). It is often difficult to decide upon a fair distribution of expenses in this situation. In addition, each will have to relinquish some financial control over his or her earnings as the new family becomes an established unit. The possibility of future children will complicate the picture.                    □

# THE FINANCIAL PLAN

Since you will be responsible for the earning and spending of a great deal of money during your lifetime, you have several choices to make. You can spend this money as soon as it is earned for instant gratification or you can defer the spending in order to provide for future needs and wants. You can muddle through life, feeling that things will somehow come out all right in the end, or you can carefully plan for all aspects of your financial life, feeling confident that your needs will be covered and your wants can sometimes be realized.

Those who plan are usually more relaxed with their finances. They feel in control and less frustrated about their earning and spending. They are able to see where they have been and where they are going. A concern often expressed to financial planners is that people feel as though their money is controlling them rather than the other way around.

## Getting Started

The most common mistake made by those who would like to be involved in planning is their failure to get started. Hoping that a full-blown financial plan will somehow materialize without any effort on your part is a dream; it will not happen. "One of these days, I've got to get started" usually results in a start "none of these days." For many people, taking the first step is the most difficult.

The first step is to review the financial papers you have. Sort through all the papers you can find—keep those that are pertinent, throw out the rest, but do not be too eager to throw things away. What do you need?

***Insurance***   Locate all insurance policies—life, health, real estate, and automobile.

Review the amounts of life insurance carried; note the current beneficiaries. Is the amount carried sufficient? Plan to have an agent help you with a review of your coverage and types of policies carried. There have been many new policies brought into the marketplace during the past few years; perhaps a change is in order for you. Check policies carefully before you discard them; even those you stopped paying premiums on a couple of years ago may have some cash value or paid up coverage. Ask your agent if you do not understand the language in the policy.

Check your homeowners policy. Is the amount of coverage on your house or condominium sufficient to replace it? Do you carry enough liability protection? Special collections or furnishings may require special coverage.

Review all policies on your automobiles. Do you have enough liability coverage in case you cause an accident? Are there some areas of coverage that should be dropped or changed? Has your insurance carrier been notified of changes in your family situation (a teenage driver leaving home, for example)? You might want to investigate the possibility of combining your homeowners and auto policies into combined coverage, made available at a lower cost by some companies. There is no point in keeping a 15-year accumulation of homeowners and auto policies.

**Wills**   Where is your will kept? Does the executor or family members know where it is? When was the last time the will was updated? Are all people you want to receive bequests mentioned? Changes in federal or state estate laws sometimes make it necessary to rewrite wills in order to get the best treatment under these laws.

**Taxes**   Income tax returns should be kept for a number of years. It is possible to get copies from the IRS of old returns (at last notice, each copy cost $4.25). As life becomes more complex for you, there may be information on previous tax returns that can be used to make tax decisions for future years. Generally speaking, the IRS can audit your return for three years from the filing date. (Some exceptions allow for longer periods of time.) Some tax records, concerning the purchase of a home or capital improvements to this home, investments in an IRA, or charitable donations, for example, should be kept indefinitely.

## Determining Financial Position

Hopefully you have some sort of financial records that show your spending patterns. If not, let us take a look at how a financial planner might proceed to get you started on thinking about your money.

You will begin by finding out your current financial position. This requires that you develop a **balance sheet** (sometimes called a financial position paper), which is a financial picture of a given point in time. You will list assets, liabilities, and net worth.

An **asset** is an item that you own that has monetary value. You will note on the balance sheet illustrated in Exhibit 23–2 that assets are listed according to their liquidity (the length of time it requires to turn them into cash).

A **liability** is a debt that you owe someone. On a balance sheet, liabilities are usually listed beginning with very short-term liabilities (those normally payable during the upcoming month), followed by those which may require several months or years to eliminate.

The bottom line of a balance sheet is your **net worth** (sometimes called equity or capital). This is the amount that would be left if all assets were liquidated and all liabilities were paid off. Assets minus liabilities equals net worth.

If you have a positive net worth, you are **solvent.** If you have a negative net worth, you are **insolvent.** Insolvency may be a minor irritation or a sign of impending doom. A student who is insolvent primarily because of a student loan probably will not be very concerned. After graduation, he or she will begin to pay off this debt with current earnings. Assets will increase as the student puts money into savings and investments.

**EXHIBIT 23–2   Example of Family Balance Sheet (Financial Position)**

*Jan and Harry Miller*
*Balance Sheet as of December 31, 199n*

| Assets | | Liabilities | |
|---|---|---|---|
| Cash | $    100 | Utility bills | $    300 |
| Checking account balance | 800 | Credit card balance | 1,400 |
| Savings account balance | 500 | Insurance premium due | 700 |
| Cash value of life insurance | 900 | Installment loan for washer and | |
| Mutual funds | 2,500 | dryer | 600 |
| Appliances | 2,000 | Car loan | 4,000 |
| Furniture | 4,000 | Educational loan | 4,000 |
| Car | 5,000 | Home mortgage | 50,000 |
| Home | 65,000 | Total Liabilities | $61,000 |
| Total assets | $80,800 | Net worth | $19,800 |
| | | Liabilities plus net worth | $80,800 |

The negative net worth will disappear within a few years. The student has a long time to build assets before earnings are curtailed.

On the other hand, people approaching retirement with a negative net worth are in trouble. Their earnings years are about to stop, and they have nothing to live on in the ensuing years except Social Security and perhaps some pension money—neither of which will provide enough resources to continue their present lifestyle and to pay off their debts. Often the terms ''insolvent'' and ''bankrupt'' are used synonymously. This is technically incorrect. An individual is not bankrupt until a court has looked at his or her finances and declared him or her a ''discharged debtor.'' It is not a requirement to be insolvent before declaring bankruptcy.

## Tracking Expenditures

The second financial paper that a financial planner will require is an **income/expense statement** (sometimes called a cash flow statement). Such a statement tells you where your money came from and where it went. This may be prepared for a month's time to give you an idea of the immediate cash flow situation. It may be done for a six-month or one-year period in order to give you a long-range picture. An example of an annual statement is shown in Exhibit 23–3.

The bottom line of this statement is the amount left for savings and investments. If this is negative, you may have borrowed money to fund your spending, which will put a lien on future earnings. You may have liquidated assets by withdrawing from savings accounts or selling stock. In either case, the source of your extra money is not inexhaustible. Lines of credit will dry up, savings accounts will be closed, and other assets will be depleted.

---

**EXHIBIT 23–3  Example of a Family Income and Expense Statement (Cash Flow Statement)**

---

*Sue and Mark Johnson*
*Income and Expense Statement*
*For the period January 1 to December 31, 199n*

*Income*

| | | |
|---|---:|---:|
| Sue's salary | $16,000 | |
| Mark's salary | 21,000 | |
| Gift from Sue's parents | 1,000 | |
| Dividends | 300 | |
| Interest | 200 | |
| Total gross income | | $38,500 |
| Less: Federal income taxes | 5,615 | |
| State income taxes | 900 | |
| Social security taxes | 2,590 | |
| Total taxes | | 9,105 |
| Total net income (also called take-home pay or discretionary income) | | $29,395 |

| *Expenses* | *Fixed* | *Flexible* | |
|---|---:|---:|---:|
| Mortgage | $ 6,500 | $ | |
| Real estate taxes | 800 | | |
| Property insurance | 600 | | |
| Utilities | | | |
| electricity, phone, water | | 2,000 | |
| Food | | 3,500 | |
| Clothing | | 2,000 | |
| Car payments | 3,000 | | |
| Car insurance | 500 | | |
| Car repairs | | 500 | |
| Gasoline | | 1,500 | |
| Vacation | | 1,200 | |
| Furniture purchases | | 1,000 | |
| Payment on personal loan | 1,500 | | |
| Entertainment | | 800 | |
| Miscellaneous | | 700 | |
| Total expenses | $12,900 | $13,200 | $26,100 |
| Surplus (or deficit) | | | $ 3,295 |

An income/expense statement can give you an idea of where money is slipping away and allow you to make changes.

## Setting and Realizing Goals

Another major mistake made by individuals is a failure to set goals and follow through on them. Without clear goals in mind, you are likely to spend for today with no regard for tomorrow. When tomorrow comes, ripe with opportunities, you cannot take advantage of them because you have no resources.

Goals need to be specific. A financial planner will ask that you specify broad goals—perhaps owning a home, sending children to college, having enough cash flow to take care of your current needs, developing a nest egg for retirement. Then he or she will ask that you be more specific—you will need $10,000 for a down payment on a home in 1992; retirement in 2030 will require $100,000.

During your lifetime, goals may change as your position in the life cycle changes, experience and education are gained, or setbacks such as illness or unemployment hit you. Nevertheless, setting goals gives you something to aim for and keeps you on a straight line rather than going around in circles.

# FINANCIAL PLANNERS

If you wish to have someone advise you about finances, help is not difficult to find. One of the fastest growing areas of service employment in the past few years has been financial planning. You may see advertisements for advisors in local newspapers and national magazines. You may find their ads in the phonebook and on television.

A financial planner should be able to take an overview of your financial picture and make recommendations concerning your financial future. He or she will usually require a full disclosure of your investments, liabilities, insurance, wills, income, and goals. He or she will ask the names of other professionals you may be working with— bankers, insurance agents, accountants, attorneys, stock brokers. A few people are uneasy about having their total financial picture known by one person rather than spreading this information among all the aforementioned people.

The news about financial planners is not all good. In the majority of states, there is no definition of what a financial planner or counselor must be. Anyone can hang out a shingle and proclaim expertise. A few states require that financial planners meet certain standards, but there are no federal guidelines.

Until you can count on standardization and regulation of the industry, you must be careful when selecting a financial planner to help you. Some planners who indicate that they are "certified" may carry several designations. The most common are Certified Financial Planner (CFP), Chartered Financial Consultant (ChFC), Certified Public Accountant (CPA), Chartered Life Underwriter (CLU), and Chartered Financial Analyst (CFA).

The College for Financial Planning in Denver confers the CFP designation while the American College in Bryn Mawr confers the ChFC. These designations are conferred after an individual has completed an extensive course of study and taken examinations. Some universities offer a certificate in financial planning and/or degrees in financial planning and financial services. The International Association for Financial Planning (IAFP) admits qualified persons to its Registry of Financial Planning Practitioners. Those admitted must have practiced for three years, pass a practical knowledge examination, and hold one of several approved degrees and/or designations such as those mentioned above.

If you doubt the credentials of any planner, you may check with the granting organization to find out if they are indeed certified.

## Selecting a Financial Planner

Here are some tips in selecting a financial planner/counselor who should be able to work well with you.

- Make sure you have some idea in mind of what you want this person to do for you. Do you want him or her to look at all your financial arrangements? Are you going to ask for some specific investment possibility, insurance for example? Are you willing to do the homework necessary to get your financial picture in clear focus? If you are married, is your spouse agreeable to this arrangement?

- Ask for an initial meeting where you can discuss your needs and your planning philosophy. This session will be offered free of charge by most planners. Ask for references and check them out.

- Be sure to discuss the cost of the service offered; it will not be free. Planners are commonly paid in one of three ways: fees, commissions, or combination of fees and commissions.

Fees may be an annual charge, entitling you to receive written recommendations and to make phone calls (sometimes a limited number) asking for advice. Fees may be a percentage of your net worth or a flat fee, due in a lump sum or spread out over the year.

Commissions are charged by those planners who are selling something. The "something" may be insurance, stocks, mutual funds, tax shelters, or computer programs. An offer of "free advice" is usually an offer to sell a product. Most planners who operate on a commission basis give advice that centers on their product, usually to the exclusion of other investment possibilities.

A combination fee/commission charge would simply combine the two above costs. Some of the fee/commissions may be tax deductible if they are charges for investment or tax advice. Advice for writing a will, buying a personal home, or setting up budget are not tax deductible.

If you do not wish to consult with an outside individual, you can gain large amounts of financial advice by reading current publications. Some of the advice is very general, and you will have to make it fit your situation. Such magazines as *Changing Times* and *Money Magazine* offer timely articles covering such topics as setting up a budget, picking a financial institution, or setting up a stock portfolio. Over the course of a year, a wide range of personal financial planning information is yours.

Several personal finance computer programs are designed to help you make decisions and to keep track of your finances. You should make sure that these will give you the information you desire. Try out the software, if possible, before purchasing it.

Computer programs are designed to help set up and keep track of a budget, sort out a checkbook (reconcile and keep track of certain categories of checks such as medical expenses), keep track of your stock portfolio gains or losses, and keep tabs on your current tax situation. You can also set up your own programs to take care of individual idiosyncrasies. You still must accumulate and type in the needed data to get information out of these programs.

If your planner is using a computer program, it should be one that will take a good look at your personal figures rather than just printing a program designed for "someone in this income category."

# SUMMARY

In order to be financially secure, you must do some planning. This is true wherever you are in your life cycle. If you choose to have professional help, make sure you understand the information given to you and make sure the person is qualified to help you.

Read all information possible. Use computer software when it is appropriate. The final decisions will be made by you.

# QUESTIONS

1. Prepare a balance sheet for yourself in your current financial position. Prepare an estimated balance sheet for yourself five years from now. Analyze the changes which you believe will occur over this period.

2. Write a profile of your risk personality. What risks are you willing to accept in your investment program today? What changes do you believe will be made in this area during the next five to ten years?

3. Make a list of your lifetime financial goals. Choose one of these and indicate why this particular goal is important to you. How do you expect to realize this goal? When would you prefer to be able to accomplish this goal?

4. What are the usual stages in the life cycle? Where are you now? Do you anticipate that you will change this position during the next couple of years?

5. How does moving from married with no children to married with children at home affect the finances of a family?

6. Assume that you are single with two children. You are planning to marry an individual who has one child. What financial difficulties do you foresee in the merging of these families?

7. What are the most common letter designations given to individuals who may advertise that they are available to work as financial planners? Do you feel that such designations are important?

8. What are the three ways in which you can expect to pay a financial planner? Which would you prefer as the customer? Which would you prefer if you were the financial planner?

9. Under what circumstances would life insurance be a required part of your financial plan? Under what circumstances would life insurance not be considered necessary?

10. Why is it important to have an up-to-date will in existence at the time of your death? What happens to your assets if you die intestate?

11. What is the difference between income and growth as it relates to an investment? Under what circumstances would income be more important to you? Under what circumstances would growth be more important?

12. Visit a local computer dealer. What types of computer assisted financial planning and record keeping programs are available? Which do you feel would be beneficial to you right now? Are there some programs that might become helpful to you in the future? Are there some programs that you feel would be a waste of time and money?

## READINGS

"Building a Capital Base—A Guide to Personal Financial Planning." Atlanta, GA: International Association for Financial Planning, 1985.
> *This booklet gives advice on beginning a financial plan and selection of a professional financial planner. This organization frequently has updates and other publications available.*

"Financial Planners: Choose with Care," *U.S. News and World Report* (April 11, 1988): 7.
> *This article outlines some problems you may face when choosing a financial planner.*

Nichols, Donald R. *Life Cycle Investing—Investing for the Times of Your Life.* New York: Dow Jones-Irwin, 1985.
> *The basis of this book is to demonstrate how your investment plans should change as your life changes.*

Toole, P. O. "Picking the Right Financial Planner," *Money* (March 1984): 131–132.

"Where to Go for Financial Advice and Planning," *U.S. News and World Report* (June 4, 1984): 56.

"Where to Look for Good Financial Planning Advice," *Better Homes and Gardens* (October 1984): 199–200.
> *The preceding three articles give advice on finding the best financial planner to meet your needs.*

*Your Social Security.* Social Security Adm. Pub. #04–10035. Washington, D.C.: U.S. Government Printing Office, 1987.
> *The Social Security Administration has many publications to help you understand your rights and responsibilities concerning Social Security. They are updated frequently and are free.*

# APPENDIX 23A —
# SOCIAL SECURITY BASICS

Following are some Social Security basics with which you should be familiar. Since some of these rights and regulations change occasionally, you will need to update the information periodically.

A ''Request for a Statement of Earnings'' form is available from the Social Security Administration (see Exhibit 23A–1a and b). You are advised to submit this form about every three years during your working career. You will receive a statement of all the earnings credited to your account up to the time of the request.

---

**EXHIBIT 23A–1   *Request for Statement of Earnings***

---

*FOLD HERE*

**REQUEST FOR STATEMENT OF EARNINGS**
(PLEASE PRINT IN INK OR USE TYPEWRITER)

| FOR SSA USE ONLY | |
| --- | --- |
| **AX** | • |
| **SP** | • |

**I REQUEST A SUMMARY STATEMENT OF EARNINGS FROM MY SOCIAL SECURITY RECORD**

**NH** | Full name you use in work or business
First | Middle Initial | Last

**SN** | Social Security number shown on your card | **DB** Your date of birth Month Day Year | **A**

**MA** | Other Social Security number(s) you have used | **SX** Your Sex ☐ Male  ☐ Female

**AK** | Other name(s) you have used (Include your maiden name)

*FOLD HERE*

**PRIVACY STATEMENT**

The Social Security Administration (SSA) is authorized to collect information asked on this form under section 205 of the Social Security Act. It is needed so SSA can quickly identify your record and prepare the earnings statement you requested. While you are not required to furnish the information, failure to do so may prevent your request from being processed. The information will be used primarily for issuing your earnings statement.

I am the individual to whom the record pertains. I understand that if I knowingly and willingly request or receive a record about an individual under false pretenses I would be guilty of a Federal crime and could be fined up to $5000.

Sign your name here: (Do not print) | TELEPHONE NO. (Area Code) | DATE

SEND THE STATEMENT TO:          (to be completed in ALL cases )

**PN** | Name

**AD** | Address (Number and Street, Apt. No., P.O. Box, or Rural Route)
City and state | **ZP** Zip Code

Form **SSA-7004-PC-OP1** (9/85)

(a) Inside

---

**EXHIBIT 23A–1  Continued**

---

POSTAGE
REQUIRED

**SOCIAL SECURITY ADMINISTRATION**
**WILKES-BARRE DATA OPERATIONS CENTER**
**P.O. BOX 20**
**WILKES-BARRE, PA 18703**

**YOUR SOCIAL SECURITY EARNINGS RECORD**

▸ For a *free* statement of earnings credited to your Social Security record, complete other side of this card. Use card for only *one* person.

▸ All covered wages and self-employment income are reported under your *name* and Social Security *number.* So show your name and number *exactly* as on your card. If you ever used another name or number, show this too.

▸ Be sure to put a stamp on this card or it won't be delivered.

▸ The name and address blocks *must* be completed in order to receive a statement of your earnings.

▸ If you have a separate question about Social Security, or want to discuss your statement when you get it, the people at any Social Security office will be glad to help you.

(b) Outside

---

By making this request frequently, any errors can be caught and corrected while employer records are easily accessible. There is no charge for this information.

Before you can draw a Social Security retirement check, you need to have credit for a certain amount of work under social security. The amount you need will depend on the year in which you reach age 62. Generally speaking, you will never need more than ten years of work to receive some benefits.

If you are employed, your Social Security tax is deducted from your wages each pay period. The withholding rate and the maximum covered wages change frequently. For 1989 the withholding rate was 7.51 percent (scheduled to increase to 7.65 percent for 1990), and the maximum covered wage was $48,000. Your employer matches this payment and sends the combined amount to the IRS. If you are self-employed and your net earnings are $400 or more in a year, you must report your earnings and pay self-employment taxes each year when you file your income taxes. Use Schedule SE; the self-employed tax rate for 1989 was 13.2 percent. The self-employment tax is due even if you owe no income tax. Both wages and self-employment income are entered into your Social Security record throughout your working years. This record will be used to determine eligibility for benefits and the amount of benefits you and your dependents can receive.

Your retirement check is based on your average earnings over a period of years. If you retire at age 62 (early retirement), your monthly benefits will be reduced to reflect the longer period of time you will be receiving money. Starting in the year 2000, the age at which full benefits can be paid, now 65, will be gradually increased until it reaches 67 in 2027.

In addition to the covered worker, his or her spouse may receive retirement benefits based on the retired worker's work record. The spouse will generally receive 50 percent of the worker's benefit. A covered spouse may also elect to receive benefits based on his or her own work record. A spouse is entitled to receive the larger of the two amounts but not both amounts. Checks can go to a divorced spouse at age 60 or to a disabled surviving divorced spouse aged 50 or older if the marriage lasted at least ten years. Beginning in 1985, a divorced spouse who was divorced at least two years could receive benefits at age 62 whether or not the former spouse chose to receive them. The former spouse must be eligible for Social Security benefits regardless of whether he or she has actually retired.

Unmarried children under 18 (under 19 if a full-time high school student) may receive dependents benefits. Unmarried severely disabled children may continue to receive benefits if they were disabled before 22 and continue to be disabled.

Normally, survivor benefits stop when the individual marries. However, benefits can continue to a widow(er) or surviving divorced spouse who remarries after age 60. If the new spouse receives Social Security,

you can take the spouse's benefit based on his/her record if it would be larger than the current widow's or widower's benefit. (It rarely is.)

If you choose to work until later than the traditional age for retiring, you might still be eligible to receive some Social Security benefits. In 1989, the earnings limit for people aged 65 to 69 was $8,880 and $6,480 for people under 65. These amounts will increase in future years. If your earnings go over the annual earnings limit, you will have $1 deducted from your benefits for each $2 you earn over the exempt amount. Beginning in 1990, $1 in benefits will be withheld for each $3 in earnings above the annual limit for people 65 and over.

At age 70, an individual may earn any amount of money and still be entitled to full Social Security benefits. However, the total earnings might mean that some part of the Social Security would become taxable income.

Starting in 1984, up to half of your benefits would be subject to federal income taxes for each year in which your adjusted gross income plus nontaxable interest income and half of your Social Security benefits exceeded a base amount. Currently this base amount is $25,000 for a single individual, $32,000 for a couple filing jointly, and $0 for a couple filing separately if they live together any part of the year. Complete taxing information can be obtained from the Internal Revenue Service.

As indicated in Chapter 24, you can save on Social Security taxes if you operate a business and hire your family members to work for you. No Social Security taxes have to be paid for your spouse (you do not have to withhold the tax or match the tax). In addition, no Social Security taxes will have to be paid for family members under the age of 21. While this can be a savings for the employer, it may affect social security benefits to which the spouse or other family members may be entitled in the future.

# Tax Planning

## OUTLINE

## OBJECTIVES

When you have finished studying this chapter, you should understand

1. The reasons for the federal personal income tax.

2. The purpose of tax planning and strategies for its implementation.

3. How to calculate personal income tax liability.

4. What abuses the Tax Reform Act of 1986 attempted to correct and how it corrected them.

5. Which types of investments are tax-advantaged and why.

6. How the sale of securities is taxed.

7. The importance of estate tax planning and strategies for its implementation.

# 24

## A Simple Estate Plan

In 1914 a bond was recorded along with a deed that transferred ownership of a Michigan farm from parents to their son and his wife. The bond gave the parents the right to live in the same dwelling and to eat at the same table as the son and his wife. The son and wife were to provide the parents with good wholesome food, with a doctor in case of sickness, and with transportation to and from church.

If the parents were to move to town they were to receive annually $50 in currency, three bags of apples, five bags of potatoes, and two tons of hay. If one of the parents died, the other was to receive one half of the benefits.

## INTRODUCTION

In the early years of our nation, the federal government was relatively small and financed mainly by tariffs and excise taxes. A personal income tax law was instituted several times, for instance, during the Civil War and again in 1894. In 1895, however, the Supreme Court ruled the income tax unconstitutional because the taxes were not proportional to each state's population. Thus, in order to have a personal income tax, it was necessary to amend the Constitution.

In 1909, Congress passed the Sixteenth Amendment, and by February 1913, enough states had ratified it to make it part of the Constitution. The Sixteenth Amendment states, "The Congress shall have the power to lay and collect taxes on incomes, from whatever source derived, without apportionment among the several states, and without regard to any census or enumeration."

In October 1913, Congress passed a new personal income tax law that introduced the Form 1040, the first page of which is shown in Exhibit 24–1. Some features from that law, such as deductions and exemptions, are still used today (see lines 2 and 6 in Exhibit 24–1). The law provided for a progressive tax rate based on ability to pay rather than a flat tax rate. The 1913 income tax did not apply to people with incomes under $20,000. A 1 percent rate was levied on the next $30,000 of taxable income, a 2 percent rate was levied on the next $50,000, while a maximum 6 percent rate was

---

**EXHIBIT 24–1   *1913 Income Tax Form (due on March 1, 1914)***

---

| TO BE FILLED IN BY COLLECTOR. | Form 1040. | TO BE FILLED IN BY INTERNAL REVENUE BUREAU. |
|---|---|---|

**INCOME TAX.**

List No. .........................

.............. District of .........................

Date received .........................................

**THE PENALTY**
FOR FAILURE TO HAVE THIS RETURN IN
THE HANDS OF THE COLLECTOR OF
INTERNAL REVENUE ON OR BEFORE
MARCH 1 IS $20 TO $1,000.
(SEE INSTRUCTIONS ON PAGE 4.)

File No. ...........................................

Assessment List ...................................

Page .................... Line ....................

**UNITED STATES INTERNAL REVENUE.**

## RETURN OF ANNUAL NET INCOME OF INDIVIDUALS.

(As provided by Act of Congress, approved October 3, 1913.)

---

**RETURN OF NET INCOME RECEIVED OR ACCRUED DURING THE YEAR ENDED DECEMBER 31, 191....**

(FOR THE YEAR 1913, FROM MARCH 1, TO DECEMBER 31.)

*Filed by (or for)* ..................................................... *of* .......................................
                  (Full name of individual.)                              (Street and No.)

*in the City, Town, or Post Office of* ........................................ *State of* ...........................

(Fill in pages 2 and 3 before making entries below.)

1. GROSS INCOME (see page 2, line 12) ........................................................ $..............

2. GENERAL DEDUCTIONS (see page 3, line 7) ............................................... $..............

3. NET INCOME ............................................................................... $..............

**Deductions and exemptions allowed in computing income subject to the normal tax of 1 per cent.**

4. Dividends and net earnings received or accrued, of corporations, etc., subject to like tax. (See page 2, line 11).......... $..............

5. Amount of income on which the normal tax has been deducted and withheld at the source. (See page 2, line 9, column A)...

6. Specific exemption of $3,000 or $4,000, as the case may be. (See Instructions 3 and 19)

Total deductions and exemptions. (Items 4, 5, and 6) ........ $..............

7. TAXABLE INCOME on which the normal tax of 1 per cent is to be calculated. (See Instruction 3). $..............

8. When the net income shown above on line 3 exceeds $20,000, the additional tax thereon must be calculated as per schedule below:

|  | INCOME. | TAX. |
|---|---|---|
| 1 per cent on amount over $20,000 and not exceeding $50,000.... | $.............. | $.............. |
| 2  "  "  50,000  "  "  75,000.... |  |  |
| 3  "  "  75,000  "  "  100,000.... |  |  |
| 4  "  "  100,000  "  "  250,000.... |  |  |
| 5  "  "  250,000  "  "  500,000.... |  |  |
| 6  "  "  500,000.... |  |  |
| Total additional or super tax | $.............. |  |
| Total normal tax (1 per cent of amount entered on line 7).... | $.............. |  |
| Total tax liability | $.............. |  |

levied on income over $500,000. (See line 8). Since few people in 1913 had incomes of more than $20,000, only 1 percent of the population was required to pay taxes.

Taxes were increased in 1916 to raise revenue for World War I and again in 1940 and 1941 for World War II. In 1943, employers were first required to withhold taxes from employees' paychecks. Indeed, it can be said that by 1945 the personal income tax had changed from "taxes of classes" to "taxes of masses."

Raising revenue is not the only purpose of the personal income tax law. If it were, taxes could be raised to reduce the federal deficit. Tax laws can be used to gain economic objectives such as price stability and economic growth. For instance, during the Kennedy administration, the top tax bracket was reduced from 91 percent to 70 percent. During the Reagan administration, it was reduced to 50 percent and later to 28 percent plus a 5 percent surtax on some income. This was done in part to stimulate the economy and increase savings.

Taxation can also be used to achieve socially desirable goals, such as encouraging people to support charitable organizations by allowing them to deduct their contributions. Another example is the tax credit for renovating historical buildings, which helps maintain our historical heritage. There are also relief provisions like the increased standard deduction for the blind and elderly.

---

# INCOME TAX PLANNING

It is possible to reduce your tax bracket by the judicial use of tax planning strategies. Income taxes consume a large portion of a person's income that could be invested or used to attain some other financial goal. Therefore, it is in the best interests of everyone to minimize tax liability consistent with personal goals. Before attempting to understand tax planning strategies, it is important to know how tax liability is calculated.

## Calculating Tax Liability

Calculating tax liability starts with gross income. Gross income includes income from all sources that is not expressly excluded by tax law. Gross income includes salaries, dividends, interest, capital gains, income from business, and so on. Some sources of income that are excluded are municipal bond interest, inheritances, proceeds from life insurance policies, and nontaxable portions of Social Security payments.

Adjustments to gross income are subtracted from the total gross income in order to arrive at adjusted gross income (see Exhibit 24–2). Adjustments to gross income include alimony paid, contributions to a Keogh Plan (for the self-employed), IRA contributions and penalties on early withdrawal of savings. The next step is to subtract either the standard deduction or itemized deductions, whichever is greater. The 1986 tax law set the 1988 standard deduction at $3,000 for a single person and $5,000 for a married couple filing jointly. The standard deduction after 1988 is indexed to inflation. That means that if there is 5 percent inflation, the standard deduction will be increased

---

**EXHIBIT 24–2   Tax Liability Calculation**

---

|        | Gross income |
| ------ | ------------ |
| Less   | Adjustments to income |
| Equals | Adjusted gross income |
| Less   | Standard deduction or itemized deductions |
| Less   | Exemptions |
| Equals | Taxable income |
|        |              |
|        | Taxes (calculation based on taxable income) |
| Less   | Tax credits |
| Equals | Tax liability |

---

by 5 percent. There is a separate standard deduction for a child or other taxpayer who can be claimed as a dependent on another return and an additional standard deduction for the elderly (over 65) and the blind.

Itemized deductions include deductions for home mortgage interest, charitable contributions, state and local income taxes, certain medical expenses that exceed 7.5 percent of the adjusted gross income, and moving expenses. The itemized deductions are totaled and compared with the standard deduction. The greater of the itemized deductions or standard deduction is subtracted from the adjusted gross income.

Exemptions are then subtracted (see Exhibit 24–2). Taxpayers can claim one exemption each for themselves, their spouse, and each of their dependents (a person

---

**EXHIBIT 24–3   1988 Tax Rate Schedule Set by Tax Reform Act 1986**

---

| *Taxable Income (TI)* | *Tax* |
| --------------------- | ----- |
| *Single Taxpayers* |  |
| $0–$17,850 | 15% |
| $17,850–$43,150 | $2,677.50 + 28% of amount over $17,850 |
| $43,150–$89,560 | $9,761.50 + 33%[a] of amount over $43,150 |
| $89,560 + | 28%[b] |
| *Married Taxpayers Filing Jointly* |  |
| $0–$29,750 | 15% |
| $29,750–$71,900 | $4,462.50 + 28% of amount over $29,750 |
| $71,900–$149,250 | $16,264.50 + 33%[a] of amount over $71,900 |
| $149,250 + | 28%[c] |

[a] Reflects the first surtax of 5% which phases out the 15% bracket.

[b] Plus lesser of (1) 28% of total exemptions or (2) 5% of (TI − $89,560).

[c] Plus lesser of (1) 28% of total exemptions or (2) 5% of (TI − $149,250).

cannot claim an exemption for himself if he is claimed as a dependent on another taxpayer's return). A taxpayer's total exemption is equal to the number of exemptions that person is allowed times the exemption allowance. The 1986 tax law set the value of one exemption as $1,950 in 1988 and $2,000 in 1989. After 1989, the amount will be indexed to inflation.

Adjusted gross income minus the standard deduction or itemized deductions and minus exemptions is equal to taxable income (see Exhibit 24–2). Taxable income is the income on which tax liability is computed. Exhibit 24–3 shows the 1988 Tax Rate Schedule set by the 1986 Tax Reform Act. Figures are shown for single taxpayers and married taxpayers filing jointly.

There are two tax brackets (15 percent and 28 percent) with two five percent surtaxes on some incomes making a third tax bracket of 33 percent. The first surtax is on incomes over $43,150 for single and $71,900 for married filing jointly and phases out the 15 percent tax bracket. The second 5 percent surtax phases out the personal and dependency exemptions. Therefore, on very high incomes there is effectively a flat tax of 28 percent with no exemptions.

The tax liability may be reduced by subtracting tax credits from it. Tax credits are usually used by Congress as a means of achieving a social or economic objective. Expenditures for investment in low-income housing, certain real estate rehabilitation, and qualified research are examples that give rise to a tax credit. The amount of the tax credit is usually a specified percentage of the expenditure.

---

**PRACTICE PROBLEM 1**

Clara and Max Simon earned salaries of $25,000 and $35,000, respectively, in 1988. They also received interest of $1,200 and dividends of $850. Max paid $2,400 in alimony to his ex-wife. The Simons could claim $4,500 in itemized deductions but no tax credits. Max supported his two children from his former marriage. For the Simons, calculate

  **a.** Gross income

  **b.** Adjusted gross income

  **c.** Total exemptions

  **d.** Taxable income

  **e.** 1988 tax liability

*Solution*

a. 

| | |
|---|---|
| Clara's Salary | $25,000 |
| Max's Salary | 35,000 |
| Interest | 1,200 |
| Dividends | 850 |
| Gross Income | 62,050 |

b. Alimony of $2,400 is an adjustment to income.

| | |
|---|---|
| Gross income | $62,050 |
| Minus adjustments | 2,400 |
| Adjusted gross income | $59,650 |

c. Clara and Max each claim an exemption. Max can also claim exemptions for each of his two dependent children. Total exemptions = 4 × $1,950 = $7,800.

d. The Simons use the standard deduction of $5,000 because that is more than the $4,500 of itemized deductions they can claim.

| | |
|---|---|
| Adjusted gross income | $59,650 |
| Minus standard deduction | − 5,000 |
| Minus total exemptions | − 7,800 |
| Taxable income | $46,850 |

e. Tax liability = $4,462.50 + 28% ($46,850 − $29,750) = $4,462.50 + $4,788.00 = $9,250.50

## Tax Planning Strategies

Three basic strategies can be used to manage your personal income tax liability: (1) avoidance of taxes, (2) deferral of taxes, and (3) conversion of income.

***Avoidance of Taxes***    Avoiding taxes is different from evading taxes. Tax evasion is the nonpayment of taxes that are legally owed; this is a criminal offense. Tax avoidance is reducing your tax liability by using all possible legal exemptions, exclusions, deductions, credits, and losses.

**1.** Exemptions. Each taxpayer can claim one exemption each for himself, his spouse, and each of his dependents. Because the amount of the exemptions is subtracted from income before the tax rate is applied, it reduces tax liability.

**2.** Exclusions. From time to time, tax laws have excluded income derived from certain sources from taxable income. For instance, no income tax is owed on inheritances or interest income from municipal bonds.

**3.** Deductions. There are two kinds of deductions: deductions "for" adjusted gross income (also called adjustments) and deductions "from" adjusted gross income. Deductions "for" adjusted gross income are deductions subtracted from gross income in order to arrive at adjusted gross income (See Exhibit 24–2). Since these deductions are subtracted from adjusted gross income before the tax rate is applied, they reduce tax liability.

**4.** Credits. A tax credit is a dollar-for-dollar reduction of tax liability. Therefore, it is more beneficial than exemptions or deductions. Tax credits may be allowed for investments in low-income housing, certain real estate rehabilitation expenditures, and qualified research expenditures.

It is possible to compare the effect of a tax credit with an exemption, deduction, or loss by using Equation 24–1.

$$TC = B \times t \tag{24-1}$$

where:  $TC$ = the amount of the tax credit

$B$ = the amount of the before tax exemption, deduction, or loss

$t$ = the marginal tax rate

---

**PRACTICE**
**PROBLEM 2**
At a 28% marginal tax rate, a $100 tax credit would be equivalent to what amount of deductions?

*Solution*

$$TC = B \times t$$
$$\$100 = B \times 28\%$$
$$B = \$357.14$$

---

**5.** Losses. Income is divided into three types: active, portfolio, and passive. Active income is income you earn such as salary or commissions. Portfolio income is income from financial securities such as stocks, bonds, and mutual funds. Passive income is income from investments such as limited partnerships and real estate where you do not actively participate in the operations. It is possible for many activities to generate a loss instead of a profit.

The loss from a passive investment can be used only to offset income from other passive investments. Unused losses can be carried forward to the next year. Passive losses carried forward can be subtracted from passive income in the next year. However, the amount of the loss on a particular passive investment cannot exceed the amount ''at risk'' (the amount invested in that passive investment).

A portfolio loss can result from selling stocks or bonds for less than their cost. This capital loss must first offset any capital gain. Then, up to $3,000 of the remaining capital loss can be used to offset other income. If there is more than $3,000, the remaining loss can be carried forward to the following years.

An active income loss such as the operation of a small business or rental property management can offset any other income.

---

**PRACTICE**
**PROBLEM 3**
Mark Jackson had a job with an engineering firm where he earned $80,000 in 1988. Since he was single, he was able to invest a good portion of his income. He invested in two limited partnerships. One resulted in an income of $5,000, the other a loss of $8,000. During the year, he sold his stock in Advanced Microwave Inc. and made a capital gain of $1,000. He received a capital loss of $5,000, however, when he sold his stock in American Tobacco Co.

What is Mark's gross income in 1988 and what losses will he be able to carry over to 1989?

*Solution*

Passive income: Zero. Income of $5,000 minus loss of $8,000 equals loss of $3,000. Mark reports a passive income of zero with a passive loss of $3,000, which he can carry forward to offset passive income in 1989.

Portfolio income:   − $3,000. Capital gain of $1,000 minus capital loss of $5,000 equals capital loss of $4,000. Only $3,000 of a capital loss can be used to offset other income. A loss of $1,000 may be carried forward.

Active income:   $80,000

Total gross income:   $77,000 ($80,000 active income − $3,000 capital loss). He can carry forward a passive loss of $3,000 and a capital loss of $1,000.

---

**Deferral of Taxes**   Taxpayers can sometimes defer the paying of taxes on income to a later time. This is nearly always a good strategy because of the time value of money. Paying a tax in a future year has a lower present value than paying the tax now. It may also be possible to defer paying tax on income to a time when the taxpayer maybe in a lower tax bracket (when you are retired for example). Thus, the taxpayer takes advantage not only of the time value of money but an anticipated lower tax rate.

An individual retirement account (IRA) is a good example of tax deferral. Anyone with earned income may make a deposit into an IRA account. The income earned on this deposit is not taxed until withdrawn. Some taxpayers qualify to have all or a portion of their IRA deposits deducted from their income before paying taxes. For these taxpayers, the tax on the initial deposit is also deferred.

**Conversion of Income**   It may be possible to convert income taxed at a high rate to income taxed at a lower rate. Corporations are taxed at different rates than individuals. Therefore, if a family owns a business, by choosing the correct form of business organization they can sometimes convert highly taxed income to more favorably taxed income. Another way of using this tax planning strategy is by giving an income producing investment to a family member who is in a lower tax bracket, although this is more difficult to do effectively since the 1986 tax reform.

# TAX-ADVANTAGED INVESTMENTS

In the 1980s, Congress did three things to address the concerns that taxpayers felt about the unfairness of the tax laws and about abuses of tax shelters in particular. First, as early as 1981 it attempted to limit losses created by tax shelters by passing a law that said that the loss generated by a particular passive investment could not exceed the amount the investor had "at risk." The amount "at risk" is the total amount the investor has invested in a particular investment.

Second, the Tax Reform Act of 1986 divided income into three types—active, passive, and portfolio. The act limited the amount of possible losses even more by requiring that a passive loss could offset only other passive income, not active or portfolio income. The law did allow any unused passive losses to be carried forward to subsequent years.

Third, the tax law of 1986 made the tax sheltering of income less effective by lowering the top tax bracket to 28 percent (plus a 5 percent surtax in some cases).

Soon after the passage of the Tax Reform Act of 1986, many passive income generators (PIGs) appeared on the market. These were marketed to those investors who had previously invested in passive investments that generated high losses. These losses would do these investors no good unless they also had passive investments that generated income.

Despite the Tax Reform Act of 1986, there are still some tax-advantaged investments.

## Tax Shelters

Tax shelters are investments that generate losses and tax credits while also returning a positive cash flow to investors. While it is still possible to invest in the tax shelters of the type that were marketed extensively before the Tax Reform Act of 1986, the losses from these tax shelters are not useful unless investors also have passive income against which they can offset losses.

It is constructive to understand how tax shelters generate losses. Many tax shelters are in the form of a limited partnership. The limited partner has limited liability and the partnership form of business acts as a conduit, in that certain items of income, deduction, and tax credit are passed through to the partners. Most tax shelters invest in things such as real estate and oil production, which can produce high amounts of depreciation, depletion allowances, and investment tax credits. The 1986 tax law eliminated investment tax credit and reduced the amount of depreciation that could be claimed in the early years of investment.

The best tax shelters produce an actual positive cash flow to the investor while generating losses that could lower the investor's taxes.

---

**PRACTICE PROBLEM 4**

A limited partnership investing in the retailing of automotive products had $100,000 in revenues, $20,000 in expenses, and $130,000 in depreciation. Carla Thomas, a limited partner, owns 20% of the partnership. What cash flow will she receive from this investment? What loss flows through to her from the partnership?

*Solution*

|  | Partnership Income Statement | Cash Flow Statement |
|---|---|---|
| Rental revenue | $100,000 | $100,000 |
| Expenses | − 20,000 | − 20,000 |
| Depreciation | − 130,000 |  |
|  | $− 50,000 | $ 80,000 |
| 20% ownership | $− 10,000 | $ 16,000 |

Carla can claim a loss of $10,000 to offset any other passive income but she receives $16,000 in cash that she can invest or spend.

---

## Working Interest in Oil and Gas

A working interest in oil and gas was exempted from the 1986 passive loss rules. A working interest refers to a taxpayer who owns a working interest individually or as a general partner (but not as a limited partner). Any losses from a working interest in oil and gas can be used to offset portfolio and active income as well as passive income.

## Real Estate

There is also an exception to the passive loss rules for real estate investments. If an investor has an adjusted gross income of less than $100,000, owns more than 10 percent of the property, and participates actively in the management, losses up to $25,000 can be used to offset portfolio and active income. For investors whose adjusted gross income is more than $100,000 but less than $150,000, the loss limitation of $25,000 is phased out. Because of the "active participation" criterion, the investment cannot be in a limited partnership.

## IRAs, Keogh Plans, TSAs

Any taxpayer with earned income may deposit his total earned income or $2,000, whichever is less, into an IRA (individual retirement account). This account may be at a bank, savings and loan, or a credit union. The account may also be with a broker, mutual fund, or life insurance company. The earnings of the account are not taxed until they are withdrawn. For some taxpayers, the initial contribution is also tax deductible. Taxpayers who can deduct the initial contribution are those who are not active in a qualified pension plan and whose spouses also are not active in a qualified pension plan. Also, single taxpayers whose adjusted gross income is less than $25,000 or married taxpayers whose joint income is less than $40,000 can deduct their entire initial contribution. If withdrawals are made before age $59\frac{1}{2}$, the taxpayer will pay taxes on the amount withdrawn (if not previously taxed) and will also be subjected to a 10 percent surcharge penalty by the IRS. For example, you withdraw $5,000 from your IRA at age 50. The penalty is $500. In addition, you will pay taxes on the $5,000 according to your tax bracket. Withdrawals after age $59\frac{1}{2}$ will result in taxes due only on the amount withdrawn.

A Keogh Plan is a retirement plan for people who are self-employed. The lesser of $30,000 or 20 percent of earned income can be contributed to a Keogh Plan. Neither the initial contribution nor the earnings are taxed until they are withdrawn.

A TSA (tax sheltered annuity) is another retirement plan that is available to employees of public schools and tax-exempt organizations. Depending on the amount also contributed to other pension plans, a specified proportion of earned income can be contributed to a TSA. Neither the initial contribution nor the earnings are taxed until withdrawal.

## Gifts

Giving to a family member is a method of converting income from a high tax bracket to a lower one. Each taxpayer can make a gift of up to $10,000 a year to any number of people without having to pay a gift tax. If the $10,000 is invested, the earnings are taxed to the recipient of the gift unless it is a child under age 14. Any passive or portfolio income over $1,000 is taxed at the parents' rate if a child is under age 14.

## Family Businesses

A family who owns a business can shelter some income by employing family members in the business. Salary paid to family members is a deductible expense to the business owner and is taxed to the employee at the employee's tax rate. Often the family member employee is taxed at a lower rate than the owner of the business. Also each taxpayer, even a child, can use the standard deduction to offset earned income. Furthermore, it is not necessary to pay Social Security taxes for a spouse or for family member employees under age 21. This can be a considerable savings. However, a person who does not pay Social Security taxes might not be entitled to receive Social Security benefits when needed.

## Municipal Bonds

Historically, municipal bonds have been tax-advantaged investments because the interest income from municipal bonds was tax exempt. Due to widespread misuse by municipalities, the Tax Reform Act of 1986 has tightened up its definition of what constitutes a tax exempt municipal bond. In order to retain its tax exempt status, a municipal bond must be used for a government function or used in a private activity on behalf of a governmental unit.

Since tax exempt bonds traditionally offer lower rates of interest than similar quality taxable bonds, the tax exempt bonds are tax-advantaged only for taxpayers in higher tax brackets.

## Insurance Products

Life insurance products have been left relatively untouched by the recent tax laws. In fact, with the removal of the tax advantages of many types of investments, life insurance has grown in importance. Money earned on investments in life insurance products is allowed to accumulate tax free. When the accumulated earnings are withdrawn, they are taxed. If the accumulated earnings are not withdrawn, but passed to a beneficiary at the death of the insured, no income tax is ever paid on the earnings. The proceeds from the life insurance policy become part of the estate of the insured and are subject to federal estate taxes, but only if the total estate is larger than $600,000. Some life insurance products are discussed in Chapter 23.

# TAXES ON THE SALE OF SECURITIES

Since the Tax Reform Act of 1986 removed the distinction between short- and long-term capital gains and losses, timing of the sale of securities is not as important a tax planning consideration as it was before 1986. However, there are some points that still should be considered. When a security is sold, the gain or loss on the sale is a capital gain or loss. Capital gains and losses are categorized as portfolio income. To compute gross income, capital losses are subtracted from capital gains. If capital losses are greater than capital gains, the net capital loss up to $3,000 can be used to offset other income. If the net capital loss exceeds $3,000, the loss exceeding $3,000 can be carried forward to later years.

Because of these rules, it is usually advantageous for an investor to plan the sale of securities so that he or she does not incur a net capital loss of more than $3,000.

---

**PRACTICE PROBLEM 5**    Mrs. Richard sold her stock in Hi Tech Corporation for $10,000. She had paid $6,000 for it two years earlier. In the same year she also sold her stock in Capital Ventures, Inc., for $3,000. She had paid $11,000 for it five months earlier. Her only other income is a salary of $35,000.

    **a.**  What is Mrs. Richard's net capital loss?

    **b.**  How much of the loss can she apply toward her active income this year?

    **c.**  What is Mrs. Richard's gross income?

*Solution*

a.  Hi Tech                     $10,000 − $6,0000 =    $4,000 (gain)
    Capital Venture           $3,000 − $11,000 =   − $8,000 (loss)
    Net capital loss                            $ − 4,000

b.  She can apply $3,000 to offset her active income. The remaining $1,000 capital loss can be carried forward to the next year to offset income.

c.  Salary                $35,000
    − Capital loss          − 3,000
    Gross income          $32,000

---

When selling mutual fund shares, a tax is owed on any capital gain. The capital gain is equal to the sale proceeds minus the cost of the shares. The cost of the shares may be difficult to determine if shares were bought at different times and prices. Three methods can be used to determine the cost. The first method is to keep detailed records of the cost of each share and specifically identify which shares are sold. The second method is to use the average cost as the cost of the shares sold. The average cost is computed by dividing the total cost of all the shares by the number of shares. The third method is to assume that the shares first-in are the shares first-out (FIFO). This method is usually the least advantageous because the shares first bought are usually the shares with the lowest cost. Using shares with the lowest cost would cause the capital gain (and hence the tax liability) to be greater.

# ESTATE TAX PLANNING

Since there is a tax levied on a person's estate at the time of death, estate planning is an important part of tax planning. In 1977 Congress passed a Unified Estate and Gift Tax Law. Before this law, individuals who wished to distribute part of their estate before death could make a gift that was taxed at the gift tax rate. At their death, whatever remained in the estate was taxed at the estate tax rate before being distributed to the heirs. The Unified Estate and Gift Tax Law applied the same rate to gifts and to estates. The estate and gift tax is a progressive tax requiring that at an individual's death, all gifts made prior to death are added back into the estate before the estate and gift tax is calculated.

One important feature of the current law is that a person can gift up to $10,000 a year to any number of individuals without owing a gift tax. There is no limit on the amount one can gift to his or her spouse. Anyone, then, with a large estate could begin to distribute it before death, estate tax free, by making annual gifts of $10,000 or less. This is an important estate tax planning technique.

Another feature of the current law is that any portion of an estate that is willed to a spouse is exempt from estate taxes.

Only estates exceeding $600,000 are subject to the estate tax. Therefore, a married couple could shelter $1,200,000 of their estate from taxes by proper planning. If the first spouse to die leaves $600,000 to relatives or friends, and the remainder to his spouse, there is no estate tax owed at his death. At the death of the second spouse, another $600,000 is exempt from estate tax. Therefore, a total of $1,200,000 escaped estate taxes. If the first spouse to die had left his entire estate to the surviving spouse, there would have been no estate taxes due at that time. However, upon the death of the second spouse, only $600,000 of the total estate would have escaped estate taxes. Exhibit 24–4 shows the Unified Estate and Gift Tax schedule.

---

**EXHIBIT 24–4   *Unified Federal Estate and Gift Tax Rates***

| *Estate Plus Prior Gifts* | *Tax* |
|---|---|
| $0–$600,000 | 0 |
| $600,000–$750,000 | 37% of amount over $600,000 |
| $750,000–$1,000,000 | $55,500 + 39% of amount over $750,000 |
| $1,000,000–$1,250,000 | $153,000 + 41% of amount over $1,000,000 |
| $1,250,000–$1,500,000 | $255,500 + 43% of amount over $1,250,000 |
| $1,500,000–$2,000,000 | $363,000 + 45% of amount over $1,500,000 |
| $2,000,000–$2,500,000 | $588,000 + 49% of amount over $2,000,000 |
| $2,500,000–$3,000,000 | $833,000 + 53% of amount over $2,500,000 |
| Over $3,000,000 | $1,098,000 + 55% of amount over $3,000,000 |

# SUMMARY

The federal government passed a personal income tax law after the Sixteenth Amendment to the Constitution was ratified in 1913. The purpose of the income tax is not only to raise revenue, but to gain economic objectives and socially desirable goals. Tax planning minimizes your income and estate taxes consistent with your personal goals.

Income tax liability is figured on the basis of your taxable income. Taxable income is gross income minus adjustments, minus the standard deduction or itemized deductions and also minus exemptions.

Three basic strategies can be used to manage personal income tax liability. Tax avoidance is reducing your tax liability by using all possible legal exemptions, exclusions, deductions, credits, and losses. Tax deferral is deferring the paying of taxes on income to a later time. Conversion of income is converting income taxed at a higher rate to income taxed at a lower rate.

By 1986 the U.S. people felt that the tax laws were unfair and that tax shelters, in particular, were being abused. An attempt was made to correct this by not allowing losses generated by passive investments to exceed the amount "at risk," by limiting passive losses to passive income, and by lowering the top tax bracket to 28 percent plus a 5 percent surtax. The investments that can still be tax-advantaged are tax shelters, working interests in oil and gas, real estate, IRAs, Keoghs, TSAs, gifts, family businesses, and some insurance products. The Tax Reform Act of 1986 taxes all capital gains as regular income and limits capital losses to $3,000 per year.

Estate planning is an important part of tax planning. Strategies that can be utilized are distribution of assets before death by gifting and use of the $600,000 exemption by both spouses.

## QUESTIONS

1. In the early years of our nation how was the government financed?
2. Why was the income tax ruled unconstitutional in 1895?
3. What is the Sixteenth Amendment to the Constitution and why was it passed?
4. What are some of the features of the 1913 personal income tax that are still used today?
5. What was the top tax bracket in 1913? What is the highest historical level of the top tax bracket? What is the top tax bracket today?
6. What percentage of the U.S. population paid personal income taxes in 1913? What percentage pays today?
7. What is the purpose of tax laws?
8. Why should a person indulge in tax planning?
9. Define the following terms: gross income, adjustments, adjusted gross income, standard deduction, itemized deductions, exemptions, taxable income, tax credits, tax liability.
10. Explain how to calculate income tax liability.
11. What are the three basic strategies that can be used to manage your personal income tax liability?
12. What is the difference between tax avoidance and tax evasion?

13. Define each of the following and explain how each can be used to avoid taxes: exemptions, exclusions, deductions, credits, and losses.

14. Define active income, portfolio income, and passive income.

15. How are losses handled from passive income, from portfolio income, and active income?

16. Explain how a deferral of taxes can result in a lower tax liability. Explain some ways one can defer taxes.

17. What is an IRA? Who can contribute?

18. Explain how conversion of income reduces tax liability. Explain two methods of converting income.

19. What were some of the concerns that people had about the unfairness of the tax law in 1986? What are the three ways in which Congress attempted to solve these problems?

20. What are PIGs and why were they popular in 1987?

21. What are tax shelters? Explain how they can generate losses while returning a positive cash flow to the investor.

22. What is a limited partnership?

23. Name some tax-advantaged investments.

24. Why are life insurance products considered tax-advantaged investments?

25. Briefly describe each of the following types of life insurance: whole life, single premium life, universal life, tax-deferred annuities.

26. How are short- and long-term capital gains taxed?

27. Explain how the Unified Estate and Gift Tax Law unifies the estate and gift taxes.

28. What amount can be gifted annually without paying a gift tax?

29. Explain two estate tax planning strategies.

## PROBLEMS

1. Herb Sorenson, a single taxpayer, earned $45,000 as an accountant. He also received $1,500 in dividends and $450 in interest. He had no adjustments or tax credits and claimed the standard deduction. Calculate Herb's taxable income and tax liability.

2. Mary Swinger, a single taxpayer, earned $60,000 as a research physicist in 1988. She also received $3,400 in dividends and $1,250 in interest. She had no adjustments or tax credits and claimed the standard deduction. Calculate Ms. Swinger's taxable income and tax liability.

3. Todd and Mary Stapleton had a combined income of $95,000 from salary and investments. They could claim adjustments of $4,000, itemized deductions of $7,000, and tax credits of $800. They have 3 dependent children. Calculate the Stapletons' taxable income and tax liability.

4. Margaret and Larry Henry had a combined income of $75,000 from salary and investments. They could claim adjustments of $1,000, itemized deductions of $6,500, and tax credits of $400. They have 2 dependent children. Calculate Margaret and Larry's taxable income and tax liability.

5. If Albert is in the 28% income tax bracket, which would give him a lower tax liability: a tax credit of $1,000 or a capital loss of $3,000?

6. If Maurine is in the 33% income tax bracket, which would give her a lower tax liability: a tax credit or $500 or a deduction of $2,000?

7. Helen and Kent Turner had a combined salary income of $100,000. From investments they received $3,000 in dividends, $1,700 in interest, $1,500 in capital gains, $5,000 in capital losses, $8,000 income from one limited partnership, and a $9,500 loss from another limited partnership. What is the Turners' gross income and what losses will they be able to carry over to the next year?

8. Richard Kennedy earned $65,000 as the financial officer in a small firm. He also received $3,500 in stock dividends, $1,400 in bond interest, $500 in capital gains, $4,000 in capital losses, $3,500 from one limited partnership, and a $4,200 loss from another limited partnership. What is Richard's gross income, and what losses will he be able to carry forward to the next year?

9. A limited partnership had revenues of $400,000, $80,000 in expenses, and $370,000 in depreciation. Nick Nelson owned 10% of the partnership as a limited partner. What cash flow will he receive from this investment? What loss flows through to him from the partnership?

10. A limited partnership that invests in rental property had rental revenues of $200,000, expenses of $50,000, and depreciation of $190,000. Bess Aakerson, as a limited partner, owns 20% of the partnership. What cash flow will she receive from the investment? What loss flows through to her from the partnership?

11. Mr. Harrison sold his stock in American Microcomputers for $12,000. He had bought it eight months earlier for $9,000. That same year he sold National Candy Inc. for $4,000. He had bought that three years earlier for $11,000. Mr. Harrison's only other income is a salary of $40,000.
    a. What is Mr. Harrison's net capital loss?
    b. How much of the loss can he apply to reduce his active income this year?
    c. What is Mr. Harrison's gross income this year?

12. Ms. Henry sold the stock she owned in State Linen Supply for $5,000. She paid $10,000 for it 10 months ago. She also sold her stock in Federal Appliance Stores for $9,000. She bought that 18 months ago for $10,500. Her only other income is a salary of $27,000.
    a. What is Ms. Henry's net capital loss?
    b. How much of the loss can be applied to reduce her other income this year?
    c. What is Ms. Henry's gross income?

*13. Loretta Ford, a TV actress, had a taxable income of $127,000. As a single taxpayer, what is her tax liability?

*14. Phyllis and Henry Dodge had a joint taxable income of $170,000. They had three dependent children. What is their tax liability?

# READINGS

Internal Revenue Service. *Your Federal Income Tax*. Publication 17. Washington, D.C. annual.
    *This free publication is the basic reference for most individuals when preparing their federal income tax.*

Pechman, Joseph A. *Federal Tax Policy,* 5th ed. Washington, D.C.: The Brookings Institution, 1987.
    *This classic book on tax policy reflects the changes brought about by the Tax Reform Act of 1986.*

---

*More difficult.

# APPENDICES

# Appendix A
# Time Value of Money

## OBJECTIVES

When you have finished studying this appendix, you should understand

1. The future value of a single amount, of an annuity due, and of a regular annuity.
2. The present value of a single amount, of an annuity due, and of a regular annuity.

## INTRODUCTION

Money invested over a period of time grows in value because it earns interest or dividends or because the investment appreciates in value. Money invested in a bank account or bonds grows because of interest earned. Money invested in common stock grows because of both dividends and appreciation in stock value.

It is possible to look at the investment's value at the beginning of the investment or at the end of the investment. The value at the beginning of the investment is called the *present value* (*PV*); the value at the end is called the *future value* (*FV*). Determining the future value will be discussed first because it is easier to conceptualize. Accruing interest will be used to illustrate the growth of invested money.

Following are definitions of terms that will be used throughout this appendix.

- *Period*. The period is the length of time until the amount of interest is computed on the principal. For instance, if a bank computed interest once a year, the period would be one year. If the bank computed interest once a month, the period would be one month. If the bank computed interest daily, the period would be one day.
- *Number of Periods* (*n*). This is the number of periods that money is invested. For example, money is invested for three years and the period is a year. Therefore, the number of periods would be three. If money is invested for three years where the period is a month, the number of periods would be 36 (3 × 12 months in a year).
- *Interest Rate* (*i*). The interest rate is the rate per period that is applied to the principal. Interest rates are usually quoted as annual rates. If the period is not one year, the annual rate has to be converted to the interest rate per period. For instance,

an annual rate of 12 percent is 3 percent per quarter (12/4 quarters in a year), or 1 percent per month (12 months in a year).

- *Payment* (*PMT*). The payment is the amount of money added to or subtracted from the investment each period. For example, you may wish to add $50 to your bank account each month. Alternatively, you may wish to withdraw $50 from your bank account each month. In either case, the payment would be $50.

# FUTURE VALUE

If money is kept in an interest bearing investment for more than one period, interest is paid on the principal and also on interest previously earned. That is, the interest earned in the first period earns interest in the second period. During the third period interest is paid on the principal and all previously accumulated interest. Interest paid on interest is said to be "compounded."

The amount originally invested is called the present value (*PV*) and the value at the end of the investment time period is the future value (*FV*). The future value of an investment when interest is compounded can be found by Equation A–1.

$$FV = PV(1 + i)^n \qquad \text{(A–1)}$$

where

$PV$ = the principal originally invested or the present value

$n$ = the number of periods

$FV$ = the total amount of principal and accumulated interest at the end of the $n$th period or the future value

$i$ = interest rate per period

This equation is derived in Appendix B. The future value can be computed using a regular calculator or a business calculator.

---

**PRACTICE PROBLEM 1**

Ethan put $100 in a bank for 5 years. The bank pays 6% annual interest and compounds yearly (that is, computes interest once a year). How much will he have in the account at the end of five years?

*Solution*

$$FV = PV (1 + i)^n$$

$$FV = \$100 (1 + .06)^5$$

$$FV = \$100 (1.06)^5 = \$100 (1.3382) = \$133.82$$

**PRACTICE PROBLEM 2**    Alice put $100 in another bank for 5 years. This bank also pays 6% annual interest but compounds monthly. How much will she have in her account at the end of five years?

*Solution*

$$FV = PV (1 + i)^n$$

$$n = 5 \times 12 = 60$$

$$i = \frac{.06}{12} = .005$$

$$FV = \$100 (1 + .005)^{60}$$

$$FV = \$100 (1.005)^{60} = \$100 (1.34885) = \$134.89$$

**PRACTICE PROBLEM 3**    Dorothy borrowed $1,000 for 3 months from a finance company that charged $1\frac{1}{2}$% interest per month (that is, equivalent to 18% annual interest compounded monthly).

(a)  How much will she have to pay back at the end of the 3 month period?
(b)  How much interest will she have to pay?

*Solution*

(a) $FV = PV (1 + i)^n$

$$n = 3, i = .015, PV = \$1,000$$

$$FV = \$1,000 (1 + .015)^3$$

$$FV = \$1,000 (1.015)^3 = \$1,000 (1.045678) = \$1,045.68$$

(b) $\$1,045.68 - \$1,000 = \$45.68$

---

## Future Value of an Annuity

If you were to make a payment of $50 every month into your investment, this would be an annuity. An *annuity* is a series of equal payments for a specified number of periods at a specified rate of interest per period. Interest will be compounded on each payment and the value of the investment at the end of the specified number of periods is the future value.

The payments can be made at the beginning of each period or at the end of each period. If the payments are made at the beginning of each period, there is an *annuity due*. If the payments are made at the end of each period, there is a *regular annuity*. When the period, the interest rate, and payments are the same, the future value of an annuity due will be larger than the future value of a regular annuity, because each payment has been accruing interest for one period longer.

The sum of the future value of each payment or the formula for the future value of an annuity due is

$$FV = PMT [(1 + i)^n + (1 + i)^{n-1} + (1 + i)^{n-2} + \ldots (1 + i)] \quad \textbf{(A–2)}$$

or

$$FV = PMT \sum_{m=1}^{n} (1 + i)^m$$

This is derived in Appendix B. Also, derived is Equation A–3

$$FV = PMT \left( \frac{(1 + i)^{n+1} - (1 + i)}{i} \right) \qquad \text{(A–3)}$$

The formula for the future value of a regular annuity is

$$FV = PMT [(1 + i)^{n-1} + (1 + i)^{n-2}$$
$$+ (1 + i)^{n-3} + \ . \ . \ . \ (1 + i) + 1] \qquad \text{(A–4)}$$

or

$$FV = PMT \sum_{m=0}^{n-1} (1 + i)^m$$

This also is derived in Appendix B, along with the equivalent formula, Equation A–5

$$FV = PMT \left( \frac{(1 + i)^n - 1}{i} \right) \qquad \text{(A–5)}$$

With Equation A–3 or A–5 it is fairly easy to compute the future value of an annuity or the payment using your calculator. The values of $i$ or $n$ can be found using successive approximations. However, it is even easier to compute on a business calculator. Also, on a business calculator any one of the variables can be found if the other three are known.

---

**PRACTICE PROBLEM 4**  Every year for her birthday Susanne receives a check for $100 from her grandmother, which she plans to save for her college education. If she deposits the $100 at the beginning of each year for the next eight years, how much will she have for college at the end of the eighth year? She will put her money in a savings account that pays 6% interest compounded annually.

*Solution*
$$PMT = \$100, i = 6\%, n = 8, FV = ?$$

This is an annuity due. Using Equation A–3,

$$FV = \$100 (10.491316) = \$1049.13$$

**PRACTICE**
**PROBLEM 5**

Mr. Summers is 45 years old and plans to retire when he is 65. If he takes $150 out of his paycheck at the beginning of every month and deposits the money in his credit union, how much will he have in 20 years when he retires? His credit union pays 8% annual interest compounded monthly.

*Solution*

$$PMT = \$150, i = 8\%/12, n = 12 \times 20 = 240, FV = ?$$

This is an annuity due. Using Equation A–3,

$$FV = \$150 \,(592.947218) = \$88,942.08$$

**PRACTICE**
**PROBLEM 6**

Ella Edmunson, who is now 20 years from retirement, wishes to accumulate $500,000 by the end of her 64th year to supplement her pension and Social Security income. How much would she have to deposit at the end of each month if her bank account paid 10% annual interest compounded monthly?

*Solution*

$$FV = \$500,000, i = 10\%/12, n = 12 \times 20 = 240, PMT = ?$$

This is a regular annuity. Using Equation A–5 and solving for *PMT*,

$$PMT = \$500,000/759.3688 = \$658.44$$

# PRESENT VALUE

The section on future value showed how to compute the future value of a single amount (called the present value) invested for *n* periods at *i* rate of interest. If the future value, the number of periods, and the rate of interest are known, it is also possible to compute the present value or amount originally invested.

Solving Equation A–1 for the present value (*PV*) gives

$$PV = \left[ \frac{FV}{(1 + i)^n} \right] \qquad \textbf{(A–6)}$$

It is easy to compute the present value using either a regular calculator or a business calculator.

**PRACTICE**
**PROBLEM 7**

Mary's rich uncle Jacob wishes to give her a $10,000 car when she graduates in 4 years. In order to have $10,000 in 4 years how much should Jacob invest now if he can earn 10% interest compounded annually?

*Solution*

$$FV = \$10,000, i = 10\%, n = 4, PV = ?$$

Using Equation A–6,

$$PV = \$10,000/1.4641 = \$6,830.13$$

**PRACTICE PROBLEM 8**  An investment at 12% per year will have a value of $5,000 at the end of 5 years. What is the present value of the investment?

*Solution*

$$FV = \$5,000, \, i = 12\%, \, n = 5, PV = ?$$

Using Equation A–6,

$$PV = \$5,000/1.762341 = \$2,837.13$$

**PRACTICE PROBLEM 9**  Jack has some money he wishes to invest in either Investment A or Investment B. Both Investments A and B require the same initial outlay of $2,000. Investment A could be sold after 4 years for $5,000; Investment B could be sold after 5 years for $5,500. At an annual interest rate of 11%, which investment should Jack make?

*Solution*

For A,

$$FV = \$5,000, \, i = 11\%, \, n = 4, PV = ?$$

Using Equation A–6,

$$PV = \$5,000/1.51807 = \$3,293.65$$

For B,

$$FV = \$5,500, \, i = 11\%, \, n = 5, PV = ?$$

Using Equation A–6,

$$PV = \$5,500/1.68506 = \$3,263.98$$

The present value for Investment A is greater; therefore, he should invest in A.

## Present Value of an Annuity

The present value (*PV*) of an annuity is the amount that, if invested now at the stated rate of interest, will provide the annuity payments. For instance, if you invested $20,000 in a bank account paying 9 percent annual interest (.75 percent monthly interest), you could draw a payment of $415.16 out of your account for five years. After the last payment there would be no money left. The $20,000 originally invested is the present value of the annuity of monthly payments of $415.16 for five years at .75 percent interest per month.

It is often more convenient to compare the present values of two annuities than the future values when making an investment decision. You can find the present value of an annuity due (for which payments occur at the beginning of each period) or of a regular annuity (for which payments occur at the end of each period). The example above was of a regular annuity because the payments occurred at the end of each month.

The formula for the present value of a regular annuity is the sum of the present values of each of the payments

$$PV = PMT \left[ \frac{1}{(1 + i)^1} + \frac{1}{(1 + i)^2} + \frac{1}{(1 + i)^3} + \cdots \frac{1}{(1 + i)^n} \right] \quad \text{(A–7)}$$

or

$$PV = PMT \sum_{m=1}^{n} \frac{1}{(1 + i)^m}$$

Another formula for the present value of an annuity that makes computation easy is derived in Appendix B.

$$PV = PMT \left[ \frac{1 - \dfrac{1}{(1 + i)^n}}{i} \right] \quad \text{(A–8)}$$

The formula for the present value of an annuity due is also the sum of the present values of each of the payments or

$$PV = PMT \left[ 1 + \frac{1}{(1 + i)^1} + \frac{1}{(1 + i)^2} + \frac{1}{(1 + i)^3} + \cdots \frac{1}{(1 + i)^{n-1}} \right] \quad \text{(A–9)}$$

or

$$PV = PMT \sum_{m=0}^{n-1} \frac{1}{(1 + i)^m}$$

A formula for easier computation derived in Appendix B is

$$PV = PMT \left[ \frac{(1 + i) - \dfrac{1}{(1 + i)^{n-1}}}{i} \right] \quad \text{(A–10)}$$

Equations A–8 and A–10 can be used to compute *PV* or *PMT* easily on a regular calculator. The variables *i* or *n* can be found using successive approximations. A business calculator can be used to find any variable if the other three are known.

---

**PRACTICE PROBLEM 10**

What is the present value of an annuity that returns $200 per period for 8 periods? The interest rate is 9% per period.

*Solution*

$$PMT = \$200, i = 9\%, n = 8, PV = ?$$

This is a regular annuity. Using Equation A–8,

$$PV = \$200 \,(5.534819) = \$1,106.96$$

**PRACTICE PROBLEM 11**

What is the present value of an annuity which returns $500 per month for 5 years when the annual interest rate is 8%?

*Solution*

$$PMT = \$500, i = 8\%/12, n = 5 \times 12 = 60, PV = ?$$

This is a regular annuity. Using Equation A–8,

$$PV = \$500 \,(49.318432) = \$24,659.22$$

---

**PRACTICE PROBLEM 12**

Jennifer Pratt is currently an executive secretary who yearns to write novels. She figures that if she were to quit her job to write full-time, it would take about 3 years before she could make a living at writing. Jennifer thinks she could live comfortably on $600 per month. If she can invest her money at a 10% annual rate, how much will she have to save before she can quit her job? She would withdraw her $600 payments at the beginning of each month.

*Solution*

This is a present value of an annuity due problem with monthly compounding.

$$PMT = \$600, i = 10\%/12, n = 3 \times 12 = 36, PV = ?$$

Using Equation A–10,

$$PV = \$600 \,(31.249496) = \$18,749.70$$

**PRACTICE PROBLEM 13**

Mr. MacDonald has just retired at the age of 65 after working for 40 years as a production engineer. He has saved $100,000, which he will invest in a money market mutual fund. He plans to withdraw a sum of money at the end of each month to supplement his pension and Social Security. He feels he will not live past age 90 and the mutual fund pays 11.5% interest compounded monthly. How much can he withdraw each month?

*Solution*

$$PV = \$100,000, i = 11.5\%/12, n = 25 \times 12 = 300, PMT = ?$$

This is a regular annuity. Using Equation A–8,

$$PMT = \$100,000/98.379787 = \$1,016.47$$

**PRACTICE**  Tom bought a new car for \$9,000. He had saved \$2,000 for a down payment and planned to
**PROBLEM 14**  borrow the remainder. If he could borrow at 8.8% for 4 years, what would his monthly payment
be?

*Solution*

An installment loan is a regular annuity where the amount borrowed is the present value.

$$PV = \$9,000 - \$2,000 = \$7,000, i = 8.8\%/12, n = 4 \times 12 = 48, PMT = ?$$

Using Equation A–8

$$PMT = \$7,000/40.338546 = \$173.53$$

# SUMMARY

Future value:

$$FV = PV(1 + i)^n \tag{A–1}$$

Future value of an annuity due:

$$FV = PMT \, [(1 + i)^n + (1 + i)^{n-1} \\ + (1 + i)^{n-2} + \ldots (1 + i)] \tag{A–2}$$

$$FV = PMT \left[ \frac{(1 + i)^{n+1} - (1 + i)}{i} \right] \tag{A–3}$$

Future value of a regular annuity:

$$FV = PMT \, [(1 + i)^{n-1} + (1 + i)^{n-2} \\ + (1 + i)^{n-3} + \ldots (1 + i) + 1] \tag{A–4}$$

$$FV = PMT \left[ \frac{(1 + i)^n - 1}{i} \right] \tag{A–5}$$

Present value:

$$PV = \frac{FV}{(1 + i)^n} \tag{A–6}$$

Present value of a regular annuity:

$$PV = PMT \left[ \frac{1}{(1+i)^1} + \frac{1}{(1+i)^2} + \frac{1}{(1+i)^3} + \cdots \frac{1}{(1+i)^n} \right] \quad \text{(A–7)}$$

$$PV = PMT \left[ \frac{1 - \dfrac{1}{(1+i)^n}}{i} \right] \quad \text{(A–8)}$$

Present value of an annuity due:

$$PV = PMT \left[ 1 + \frac{1}{(1-i)^1} + \frac{1}{(1+i)^2} \right.$$

$$\left. + \frac{1}{(1+i)^3} + \cdots \frac{1}{(1+i)^{n-1}} \right] \quad \text{(A–9)}$$

$$PV = PMT \left[ \frac{(1+i) - \dfrac{1}{(1+i)^{n-1}}}{i} \right] \quad \text{(A–10)}$$

## PROBLEMS

1. Mrs. Thorpe put $5,000 in an account that paid 7% annual interest compounded yearly. How much will she have at the end of 5 years?

2. Mrs. Jackson also put $5,000 into an account that paid 7% annual interest; however, her bank compounded monthly. How much will Mrs. Jackson have at the end of 5 years?

3. Phil borrowed $2,500 for 8 months from a bank that charged 11% annual interest compounded monthly. He intended to pay the amount he borrowed and all of the interest at the end of the 8 month period.

    (a) How much will he pay back at the end of the 8 months?
    (b) How much of the payment will be interest?

4. How much will Mr. Beacon have to invest now if he wishes to have $5,000 at the end of 5 years? He can invest his money at 9% interest compounded annually.

5. An investment at 13% interest compounded monthly will have a value of $8,000 at the end of 8 years. What is the present value of the investment?

6. Jill has $3,000 she wishes to invest in either Investment X or Investment Y. Investment X could be sold after 5 years for $7,000; Investment Y could be sold after 6 years for $8,000. At an annual interest rate of 10%, which investment should Jill make?

7. What is the present value of an annuity that returns $1,000 per year for 10 years if the interest rate is 10% per year?

8. What is the present value of an annuity that returns $400 per month for 8 years if the annual interest rate is 9% compounded monthly?

9. Maria wishes to retire at age 55. She figures she needs $1,000 per month for 10 years until she can qualify for Social Security and her pension fund. If she can earn an annual interest rate of 9% compounded monthly, how much will she have to invest at age 55 to receive $1,000 per month for 10 years?

10. Craig borrowed $800 for 8 months from a bank that charged 14% annual interest compounded monthly. What was his monthly installment payment?

11. Mr. Donahue borrowed $50,000 for 25 years to buy a house. The Savings and Loan charged him $12\frac{1}{2}\%$ annual interest compounded monthly.

    (a) What was his monthly installment payment?
    (b) What is the total amount he paid on the loan during the 25 year period?

12. Roger plans to deposit $100 into his account at the beginning of every month for the next five years. If his account pays 8% annual interest compounded monthly, how much will he have at the end of 5 years?

13. Peggy wishes to invest $1,000 at the beginning of each of the next 8 years for her son's college education. If she can earn $10\frac{1}{2}\%$ per year on her investment, how much will she have at the end of 8 years?

14. At age 45, Ron inherited $20,000 from his father. If he can invest this money at $12\frac{1}{2}\%$ annual interest, how much will he have by the time he retires at age 65?

15. Pam wishes to have $100,000 when she retires at age 65. How much will she have to invest at the end of each month starting at age 35 if she can invest at 10.4% annual interest compounded monthly?

16. Larry borrowed $8,000 for 3 years at $15\frac{1}{4}\%$ annual interest compounded monthly.

    (a) What was his monthly installment payment?
    (b) What is the total amount of interest he paid?

17. Lou Ceil is 65 years old. She just received $90,000 cash from the sale of her home. If she can deposit this money in an account paying 9.6% annual interest compounded monthly, how much can she withdraw from her account at the end of each month for the next 30 years?

18. Fred can deposit his money in an account at the First National Bank, which pays $8\frac{1}{2}\%$ annual interest compounded daily, or he can deposit his money in the First American Bank, which pays $8\frac{3}{4}\%$ annual interest compounded monthly. In which bank should he deposit his money?

# Appendix B
# Derivations

## FUTURE VALUE

Define

$P_0$ = the principal at time zero

$n$ = the number of periods

$P_n$ = the total amount of principal and accumulated interest at the end of the $n$th period

$i$ = interest rate per period

$I_n$ = the amount of interest earned in the $n$th period

$P_1 = P_0 + I_1$, but $I_1 = P_0 i$

therefore,

$$P_1 = P_0 + P_0 i = P_0 (1 + i)$$
$$P_2 = P_1 + I_2, \text{ but } I_2 = P_1 i$$

therefore,

$$P_2 = P_1 + P_1 i = P_1 (1 + i), \text{ but } P_1 = P_0 (1 + i)$$

therefore,

$$P_2 = P_0 (1 + i) (1 + i) = P_0 (1 + i)^2$$
$$P_3 = P_2 + I_3, \text{ but } I_3 = P_2 i$$

therefore,

$$P_3 = P_2 + P_2 i = P_2 (1 + i), \text{ but } P_2 = P_0 (1 + i)^2$$

therefore,

$$P_3 = P_0 (1 + i)^2 (1 + i) = P_0 (1 + i)^3$$

$$\vdots$$

$$P_n = P_0 (1 + i)^n$$

If you let $P_n = FV$ and $P_0 = PV$ the formula becomes

$$FV = PV (1 + i)^n \hspace{4cm} \textbf{(A–1)}$$

# FUTURE VALUE OF AN ANNUITY DUE

Period 1: From the future value formula, $FV = PV (1 + i)^n$, an amount $PMT$ invested at the beginning of the first period will grow to an amount $PMT$ $(1 + i)^n$ by the end of the $n$th period.

Period 2: The amount $PMT$ invested at the beginning of the second period will grow to the amount $PMT (1 + i)^{n-1}$, since it will be invested for one period less than $n$.

Period 3: The amount $PMT$ invested at the beginning of the third period will grow to $PMT (1 + i)^{n-2}$ by the end of the $n$th period.

$$\vdots$$

Period $n$: The amount $PMT$ invested at the beginning of the $n$th period will grow for only one period to become $PMT (1 + i)^1$.

If we sum up the future value of each investment $PMT$ we get

$$FV = PMT (1 + i)^n + PMT (1 + i)^{n-1}$$
$$+ PMT (1 + i)^{n-2} + \ldots PMT(1 + i)^1$$

where $FV$ is the future value of an annuity due. Factoring out $PMT$ we get

$$FV = PMT [(1 + i)^n + (1 + i)^{n-1}$$
$$+ (1 + i)^{n-2} + \ldots (1 + i)^1] \hspace{1cm} \textbf{(A–2)}$$

Multiply Equation A–2 by $(1 + i)$.

$$(1) \; FV(1 + i) = PMT [(1 + i)^{n+1}$$
$$+ (1 + i)^n + (1 + i)^{n-1} + \ldots (1 + i)^2]$$

Subtract Equation A–2 from (1).

$$(2) \; FV(1 + i) - FV = PMT [(1 + i)^{n+1} - (1 + i)]$$

Notice that all the intermediate terms

$$(1 + i)^n, (1 + i)^{n-1}, (1 + i)^{n-2}, \ldots , (1 + i)^2$$

are contained in both Equations A–2 and (1) and, therefore, subtract out. Simplify (2).

$$(3) \ FV + iFV - FV = PMT\,[(1 + i)^{n+1} - (1 + i)] \qquad \text{(A–3)}$$

$$FV = PMT\left[\frac{(1 + i)^{n+1} - (1 + i)}{i}\right]$$

# FUTURE VALUE OF A REGULAR ANNUITY

Period 1: From the future value formula, $FV = PV(1 + i)^n$, an amount $PMT$ invested at the end of the first period will grow to an amount $PMT$ $(1 + i)^{n-1}$ by the end of the $n$th period. It will have been invested for only $n - 1$ periods since it was not invested until the end of the first period.

Period 2: The amount $PMT$ invested at the end of the second period will grow to an amount $PMT(1 + i)^{n-2}$ by the end of the $n$th period, since it will be invested for one period less than the first period investment.

Period 3: The amount $PMT$ invested at the end of the third period will grow to $PMT\,(1 + i)^{n-3}$ by the end of the $n$th period.
$$\vdots$$

Period $n$: The amount $PMT$ invested at the end of the $n$th period will be invested for zero time and, therefore, will not grow. It will remain $PMT$.

If we sum up the future value of each investment $PMT$ we get

$$FV = PMT(1 + i)^{n-1} + PMT(1 + i)^{n-2}$$
$$+ PMT\,(1 + i)^{n-3} + \ldots PMT$$

where $FV$ is the future value of a regular annuity. Factoring out $PMT$ we get

$$FV = PMT\,[(1 + i)^{n-1} + (1 + i)^{n-2} + (1 + i)^{n-3} + \ldots 1] \qquad \text{(A–4)}$$

Multiply Equation A–4 by $(1 + i)$.

$$(1) \ FV(1 + i) = PMT\,[(1 + i)^n + (1 + i)^{n-1}$$
$$+ (1 + i)^{n-2} + \ldots (1 + i)]$$

Subtract Equation A–4 from (1).

$$(2)\ FV(1 + i) - FV = PMT\,[(1 + i)^n - 1]$$

Notice that all the intermediate terms

$$(1 + i)^{n-1}, (1 + i)^{n-2}, (1 + i)^{n-3}, \ldots, (1 + i)$$

are contained in both Equations A–4 and (1) and, therefore, subtract out. Simplify (2).

$$(3)\ FV + iFV - FV = PMT\,[(1 + i)^n - 1)]\qquad\text{(A–5)}$$

$$FV = PMT \left[\frac{(1 + i)^n - 1}{i}\right]$$

# PRESENT VALUE OF A REGULAR ANNUITY

Define

$PV$ = the present value of an annuity

$PMT$ = the payment at the end of each period

$n$ = the number of periods

$i$ = the rate per period

Period 1: Using the equation $PV = FV/(1 + i)^n$ the present value of the payment $PMT$ at the end of the first period is $PMT/(1 + i)^1$, where $FV = PMT$.

Period 2: The present value of the payment $PMT$ at the end of the second period is $PMT/(1 + i)^2$.

Period 3: The present value of the payment $PMT$ at the end of the third period is $PMT/(1 + i)^3$.

$\vdots$

Period $n$: The present value of the payment $PMT$ at the end of the $n$th period = $PMT/(1 + i)^n$.

The present value of all the payments is the sum:

$$PV = \frac{PMT}{(1 + i)^1} + \frac{PMT}{(1 + i)^2} + \frac{PMT}{(1 + i)^3} + \cdots \frac{PMT}{(1 + i)^n}$$

Factor out the $PMT$.

$$PV = PMT \left[\frac{1}{(1 + i)^1} + \frac{1}{(1 + i)^2} + \frac{1}{(1 + i)^3} + \cdots \frac{1}{(1 + i)^n}\right]\qquad\text{(A–7)}$$

Multiply Equation A–7 by $(1 + i)$.

$$(1) \quad PV(1 + i) = PMT \left[ 1 + \frac{1}{(1 + i)^1} + \frac{1}{(1 + i)^2} + \cdot \cdot \cdot \frac{1}{(1 + i)^{n-1}} \right]$$

Subtract Equation A–7 from (1).

$$(2) \quad PV(1 + i) - PV = PMT \left[ 1 - \frac{1}{(1 + i)^n} \right]$$

Notice that all the intermediate terms

$$\left( \frac{1}{(1 + i)^1}, \frac{1}{(1 + i)^2}, \frac{1}{(1 + i)^3}, \cdot \cdot \cdot \frac{1}{(1 + i)^{n-1}} \right)$$

are contained in both Equations A–7 and (1) and, therefore, subtract out. Simplify (2).

$$(3) \quad PV + iPV - PV = PMT \left[ 1 - \frac{1}{(1 + i)} \right] \tag{A–8}$$

$$PV = PMT \frac{\left[ 1 - \frac{1}{(1 + i)^r} \right]}{i}$$

# PRESENT VALUE OF AN ANNUITY DUE

Period 1: The present value of the payment $PMT$ at the beginning of the first period is $PMT$ since no time has elapsed.

Period 2: Using the equation $PV = FV/(1 + i)^n$, the present value of the payment at the beginning of the second period is $PMT/(1 + i)^1$ since one period has elapsed. Note that $FV = PMT$.

Period 3: The present value of the payment $PMT$ at the beginning of the third period is $PMT/(1 + i)^2$ since two periods have elapsed.

$\vdots$

Period $n$: The present value of the payment $PMT$ at the beginning of the $n$th period is $PMT/(1 + i)^{n-1}$ since $n - 1$ periods have elapsed.

The present value of all of the payments is the sum

$$PV = PMT + \frac{PMT}{(1 + i)^1} + \frac{PMT}{(1 + i)^2} + \cdot \cdot \cdot \frac{PMT}{(1 + i)^{n-1}}$$

Factor out *PMT*.

$$PV = PMT \left[ 1 + \frac{1}{(1 + i)^1} + \frac{1}{(1 + i)^2} + \cdots \frac{1}{(1 + i)^{n-1}} \right] \tag{A-9}$$

Multiply Equation A–9 by $(1 + i)$.

$$(1) \; PV(1 + i) = PMT \left[ (1 + i) + 1 + \frac{1}{(1 + i)^1} \right.$$
$$\left. + \frac{1}{(1 + i)^2} + \cdots \frac{1}{(1 + i)^{n-2}} \right]$$

Subtract Equation A–9 from (1).

$$(2) \; PV(1 + i) - PV = PMT \left[ (1 + i) - \frac{1}{(1 + i)^{n-1}} \right]$$

Notice that all the intermediate terms

$$1, \frac{1}{(1 + i)^1}, \frac{1}{(1 + i)^2}, \cdots, \frac{1}{(1 + i)^{n-2}}$$

are contained in both Equations A–9 and (1) and therefore subtract out. Simplify (2).

$$(3) \; PV + iPV - PV = PMT \left[ (1 + i) - \frac{1}{(1 + i)^{n-1}} \right]$$

$$PV = PMT \left[ \frac{(1 + i) - \dfrac{1}{(1 + i)^{n-1}}}{i} \right] \tag{A-10}$$

# Appendix C
# Compound Interest and Annuity Tables

Appendix tables are reprinted from Carlene Creviston et al., *Contemporary Personal Finance* (Boston: Allyn and Bacon, 1985), pp. 582–589. Used with permission of Allyn and Bacon.

# TABLE C–1 Present Value of One Dollar—Annual Compounding: [$PVF_{i,n}$]

| PERIOD | 1% | 2% | 3% | 4% | 5% | 6% | 8% | 10% | 12% | 14% | 16% | 18% | 20% | 22% | 24% |
|---|---|---|---|---|---|---|---|---|---|---|---|---|---|---|---|
| 1 | 0.9901 | 0.9804 | 0.9709 | 0.9615 | 0.9524 | 0.9434 | 0.9259 | 0.9091 | 0.8929 | 0.8772 | 0.8621 | 0.8475 | 0.8333 | 0.8197 | 0.8065 |
| 2 | 0.9803 | 0.9612 | 0.9426 | 0.9246 | 0.9070 | 0.8900 | 0.8573 | 0.8264 | 0.7972 | 0.7695 | 0.7432 | 0.7182 | 0.6944 | 0.6719 | 0.6504 |
| 3 | 0.9706 | 0.9423 | 0.9151 | 0.8890 | 0.8638 | 0.8396 | 0.7938 | 0.7513 | 0.7118 | 0.6750 | 0.6407 | 0.6086 | 0.5787 | 0.5507 | 0.5245 |
| 4 | 0.9610 | 0.9238 | 0.8885 | 0.8548 | 0.8227 | 0.7921 | 0.7350 | 0.6830 | 0.6355 | 0.5921 | 0.5523 | 0.5158 | 0.4823 | 0.4514 | 0.4230 |
| 5 | 0.9515 | 0.9057 | 0.8626 | 0.8219 | 0.7835 | 0.7473 | 0.6806 | 0.6209 | 0.5674 | 0.5194 | 0.4761 | 0.4371 | 0.4019 | 0.3700 | 0.3411 |
| 6 | 0.9420 | 0.8880 | 0.8375 | 0.7903 | 0.7462 | 0.7050 | 0.6302 | 0.5645 | 0.5066 | 0.4556 | 0.4104 | 0.3704 | 0.3349 | 0.3033 | 0.2751 |
| 7 | 0.9327 | 0.8706 | 0.8131 | 0.7599 | 0.7107 | 0.6651 | 0.5835 | 0.5132 | 0.4523 | 0.3996 | 0.3538 | 0.3139 | 0.2791 | 0.2486 | 0.2218 |
| 8 | 0.9235 | 0.8535 | 0.7894 | 0.7307 | 0.6768 | 0.6274 | 0.5403 | 0.4665 | 0.4039 | 0.3506 | 0.3050 | 0.2660 | 0.2326 | 0.2038 | 0.1789 |
| 9 | 0.9143 | 0.8368 | 0.7664 | 0.7026 | 0.6446 | 0.5919 | 0.5002 | 0.4241 | 0.3606 | 0.3075 | 0.2630 | 0.2255 | 0.1938 | 0.1670 | 0.1443 |
| 10 | 0.9053 | 0.8203 | 0.7441 | 0.6756 | 0.6139 | 0.5584 | 0.4632 | 0.3855 | 0.3220 | 0.2697 | 0.2267 | 0.1911 | 0.1615 | 0.1369 | 0.1164 |
| 11 | 0.8963 | 0.8043 | 0.7224 | 0.6496 | 0.5847 | 0.5268 | 0.4289 | 0.3505 | 0.2875 | 0.2366 | 0.1954 | 0.1619 | 0.1346 | 0.1122 | 0.0938 |
| 12 | 0.8874 | 0.7885 | 0.7014 | 0.6246 | 0.5568 | 0.4970 | 0.3971 | 0.3186 | 0.2567 | 0.2076 | 0.1685 | 0.1372 | 0.1122 | 0.0920 | 0.0757 |
| 13 | 0.8787 | 0.7730 | 0.6810 | 0.6006 | 0.5303 | 0.4688 | 0.3677 | 0.2897 | 0.2292 | 0.1821 | 0.1452 | 0.1163 | 0.0935 | 0.0754 | 0.0610 |
| 14 | 0.8700 | 0.7579 | 0.6611 | 0.5775 | 0.5051 | 0.4423 | 0.3405 | 0.2633 | 0.2046 | 0.1597 | 0.1252 | 0.0985 | 0.0779 | 0.0618 | 0.0492 |
| 15 | 0.8613 | 0.7430 | 0.6419 | 0.5553 | 0.4810 | 0.4173 | 0.3152 | 0.2394 | 0.1827 | 0.1401 | 0.1079 | 0.0835 | 0.0649 | 0.0507 | 0.0397 |
| 16 | 0.8528 | 0.7284 | 0.6232 | 0.5339 | 0.4581 | 0.3936 | 0.2919 | 0.2176 | 0.1631 | 0.1229 | 0.0930 | 0.0708 | 0.0541 | 0.0415 | 0.0320 |
| 17 | 0.8444 | 0.7142 | 0.6050 | 0.5134 | 0.4363 | 0.3714 | 0.2703 | 0.1978 | 0.1456 | 0.1078 | 0.0802 | 0.0600 | 0.0451 | 0.0340 | 0.0258 |
| 18 | 0.8360 | 0.7002 | 0.5874 | 0.4936 | 0.4155 | 0.3503 | 0.2502 | 0.1799 | 0.1300 | 0.0946 | 0.0691 | 0.0508 | 0.0376 | 0.0279 | 0.0208 |
| 19 | 0.8277 | 0.6864 | 0.5703 | 0.4746 | 0.3957 | 0.3305 | 0.2317 | 0.1635 | 0.1161 | 0.0829 | 0.0596 | 0.0431 | 0.0313 | 0.0229 | 0.0168 |
| 20 | 0.8195 | 0.6730 | 0.5537 | 0.4564 | 0.3769 | 0.3118 | 0.2145 | 0.1486 | 0.1037 | 0.0728 | 0.0514 | 0.0365 | 0.0261 | 0.0187 | 0.0135 |
| 21 | 0.8114 | 0.6598 | 0.5375 | 0.4388 | 0.3589 | 0.2942 | 0.1987 | 0.1351 | 0.0926 | 0.0638 | 0.0443 | 0.0309 | 0.0217 | 0.0154 | 0.0109 |
| 22 | 0.8034 | 0.6468 | 0.5219 | 0.4220 | 0.3419 | 0.2775 | 0.1839 | 0.1228 | 0.0826 | 0.0560 | 0.0382 | 0.0262 | 0.0181 | 0.0126 | 0.0088 |
| 23 | 0.7954 | 0.6342 | 0.5067 | 0.4057 | 0.3256 | 0.2618 | 0.1703 | 0.1117 | 0.0738 | 0.0491 | 0.0329 | 0.0222 | 0.0151 | 0.0103 | 0.0071 |
| 24 | 0.7876 | 0.6217 | 0.4919 | 0.3901 | 0.3101 | 0.2470 | 0.1577 | 0.1015 | 0.0659 | 0.0431 | 0.0284 | 0.0188 | 0.0126 | 0.0085 | 0.0057 |
| 25 | 0.7798 | 0.6095 | 0.4776 | 0.3751 | 0.2953 | 0.2330 | 0.1460 | 0.0923 | 0.0588 | 0.0378 | 0.0245 | 0.0160 | 0.0105 | 0.0069 | 0.0046 |
| 26 | 0.7720 | 0.5976 | 0.4637 | 0.3607 | 0.2812 | 0.2198 | 0.1352 | 0.0839 | 0.0525 | 0.0331 | 0.0211 | 0.0135 | 0.0087 | 0.0057 | 0.0037 |
| 27 | 0.7644 | 0.5859 | 0.4502 | 0.3468 | 0.2678 | 0.2074 | 0.1252 | 0.0763 | 0.0469 | 0.0291 | 0.0182 | 0.0115 | 0.0073 | 0.0047 | 0.0030 |
| 28 | 0.7568 | 0.5744 | 0.4371 | 0.3335 | 0.2551 | 0.1956 | 0.1159 | 0.0693 | 0.0419 | 0.0255 | 0.0157 | 0.0097 | 0.0061 | 0.0038 | 0.0024 |
| 29 | 0.7493 | 0.5631 | 0.4243 | 0.3207 | 0.2429 | 0.1846 | 0.1073 | 0.0630 | 0.0374 | 0.0224 | 0.0135 | 0.0082 | 0.0051 | 0.0031 | 0.0020 |
| 30 | 0.7419 | 0.5521 | 0.4120 | 0.3083 | 0.2314 | 0.1741 | 0.0994 | 0.0573 | 0.0334 | 0.0196 | 0.0116 | 0.0070 | 0.0042 | 0.0026 | 0.0016 |

## TABLE C–2 Future Value of One Dollar—Annual Compounding: [FVF$_{i,n}$]

| PERIOD | 1% | 2% | 3% | 4% | 5% | 6% | 8% | 10% | 12% | 14% | 16% | 18% | 20% | 22% | 24% |
|---|---|---|---|---|---|---|---|---|---|---|---|---|---|---|---|
| 1 | 1.0100 | 1.0200 | 1.0300 | 1.0400 | 1.0500 | 1.0600 | 1.0800 | 1.1000 | 1.1200 | 1.1400 | 1.1600 | 1.1800 | 1.2000 | 1.2200 | 1.2400 |
| 2 | 1.0201 | 1.0404 | 1.0609 | 1.0816 | 1.1025 | 1.1236 | 1.1664 | 1.2100 | 1.2544 | 1.2996 | 1.3456 | 1.3924 | 1.4400 | 1.4884 | 1.5376 |
| 3 | 1.0303 | 1.0612 | 1.0927 | 1.1249 | 1.1576 | 1.1910 | 1.2597 | 1.3310 | 1.4049 | 1.4815 | 1.5609 | 1.6430 | 1.7280 | 1.8158 | 1.9066 |
| 4 | 1.0406 | 1.0824 | 1.1255 | 1.1699 | 1.2155 | 1.2625 | 1.3605 | 1.4641 | 1.5735 | 1.6890 | 1.8106 | 1.9388 | 2.0736 | 2.2153 | 2.3642 |
| 5 | 1.0510 | 1.1041 | 1.1593 | 1.2167 | 1.2763 | 1.3382 | 1.4693 | 1.6105 | 1.7623 | 1.9254 | 2.1003 | 2.2878 | 2.4883 | 2.7027 | 2.9316 |
| 6 | 1.0615 | 1.1262 | 1.1941 | 1.2653 | 1.3401 | 1.4185 | 1.5869 | 1.7716 | 1.9738 | 2.1950 | 2.4364 | 2.6996 | 2.9860 | 3.2973 | 3.6352 |
| 7 | 1.0721 | 1.1487 | 1.2299 | 1.3159 | 1.4071 | 1.5036 | 1.7138 | 1.9487 | 2.2107 | 2.5023 | 2.8262 | 3.1855 | 3.5832 | 4.0227 | 4.5077 |
| 8 | 1.0829 | 1.1717 | 1.2668 | 1.3686 | 1.4775 | 1.5938 | 1.8509 | 2.1436 | 2.4760 | 2.8526 | 3.2784 | 3.7589 | 4.2998 | 4.9077 | 5.5895 |
| 9 | 1.0937 | 1.1951 | 1.3048 | 1.4233 | 1.5513 | 1.6895 | 1.9990 | 2.3579 | 2.7731 | 3.2519 | 3.8030 | 4.4355 | 5.1598 | 5.9874 | 6.9310 |
| 10 | 1.1046 | 1.2190 | 1.3439 | 1.4802 | 1.6289 | 1.7908 | 2.1589 | 2.5937 | 3.1058 | 3.7072 | 4.4114 | 5.2338 | 6.1917 | 7.3046 | 8.5944 |
| 11 | 1.1157 | 1.2434 | 1.3842 | 1.5395 | 1.7103 | 1.8983 | 2.3316 | 2.8531 | 3.4785 | 4.2262 | 5.1173 | 6.1759 | 7.4301 | 8.9117 | 10.6571 |
| 12 | 1.1268 | 1.2682 | 1.4258 | 1.6010 | 1.7959 | 2.0122 | 2.5182 | 3.1384 | 3.8960 | 4.8179 | 5.9360 | 7.2876 | 8.9161 | 10.8722 | 13.2148 |
| 13 | 1.1381 | 1.2936 | 1.4685 | 1.6651 | 1.8856 | 2.1329 | 2.7196 | 3.4523 | 4.3635 | 5.4924 | 6.8858 | 8.5994 | 10.6993 | 13.2641 | 16.3863 |
| 14 | 1.1495 | 1.3195 | 1.5126 | 1.7317 | 1.9799 | 2.2609 | 2.9372 | 3.7975 | 4.8871 | 6.2613 | 7.9875 | 10.1473 | 12.8392 | 16.1822 | 20.3191 |
| 15 | 1.1610 | 1.3459 | 1.5580 | 1.8009 | 2.0789 | 2.3966 | 3.1722 | 4.1772 | 5.4736 | 7.1379 | 9.2655 | 11.9738 | 15.4070 | 19.7423 | 25.1956 |
| 16 | 1.1726 | 1.3728 | 1.6047 | 1.8730 | 2.1829 | 2.5404 | 3.4259 | 4.5950 | 6.1304 | 8.1372 | 10.7480 | 14.1290 | 18.4884 | 24.0856 | 31.2426 |
| 17 | 1.1843 | 1.4002 | 1.6528 | 1.9479 | 2.2920 | 2.6928 | 3.7000 | 5.0545 | 6.8660 | 9.2765 | 12.4677 | 16.6723 | 22.1861 | 29.3844 | 38.7408 |
| 18 | 1.1961 | 1.4282 | 1.7024 | 2.0258 | 2.4066 | 2.8543 | 3.9960 | 5.5599 | 7.6900 | 10.5752 | 14.4625 | 19.6733 | 26.6233 | 35.8490 | 48.0386 |
| 19 | 1.2081 | 1.4568 | 1.7535 | 2.1068 | 2.5269 | 3.0256 | 4.3157 | 6.1159 | 8.6128 | 12.0557 | 16.7765 | 23.2145 | 31.9480 | 43.7358 | 59.5679 |
| 20 | 1.2202 | 1.4859 | 1.8061 | 2.1911 | 2.6533 | 3.2071 | 4.6610 | 6.7275 | 9.6463 | 13.7435 | 19.4607 | 27.3931 | 38.3376 | 53.3577 | 73.8642 |
| 21 | 1.2324 | 1.5157 | 1.8603 | 2.2788 | 2.7860 | 3.3996 | 5.0338 | 7.4003 | 10.8038 | 15.6676 | 22.5745 | 32.3238 | 46.0051 | 65.0964 | 91.5916 |
| 22 | 1.2447 | 1.5460 | 1.9161 | 2.3699 | 2.9253 | 3.6035 | 5.4365 | 8.1403 | 12.1003 | 17.8610 | 26.1864 | 38.1421 | 55.2061 | 79.4176 | 113.5736 |
| 23 | 1.2572 | 1.5769 | 1.9736 | 2.4647 | 3.0715 | 3.8198 | 5.8715 | 8.9543 | 13.5523 | 20.3616 | 30.3762 | 45.0077 | 66.2474 | 96.8894 | 140.8312 |
| 24 | 1.2697 | 1.6084 | 2.0328 | 2.5633 | 3.2251 | 4.0489 | 6.3412 | 9.8497 | 15.1786 | 23.2122 | 35.2364 | 53.1091 | 79.4968 | 118.2051 | 174.6307 |
| 25 | 1.2824 | 1.6406 | 2.0938 | 2.6658 | 3.3864 | 4.2919 | 6.8485 | 10.8347 | 17.0001 | 26.4619 | 40.8742 | 62.6687 | 95.3962 | 144.2103 | 216.5421 |
| 26 | 1.2953 | 1.6734 | 2.1566 | 2.7725 | 3.5557 | 4.5494 | 7.3964 | 11.9182 | 19.0401 | 30.1666 | 47.4141 | 73.9491 | 114.4755 | 175.9365 | 268.5122 |
| 27 | 1.3082 | 1.7069 | 2.2213 | 2.8834 | 3.7335 | 4.8224 | 7.9881 | 13.1100 | 21.3249 | 34.3899 | 55.0003 | 87.2599 | 137.3706 | 214.6425 | 332.9552 |
| 28 | 1.3213 | 1.7410 | 2.2879 | 2.9987 | 3.9201 | 5.1117 | 8.6271 | 14.4210 | 23.8839 | 39.2045 | 63.8004 | 102.9667 | 164.8447 | 261.8640 | 412.8644 |
| 29 | 1.3345 | 1.7758 | 2.3566 | 3.1186 | 4.1161 | 5.4184 | 9.3173 | 15.8631 | 26.7499 | 44.6931 | 74.0084 | 121.5007 | 197.8136 | 319.4740 | 511.9519 |
| 30 | 1.3478 | 1.8114 | 2.4273 | 3.2434 | 4.3219 | 5.7435 | 10.0627 | 17.4494 | 29.9599 | 50.9502 | 85.8498 | 143.3709 | 237.3763 | 389.7583 | 634.8203 |

## TABLE C-3  Present Value of One Dollar per Period—Annual Compounding: [PVA$_{i,n}$]

| PERIOD | 1% | 2% | 3% | 4% | 5% | 6% | 8% | 10% | 12% | 14% | 16% | 18% | 20% | 22% | 24% |
|---|---|---|---|---|---|---|---|---|---|---|---|---|---|---|---|
| 1 | 0.9901 | 0.9804 | 0.9709 | 0.9615 | 0.9524 | 0.9434 | 0.9259 | 0.9091 | 0.8929 | 0.8772 | 0.8621 | 0.8475 | 0.8333 | 0.8197 | 0.8065 |
| 2 | 1.9704 | 1.9416 | 1.9135 | 1.8861 | 1.8594 | 1.8334 | 1.7833 | 1.7355 | 1.6901 | 1.6467 | 1.6052 | 1.5656 | 1.5278 | 1.4915 | 1.4568 |
| 3 | 2.9410 | 2.8839 | 2.8286 | 2.7751 | 2.7232 | 2.6730 | 2.5771 | 2.4869 | 2.4018 | 2.3216 | 2.2459 | 2.1743 | 2.1065 | 2.0422 | 1.9813 |
| 4 | 3.9020 | 3.8077 | 3.7171 | 3.6299 | 3.5459 | 3.4651 | 3.3121 | 3.1699 | 3.0373 | 2.9137 | 2.7982 | 2.6901 | 2.5887 | 2.4936 | 2.4043 |
| 5 | 4.8534 | 4.7134 | 4.5797 | 4.4518 | 4.3295 | 4.2124 | 3.9927 | 3.7908 | 3.6048 | 3.4331 | 3.2743 | 3.1272 | 2.9906 | 2.8636 | 2.7454 |
| 6 | 5.7955 | 5.6014 | 5.4172 | 5.2421 | 5.0757 | 4.9173 | 4.6229 | 4.3553 | 4.1114 | 3.8887 | 3.6847 | 3.4976 | 3.3255 | 3.1669 | 3.0205 |
| 7 | 6.7282 | 6.4720 | 6.2303 | 6.0021 | 5.7864 | 5.5824 | 5.2064 | 4.8684 | 4.5638 | 4.2883 | 4.0386 | 3.8115 | 3.6046 | 3.4155 | 3.2423 |
| 8 | 7.6517 | 7.3255 | 7.0197 | 6.7327 | 6.4632 | 6.2098 | 5.7466 | 5.3349 | 4.9676 | 4.6389 | 4.3436 | 4.0776 | 3.8372 | 3.6193 | 3.4212 |
| 9 | 8.5660 | 8.1622 | 7.7861 | 7.4353 | 7.1078 | 6.8017 | 6.2469 | 5.7590 | 5.3283 | 4.9464 | 4.6065 | 4.3030 | 4.0310 | 3.7863 | 3.5655 |
| 10 | 9.4713 | 8.9826 | 8.5302 | 8.1109 | 7.7217 | 7.3601 | 6.7101 | 6.1446 | 5.6502 | 5.2161 | 4.8332 | 4.4941 | 4.1925 | 3.9232 | 3.6819 |
| 11 | 10.3676 | 9.7868 | 9.2526 | 8.7605 | 8.3064 | 7.8869 | 7.1390 | 6.4951 | 5.9377 | 5.4527 | 5.0286 | 4.6560 | 4.3271 | 4.0354 | 3.7757 |
| 12 | 11.2551 | 10.5753 | 9.9540 | 9.3851 | 8.8632 | 8.3839 | 7.5361 | 6.8137 | 6.1944 | 5.6603 | 5.1971 | 4.7932 | 4.4392 | 4.1274 | 3.8514 |
| 13 | 12.1337 | 11.3483 | 10.6350 | 9.9856 | 9.3936 | 8.8527 | 7.9038 | 7.1034 | 6.4235 | 5.8424 | 5.3423 | 4.9095 | 4.5327 | 4.2028 | 3.9124 |
| 14 | 13.0037 | 12.1062 | 11.2961 | 10.5631 | 9.8986 | 9.2950 | 8.2442 | 7.3667 | 6.6282 | 6.0021 | 5.4675 | 5.0081 | 4.6106 | 4.2646 | 3.9616 |
| 15 | 13.8650 | 12.8492 | 11.9379 | 11.1184 | 10.3796 | 9.7123 | 8.5595 | 7.6061 | 6.8109 | 6.1422 | 5.5755 | 5.0916 | 4.6755 | 4.3152 | 4.0013 |
| 16 | 14.7179 | 13.5777 | 12.5611 | 11.6523 | 10.8378 | 10.1059 | 8.8514 | 7.8237 | 6.9740 | 6.2651 | 5.6685 | 5.1624 | 4.7296 | 4.3567 | 4.0333 |
| 17 | 15.5622 | 14.2918 | 13.1661 | 12.1657 | 11.2741 | 10.4773 | 9.1216 | 8.0216 | 7.1196 | 6.3729 | 5.7487 | 5.2223 | 4.7746 | 4.3908 | 4.0591 |
| 18 | 16.3983 | 14.9920 | 13.7535 | 12.6593 | 11.6896 | 10.8276 | 9.3719 | 8.2014 | 7.2497 | 6.4674 | 5.8178 | 5.2732 | 4.8122 | 4.4187 | 4.0799 |
| 19 | 17.2260 | 15.6784 | 14.3238 | 13.1339 | 12.0853 | 11.1581 | 9.6036 | 8.3649 | 7.3658 | 6.5504 | 5.8775 | 5.3162 | 4.8435 | 4.4415 | 4.0967 |
| 20 | 18.0455 | 16.3514 | 14.8775 | 13.5903 | 12.4622 | 11.4699 | 9.8181 | 8.5136 | 7.4694 | 6.6231 | 5.9288 | 5.3527 | 4.8696 | 4.4603 | 4.1103 |
| 21 | 18.8570 | 17.0112 | 15.4150 | 14.0292 | 12.8211 | 11.7641 | 10.0168 | 8.6487 | 7.5620 | 6.6870 | 5.9731 | 5.3837 | 4.8913 | 4.4756 | 4.1212 |
| 22 | 19.6604 | 17.6580 | 15.9369 | 14.4511 | 13.1630 | 12.0416 | 10.2007 | 8.7715 | 7.6446 | 6.7429 | 6.0113 | 5.4099 | 4.9094 | 4.4882 | 4.1300 |
| 23 | 20.4558 | 18.2922 | 16.4436 | 14.8568 | 13.4886 | 12.3034 | 10.3711 | 8.8832 | 7.7184 | 6.7921 | 6.0442 | 5.4321 | 4.9245 | 4.4985 | 4.1371 |
| 24 | 21.2434 | 18.9139 | 16.9355 | 15.2470 | 13.7986 | 12.5504 | 10.5288 | 8.9347 | 7.7843 | 6.8351 | 6.0726 | 5.4509 | 4.9371 | 4.5070 | 4.1428 |
| 25 | 22.0232 | 19.5234 | 17.4131 | 15.6221 | 14.0939 | 12.7834 | 10.6748 | 9.0770 | 7.8431 | 6.8729 | 6.0971 | 5.4669 | 4.9476 | 4.5139 | 4.1474 |
| 26 | 22.7952 | 20.1210 | 17.8768 | 15.9828 | 14.3752 | 13.0032 | 10.8100 | 9.1609 | 7.8957 | 6.9061 | 6.1182 | 5.4804 | 4.9563 | 4.5196 | 4.1511 |
| 27 | 23.5596 | 20.7069 | 18.3270 | 16.3296 | 14.6430 | 13.2105 | 10.9352 | 9.2372 | 7.9426 | 6.9352 | 6.1364 | 5.4919 | 4.9636 | 4.5243 | 4.1542 |
| 28 | 24.3164 | 21.2812 | 18.7641 | 16.6631 | 14.8981 | 13.4062 | 11.0511 | 9.3066 | 7.9844 | 6.9607 | 6.1520 | 5.5016 | 4.9697 | 4.5281 | 4.1566 |
| 29 | 25.0658 | 21.8443 | 19.1885 | 16.9837 | 15.1411 | 13.5907 | 11.1584 | 9.3696 | 8.0218 | 6.9830 | 6.1655 | 5.5098 | 4.9747 | 4.5312 | 4.1585 |
| 30 | 25.8077 | 22.3964 | 19.6004 | 17.2920 | 15.3724 | 13.7648 | 11.2578 | 9.4269 | 8.0552 | 7.0027 | 6.1772 | 5.5168 | 4.9789 | 4.5338 | 4.1601 |

**TABLE C-4  Future Value of Annuity Due—Annual Compounding: [FVA₁,ₙ]**

| PERIOD | 1% | 2% | 3% | 4% | 5% | 6% | 8% | 10% | 12% | 14% | 16% | 18% | 20% | 22% | 24% |
|---|---|---|---|---|---|---|---|---|---|---|---|---|---|---|---|
| 1 | 1.010 | 1.020 | 1.030 | 1.040 | 1.050 | 1.060 | 1.080 | 1.100 | 1.120 | 1.140 | 1.160 | 1.180 | 1.200 | 1.220 | 1.240 |
| 2 | 2.030 | 2.060 | 2.091 | 2.122 | 2.152 | 2.184 | 2.246 | 2.310 | 2.374 | 2.440 | 2.506 | 2.572 | 2.640 | 2.708 | 2.778 |
| 3 | 3.060 | 3.122 | 3.184 | 3.246 | 3.310 | 3.375 | 3.506 | 3.641 | 3.779 | 3.921 | 4.066 | 4.215 | 4.368 | 4.524 | 4.684 |
| 4 | 4.101 | 4.204 | 4.309 | 4.416 | 4.526 | 4.637 | 4.867 | 5.105 | 5.353 | 5.610 | 5.877 | 6.154 | 6.442 | 6.740 | 7.048 |
| 5 | 5.152 | 5.308 | 5.468 | 5.633 | 5.802 | 5.975 | 6.336 | 6.716 | 7.115 | 7.536 | 7.977 | 8.442 | 8.930 | 9.442 | 9.980 |
| 6 | 6.214 | 6.434 | 6.662 | 6.898 | 7.142 | 7.394 | 7.923 | 8.487 | 9.089 | 9.730 | 10.414 | 11.142 | 11.916 | 12.740 | 13.615 |
| 7 | 7.286 | 7.583 | 7.892 | 8.214 | 8.549 | 8.897 | 9.637 | 10.436 | 11.300 | 12.233 | 13.240 | 14.327 | 15.499 | 16.762 | 18.123 |
| 8 | 8.369 | 8.755 | 9.159 | 9.583 | 10.027 | 10.491 | 11.488 | 12.579 | 13.776 | 15.085 | 16.518 | 18.086 | 19.799 | 21.670 | 23.712 |
| 9 | 9.462 | 9.950 | 10.464 | 11.006 | 11.578 | 12.181 | 13.487 | 14.937 | 16.549 | 18.337 | 20.321 | 22.521 | 24.959 | 27.657 | 30.643 |
| 10 | 10.567 | 11.169 | 11.808 | 12.486 | 13.207 | 13.972 | 15.645 | 17.531 | 19.655 | 22.045 | 24.733 | 27.755 | 31.150 | 34.962 | 39.238 |
| 11 | 11.682 | 12.412 | 13.192 | 14.026 | 14.917 | 15.870 | 17.977 | 20.384 | 23.133 | 26.271 | 29.850 | 33.931 | 38.580 | 43.874 | 49.895 |
| 12 | 12.809 | 13.680 | 14.618 | 15.627 | 16.713 | 17.882 | 20.495 | 23.523 | 27.029 | 31.089 | 35.786 | 41.219 | 47.497 | 54.746 | 63.110 |
| 13 | 13.947 | 14.974 | 16.086 | 17.292 | 18.599 | 20.015 | 23.215 | 26.975 | 31.393 | 36.581 | 42.672 | 49.818 | 58.196 | 68.010 | 79.496 |
| 14 | 15.097 | 16.293 | 17.599 | 19.024 | 20.579 | 22.276 | 26.152 | 30.772 | 36.280 | 42.842 | 50.659 | 59.965 | 71.035 | 84.192 | 99.815 |
| 15 | 16.258 | 17.639 | 19.157 | 20.825 | 22.657 | 24.673 | 29.324 | 34.950 | 41.753 | 49.980 | 59.925 | 71.939 | 86.442 | 103.935 | 125.011 |
| 16 | 17.430 | 19.012 | 20.762 | 22.697 | 24.840 | 27.213 | 32.750 | 39.545 | 47.884 | 58.118 | 70.673 | 86.068 | 104.931 | 128.020 | 156.253 |
| 17 | 18.615 | 20.412 | 22.414 | 24.645 | 27.132 | 29.906 | 36.450 | 44.599 | 54.750 | 67.394 | 83.141 | 102.740 | 127.117 | 157.405 | 194.994 |
| 18 | 19.811 | 21.840 | 24.117 | 26.671 | 29.539 | 32.760 | 40.446 | 50.159 | 62.440 | 77.969 | 97.603 | 122.414 | 153.740 | 193.254 | 243.033 |
| 19 | 21.019 | 23.297 | 25.870 | 28.778 | 32.066 | 35.786 | 44.762 | 55.275 | 71.052 | 90.025 | 114.380 | 145.628 | 185.688 | 236.989 | 302.601 |
| 20 | 22.239 | 24.783 | 27.676 | 30.969 | 34.719 | 38.993 | 49.423 | 63.003 | 80.699 | 103.768 | 133.840 | 173.021 | 224.026 | 290.347 | 376.465 |
| 21 | 23.472 | 26.299 | 29.537 | 33.248 | 37.505 | 42.392 | 54.457 | 70.403 | 91.503 | 119.436 | 156.415 | 205.345 | 270.031 | 355.443 | 468.056 |
| 22 | 24.716 | 27.845 | 31.453 | 35.618 | 40.430 | 45.996 | 59.893 | 78.543 | 103.603 | 137.297 | 182.601 | 243.487 | 325.237 | 434.861 | 581.630 |
| 23 | 25.973 | 29.422 | 33.426 | 38.083 | 43.502 | 49.816 | 65.765 | 87.497 | 117.155 | 157.659 | 212.977 | 288.495 | 391.484 | 531.750 | 722.461 |
| 24 | 27.243 | 31.030 | 35.459 | 40.646 | 46.727 | 53.865 | 72.106 | 97.347 | 132.334 | 180.871 | 248.214 | 341.604 | 470.981 | 649.956 | 897.092 |
| 25 | 28.526 | 32.671 | 37.553 | 43.312 | 50.113 | 58.156 | 78.954 | 108.182 | 149.334 | 207.333 | 289.088 | 404.273 | 566.377 | 794.166 | 1113.634 |
| 26 | 29.821 | 34.344 | 39.710 | 46.084 | 53.669 | 62.706 | 86.351 | 120.100 | 168.374 | 237.499 | 336.502 | 478.222 | 680.853 | 970.102 | 1382.146 |
| 27 | 31.129 | 36.051 | 41.931 | 48.968 | 57.402 | 67.528 | 94.339 | 133.210 | 189.699 | 271.889 | 391.502 | 565.482 | 818.223 | 1184.745 | 1715.101 |
| 28 | 32.450 | 37.792 | 44.219 | 51.966 | 61.323 | 72.640 | 102.966 | 147.631 | 213.583 | 311.094 | 455.303 | 668.448 | 983.068 | 1446.609 | 2127.966 |
| 29 | 33.785 | 39.568 | 46.575 | 55.085 | 65.439 | 78.058 | 112.283 | 163.494 | 240.333 | 355.787 | 529.311 | 789.949 | 1180.882 | 1766.083 | 2639.917 |
| 30 | 35.133 | 41.379 | 49.003 | 58.328 | 69.761 | 83.802 | 122.346 | 180.944 | 270.293 | 406.737 | 615.161 | 933.320 | 1418.258 | 2155.841 | 3274.737 |

## TABLE C-5  Present Value of One Dollar—Monthly Compounding: [PVF$_{i/12,n}$]

| YR | MO | 5% | 6% | 7% | 8% | 9% | 10% | 11% | 12% | 13% | 14% | 15% | 16% | 17% | 18% | 20% |
|---|---|---|---|---|---|---|---|---|---|---|---|---|---|---|---|---|
| | 1 | 0.9959 | 0.9950 | 0.9942 | 0.9934 | 0.9926 | 0.9917 | 0.9909 | 0.9901 | 0.9893 | 0.9885 | 0.9877 | 0.9868 | 0.9860 | 0.9852 | 0.9836 |
| | 2 | 0.9917 | 0.9901 | 0.9884 | 0.9868 | 0.9852 | 0.9835 | 0.9819 | 0.9803 | 0.9787 | 0.9771 | 0.9755 | 0.9739 | 0.9723 | 0.9707 | 0.9675 |
| | 3 | 0.9876 | 0.9851 | 0.9827 | 0.9803 | 0.9778 | 0.9754 | 0.9730 | 0.9706 | 0.9682 | 0.9658 | 0.9634 | 0.9610 | 0.9587 | 0.9563 | 0.9516 |
| | 4 | 0.9835 | 0.9802 | 0.9770 | 0.9738 | 0.9706 | 0.9673 | 0.9642 | 0.9610 | 0.9578 | 0.9547 | 0.9515 | 0.9484 | 0.9453 | 0.9422 | 0.9360 |
| | 5 | 0.9794 | 0.9754 | 0.9713 | 0.9673 | 0.9633 | 0.9594 | 0.9554 | 0.9515 | 0.9476 | 0.9437 | 0.9398 | 0.9359 | 0.9321 | 0.9283 | 0.9207 |
| | 6 | 0.9754 | 0.9705 | 0.9657 | 0.9609 | 0.9562 | 0.9514 | 0.9467 | 0.9420 | 0.9374 | 0.9328 | 0.9282 | 0.9236 | 0.9191 | 0.9145 | 0.9056 |
| | 7 | 0.9713 | 0.9657 | 0.9601 | 0.9546 | 0.9490 | 0.9436 | 0.9381 | 0.9327 | 0.9273 | 0.9220 | 0.9167 | 0.9115 | 0.9062 | 0.9010 | 0.8907 |
| | 8 | 0.9673 | 0.9609 | 0.9545 | 0.9482 | 0.9420 | 0.9358 | 0.9296 | 0.9235 | 0.9174 | 0.9114 | 0.9054 | 0.8995 | 0.8936 | 0.8877 | 0.8761 |
| | 9 | 0.9633 | 0.9561 | 0.9490 | 0.9420 | 0.9350 | 0.9280 | 0.9212 | 0.9143 | 0.9076 | 0.9009 | 0.8942 | 0.8876 | 0.8811 | 0.8746 | 0.8618 |
| | 10 | 0.9593 | 0.9513 | 0.9435 | 0.9357 | 0.9280 | 0.9204 | 0.9128 | 0.9053 | 0.8979 | 0.8905 | 0.8832 | 0.8759 | 0.8688 | 0.8617 | 0.8476 |
| | 11 | 0.9553 | 0.9466 | 0.9380 | 0.9295 | 0.9211 | 0.9128 | 0.9045 | 0.8963 | 0.8882 | 0.8802 | 0.8723 | 0.8644 | 0.8566 | 0.8489 | 0.8337 |
| 1 | 12 | 0.9513 | 0.9419 | 0.9326 | 0.9234 | 0.9142 | 0.9052 | 0.8963 | 0.8874 | 0.8787 | 0.8701 | 0.8615 | 0.8530 | 0.8447 | 0.8364 | 0.8201 |
| | 18 | 0.9279 | 0.9141 | 0.9006 | 0.8873 | 0.8742 | 0.8612 | 0.8485 | 0.8360 | 0.8237 | 0.8116 | 0.7996 | 0.7879 | 0.7763 | 0.7649 | 0.7427 |
| 2 | 24 | 0.9050 | 0.8872 | 0.8697 | 0.8526 | 0.8358 | 0.8194 | 0.8033 | 0.7876 | 0.7721 | 0.7570 | 0.7422 | 0.7277 | 0.7135 | 0.6995 | 0.6725 |
| | 30 | 0.8827 | 0.8610 | 0.8399 | 0.8193 | 0.7992 | 0.7796 | 0.7605 | 0.7419 | 0.7238 | 0.7061 | 0.6889 | 0.6721 | 0.6557 | 0.6398 | 0.6090 |
| 3 | 36 | 0.8610 | 0.8356 | 0.8111 | 0.7873 | 0.7641 | 0.7417 | 0.7200 | 0.6989 | 0.6785 | 0.6586 | 0.6394 | 0.6207 | 0.6026 | 0.5851 | 0.5515 |
| 4 | 48 | 0.8191 | 0.7871 | 0.7564 | 0.7269 | 0.6986 | 0.6714 | 0.6453 | 0.6203 | 0.5962 | 0.5731 | 0.5509 | 0.5295 | 0.5090 | 0.4894 | 0.4523 |
| 5 | 60 | 0.7792 | 0.7414 | 0.7054 | 0.6712 | 0.6387 | 0.6078 | 0.5784 | 0.5504 | 0.5239 | 0.4986 | 0.4746 | 0.4517 | 0.4300 | 0.4093 | 0.3709 |
| 6 | 72 | 0.7413 | 0.6963 | 0.6578 | 0.6198 | 0.5839 | 0.5502 | 0.5184 | 0.4885 | 0.4603 | 0.4338 | 0.4088 | 0.3853 | 0.3632 | 0.3423 | 0.3042 |
| 7 | 84 | 0.7052 | 0.6577 | 0.6135 | 0.5723 | 0.5338 | 0.4980 | 0.4646 | 0.4335 | 0.4045 | 0.3774 | 0.3522 | 0.3287 | 0.3068 | 0.2863 | 0.2495 |
| 8 | 96 | 0.6709 | 0.6195 | 0.5721 | 0.5284 | 0.4881 | 0.4508 | 0.4164 | 0.3847 | 0.3554 | 0.3284 | 0.3034 | 0.2804 | 0.2591 | 0.2395 | 0.2046 |
| 9 | 108 | 0.6382 | 0.5835 | 0.5336 | 0.4879 | 0.4462 | 0.4081 | 0.3733 | 0.3414 | 0.3123 | 0.2857 | 0.2614 | 0.2392 | 0.2189 | 0.2003 | 0.1678 |
| 10 | 120 | 0.6072 | 0.5496 | 0.4976 | 0.4505 | 0.4079 | 0.3694 | 0.3345 | 0.3030 | 0.2744 | 0.2486 | 0.2252 | 0.2040 | 0.1849 | 0.1675 | 0.1376 |
| 11 | 132 | 0.5776 | 0.5177 | 0.4641 | 0.4160 | 0.3730 | 0.3344 | 0.2998 | 0.2689 | 0.2412 | 0.2163 | 0.1940 | 0.1741 | 0.1562 | 0.1401 | 0.1128 |
| 12 | 144 | 0.5495 | 0.4876 | 0.4328 | 0.3841 | 0.3410 | 0.3027 | 0.2687 | 0.2386 | 0.2119 | 0.1882 | 0.1672 | 0.1485 | 0.1319 | 0.1172 | 0.0925 |
| 13 | 156 | 0.5228 | 0.4593 | 0.4036 | 0.3547 | 0.3117 | 0.2740 | 0.2409 | 0.2118 | 0.1862 | 0.1637 | 0.1440 | 0.1267 | 0.1114 | 0.0980 | 0.0759 |
| 14 | 168 | 0.4973 | 0.4326 | 0.3764 | 0.3275 | 0.2850 | 0.2480 | 0.2159 | 0.1879 | 0.1636 | 0.1425 | 0.1241 | 0.1080 | 0.0941 | 0.0820 | 0.0622 |
| 15 | 180 | 0.4731 | 0.4075 | 0.3510 | 0.3024 | 0.2605 | 0.2245 | 0.1935 | 0.1668 | 0.1438 | 0.1240 | 0.1069 | 0.0922 | 0.0795 | 0.0686 | 0.0510 |
| 20 | 240 | 0.3686 | 0.3021 | 0.2476 | 0.2030 | 0.1664 | 0.1365 | 0.1119 | 0.0918 | 0.0753 | 0.0618 | 0.0507 | 0.0416 | 0.0342 | 0.0281 | 0.0189 |
| 25 | 300 | 0.2872 | 0.2240 | 0.1747 | 0.1362 | 0.1063 | 0.0829 | 0.0647 | 0.0505 | 0.0395 | 0.0308 | 0.0241 | 0.0188 | 0.0147 | 0.0115 | 0.0070 |
| 30 | 360 | 0.2238 | 0.1660 | 0.1232 | 0.0914 | 0.0679 | 0.0504 | 0.0374 | 0.0278 | 0.0207 | 0.0154 | 0.0114 | 0.0085 | 0.0063 | 0.0047 | 0.0026 |
| 35 | 420 | 0.1744 | 0.1231 | 0.0869 | 0.0614 | 0.0434 | 0.0306 | 0.0217 | 0.0153 | 0.0108 | 0.0077 | 0.0054 | 0.0038 | 0.0027 | 0.0019 | 0.0010 |

## TABLE C–6  Future Value of One Dollar—Monthly Compounding: [FVF $_{i/12,n}$]

ANNUAL PERCENTAGE RATE

| YR | MO | 5% | 6% | 7% | 8% | 9% | 10% | 11% | 12% | 13% | 14% | 15% | 16% | 17% | 18% | 20% |
|---|---|---|---|---|---|---|---|---|---|---|---|---|---|---|---|---|
| | 1 | 1.0042 | 1.0050 | 1.0058 | 1.0067 | 1.0075 | 1.0083 | 1.0092 | 1.0100 | 1.0108 | 1.0117 | 1.0125 | 1.0133 | 1.0142 | 1.0150 | 1.0167 |
| | 2 | 1.0084 | 1.0100 | 1.0117 | 1.0134 | 1.0151 | 1.0167 | 1.0184 | 1.0201 | 1.0218 | 1.0235 | 1.0252 | 1.0268 | 1.0285 | 1.0302 | 1.0336 |
| | 3 | 1.0126 | 1.0151 | 1.0176 | 1.0201 | 1.0227 | 1.0252 | 1.0278 | 1.0303 | 1.0329 | 1.0354 | 1.0380 | 1.0405 | 1.0431 | 1.0457 | 1.0508 |
| | 4 | 1.0168 | 1.0202 | 1.0235 | 1.0269 | 1.0303 | 1.0338 | 1.0372 | 1.0406 | 1.0440 | 1.0475 | 1.0509 | 1.0544 | 1.0579 | 1.0614 | 1.0684 |
| | 5 | 1.0210 | 1.0253 | 1.0295 | 1.0338 | 1.0381 | 1.0424 | 1.0467 | 1.0510 | 1.0554 | 1.0597 | 1.0641 | 1.0685 | 1.0729 | 1.0773 | 1.0862 |
| | 6 | 1.0253 | 1.0304 | 1.0355 | 1.0407 | 1.0459 | 1.0511 | 1.0563 | 1.0615 | 1.0668 | 1.0721 | 1.0774 | 1.0827 | 1.0881 | 1.0934 | 1.1043 |
| | 7 | 1.0295 | 1.0355 | 1.0416 | 1.0476 | 1.0537 | 1.0598 | 1.0660 | 1.0721 | 1.0783 | 1.0846 | 1.0909 | 1.0972 | 1.1035 | 1.1098 | 1.1227 |
| | 8 | 1.0338 | 1.0407 | 1.0476 | 1.0546 | 1.0616 | 1.0686 | 1.0757 | 1.0829 | 1.0900 | 1.0972 | 1.1045 | 1.1118 | 1.1191 | 1.1265 | 1.1414 |
| | 9 | 1.0381 | 1.0459 | 1.0537 | 1.0616 | 1.0696 | 1.0775 | 1.0856 | 1.0937 | 1.1018 | 1.1100 | 1.1183 | 1.1266 | 1.1350 | 1.1434 | 1.1604 |
| | 10 | 1.0425 | 1.0511 | 1.0599 | 1.0687 | 1.0776 | 1.0865 | 1.0955 | 1.1046 | 1.1138 | 1.1230 | 1.1323 | 1.1416 | 1.1510 | 1.1605 | 1.1797 |
| | 11 | 1.0468 | 1.0564 | 1.0661 | 1.0758 | 1.0857 | 1.0956 | 1.1056 | 1.1157 | 1.1258 | 1.1361 | 1.1464 | 1.1568 | 1.1674 | 1.1779 | 1.1994 |
| 1 | 12 | 1.0512 | 1.0617 | 1.0723 | 1.0830 | 1.0938 | 1.1047 | 1.1157 | 1.1268 | 1.1380 | 1.1493 | 1.1608 | 1.1723 | 1.1839 | 1.1956 | 1.2194 |
| | 18 | 1.0777 | 1.0939 | 1.1104 | 1.1272 | 1.1440 | 1.1611 | 1.1785 | 1.1961 | 1.2140 | 1.2322 | 1.2506 | 1.2692 | 1.2882 | 1.3073 | 1.3465 |
| 2 | 24 | 1.1049 | 1.1272 | 1.1498 | 1.1729 | 1.1964 | 1.2204 | 1.2448 | 1.2697 | 1.2951 | 1.3210 | 1.3474 | 1.3742 | 1.4016 | 1.4295 | 1.4869 |
| | 30 | 1.1329 | 1.1614 | 1.1906 | 1.2206 | 1.2513 | 1.2827 | 1.3149 | 1.3478 | 1.3816 | 1.4162 | 1.4516 | 1.4879 | 1.5250 | 1.5631 | 1.6419 |
| 3 | 36 | 1.1615 | 1.1967 | 1.2329 | 1.2702 | 1.3086 | 1.3482 | 1.3889 | 1.4308 | 1.4739 | 1.5183 | 1.5639 | 1.6110 | 1.6593 | 1.7091 | 1.8131 |
| 4 | 48 | 1.2209 | 1.2705 | 1.3221 | 1.3757 | 1.4314 | 1.4894 | 1.5496 | 1.6122 | 1.6773 | 1.7450 | 1.8154 | 1.8885 | 1.9645 | 2.0435 | 2.2109 |
| 5 | 60 | 1.2834 | 1.3489 | 1.4176 | 1.4898 | 1.5657 | 1.6453 | 1.7289 | 1.8167 | 1.9089 | 2.0056 | 2.1072 | 2.2138 | 2.3257 | 2.4432 | 2.6960 |
| 6 | 72 | 1.3490 | 1.4320 | 1.5201 | 1.6135 | 1.7126 | 1.8176 | 1.9290 | 2.0471 | 2.1723 | 2.3051 | 2.4459 | 2.5952 | 2.7534 | 2.9212 | 3.2874 |
| 7 | 84 | 1.4180 | 1.5204 | 1.6300 | 1.7474 | 1.8732 | 2.0079 | 2.1522 | 2.3067 | 2.4722 | 2.6494 | 2.8391 | 3.0423 | 3.2597 | 3.4926 | 4.0087 |
| 8 | 96 | 1.4906 | 1.6141 | 1.7478 | 1.8925 | 2.0489 | 2.2182 | 2.4013 | 2.5993 | 2.8134 | 3.0450 | 3.2955 | 3.5663 | 3.8592 | 4.1758 | 4.8881 |
| 9 | 108 | 1.5668 | 1.7137 | 1.8742 | 2.0495 | 2.2411 | 2.4504 | 2.6791 | 2.9289 | 3.2018 | 3.4998 | 3.8253 | 4.1807 | 4.5689 | 4.9927 | 5.9606 |
| 10 | 120 | 1.6470 | 1.8194 | 2.0097 | 2.2196 | 2.4514 | 2.7070 | 2.9891 | 3.3004 | 3.6437 | 4.0225 | 4.4402 | 4.9009 | 5.4090 | 5.9693 | 7.2683 |
| 11 | 132 | 1.731 | 1.932 | 2.155 | 2.404 | 2.681 | 2.991 | 3.335 | 3.719 | 4.147 | 4.623 | 5.154 | 5.745 | 6.404 | 7.137 | 8.863 |
| 12 | 144 | 1.820 | 2.051 | 2.311 | 2.603 | 2.933 | 3.304 | 3.721 | 4.191 | 4.719 | 5.314 | 5.983 | 6.735 | 7.581 | 8.533 | 10.807 |
| 13 | 156 | 1.913 | 2.177 | 2.478 | 2.819 | 3.208 | 3.650 | 4.152 | 4.722 | 5.370 | 6.107 | 6.944 | 7.895 | 8.975 | 10.202 | 13.178 |
| 14 | 168 | 2.011 | 2.312 | 2.657 | 3.053 | 3.509 | 4.032 | 4.632 | 5.321 | 6.112 | 7.019 | 8.061 | 9.255 | 10.626 | 12.198 | 16.069 |
| 15 | 180 | 2.114 | 2.454 | 2.849 | 3.307 | 3.838 | 4.454 | 5.168 | 5.996 | 6.955 | 8.068 | 9.356 | 10.850 | 12.580 | 14.584 | 19.595 |
| 20 | 240 | 2.713 | 3.310 | 4.039 | 4.927 | 6.009 | 7.328 | 8.935 | 10.893 | 13.277 | 16.180 | 19.715 | 24.019 | 29.258 | 35.633 | 52.828 |
| 25 | 300 | 3.481 | 4.465 | 5.725 | 7.340 | 9.408 | 12.057 | 15.448 | 19.788 | 25.343 | 32.451 | 41.544 | 53.174 | 68.046 | 87.059 | 142.461 |
| 30 | 360 | 4.466 | 6.023 | 8.116 | 10.936 | 14.731 | 19.837 | 26.708 | 35.950 | 48.377 | 65.085 | 87.541 | 117.717 | 158.256 | 212.704 | 383.464 |
| 35 | 420 | 5.734 | 8.124 | 11.506 | 16.293 | 23.063 | 32.639 | 46.176 | 65.310 | 92.345 | 130.534 | 184.465 | 260.602 | 368.061 | 519.682 | 1035.156 |

# TABLE C–7 Present Value of One Dollar per Period—Monthly Compounding: $[PVA_{i/12, n}]$

| YR | MO | 5% | 6% | 7% | 8% | 9% | 10% | 11% | 12% | 13% | 14% | 15% | 16% | 17% | 18% | 20% |
|---|---|---|---|---|---|---|---|---|---|---|---|---|---|---|---|---|
| | | | | | | | ANNUAL PERCENTAGE RATE | | | | | | | | | |
| | 1 | 0.9959 | 0.9950 | 0.9942 | 0.9934 | 0.9926 | 0.9917 | 0.9909 | 0.9901 | 0.9893 | 0.9885 | 0.9877 | 0.9868 | 0.9860 | 0.9852 | 0.9836 |
| | 2 | 1.9876 | 1.9851 | 1.9826 | 1.9802 | 1.9777 | 1.9753 | 1.9728 | 1.9704 | 1.9680 | 1.9655 | 1.9631 | 1.9607 | 1.9583 | 1.9559 | 1.9511 |
| | 3 | 2.9752 | 2.9702 | 2.9653 | 2.9604 | 2.9556 | 2.9507 | 2.9458 | 2.9410 | 2.9362 | 2.9313 | 2.9265 | 2.9217 | 2.9170 | 2.9122 | 2.9027 |
| | 4 | 3.9587 | 3.9505 | 3.9423 | 3.9342 | 3.9261 | 3.9180 | 3.9100 | 3.9020 | 3.8940 | 3.8860 | 3.8781 | 3.8701 | 3.8622 | 3.8544 | 3.8387 |
| | 5 | 4.9381 | 4.9259 | 4.9137 | 4.9015 | 4.8894 | 4.8774 | 4.8654 | 4.8534 | 4.8415 | 4.8297 | 4.8178 | 4.8061 | 4.7943 | 4.7826 | 4.7594 |
| | 6 | 5.9135 | 5.8964 | 5.8794 | 5.8625 | 5.8456 | 5.8288 | 5.8121 | 5.7955 | 5.7789 | 5.7624 | 5.7460 | 5.7297 | 5.7134 | 5.6972 | 5.6650 |
| | 7 | 6.8848 | 6.8621 | 6.8395 | 6.8170 | 6.7946 | 6.7724 | 6.7502 | 6.7282 | 6.7063 | 6.6844 | 6.6627 | 6.6411 | 6.6196 | 6.5982 | 6.5557 |
| | 8 | 7.8521 | 7.8230 | 7.7940 | 7.7652 | 7.7366 | 7.7081 | 7.6798 | 7.6517 | 7.6237 | 7.5958 | 7.5681 | 7.5406 | 7.5132 | 7.4859 | 7.4319 |
| | 9 | 8.8153 | 8.7791 | 8.7430 | 8.7072 | 8.6716 | 8.6362 | 8.6010 | 8.5660 | 8.5313 | 8.4967 | 8.4623 | 8.4282 | 8.3943 | 8.3605 | 8.2936 |
| | 10 | 9.7746 | 9.7304 | 9.6865 | 9.6429 | 9.5996 | 9.5565 | 9.5138 | 9.4713 | 9.4291 | 9.3872 | 9.3455 | 9.3041 | 9.2630 | 9.2222 | 9.1413 |
| | 11 | 10.7299 | 10.6770 | 10.6245 | 10.5724 | 10.5207 | 10.4693 | 10.4183 | 10.3676 | 10.3173 | 10.2674 | 10.2178 | 10.1686 | 10.1197 | 10.0711 | 9.9750 |
| 1 | 12 | 11.6812 | 11.6189 | 11.5571 | 11.4958 | 11.4349 | 11.3745 | 11.3146 | 11.2551 | 11.1960 | 11.1375 | 11.0793 | 11.0216 | 10.9643 | 10.9075 | 10.7951 |
| | 18 | 17.3069 | 17.1728 | 17.0401 | 16.9068 | 16.7792 | 16.6508 | 16.5239 | 16.3983 | 16.2740 | 16.1511 | 16.0295 | 15.9093 | 15.7903 | 15.6726 | 15.4409 |
| 2 | 24 | 22.7939 | 22.5629 | 22.3351 | 22.1105 | 21.8891 | 21.6709 | 21.4556 | 21.2434 | 21.0341 | 20.8277 | 20.6242 | 20.4235 | 20.2256 | 20.0304 | 19.6480 |
| | 30 | 28.1457 | 27.7941 | 27.4485 | 27.1088 | 26.7751 | 26.4470 | 26.1246 | 25.8077 | 25.4962 | 25.1900 | 24.8889 | 24.5929 | 24.3019 | 24.0158 | 23.4579 |
| 3 | 36 | 33.3657 | 32.8710 | 32.3865 | 31.9118 | 31.4468 | 30.9912 | 30.5449 | 30.1075 | 29.6789 | 29.2589 | 28.8473 | 28.4438 | 28.0483 | 27.6607 | 26.9081 |
| 4 | 48 | 43.4230 | 42.5803 | 41.7602 | 40.9619 | 40.1848 | 39.4282 | 38.6914 | 37.9740 | 37.2752 | 36.5945 | 35.9315 | 35.2855 | 34.6560 | 34.0426 | 32.8619 |
| 5 | 60 | 52.9907 | 51.7256 | 50.5020 | 49.3184 | 48.1734 | 47.0654 | 45.9930 | 44.9550 | 43.9501 | 42.9770 | 42.0346 | 41.1217 | 40.2373 | 39.3803 | 37.7446 |
| 6 | 72 | 62.0928 | 60.3395 | 58.6544 | 57.0345 | 55.4768 | 53.9787 | 52.5373 | 51.1504 | 49.8154 | 48.5302 | 47.2925 | 46.1003 | 44.9516 | 43.8447 | 41.7487 |
| 7 | 84 | 70.7518 | 68.4530 | 66.2573 | 64.1593 | 62.1540 | 60.2367 | 58.4029 | 56.6485 | 54.9693 | 53.3618 | 51.8222 | 50.3472 | 48.9337 | 47.5786 | 45.0325 |
| 8 | 96 | 78.9894 | 76.0952 | 73.3476 | 70.7380 | 68.2584 | 65.9015 | 63.6601 | 61.5277 | 59.4981 | 57.5655 | 55.5724 | 53.9701 | 52.2973 | 50.7017 | 47.7254 |
| 9 | 108 | 86.8261 | 83.2934 | 79.9558 | 76.8125 | 73.8394 | 71.0294 | 68.3720 | 65.8578 | 63.4776 | 61.2231 | 59.0865 | 57.0605 | 55.1384 | 53.3137 | 49.9338 |
| 10 | 120 | 94.2813 | 90.0735 | 86.1264 | 82.4215 | 78.9417 | 75.6712 | 72.5953 | 69.7005 | 66.9744 | 64.4054 | 61.9828 | 59.6968 | 57.5382 | 55.4985 | 51.7449 |
| 11 | 132 | 101.374 | 96.460 | 91.877 | 87.601 | 83.606 | 79.873 | 76.380 | 73.111 | 70.047 | 67.174 | 64.478 | 61.946 | 59.565 | 57.326 | 53.230 |
| 12 | 144 | 108.121 | 102.475 | 97.240 | 92.383 | 87.871 | 83.677 | 79.773 | 76.137 | 72.747 | 69.583 | 66.628 | 63.864 | 61.277 | 58.854 | 54.448 |
| 13 | 156 | 114.540 | 108.140 | 102.242 | 96.798 | 91.770 | 87.120 | 82.814 | 78.823 | 75.120 | 71.679 | 68.480 | 65.501 | 62.724 | 60.132 | 55.441 |
| 14 | 168 | 120.640 | 113.477 | 106.906 | 100.876 | 95.335 | 90.236 | 85.539 | 81.206 | 77.204 | 73.503 | 70.075 | 66.897 | 63.945 | 61.201 | 56.266 |
| 15 | 180 | 126.455 | 118.504 | 111.256 | 104.641 | 98.593 | 93.057 | 87.982 | 83.322 | 79.036 | 75.090 | 71.450 | 68.087 | 64.977 | 62.096 | 56.938 |
| 20 | 240 | 151.525 | 139.581 | 128.983 | 119.554 | 111.145 | 103.625 | 96.882 | 90.819 | 85.355 | 80.417 | 75.942 | 71.877 | 68.176 | 64.796 | 58.864 |
| 25 | 300 | 171.060 | 155.207 | 141.487 | 128.565 | 119.162 | 110.047 | 102.029 | 94.947 | 88.665 | 83.073 | 78.074 | 73.590 | 69.551 | 65.901 | 59.579 |
| 30 | 360 | 186.282 | 166.792 | 150.305 | 136.283 | 124.282 | 113.951 | 105.006 | 97.218 | 90.400 | 84.397 | 79.086 | 74.363 | 70.142 | 66.353 | 59.844 |
| 35 | 420 | 198.142 | 175.380 | 156.530 | 140.793 | 127.552 | 116.323 | 106.728 | 98.469 | 91.308 | 85.058 | 79.566 | 74.712 | 70.396 | 66.538 | 59.942 |

## TABLE C–8 Future Value of Annuity Due—Monthly Compounding: [FVA_{I/12,n}]

| YR | MO | 5% | 6% | 7% | 8% | 9% | 10% | 11% | 12% | 13% | 14% | 15% | 16% | 17% | 18% | 20% |
|---|---|---|---|---|---|---|---|---|---|---|---|---|---|---|---|---|
| | 1 | 1.0042 | 1.0050 | 1.0058 | 1.0067 | 1.0075 | 1.0083 | 1.0092 | 1.0100 | 1.0108 | 1.0117 | 1.0125 | 1.0133 | 1.0142 | 1.0150 | 1.0167 |
| | 2 | 2.0125 | 2.0150 | 2.0175 | 2.0200 | 2.0226 | 2.0251 | 2.0276 | 2.0301 | 2.0326 | 2.0351 | 2.0377 | 2.0402 | 2.0427 | 2.0452 | 2.0503 |
| | 3 | 3.0251 | 3.0301 | 3.0351 | 3.0402 | 3.0452 | 3.0503 | 3.0553 | 3.0604 | 3.0655 | 3.0705 | 3.0756 | 3.0807 | 3.0858 | 3.0909 | 3.1011 |
| | 4 | 4.0418 | 4.0503 | 4.0587 | 4.0671 | 4.0756 | 4.0840 | 4.0925 | 4.1010 | 4.1095 | 4.1180 | 4.1266 | 4.1351 | 4.1437 | 4.1523 | 4.1695 |
| | 5 | 5.0628 | 5.0755 | 5.0882 | 5.1009 | 5.1136 | 5.1264 | 5.1392 | 5.1520 | 5.1649 | 5.1777 | 5.1907 | 5.2036 | 5.2166 | 5.2296 | 5.2556 |
| | 6 | 6.0881 | 6.1059 | 6.1237 | 6.1416 | 6.1595 | 6.1775 | 6.1955 | 6.2135 | 6.2317 | 6.2498 | 6.2680 | 6.2863 | 6.3046 | 6.3230 | 6.3599 |
| | 7 | 7.1176 | 7.1414 | 7.1653 | 7.1892 | 7.2132 | 7.2373 | 7.2614 | 7.2857 | 7.3100 | 7.3344 | 7.3589 | 7.3835 | 7.4081 | 7.4328 | 7.4826 |
| | 8 | 8.1515 | 8.1821 | 8.2129 | 8.2438 | 8.2748 | 8.3059 | 8.3371 | 8.3685 | 8.4000 | 8.4316 | 8.4634 | 8.4952 | 8.5272 | 8.5593 | 8.6239 |
| | 9 | 9.1896 | 9.2280 | 9.2666 | 9.3054 | 9.3443 | 9.3835 | 9.4227 | 9.4622 | 9.5019 | 9.5417 | 9.5817 | 9.6218 | 9.6622 | 9.7027 | 9.7843 |
| | 10 | 10.2321 | 10.2796 | 10.3266 | 10.3741 | 10.4219 | 10.4700 | 10.5183 | 10.5668 | 10.6156 | 10.6647 | 10.7139 | 10.7635 | 10.8132 | 10.8633 | 10.9641 |
| | 11 | 11.2789 | 11.3356 | 11.3926 | 11.4499 | 11.5076 | 11.5656 | 11.6239 | 11.6825 | 11.7415 | 11.8007 | 11.8604 | 11.9203 | 11.9806 | 12.0412 | 12.1635 |
| 1 | 12 | 12.3300 | 12.3972 | 12.4649 | 12.5329 | 12.6014 | 12.6703 | 12.7396 | 12.8093 | 12.8795 | 12.9501 | 13.0211 | 13.0926 | 13.1645 | 13.2368 | 13.3829 |
| | 18 | 18.7296 | 18.8797 | 19.0313 | 19.1842 | 19.3387 | 19.4946 | 19.6520 | 19.8109 | 19.9713 | 20.1333 | 20.2968 | 20.4618 | 20.6285 | 20.7967 | 21.1180 |
| 2 | 24 | 25.2309 | 25.5591 | 25.8306 | 26.1061 | 26.3849 | 26.6673 | 26.9534 | 27.2432 | 27.5368 | 27.8342 | 28.1354 | 28.4406 | 28.7498 | 29.0630 | 29.7018 |
| | 30 | 32.0179 | 32.4414 | 32.8719 | 33.3094 | 33.7542 | 34.2062 | 34.6657 | 35.1327 | 35.6075 | 36.0901 | 36.5807 | 37.0794 | 37.5864 | 38.1018 | 39.1584 |
| 3 | 36 | 38.9148 | 39.5328 | 40.1630 | 40.8058 | 41.4614 | 42.1300 | 42.8120 | 43.5076 | 44.2172 | 44.9411 | 45.6794 | 46.4327 | 47.2011 | 47.9851 | 49.6010 |
| 4 | 48 | 53.2358 | 54.3683 | 55.5313 | 56.7256 | 57.9521 | 59.2118 | 60.5057 | 61.8348 | 63.2001 | 64.6027 | 66.0437 | 67.5243 | 69.0455 | 70.6087 | 73.8658 |
| 5 | 60 | 68.2894 | 70.1189 | 72.0105 | 73.9667 | 75.9898 | 78.0824 | 80.2470 | 82.4864 | 84.8033 | 87.2007 | 89.6817 | 92.2493 | 94.9069 | 97.6579 | 103.4542 |
| 6 | 72 | 84.11 | 86.84 | 89.68 | 92.64 | 95.72 | 98.93 | 102.27 | 105.76 | 109.39 | 113.17 | 117.12 | 121.23 | 125.52 | 130.00 | 139.53 |
| 7 | 84 | 100.75 | 104.59 | 108.63 | 112.86 | 117.30 | 121.96 | 126.85 | 131.98 | 137.37 | 143.03 | 148.97 | 155.21 | 161.77 | 168.67 | 183.53 |
| 8 | 96 | 118.23 | 123.44 | 128.95 | 134.76 | 140.91 | 147.40 | 154.27 | 161.53 | 169.21 | 177.33 | 185.94 | 195.04 | 204.68 | 214.90 | 237.18 |
| 9 | 108 | 136.61 | 143.45 | 150.73 | 158.48 | 166.72 | 175.50 | 184.86 | 194.82 | 205.44 | 216.77 | 228.85 | 241.74 | 255.49 | 270.17 | 302.59 |
| 10 | 120 | 155.93 | 164.70 | 174.09 | 184.17 | 194.97 | 206.55 | 218.99 | 232.34 | 246.68 | 262.09 | 278.66 | 296.47 | 315.64 | 336.26 | 382.36 |
| 11 | 132 | 176.24 | 187.25 | 199.14 | 211.98 | 225.86 | 240.85 | 257.07 | 274.61 | 293.61 | 314.18 | 336.47 | 360.64 | 386.84 | 415.27 | 479.63 |
| 12 | 144 | 197.58 | 211.20 | 226.01 | 242.11 | 259.64 | 278.74 | 299.56 | 322.25 | 347.02 | 374.05 | 403.58 | 435.86 | 471.14 | 509.74 | 598.24 |
| 13 | 156 | 220.02 | 236.62 | 254.81 | 274.74 | 296.60 | 320.60 | 346.96 | 375.93 | 407.80 | 442.87 | 481.48 | 524.04 | 570.95 | 622.70 | 742.88 |
| 14 | 168 | 243.61 | 263.62 | 285.69 | 310.08 | 337.03 | 366.84 | 399.85 | 436.42 | 476.97 | 521.95 | 571.91 | 627.40 | 689.10 | 757.74 | 919.24 |
| 15 | 180 | 268.40 | 292.27 | 318.81 | 348.35 | 381.24 | 417.92 | 458.86 | 504.58 | 555.68 | 612.85 | 676.86 | 748.58 | 828.99 | 919.21 | 1134.30 |
| 20 | 240 | 412.75 | 464.35 | 523.97 | 592.95 | 672.90 | 765.70 | 873.57 | 999.15 | 1145.52 | 1316.35 | 1515.96 | 1749.06 | 2022.92 | 2343.49 | 3161.48 |
| 25 | 300 | 597.99 | 696.46 | 814.80 | 957.37 | 1129.53 | 1337.89 | 1590.58 | 1897.64 | 2271.43 | 2727.26 | 3284.07 | 3965.22 | 4799.67 | 5823.31 | 8626.71 |
| 30 | 360 | 835.73 | 1009.54 | 1227.09 | 1500.30 | 1844.47 | 2279.33 | 2830.23 | 3529.91 | 4420.65 | 5557.06 | 7009.82 | 8870.48 | 11257.67 | 14325.29 | 23360.81 |
| 35 | 420 | 1140.6 | 1431.6 | 1811.6 | 2309.2 | 2963.8 | 3828.3 | 4973.5 | 6495.3 | 8523.2 | 11232.5 | 14860.6 | 19729.8 | 26277.2 | 35097.5 | 63083.5 |

515

# Glossary

**Agency relationship** (10)   A contract under which one or more principals employ another person, the agent, to perform some service and delegate some authority to that agent.

**American Depository Receipts (ADRs)** (18)   Receipts deposited with a bank (custodian) used to represent ownership of foreign securities; bought and sold on U.S. stock exchanges and OTC.

**American option** (16)   An option contract that can be exercised anytime before expiration.

**Appreciation** (19, 20)   An increase in value over time—of real estate, stock, precious metals, and so on.

**Arbitrage pricing theory** (22)   A model that explains security returns by using more than one causal factor. This theory states the market equilibrium will be characterized by a linear relationship between each security's expected return and its loading on several factors common to the returns of all securities.

**Ask price** (2)   The price at which a dealer offers to sell.

**Asset** (23)   An item you own that has monetary value.

**Auction market** (2)   Market where prices are determined by the active competition of several parties willing to buy and sell.

**Balance sheet** (23)   A financial position paper used to determine net worth at some given time.

**Basis (commodities)** (17)   Cash price minus the futures price of a particular product at a certain point in time.

**Basis (real estate)** (19)   Usually the purchase price of an asset; may also include cost of capital improvements to real property.

**Best efforts arrangement** (2)   The agreement under which the investment banking firm works as the issuing firm's agent in trying to sell a new issue of securities. The issuing firm pays the investment banking firm a commission for each share sold but the investment banking firm does not guarantee to sell a specific number of shares.

**Beta** (1)   A measure of the sensitivity of a stock to systematic risk. The beta of the stock market as a whole is one.

**Bid price** (2)   The price at which a dealer offers to buy.

**Blue chip stocks** (10)   Stocks of large well-managed firms, which can be expected to grow as the economy grows.

**Book-entry form** (6)   Securities issued with computerized ownership records; certificates are not issued.

**Book value** (5)   The value of the firm's assets minus its liabilities. By accounting definition this equals the stockholders' equity. Dividing the book value by the number of shares outstanding gives book value per share.

**Business risk** (10)   The chance that a firm will not be as successful as expected.

---

Note: The number after the term indicates chapter(s) where discussed.

**516**

**Call option** (16)  A contract that allows its holder to buy a specified security at an established exercise price anytime before the expiration date.

**Call premium** (13)  An amount in addition to the principal that an issuer is required to pay the bondholder if the bonds are called.

**Call provision** (13)  A bond feature that gives the issuer the right to redeem the bonds early.

**Capital appreciation** (1)  The gains (or losses) that occur when any investment is sold for more (or less) than it cost.

**Capital gain (loss)** (19)  When capital assets are sold for more than the purchase price. Totally taxable by 1986 tax reform. A loss is deductible within certain guidelines.

**Capital market** (2)  The market in which financial assets with a maturity of more than a year are bought and sold. Stocks and bonds are traded here.

**Capital market line** (22)  The line that describes the tradeoff between expected return and risk for various holdings of the risk-free asset and the market portfolio.

**Cash contract** (17)  A contract between a buyer and a seller of a product where the product is delivered immediately and payment is received immediately.

**Cash management bills** (6)  Short-term borrowings by the Treasury to adjust for an uneven flow of revenue from taxes.

**Classified common stock** (5)  The existence of more than one class of common stock. Usually, the different classes of common stock have different voting rights and dividend priorities.

**Closed-end investment company** (15)  An investment fund that has a fixed number of common shares which are originally sold through investment banking firms. Purchasers resell the shares in the secondary market in the same manner as any other stock.

**Collateral trust bonds** (13)  Bonds that have stocks or bonds of other firms pledged as security.

**Commodities** (17)  Homogeneous raw materials and farm products.

**Commodity Futures Trading Commission (CFTC)** (17)  Government agency which regulates futures trading.

**Competitive bidding** (2)  The arrangement under which a firm issuing securities solicits bids for the securities from investment banking firms. The investment banking firm offering the highest price purchases the securities for resale to the public.

**Contractual theory** (10  This model views the corporation as a set of explicit and implicit contracts among stockholders, debt holders, managers, and workers. These contracts define rights, obligations, and payoffs under alternative circumstances.

**Convertible security** (5)  A security (usually a bond or preferred stock) that can be exchanged for another security of the firm (usually common stock) at the option of the holder.

**Coupon rate** (13)  The amount of interest that a bond promises to pay annually divided by the face value of the bond.

**Cumulative preferred stock** (5)  A feature that preferred stock can have under which if the stated dividend is not paid, the dividends accrue and must be paid before any subsequent common stock dividends are paid. Opposite of noncumulative preferred stock.

**Current income** (19)  A cash flow from investments that occurs on a predictable basis—rent, dividends, interest.

**Current yield** (13)  The current rate of return on a bond. It is computed by dividing the annual coupon interest by the current price of the bond.

**Cyclical indicators** (9)  Economic series that tend to lead, coincide with, or lag behind broad movements in aggregate economic activity.

**Cyclical stocks** (10)  Stocks of firms that are very sensitive to economic cycles.

**Debenture** (13)  A bond secured only by the general credit of the issuer; there is no pledge of a specific asset. Unsecured bond.

**Default insurance** (6) Insurance that pays a bond's interest and principal if the bond issuer does not pay them.

**Defensive stocks** (10) Stocks of firms that continue to do well in bad economic times.

**Depreciation** (19) A decrease in value over time of real or personal intangible property.

**Direct foreign investment** (18) Ownership of foreign real assets such as land and factories.

**Discount brokerage firms** (3) Firms that charge lower commissions than full service brokers because they do not give advice.

**Diversification** (1) Distributing wealth among many assets in order to minimize the risk of loss.

**Dominant portfolio** (22) A portfolio that offers a higher return and the same risk as the other portfolio or it offers less risk and the same return.

**Duration** (13) A measure of a bond's term to maturity. It considers the amount and timing of all the cash flows (interest and principal).

**Economic earnings** (11) The maximum amount of wealth which can be consumed by the owners of the firm in any period without decreasing future consumption opportunities.

**Efficient portfolio** (23) A portfolio that offers the maximum return for a given amount of risk or the least risk for a given amount of return. The efficient frontier of the opportunity set.

**Equipment trust certificates** (13) Bonds issued to finance the purchase of equipment, and the title to that equipment is held by the bond trustee.

**Equity** (3) The market value of all securities in a margin account minus the amount borrowed.

**Equity fund REIT and RELP** (19) A REIT or RELP that is backed by real estate, such as buildings or land.

**European option** (16) An option contract that can be exercised only on the expiration date.

**Exchange controls** (18) Foreign government restrictions on converting its currency to dollars.

**Ex dividend date** (10) The stock sells without its dividend on this date. If you buy on the ex dividend date, your name will not get on the company's books by the holder-of-record date.

**External efficiency** (2) This "pricing" efficiency exists when security prices fully reflect all available information about the economy, the industry, and the specific firm.

**Fair game** (2) The environment in which investors face a common set of rules and cannot expect to outperform each other by trading practices based on existing information.

**Federal Financing Bank** (6) A bank established by Congress to issue securities or borrow from the Treasury in order to loan money to government owned agencies and other entities approved by law.

**Federally sponsored agency** (6) An independent agency established by the government in order to increase the flow of credit to desired activities, in particular agriculture, housing, and education.

**Financial assets** (1) Pieces of paper that represent claims on wealth held by others.

**Financial risk** (10) The chance that the firm's use of debt financing will adversely affect the returns to its stockholders.

**Forward contract** (17) A contract between a buyer and a seller of a product for delivery and payment at some specified future date. The product, its quality, quantity, price, and future delivery and payment dates are all negotiated elements of the contract.

**Fourth market** (2) Institutional investors buying and selling securities without using brokerage firms.

**Full service broker** (3) A brokerage firm that offers advice and, therefore, charges higher commissions than discount brokers.

**Futures contract** (17) A contract to buy or sell a product and to make payment or delivery at some specified future date. The terms of a futures contract are standardized by the futures exchange.

**Global fund** (15, 18) An investment company that invests in both U.S. and foreign securities.

**Greenmail** (10) A firm's repurchase of its stock from a potential acquirer at a price above the current market price. The firm does not offer to purchase the stock of other owners at this price.

**Guaranteed bond** (13)   A bond that has its interest and/or principal payments guaranteed by another corporation.

**Hedging** (17)   A strategy whereby prospective buyers or sellers of a product can buy or sell futures contracts to reduce their risk of price fluctuations.

**Holder-of-record date** (10)   The date on which a shareholder must be listed on the corporate books in order to obtain the dividend. Four business days after the ex dividend date.

**Income bond** (13)   A bond that has to pay interest only if the firm has enough earnings to cover the interest payment.

**Income/expense statement** (23)   A cash flow statement used to determine where money is spent for some period of time.

**Income stocks** (10)   Stocks of companies that pay high dividends and, therefore, give a high priority to maintaining their dividend records.

**Indenture** (8, 13)   The contract detailing all the provisions of a bond issue.

**Index fund** (15)   An investment fund that attempts to match the performance of a stock market index.

**Index option** (16)   An option contract that gives the holder the right to buy or sell the cash value of a market index at the exercise price in the contract.

**Indirect shareowner** (1)   Anyone who owns a life insurance policy, participates in a pension or deferred profit-sharing plan, has an account in a mutual savings bank, or receives a scholarship from a college endowment fund.

**Individual Retirement Account (IRA)** (23, 24)   Individual pension plans set up by wage earners.

**Inflation premium** (1)   The addition to the required rate of return that compensates the investor for expected inflation.

**Initial margin requirement** (3)   The percent of the total money required for purchasing securities that the customer must put up when the purchase is made; determined by the Federal Reserve; presently 50 percent for stock.

**Inside information** (8)   Information that is not available to the general public and that, therefore, could not be discovered if an investor searched for it.

**Insolvent** (23)   Net worth (assets minus liabilities) is negative.

**Interest rate risk** (10)   The chance of decrease in the value of outstanding securities because interest rates throughout the economy rise.

**Internal efficiency** (2)   This "operating" efficiency exists if a market provides the means through which investors can buy and sell securities at prices as low as possible considering the costs of the services used by them.

**International fund** (15, 18)   An investment company that invests in only foreign securities.

**Intestate** (23)   Dying without a valid will in existence.

**Investment** (1)   Foregoing current consumption of wealth in order to obtain greater future benefits.

**Investment banking firm** (2)   The middleman between firms wishing to raise money by selling securities and investors wanting to buy securities.

**Joint tenancy** (19)   Two or more owners of property. With right of survivorship, surviving owner will automatically receive property upon death. As tenants in common, each owner may determine where the property will go at death.

**Junk bond** (13)   A bond with a quality rating of BB or less at the time of issue. It offers the buyer higher returns and higher risk than better quality bonds.

**Keogh Plan** (23, 24)   Individual pension plans for self-employed individuals.

**Law of descent** (23)   A state law that determines the distribution of an estate if the person dies intestate.

**Leverage** (19)   Buying real or personal property by putting up a portion of the purchase price (or using other collateral as the down payment) and borrowing the balance.

**Liability** (23)   A debt that is owed by an individual or corporation.

**Limit order** (2)   A buy or sell order with a price restriction on it.

**Limited payment life insurance** (23, 24)   A policy where premiums are paid for a limited period of time; protection extends for the lifetime of the insured.

**Liquidity** (1)   A measure of how quickly an asset can be converted to currency with little or no loss in value. The degree of liquidity is measured on a continuum from perfectly liquid to extremely illiquid.

**Locals** (17)   Members of a futures exchange who buy and sell for their own account.

**Maintenance margin requirement** (3)   The minimum amount that must be kept in a margin account to keep the account viable; imposed by the exchanges and individual brokers.

**Management risk** (10)   The chance that the managers of the firm will not perform as well as expected.

**Margin** (3)   The down payment when stocks are bought with borrowed money.

**Margin call** (3)   Call from the broker informing a client that additional cash or securities must be deposited into the margin account; comes when the market value of securities declines. This call must be met or securities can be sold by the broker.

**Market averages** (7)   Summary measure of the movement of a segment of the financial markets.

**Market order** (2)   A buy or sell order without any price restriction.

**Market risk** (10)   The chance that investors will become less willing to hold securities, and, therefore, most securities will sell at lower prices.

**Mature growth stocks** (10)   Stocks of well-established firms in growth industries. The nature of their products combined with aggressive management should permit them to grow faster than the economy.

**Medium-term notes** (5)   Unsecured promissory notes issued by corporations. Maturities range from 9 months to 15 years, with most maturaties ranging between 1 and 7 years.

**Money market** (2)   The financial market in which large denomination debt instruments with original maturities of less than a year are bought and sold.

**Mortgage backed securities** (6)   Debt securities that represent ownership of pools of mortgages. Interest and principal payments made on the mortgages are ''passed through'' to the holder of the security.

**Mortgage bond** (13)   A bond that pledges land and/or buildings as security.

**Mortgage fund REIT and RELP** (19)   A REIT or RELP that is backed by construction or mortgage loans.

**Multinational corporation** (18)   A company headquartered in one country with operating affiliates elsewhere; it conducts business on a global scale.

**Municipal securities** (6)   Debt securities issued by state and local governments and their political subdivisions.

**Mutual fund** (15)   An investment company that sells new shares to any interested person and repurchases its outstanding shares when requested by a shareholder. An open-end investment company.

**NASD Automated Quotations (NASDAQ)** (2)   A system that electronically links brokers with OTC market makers.

**NASDAQ's National Market System list** (2)   Over 2,600 of the most actively traded stocks on the NASDAQ. The transactional information reported on these stocks is as complete as the information reported on the stocks listed on the exchanges.

**National Association of Security Dealers (NASD)** (2)   The self-regulatory organization of the securities industry that oversees the OTC market.

**Net asset value (NAV)** (15)   The value of a share of stock in a mutual fund. It is calculated by substracting fund liabilities from fund assets and dividing by the number of outstanding shares.

**Net worth** (23)   The amount remaining if all liabilities are paid from the value of your assets (assets minus liabilities equals net worth); sometimes called capital or equity.

**Nonmarketable Treasury securities** (6)   A Treasury debt that cannot be resold by the original purchaser to a third party. It is issued in specific series based on the type of purchaser.

**Odd lot** (2)   When 100 shares is a round lot, any number of shares from 1 to 99. When 10 shares is a round lot, any number of shares from 1 to 9.

**Open-end investment company** (15)   A fund that sells new shares to any interested person and repurchases its outstanding shares when requested by a shareholder. A mutual fund.

**Opportunity set** (22)   The set composed of all the available portfolios.

**Option** (16)   A contract that allows its holder to buy or sell a specified security at an established exercise price anytime before the expiration date.

**Option premium** (16)   The price of an option contract.

**Ordinary life insurance** (23)   Life insurance where premiums are paid for the entire life of the insured.

**Over-the-counter (OTC) market** (2)   This market consists of all trading of securities except that which takes place on the organized exchanges. This market does not have a specific trading location; it is made up of thousands of securities dealers and brokers located across the country.

**Participating preferred stock** (5)   A feature of preferred stock under which, in certain circumstances, the holder can receive more than the stated dividend. Most preferred stock issues are nonparticipating.

**Pegging prices** (8)   Illegal activity by which a powerful market participant buys whenever sell orders would force a stock below a certain price.

**Permanent life insurance** (23)   Life insurance designed to provide protection for an individual's entire lifetime.

**Poison pill** (10)   An agreement that destroys the value of the firm if a hostile takeover occurs.

**Pools** (8)   Illegal arrangements under which individuals put together a large sum of money to buy stock and drive up the price. When others are buying at the new high price, members of the pool sell.

**Portfolio** (1)   The combination of all the investor's assets.

**Portfolio foreign investment** (18)   Ownership of foreign financial assets such as stocks, bonds, and bank accounts.

**Preemptive right** (5, 14)   The shareholder prerogative that allows him or her to purchase enough new shares to maintain the percentage ownership he or she had before the issue of additional stock.

**Preferred stock** (5)   Equity ownership of the firm that is favored in some way over common stock. Usually, preferred stock does not vote but comes ahead of common stock in the receipt of dividends and in return of capital if the firm is liquidated.

**Primary market** (2)   The market in which the original sale of a security takes place. The money paid for the security goes to its issuer.

**Principal residence** (19)   The IRS considers this to be the house, condo, or coop in which one spends the majority of time.

**Prospectus** (8)   A pamphlet summarizing important information in the registration statement. A copy of the prospectus must be supplied to everyone solicited to buy a new issue of securities.

**Proxy** (5)   The legal instrument that allows another person to vote the shares of a stockholder.

**Purchasing power risk** (10)   The chance that the money returned on an investment will purchase less than expected because of inflation.

**Put bonds** (6, 13)   Bonds with a feature that allows the holder to redeem the bond at face value on certain dates before maturity.

**Put option** (16)   An option that allows its holder to sell a specified security at an established price anytime before the expiration date.

**Random walk** (21)   Mathematical term used to describe a price series in which each price change is independent of the price pattern which occurred previously.

**Real assets** (1)   Physical goods. Some real assets provide a current benefit, such as houses; others do not, like gold.

**Real Estate Investment Trust (REIT)** (19)   An ownership of real estate represented by shares that can be traded like stock.

**Real Estate Limited Partnership (RELP)** (19)   An ownership of real estate comprised of a general partner and a number of limited partners; ownership consists of shares or units.

**Real rate of interest** (1)   This rate compensates investors for the time value of money. It is determined by the supply and demand for investment funds.

**Registration statement** (8)   The document that must be filed with the SEC before new securities are sold to the public. It describes the security, the company, its management, its financial position, the purpose for which the money will be used, and any potential conflicts of interest.

**Reinvestment rate risk** (13)   The chance that a bondholder will not be able to reinvest interest payments at the bond's yield to maturity.

**Resistance level** (12)   The price where a price rise is expected to stop because of selling forces.

**Restricted account** (3)   A margin account that cannot make additional margin purchases without depositing more money or securities.

**Retirement Equity Act of 1984** (23)   The law granting automatic pension rights to spouses.

**Right** (5, 14)   A security issued by a corporation to its stockholders. A right gives its holder the option to buy a certain number of common shares at a specified subscription price.

**Risk** (1)   The chance that the investment will not achieve the expected return.

**Risk aversion** (1)   The dislike for risk displayed by most people. The degree of risk aversion varies from person to person.

**Risk premium** (1)   Compensation the investor demands for bearing the risk. The greater the investment risk, the greater the premium the investor demands.

**Round lot** (2)   Usually, 100 shares of stock; although for a few less actively traded, higher-price stocks, it is 10 shares. Stocks trade in round lots on exchanges.

**Secondary market** (2)   The market in which sales of a security subsequent to the original sale take place. The money paid for the security goes to its previous owner.

**Secured bond** (13)   A bond that has a specific asset pledged in addition to the pledge of the general credit of the issuer.

**Securities Investor Protection Corporation (SIPC)** (3)   The government agency that insures brokerage accounts.

**Securities market** (2)   A mechanism for bringing together people who want to buy and sell financial assets.

**Security market line** (22)   The line that describes the relationship between a security's expected return and its systematic risk.

**Selling climax** (12)   A situation where prices go down in very heavy volume just before the market starts recovering.

**Serial bond** (13)   A bond issue having several different maturity dates.

**Severalty** (19)   One owner of property.

**Short selling** (3)   Selling stock that the investor does not own but has borrowed. If the price declines, the investor can purchase at the lower price the number of shares needed to replace what was borrowed.

**Solvent** (23)   Net worth (assets minus liabilities) is positive.

**Specialists** (2)   Members of an exchange who make a continuous orderly market in stocks assigned them by the exchange.

**Speculating** (17)   A strategy of taking risk in the hopes of making a profit.

**Speculative blowoff** (12)   A situation where prices go up on very heavy volume just before a long-term price decline starts.

**Speculative growth stocks** (10)   Stocks of unproven young firms with the potential for spectacular growth.

**Split rating** (13)   A situation where a bond is given different ratings by different bond rating agencies.

**Spread** (2)   In underwriting, the difference between the gross proceeds from selling the securities to the public and the net amount paid by the investment banking firm to the issuer. In market making, the difference between the dealer's bid and ask prices.

**Standby offering** (2)  The agreement between an issuing firm and an investment banking firm under which the investment banking firm agrees to underwrite and sell any portion of a new issue not purchased by existing shareholders.

**Stock exchange** (2)  A not-for-profit corporation that provides a place where its members can come together for the purpose of buying and selling securities.

**Stock index bond** (13)  A bond that promises to pay at maturity the greater of the par value or a dollar amount based on stock index.

**Stop loss order** (2)  An order to sell stock if the market price drops to the price specified.

**Street name** (3)  When brokerage firms store customers' securities, they keep them registered in the name of the brokerage firm.

**Subordinate debenture** (13)  A bond having a claim on earnings and assets which ranks after secured debt, debentures, and sometimes general creditors.

**Support level** (12)  The price where a price decline is expected to stop because of buying forces.

**Syndicate** (2)  A group of investment banking firms that share the risk of underwriting a new issue of securities and the task of selling it to the public.

**Systematic risk** (1, 22)  The risk that originates in the general economy and affects all stocks. It cannot be diversified away.

**Tax deferment** (19)  An opportunity to defer taxation in capital gains from the sale of a principal residence.

**Tax exclusion** (19)  Opportunity to exclude from taxation up to $125,000 capital gains from the sale of a personal residence (one time only after age 55).

**Technical analaysis** (12)  The use of market generated data, such as prices and volume, to forecast future price.

**Tender offer** (8)  An invitation to stockholders to offer their shares for purchase at a specified price.

**Term bond** (13)  A bond issue having one single maturity date. All bonds will be paid off at the same time.

**Term insurance** (23)  Life insurance designed to provide protection for a predetermined period of time.

**Third market** (2)  OTC trading of securities that are listed on the exchanges. This trading is carried out by broker dealer firms that are not exchange members.

**Time share** (19)  A method of ownership (usually vacation/resort property) allowing a person to use property for a prespecified period every year.

**Treasury bills** (6)  Short-term debt of the U.S. government. It is issued with 91, 182, and 364 day maturities.

**Treasury bonds** (6)  Borrowings by the U.S. Treasury having maturities of 10 to 30 years.

**Treasury Direct account** (6)  An individual's account at the Treasury that keeps a record of the Treasury securities he or she owns.

**Treasury notes** (6)  Borrowings by the U.S. Treasury having maturities of one to ten years.

**Trustee** (13)  Financial institution that represents corporate bond holders and enforces the indenture agreement.

**Underwriting** (2)  The process in which the investment banking firm bears the risk of the sale of new securities by purchasing them from the issuer and then reselling them to the public.

**Unit trust** (15)  An investment fund that is not actively managed. After money is raised through the sale of the investment trust units, the trust purchases securities which are held by a bank trustee.

**Universal life insurance** (23)  Premiums and face value of the policy are both flexible to allow for changes in coverage as the life cycle changes.

**Unsystematic risk** (1, 22)  The risk that is unique to a particular stock. It can be diversified away by holding many stocks.

**Variable life insurance** (23)   Final face value of the insurance is determined by the performance of a stock portfolio; minimum face value guaranteed.

**Warrant** (5, 14)   A security which gives the holder the option of purchasing from the issuing company a given number of shares of a specified security at a stated price for a specified time period.

**Wash sales** (8)   Security sales that are executed only to create the appearance of more sales activity. Wash sales combined with rumors deceive other investors into buying or selling.

**Yield spreads** (13)   The differences between the yields on bonds of different quality. Usually, a yield spread is measured between bonds of a given quality and Treasury securities of the same maturity.

**Yield curve** (13A)   A graphic representation of the relationship between maturity and yield for bonds.

# INDEX